MICROCOMPUTERS:

Concepts and Applications

Randolph Johnston

M|P *Mitchell Publishing, Inc.*
Innovators in Computer Education
915 River Street • Santa Cruz, California 95060
(800) 435-2665 • In California (408) 425-3851

This book is in compliance with the Level One provisions of the DPMA Associate-Level Model Curriculum in Computer Information Systems. This work has been reviewed by and awarded the exclusive endorsement of DATA PROCESSING MANAGEMENT ASSOCIATION February, 1987

Dedication to Quality Publishing: All employees of Mitchell Publishing, Inc.

Sponsoring Editor: Raleigh Wilson

Director of Product Development: Raleigh Wilson

Production Management: i/e inc.

Interior and Cover Design: Gary Palmatier

Printing: R. R. Donnelly and Sons Company

© 1987

Mitchell Publishing, Inc., a division of Random House, Inc., New York City.
Innovators in Computer Education
915 River Street
Santa Cruz, CA. 95060
(800)435-2665; in California (408)425-3851

SOFTWARE VERSION:
ISBN: 0-394-39059-8   Library of Congress Catalog Card No.: 86-062004

NON-SOFTWARE VERSION:
ISBN: 0-394-39160-8   Library of Congress Catalog Card No.: 86-063827

Brief Table of Contents

Application Software Tutorial following page 522

Contents

PART III. MICROCOMPUTER SOFTWARE: DATABASES

8. Microcomputer Systems Development 224

9. Working With Databases 256

PART IV. MICROCOMPUTER SOFTWARE: ELECTRONIC SPREADSHEETS

Preface

THE VALUE OF THIS TEXT

Microcomputers are everywhere. Already, more than 10 million microcomputers are being used by business organizations and individuals. Eventually, the number of microcomputers in use may rival the number of automobiles.

This text recognizes the realities of the microcomputer impact on society and provides a unique basis for matching educational curricula to the realities of present-day student needs.

MICROCOMPUTERS: Concepts and Applications may be used for virtually any course that teaches the use of microcomputer software. Students with little or no computer experience will profit from the hardware and software concepts emphasized throughout the text.

SPECIAL GOALS OF THIS TEXT

After completing use of this text, the author hopes that you will be able to:

- Apply the hardware and software concepts of information systems and, more particularly, of microcomputers.
- Develop skills necessary to use major commercial microcomputer software.
- Understand the capabilities and limitations of current microcomputer systems, software, and hardware.
- Select appropriate microcomputer software and hardware to help you solve problems.
- Develop an understanding of computer and microcomputer terminology.

Computers are no longer new or novel. Today's educators and students are aware that computers are a pervading part of their environment, a challenge with which they must learn to deal. This book is filled with cases that relate computers to life experiences with which students already are familiar.

Most existing texts are dominated by a large-system viewpoint and large-system thinking. As one example, descriptions of systems development methodologies in most existing introductory texts feature a life-cycle approach. This methodology grew up around and is applicable almost exclusively to systems involving mainframe computers, large user populations, and teams of programmers developing tailored application software. Realities of computer utilization look different today and students should be accorded a view of things the way they are and will be when they enter the job market.

The current workplace is dominated by managers and other computer users who interact with the world of computers through small, relatively simple microcomputers. Millions of microcomputers are standard working tools found on desks of executives, middle managers, secretaries, and other clerical personnel. Many thousands of salespeople carry microcomputers that permit recording of orders right in customer facilities. Doctors and nurses now annotate patient diagnoses and treatments directly on microcomputer keyboards. This book will help you acquire the necessary tools to work with the microcomputer.

It is true that large computers are getting bigger and more powerful and that the databases they manage are more inclusive. But the threshold that provides the most common avenue of access to computer power is the microcomputer.

AN EFFECTIVE STUDENT PERSPECTIVE

This isn't to say that microcomputers represent the whole story or the total picture that students need to master to gain necessary computer application proficiency. Rather, the point is that the time has come when microcomputers hold the key to the perspective on computing that should be the focal point of introductory-level courses.

This text establishes a realistic outlook that builds understanding from the student's vantage point. This perspective holds that a microcomputer is a full-scale computer that contains all of the components and characteristics of any other computer system. Therefore, the microcomputer, rather than the mainframe, is used to establish the frame of reference within which students are encouraged to make themselves comfortable in the world of computing. Mainframe computers and large-scale systems are present, and are seen from the vantage point occupied by the typical user who is not a computer professional.

Because of the microcomputer-based vantage point, this book is appropriate for introductory courses that serve either prospective computer information system (CIS) or management information system (MIS) majors. Yet, the text is equally appropriate for students majoring in other areas that can range from business to general education and can include persons whose dominant interests lie in social sciences, humanities, or language-based disciplines.

SPECIAL FEATURES

This book has been developed from a strong, systems-oriented perspective. That is, emphasis is less on what microcomputers are and more on what they can do for people in a variety of situations.

Throughout the book, heavy use is made of case scenarios that enable students to "walk through" realistic situations involving development and use of microcomputer-based systems. The narratives are interspersed heavily with illustrations of menus, screen prompts, and other software-implemented tools that hold the key to effective microcomputer utilization. This approach is part of a recognition that users encounter and master applications of microcomputers through the features implemented by standard software packages. Further, the successful penetration of microcomputers into the business market has been based primarily on the availability of software packages that enable the machines to do what large numbers of people want.

Because of this perspective, separate, complete sections of the text are devoted to sequences of chapters that introduce and present cases on the major categories of software: word processing, databases, and electronic spreadsheets. A separate sequence of chapters covers other categories of software tools, including operating systems, integrated packages, desktop publishing and graphics, data communication, and decision support and expert systems.

Pedagogical Features

Complete sets of study and reinforcement aids are incorporated within all chapters of the text:

- Each chapter begins with a review of KEY IDEAS. This summary provides a conceptual overview of the content within the chapter and the learning experiences that can be anticipated.

- At the conclusion of each chapter is a list of key terms that students should have mastered. In turn, all the terms on these lists are defined in the glossary at the end of the text. Thus, the lists of terms provide a significant key to learning potential.

- End-of-chapter review materials include quizzes involving definitions of terms, true/false questions, short essay/discussion questions, and research- or reference-based projects.

Software Tutorial

The software version of this text includes a tutorial by Keiko M. Pitter. Four diskettes are included in the software version. These present educational versions of three popular, commercial packages for use on IBM PC and compatible microcomputers:

- WordPerfect (4.2)
- SuperCalc3 (3.0)
- dBASE III PLUS.

In addition, an introductory module of the software tutorial covers the features of DOS that students must master for effective use of IBM PC or compatible microcomputers.

To complete the tutorial, each student also must have a formatted, blank disk for storage of personally produced data.

The hardware requirement for the software programs is an IBM PC or compatible system with two disk drives and 256K of RAM memory.

Microcomputer Lab Manual

The text also is compatible with a companion lab manual that provides an in-depth series of microcomputer laboratory assignments through use of generic, easily mastered software. The software, designed especially for student skill-building, is called LEARNware. The companion lab manual is entitled **USING LEARNware.**

CONTENT ORGANIZATION

Content of this text is organized into five parts, plus the software tutorial addendum to the software edition.

Part One—Microcomputers

The initial part of your text is for getting acquainted. The cumulative effect of the content of the chapters in this part should be to establish a personal comfort level.

The first chapter deals with the impact and importance of computers. Computers are here. It is almost as likely that you will have to learn to use a microcomputer as it is that you will learn to drive a car.

Chapters 2 and 3 deal with what microcomputers do and how they are used. Chapters 4 and 5 round out this first part of your text by describing the units of equipment, or devices, that make up a computer system. The functions and interactions of these devices are covered.

Part Two—Microcomputer Software: Word Processors

Word processing software packages were the first to establish popularity and promote widespread sales of microcomputers. This part of the book contains two chapters that describe the elements of word processing packages and illustrate how word processing programs are put to use through an in-depth case study. The examples presented might well fit into your own requirements as a student or in a later career. A final, useful element of the presentations in this part is a description of techniques that you can apply in evaluating and purchasing a word processing package for your own use.

Part Three—Microcomputer Software: Databases

Database software occupies a special niche in promoting the use of microcomputers. This is because virtually all computer-based information systems, of all sizes, center around the organization, collection, storage, and use of data.

Because of this importance, the initial chapter in this part of your text describes the processes for developing computer systems generally and also the special considerations associated with development of microcomputer-based systems. This discussion of systems development helps to establish a basis for understanding and use of database packages.

The remaining two chapters in this part cover the principles of database management systems (DBMS) for microcomputers and also present case situations to demonstrate the place for DBMS software and realistic techniques for building systems. An in-depth discussion deals with techniques for evaluating and buying DBMS application packages for your microcomputer.

Part Four—Microcomputer Software: Electronic Spreadsheets

Spreadsheet software is responsible for a major breakthrough that has been achieved by microcomputers: Spreadsheets have been the main justification for putting microcomputers on desks of executives and managers.

The chapters in this part of your text deal with spreadsheet capabilities and provide extensive examples of spreadsheet applications. In addition, there is a set of guidelines you can use for evaluating and purchasing spreadsheet software packages.

Part Five—More Microcomputer Software

The chapters in this part of your text deal with a variety of other microcomputer software packages that you may encounter in the workplace or may find personally useful.

Chapter 13 is about microcomputer operating systems, their role, capabilities, and features that you must master to use microcomputer application programs.

Chapter 14 deals with software integration, the special packages that make it possible for a user to switch from one job to another—conveniently and without loss of data.

Chapter 15 is about the growing field of desktop publishing, the ability to create entire publications with microcomputer systems. Also covered are the capabilities of graphics software packages available for use on microcomputers.

Chapter 16 reviews capabilities of hardware devices and software packages that, together, turn a microcomputer into a data communication system. Communication is an important and growing aspect of microcomputer use.

Chapter 17 covers specialized management uses of microcomputer software packages. The discussion deals with management information systems, decision support systems, and expert or knowledge-based systems.

Instructor's Manual

A comprehensive set of classroom management tools is included in the Instructor's Manual that accompanies this text. The Instructor's Manual corresponds closely with the text. For each text chapter, a corresponding chapter of the Instructor's Manual contains:

- An extensive set of review/lecture notes begins each chapter of the Instructor's Manual. These notes are built around the student knowledge base. That is, the set of KEY IDEAS at the beginning of each chapter of the student text are incorporated in the lecture notes for ease of reference. In this way, the instructor can build presentations from a base of student familiarity. In addition, however, the lecture notes are supplemented with materials that add to the content of the student notes and also suggest points of emphasis or questions that can be used as classroom discussion starters.

- Answers to all questions included in the text are provided within each corresponding chapter of the Instructor's Manual.

In addition, general content provided at the end of the Instructor's Manual includes:

- An extensive test bank for instructor use
- Transparency masters for key illustrations within the text, provided both in the Instructor's Manual and as a separate set of overhead projection transparencies ready for your use.

STUDENT BENEFITS

The main benefit to students to be derived from use of this text is ***confidence.*** This text puts the world of computers generally and microcomputers in particular into a framework that students can understand. Any technical terms used are defined in context at the point of introduction. The abundance of cases are selected and built to promote comprehension.

If this text is used in conjunction with the integrated application software or accompanying lab materials, students can move a long way toward the building of employable skills.

ACKNOWLEDGMENTS

An important contribution to the quality of this book came from Dr. Don B. Medley, Chairman, Computer Information Systems, California State Polytechnic Institute, Pomona. Dr. Medley contributed far more than the requirements of his accepted assignment, a compliance review on behalf of DPMA. His great store of knowledge, both technical and application-oriented, enhanced the quality of the text.

Many other reviewers helped in the early shaping and development of **MICROCOMPUTERS.** A very special thanks is due for the creative work of the following persons: Denise Avinger, Texas State Technical Institution; Marilyn Bohl, IBM; Barbara B. Denison, Wright State University; E. James Dunne, University of Dayton; Donald L. Haney, St. Mary's University; Milton W. Harden, University of South Carolina, Salkehatchie University Campus; Dr. Thomas E. Herbert, California State University, Sacramento; Sue Krimm, Pierce College, Los Angeles; Donald C. Lyndahl, Milwaukee Area Technical College; William L. O'Hare, Prince George's Community College; Herbert F. Rebhun,

University of Houston, Downtown; and Carol Saunders, Texas Christian University.

Benedict Kruse of i/e, inc., Arleta, California, supervised development and editing of the manuscript for this text. His editorial contributions have helped both to make this book possible and to assure a high level of quality.

Production supervision that helped to maintain the high standards targeted for this book and also to bring the project to completion on time was provided by Karon Morgan French of i/e, inc.

DPMA Endorsement

Completeness of topical coverage for this text is assured by its endorsement by the Data Processing Management Association (DPMA). The book is designed to support the CIS-2 course in DPMA CURRICULUM '86. The text has been developed under guidelines established by DPMA and has undergone a review designed specifically to establish its suitability for support of the CIS-2 course.

The CIS-2 course description itself represents a departure for information systems education. The course supported by this book can be recognized either as a second offering that supplements a general introduction or as an alternative. That is, the CIS-2 course can be substituted for the traditional, general introduction. The content of this text is strong enough and inclusive enough for use with either an introductory course in computer applications or a second course that stresses microcomputer-based skills.

Trademarks

Apple and the Apple logo are registered trademarks of Apple Computer, Inc.
CompuServe Information Service is a registered trademark of CompuServe, Inc.
dBase III PLUS is a registered trademark of Ashton-Tate.
Dow-Jones News/Retrieval is a registered trademark of Dow-Jones & Company, Inc.
Hayes Smartmodem and Smartcom II are trademarks of Hayes Microcomputer Products, Inc.
IBM and IBM PC are registered trademarks of International Business Machines Corporation.
Lotus and 1-2-3 are registered trademarks of Lotus Development Corporation.
Macintosh is a trademark licensed to Apple Computer, Inc.
MacLink is a trademark of Dataviz, Inc.

Photo Essay Credits

Hardware

Page 1: Anacomp, Inc. **Page 3:** Universal Data Systems, Hewlett Packard. **Pages 4–5:** Prime Computer, Inc., American Airlines, Apple Computer, Inc., International Business Machines Corporation, American Airlines. **Pages 6–7:** Ramtek Corporation, Hewlett Packard, International Business Machines Corporation, Apple Computer, Inc. **Pages 8–9:** Apple Computer, Inc., Apple Computer, Inc., Digital Equipment Corporation, Sun Microsystems. **Pages 10–11:** Digital Equipment Corporation, CRAY Research, Inc., Interleaf, Inc. **Pages 12–13:** Anacomp, Inc., Xerox Corporation, Xerox Corporation, Hewlett Packard. **Pages 14–15:** L.A. Schwaber-Barzilay, AT&T Company, Hewlett Packard.

The Chip

Page 1: International Business Machines Corporation. **Pages 2–3:** Chuck O'Rear, Chuck O'Rear, Chuck O'Rear, Ramtek Corporation. **Pages 4–5:** Chuck O'Rear, Intel Corporation, Intel Corporation, Chuck O'Rear. **Pages 6–7:** Chuck O'Rear, Intel Corporation, Intel Corporation, Intel Corporation. **Pages 8–9:** Intel Corporation, AT&T Company, Intel Corporation, Intel Corporation, Intel Corporation, Chuck O'Rear, Hewlett Packard. **Pages 10–11:** Hewlett Packard, AT&T Company, Intel Corporation, Hewlett Packard. **Pages 12–13:** RCA, National Semiconductor Corporation, Intel Corporation, L.A. Schwaber-Barzilay. **Pages 14–15:** Motorola, L.A. Schwaber-Barzilay, L.A. Schwaber-Barzilay, Hewlett Packard, Hewlett Packard. **Page 16:** National Semiconductor Corporation.

Microcomputers

All photos for this section are by Liane Enkelis.

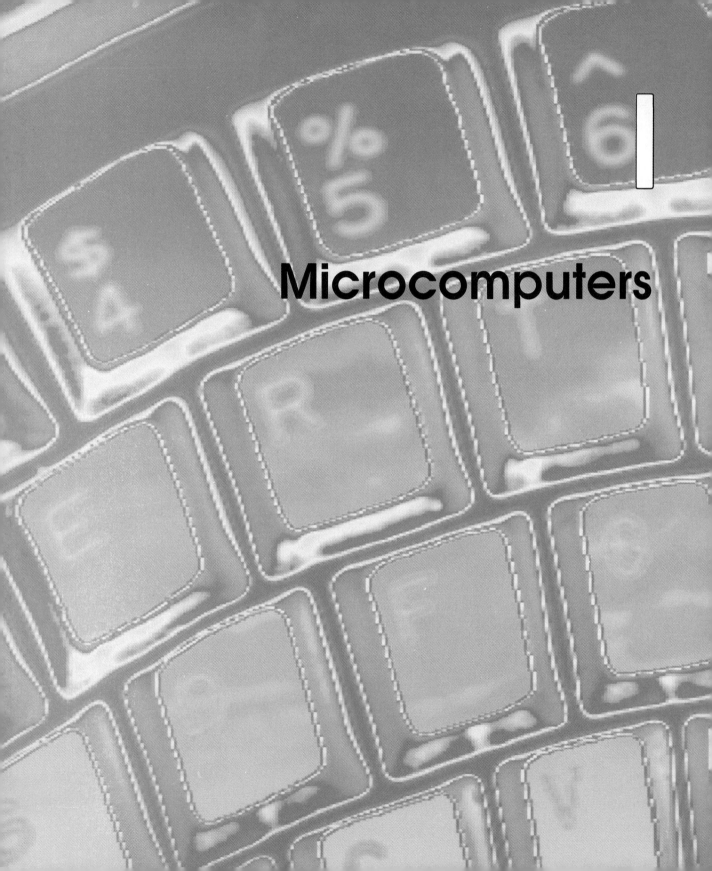

Microcomputers

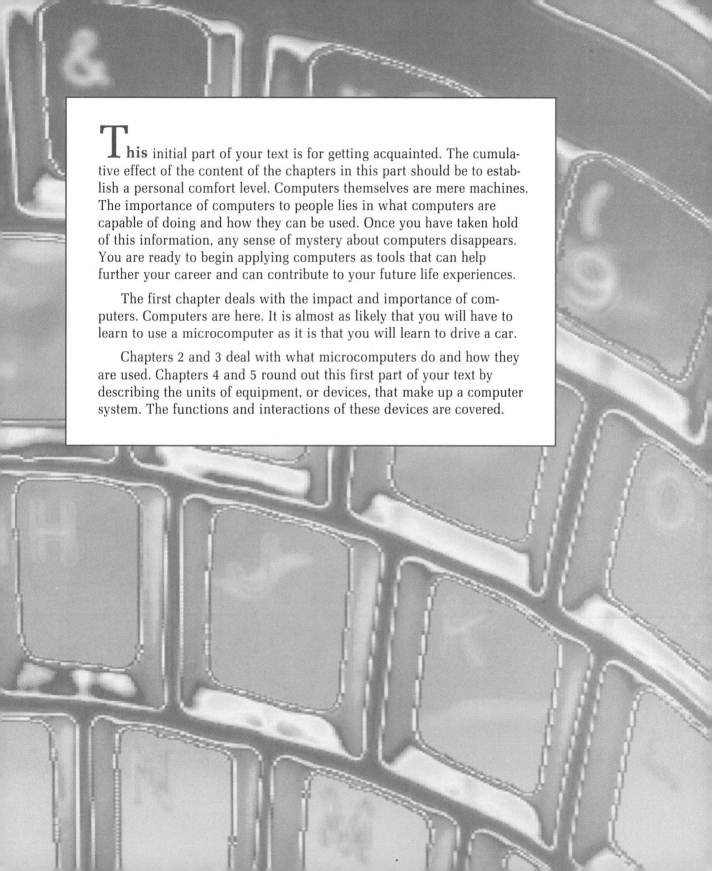

This initial part of your text is for getting acquainted. The cumulative effect of the content of the chapters in this part should be to establish a personal comfort level. Computers themselves are mere machines. The importance of computers to people lies in what computers are capable of doing and how they can be used. Once you have taken hold of this information, any sense of mystery about computers disappears. You are ready to begin applying computers as tools that can help further your career and can contribute to your future life experiences.

The first chapter deals with the impact and importance of computers. Computers are here. It is almost as likely that you will have to learn to use a microcomputer as it is that you will learn to drive a car.

Chapters 2 and 3 deal with what microcomputers do and how they are used. Chapters 4 and 5 round out this first part of your text by describing the units of equipment, or devices, that make up a computer system. The functions and interactions of these devices are covered.

1 The Microcomputer Revolution

KEY IDEAS

SMALL COMPUTERS, BIG IMPACT

A knowledge of microcomputers and their uses has become a requirement for most working people.

A Matter of Scale

Microcomputers have simplified computerized information processing; anyone with basic skills can generate results from a microcomputer.

A TOOL FOR WHAT?

Microcomputers have succeeded, in part, because the range of requirements to which they can be applied is so vast.

THE PLACE FOR MICROCOMPUTERS

Microcomputer evolution has been cyclical: Demands lead to hardware or software developments which, in turn, lead to further demand-solution cycles.

Introduction and Acceptance

The breakthrough development for microcomputers has been the microprocessor, a complete computer processor on a fingernail-size chip.

MICROCOMPUTERS FOR MEETING NEEDS

The microcomputer revolution has been motivated by the successful application of microcomputer tools to three major requirements: correspondence, organizational planning, and decentralized processing.

CORRESPONDENCE

Microcomputer tools can streamline the process of creating and producing documents.

Word Processing

Storage inefficiencies inherent with using mainframe computers to handle text are inconsequential for microcomputer systems.

ORGANIZATIONAL BUDGETING, PLANNING, AND DECISION MAKING

Spreadsheets are tools for presenting data in comparative formats and have been used for many decades as planning and budgeting tools.

Electronic Spreadsheets

Electronic spreadsheet packages have streamlined the process of producing spreadsheets and have introduced microcomputers to decision makers.

DECENTRALIZED PROCESSING

Computer tools are most effective when implemented by people who produce information or use processing results.

Microcomputers are inexpensive and compact enough to be installed at virtually any location at which data-handling requirements exist.

SMALL COMPUTERS, BIG IMPACT

The early space missions of the late 1950s and early 1960s were supported by the largest computer systems available at the time. Behemoth computers occupied multiple rooms, occasionally entire buildings. These systems, regarded as large-scale marvels, were delivered with 64,000 characters (64K) of main memory and perhaps 50 million characters (megabytes) of storage. In the early 1960s, each large computer represented an investment that could run into millions of dollars.

Today, you may well be harnessing processing capacities like those described above in the ignition and suspension systems of your automobile. Certainly, you can put many times that capacity into a microcomputer that fits onto a desk top or into a compact work station. As a further comparison, consider this: Today, for roughly $2,000, you can go to a retail store and buy a microcomputer that has equivalent or greater capabilities than the computers that supported the launch of the first space satellites. (See Figure 1-1.)

The connection between computers and automobiles makes for an interesting comparison. In the United States and other industrial nations, microcomputers are being delivered in greater numbers than automobiles. Ultimately, microcomputers may well outnumber automobiles. Microcomputers also will affect the lives of most people at least as dramatically as did the automobile.

The automobile has shaped the development of the United States and the lifestyles of its people. Similarly, microcomputers already have generated many changes in the workplace. The majority of microcomputers are sold to businesses. Most people who work now use computers or the information generated by computers. This trend is so strong that the United States often is called an Information Society.

In this sense, the impacts of the automobile and the microcomputer have some parallels. The great majority of adults regard driving as a necessary skill. In the same way, a knowledge of microcomputers and their uses is becoming a requirement for the majority of successful people.

A Matter of Scale

One reason why microcomputers have achieved universal success is that they are understandable. Computers are relatively new on the business and technology scenes. An early electronic computer handled calculations for the 1950 census. It is considered the first time computer capabilities were applied to a practical *application,* or task. The first computer to handle commercial processing was installed by General Electric in 1952. Figure 1-2 shows a computer installation of the 1950s.

Figure 1-1.

A typical microcomputer provides capabilities equivalent to systems that supported satellite launches in the 1950s.
COURTESY OF INDEX TECHNOLOGY CORPORATION

From this starting point through the decade of the 1960s, computers maintained their image as large, forbidding technological giants. Working with computers was considered a specialty of technical wizards and beyond the understanding of regular people. The computers themselves were surrounded by a mystique that made them unapproachable to home or office users.

Even with the introduction of so-called minicomputers in the late 1960s and early 1970s, computers retained their forbidding image. In part, this was because of the difficulties involved in putting a computer to work. Before people and computers could come together, special **programs** had to be written. Programs are sets of instructions that direct the operation of computers. Cumulatively, sets of programs are called **software** while computer equipment is known as **hardware.**

Writing software and installing hardware for a major computer system could take one to two years. Once a system was installed, operators were limited to performing specific tasks. That is, large systems were set up to produce specific results according to a designated sequence of processing tasks. To alter or direct this sequence as needs arose—or according to the needs of different applications—was impractical.

Microcomputers broke these barriers of inaccessibility. Microcomputers didn't require a platoon of experts between the equipment and its prospective users. To the contrary, microcomputers could be bought in retail computer stores that quickly became as familiar as automotive showrooms.

Along with the microcomputer, the market was swept by a new kind of technology that served to make computers understandable to people. This new development took the form of packaged software. It became possible simply to load a diskette into the computer and tell the machine what to do. This simple task is illustrated in Figure 1-3. Computers were ready to serve people. This was a major reversal of roles in the eyes of many people who saw computers as forbidding technical giants.

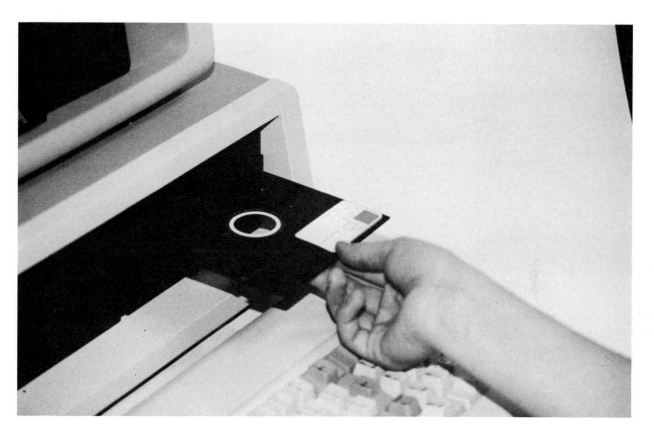

Here again, the comparison of the automobile and the computer holds up. Early automobiles were engineering and technical complexities. Before an early-day driver could go anywhere, he or she had to set several controls, then heave on a large crank that started the engine. The automobile needed friendly technology before it could gain universal acceptance. This came when Charles F. "Boss" Kettering, one of the founders of General Motors, invented the self-starter. Starting an automobile became as easy as turning a switch. The barriers fell and the automobile quickly became a necessity of modern life.

In a similar breakthrough, George Eastman introduced a concept for roll film that could be carried into a store for others to develop. This eliminated the need to coat glass photographic plates individually, by hand. Eastman sold simplicity. His slogan for the Eastman Kodak Company became: "You press the button. We do the rest."

Microcomputers, basically, have taken the mystery out of information processing. (See Figure 1-4.) Anyone with basic capabilities to read, write, and use numbers can get results from a microcomputer. All it takes is an understanding of the processes you control. If you can understand that an accelerator pedal

Figure 1-3.

Software packages contain instructions recorded on diskettes; users simply insert a diskette and they are ready to produce results.

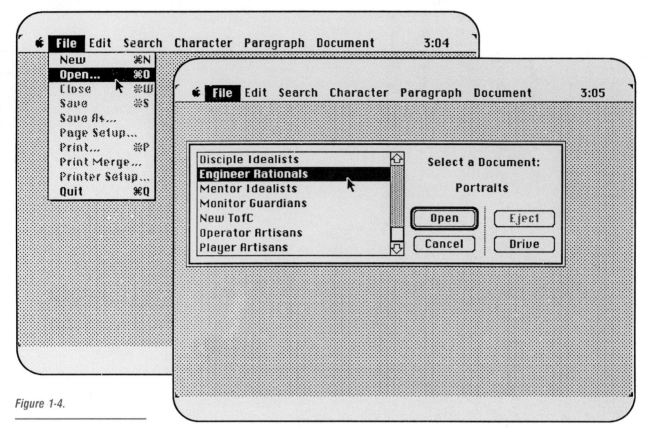

Figure 1-4.

Microcomputer software is designed to provide users with processing choices, through displays called menus. Users implement services by making selections from among these choices.

makes a car go faster and a brake pedal makes it slow down, you can build an understanding of computers and put them to work in building yourself a better, more secure future. That's what this book is all about.

A TOOL FOR WHAT?

Microcomputers, first and foremost, are tools. As tools, the special characteristic about microcomputers is that you can master them.

To master the use of microcomputers, it is necessary to understand what kind of work microcomputers do, and for whom. At a basic level, the power of any computer lies in its ability to store and process data. Data items take the form of letters of the alphabet, numbers, and special characters such as punctuation marks and symbols ($, %, +, -, <, >, @, and others). Individually or in small, related sets, these characters represent people, places, things, or events and are known as *items* of data. Examples of *data items* include names, addresses, prices, part numbers, and so on.

A list of names and addresses on the back of an envelope is a collection of data items. Similar listings in an address book also are a collection of data items.

Both can be used for the same purpose: to store names, addresses, and telephone numbers of friends or other important people.

Address books and envelopes can be used as tools for storing data items. Tools are chosen according to the requirements of the job to be performed. The capacity of an envelope is limited. As the number of listings grows, an address book becomes more suitable. In addition, the listings in an address book can be indexed for easy access. An address book might be replaced with a card file if further entries exceed the capacity of the book.

However, consider the requirements for maintaining collections of data items in a company with 50,000 customers who buy any of 300,000 products. A typical description of a customer might contain several items of data: name, street address, city, state, ZIP code, name of contact person, telephone number, and the amount of credit the customer has established. Each of these is a separate data item, also known as a **data element** or **field.** A set of elements or fields may be needed to describe a single customer or product. This collection of data elements about the same person, event, or thing is known as a **record.** Collections of related records are grouped to form **files.** That is, the collection of customer records makes up a customer file. The relationship among characters, fields, records, and files is illustrated in Figure 1-5.

Continuing the example, a record would be set up within a computer system for each of the 50,000 customers and 300,000 products. Records would be grouped to form files. The organization using the system then would establish performance standards for handling these files. For example, it might be standard to expect to be able to retrieve any given record from a massive computer file in one-quarter to one-half second.

Maintaining and using files of this magnitude add up to a big job. Therefore, a company with this many records to maintain and process would need a big computer. In data processing terminology, jobs with massive file and transaction volumes need a large-scale, or **mainframe,** computer.

Notice the difference in scale between the capacities of a mainframe and the capacities of an address book or card file. Business tools—which range from address books to mainframe computers—are implements for solving business problems or meeting business needs. There is an enormous range of requirements for which manual methods (address books and card files) and mainframes are inappropriate. It is within this range that smaller computers have been introduced and have been accepted in great numbers.

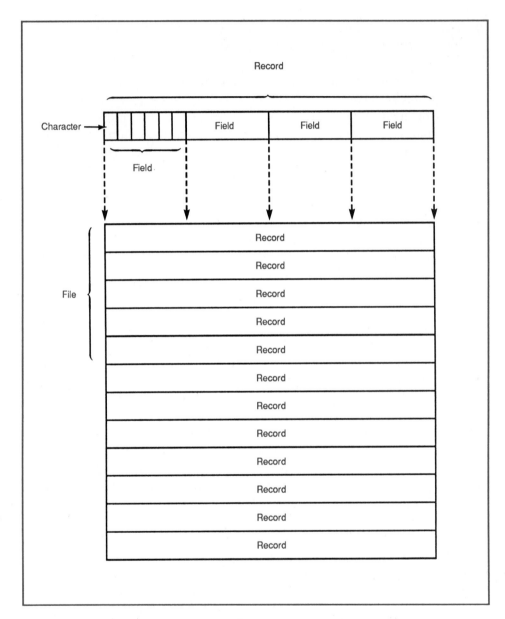

Figure 1-5.

Data items consist of letters, numbers, and special characters. In turn, data items are used to create records. Files are made up of groups of related records.

One intermediate size of computer, which enjoyed great success during the 1960s, is the minicomputer. A minicomputer, in effect, occupies the high end of the gap between the mainframe and the lead pencil. However, minicomputers still can run up costs of tens or hundreds of thousands of dollars. Also, as is the case with mainframes, systems that lend themselves to operation on minicomputers tend to require extensive planning and programming before they can be put to work.

Figure 1-6.

Microcomputers meet a wide range of needs. This system is used in hospitals to support the patients' diagnosis and treatment.

COURTESY OF HEWLETT PACKARD

THE PLACE FOR MICROCOMPUTERS

After minicomputers were introduced, a need emerged in the low end of the gap between mainframes and lead pencils. Users wanted simple electronic systems that could be implemented inexpensively and with the simplicity of a toaster or refrigerator. When microcomputers filled this need, it turned out that the total market for small systems was possibly as large as for minicomputers and mainframes combined.

Another reason for the universal acceptance of microcomputers is that the range of requirements to which they can be applied is so vast. In other words, the microcomputer is the right tool for countless business jobs. This point, illustrated in Figure 1-6, is given major emphasis throughout this text. That is, microcomputers, like mainframes or minicomputers, are tools for solving problems and meeting needs.

Similarly, there are jobs that might take a microcomputer hours that can be completed in minutes on a mainframe. Thus, microcomputers and mainframes often are used by businesses in the same way. Mainframes are appropriate for tasks that require large capacities. For smaller, lower-volume tasks, microcomputers are the right tool.

From mainframes to microcomputers, the evolution of computer technology has been driven by the needs of people to do jobs. Typically, technological development evolves through repetitions of what can be called a demand-solution cycle. The cycle begins when people realize that their job performance can be improved by improving the capabilities of their tools. That is, people express a demand for better technology than is available currently.

At the next stage in the cycle, existing technology is improved or new technology is developed to meet the demand. As users become experienced with the new tool, their proficiency increases, as well as their demands for additional capabilities. The cycle then repeats.

Consider again the automobile. The first automobiles traveled at roughly 20 miles per hour, on primitive roads built originally for horsedrawn carriages. As the convenience and advantages of automobile travel became apparent, people wanted to travel farther, in less time. Faster automobiles were built, demands increased further. Roads were improved. Smoother roads meant that automobiles could be made more comfortable and even faster. The demand-solution cycle reiterated until it became possible to travel from Boston to San Francisco on a four-lane concrete superhighway. Although speeds are legislated, most automobiles are capable of attaining speeds exceeding 100 miles per hour.

Introduction and Acceptance

In many respects, the evolution of microcomputers has been even more dramatic than the evolution of the automobile. In 1975, an advertisement in *Popular Electronics* magazine offered an early microcomputer. The machine, the Altair 8800 had 256,000 **bytes,** or characters, of internal memory, no external storage, no keyboard, and no display screen. To operate this machine, data and programs were entered in code, through a series of toggle switches. Results, or **outputs,** took the form of blinking lights that had to be decoded, or interpreted, to be useful.

External storage refers to the capability for storing data and/or programs in a permanent or semi-permanent form. The lack of external storage in the Altair 8800 meant that every time the machine was turned off, the content of internal memory was lost. There was no way to store data and/or programs electronically. To complicate matters further, Altair machines were delivered in kit form, connections were soldered and machines assembled by buyers. See Figure 1-7.

ALTAIR 8800
The most powerful minicomputer project ever presented—can be built for under $400

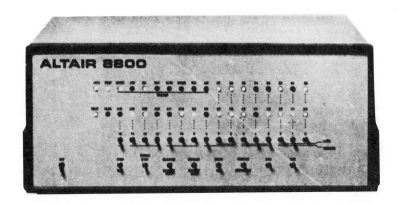

Figure 1-7.

The Altair, an early microcomputer, was purchased as a kit, assembled by users, and was operated through complicated encoding and decoding of switches and lights.

During this same time frame, a major new technology set the stage for mass production of microcomputers. Intel Corporation announced the availability of its "computer on a chip." The breakthrough lay in the fact that microcircuits had been reduced in size so that a complete computer processor could be packaged on a wafer of silicon smaller than one of your fingernails. The compression of size for computer processors also led to a compression of costs for complete computers. With the advent of the microprocessor, a situation developed in which, it seemed, the microcomputer was waiting to be invented.

Shortly thereafter, two teenagers named Steve—Wozniak and Jobs—developed the Apple I microcomputer in a garage in Northern California. The Apple I featured a keyboard for input, a display screen, external storage, and an optional printer to produce outputs. In short, the Apple I was a computer that you could plug in, insert a **disk** (for external storage), and begin to generate results. The Apple I was an unprecedented success—and signaled the beginning of the microcomputer revolution.

Since that time, computer technology has evolved rapidly. Microcomputer systems currently are available with up to a megabyte (one million bytes) of internal memory, 40 or more megabytes of external storage, and a wide variety of input and output devices. In fact, the availability and variety of **peripheral devices** has reduced the process of designing microcomputer **systems** to a series of equipment and software selections.

The term, system, refers to a collection of people, data, equipment, programs, and procedures that are brought together to produce desired results. Note that people come first. People develop and use computer systems to meet human needs. Computers—any computers of any size—are tools for people. It also is true that different people, and different organizations need different tools. People develop needs; systems using microcomputers often provide solutions.

MICROCOMPUTERS FOR MEETING NEEDS

Three major needs have led to the sales avalanche that has seen microcomputers installed in business offices by the millions. These needs include:

- Correspondence
- Organizational budgeting, planning, and decision making
- Decentralized processing, or the distribution of processing capabilities to points at which data items are created and handled.

CORRESPONDENCE

In a basic sense, virtually all people and organizations are required to communicate. An organization must maintain relationships with vendors, creditors, employees, and customers. For example, to offer a product or service for sale, descriptions must be prepared for potential customers. Raw materials or supplies must be purchased from vendors. Employees must be instructed to produce and/or prepare the goods and services involved. All these activities involve communication.

Business communication takes two forms: oral and written. Oral communication is through spoken words. For example, a manager informs employees of their daily assignments. A salesperson might call a customer to set up an appointment for a sales demonstration. A customer might call a vendor for information concerning a new product line. This type of oral exchange is vital to the conduct of any business. In fact, spoken words are the most common form of business communication, and the most common communication tool in businesses is the telephone.

Oral communication meets transient needs. That is, spoken words are impermanent and may not carry the same weight as written or printed words—**text.** Many situations require permanent or semi-permanent records of communicated messages. Under different circumstances, text documents can be used to reinforce spoken communication.

The production of text on documents is a major requirement—and expense—for businesses. Sales letters, internal memos, contracts, and any type of business

May 12, 1987

Mr. John Moreno
1511 Monte Vista
San Diego, CA 92565

Dear Mr. Moreno:

Thank you for your recent order for our home improvement
catalog. In it, you will find hundreds of ideas and products
for improving the ~~quality~~ and safety of your home.

When ordering products from the catalog, just use the order
form provided at the end of the catalog. If you have any
questions about billing or payments, just call our home
office in Chicago (TOLL FREE: 1-800-555-1234). We guarantee
your order will be filled in four to six weeks.

Thank you again. We look forward to doing business with you.

Sincerely,

Rhonda Gardner
Director of Sales

Editing changes

used to require that documents
be retyped completely. With
microcomputer word processing
packages, only the changes
need be entered. Retyping is
automatic.

letter involves the production of textual documents. Before computers were developed, the main method for producing text involved manual or electric typewriters.

Typewriters provide major advantages over pens and pencils. Typewritten characters are consistent, neat, and easy to read. Typewriters also have limited capabilities for producing multiple copies of the same document.

On the other hand, typewriter-based document production can be a repetitive, costly process. The creation of text documents usually involves a series of *drafts.* A draft is a preliminary version of a document subject to changes, revisions, and corrections.

Several drafts may be required before an acceptable final version is produced. Initially, an executive might dictate the content of a document to an administrative assistant. The assistant then types a first draft and presents it to the executive for editing. During the editing process, several drafts may be produced and revised. Succeeding drafts also are typewritten. Each retyping operation increases the chances of human errors. Errors, of course, are unacceptable, and with each error the entire draft may be retyped still again. In other words, manual production methods are repetitive and inefficient. Under these methods, a text document may be typed and retyped four or six times before a final version is accepted.

Computers provide capabilities to streamline this process. With computerized tools, documents are **keyed,** or captured, once. Changes, revisions, and corrections can be made electronically. The editing process involves only the pertinent portions of text—the need to re-key the entire document is eliminated.

Figure 1-8.

Use of storage capacity is efficient when the objects to be stored are of uniform shapes and sizes.

COURTESY OF SPACESAVER
CORPORATION

Word Processing

The creation and handling of text documents with computer tools is known as **word processing** or **text processing.** However, computers had been available for almost two decades before word processing gained wide acceptance in business organizations. Storage considerations delayed the development of word processing applications until microcomputers solved a storage problem.

To illustrate, consider the difference between stacking regularly shaped boxes and stacking objects of indeterminate shapes. See Figure 1-8. Square boxes can be stacked alongside and on top of each other with minimal wasted space. Objects that lack uniformity, however, do not stack neatly and use of storage area is inefficient and wasteful.

This principle also applies to the storage of data and text with microcomputer tools. Data items are predictable in terms of length and structure. For example, a social security number consists of nine numeric characters. A ZIP code has either five or nine numbers. A one-letter designation can be used to describe the sex of a person (M or F). Even names can be accommodated in fixed-length spaces. For example, 25 character positions can be set aside for names. If names have fewer than 25 characters, blank spaces exist; longer names can be abbreviated. The point is that data items fit fixed spaces. Each item has a **fixed length.** Storage requirements are relatively predictable and manageable.

In contrast, consider the haphazard nature of the use of words, or text, for human communication. Words are collections of letter characters. Words, in

Floppy disks

made it economical and feasible to produce and store text documents on microcomputers.

Figure 1-9.

Floppy disks make it possible to store and find massive collections of information in ordinary office files.

turn, are grouped to form other structures, such as sentences and paragraphs, to convey a message. Unlike data, text is stored in areas of unpredictable, or variable, lengths. Because of these irregularities, text storage in computer systems is less efficient than data storage. See Figure 1-9.

The cost of microcomputer storage, however, fell within a range at which cost inefficiencies were offset by increases in production and convenience. Microcomputers do not store text any more efficiently than large computers. However, microcomputers store data and text on relatively inexpensive—and compact—floppy or hard disks. Economies of scale were achieved by implementing word processing on small systems. That is, the inefficiency of text storage became inconsequential—and word processing applications were implemented in business offices worldwide.

The section that follows presents a scenario of microcomputer tools applied to the creation and production of text documents.

```
DOCUMENT: fig1-10                    |PAGE:  1|LINE:  1|COL:  1|
|1..».....».....»...........................................«
«
«
«
├date┤«
«
«
├title┤ ├first name┤ ├last name┤«
├street address┤«
├city state zip┤«
«
Dear ├title┤ ├last name┤«
«
Welcome to the neighborhood!  Now that you have settled into your new
home, you probably will be digging into the yard work that your home
demands.  We'd like to help you with the chores faced by all homeowners:
landscaping, yard maintenance, and gardening care.«
«
Morgan's Landscaping has been serving this community for over 15 years.
We provide regular gardening and yard maintenance services to our
customers, as well as landscape and garden consulting services.  We feel
we can meet any needs you may have as a homeowner--whether you like to do
your own gardening or have professionals do the work.«
```

Figure 1-10.

A microcomputer-based word processing system provides capabilities for producing form letters with "personalized" references to the addressee.

Word processing/power typing. As stated previously, word processing was a major factor for acceptance of microcomputers in businesses. The capabilities of word processors are dramatized by a type of application known as ***power typing,*** or ***mail merge.*** Power typing is an efficient method for creating form letters, or letters that convey the same message to multiple people. Because the body of a form letter is identical or closely similar for all parties, it becomes highly efficient to produce these letters with microcomputer tools.

For example, suppose you are appointed to a committee for organizing a "Getting Acquainted" luncheon for the parents of incoming freshmen to your school. A letter is written extending the invitation and providing other pertinent details. As a personal touch, all parents should receive individually typed letters.

Consider the performance of this task under manual methods. To eliminate the enormous task of retyping each letter, the body of the letter might be copied xerographically. This operation would save substantial amounts of time. However, parent names and addresses still would have to be typed individually on each letter and on each envelope. Consider also the appearance of a letter in which the heading is typed and the body is a xerographic copy.

Most word processors provide power typing capabilities. This feature allows a user to set up a file for the body of the letter and a secondary file for names and addresses. The system then is instructed to pull entries from the secondary file, and to insert each entry into a complete, individually printed letter. See Figure 1-10.

The entire process can be completed within a few hours. The finished letter sets a warm feeling, referring to addressees by name. Power typing also provides a method for printing names and addresses from the master file onto envelopes.

Microcomputer-based word processing tools succeeded, in part, because of the capabilities they provide. Similar capabilities spurred the development of other types of tools, such as electronic spreadsheets, discussed in the section that follows.

ORGANIZATIONAL BUDGETING, PLANNING, AND DECISION MAKING

As costs fell for both internal and external storage, it became practical to apply microcomputers to other tasks. For instance, the ability to edit data displayed on terminal screens simplifies the preparation of financial worksheets. Worksheets, or *spreadsheets,* are a means for presenting numeric data in comparative formats.

Spreadsheets have been prepared in business organizations for many decades. Before microcomputers entered the scene, spreadsheets were prepared on handwritten forms like the one in Figure 1-11. Like correspondence, spreadsheets usually are revised repeatedly. The work can be tedious—and becomes easier through use of electronic techniques and microcomputers.

At top organizational levels, executives and managers can be classified loosely as decision makers. That is, a major part of the activities of these personnel involve making decisions and plans that determine courses of action for the business. Many organizational plans involve receiving or spending money. Plans involving money are called *budgets* and are organized on spreadsheets.

Budgets present figures that reflect expected performance for a specific period. At the end of the budgeting period, these figures can be compared with other figures that represent actual performance during the period. Suppose, for example, that $500 is budgeted for raw materials during a 30-day period. At the end of 30 days, receipts for raw materials total $780. Actual performance exceeds expectations by more than 50 percent. This type of comparison gives decision makers a basis for identifying problem areas. Figure 1-12 shows a spreadsheet display on a microcomputer screen.

Spreadsheets are set up as vertical columns and horizontal rows. At the intersections of rows and columns, called *cells,* data items are entered. Notice that columns and rows are designated by *labels,* or *headings.* Labels identify entries that appear within the column or row. That is, the first row in Figure 1-12 is

	JANUARY	FEBRUARY	MARCH	APRIL	MAY
SALES	$94,587.92	$88,742.92	$93,821.88	$82,987.34	$95,875.23
COST OF GOODS SOLD	$31,764.34	$33,875.98	$34,342.82	$27,340.34	$34,582.77
GROSS INCOME	$62,823.58	$54,866.94	$59,479.06	$55,647.00	$61,292.46
MATERIALS	$2,345.55	$4,232.81	$1,874.44	$2,321.84	$4,875.33
LABOR	$18,428.44	$13,759.39	$21,234.33	$17,653.98	$19,876.35
EQUIPMENT	$12,874.22	$14,329.86	$13,654.97	$11,986.55	$13,629.07
OVERHEAD	$10,874.22	$9,654.45	$9,976.64	$10,943.92	$11,238.55
TOTAL COSTS	$44,522.43	$41,971.51	$46,640.38	$42,906.29	$49,619.30
NET INCOME	$18,301.15	$12,895.43	$12,838.68	$12,740.71	$11,673.16

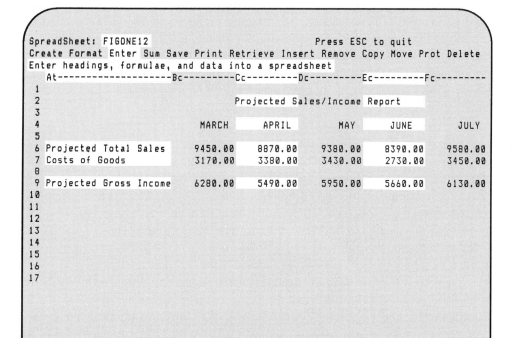

Figure 1-11.

The production of manual spreadsheets is a tedious task; erasures and corrections may create a sloppy appearance.

```
SpreadSheet: FIGONE12                        Press ESC to quit
Create Format Enter Sum Save Print Retrieve Insert Remove Copy Move Prot Delete
Enter headings, formulae, and data into a spreadsheet
   At--------------------Bc---------Cc---------Dc---------Ec---------Fc---------
 1
 2                        Projected Sales/Income Report
 3
 4                     MARCH      APRIL       MAY      JUNE       JULY
 5
 6  Projected Total Sales  9450.00    8870.00    9380.00    8390.00    9580.00
 7  Costs of Goods         3170.00    3380.00    3430.00    2730.00    3450.00
 8
 9  Projected Gross Income 6280.00    5490.00    5950.00    5660.00    6130.00
10
11
12
13
14
15
16
17
```

Figure 1-12.

Under electronic spreadsheet techniques, entries can be changed and recalculated before a hard-copy version is produced.

labeled PROJECTED TOTAL SALES. Notice also that the five columns in this spreadsheet are labeled according to months. Cells within this row contain figures that represent expected sales for the five months designated by column headings.

Spreadsheets are recalculated and reworked frequently. The purpose of corporate budgeting mechanisms is to monitor activities, to identify problem areas, and to correct problem situations. Analysis of needs or problems can require considerable reworking of spreadsheets. Under manual methods, figures have to be erased and reentered. Unavoidably, the appearance of the spreadsheet suffers. Spreadsheets may contain hundreds of cells, and many cell entries may be derived by applying *formulas* for computations involving other entries. For this type of spreadsheet, even simple changes might affect large numbers of cell entries.

Electronic Spreadsheets

Consider the process of producing spreadsheets with computer tools. Many parallels exist between this process and the production of text documents with word processing systems. **Electronic spreadsheet** packages allow the user to format and capture the spreadsheet electronically. In addition, most spreadsheet packages have capabilities for recalculating formulas. With this capability, relationships among cells described by formulas are reflected within the spreadsheet automatically. At any time, the spreadsheet can be output on a printer. That is, clean, attractive copies of succeeding spreadsheet versions are attainable with relative ease.

Electronic spreadsheet packages often are credited with opening the eyes of high-level executives to the power of microcomputers. For many executives, the decision making process involves asking and answering series of "What if . . . ?" questions. Examples of these questions might include: "What if material costs surpass expectations by 50 percent? What if the new labor agreement raises wages of line employees by $1.05 an hour? What if tax deductions for entertainment expenses are eliminated?

To answer these questions, executives derive projected figures by applying calculations to actual figures. Before microcomputers, executive analyses of this type were limited by time and cost factors of manual production. However, spreadsheet systems are easy to use and virtually unlimited in their ability to manipulate entries. These capabilities proved to be major factors in placing microcomputers on executive desks—and in increasing demands for people who

```
SpreadSheet: FIGONE13                    Press ESC to quit
Create Format Enter Sum Save Print Retrieve Insert Remove Copy Move Prot Delete
Enter headings, formulae, and data into a spreadsheet
   At----------Bn------------Cn------------Dn------------En----------Fn
 1
 2                  TEXTBOOK STATUS REPORT
 3
 4  Class          BookNumber    Registration        On Hand       Needed
 5
 6 HISTORY101       HC1256     .     357               143          C6-D6
 7
```

Figure 1-13.

Calculations are described as formulas, entered into spreadsheet cells, and executed under program control.

can understand and use microcomputer capabilities. This concept is illustrated in the case scenario in the section that follows.

Spreadsheets for inventory control. Suppose you are working in a college bookstore. The operations of this store are supported by a microcomputer system that maintains and monitors inventory levels and is linked with enrollment records. The system is set up to signal managers when orders are needed to bring inventories to satisfactory levels. The number of students enrolled for a specific class is compared with the present inventory level for its textbook. If the number of registered students for any class exceeds the number of books on hand, additional books must be ordered. To determine whether additional books are needed, and the quantity needed, an electronic spreadsheet can be set up, as shown in Figure 1-13.

The spreadsheet in Figure 1-13 presents inventory information about a textbook used for a history class. Data items within the the first row reflect the name of the class, a numeric identifier for the textbook, the number of students registered, and the number of texts on hand. The entry in the last cell in the row (E6) is calculated from the formula C6 – D6.

In this way, texts on hand are related to current registration figures for the current school period—and the difference is reflected in cell E6. This difference, or result, indicates the inventory status of the history book. A positive number in cell E6 indicates a low inventory situation, and the quantity of books that should be ordered. A negative number in the same cell indicates sufficient available quantities—and the amount of excess books that should be left over after registration is completed.

To appreciate the power of this application, consider that a bookstore normally sells thousands of books and other items. Stock items held in inventory represent cash that cannot be spent. Therefore, by keeping inventory at minimum levels, the cash flow of a business is improved. Spreadsheet packages can help achieve this result.

The simple operation described above can be applied to the thousands of books and other items normally sold in a bookstore. In addition, this application can be executed weekly or daily according to requirements for inventory control. Further, data files that support this application can be updated to reflect new items received, depletion of inventory levels due to sales, and new registration periods. Inventory items, and the cash they represent, can be held to minimum-but-efficient levels. The risk of running out of stock items is reduced as well. Under manual methods, inventory levels usually were counted only prior to each semester. Managers tended to tie up cash needlessly in high inventory levels as a cushion against out-of-stock situations.

The above example illustrates a concept that is central to this text. That is, microcomputer tools reflect the people or organization they serve. Regardless of sophistication, tools should fit existing methods and procedures. People should not have to change to fit their tools. A similar concept, also stressed in this book, is that tools should be in the hands of people who use them. This second concept reflects another requirement that—when met effectively by microcomputer tools—accelerated demand-solution cycles in the microcomputer evolution.

DECENTRALIZED PROCESSING

Decentralized processing means that processing capabilities are given to people who produce information and who need processing results to do their work. Microcomputers are small and inexpensive enough to be applied to previously unmet demands. In turn, the ability to place microcomputer tools into the hands of people who create and/or use data elements provided additional impetus to the microcomputer revolution.

At a basic level, processing is decentralized every time a microcomputer is installed within a business. The reasoning behind this concept (repeated here)

Figure 1-14.

Fingertip control becomes possible with restaurant microcomputer systems, on which servers enter orders by touching points on screen displays.

is straightforward: Tools should be placed in the hands of people who are doing the work.

Point-of-Sale Processing

A microcomputer places processing control in the hands of people who are doing business. This concept differs from early mainframe-based systems, in which processing control, as well as data, were held in a centralized facility. People who needed data, or data to be processed, submitted formal requests for service. Requests were filled according to organizational priorities. This arrangement created many problems. In effect, a separation existed between the **owners** and **custodians** of data. An analogy can be drawn between this situation and a large construction company. A construction company does not keep hammers in a central facility and distribute them to carpenters in response to formal requests. Hammers belong in the hands of carpenters at construction sites.

Similarly, computers meet needs most effectively in the hands of the people who create and/or use data to perform their jobs. Consider Figure 1-14. The microcomputer in this photograph uses a technology known as a **touch screen.** A touch screen is a type of **input device,** or a device used to enter data or programs into a computer system. To perform input through a touch screen, operators point to screen locations at which representations of data items or processing routines are displayed. The actual screen is sensitized and input operations are activated in response to pressure.

In this example, servers point to screen locations at which representations of food items are displayed. In this way, customer orders are entered to the system. A succeeding display image simulates a 10-character numeric keypad, such as is found on cash registers or adding machines. Servers use this display to enter numeric information, such as their employee number, the number of guests at the table, and table location.

The system accepts and combines these data to produce a guest check for the order. The guest check contains data items described above, as well as entries for applicable taxes and an overall total for the order. The system inserts prices for food items ordered, sums these prices, adds taxes, and generates the overall total automatically. In this way, manual entries effectively are eliminated and the accuracy of calculations is ensured.

The important point here, however, is the location at which microcomputers are used to produce results. As servers take customer orders at tables, requirements arise for creating and handling data. In this system, the terminal is located in the restaurant dining room. Data items are created and introduced to the system within minutes of the order. That is, processing capabilities are installed where they are needed, rather than in a central facility. Results are produced quickly and can be applied to real-life situations. Further, the separation of ownership and custody of data is eliminated effectively.

By performing entry at the point of sale, data items can be shared by related functions within the organization. For instance, in the restaurant example, data representing food items are used by kitchen personnel to prepare the order. These data can be sent over cable to a printer or display in the kitchen, where they are used as needed. In addition, data items from customer orders can be applied to files containing inventory records. In this way, inventory records are kept accurate and up-to-date, and stock items can be maintained at efficient levels.

In summary, microcomputers produce results by applying the same basic functions and capabilities of computers many times as large. The success of microcomputers can be attributed to the flexibility with which these functions and capabilities can be installed, and the wide range of requirements to which they can be applied. The chapter that follows discusses the basic functions and capabilities that give microcomputers their power as data-handling tools.

KEY TERMS

application	key
program	word processing
software	text processing
hardware	fixed length
data item	power typing
data element	mail merge
field	spreadsheet
record	budget
file	cell
mainframe	label
byte	heading
output	formula
external storage	electronic spreadsheet
disk	owner
peripheral device	custodian
system	touch screen
draft	input device

DEFINITIONS

Instructions: On a separate sheet, define each term according to its use in this chapter.

1. application

2. program

3. mainframe

4. external storage

5. word processing

6. system

7. mail merge

8. file

T R U E / F A L S E

Instructions: For each statement, write T for true or F for false on a separate sheet.

1. A microcomputer provides the same basic processing capabilities as a mainframe computer.

2. Text files have unpredictable lengths; data files usually are predictable or fixed in length.

3. Power typing is a method for inserting variable data elements into form letters for efficient mass production.

4. Examples of data items include names, ages, and social security numbers.

5. Microcomputers now have capabilities roughly equal to or greater than early machines that occupied entire rooms.

6. Word processing applications cannot be run on mainframes because mainframes have insufficient capabilities.

7. Electronic spreadsheets provide capabilities for producing form letters.

8. Oral communication meets transient needs, written communication is more permanent.

9. Technology usually is developed in response to demands by people.

10. A set of programs comprises the hardware component of a computer system.

11. The Apple I computer featured a keyboard and display screen, but no external storage.

12. The first microcomputer handled calculations for the 1950 census.

13. Designing microcomputer systems effectively has been reduced to a series of decisions regarding available software and peripheral devices.

14. A record is a collection of related files.

15. The evolution of computer technology has been driven by demand-solution cycles.

Instructions: On a separate sheet of paper, answer each question in one or two brief sentences.

1. List and explain three business requirements that have led to increased microcomputer sales.

2. Explain the data storage problem which microcomputers had to solve before word processing gained wide acceptance.

3. Explain why financial spreadsheets are important tools for organizations.

4. Describe the similarities between the evolution of the computer and of the automobile.

5. Compare and contrast external storage for mainframes and microcomputers.

6. How do electronic spreadsheet packages support planning, budgeting, and decision-making activities for executives? What effect has this had on the role of microcomputers in business organizations?

R E S E A R C H   P R O J E C T

What would your life be like without computers? Write a short report describing how computers—especially microcomputers—affect your daily activities. Then, speculate how your activities would change if there were no computers.

2 Microcomputer Functions and Capabilities

WHAT IS A COMPUTER?

Microcomputers and larger computers have the same basic parts and provide the same basic capabilities: arithmetic, logic, data storage, and programmability.

THE INFORMATION PROCESSING CYCLE

Results are obtained from computers through the functions of the information processing cycle: input, processing, output, and storage.

Information processing is essential to survival and is performed universally by people and systems.

INFORMATION PROCESSING SYSTEMS

An information processing system comprises components set up to process data and deliver information to people.

People

People must write programs, compile data, operate equipment, and interpret and apply outputs.

Data

Data are the ''raw materials'' of information processing systems.

Hardware

Microcomputer hardware can be classified according to the functions in the information processing cycle.

Programs

Microcomputer software is made up of two levels: system software, which includes operating systems and utility programs, and application programs.

Procedures

Procedures, usually outlined in a set of manuals, describe operations and methods for achieving results.

WHAT MICROCOMPUTERS DO

System implementation parallels the information processing cycle, and usually requires extensive design and development.

Input—Creating files

The initial step in systems implementation is to create data resources to support applications.

Storage

Storage often is said to be at the hub of an information system; all input, processing, and output operations involve data stored within files.

Processing

Operational support for organizations is derived from files by applying processing functions to data.

Output

The requirements for output should be met by the capabilities of output devices.

MICROCOMPUTER WORK SESSION

Data, once accessed, can be manipulated and/or output as meaningful information.

WHAT IS A COMPUTER?

Microcomputers are tools that should produce meaningful results to solve problems and/or meet requirements. To obtain results from a microcomputer, it is helpful to know what a computer is and how computers handle data. Microcomputers are computers with capabilities and features common to computers of any size. A good way to define computers is by their capabilities, which include the following:

- A computer performs arithmetic operations on data through electronic processing. Functional results of these operations include addition, subtraction, multiplication, and division.

- A computer performs *logic operations.* That is, a computer can compare data items to determine whether they are equal or unequal and whether one is smaller or larger than the other. A computer also uses the results of comparisons to select processing options included in programs.

- A computer can be programmed to perform different tasks. That is, a computer can follow a predetermined set of instructions from startup to conclusion without human intervention.

- A computer can *store* programs and data. A computer stores programs internally during processing. Most computers also provide capabilities for *external storage,* or storage in permanent or semi-permanent form.

Any computer has these capabilities, regardless of size. Microcomputers have the same basic parts and perform the same basic functions as larger computers. People choose between computers of different sizes and capacities according to job requirements. An analogy can be drawn between the requirements that can be met by a passenger automobile and a 40-foot moving truck. To move large collections of furniture and appliances, the truck is the better tool. However, the passenger automobile is more appropriate for moving passengers or small, delicate articles and for maneuvering through heavy traffic. Even if the materials to be moved could be handled in the automobile in dozens of trips, the operation obviously is performed more efficiently with the truck.

The analogy can be extended: Just as the internal combustion engines that power trucks and automobiles operate under the same basic principles, the data processing functions through which large and small computers deliver results also are fundamentally the same. The processing of data involves a cyclical series of functions. This cycle is the subject of the section that follows.

Regardless of size, computers

consist of the same basic components and provide the same
basic capabilities. These photos,
top to bottom, show a large
mainframe, a desktop
microcomputer, and a lap-top
portable microcomputer.

TOP PHOTO COURTESY OF LAWRENCE
LIVERMORE NATIONAL LABORATORY.
MIDDLE PHOTO COURTESY OF
OEMTEK, INC. BOTTOM PHOTO
COURTESY OF EPSON AMERICA, INC.

THE INFORMATION PROCESSING CYCLE

Results are obtained from computers through a series of functional stages, or steps. Again, these functions apply to all computers, no matter how large or small. Meaningful results are delivered to people through the functions of the information processing cycle, which include:

- The *input* function involves converting data into computer-readable format and entering the data for processing. These two functions, known respectively as *data capture* and *data entry,* may be performed simultaneously by microcomputers. The combination of these two functions often is called *direct data entry.* Direct data entry is achieved on most microcomputers through a keyboard device.

- The *processing* function involves the manipulation of data to add to or change their meaning. All processing operations are based on two basic capabilities. The arithmetic capability executes calculations. The logic capability directs processing through simple comparisons of two values.

- The *output* function refers to the delivery of processing results to people in an understandable form. Data are handled by computers as electronic signals. These signals are presented in human-readable form—such as words or pictures—by output devices.

- The *storage* function involves maintaining the availability of data for processing. In this sense, the storage function usually refers to external storage, or data maintained in some type of permanent or semi-permanent form. Magnetic disks are the most common form of external storage used for microcomputers.

Using the Information Processing Cycle

This cycle, diagrammed in Figure 2-1, applies to computerized systems as well as to systems that use common tools, such as pencils and paper. For example, you process information every time you record notes and study for a test. In addition, you are able to utilize the most sophisticated information processor there is—the human mind.

Notice how the information processing cycle applies to note taking:

- The input function is performed as you listen to a lecture and write, or *record,* notes on notebook paper.

- Processing takes place throughout the experience—as you listen to the lecture and, later, as you study your notes. Processing involves decisions you

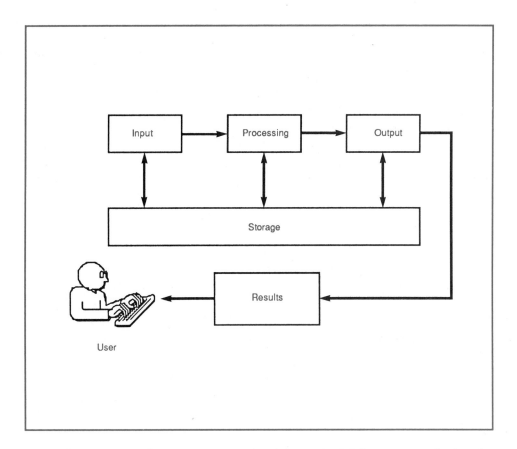

Figure 2-1.

The information processing
cycle establishes a series of
steps—insert, processing, output, and storage—for processing data and delivering
information.

make—consciously or not—as to what is meaningful for your needs. In addition, processing might involve reorganizing your notes after the lecture to
emphasize or clarify important points.

- Storage is implemented in two ways: Pertinent information is recorded in
your notebook and also held in your own memory. Storage is organized
through selections and decisions made during processing.

- Finally, the output phase occurs as you answer test questions, either orally
or in writing.

Information processing is a universal requirement. Survival is impossible unless
people can store and use important information. Early people recorded and communicated important information—such as how and where to hunt for food—
as crude drawings on cave walls. In fact, the entire evolution of technology,
culminating in the development of the computer, is driven by the human need
for information.

INFORMATION PROCESSING SYSTEMS

The important point throughout this discussion is this: The purpose of information processing is to meet the needs and wants of *people.* Ultimately, businesses produce goods and/or provide services for people. People are a vital component of computerized *information processing systems.* The term, *system,* refers to an interrelated, coordinated collection of procedures and other components that deliver specific results. An information processing system, then, consists of components that are set up to process data and deliver meaningful information to people. Information processing systems are discussed in the section that follows.

The role of microcomputers as a component of information systems illustrates their most powerful business capability. The major components in an information processing system include:

- People
- Data
- Hardware
- Programs
- Procedures.

People

People play an obvious role in information processing systems. People are needed to write programs, compile data for input, operate equipment, and interpret and apply outputs. In short, nothing happens until people make it happen.

Data

Data are the "raw materials" of information processing systems. By themselves, data items have little meaning and utility for people. For example, suppose you were reading a restaurant menu, deciding what to have for lunch. The items on the menu read: cheese, pickles, onions, ketchup, mayonnaise, ground beef, and bun.

As individual menu entries, these items have little value. However, combining these items results in a recognizable (meaningful) and useful luncheon entree—a cheeseburger. Data play a similar role in information systems. Data have little value, or meaning, for users until they have been combined and/or manipulated in some way.

In the above example, cheese, pickles, onions, and so on represent *data items.* The terms, *data elements,* or *fields,* are used throughout this text interchangeably with data items. By themselves, data items have little meaning for

people. Data items are combined to make up **records** that describe a person, thing, place, or event, just as the food items above combine to describe a cheeseburger.

As another example, a social security number means virtually nothing by itself. A social security number must be linked to a person before it can be put to meaningful use. In many types of information systems, social security numbers are combined with names and addresses to create records that identify related groups of people, such as customers or employees.

Groups of related data records make up *files.* A file is a collection of records that is organized for ease of use. For example, a payroll master file might consist of records for each person employed by an organization. Data items within

People play

vital roles in computer systems; nothing happens until people make it happen.

COURTESY OF XEROX CORPORATION

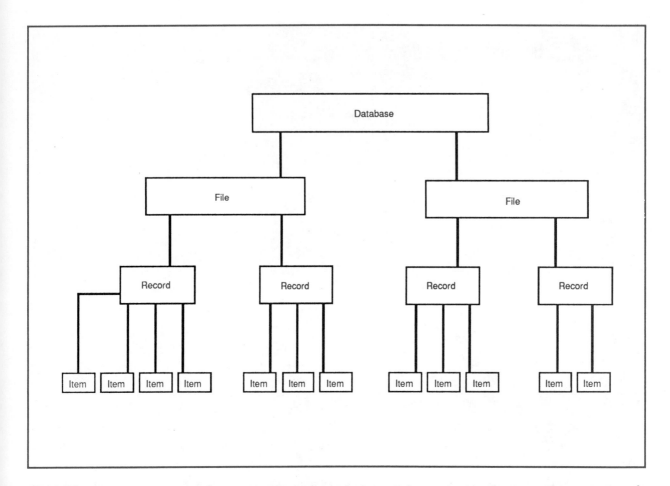

Figure 2-2.

Data structures are built as a hierarchy to organize data items, records, files, and databases for ease of storage and retrieval.

employee records might include social security numbers, employee name, address, and pertinent wage or salary figures. The payroll master file is processed each pay period to deliver meaningful results to people—in the form of employee paychecks.

Data are organized, or **structured,** in information systems as data items, data records, and files. See Figure 2-2. In the past, separate files were needed for each application run by an organization. That is, data items used for multiple applications, such as customer identifications and product descriptions, would be duplicated and stored in separate files for each application.

Recent developments in hardware and software have made it possible to integrate file structures, or organization schemes, to reduce or eliminate redundant occurrences of stored data items. A collection of files organized to support multiple applications is called a **database.** Databases are discussed later in this chapter and in other chapters throughout this text.

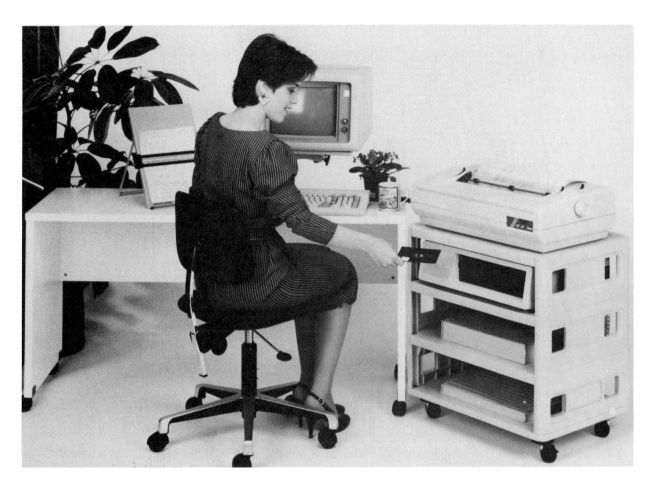

Hardware

The hardware components of microcomputer systems, or work stations, are configured according to the needs of the job to be performed. Microcomputer devices are available to meet a wide variety of needs. For instance, an engineering system that produces graphic outputs might include a **plotter,** an output device for producing line drawings, instead of a printer. Regardless of application, the devices of a microcomputer work station correspond roughly with the steps in the information processing cycle. Typical system configurations include the following devices (see Figure 2-3):

- Input is performed through a typewriter-style **keyboard.** Keyboard entries are converted into computer-readable data ready to be processed.

- Processing falls within the range of operations performed by the **processing unit.** The processing unit executes arithmetic and logic operations and controls the transference of data to and from other system devices.

Figure 2-3.

In a typical microcomputer system, input is performed through a keyboard; entered data are routed through the processing unit; a printer is used to present outputs; and one or more disk drives are used for storage.

COURTESY OF INMAC

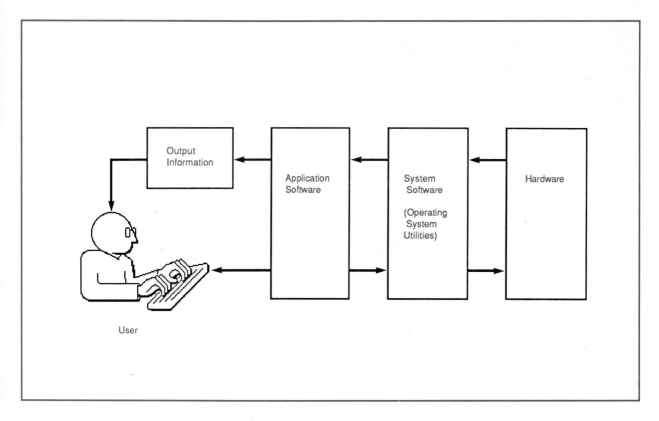

Figure 2-4.

The software component of a microcomputer system consists of multiple programs integrated to meet user needs.

- **Disk drives** are the most common data storage device used in microcomputer work stations. Disk drives house magnetic disks and implement the reading and writing of data to and from these disks.

- The output device most often used for microcomputers is a **printer.** A printer resembles a computer-driven typewriter. That is, printers are used mainly to produce text outputs. There are many styles and classifications of microcomputer printers, most of which are discussed in a later chapter.

Programs

In an earlier section, computers are defined by their ability to interpret and follow **programs.** Programs consist of sequences of instructions followed by computers to produce a desired result. The program, or software, component of microcomputer systems is made up of two basic levels. See Figure 2-4. At the lower level (closest to hardware), **system software** controls and monitors the operations of hardware and other software. An **operating system,** a subset of system software, provides most of these capabilities. In addition, system software may include several **utility programs,** or **utilities.** Utilities are programs that provide standard functions, such as copy or print, in support of higher-level programs.

At the higher of the two basic levels, **application programs** consist of instructions and routines by which specific tasks are performed. Application programs, or packages, control production of results required by people, or computer **users.** As discussed in Chapter 1, the development of application programs such as electronic spreadsheets and word processors had a direct effect on the microcomputer revolution.

Procedures

Procedures refer to methods for operating equipment, running software, and implementing a system. To ensure uniformity, procedures usually are outlined in a set of reference books, or manuals.

An **operations manual** describes the commands and actions for operating hardware devices or for running application programs.

A **training manual** orients people to an information system. That is, a training manual should smooth user transitions from manual to computerized operations, or from the operations of an existing system to those of a new system. Training manuals might guide users through the process of installing and implementing a system. Implementation involves bringing a system into regular operation. Systems are rooted in the functions of the information processing cycle. For this reason, the discussion of system implementation that follows is based loosely on the functions of input, processing, output, and storage.

WHAT MICROCOMPUTERS DO

Information systems provide significant capabilities for delivering results. In turn, information represents and supports virtually all organizational activities. In this role, information—especially information stored in files—becomes a **resource.** A resource is anything that is manipulated or applied to obtain results. Further, because of their value as resources, the allocation and distribution of resources are monitored closely within most organizations.

To appreciate the value of information, picture what would occur if different organizations lost their information resources. If your school's information resources were lost, there would be no records to prove that you had earned credit for previous courses. All your work, and that of other students, could be lost. A business that lost its information could not pay employees or outstanding bills. Neither could the company collect amounts due from customers, or even collect insurance without proof of ownership for lost valuables.

Information systems are set up to build and process information resources—data and information stored in files. Information processing, as stated previously, involves a cycle of functions: input, processing, output, and storage. System implementation sets up these functions for execution. Similarly, a discussion of system implementation, presented in the section that follows, can be based loosely upon the information processing cycle.

The process of building information systems for microcomputers is simplified by the availability of application packages, discussed earlier. Application packages are programs for executing standard processing functions. The scenario that follows is based upon a type of package known as a ***database management system (DBMS).*** As the name implies, a DBMS is a software tool for building and manipulating a database. A database is a collection of files organized to support multiple applications. Databases and DBMSs are covered extensively throughout this text. For immediate purposes, a typical DBMS is presented to illustrate the processes of building information systems. Regardless of package, systems are implemented through generic functions. For example, virtually all packages provide a function for creating a file, another function for changing or editing a file, and for manipulating data within files.

Similarly, most application packages implement an operational method known as ***interactive processing.*** Under interactive methods, processing is carried out through a continuing dialog between a user and the system. A user communicates through keyboard entries. The system communicates by displaying either ***prompts,*** or ***menus.*** A prompt is a displayed request for user input. Typically, prompts are used in conjunction with menus. A menu is a list of processing options from which a user makes selections to direct processing.

Figure 2-5 presents a ***main menu*** for a model DBMS package. Notice the prompt at the bottom of the screen, which reads:

ENTER NUMBER OF SELECTION AND PRESS RETURN >

This type of interaction allows a user to structure work for achievement of specific results. That is, the system responds to user input by displaying succeeding menus or prompts. Additional user input initiates further processing routines until desired results are achieved. This concept of interactive processing is demonstrated in the system implementation discussions that follow.

For the purposes of illustration, assume that the needs of users have been studied and that files, input records, and output displays and reports have been developed. Extensive design and development should precede implementation of any system. In effect, a detailed design is the plan followed in system implementation. Conversely, systems design requires knowledge of and experience

```
LEARNware : DB :::::::::::::::::::::::::::::::::::::::::::::::::::::
E                                                                 ::
A              DATABASE MANAGEMENT MAIN MENU                       ::
R                                                                 ::
N                                                                 ::
W      1.   FILE SPECIFICATION/MAINTENANCE MENU                    ::
a      2.   MANIPULATION/QUERY COMMAND MENU                        ::
r      3.   DATA ENTRY AND PROCESSING MENU                         ::
e                                                                 ::
::     4.   CHANGE SYSTEM DATE -> 000000                           L
::                                                                 E
::                                                                 A
::                                                                 R
::                                                                 N
::                                                                 W
::           ENTER NUMBER OF SELECTION AND PRESS [RETURN] >        a
::                                                                 r
:::::::::::::::::::::::::::::::::::::::::::::::::::::::::::::LEARNware
Press [Esc] and [Return] to quit menu.
```

Figure 2-5.

The main menu of an application package provides standard processing functions; users select options by entering the appropriate number and pressing the RETURN key.

in implementation and use of computer systems. In practice, the ability to understand and use computers is a prerequisite to design and development of information systems. This is the reason for reviewing implementation and use of systems in the presentation that follows.

Input—Creating Files

The initial step in the processing cycle is input. The input of data also is the initial step in implementing systems. In both instances, input involves data entry through computer devices. In a strict sense, though, input in the processing cycle involves data entry into computer memory. For building systems, input involves the creation of semipermanent processing entities, or externally stored files.

To initiate the input stage of system implementation using the main menu shown in Figure 2-5, the user simply selects the FILE SPECIFICATION/MAINTENANCE MENU option. The user presses number 1 and the enter key (RETURN). In response to this input, the computer locates and follows a set of instructions through which files are created.

All files must be given names. The system prompts the user to enter a file name. In this example, the file is to be a set of customer identification records—so

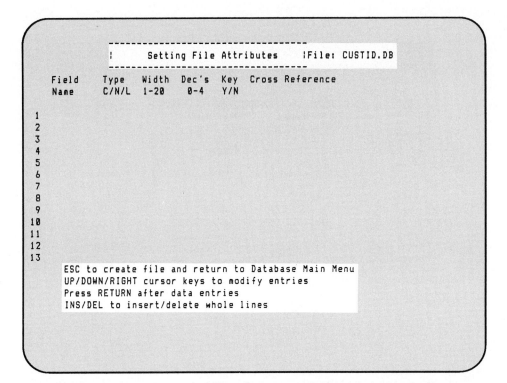

Figure 2-6.

Data descriptions are entered and displayed, then recorded by the system to support access and retrieval operations. This screen display is used to specify formats for records that will make up a file.

the file is labeled CUSTID. This name is keyed and entered. The system records the entry and then displays a screen, shown in Figure 2-6, through which the fields in the CUSTID files are defined. Database systems use these definitions to organize storage files for easy access and use.

Several terms used on this screen may be unfamiliar to you. Fields are named according to the type of entries they are to hold. Data type refers to the characters that make up the entry. In this example, three types of entries are specified:

- A C indicates a character field, also called an **alphanumeric field.** This field will accept entries of letters and numbers.

- An N indicates numeric entries. Numeric entries are numbers that have significant value. In this example, numeric entries are used only for dollar amounts.

- An L indicates a **logic field**. A logic entry is a coded selection, in this case yes or no (Y/N)—indicating the presence or absence of a credit account.

The CUSTID file also is set up with a five-digit customer number designated as a **record key.** A record key is a data item that is unique to a record and is used to identify and locate the record within a file. Figure 2-7 shows the display screen for the record entry operation described above.

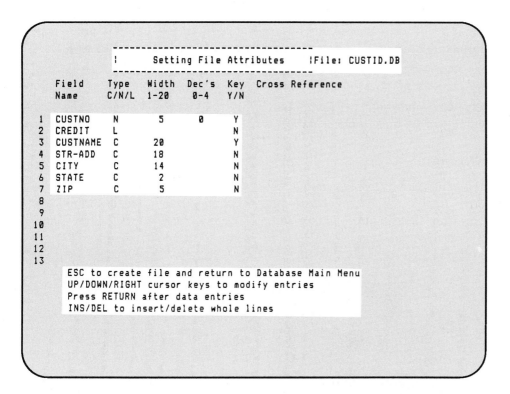

```
 ------------------------------------------
 !       Setting File Attributes     !File: CUSTID.DB
 ------------------------------------------
     Field    Type   Width   Dec's  Key  Cross Reference
     Name     C/N/L  1-20    0-4    Y/N

  1  CUSTNO    N        5       0     Y
  2  CREDIT    L                      N
  3  CUSTNAME  C       20             Y
  4  STR-ADD   C       18             N
  5  CITY      C       14             N
  6  STATE     C        2             N
  7  ZIP       C        5             N
  8
  9
 10
 11
 12
 13

     ESC to create file and return to Database Main Menu
     UP/DOWN/RIGHT cursor keys to modify entries
     Press RETURN after data entries
     INS/DEL to insert/delete whole lines
```

Figure 2-7.

This display shows a series of entries for items that make up a data record.

Record keys establish a basis for organizing storage files for easy access. For example, records can be sorted numerically according to the values of their record keys. Files also can be sorted alphabetically and both types of sorts can be designated as ascending (A – Z, 1 – number of last record) or descending (Z – A, number of last record – 1). Sort procedures are executed easily. The CUSTNO field has been designated as record key. Usually, all that is required is to enter a simple command, such as SORT, the name of the file, and the sequence (ascending/descending) to be followed.

Suppose, in this example, that customer names and addresses are needed to produce *invoices,* or documents describing sales orders. Invoices contain selected data items from several sources. Order files might contain information concerning sales and the number of the customers making purchases. Data items within product description files usually are needed for pricing and other information. To produce invoices, then, the system needs to access customer name and address from the CUSTID file as well as order and product information from those files.

To facilitate this kind of access operation, all files can be sorted in identical sequences, according to customer number. Notice the correlation here between the input of records and their storage and retrieval. The input function is performed to create stored files. Files are organized to support processing.

Storage files support processing most effectively when they are organized for easy access. Because of this relationship, the discussions in this section—and in the two chapters on hardware that follow—link input with storage. The role of storage in systems implementation is the subject of the section that follows.

Storage

When all records have been entered, the file can be **saved,** or written to disk. Saving a file usually involves a simple command, or a single function key. However, this simple command initiates the creation of storage files, valuable information resources.

Storage plays an important

role within information systems; stored files keep data records available for processing or reference.

PHOTO BY LISA SCHWABER-BARZILAY

Storage often is said to be positioned at the hub of an information system. That is, the functions of input, processing, and output revolve around storage files—more specifically, the data records within them. In simple terms, the processing cycle involves taking data from stored files, manipulating them in some way to give them meaning, delivering the results to people, and sending the results back to files.

The true importance of business files, however, becomes clear when you consider what the data within files represent. Typically, files maintained for organizational entities include:

- Sources of income, or customers
- Products and/or services sold by the business
- Suppliers
- Money owed to the business by customers
- Money owed by the business to vendors
- Acts of doing business, or **transactions.**

In effect, everything that makes a business what it is—how and from where it gets its money and where the money goes—is represented in stored files. This fact is central to the emergence of files as information resources. Because of this fact, the storage function presents some special considerations for system implementation projects.

Resources must be protected. Part of the job of building systems is to establish methods for creating **backups** of information resources. That is, copies of stored files and alternate hardware and software should be secured. The creation of backup systems and files is discussed in later chapters. For present purposes, keep in mind that the concept of information resources is central to systems implementation. For reinforcement, imagine the consequences of losing your lecture notes the night before a big test. Remember: The loss of information resources can mean the end of operations.

Processing

Return to the example of the CUSTID file. Suppose the business gains a new customer. A new record must be added to the file. In strict terms, this procedure involves input rather than processing. But operations of this type usually are executed after files have been created and systems implemented.

Regardless of function, the operation is performed easily in a matter of minutes. The function, DATA ENTRY AND PROCESSING, is selected from the main menu (see Figure 2-5). The appropriate entries are keyed and the record is added to the file. If the system requires that the record be placed within the proper sequence of customer numbers, a SORT operation can be evoked. Most systems implement some type of method for leaving gaps in record-numbering sequences for this purpose.

Now, suppose that one of the records has to be changed. Perhaps a business customer changes its name or location. This change must be reflected within the appropriate fields of the customer record.

The DBMS package provides a menu selection for implementing this operation. That is, the user selects the MAINTENANCE OF DATA RECORDS option and follows prompts to identify and display the appropriate record. Changes are made in memory and displayed on the screen. See Figure 2-8. The entire file—with required changes—now can be written back to its original disk location. It's just that simple.

Other types of processing operations permit users to produce outputs, such as invoices. Output documents usually are compiled from data that are combined and/or manipulated to achieve desired results. The SORT operation described above is one of several basic functions performed by computers to add meaning to data. A list of these functions includes:

- To *classify* means to put into categories. That is, records with similar characteristics are put into categories. For example, a customer identification file might be classified according to geographic location, indicated by ZIP codes.

- *Sort* operations (discussed above) arrange data items in a desired sequence.

- The *calculate* function refers to the application of arithmetic operations to data items. Arithmetic operations include addition, subtraction, multiplication, and division. To illustrate, consider a list of purchases on an order form. To obtain an overall price for the order, the prices of individual items must be multiplied by quantities ordered, and these subtotals added to derive a total.

- To *summarize* is to reduce the volume of a group of data items, while enhancing their meaning. For instance, the sales figures for a dozen fast food outlets might be summarized each week to give managers a picture of the overall performance of the organization.

- The *compare* function is the basis of what is known as computer logic. Computer logic is based upon the ability of a computer to compare two data items and to direct processing on the basis of the results. Comparisons are used extensively in programs. The level of stock items, for example, can be monitored by comparison. Stock items are depleted by outgoing deliveries or increased by incoming shipments. An inventory control system can be set up

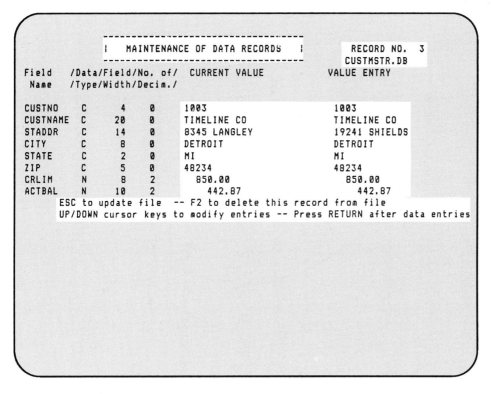

```
        ---------------------------------------
        I   MAINTENANCE OF DATA RECORDS    I        RECORD NO.  3
        ---------------------------------------         CUSTMSTR.DB
Field   /Data/Field/No. of/  CURRENT VALUE        VALUE ENTRY
Name    /Type/Width/Decim./

CUSTNO     C    4    0    1003                     1003
CUSTNAME   C   20    0    TIMELINE CO              TIMELINE CO
STADDR     C   14    0    8345 LANGLEY             19241 SHIELDS
CITY       C    8    0    DETROIT                  DETROIT
STATE      C    2    0    MI                       MI
ZIP        C    5    0    48234                    48234
CRLIM      N    8    2       850.00                   850.00
ACTBAL     N   10    2       442.87                   442.87
        ESC to update file  -- F2 to delete this record from file
        UP/DOWN cursor keys to modify entries -- Press RETURN after data entries
```

Figure 2-8.

Menu selections within application packages guide access to and modification of stored files.

to compare individual levels with ***reorder levels*** established by managers. If stock levels fall below reorder levels, the system generates a signal indicating a low-stock condition for those items.

The functions described here pertain only to the processing step of the information processing cycle. Other basic functions (discussed earlier) include the record function of the input phase, and the store and retrieve functions of the storage phase. The output phase is based upon the ability of computers to deliver meaningful results to people. Output, as it pertains to information systems, is discussed in the section that follows. The interrelation of these functions is diagrammed in Figure 2-9.

The important point in this discussion is that records within files provide support to businesses. This support is derived from files by executing the basic functions described above. To illustrate, return to the CUSTID file.

This file contains the names and addresses of an organization's customers. Suppose managers decide to derive specialized mailing lists from this file. Perhaps the organization realizes that many of its products have utility only in certain areas. A need is identified to produce and mail sales letters that are applicable to customers in specific areas.

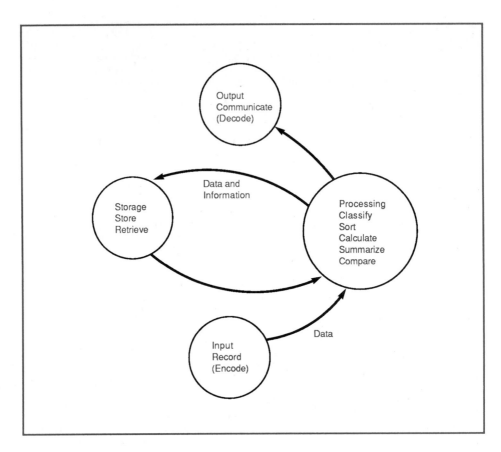

Figure 2-9.

Elements of the information processing cycle interact to produce desired results.

Given a system with the basic capabilities, the CUSTID file could be sorted according to ZIP codes for efficient mailing. As an alternative, customer records could be matched with order files to determine which customers purchased specific products. The dates on order records would indicate the frequency of purchases. These dates could be compared with corresponding product prices to determine any correlation between price and purchase, or purchase quantity, and so on. All these analyses can enhance the decision making capabilities of organizational managers—but only if results are applied to actual situations. Most often, applying results involves producing some type of output.

Output

The analyses described above are performed for a specific purpose: To produce a mailing list that is tailored to the needs of customers in different geographic areas. This list has little value unless it is applied to a mailing operation.

In many cases, output considerations in building information systems involve hardware selections. The requirements for output must be matched by the capabilities of output devices. For example, the mailing list that results from analyses of the customer file can be output as mailing labels, printed on special paper fed through a printer.

Once again, these sophisticated operations are performed with relative ease, usually a simple matter of directing processing through menu and prompt responses. Further, the capabilities required to perform this type of processing are available in relatively inexpensive microcomputers. Once these capabilities are in place, obtaining and applying results can become understandable to non-technical users.

This concept is illustrated in the scenario that follows. At a basic level, the scenario is meant to familiarize you with a microcomputer work session. However, at another level, this simple operation—accessing data within files—is the basis of a new world of microcomputer applications.

MICROCOMPUTER WORK SESSION

Jane Daniels is a part-time employee in the administrative offices of a local community college. Administrative personnel perform many duties—one of which is the maintenance and handling of student records and files. Files are collections of related records. In this scenario, student records are organized into the following classifications, or files:

- Student identification records are grouped into a file labeled STUDENTID. Data items within these records include student name, address, and an identification number. Social Security numbers often are used as student identification numbers.

- Records of student grades are collected into a file labeled GRADES. Records within this file are identified by the student identification number from the STUDENTID file. That is, the student identification number is used by the system as a record key to locate specific records within the file. Data items in these records include—in addition to the student identification number—class name, grade in each class, a two-character designation of student status (FR = freshman; SO = sophomore) for each class attended, and grade points earned toward graduation.

Students often come to the administrative offices with requests for information concerning their records. Students may want printed transcript reports to be sent to universities, or may wish simply to verify their current course credits or grade

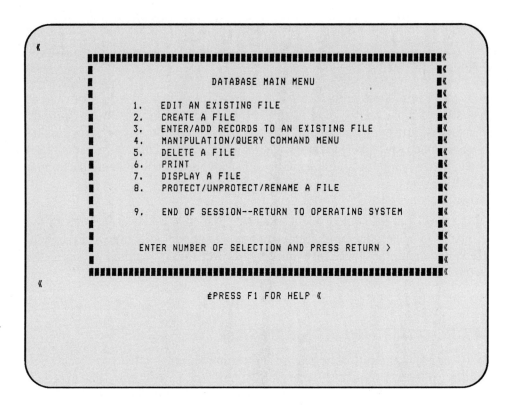

Figure 2-10.

The DISPLAY A FILE option is used to access stored records for presentation on a terminal screen.

point averages. In the latter situation, the student GRADES record need not be output as a printed document. The record can be accessed and displayed on a terminal screen.

Before a microcomputer can be put to work to solve problems or meet needs, a series of initial startup procedures must be executed. Startup procedures are discussed in a later chapter. For this discussion, assume that an operational microcomputer system is available. In this fictional system, as well as in many actual business systems, programs and data are stored on a **hard disk.** A hard disk is a high-capacity, high-speed magnetic storage device for microcomputers.

Daniels is currently handling a request from Dennis Vaughan, a second-year student. Vaughan wants to verify his status and grade point average to be sure that he will qualify for admission next year to a four-year university. To fill this request, Daniels calls up the application main menu, shown in Figure 2-10. For continuity, the DBMS package from the previous example is used.

Daniels then follows the displayed prompt at the bottom of the screen. She presses the key for number 7 to select the processing option: DISPLAY A FILE. She then presses the RETURN key to enter this selection. The system then displays the first record within the file. See Figure 2-11.

```
    Adams                           FR


    --------------------------------------------------------
    CLASS                 CREDITS              GRADE

    English 101              3                  2.6
    Algebra 100              3                  3.6
    History 122              3                  2.8
    Biology 100              3                  3.0


       TOTAL CREDITS        12       CURRENT GPA   3.0


USE PgUp or PgDn TO DISPLAY PREVIOUS OR NEXT RECORD
PRESS F10 TO RETURN TO MAIN MENU
>
```

Figure 2-11.

To support inquiry, the computer generates a display that requests appropriate user entries.

Notice the > prompt at the bottom of the screen. This prompt is an entry area through which commands are executed. For example, Daniels keys in the command:

DISPLAY VAUGHAN.

The microcomputer does the rest of the work. Under control of the DBMS, Vaughan's record is located and displayed on the terminal screen. This operation should be completed in a fraction of a second, depending upon the size of the database. The student record display is shown in Figure 2-12.

The operation described above is completed quickly. Daniels relays the information to Vaughan. Of course, this is a simple example of computer processing, meant to give you an idea of how applications are executed. Keep in mind, however, that the basis for most computer applications is access to data. The differences, again, are a matter of scale.

Databases may involve millions of records stored in the central facility of a large organization. This type of database usually can be accessed from remote microcomputer work stations. Or, there are literally thousands of databases that

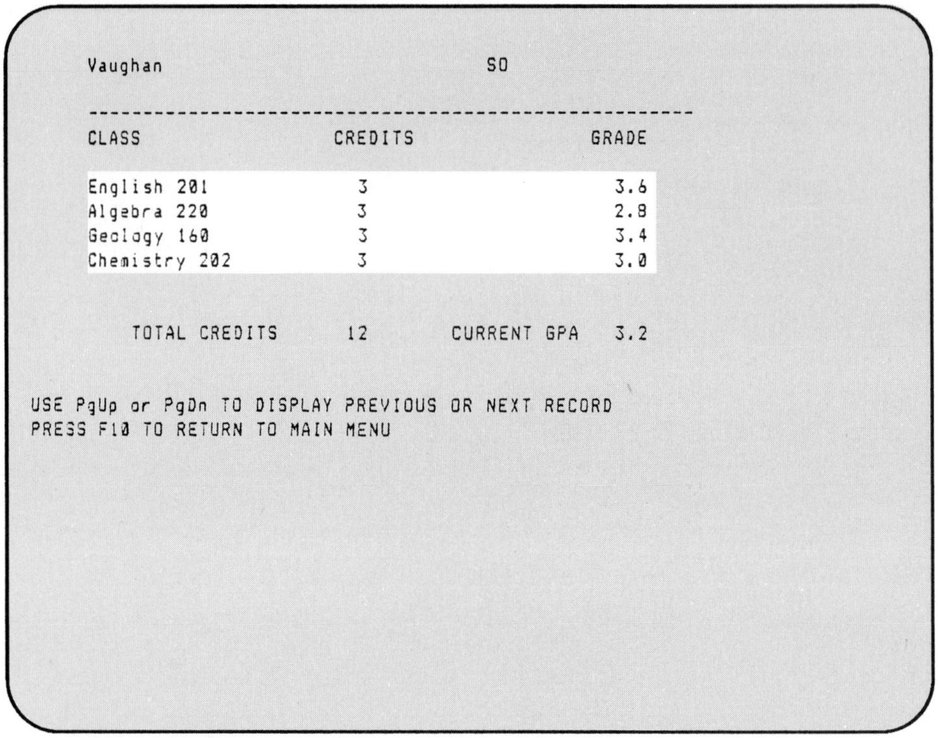

```
Vaughan                              SO

-----------------------------------------------------------

CLASS                    CREDITS              GRADE

English 201                 3                   3.6
Algebra 220                 3                   2.9
Geology 160                 3                   3.4
Chemistry 202               3                   3.0


     TOTAL CREDITS          12        CURRENT GPA    3.2


USE PgUp or PgDn TO DISPLAY PREVIOUS OR NEXT RECORD
PRESS F10 TO RETURN TO MAIN MENU
```

Figure 2-12.

Records are displayed in response to user queries.

can be accessed from any properly equipped microcomputer linked with a telephone. Such services run a broad gamut of content, from special interest automobiles, to technological developments, to research libraries, to career placement services, even to dating services. In effect, the world is at the fingertips of anyone familiar with the concepts and operations of microcomputers.

Much of this information was available before the invention of the microcomputer. The microcomputer, however, is the most advanced tool yet developed for achieving this level of universal access. In addition, the microcomputer allows a user to organize and analyze information to support job performance.

The important point: Once data are accessed, they can be manipulated and/or output as meaningful information. In businesses, information is the foundation upon which decisions are made and problems solved. Remember, a microcomputer is a tool. Information is a resource, or "raw material," that is shaped by this tool. This concept is central to this text: Information is a business resource. The next chapter discusses hardware considerations in managing this resource.

KEY TERMS

logic operation

store

external storage

input

data capture

date entry

direct data entry

processing

output

storage

record

people

information processing system

system

data item

data element

field

record

file

data structure

database

plotter

keyboard

processing unit

disk drive

printer

program

system software

operating system

utility program

utility

application program

user

operations manual

training manual

resource

database management system
   (DBMS)

interactive processing

prompt

menu

main menu

alphanumeric field

logic field

record key

invoice

save

transaction

backup

classify

sort

calculate

summarize

compare

reorder level

hard disk

DEFINITIONS

Instructions: On a separate sheet, define each term according to its use in this chapter.

1. disk drive

2. database

3. backup

4. interactive processing

5. application program

6. plotter

7. save

8. logic operation

T R U E / F A L S E

Instructions: For each statement, write T for true or F for false on a separate sheet.

1. Programs are the "raw materials" of information processing systems.

2. Basically, microcomputers perform the same functions as minicomputers or mainframes.

3. Processing operations are based on two capabilities: input and output.

4. Keyboards are the most common information storage device used in microcomputers.

5. Information systems often are said to revolve around storage.

6. The calculate function is part of the input phase of the information processing cycle.

7. Building information systems for microcomputers is made more complex by the availability of application packages.

8. An arithmetic operation determines whether one data item is equal to, greater than, or less than another item.

9. The input phase of the information processing cycle involves two operations: data capture and data entry.

10. A record key is used to delete records within files.

11. Writing answers to questions on an exam is an example of data output.

12. Stored data files are important business resources.

13. People are only a minor component of information processing systems.

14. Placing a set of files in alphabetical order (A – Z) is an example of a descending sort operation.

15. Microcomputers can hold data internally during processing.

SHORT ANSWER QUESTIONS

Instructions: On a separate sheet of paper, answer each question in one or two brief sentences.

1. List and describe the phases of the information processing cycle.

2. Describe the difference between an operations manual and a training manual.

3. What are the basic capabilities of any computer, regardless of size?

4. Describe direct data entry.

5. How does interactive processing work?

6. Explain the meaning of the statement: Data are the "raw materials" of information processing systems.

RESEARCH PROJECT

The next time you visit a fast-food outlet, pay particular attention to the way in which your order is taken. Observe closely the cash register and the labels affixed to the buttons or keys. If necessary, ask the manager to explain the procedure for taking and filling your order and the way in which the computer assists in order processing. Write a report describing your experience and how it relates to the information processing cycle.

3 Putting Microcomputers to Work

THE ROLE OF MICROCOMPUTERS

Microcomputers place both ownership and custody of data resources in the hands of people performing work.

MICROCOMPUTERS AND TRANSACTIONS

Microcomputer-based transaction processing systems mirror the way an organization does business.

Microcomputers are powerful enough to provide support for small organizations, yet flexible enough to fit into the schemes of large organizations.

MICROCOMPUTERS FOR TRANSACTION ANALYSIS

As tools for analyzing transaction data, microcomputers provide a means for managing an organization and plotting its future course.

The Transaction Path

Using a fictional company, the transaction documents created to support business and management functions are described.

MICROCOMPUTERS AND TRANSACTION PROCESSING SYSTEMS

With microcomputers, transaction data can be created and input to a processing system at the point of transaction.

Master Files

Master files reflect the current and past history of business activities.

Transaction Files

Transaction files are accumulations of data items from individual transactions, recorded as they occur.

CASE SCENARIO: GENERATING INVOICES WITH MICROCOMPUTER TOOLS

Capabilities for gathering data from files to produce transaction documents are provided effectively by microcomputer tools.

Status and Condition: A Study in Transactions

Transaction data can be summarized to generate a financial "snapshot" of an organization.

Financial Statements

Standard reports of transaction data also may be required by government agencies, creditors, vendors, and so on.

THE ROLE OF MICROCOMPUTERS

A tool helps perform a job and produce desired results. A tool cannot make decisions on what is to be done or how to do anything. Computers are tools for operating and managing organizations. Computers are used to create and manipulate data resources to support transaction processing and analyses of transaction data. Every organization is set up and run differently, individually. In this role, therefore, microcomputers must fit in with the events that take place and results that are produced by organizations as a whole.

Systems based on mainframe computers and centralized processing techniques typically created a separation between **owners** and **custodians** of data resources. That is, data owners, the people who create and use data or the results of processing for performing work, often had little or no control over these resources. Because of the centralized nature of these systems, data custody was entrusted to specialists within the central facility. Microcomputers are tools that place both ownership and custody of data resources in the hands of people performing work.

To understand the role of microcomputers within a business, it is necessary to know what that business does. Every organization is motivated by an underlying purpose, or **driving force.** The driving force also may be called the mission of a business. Regardless of name, the basis for understanding is the same: Every business organization is established to provide certain, specific products or services to an identified market (or public).

Any exchanges of services or products between an organization and its customers are called **transactions.** Putting it simply, a transaction is any act of doing business. Generally, transactions are recorded and/or **documented.** Part of each transaction involves an **exchange of value.** That is, an organization supplies goods or services in exchange for something that has value in return.

Before commerce evolved, for example, a farmer might have exchanged crops for necessities such as clothes or tools. This method is known as the **barter system.** As people began to live in cities, a **medium of exchange** was needed that was portable and had a standard, recognized value. Farmers could not always bring their crops to markets in distant cities. So farmers sold their crops to a middleman for money. The middleman transported goods to markets and resold them at a higher price.

The nature of transactions has not changed essentially since these simple beginnings. However, as businesses have grown larger and increasingly complex, transaction patterns have kept pace. In modern business organizations, transactions can be comprised of several components and can exhibit a wide range

of characteristics. In turn, just as society and businesses have grown in sophistication, so have their tools.

The strength of microcomputers as transaction processing tools lies in two significant factors. First, microcomputers are compact and inexpensive enough to be installed at the **point of transaction,** also called the **source** of the transaction. Second, microcomputers provide a full range of information-handling capabilities for managers and other personnel who analyze transaction data to support decision making activities. To illustrate, the section that follows discusses transaction processing with microcomputer tools.

MICROCOMPUTERS AND TRANSACTIONS

Transactions may be simple or complex. For example, you may be asked to sign a receipt for a package delivered to your home by the post office or a parcel delivery service. The delivery marks the completion of a transaction. That is, the post office or carrier has been paid through stamps or fees to get the package to you. Part of the transaction, for which the customer may pay an extra fee, is to provide proof of delivery. Your signature on a receipt slip serves as that proof.

Transaction processing

has been streamlined and accelerated through use of microcomputer devices at point of sale.

Transactions can be as straightforward as an exchange of a parcel for a signature. Many transactions, however, are multifaceted. In the above example, the delivery company is engaged in another transaction with the sender. Your signature represents proof of delivery and, therefore, the documentation that is required for the delivery company to collect payment.

Regardless of complexity, transactions invariably reflect the nature and requirements of organizations conducting them. In turn, microcomputer-based transaction processing systems also mirror the way an organization does business. The section that follows illustrates this concept.

Transaction Complexity

Picture yourself as a restaurant customer. You are escorted to a table and presented a menu. After a short period, a server takes your order. The server records your order manually on a guest check designed for this purpose. The guest check is used to record data that represent the transaction. For this reason, the guest check—and any document that is used to record transaction data—is called a ***transaction document.***

In microcomputer-based transaction processing systems, transaction documents often are created at source points for documents. Data created in conjunction with production of source documents serves as initial input for transaction processing activities. For these reasons, transaction documents also are referred to as ***source documents*** throughout this text.

The guest check marks the starting point of a ***transaction flow*** through the organization. That is, in many organizations, products or services are delivered through a series of internal transactions. Transaction documents follow a path through the organization defined by these internal exchanges.

For example, in restaurants like the one described above, beverages typically are ordered and delivered prior to the main course. The server presents the check at a beverage station. In effect, the check is exchanged for beverage items described on the check. However, it would not be feasible for the server to write two checks—one for beverages and one for food items—and a third check to present total price. To confirm delivery, beverage personnel might sign or mark the check in some way. As an alternative, some guest checks are designed with overlay copies; the copy containing the beverage order can be removed and retained at the beverage station.

In the kitchen, a similar exchange takes place. The guest check is presented by the server. Information on the check is used to prepare the food items that comprise your order. Again, a copy of the check is retained or a confirming notation is made.

```
                THE
                BACK
                PORCH

                                    126280
        SHERATON GRANDE

   DANNY                  CK# 2434
   10/20/86  12:47PM  05  TABLE- 20  COVERS-5

    6  FOOD         DOWNTOWNER      7.25
    7               PARADISE SALAD  4.50
    8               HOT ENCROUTE    8.95
    9               SUPER CLUB      6.50
   10               SWORDFISH LBP   9.25
   15       5       COFFEE          5.00
   16       5       PATISSERIES    18.75
        *****TOTAL FOOD        60.20
    1  BEVERAGE     IMPORTED BEER   3.00
   14               IMPORTED BEER   3.00
        *****TOTAL BEVERAGE      6.00
    2  WINE         GL BEAUL CHARD  3.50
    3               GL BEAUL CHARD  3.50
    4               GL ZINFANDEL YC 3.50
    5               GL CHENIN BLANC 3.50
   11               GL BEAUL CHARD  3.50
   12               GL CHENIN BLANC 3.50
   13               GL ZINFANDEL YC 3.50
        *****TOTAL WINE        24.50

     90.70 SBTL     5.90 TX    96.60 TTL

   Amount_____   THE
   Room_____   BACK
   Guest_____   PORCH
   Date_____   126280
```

Figure 3-1.

A meal check in a restaurant is a good example of a transaction document that represents an exchange of value.

So far, several steps have taken place. Beverages and food items have been delivered to the server separately, in exchange for something of value—the guest check. The guest check represents money that is to be collected from you before you leave. In business, transaction documents often are used to represent the exchange value of a transaction until payment is made. This concept is illustrated in Figure 3-1.

When you finish, the server totals, or summarizes, the original guest check. Individual items and prices now are described as a single data item, the price of your meal. The completed guest check is presented to you by the server.

You take the check to a cashier station, where you make payment. The overall transaction is completed. You have received a meal, and the restaurant has collected payment. Notice that product delivery and customer payment in this example are separated, by both time and physical location.

The nature of the restaurant dictates this practice. A customer does not receive full value until he or she has finished—and is satisfied—with both service and food. Thus, a transaction document is used to represent value until the exchange is completed.

The separation of delivery of service and/or product from exchange of value is typical of transactions among organizations. Services and goods often are provided in exchange for a promise to pay at a later date, such as 30 days from delivery. Businesses also use transaction documents to represent internal transactions. The exchange described above between server and chef is an example of an internal transaction in a restaurant. In a manufacturing business, transactions occur between purchasing and warehousing functions, warehousing and manufacturing functions, manufacturing and shipping functions, and so on.

Microcomputers provide capabilities for meeting the various data-handling requirements for organizations. Any organization, regardless of size, has requirements for creating and processing transaction data. **Transaction processing** refers to collecting and maintaining transaction data and manipulating that data to produce information about the status of the organization. Transaction processing usually involves the use of some kind of tools. In the above example, pencils and guest checks are used to record data. These data are entered into the restaurant's processing system at some later time. When a transaction is completed, it is reflected within the processing system of the organization. In the above example, transactions are not completed at the time they occur: The information recorded on the guest check is not entered into the restaurant's processing system until later.

Microcomputers make it possible to *perfect,* or complete, transactions at the time of occurrence. That is, data are entered into a system at the time of a transaction. For example, microcomputer-based transaction processing systems, allow store clerks to enter purchase data directly into transaction processing systems at the time of a customer's purchase. Purchase data then are transferred automatically to other points at which they are needed. Under these microcomputer-based systems, customers receive outputs similar to the one pictured in Figure 3-2.

In large organizations, microcomputer capabilities can be incorporated into overall, mainframe-based systems as well. In this context, microcomputers create and input data at points of transaction. This data can be shared throughout the

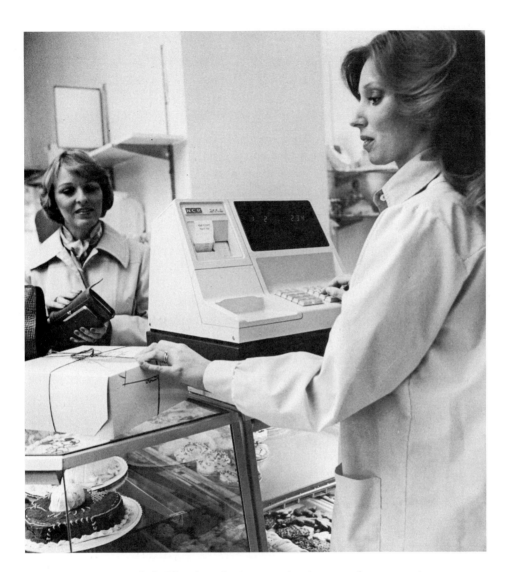

Figure 3-2.

In microcomputer-based transaction systems, data are entered directly, and support documents produced as needed, at the point of occurrence.

organization as needed. That is, a large organization may have massive accumulations of data files representing historical transaction activities. Microcomputers can be used to build or update these files at points of transactions. Further, managers may use microcomputers to **download,** or transfer from a mainframe, specified data entities for analyses and decision making support.

In effect, microcomputers run the gamut of information-handling needs. Microcomputers are powerful enough to provide a full range of support for small organizations, yet flexible enough to fit into overall systems schemes of large organizations. The value of these tools becomes increasingly apparent when seen in light of their role in transaction analysis, discussed in the section that follows.

MICROCOMPUTERS FOR TRANSACTION ANALYSIS

Suppose the restaurant in the above example features a special for the day—poached salmon. Managers know that 20 orders of the salmon have been purchased by the restaurant. This information may be presented on other transaction documents, called *invoices,* that are discussed later in this chapter.

At the end of the business day, managers can compare the number of salmon dishes ordered with the number of specials ordered and paid for by customers. This information is derived from data on guest checks. Managers also can compare the number of salmon orders from guest checks with the remaining supply, or physical inventory. Discrepancies will be investigated, and corrective action may be required. Figure 3-3 illustrates this control procedure.

Collectively, transaction data provides a basis for monitoring and controlling an organization's operations. This support capability, combined with the representation of exchange value discussed above, again illustrates the importance of data resources to businesses. As tools for handling data resources, microcomputers provide a means for managing an organization and plotting its future course.

Keep this point in mind as you read the section that follows. To enhance the discussion of transaction processing, this chapter now moves to a specific review of the execution of a business purchase. The internal transactions and documentation activities involved with the purchase also are covered.

The driving force of any organization is transactions. A business initiates transactions to obtain the raw materials and/or supplies from which it produces and delivers products or services. Additional transactions involve exchanges of products or services for money from customers. The data recorded with each exchange establish a control mechanism for the business. However, nothing happens until a need is present and identified.

The Transaction Path

In any organization, a need is identified when a worker or manager requires a product or service to perform a job. If that product or service is not available from present resource inventories, the business has to purchase it from an outside supplier. In business, needs of this type are known cumulatively as *demand.* In large organizations, the person with the identified need might prepare a *requisition.*

A requisition is a transaction document that describes a need and requests that the required good or service be purchased. A requisition is forwarded to the purchasing department of an organization, where it must be approved by someone authorized to spend money on behalf of the company. Data contained on this

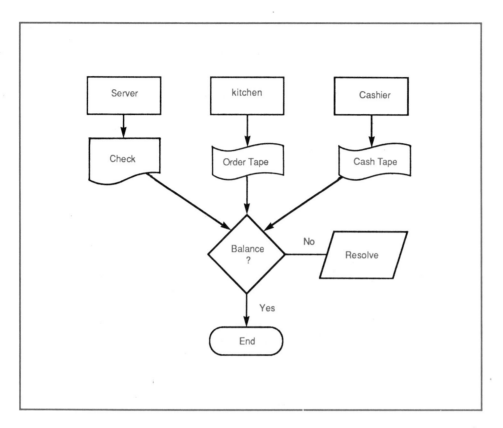

Figure 3-3.

Organizations can be monitored through comparisons and evaluations of transaction data.

type of document describe what is needed, how much is needed, and where or how it can be obtained. Figure 3-4 illustrates a typical requisition document.

For example, consider a fictional clock manufacturing company, Big Time, Inc. Mary Stewart, the manufacturing manager at Big Time, discovers that inventory levels of solder are low. Solder is a metallic alloy that is melted to join metal surfaces. Big Time uses solder to make electrical wiring connections in clocks.

Stewart realizes that, unless purchasing procedures for solder are implemented quickly, the supply of solder will be depleted and the entire manufacturing operation may be brought to a halt. She fills out a requisition for solder and forwards it to the purchasing department marked "Rush!"

Authorization for the purchase of solder is the responsibility of the purchasing manager. This manager also sees the urgency of the situation and wastes no time in granting approval by signing it. The purchasing manager then issues a **purchase order** for the solder. A purchase order is a transaction document that orders goods or services. (See Figure 3-5.) The purchasing manager sends the purchase order to a solder distributor by overnight mail.

```
┌─────────────────────────────────────────────────────────────────┐
│                                                                   │
│              DEPARTMENTAL REQUISITION                             │
│                                                                   │
│                                                                   │
│   DATE: 11/17/87                                                  │
│                                                                   │
│   DEPT: 38                                                        │
│                                                                   │
│   REQUESTED BY: B. Badger                                         │
│                                                                   │
│   AUTHORIZED BY (Purchasing agent): _____      │
│                                                                   │
│                                        Signature                  │
│                                                                   │
└─────────────────────────────────────────────────────────────────┘
```

STOCK#	ITEM DESCRIPTION	QTY	VENDOR
38912-4	3/4" Dowels	10 cases	Rollins Supply
87452-4	Brooms	2 dozen	Sweep n' Such
38847-2	4hp Electric Motor	3	Motor Works

Figure 3-4.

Data presented on requisition documents describe types and quantities of needed articles, and where the articles may be purchased.

The company that receives a purchase order can be referred to as the seller, or **vendor.** The vendor usually documents the transaction further by preparing its own paperwork. The vendor might first prepare a **picking order** that is used to assemble or gather ordered merchandise for shipment. Then, a **shipping order** might be issued to the shipping department or to an independent carrier that makes the delivery.

These documents serve many purposes. First, data contained on the documents is used to prepare and ship the correct order to the correct customer and address. Second, both of these documents are signed by appropriate personnel, which serves to confirm that the stage of the transaction reflected by the document has been completed. This type of confirmation mechanism represents a major reason for using transaction documents.

The solder supplier then produces and issues an invoice to the buying company, or customer—Big Time, Inc. An invoice serves many functions. Data items contained on an invoice identify the seller and the buyer and describe products and/or services to be exchanged. In addition, an invoice details prices for exchanged items, including taxes when necessary, and an overall amount owed by the buyer is calculated. Finally, an invoice represents a demand for payment for delivered goods or services and specifies **terms of payment.** Terms of payment

Carmello's Bakery

2893 Corvette Street

Seattle, WA   92874

SOLD TO: Manhattan Restaurant   SHIP TO: Same

12873 Occidental Road

Seattle, WA   92833

CUSTOMER NUMBER: 828432

PURCHASE ORDER NUMBER	ORDER DATE	SALESPERSON
8342	1/8/87	G. PALMATIER

QTY ORDERED	QTY SHIPPED	ITEM NUMBER	DESCRIPTION	UNIT PRICE	EXTENDED PRICE
3 dozen			Apricot Danish		
6 loaves			French Sourdough		
20 cases			After-dinner mints		

Figure 3-5.

A buyer sends a purchase order document to a vendor; the purchase order describes goods and services to be delivered to the buyer.

indicate when and how the buyer is asked to pay for goods or services received. Figure 3-6 illustrates a typical invoice form.

An invoice accompanies a delivery of goods or services. Upon delivery, the buyer signs the invoice and retains a copy. The signature confirms delivery and represents the buyer's agreement to the payment terms described on the invoice. For example, "net 30 days" are common terms of payment on business invoices. This means that the company can pay the indicated amount within 30 days and no interest or late charges will be added. The invoice also may describe interest or late charges that are accrued after the original 30-day period.

The receiving manager at Big Time, Inc., signs the invoice when the solder is delivered. The signed invoice represents a promise to pay for the solder. The purchasing manager retains a copy of the invoice, and the document moves further along the "path" initiated by the requisition for solder.

Data items from the invoice are entered into accounting and financial records. On a specified date, the accounting function issues another transaction document, a check, in payment for the solder. Information on the check describes the transaction, usually in terms of order number and amount of purchase. The accounting department retains a record of the check for this reason. When the vendor receives and deposits the check, the transaction is completed.

DONNY'S RECORDS AND CASSETTES

Customer Invoice

SOLD TO: James Funkhouser

Item No.	Qty Ordered	Unit	Item Description	Unit Price	Item Amount
1321	3	box	Album sleeves	8.49	25.47
1894	1	ea.	Diskcleaner	11.83	11.83
8323	2	ea.	Cassette racks	6.44	12.88

SUBTOTAL	50.18
TAX	3.10
TOTAL	53.28

TERMS: Net 30 days

RECEIVED BY: _____

Signature

Figure 3-6.

Data contained on invoices describe purchases, prices, and terms of payment.

Notice in this example that transaction documents are created at every step. These documents contain information used to support business and management functions. In addition, records handled by the accounting and financial functions accumulate to form a picture of the operating status and financial condition of the organization.

Transactions affect a business in one of two ways. Either the business has more money or less goods or services. Thus, the business changes with each transaction. For this reason, the currency with which transaction data can be maintained largely determines the value of support that decision makers can derive from its information systems. The section that follows discusses the functions and features of information systems set up to handle transactions.

MICROCOMPUTERS AND
TRANSACTION PROCESSING SYSTEMS

To repeat an earlier point, microcomputers are business tools that perform basic information-handling functions: input, processing, output, and storage. Data are transformed into information through applications of these functions. In a transaction processing system, for example, the data items, $4,500, or ORDER #12255, are meaningless by themselves. These data items must be combined with others before meaning is derived. For example, the data items, $4,500, RECEIVED, ORDER #12255, 5 CASES, ALMONDS, might indicate that $4,500 has been received for an order of almonds.

In a basic sense, this function is performed by computers in transaction processing systems. Transaction processing may be performed manually, or with the support of computers. When microcomputers are used, transaction data can be input at the source of the transaction. For this reason, transaction documents often are called source documents.

Entering data into a processing system involves converting entries into formats that can be handled by computers. Refer to the discussion in the first chapter concerning data items, data elements, and fields as the basic units of data. Data elements relating to a specific entity form a data record. Data records are combined into files. In transaction processing sytems, data files can be grouped into two main categories:

- Master files
- Transaction files.

Master Files

Master files contain information that reflects the current and past history of business activities. Master files are retained for long periods, sometimes permanently. Customer accounts represent a common type of master file. In a customer master file, separate account records are maintained for individual customers. Data items within these records reflect names, addresses, credit information, contact personnel, and other pertinent data items about customers.

In addition, the current and past balances, or amounts of money owed, are reflected by data items in the master record for each customer. Thus, each transaction conducted with a customer affects data items within that customer master record. Thus, master files must be ***updated*** periodically to reflect the impacts of ongoing transactions. As master files are updated, historic, or outdated, versions of the files are stored ***off-line*** for backup purposes. Off-line storage removes files from ready accessibility by a computer and holds them for possible future use.

Master files

*contain historical data and are
maintained for long periods.
This photo shows system files in
hard copy and in magnetic
media.*

COURTESY OF ACME VISIBLE RECORDS

Transaction Files

In contrast, ***transaction files*** are collected and retained for relatively short periods. The data items within transaction files usually are recorded in the order in which transactions take place; no specific order or organization scheme generally is possible. Transaction files simply are accumulations of data items from individual transactions. Then, transaction files are ***posted*** to, or used to update, master files.

For example, records from a cash receipts transaction file are posted against the corresponding records in the customer accounts master file. A cash receipt is a payment against an amount owed. Thus, a cash receipt transaction is posted to the data field for current balance in the appropriate customer record. In this way, current balances in customer account files are reduced and kept current.

Often—especially when microcomputers are used at the point of sale—transaction entries are created randomly, as they occur. Posting of transactions to master files usually occurs at regular intervals. Again, the posting of transaction files keeps master files up-to-date. Master files, in turn, reflect the condition of the business. This is one of the main functions of a transaction processing system. Recall that transactions, especially within large organizations, vary in complexity and nature. In addition, transaction processing activities vary for different organizations. Common categories for transaction processing do exist, however, and include:

- Purchasing and receiving

- Order entry, invoicing, and accounts receivable

- Accounts payable

- Inventory control

- Payroll and personnel.

In effect, each transaction processing system has one or more **subsystems.** Another transaction processing subsystem, called the general ledger, deals with using the transaction information for monitoring, controlling, and reporting on the status and condition of a business. Seen in this light, transaction processing takes on new meaning as a business resource.

Purchasing and Receiving.　Business organizations purchase goods and services to support their operations. Part of the responsibility of the purchasing and receiving function is to order needed supplies. Orders must be authorized by appropriate personnel, who are responsible for the money expended to make the purchase. Items to be purchased are documented on purchase orders—which represent formal commitment to future payments.

As the name implies, the purchasing and receiving department's duties also include inspections of incoming deliveries to confirm that items ordered, delivered, and described on invoices match purchasing commitments. Incorrect items and shipments must be caught to avoid paying for goods that have not been ordered or fail to meet specifications.

Order Entry, Invoicing, and Accounts Receivable.　Incoming orders for goods and services must be recorded and entered into the transaction processing system. The purchase order from the buying company usually serves as a source document for this operation, known as ***order entry.***

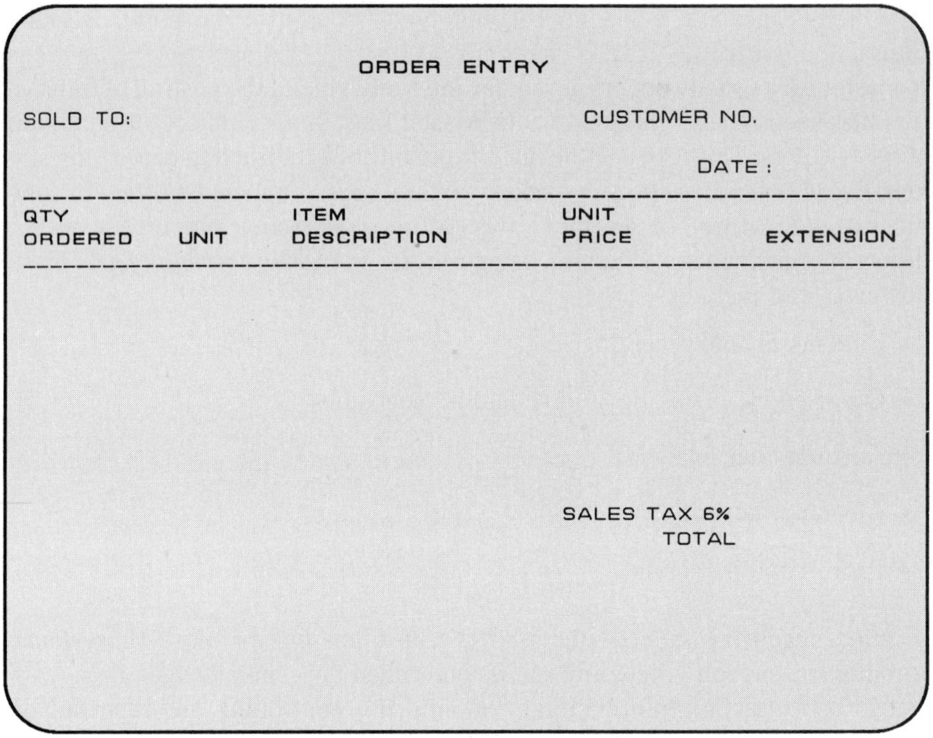

ORDER ENTRY

SOLD TO: CUSTOMER NO.

                                                DATE :

QTY   ITEM   UNIT
ORDERED   UNIT   DESCRIPTION   PRICE   EXTENSION

                                           SALES TAX 6%
                                                TOTAL

Figure 3-7.

Entry screens can streamline order entry operations; transaction data are entered into spaces provided on screens and input directly into the processing system.

Often, order entry is performed over the telephone. A purchasing company calls a vendor, and specifies items for order. A salesperson for the vendor organization confirms the order and immediately enters the data into the transaction processing system. Figure 3-7 shows a microcomputer terminal screen that might be used for an order entry application.

Microcomputers can streamline the order entry function significantly. For example, a credit check for the purchasing company can be generated automatically within these systems. If the purchase amount causes the buying company's balance to exceed established limits, the situation can be dealt with immediately.

The processing that is initiated by order entry activities usually results in an invoice that accompanies delivery of the order. Remember that an employee in the purchasing and receiving department at Big Time, Inc., signs the invoice upon delivery.

Big Time then owes money to the distributor for the solder. It is important that the distributor be able to monitor and control this source of income. Thus, a master file is maintained that includes current balances for all customers. Records for amounts owed by customers form an *accounts receivable* file. Transaction records are posted periodically against accounts receivable master files to reflect new additions or diminished balances.

```
Report Date:  10/28/87              Big Time, Inc.
                                    AGED TRIAL BALANCE


     Customer        Credit  Current   Over 18     Over 30     Total
     Name            Status  Billing   Days        Days        Due


  1. Hy Jewelers       B    $ 2,398.44 $ 1,094.44              $  3,492.88
  2. Dandy Drugs       A    $ 1,254.99 $ 2,358.7   $ 1,459.82  $  5,073.52
  3. Timeline Co.      C    $   526.99 $ 5,468.04  $ 1,258.76  $  7,253.79
  4. The Clockworks    A    $ 1,589.47 $ 3,654.20  $ 2,584.31  $  7,827.98
  5. Ferris Jewelers   B    $ 1,258.46 $ 2,365.84              $  3,624.30
  6. ABC Store         A    $ 2,548.76 $ 3,256.84  $ 2,365.84  $  8,171.44
  7. Ben's Market      C    $ 4,568.72 $ 3,654.98  $ 2,468.72  $ 10,692.42


                           $14,145.83 $21,853.05  $10,137.45  $46,136.33
```

Figure 3-8.

An aged trial balance document describes amounts owed by customers, organized according to payment due dates.

Accounts receivable files are used to follow up on payments due and to collect customer payments. Typically, a program is run that results in a report known as an *aged trial balance* of accounts receivable. This report shows amounts owed by all customers according to payment due dates. Figure 3-8 presents a typical aged trial balance. This report can be an effective tool for managing an organization's cash flow.

Accounts Payable. An account payable is established by a purchaser after a delivery has been received. The invoice that accompanies the delivery often is used as a source document for input to *accounts payable* files. An accounts payable file reflects money owed by an organization to its vendors.

Big Time, Inc., would post the purchase amount of the solder order to the account payable for that vendor. That amount is added to the previous amount owed to reflect the current balance. Outputs of this transaction processing subsystem are payments for ordered goods and services—usually in the form of a check. Payment cycles usually are set up according to payment terms described on invoices. Thus, an organization might establish a 10-day payment cycle for one vendor and a 30-day cycle for another.

Many vendors provide structured discounts to encourage early payments. For example, the solder vendor might stipulate "30-days net; 2 percent 10 days." This means that the net, or full, amount is due in 30 days and that a 2 percent discount may be taken if the bill is paid within 10 days. Computer systems can be programmed to generate outputs at times that take maximum advantage of such discounts.

Inventory Control. In the scenario of Big Time, Inc., the manufacturing manager discovers that inventory levels of solder are dangerously low. The urgency of this situation indicates a possible problem in the ***inventory control*** function. Inventory control is set up to establish and maintain appropriate stock levels.

Inventory levels of stock items should not go below or above established limits. The situation at Big Time illustrates potential negative effects if proper levels of solder are not maintained. In addition, stock items that exceed established limits can tie up the cash resources of a business. In this situation, stock items are paid for but will not be sold until a later period. In determining appropriate stock levels, then, managers evaluate the rate at which each product is selling, how long a product can be held in storage, and how long it takes for new supplies of a product to be delivered.

Payroll and Personnel. The payroll and personnel function handles transactions that involve employers and employees. Any time you go to work for a company, you enter into a transaction with that company. That is, you exchange something of value—your time, skills, and effort—for a specific wage or salary. The company pays the wage or salary in exchange for the value you deliver.

As with other types of transactions, payroll and personnel requires documentation. For example, when you go to work you might punch a time clock or enter IN and OUT times on a time sheet. These source documents provide information about when you arrive, how long you work, and when you leave. During processing, these and other data items that reflect your pay scale, tax status, and other deductions are processed to produce meaningful documents—your paycheck.

A single, overall transaction might follow a path that winds through many or all of the subsystems described above. Data items that reflect the transaction are recorded and processed at each step. Sometimes, the same data items are handled at several points along the transaction path. Such situations can create inefficiencies and other problems in information systems. Fortunately, microcomputers provide capabilities for solving these problems—especially microcomputers in conjunction with database software (the subject of a later chapter).

A database is a collection of data organized to support multiple applications. Further, databases can be accessed at the level of individual data items. This means that a user can retrieve specific elements within files as needed. Keep this in mind as you read the section that follows.

CASE SCENARIO: GENERATING INVOICES WITH MICROCOMPUTER TOOLS

Transaction processing requirements vary within businesses according to internal functions and departments. For efficient transaction processing, microcomputer systems should provide enough flexibility to execute multiple applications and to support the activities of multiple users. The same systems, however, also should provide mechanisms for effective control and maintenance of stored data.

To illustrate, consider the data items needed to produce an invoice. An invoice is a type of transaction document used by most businesses. Data items on an invoice identify the buyer, seller, products and/or services to be exchanged, unit prices, extended prices, taxes, and a total amount owed. In addition, an invoice represents a demand for payment and describes terms for which payment is expected.

Business documents,

such as invoices, result from processing of data on sales transactions.

COURTESY OF FACIT, INC.

```
                              ORDER  ENTRY

   SOLD TO:                                   CUSTOMER NO.

                                                 DATE :
   -----------------------------------------------------------------
   QTY                        ITEM              UNIT
   ORDERED      UNIT          DESCRIPTION       PRICE          EXTENSION
   -----------------------------------------------------------------
   10           case          Solder           $12.45         $124.50




                                              SALES TAX 6%    $7.47
   Big Time, Inc.                                    TOTAL    $131.97
   225 Hourglass Lane
   Milwaukee, WI 45987

   22378

   22 Jan 87
```

Figure 3-9.

Data for invoice documents are created and input during the order entry application.

Invoices are produced in response to orders from customers. Recall that the purchasing manager at Big Time, Inc. filled out a purchase order for solder. Continuing this scenario, suppose this purchase order was sent to a fictional vendor, Dragon Electrical Supply Company, referred to in this discussion as DESC.

The order department at DESC prides itself on providing quick service to customers. A microcomputer-based transaction processing system has been implemented to enhance this service.

In this system, order requests initially are entered into a transaction file of customer accounts. For example, the order from Big Time, Inc., is presented on a source document, the purchase order described in the previous section. This document is used to support order entry at DESC. Data items from the order are entered through a special terminal screen designed for this purpose, shown in Figure 3-9.

Notice the entry screen resembles an invoice form. This entry method is designed to facilitate operations. The operator first enters a customer identification in the field labeled SOLD TO. Entry of a customer identification (in this example the name of the company) triggers an access and retrieval operation. That is, the system locates the appropriate record in a customer master file and brings that record into the invoice file. This record includes data such as customer address, customer number, and credit status. The credit status data item indicates whether the customer has a credit account with DESC. In this case, Big Time has established a credit account with DESC, indicated by the word "OPEN" in the credit status field.

The invoice number and data shown on the entry screen are generated automatically by the system. Thus, the operator is ready now to enter items describing the purchase. The operator enters a code, or identifying number, for the solder and a quantity ordered, 10 cases. The system automatically locates and triggers the entry of product descriptions, such as name and **unit price.** Unit price is the amount charged for a single unit of a specific product. For each **line item,** or product description, on an invoice, the system also generates an **extended price.** An extended price is derived by multiplying unit price by number of units ordered.

Upon completion of order entry, indicated to the computer by the operator, the system computes any taxes and develops a total price for the order. The operator then compares the data displayed on the screen with the data from the purchase order. Any mistakes are corrected until the accuracy of the order has been confirmed.

A file has been created that can be output as an invoice document. This file is processed against master files to create, or update, an accounts receivable file that reflects money owed for the order. First, however, the invoice is output and used by the shipping department to compile and deliver the order to Big Time, Inc.

The shipping department retains a copy of the invoice as proof that the order has been filled. Additional copies are sent along with the order to Big Time, Inc. One copy is signed by an authorized person at Big Time to confirm delivery. One or more additional copies are retained at Big Time to establish or update an account payable. That is, the invoice is used as a basis of payment for delivered goods—the 10 cases of solder. An invoice, remember, represents a demand for payment. Figure 3-10 presents the finished invoice for this scenario. Notice the terms of payment at the bottom of the document.

To generate this invoice document, data items were drawn from multiple master files. This processing capability is provided partly by the organization scheme of the system at DESC. In this example, there is a logical relationship between the customer, Big Time, Inc., and the product, solder. This relationship is reflected within the organization's data resources.

DRAGON ELECTRICAL
SUPPLY COMPANY

321 St. George Boulevard
Milwaukee, Wisconsin 45987

INVOICE

SOLD TO:. Big Time, Inc.   NO. 22378
           225 Hourglass Lane
           Green Bay, Wisconsin 45703   DATE: 22JAN 1986

QTY	UNIT	NUMBER	DESCRIPTION	UNIT PRICE	EXTENSION
10	Box	5812	Solder	12.45	124.50
				SALES TAX 6%	$7.47
				TOTAL	$131.97

TERMS: Net 10 days
        Add 1% each 30 days past due
        Deduct 2% if mailed within 10 days.

Figure 3-10.

Data elements are pulled from multiple sources and presented as a finished output, the invoice.

Recall that business files represent the following entities:

- Sources of income, or customers

- Products and/or services sold by the business

- Suppliers

- Money owed to the business by customers

- Money owed by the business to vendors

- Acts of doing business.

This description illustrates the importance of files as resources. The addition of logical relationships adds another dimension to these resources. In effect, relationships are the "glue" that holds a business together. In this light, information resources can be said to create a **model** of the business.

A model provides many powerful capabilities for business managers. The model can be studied to determine the current status or condition of the business. In addition, the model can be manipulated to project, or **forecast,** the results of decisions or actions. Microcomputer tools provide these capabilities, as is discussed in the section that follows.

Status and Condition: A Study in Transactions

Business organizations need computer-maintained files, in part to produce information on status or condition. For most businesses, periodic status reports are required by government agencies. In addition, managers need to know whether more money is coming in (income) than going out (expenses).

Medium- to large-sized businesses engage in large volumes and varieties of transactions. Further, transactions are completed in stages. The period between order and payment may be 30 days or more—and may involve intermediate delivery and billing events. In such businesses, the ability to derive accurate determinations of income and expenses may stem from summary reports of transaction activities.

Detailed summaries of transactions can identify areas of strengths and problems for the business. The decision making activities of managers are supported by these status reports. In turn, the information accumulated in support of transactions and for status reporting is needed for planning. In this way, data resources also impact future operations of a business. Given this type and scope of impact, data files become central to the organization they support.

As a point of reference, the status of a business is related to its financial standing at a given time. For this reason, status reports are often called financial "snapshots" of a business. By definition, every transaction conducted by a business affects its financial status. The condition of a business is an indication of a company's overall worth. Information on both status and condition is derived from master files and/or the company's database. Special reporting programs extract information on financial status and condition to generate a series of documents that form the general ledger of the organization.

General ledger.   The general ledger application produces reports that summarize and provide a basis for analyzing business transactions. Data records and files from all of an organization's transaction processing applications (including order entry, invoicing, accounts receivable, payroll and personnel, and others described earlier in this chapter) are consolidated to produce general ledger reports.

The general ledger application organizes and summarizes transaction information according to importance to the operating success of the business. Since a key measure of the success of a business is the profit it produces, general ledger reports are organized accordingly.

A series of records, known as general ledger accounts, is established within a stored file. These records, or accounts, are organized under a plan known as a ***chart of accounts.*** See Figure 3-11. The chart of accounts is a list that separates and organizes the effects of transactions to reflect their impact upon the financial condition of the company. General ledger accounts are categorized according to income or expense. In this way, the differences between income and expenses reflect the profit position of the company.

Within the income portion of the general ledger, accounts are established to identify the sources of money received by the company. The level of detail in account breakdowns depends on the needs and interests of managers. For example, all sales income might be recorded in a single account. Or, under another approach, separate income accounts can be set up according to type of customer, geographic area, state, or other classification.

Accounts used for recording expenses typically are organized according to categories such as labor, materials, and overhead (the costs of running a company). Within these categories, accounts often are set up to record expenses according to department, product, or other classification.

All told, a general ledger may have hundreds of accounts that summarize income and expense items included in transactions. General ledger reports are produced periodically, usually monthly. Totals on the general ledger, in turn, are

```
                              Spinamar Inc.
                           CHART OF ACCOUNTS


      ACCT        DESCRIPTION          ACCT          DESCRIPTION

      100    ASSETS                    200     LIABILITIES & EQUITY
      102    Liquid Assets             201     Liabilities
      104       CASH                   202         ACCOUNTS PAYABLE
      106       CASH-City Bank         203         TAXES PAYABLE
      105       CASH-State Bank        204         SALARIES PAYABLE
      110       ACCOUNTS RECEIVABLE    207         PAYROLL TAXES PAYABLE
      111       Open/Unpaid Invoices   219           TOTAL LIABILITIES
      118       PREPAID EXPENSES       221     Equity
      127       Prepaid Insurance      230         RETAINED EARNINGS
      134       Prepaid Taxes          233         CURRENT EARNINGS
      135       Prepaid Rent           299     TOTAL LIABILITIES & EQUITY
      140       INVENTORY              300     INCOME
      141          TOTAL LIQUID ASSETS 301         CURRENT SALES
      145    Fixed Assets              401     EXPENSES
      147       Furniture & Equipment  403     Costs of Goods
      149       Less Depreciation      405     Rent
      150       TOTAL FIXED ASSETS     407     Utilities
      199    TOTAL ASSETS              499     TOTAL EXPENSES
```

matched against and must balance with controls established within transaction processing systems. Specifically, the total of income must equal the total for expenses and profits.

As a management tool, general ledger reports provide a basis for monitoring the current, ongoing operations of the organization. General ledger reports break down income and expenses in enough detail to establish controls over the individual parts of an organization to the level of sales regions, individual products, operating departments, rent, utilities, maintenance, etc. This information is important and valuable, but is too detailed to provide an overview of company status.

For example, a general ledger report may contain enough detail to occupy 20 or 30 pages of account detailing. However, for top managers, government agencies, banks, and others it is useful to compress overall status information into two or three pages. To accomplish this, the detailed account listings of the general ledger are consolidated into a smaller number of accounts. These items, in turn, are listed on a set of documents known as *financial statements.*

Figure 3-11.

A chart of accounts organizes transactions according to their effects on the financial status of the organization.

Financial Statements

A set of financial statements consists of three documents:

- Income statement
- Balance sheet
- Statement of changes in financial condition.

Income statement.   An *income statement* presents a summary of money coming in and money going out. Data items on an income statement are separated
into two categories: income and expenses. Income items deal with money
received or promises to pay and may be derived from general ledger accounts
for cash receipts or accounts receivable.

Expense items represent money that the company pays for resources, facilities, and personnel, and for any cost incurred to support business operations.
Data items in this category stem from purchase orders, accounts payable, payroll and personnel, and other general ledger expense totals.

Totals are calculated for both categories and then the expense total is subtracted from the income total. The resulting value is the net income or loss the
organization has realized from operations.

An income statement provides managers with an indication of the relative
success of their operations. Figure 3-12 presents a sample income statement from
a fictional business organization. It often is said that the "bottom line" goal of
a business is to make a profit. The bottom line may stem from the location of
profit or loss figures on business income statements. In simple terms, profit is
the difference between income, the money coming in, and expenses, the money
going out—given that more money is taken in than paid out. If expenses exceed
income, a loss situation results.

Balance sheet.   A *balance sheet* is a report that describes the worth of a business. A balance sheet involves data items that represent what the business has,
what it owes, and the difference between the two. Balance sheet entries are
categorized according to *assets, liabilities,* and *equity.*

Assets are items that represent the value of an organization. Thus, money in
the bank is an asset. Because money and certain securities are easily spent, they
are known as *liquid assets.* Other items of value, such as land, buildings, and
heavy machinery, are known as *fixed assets* because it would take time to realize cash from these items.

Randazzo Food Market

Run Date: 04/22/87

INCOME	March 1987	March 1986	YTD 1987	YTD 1986
Grocery	$ 83,482.93	$ 79,374.22	$ 984,298.33	$ 883,232.22
Meats	$ 11,289.33	$ 14,232.33	$ 184,520.74	$ 157,320.28
Dairy	$ 22,984.10	$ 24,873.93	$ 258,284.23	$ 304,872.32
Produce	$ 18,329.33	$ 16,824.20	$ 248,528.47	$ 228,375.92
Frozen Foods	$ 31,842.88	$ 29,472.84	$ 329,462.88	$ 318,428.28
Deli	$ 12,984.22	$ 10,324.48	$ 153,823.82	$ 119,823.84
Paper Goods	$ 8,428.74	$ 6,087.34	$ 96,263.85	$ 78,185.34
Soft Goods	$ 5,620.64	$ 5,319.47	$ 58,453.97	$ 49,762.99
Stationery	$ 2,843.09	$ 1,952.22	$ 29,653.97	$ 27,482.85
Gross Income	$ 197,805.26	$ 188,461.03	$2,343,290.26	$2,167,484.04

EXPENSES				
Costs of Goods	$ 83,753.93	$ 79,284.34	$ 996,231.49	$ 851,285.35
Payroll	$ 28,482.27	$ 27,932.46	$ 345,681.39	$ 359,835.26
Rent	$ 3,573.39	$ 3,462.95	$ 35,654.18	$ 37,408.45
Utilities	$ 489.23	$ 524.83	$ 58,248.24	$ 61,283.28
Equipment	$ 264.98	$ 1,832.94	$ 1,966.43	$ 4,283.28
Advertising	$ 832.74	$ 793.64	$ 2,387.64	$ 2,793.62
Administration	$ 384.29	$ 857.25	$ 2,793.75	$ 9,732.98
Insurance	$ 2,483.83	$ 4,287.47	$ 11,468.96	$ 65,843.44
Depreciation	$ 387.52	$ 403.74	$ 1,583.85	$ 1,646.98
Total Expenses	$ 120,652.18	$ 119,379.62	$1,456,015.93	$1,394,112.64
NET INCOME	$ 77,153.08	$ 69,081.41	$ 887,274.33	$ 773,371.40

Figure 3-12.

Data included in income statements describe the relative success (profit) or failure (loss) of an organization during the reporting period.

Liabilities are amounts owed—such as unpaid taxes, loans from banks or other financial institutions, and accounts payable. A balance sheet gets its name from the practice of balancing assets against liabilities and equity. Equity represents the worth of a business. Equity is calculated by subtracting the value of liabilities from the value of assets. In theory, if all assets were converted to cash and used to pay off all liabilities, the remaining money would represent equity, the business' worth. Figure 3-13 presents a sample balance sheet.

Income statements and balance sheets, then, are effective tools for describing the status and/or condition of a business. Income statements can be thought of as summaries of the results of operations. Balance sheets focus on the financial condition of a company. Managers or other decision makers also can benefit from a third type of financial statement that describes changes in financial conditions.

Statement of changes in financial condition.   A *statement of changes in financial condition* is a report that presents a picture of the flow of financial resources during a given period. Thus, this report summarizes income and expenses. The report also describes money brought into a company by investors, stockholders, or sales of fixed assets. Collectively, these financial resources and operational income are known as *working capital.*

In effect, a statement of changes in financial condition details the sources of working capital and the areas in which it is applied. A typical statement of changes in financial condition is presented in Figure 3-14. Working capital is decreased by expenditures applied to equipment and land purchases, dividends paid to stockholders, and profits retained by owners.

A statement of financial condition is useful to managers as well as to creditors and financial analysts. This type of report presents the answers to questions such as: What use was made of net income? Why have assets declined even though income has increased? The ability to pose and to answer these questions can be enhanced by using microcomputer tools.

In summary, all three of the financial reports described above stem from master files updated through transaction processing. General ledger reports are derived from the files and, in turn, serve as the basis for financial reports. Financial reports for management are among a variety of end products developed from what are known as an organization's information resources. Collectively, these information resources create a model of the organization. The model is applied in a variety of situations to support managerial decision making and organizational planning.

```
                        Spinamar Inc.
                        March 1, 1987

    GENERAL LEDGER
    BALANCE SHEET

                             ASSETS
    ================================================================

    Liquid Assets
    ----------------------------------------------------------------

    CASH                        $4,234.88
    ACCOUNTS RECEIVABLE         $81,349.84
    PREPAID EXPENSES            $1,299.42
    INVENTORY                   $28,349.22

         TOTAL LIQUID ASSETS                   $115,233.36


    Fixed Assets
    ----------------------------------------------------------------

    FURNITURE & EQUIPMENT       $135,628.65
    LESS DEPRECIATION           $30,873.75

         TOTAL FIXED ASSETS                    $104,754.90

         TOTAL ASSETS                                $219,988.26
                                                     ============



                        LIABILITIES & EQUITY
    ================================================================

    Liabilities
    ----------------------------------------------------------------

    ACCOUNTS PAYABLE            $79,417.49
    TAXES PAYABLE               $2,514.39
         TOTAL CURRENT LIABILITIES            $81,931.88

    NOTE PAYABLE-BANK           $55,332.96
         TOTAL LONG-TERM LIABILITIES          $55,332.96

         TOTAL LIABILIIES                           $135,264.84
                                                     ============


    Equity
    ----------------------------------------------------------------

    EQUITY                      $52,146.42
    RETAINED EARNINGS           $2,578.03
    CURRENT EARNINGS            $29,998.97

         TOTAL EQUITY                          $84,723.42

         TOTAL LIABILITIES & EQUITY                 $219,988.26
                                                     ============
```

Figure 3-13.

A balance sheet describes the condition, or overall worth, of an organization in terms of assets, liabilities, and equity, or worth of the business.

```
                              ACME, Inc.

              STATEMENT_OF_CHANGES_IN_FINANCIAL_CONDITION


                                            Year Ended June 30,
                                              1987        1986
                                            ---------   ---------
SOURCE OF FUNDS:
   Net income before extraordinary
      item                                  $ 25,492    $ 20,996
   Item not requiring outlay of working
      capital:
         Depreciation                          2,968         960
   Extraordinary item:
      Reduction of federal taxes on income
         through utilization of operating
         loss carryover                      -------     ----434
   Working capital provided from operations   28,460      22,390


APPLICATION OF FUNDS:
   Purchase of furniture and equipment         6,277      13,204
   Increase (decrease) in deposit          (___150)      ----40
                                              _6,127      13,244

INCREASE IN WORKING CAPITAL                 $ 22,333    $  9,146
                                            ======      ======

              SUMMARY OF CHANGES IN WORKING CAPITAL

CURRENT ASSETS - INCREASE (DECREASE):
   Cash                                     $ 24,936    $  8,335
   Accounts Receivable                        22,777       7,962
   Royalty advances to authors                 1,700       2,000
   Refundable federal and state taxes on income 2,565         -
   Due from stockholder                          967         -
   Inventory                                   2,935         261
   Prepaid expenses                          --:----    (_1,919)
                                              55,880      16,639

CURRENT LIABILITIES - INCREASE (DECREASE):
   Note payable to bank                       50,000         -
   Accounts payable                             718      ( 1,666)
   Royalty advances from publishers            2,879       2,905
   Notes payable to stockholders             (13,070)    (18,930)
   Federal and state taxes on income        ( 4,210)       4,037
   Deferred income                           (_2,770)     21,147
                                              33,547      _7,493

INCREASE IN WORKING CAPITAL                 $ 22,333       9,146
                                            =======      ======
```

Figure 3-14.

A statement of changes in financial condition presents data that describe the flow of working capital for an organization.

Capabilities required to create and manipulate the data resources that make up this model are provided most effectively by microcomputers. Microcomputers have come of age as tools for supporting both ongoing operations and planning future-related activities. To best use these tools, an understanding of the technology behind microcomputers often is helpful. Technology-related topics comprise the two chapters that follow.

KEY TERMS

owner	demand	inventory control
custodian	requisition	unit price
driving force	purchase order	line item
transaction	vendor	extended price
document	picking order	model
exchange of value	shipping order	forecast
barter system	terms of payment	chart of accounts
medium of exchange	master file	financial statement
point of transaction	update	income statement
transaction source	off-line	balance sheet
transaction document	transaction file	asset
source document	post	liability
transaction flow	subsystem	equity
transaction processing	order entry	liquid asset
perfect	accounts receivable	fixed asset
download	aged trial balance	statement of changes in financial condition
invoice	accounts payable	working capital

DEFINITIONS

Instructions: On a separate sheet, define each term according to its use in this chapter.

1. transaction

2. source document

3. order entry

4. chart of accounts

5. asset

6. point of transaction

7. accounts payable

8. aged trial balance

T R U E / F A L S E

Instructions: For each statement, write T for true or F for false on a separate sheet.

1. Mainframe computers and centralized processing systems tend to create a separation between owners and custodians of data.

2. As people began to live in cities, a simple system of barter was no longer sufficient for business transactions.

3. An invoice is a transaction document that orders goods or services.

4. A chart of accounts is a report that summarizes inventory data.

5. The company that receives a purchase order is known as the vendor.

6. By signing a requisition, a buyer confirms a delivery and agrees to the terms of payment.

7. One advantage of using microcomputers for transaction processing is that data can be input to the system at the source of transactions.

8. Transaction processing categories include accounts payable, inventory control, and payroll/personnel.

9. Order entry often is performed by telephone.

10. Not every transaction conducted by a business affects its financial status.

11. The production of a general ledger report involves records and files from all of an organization's transaction processing applications.

12. A balance sheet describes the flow of financial resources during a given period.

13. Microcomputers cannot be used to download data from a mainframe.

14. An accounts payable file is comprised of records for amounts owed by customers.

15. The net income of an organization can be derived from the formula: income minus expenses.

SHORT ANSWER QUESTIONS

Instructions: On a separate sheet of paper, answer each question in one or two brief sentences.

1. Explain the difference between ownership and custody of data resources.

2. List and describe the three documents which make up a set of financial statements.

3. What are the functions served by an invoice?

4. List and describe the two categories into which data files are grouped in transaction processing systems.

5. What are the two significant factors contributing to the strength of microcomputers as transaction processing tools?

6. Has the nature of transactions changed since the beginnings of commerce? If so, how?

RESEARCH PROJECT

Think about the concepts of transaction flow and flow of data within systems. Then describe a transaction processing system with which you are familiar. Explain the sequence of transactions and the flow of data within this system. Also include descriptions of any source documents, transaction documents, or summary documents that are a part of the system. Suggestions for transaction processing systems that you may be familiar with include your personal checking account, your school's bookstore, or your place of work.

4 Microcomputer Hardware: Input and Storage

SCOPE

An understanding of technical principles helps to make educated use of and/or decisions relating to microcomputers.

INFORMATION OWNERSHIP

When ownership and custody of information are shared and distributed among users, the efficiency of information processing is greatest.

PROCESSING TECHNOLOGY

Computer processing involves routing electronic impulses that represent data through a collection of switching devices within the computer.

Any data item or program instruction must be encoded into a two-state, or binary, format; all data values are coded as collections of bits representing combinations of zeros and ones.

HARDWARE EVOLUTION

Developments in hardware technology have occurred in response to user demand for increased performance and capacity.

Vacuum Tubes

The first generation of computers used vacuum tubes as switching devices; the size of these devices made computers extremely large and bulky, requiring extensive maintenance.

Transistors

Transistors are made of special solid materials called semiconductors, generating less heat and consuming less electricity than vacuum tubes.

Integrated Circuits

Integrated circuits, consisting of silicon chips layered with semiconductor materials, marked a major advance in computer technology, leading to the development of the microchip.

Microchips

Very large-scale integration resulted in the development of microchips that could perform the entire range of processing functions (microprocessors) and made possible the development of the microcomputer.

Types of Memory

Microchip technology has had a profound impact on random access memory, and also has led to the development of read-only memory and programmable read-only memory.

INPUT DEVICES

A variety of devices for entering data into microcomputers are available to meet a wide range of needs.

Keyboards

Keyboards are the most common input device for microcomputers; they provide capabilities for controlling cursor movement, initiating standard processing operations, and selecting processing options.

Mouse Devices

A mouse is a pointing device that is maneuvered manually across a surface to control cursor movement; mouse devices are especially useful for graphics and electronic publishing applications.

Touch Screens

A touch screen allows users to make menu selections by touching its special, sensitized terminal screen with a variety of pointing devices.

Electronic Tablets

An electronic tablet enables users to input images by moving a pen-like device on a touch-sensitive surface.

Voice Input

Voice recognition devices are still in the developmental stages, although voice input may someday become a highly popular method of data entry.

Optical Devices

Optical devices convert visual images into digital signals; reading devices called scannners are the most popular tools for optical input.

DISPLAYS

Display devices serve both input and output functions within computer systems.

Graphic Displays

CAD/CAM applications make use of graphics capabilities, in which pictorial images are digitized for display and can be manipulated visually.

STORAGE DEVICES

Processing revolves around the storage function, so the speed with which data and programs can be accessed is a significant factor in determining system performance.

Magnetic Disks

Magnetic disks—which include floppy diskettes and hard disks—are the most common storage media for microcomputers.

Tape Storage

Magnetic tape is convenient for creating backup versions of software and stored files that must be kept for long periods.

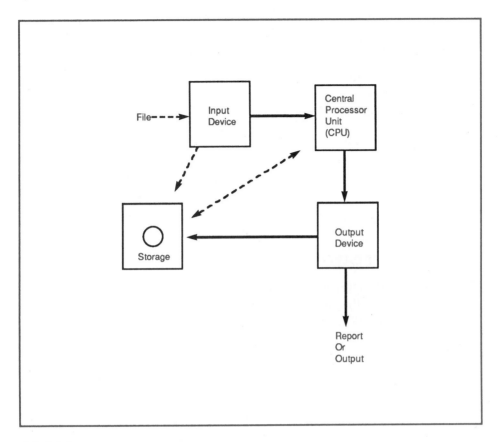

Figure 4-1.

A ''black box'' view of information processing systems describes the functions performed by, and the flow of data into and out of, hardware devices.

SCOPE

Earlier chapters in this text have stressed that all computers, large or small, perform the same basic processing functions. Similarly, all computers, regardless of their size, operate under the same basic technological principles. For many people, solving business problems with computer tools can be accomplished without understanding the underlying technologies.

Most computer devices can be viewed as ''black boxes'' into which source data are entered and from which specific results are derived. That is, the internal processes are out of sight of (and need not concern) the user. Computer systems often are portrayed as collections of black boxes. For example, in a processing diagram, data files are depicted as being entered into a processor that generates outputs. See Figure 4-1. Notice in the diagram that the internal operations by which data are manipulated within the processor are not described or represented.

For instruction purposes, this approach is practical and convenient—and can establish a fundamental understanding of system functions. However, knowledge about the equipment you are using can make you a more effective user. For example, it is possible to drive a car with no knowledge whatsoever of engine operation and maintenance or of tire care. It is clear, though, that an understanding of these topics will make you a better, safer driver. The same principle applies to microcomputers. The greater your knowledge base, the more effective and sophisticated a user you can become.

The discussions in this chapter and in the one that follows are oriented toward imparting a level of technical understanding that can be applied to business decisions and operations. This approach can be summarized with the statement: An understanding of technical principles can enhance your abilities to make educated use of and/or decisions relating to microcomputers.

INFORMATION OWNERSHIP

A major challenge in microcomputer use lies in matching the capabilities of system components to the requirements of individual jobs. If mismatches occur between requirements and capabilities, problems can be compounded rather than solved.

Just as the range of business functions and requirements is broad and varied, so are the computer systems implemented to perform the functions and to meet the requirements. At one extreme, large, centralized systems feature multiple computers or configurations involving mainframes and one or more *front-end* machines. In these multi-computer installations, the front-end machine handles communication and processing setup (housekeeping) chores. The large-scale system then is free to dedicate all of its power to actual processing. It is not unusual for centralized systems to handle 100 or more files—each containing up to 40 million bytes of data.

Under this type of system, data from user departments are transferred to a computer center for processing. User data files become part of central data resources. For example, a sales department might create source documents as customer orders are received. A source document is a form used for initial recording of data to be input to a computer or system. Source documents for customer orders would be sent to the central facility and source data would be input to the computer for processing. After processing, invoice outputs are forwarded to the accounts receivable and warehousing functions to complete the transaction.

As an alternative, source documents might be processed in a sales department through the use of microcomputers or computer terminals. This means each transaction is completed, or perfected, at its point of origin. However, data

about the transaction still are transmitted to and maintained by a central computer. Only the point of input moves when an organization maintains a single, central, massive computer facility.

In centralized systems, data are recorded, processed, stored, and accessed from the central facility. This approach provides many advantages. System performance often is measured in costs per byte of storage. In these terms, large systems provide efficiency through economies of scale. In a large system, unit costs of data storage and processing are lower, proportionately, than for smaller computers or manual methods. Centralization also facilitates the uniformity needed for consolidated corporate reporting.

However, the separation of data resources from the points at which data are created and used can lead to problems. A sales department, for example, relies on customer, product, and sales history information to do its job. The sales department generates these data and relies on the resulting files for day-to-day operations and decisions. The sales department, then, functions as creator and

Many large corporations

maintain enormous libraries of stored data.
PHOTO BY LIANNE ENKELIS

primary user of marketing and product data. Such a user group is said to be the **owner** of the data resources they create and on which they rely. When the data reside on an electronic file in another location, **custody** of the data is separated from ownership. Managers in the marketing department, in effect, surrender some control over the resources they own.

To illustrate, customers often revise orders. Salespeople cannot afford to be unable to accommodate customer requests because of limitations to their ability to access data. The efficiency of information processing—and, in turn, the functioning of the entire organization—is greatest when both ownership and custody of information are shared by, or distributed to, users.

The hardware configuration of **distributed systems**, for example, illustrates one method for sharing data resources. In a distributed system, remote or outlying work stations are linked to a central computer facility. In this way, an organization's executives have access to a composite information "picture" while users retain ownership, and possibly custody, of needed information resources. Microcomputers play major roles in the implementation of distributed systems. Either of two approaches can be used.

Under one method, microcomputer users retain both ownership and custody of data. That is, transactions are processed to completion at the point of occurrence. In addition, the microcomputers retain files that are updated at the time transactions take place. The microcomputer files are used periodically to update the central files for the company as a whole. This type of arrangement implements **standalone** processing by microcomputers.

Under the alternative method, the microcomputer is linked, through communication lines, with the central computer. The microcomputer draws upon the master files in the central computer. Transactions processed on the microcomputer update the master files in the central computer. This type of processing is said to be **interactive.** The microcomputer user has ready access to data files, and, thus, shares custody with the central facility.

With either approach, the microcomputer has a major impact on the way an organization does business. Control and decision power are placed in the hands of the managers who transact a given type of business. The capabilities and configurations of the microcomputers can differ extensively for each type of application. These differences represent a basis for understanding microcomputer equipment and operations.

PLACE VALUES	BINARY SYSTEM					DECIMAL SYSTEM			
	8	4	2	1		1000	100	10	1
	0	0	0	0	=	0	0	0	0
	0	0	0	1	=	0	0	0	1
	0	0	1	0	=	0	0	0	2
	0	0	1	1	=	0	0	0	3
	0	1	0	0	=	0	0	0	4
	0	1	0	1	=	0	0	0	5
	0	1	1	0	=	0	0	0	6
	0	1	1	1	=	0	0	0	7
	1	0	0	0	=	0	0	0	8
	1	0	0	1	=	0	0	0	9

Figure 4-2.

The decimal system assigns place values for numbers in powers of 10; in the binary system, place values are assigned in powers of 2.

PROCESSING TECHNOLOGY

One key function of hardware, as illustrated in the above example, is to establish access to data for users. The success of microcomputers is due partly to their ability to distribute data access throughout business organizations. Microcomputers also are cost-effective enough to allow the distribution of processing capabilities as well. A full-service processing facility configured to sit on a desktop can be relatively inexpensive.

In a basic sense, a computer is a complex collection of electronic switching devices, or *gates,* that are arranged to reflect processing operations. Processing involves routing (under program control) electronic impulses, or signals, that represent data through these gates. The signals change the condition of the electronic switches to achieve processing results. Other components convert these electronic signals into some type of human-readable output.

Data Representation

A switch has two states: off and on. Therefore, any data item or program instruction entered into main memory or processed must be *encoded* into a two-state, or *binary,* format. Encoding is a process for recording, or *capturing,* information in a specific, machine-readable pattern through use of a given set of symbols of values. In binary, or two-state, coding, these values are zero (0) and one (1). Computer data representation, then, is based on the two states or conditions of binary signals. The on and off, or positive and negative, states parallel the numeric values of 1 and 0 that make up the *binary number system.* See Figure 4-2.

As shown, numbers written in binary notation are expressed as sets of zeros and ones. Within computer processors, each gate, or switch, is either off or on, depending on whether current has been applied. An "off" condition is given a zero value; an "on" condition is given a value of one. Binary recording in electronic memories is based on the presence of positive or negative values for transistors built into microchips. A negative charge is treated as a 0 value, a positive charge as a 1. Each gate or memory position is said to represent one ***bit (Binary digIT)*** of data.

Data values are represented, or ***coded,*** as collections of bits, or combinations of zeros and ones. Letters, numbers, punctuation marks, and special codes all can be represented in binary format. Each of these ***characters*** is coded as a series of bits. A ***byte*** is a collection of bits that represents a single data character. Each data character is represented by a specific pattern of bits, one byte in length.

The number of bits per byte may vary. However, many computers use coding schemes that include eight bits per byte. Under this scheme, 256 different bit patterns (combinations of 0 and 1 values) are possible within a single recording position. Each bit combination is assigned to a specific data character. With an eight-bit byte, 256 different characters can be represented.

The most popular coding schemes for data representation include:

- ***Extended Binary Coded Decimal Interchange Code (EBCDIC)*** which is based on an eight-bit byte.

- ***American Standard Code for Information Interchange (ASCII)*** which was based originally on seven bits per byte. A newer version uses eight-bit bytes.

Figures 4-3 and 4-4 present listings of EBCDIC and ASCII coding schemes and a brief explanation of their coding conventions. The EBCDIC system was developed by IBM for use on mainframe systems. This format has been adopted as the internal language for a number of computers, particularly large systems. ASCII was developed before the introduction of computers. Originally, this coding scheme was used for communication between teletypewriters. ASCII also is the internal language for a number of minicomputers and for many microcomputers.

ASCII has remained the standard for data communication, since this language is compatible with equipment of the telephone industry. To implement communication among computers, devices that use EBCDIC or other coding schemes, require translation capabilities. That is, EBCDIC must be converted to ASCII, transmitted from point of origin to destination, then converted to the language of the receiving computer. ASCII transmission also makes it possible to link computers that have different, basically incompatible internal coding schemes. See Figure 4-5.

CHARACTER	EBCDIC ZONE	EBCDIC DIGIT	CHARACTER	EBCDIC ZONE	EBCDIC DIGIT	CHARACTER	EBCDIC ZONE	EBCDIC DIGIT
a	1000	0001	A	1100	0001	0	1111	0000
b	1000	0010	B	1100	0010	1	1111	0001
c	1000	0011	C	1100	0011	2	1111	0010
d	1000	0100	D	1100	0100	3	1111	0011
e	1000	0101	E	1100	0101	4	1111	0100
f	1000	0110	F	1100	0110	5	1111	0101
g	1000	0111	G	1100	0111	6	1111	0110
h	1000	1000	H	1100	1000	7	1111	0111
i	1000	1001	I	1100	1001	8	1111	1000
j	1001	0001	J	1101	0001	9	1111	1001
k	1001	0010	K	1101	0010	(space)	0100	0000
l	1001	0011	L	1101	0011	.	0100	1011
m	1001	0100	M	1101	0100	<	0100	1100
n	1001	0101	N	1101	0101	(	0100	1101
o	1001	0110	O	1101	0110	+	0100	1110
p	1001	0111	P	1101	0111	&	0101	0000
q	1001	1000	Q	1101	1000	!	0101	1010
r	1001	1001	R	1101	1001	$	0101	1011
s	1010	0010	S	1110	0010	*	0101	1100
t	1010	0011	T	1110	0011	)	0101	1101
u	1010	0100	U	1110	0100	;	0101	1110
v	1010	0101	V	1110	0101	/	0110	0001
w	1010	0110	W	1110	0110	,	0110	1011
x	1010	0111	X	1110	0111	%	0110	1100
y	1010	1000	Y	1110	1000	?	0110	1111
z	1010	1001	Z	1110	1001	#	0111	1011

Figure 4-3.

The Extended Binary Coding System (EBCDIC) represents characters by designating zone and digit portions of an eight-bit byte. The zone portion indicates the type of character. The uppercase alphabet is divided into three groups: A through I (1100), J through R (1101), and S through Z (1110). Other character groups, such as numbers and lowercase alphabet, are designated by bit codes within the zone portion of the byte. The digit portion specifies individual characters within each of these groups.

CHARACTER	ASCII BINARY	ASCII DECIMAL	CHARACTER	ASCII BINARY	ASCII DECIMAL	CHARACTER	ASCII BINARY	ASCII DECIMAL
a	1100001	97	A	1000001	65	0	0110000	48
b	1100010	98	B	1000010	66	1	0110001	49
c	1100011	99	C	1000011	67	2	0110010	50
d	1100100	100	D	1000100	68	3	0110011	51
e	1100101	101	E	1000101	69	4	0110100	52
f	1100110	102	F	1000110	70	5	0110101	53
g	1100111	103	G	1000111	71	6	0110110	54
h	1101000	104	H	1001000	72	7	0110111	55
i	1101001	105	I	1001001	73	8	0111000	56
j	1101010	106	J	1001010	74	9	0111001	57
k	1101011	107	K	1001011	75	(space)	0100000	32
l	1101100	108	L	1001100	76	.	0100001	33
m	1101101	109	M	1001101	77	"	0100010	34
n	1101110	110	N	1001110	78	#	0100011	35
o	1101111	111	O	1001111	79	$	0100100	36
p	1110000	112	P	1010000	80	%	0100101	37
q	1110001	113	Q	1010001	81	&	0100110	38
r	1110010	114	R	1010010	82	(	0101000	40
s	1110011	115	S	1010011	83	)	0101001	41
t	1110100	116	T	1010100	84	*	0101010	42
u	1110101	117	U	1010101	85	+	0101011	43
v	1110110	118	V	1010110	86	.	0101110	46
w	1110111	119	W	1010111	87	/	0101111	47
x	1111000	120	X	1011000	88	<	0111100	60
y	1111001	121	Y	1011001	89	>	0111110	62
z	1111010	122	Z	1011010	90	?	0111111	63

Figure 4-4.

The American Standard Code for Information Interchange (ASCII) represents characters as seven-bit bytes.

Figure 4-5.

To produce results, people working together must be able to communicate with each other. Similarly, computers must be able to ''speak,'' or at least understand, the same language to complete data transfers.

To write data to external storage, electrical impulses are converted to magnetic spots on disk or tape in the same bit and byte patterns used by the computer. These patterns are read from disk or tape in the same way for input to the computer. Storage technology is discussed in depth later in this chapter.

Regardless of the coding scheme used, the principle of computer processing is the same. Electricity flows through a circuit (a complete path followed by current) each time it passes through a gate, or switch. Each gate represents a specific processing function. Since the 1950s, the electronic switching devices used in computers have evolved from vacuum tubes to the microchips from which microcomputers derive their name.

Thousands of vacuum tubes

and rooms full of hardware handled processing on early computers. This is ENIAC, the first electronic computer.

HARDWARE EVOLUTION

Throughout the evolution of computers, hardware developments have resulted in capabilities for building smaller processing components with increased capacities. Every development has been a response to the continuing demand of computer users for increased performance and capacity, at decreased costs. The section that follows describes this evolution.

Vacuum Tubes

Vacuum tubes are a type of switching device that was used through the 1950s in machines that came to be known as *first-generation* computers. Vacuum tubes are similar in construction to incandescent light bulbs. A glowing *filament,* or wire, through which electricity is flowing, gives off electrons when voltage is applied. For this reason, the filament—or a separate metal plate heated by the filament—in this type of switch serves as an *emitter.* Another metal plate, called the *anode,* picks up electrons from the emitter to complete, or close, the circuit. When no voltage is applied to the emitter, no electrons flow and the circuit is incomplete, or open.

Electronic devices that perform this kind of binary, or two-state, switching are known as *diodes.* A switch has two states, open and closed. A vacuum tube is switched on and off by applying or removing voltage, creating positive or negative conditions respectively.

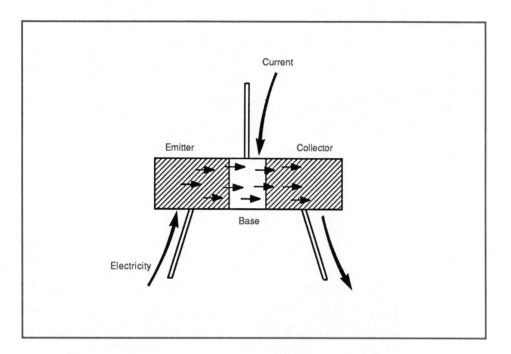

Figure 4-6.

Electrical signals passed through a transistor are "switched," or routed, according to the positive or negative condition of the signal.

As computer components, vacuum tubes were bulky and gave off tremendous amounts of heat. The size of these devices meant that early computers occupied areas as large as auditoriums. For example, the ENIAC, built in 1946, perhaps the first large-scale computer, contained about 19,000 vacuum tubes. The heat emitted by tubes caused frequent failures. Early computer technicians spent much of their time changing tubes. Because of these maintenance requirements, early computers were highly unreliable by today's standards.

Transistors

In the 1950s, efficiency and reliability increased with the development of **transistors.** In transistors, electricity is passed through a special, solid material, called a **semiconductor.** For this reason, transistors and other semiconductor devices are known as **solid-state devices.** Solid-state devices generate less heat and consume less electricity than vacuum tubes. See Figure 4-6.

The electrical conducting properties of semiconductors vary with the electrical inputs applied. Variations in conducting states provide the switching action in computers.

Transistors enhanced the ability to use computer circuits to perform logic operations. Transistors can be designed to perform as **logic gates.** Logic gates are switching devices that perform basic transformations on the electronic signals representing encoded data. In effect, a computer processor is a set of logic gates

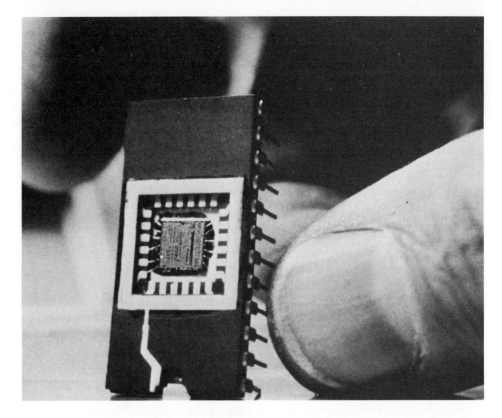

through which signals are passed to perform arithmetic and logic operations. Processing operations, then, are broken down into complex patterns of simple yes/no, true/false, or on/off transformations.

Similar principles are used to establish storage positions within main memory. Both logic gates and memory cells are two-state, or binary, devices. Again, they may be on or off, open or closed, or positive or negative. Memory cells retain the value of a data signal and logic gates transform those values.

Integrated Circuits

In the early 1960s, technology was developed for layering semiconductor materials on tiny, thin, silicon chips. Different layers have different electrical properties. Several gates and their interconnections can be built into a single chip to form an **integrated circuit (IC),** as shown in Figure 4-7. Layers of integrated circuits are used to position large numbers of switching components.

Integrated circuits are compact, efficient memory devices and mark a major advance in computer technology. The ability to manufacture memory devices on chips generates major savings in the manufacture of computers. Many chips are produced in a single sheet, or **wafer,** then cut apart into individual circuits. In addition, the combining of multiple gates on a single chip reduces the cost of each gate.

Other advantages stem from the physical characteristics of integrated circuit chips. Chips can be designed as compact modules that are more reliable than a configuration of separate components and interconnections. Because all circuits are sealed within a single component, chances of failure are decreased.

Microchips

As manufacturing techniques improved, increasing numbers of gates and/or memory cells were put on IC chips. Originally, integrated circuits contained four, 10, and 100 gates per chip. A later generation of IC technology, described as **medium-scale integration,** housed 100 to 1,000 gates per chip. **Large-scale integration (LSI)** technology exceeds 1,000 gates per chips. With each of these generations, integrated circuits have decreased in size, and provided increases in processing speed and storage capacity.

Within computers, size and speed are related through the factor of travel time for electrical current. Electricity travels at a speed of approximately 186,000 miles per second. In early computers, size was not considered to be a factor because of this inherent speed. However, as demands increased for processing speeds and capacities, the size of components and circuits became critical. Electricity travels approximately 11 inches in one billionth of a second, or a nanosecond. On modern computers, reduction in the lengths of electrical paths has been a major factor in improving performance.

At levels above 10,000 gates, representing **very large-scale integration (VLSI),** the term, **microchip,** is applied. At these levels, single microchips, called **microprocessors,** or chips that perform the entire range of processing functions (input, processing, output, and storage), can be made.

The development of microprocessors made it possible to build full-function computers small enough to sit on a desktop. In fact, the microcomputer derives its name from the microprocessor. Microprocessors provide complete processing control for typical microcomputers.

Types of Memory

VLSI technology has had a profound impact on electronic **random-access memory (RAM).** RAM, or main memory, is used to store programs and data temporarily during processing operations. Random-access memory is volatile; if power is lost, the content of memory also is lost.

In RAM, program instructions are executed at the speed of electricity. If the size of programs and/or data exceeds the capacity of main memory, the system must perform separate, relatively slow, mechanical tasks associated with bringing data from external storage. Therefore, computing efficiency tends to increase

The microchip

made it possible to build full-function computers that could fit on a desktop. A chip this size may contain hundreds of thousands of memory bits.

with the addition of memory capacity. VLSI technology has established a standard for microcomputers of 256,000 (256K) bytes of RAM. Modules of 256K chips can be combined for increased capacity. Many microcomputers have memory capacities of 1 million bytes (1 megabyte) or more.

The microchip has provided many other benefits in terms of cost and reliability. In addition to increasing the efficiency of random-access memory, the cost-per-bit of RAM has gone down. In the mid-1980s, costs for 256K chips are about the same as for the 64K chips they replaced. Microchip technology also has given rise to different types of memory chips:

- *ROM (read-only memory)* chips are preprogrammed with instructions to perform specific tasks, such as starting the computer when power is supplied, or handling specific input or output tasks. The programs in ROM are recorded permanently; the user may access these programs but cannot change or erase them. ROM is non-volatile; its content is not lost when power is removed.

- *PROM (programmable read-only memory)* and *EPROM (erasable programmable read-only memory)* are ROM chips that provide limited capabilities to alter the programs they contain. Reprogramming these chips requires different techniques and devices, usually involving ultraviolet light. PROM and EPROM chips can be used to control the actions of hardware devices. Reprogramming allows manufacturers to update machines to keep pace with technological developments.

Microchips also are used throughout the processing component of microcomputers. For example, the two basic components of computers—the processor and memory—use different types of chips. Memory chips hold data and programs temporarily to support processing. Processing chips house the gates, or switches, that manipulate electrical signals representing data. Both chips perform the same functions as predecessor technologies—vacuum tubes and single-circuit boards.

In microcomputers, processing and memory chips are housed on the main circuit board, called a **motherboard.** Processing and memory functions of microprocessors are linked by **buses.** A bus is a high speed connector capable of transmitting one or more entire bytes of data through parallel circuits. Within computers, buses handle transfers of electrical signals throughout the processing component. The width of a bus determines the amount of signal that can be moved in one operation, a factor in determining processing speed.

Buffers.   Microchips also are installed throughout modern computer hardware to provide support and increase efficiency. For example, microchips are often used as temporary storage areas, called **buffers.** A buffer is a memory device that stores data temporarily during processing or data transfer operations. A buffer might be used to assemble and hold parts of data files awaiting printing. The buffer then feeds the printer with a steady stream of data to make maximum performance possible.

Other buffers facilitate the transfer of keystroke entries into memory. Keystrokes initiate electronic signals that are sent through microchips to memory and to display devices that form character images on screens. For many types of microcomputers, buffers hold keyboard entries made while the processor is busy with other tasks. Keyboard entry and display technology is described later in this chapter.

Given that microprocessors are the heart of microcomputer design, or **architecture,** a logical view of hardware might follow the information processing cycle, described in Chapter 2: input, processing, output, and storage. Each function establishes a separate category of hardware device. The descriptions of hardware found in this and the next chapter are categorized in this manner. Input and storage devices are linked in this chapter because their functions are central to a resource-oriented approach to business information systems.

INPUT DEVICES

The flexibility with which microcomputers meet business requirements stems largely from the variety of available input devices. The input function involves the encoding and entry of data into an information system.

Input can be performed with a variety of tools. For example, you input data every time you write lecture notes. In this case, pens and pencils are input devices. Entries are processed when you use these recorded notes to study for a test, and outputs take the form of written reports or test answers.

A microcomputer does nothing that you could not do with a pencil, eraser, paper, and time. However, microcomputer devices for handling data can offer advantages in terms of speed and convenience. Microcomputers provide capabilities for handling large amounts of data quickly.

Many types of input devices are used in microcomputer systems, including:

- Keyboards

- Mouse devices

- Touch screens

- Electronic tablets

- Voice Input

- Optical devices.

Keyboards

Typewriter-style keyboards are the most common input device for microcomputers. The basic function of keyboards is to enter human-readable data and commands into a computer. Keyboards differ slightly according to manufacturers and types of computer, but all have several important features in common.

All keyboards, for instance, include characters for the letters of the alphabet, the numeric digits 0 through 9, and other special characters (*, &, $, >, <, etc). Virtually all keyboards are set up to *echo* keystrokes on video screens. That is, keyboard entries are displayed on screens as keys are stroked. Characters are captured and displayed before they are entered and/or affect files. This feature allows the operator to verify entries visually before processing takes place. Keystroking errors can be corrected with minimal disruption and delay.

Most keyboards also provide keys for movement of the display *cursor.* A cursor is a highlighted line or block on a display screen that marks the location at

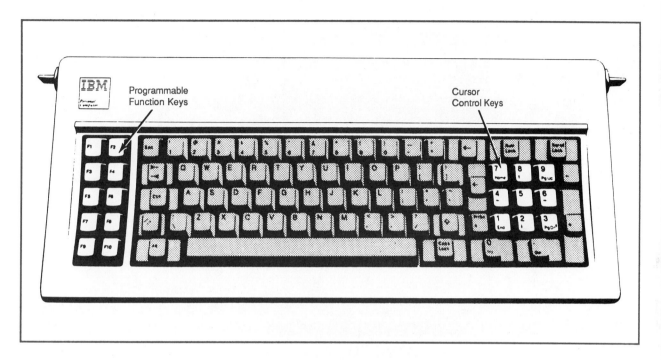

Programmable
Function Keys

Cursor
Control Keys

which the next keystroke or input entry will appear. Most keyboards contain keys labeled with directional arrows (up, down, left, and right) that control cursor movement. In addition, cursor movements to left and right margins, or beginnings and endings of displays, pages, and files usually may be implemented with specific combinations of keystrokes.

A typical microcomputer keyboard is pictured in Figure 4-8. Notice the keys on the left side labeled F1 through F10. These keys are known as *function keys.* (On some keyboards, function keys are positioned across the top.) Function keys are assigned to standard processing operations, such as executing searches or copies, or entering and exiting application programs. These keys also may be used to call up help screens, spell-check menus, printer instructions, and other kinds of auxiliary support routines. The actions initiated by function keys often can be changed and controlled by system or application software routines.

Other functions may be executed through the pressing of character keystrokes in conjunction with *control keys.* A control key signals a shift in operating mode. For some keyboards, such as the one shown in Figure 4-9, the shift into control mode is needed to perform the standard operations described above. This keyboard contains no special, programmable function keys. A user presses the control (CTRL) or alternate (ALT) key and a combination of character keys to perform cursor movements, file searches, inserts, and deletes.

Figure 4-8.

Microcomputer keyboards are designed to perform a variety of functions. Notice the function keys along the left side of this keyboard.

Figure 4-9.

Some keyboards have few function keys. This keyboard, typical
on early microcomputer systems, uses the control (CTRL)
key to enter commands for
cursor movements and other
operations.

Figure 4-10.

Manufacturers often build keyboards that are dedicated, or
designed to be used with,
specific software packages.

COURTESY OF ASHTON-TATE
COMPANY

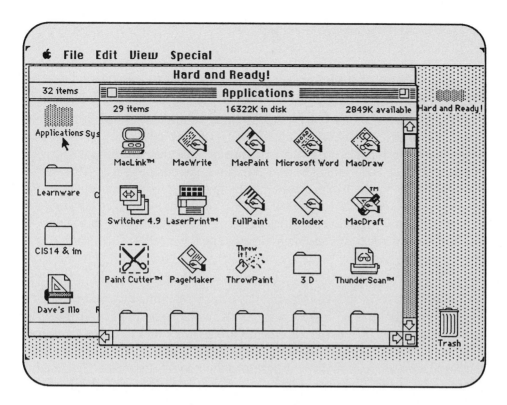

Figure 4-11.

Icons are symbols that represent processing selections. To execute a selection, the cursor is positioned over the desired icon.

Still other keyboards might be designed and built to run specific applications or application packages. To illustrate, Figure 4-10 presents a photo of a keyboard *dedicated* to the MultiMate® word processing package.

Another input method involves pointing devices for selecting processing options from menu displays. Pointing devices simplify many types of applications. In most cases, these tools are ineffective for handling large volumes of data for entry. Most often, pointing devices are used to supplement, rather than to replace keyboards. The most popular pointing device, the mouse, is discussed in the next section.

Mouse Devices

As an alternative or a supplement to keyboard commands, a pointing device called a *mouse* may be used to implement input operations. A mouse is maneuvered manually across a surface, such as a tabletop, and the cursor is positioned on the display screen relative to this movement. Menus for mouse-oriented systems generally consist of *icons,* or symbols representing processing options. The mouse is used to position the cursor at the desired selection. Buttons on the mouse are pressed to indicate selections.

Figure 4-11 illustrates the positioning of a mouse to indicate menu selections. Notice the menu icons. The hand holding the pencil represents an operation for writing data to external storage. The wastebasket symbol is used to indicate file content that can be "thrown away," or removed from memory or storage.

As input tools, mouse devices are gaining in popularity and usefulness—especially for **desktop publishing** applications. Desktop publishing packages provide capabilities for formatting document pages (margins, headings, boxes, and so on), as well as integrating text and graphics on document pages. These packages implement interactive processing techniques. The user selects options from a repeating and continuing series of menus. Menus are displayed as **windows,** or separate display frames within the overall screen. Mouse devices are used to point to desired selections and then to designate the location at which the operation is to take place.

For example, a menu might present a list of available typefaces, or styles, in which text can be produced. Moving the mouse positions the cursor first at a desired typeface, then at the text segment to be displayed in the selected style. A mouse also makes it easier to execute processing options. Users can interchange typefaces, move and alter column or margin arrangements, create boldface headlines, and manipulate the design to their own satisfaction. High-quality outputs are produced on laser printers or typesetting machines. Desktop publishing is discussed in a later chapter.

Touch Screens

Another type of input method involves the selection of processing options on **touch screens.** Touch screens let you use pointing devices such as pencils, styluses, or even fingers, to make menu selections. A special, sensitized terminal screen is required to implement this process. Touch screen technology simplifies input operations. For example, Figure 4-12 shows a touch-screen input being executed by a restaurant cashier.

The main menu for this application displays the names of all authorized cashiers. To initiate a transaction, a cashier touches the menu selection for his or her identification. For a food-ordering transaction, a menu is displayed which instructs the user to touch a position that identifies an ordered menu item. Touching the screen enters an order. The computer provides descriptions and prices. For numeric entries, a keyboard layout is displayed, and numbers are entered by touching them.

Light pens.   A **light pen** is another "through the screen" input device. A light pen senses light emitted from a display screen cursor. The movement of a light pen across a screen is tracked by the light-emitting cursor and is echoed on the display screen. The effect is that the light pen appears to be drawing lines or images directly onto the screen. These images can be converted into data for entry

to the computer. Light pens are used mainly to create graphic images, but also can be used as pointing devices.

Figure 4-12.

Touch screens simplify input. Data and commands are entered simply by pointing to appropriate display points.

Electronic Tablets

An **electronic tablet** is a touch-sensitive surface placed on a tabletop that functions like a touch screen. Pressure applied to the surface with a pen-like device is converted into images, or images of movement, on display screens. See Figure 4-13. Electronic tablets are used mainly for graphics applications. Any pointing device, however, can be used to facilitate menu selections, as described above.

Voice Input

Voice recognition devices may have a major impact on microcomputer processing in the near future. Voice input involves computers programmed to accept spoken commands and/or spoken responses to prompts to direct processing. Still in developmental stages, these devices potentially may benefit blind or other handicapped persons.

Figure 4-13.

Images ''drawn'' on electronic tablets are echoed, or displayed, on terminal screens.

PHOTO BY LISA SCHWABER-BARZILAY

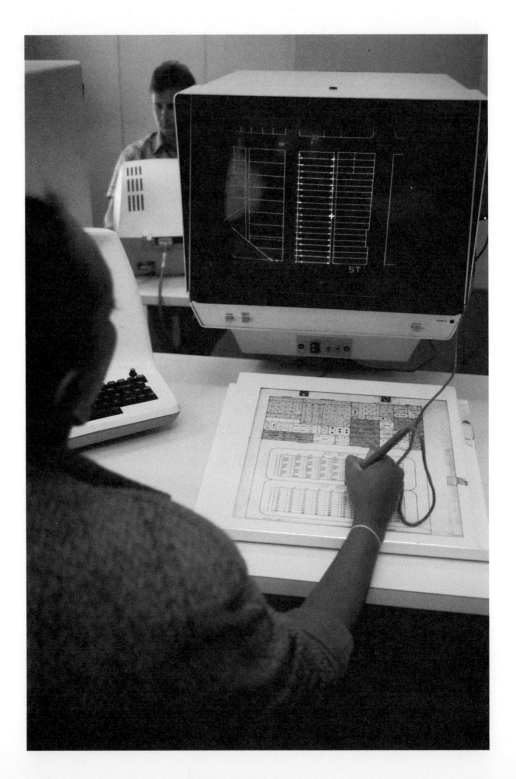

Many experts believe that voice input someday may replace keyboards as the most popular method of data entry and computer control. The challenge presently lies in that no two people speak exactly alike. Voice input computers must be able to recognize different accents, inflections, and other speech patterns. In addition, the English language contains many homonyms, ambiguities, and shades of meaning. For example, consider the inherent difficulties in instructing a computer to make the differentiations needed to understand these two sentences:

> Time flies like an arrow.
> Tiny flies like a peach.

This example also illustrates the processing performed routinely by the human brain. You probably have no difficulty interpreting the word "flies" in one sentence as a verb and as a noun in the other. In addition, the word "like" functions in different ways for both sentences. The difficulties are compounded when you consider that no two people would pronounce the sentences exactly alike.

Optical Devices

Optical input devices convert visual images into digital signals for input into computers. In supermarkets, you probably have seen cashiers passing specially coded labels over a type of window built into the checkout counter. These labels are coded in the **universal product code (UPC).** The UPC uses data encoded as patterns of lines of varying widths, or **bar codes.** Reading devices, called **scanners,** translate bar codes into input data. From these inputs, computers find and retrieve item descriptions, prices, and other information. For inventory purposes, hand-held scanners can be used to read data from items on shelves or in warehouses. Bar code scanners also have been implemented to facilitate check-out procedures for library books, and for rentals of video cassette tapes.

Scanners.   In a general sense, the term, scanner, can be applied to any type of device that converts visual images into input formats. **Character readers,** for example, read images of text for input. Character readers effectively eliminate separate keying procedures for recording data from preprinted documents. Instead, the document is fed through a reader and text content is input to memory and echoed on a display screen.

The input devices described above represent a brief overview. New and specialized input devices are introduced each year. Further, established technologies tend to mature and improve—or become obsolete.

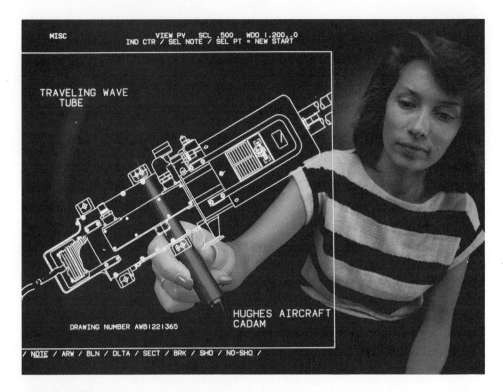

The movement of a light pen

is tracked across a screen and echoed as a display image.
COURTESY OF HUGHES AIRCRAFT CORPORATION

DISPLAYS

Displays serve dual functions within computer systems. Displays often are used to present processing results in human-readable form. By definition, then, displays can be classified as output devices. However, displays also are integral to terminal-oriented input procedures. Input data are echoed on display screens, where they can be verified and corrected by operators. In other cases, input is fed through touch screens or light pens interacting with displays. In effect, display screens can be classified as input/output (I/O) devices.

A display screen is the user's window into the processing that is taking place and the information content of computer-maintained files. Terminal displays are the most common tool for human interaction with computers. Terminal displays meet requirements for a wide range of information-handling situations. These requirements include:

- Viewing and/or manipulating information displayed on the screen— a hard copy output is unnecessary or supplementary to the immediate need.

- Rapid viewing of specific information within files.

- Interactive processing (between user and computer) directed by application programs.

Figure 4-14.

Input operations are simplified when entry screens are designed to simulate the format of paper documents from which data are taken, or to which data are output.

COURTESY OF TELEVIDEO SYSTEMS, INC.

Microcomputer terminals—which consist of display screens and keyboards linked to a processor and storage devices—often are called *video display terminals (VDTs)* or *cathode-ray tubes (CRTs).* A terminal screen is coated with a layer of phosphorus, which glows when a light source is applied. An *electron gun* within the terminal provides the light source. System software divides a terminal screen into a matrix of picture elements, or *pixels.* Then, digital signals from the processing unit are decoded into images of graphics or text on display screens.

The number of pixels in a display matrix determine the *resolution* of images presented on the screen. A large number of pixels provides a high resolution, while a small number provides a poor resolution. High resolution displays are clear, sharp, and easy to see. Poor resolution images, in which individual pixels are further apart from each other, are difficult to read—especially for long periods—and may cause user discomfort and eye strain.

Displayed images can enhance input capabilities. Consider this example: Many data entry operations use displays of input forms, which resemble paper forms used for the same purpose. See Figure 4-14. Blank spaces, or fields, on the form are filled in just as if a pen and paper form were being used. The program moves the cursor to appropriate fields for data entries. This process is known as ***direct data entry*** because data are entered directly, effectively eliminating the production of source documents.

At another level of use, a manager who needs information on a customer account could call up that file and display selected records and data fields instantly. In word processing applications, the content of text files can be displayed, edited, revised, corrected, and then written back to disk and/or produced as hard copy.

Graphic Displays

In another type of application, known as ***computer-aided design/computer-aided manufacturing (CAD/CAM),*** engineering designs of parts or products can be created, displayed, and manipulated visually. CAD/CAM systems are configured to produce graphic images of designs and to control manufacturing machinery through use of digital design information. Under CAD/CAM techniques, the screen becomes an electronic scratch pad for a draftsperson.

For example, a drawing of an engine component can be displayed, rotated 360 degrees, enlarged, and/or reduced repeatedly for complete evaluation. In the past, separate drawings from one, or perhaps a few, angles were prepared manually. This was an extremely labor-intensive task and, if corrections were required, there was no alternative but to repeat the process.

CAD/CAM systems use a special type of display terminal that has capabilities to produce ***graphic,*** or pictorial, images. Graphics are produced by ***digitizing*** images. Digitizing refers to conversions of graphic images into numeric data values and of numeric values to images represented through a series of tiny points, or pixels, on a CRT screen. Thus, images are stored and manipulated as numeric values. For instance, system software might set up horizontal and vertical coordinates for a screen and form images around the coordinates. In addition, tone values may be assigned to provide light, dark, and shaded areas within an image. See Figure 4-15.

Special microchips are used to produce graphics on display screens. These chips comprise ***graphics boards*** that translate geometric information into display images. Graphics boards work in conjunction with software tools that create this geometric information. Graphics boards are installed and operated separately from the central processing unit. This makes it possible to add graphics capabilities to systems that do not have them. In effect, a system can grow and mature with the sophistication and requirements of users.

Graphics also may be produced in single or multiple colors. Special terminals, called ***color monitors,*** create displays of images and text in different colors.

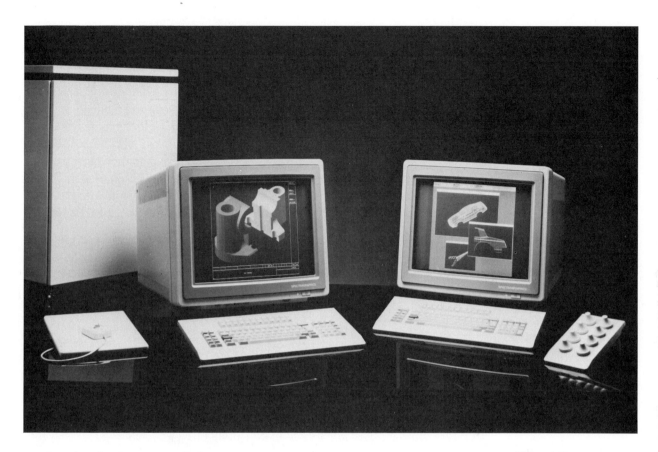

Single-color displays are called **monochrome monitors.** Color monitors usually are used in microcomputer systems that handle and produce graphics. For this reason, screen resolution is an important factor in selecting color monitors.

Notice the use of the term, monitor, referring to display devices. The use of this term refers to the service provided to users by information displayed on terminal screens. You probably have seen displays of flight information in airports. This information is updated frequently—and monitored by passengers waiting for flights to depart or arrive.

STORAGE DEVICES

All information systems need a way to store records and files that are not in active use. For example, most business managers receive mail daily. Incoming items are placed in a basket or stacked on the managers' desks. Each letter or parcel is reviewed by managers and reply letters or documents are generated as needed. Incoming letters that are important to operations or that will be needed in the future are stored in a file cabinet or similar unit. The letters are stored

Figure 4-15.

Computer aided design (CAD) systems provide capabilities for producing and manipulating graphic images to represent the appearance and performance of products under design.
COURTESY OF SPECTRA GRAPHICS CORPORATION

according to some kind of organization scheme so that they can be retrieved as required.

In a manual system, the manager's role parallels that of a computer processor. Incoming mail items form a work *queue,* or a lineup of processing tasks. The handling of these letters, first stacked on a desktop within the manager's reach, are analogous to data held in main memory. Continuing the analogy, file cabinets for holding processed mail items are the equivalent of external, or secondary, storage within a computer system. In a computer system, however, external storage files are linked with and accessed by one or more computers. Actual storage *media* (disks or tapes), however, are handled and stored with the same convenience—and often in the same file folders or cabinets—as paper documents.

External storage plays a vital role in computer systems. When computers are turned off, the content of main memory disappears. In effect, data within memory is forgotten completely if power is interrupted. Secondary storage ensures that information created and/or handled by a computer is retained for future, or continuing, use. Even systems with enormous internal memory capacities need secondary storage.

Processing, in effect, revolves around the storage function, especially in business transaction processing systems. For this reason, the storage function often is called the hub of computer systems. Virtually all programs and data, in virtually all systems, are stored externally at one time or another. Versions of programs and data for input often are created originally as stored files. In such cases, input becomes a relatively simple matter of locating and reading external files into main memory.

Further, application packages are implemented by loading data and programs from disk storage into main memory. Once a package is loaded, the first task in executing the application usually is to build storage files. From that point on, data from secondary storage are accessed and/or manipulated each time the application is run.

The speed with which data can be accessed and retrieved from storage files is a significant factor in determining system performance. Stored files are information resources. Resources have value only to the extent that they can be utilized to support business operations. The analysis of storage and retrieval requirements, therefore, should be a primary concern for decision makers building microcomputer systems.

Factors pertinent to analyses of storage requirements include the capacity of main memory in the system, and the accessibility and capacity of external storage for programs and data. Programs and data are held in main memory during processing. As memory capacities for microcomputers have grown, however,

System performance

is determined, in part, by the interaction between main memory and secondary storage (disk) devices for data and software.
COURTESY OF CDEX CORPORATION

programs also have become larger. Increases in sizes of programs reflect improvements in help menus, interfaces, and functional capabilities. Many programs have grown so large that overall programs must be broken into modules for processing. For example, a **shell** of the program, containing basic or frequently used routines, might be read into memory to control processing. As subroutines or utilities are needed, they are called up from external storage.

External storage accesses can slow processing considerably, especially when storage media, such as floppy disks, must be interchanged for access operations. Technologies have been developed, such as hard disks, for minimizing these delays. With an installed hard disk, 10 to 40 or more megabytes of storage can be accessed quickly on a single, high-speed disk drive.

The same principle—that accesses to external storage are time consuming in relation to memory operations—holds for data files as well. In other words, the more pertinent data you can load into main memory at one time, the faster the application should run. It may appear that the answer is to build computers with enormous memory capacities. In a sense, it is true that increasing memory capacities to support maximum amounts of data and programs would increase overall processing speed. However, main memory costs considerably more per bit than external storage. In addition, many developments throughout the computer evolution were seen as the answer to all needs—only to become obsolete quickly in the face of increasing sophistication of users and their requirements. This fact, combined with the universal business requirement to maintain permanent records, indicates that secondary storage will remain a significant factor for business systems.

Other factors that determine the capability of a system to access externally stored entities include software design and storage media. External accesses are executed under the control of application or system software. Access times, then, are determined partly by program schemes. However, the major factor in meeting storage requirements is the selection of storage media and supporting devices. The section that follows presents a discussion of storage equipment.

Magnetic Disks

Magnetic disks are the most common storage media for microcomputers. The two most prevalent forms of disks are **floppy disks,** or **diskettes,** and **hard disks.** Both types of disks use similar recording patterns controlled by system software. That is, both diskettes and hard disks are divided into **tracks.** Tracks are concentric, circular recording paths around the hub of a disk. Diskettes usually are divided into 40 tracks; hard disks may contain up to 400 tracks.

The tracks on a disk are divided into **sectors** that help to organize stored data for ease of access. Tracks and sectors provide the computer with a referencing system by which any record stored on disk can be accessed directly. Figure 4-16 shows a typical arrangement of tracks and sectors on a disk surface.

Disk reference is guided also by the starting point, or **home address,** for each track. **Identification fields** may be included to locate records or groups of related records stored on disk. In addition, **gaps** are used to separate data records, and to identify starting and ending locations of identification fields and home addresses. This process of establishing references on disks is known as **formatting** and is illustrated in Figure 4-17. Recording formats for diskettes and hard disks follow the same general principles. The main difference is the increased capacities and speed of hard disks.

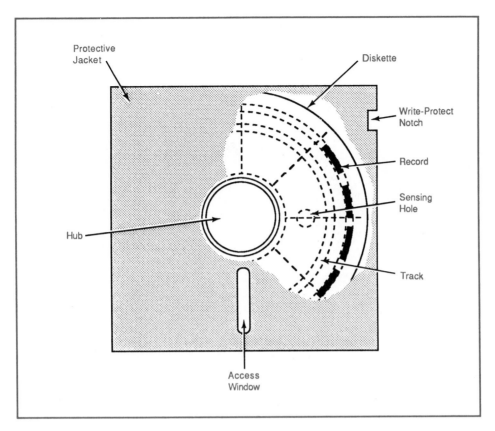

Figure 4-16.

Diskettes are divided into tracks and sectors for efficient organization and retrieval of stored data.

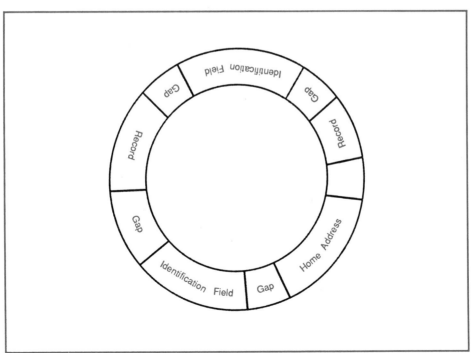

Figure 4-17.

Disk storage locations are established with home addresses, interrecord gaps, and identification fields.

Floppy disks,

also known as diskettes, provide storage capacities up to 1.2 megabytes (million bytes) of data on each diskette.

COURTESY OF SENTINEL
TECHNOLOGIES

Floppy disks. Floppy disks, or diskettes, provide storage capacities ranging from 70K to 1.5 megabytes (million bytes) of data. A 5.25 inch floppy disk has been an accepted standard since its adoption by IBM. A 3.5 inch floppy has seen continuous use with microcomputers made by Apple, Commodore, Atari, and others. Some IBM computers have used this size diskette in the past. Recent events seem to indicate that the smaller size may become the de facto standard for diskettes. In 1986, IBM introduced a laptop computer that features the smaller diskette. About the same time, Sony introduced a 3.5 inch diskette that provides 1 megabyte of storage capacity.

Hard disks. Hard disks provide substantial increases in speed and capacity over floppy disks. Hard disk capacities can range into hundreds of megabytes. **Winchester disks** are a type of hard disk adapted specifically for microcomputers. Winchester disks are housed permanently in hermetically sealed drive devices. Capacities of Winchester disks range from 10 to roughly 300 megabytes of storage for microcomputers.

Similar capacities are provided by hard disks mounted on an expansion board that is installed within the processor housing. These units are installed easily with a screwdriver and consist of the disk and drive device, and ROM chips that facilitate formatting and disk handling. The difficulty with these devices, as with hard disks in general, centers around the strain placed on internal power supplies. Hard disk devices must be able to accelerate and come

A Winchester disk

is a sealed, high-capacity disk storage device.

COURTESY OF AMPEX CORPORATION

to a complete stop in fractions of a second. This level of performance can cripple many machines, especially older machines in which a hard disk is installed to upgrade capabilities.

The advantages provided by hard disks, however, cannot be ignored. Because of the increased capacities of hard disks, processing efficiency may be increased. One reason lies in the amount of data available to the computer. Applications with large files can be processed completely through use of a single data source. Another advantage is that hard disks provide faster data access. Because Winchester disks are rigid and are housed in sealed units, they can be rotated at least 10 times as fast as floppy disks. At higher rotation speeds, access time is bound to be shorter.

Hard disks also may be required to execute high-level, integrated software packages. Such packages might contain a word processor, spreadsheet, database, and graphics programs as components within a single package. Without a hard disk, separate floppies have to be interchanged frequently. A hard disk provides sufficient capacity to load the entire package onto a single, high-speed storage device.

CDROM and optical disk. Large-capacity, high-speed storage devices are under development constantly. **CDROM (compact disk read-only memory)** and **optical disks** fall within this category. Both types of devices use technology similar to the compact disk audio recordings of popular artists. CDROM and optical disks typically store from 200 megabytes to 2 or more **gigabytes** (billion bytes) of storage. However, these technologies are "read only." That is, data cannot be written to storage. Write capabilities for these devices are under development and may be available at a later date. For this reason, CDROM and optical disks presently are excellent storehouses of archival data.

Tape Storage

Because of the importance of information resources to continuing business operations, provisions should be made for **backup** versions of software and stored files. Remember the discussion in Chapter 2 of an organization that is forced out of business when information resources are lost. Many backup systems and files are created on magnetic tape. Magnetic tape has limited uses for microcomputer applications, mainly because of the efficiencies and economies inherent in disk storage. However, tapes provide a convenient medium for writing backup copies of files that must be stored for long periods.

In transaction processing systems, tapes often are an inexpensive medium for storing backup copies of master files. In addition, many systems maintain **data logs.** These logs are used for sequential recording of all transactions handled by a system. Should the main master files be destroyed, the backup master files and transaction logs are processed to create current on-line files—and to restore operations.

Another backup method involves recording streams of keystrokes on tape. In effect, this creates a keystroke-by-keystroke record of work sessions, which can be used to recreate files.

In summary, equipment is available with which a microcomputer system can be adapted to a variety of functions and requirements. At a basic level, configuring such systems can be a simple matter of selecting the right tool for the right job. At another level, business managers and other decision makers striving to maximize system performance and productivity may need to understand how equipment is used to produce results. Of the functions in the information processing cycle—input, processing, output, and storage—input and storage are linked by their importance in creating and maintaining files. The files a business creates and maintains with microcomputers provide direct support and service to its operations. The delivery of this support is performed by the remaining functions in the cycle: processing and output. Processing refers to the transformation of data into information that has meaning to people. The results of processing must be delivered, or output, in a format that people can understand. The equipment used to implement these functions largely determines the ability of a system to serve its owners, or users. The next chapter overviews the hardware associated with the functions of processing and output.

KEY TERMS

front-end

owner

custody

distributed system

standalone

interactive

gate

encode

binary

capture

binary number system

bit (Binary digIT)

code

character

byte

Extended Binary Coded Decimal Interchange Code (EBCDIC)

American Standard Code for Information Interchange (ASCII)

vacuum tube

first-generation

filament

emitter

anode

diode

transistor

semiconductor

solid-state device

logic gate

memory cell

integrated circuit (IC)

wafer

medium-scale integration

large-scale integration (LSI)

nanosecond

very large-scale integration (VLSI)

microchip

microprocessor

random-access memory (RAM)

read-only memory (ROM)

PROM (programmable read-only memory)

EPROM (erasable programmable read-only memory)

motherboard

bus

bus width

buffer

architecture

input device

echo

cursor

function keys

control keys

dedicated

mouse

icon

desktop publishing

window

touch screen

light pen

electronic tablet

voice recognition

universal product code (UPC)

bar code

scanner

character reader

video display terminals (VDTs)

cathode ray tube (CRT)

electron gun

pixel

resolution

direct data entry

computer-aided design/computer-aided manufacture (CAD/CAM)

graphic

digitize

graphics board

color monitor

monochrome monitor

queue

media

shell

floppy disk

diskette

hard disk

track

sector

home address

identification field

gap

formatting

Winchester disk

CDROM (compact disk read-only memory)

optical disk

gigabyte

backup

data log

D E F I N I T I O N S

Instructions: On a separate sheet, define each term according to its use in this chapter.

1. standalone
2. bit
3. semiconductor
4. microprocessor
5. mouse

6. voice recognition
7. video display terminal
8. digitize
9. queue

T R U E / F A L S E

Instructions: For each statement, write T for true or F for false on a separate sheet.

1. The content of a computer's main memory disappears if power is interrupted.

2. The EBCDIC coding scheme was developed by IBM for use on mainframe systems.

3. Integrated circuit chips have a smaller chance of failure than transistors because all circuits are sealed within a single component.

4. In binary coding, information is recorded as values of 1 and 2.

5. Most keyboards are set up to echo keystrokes, or display entries on screens simultaneously as keys are stroked.

6. In CAD/CAM systems, graphic images are first translated into numeric data values before they are stored and/or processed.

7. During processing, programs and data are temporarily stored within ROM.

8. In standalone processing, a microcomputer is linked with a central computer through communication lines.

9. Each byte stored in memory represents a character of data.

10. The beginning of a sector on a magnetic disk is marked by its home address.

11. To communicate with other computers, a computer that uses ASCII coding must translate data into EBCDIC for transmission along telephone lines.

12. Sectors are concentric, circular recording paths around the hub of a disk.

13. A major obstacle to the development of voice input devices is the need for the computer to distinguish between different speech patterns.

14. A high-resolution display screen is difficult to read for long periods and may result in eye strain.

15. Identification fields on disks can be used to locate specific groups of records.

SHORT ANSWER QUESTIONS

Instructions: On a separate sheet of paper, answer each question in one or two brief sentences.

1. Explain how a distributed system resolves some of the problems associated with centralized information systems.

2. Describe how data is represented within a computer. Include in your description an explanation of what bits and bytes are.

3. Briefly summarize the evolution of hardware components, and explain how miniaturization has increased the efficiency of computers.

4. What are the functions of ROM, PROM, and EPROM chips? Explain what is different about each kind of chip.

5. What difficulties must be overcome to bring voice recognition devices into popular use for microcomputer systems?

6. How does the capacity of main memory and the speed of accessibility of external storage affect system performance?

RESEARCH PROJECT

Visit a computer store and read through several computer magazines. Select three different types of microcomputer input devices. Describe how each is used and compare specific features. Explain what kinds of tasks are accomplished and what kinds of needs are met by using each device.

5 Microcomputer Hardware: Processing and Output

INTRODUCTION

The functions of processing and output share a common purpose: to deliver meaningful information to users.

THE CENTRAL PROCESSING UNIT

A microcomputer's central processing unit (CPU) is divided into processor and main memory areas.

Arithmetic

All computer arithmetic operations are based on repeated simple addition.

Logic

Computer logic consists of comparing the values of two data items and selecting processing routines based on the result.

Control

Control circuits route signals, representing data and programs, within the CPU and to and from peripheral devices.

Primary Storage

Primary storage, or main memory, holds programs and data temporarily to keep them available for processing.

PROCESSING

Processing involves a series of signal transfers between the processor and main memory.

Operating Sequences

Operational steps for implementing and using a microcomputer application include the operations performed by users.

Performance and Architecture

Performance depends on many factors, including architecture (design), main memory capacity, and bit orientation of buses.

OUTPUT DEVICES

Output devices present processing results in readable form; common outputs are hard-copy (paper) documents consisting of graphics or alphanumeric data.

Printers and Plotters

Printers and plotters are classified according to the quality of outputs they produce, and are selected according to application requirements.

MODEMS FOR MICROCOMPUTERS

Modems perform the digital-to-analog and analog-to-digital conversions required to transfer signals between computers over communication lines.

Types of Modems

Acoustic couplers and direct-connect modems link computers to telephones; smart modems are connected directly to communication lines.

Microcomputers and Networks

Networks support the sharing of information resources and devices among computers.

Computer processing

is accomplished through arrays of chips mounted on circuit boards.

COURTESY OF MDB SYSTEMS, INC.

INTRODUCTION

The functions of the information processing cycle—input, processing, output, and storage—establish a framework for reviewing microcomputer hardware. In the previous chapter, the functions of input and storage are linked by their respective roles in creating and handling information resources. In this chapter, discussions of processing and output devices complete the function-oriented view of microcomputer hardware.

Processing and output equipment also share a common, primary role—to deliver meaningful information from computers or computer-maintained files to human users. As in the previous chapter, discussions of hardware in this chapter are aimed at enhancing your ability to make knowledgeable decisions about or effective use of microcomputers.

THE CENTRAL PROCESSING UNIT

Actual computing takes place in the *central processing unit (CPU).* A microcomputer CPU consists of two major components:

- The *processor* controls and executes computation and comparison operations, and coordinates interactions with peripheral devices. For many microcomputers, the heart of the processing component is a *microprocessor.* A microprocessor, as described in the previous chapter, can support all four information processing functions.

- *Main memory,* also called *primary storage,* stores data and programs temporarily to support processing operations. Main memory is comprised of one or more chips designed for this purpose, called memory chips.

Together, these components of the CPU perform a series of vital functions:

- Arithmetic
- Logic
- Control
- Primary storage.

Arithmetic

Computer arithmetic operations—addition, subtraction, multiplication, and division—are variations of addition. Arithmetic is performed by special circuitry called the *adder.* Suppose two values are to be added. Both numbers are read into the input storage area of main memory. The numeric values are sent through the adder, in which the arithmetic operation is performed, and the result is sent back to main memory—specifically to the output storage area. Then, the sum can be used for further processing or used as output.

The adder also performs multiplication, subtraction, and division operations—but all computer calculations are based upon simple addition. Multiplication, in effect, is repeated addition. Subtraction is negative addition; and division is repeated negative addition.

Subtraction is achieved through addition of negative numbers. For example, $64 + (-32) = 32$. To multiply the values 32 and 8,976, the adder performs 32 additions of the value 8,976—or vice versa. To divide the same numbers, the value -32 is added to 8,976 until a number less than 32 is reached. A quotient is derived by counting the number of addition operations. Each addition operation initiates an incremental increase in a memory area that serves as an *accumulator,* or counter.

Most computers can perform calculations like these in millionths, or even billionths, of a second. The true calculating power of computers lies in the speed with which a long series of computations can be executed under program control. This concept can be applied as well to computer logic capabilities, discussed in the next section.

Logic

In simple terms, computer logic refers to the capability of computers to compare two data values at a time and to direct processing on the basis of comparison results. That is, computers "look at" two data elements and determine whether the value of one element is equal to, greater than, or less than that of the other element.

This type of **condition test,** or comparison, is the basis for selecting alternate processing routines. Alternate processing sequences and/or instruction routines are written into program designs. Logic operations support selections and implementations of program routines without human intervention. This is one of the capabilities that separates computers from other electronic calculating devices.

For example, a condition test might be written into a program for establishing class schedules for your school. As students register for classes, the number of students applying for each class is compared with the total available number of openings. If both numbers are found to be equal, the class is full, and subsequent requests are rejected, or assigned to other available class sessions (according to program design).

Computer logic also can be implemented to perform sort operations. That is, data records can be placed into ascending or descending alphabetic or numeric order based upon a particular data element within those records. Sorting involves repeated comparisons; each comparison determines the relative position of one data element to another. Data records are repositioned based upon successive comparisons until the desired order is achieved. Comparisons are performed rapidly, and complex sort operations are executed quickly.

In a strict sense, then, computer arithmetic and logic both are based upon high-speed executions of relatively simple tasks. All processing operations are initiated by program instructions. Special circuits within the processor interpret program instructions and direct internal operations for their execution. These circuits implement the control function of computers, discussed in the section that follows.

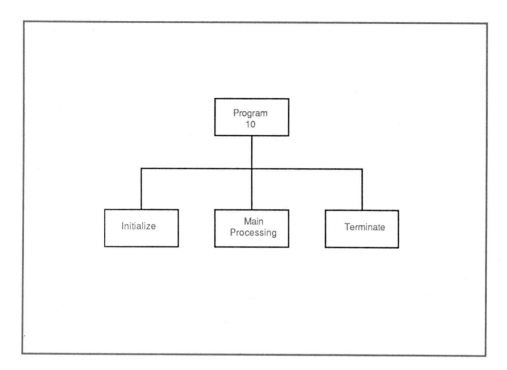

The control structure

———————————

that governs execution of all application programs divides execution into three functional segments, or legs—initialize, process, and terminate.

Control

The circuits that comprise the ***control function*** act as a "traffic cop" for signals passing through the processor and main memory. To perform this role, three capabilities are required, including:

- Select (according to program sequences) and decode processing instructions.

- Control the routing of signals between sections of the processor and main memory.

- Communicate and direct the operations of input and output devices attached or linked to the computer.

For example, consider an addition operation. The control function sends appropriate data items through arithmetic circuits. In most cases, new data items are created as a result of arithmetic operations performed upon source data. These results, or new data items, usually are needed for further processing, or for external storage or output.

At this point, the control function reads from main memory the next processing instruction within the program sequence. The instruction determines what is to be done with the data items created by arithmetic operations. These data items (results) are routed either to the working storage area (for further processing) or output storage area (for external distribution) of main memory. See Figure 5-1.

The control function provides capabilities for assigning functional areas to main memory. Working storage holds interim results—the control function can call these data again into arithmetic or logic circuits for further manipulation. Output storage holds data for distribution to **peripheral devices.** Peripheral devices are the input and output equipment attached to or linked with the computer. The interactions of peripheral devices and the CPU also are handled by the control function. For example, this function sends instructions to printers to begin or stop printing—and calls up error messages when printers malfunction.

Primary Storage

The purpose of primary storage is to hold programs and data temporarily—keeping them available for processing. In microcomputers, the primary storage function, or main memory, is housed on microchips. Memory chips typically have capacities ranging from 8 to 256K of data storage, usually in multiples of eight. Further, the main memory capacities of many microcomputers can be increased by adding more chips.

Data and programs are entered into main memory through the keyboard, the processor, or from disk storage. Program instructions and data items are transferred to the processor for execution. The results of processing are returned to main memory before they are routed to output or storage devices. Of course, all these transfer operations are directed by the control function.

For processing purposes, main memory can be viewed as being divided into four functional sections, or parts:

- Program storage
- Input (data) storage
- Working storage
- Output (data) storage.

Program storage.   The program storage section holds both system software and application programs. In microcomputer systems, both types of programs usually are stored on disk and loaded with keystroke commands. Program storage also includes startup routines stored on **read-only memory (ROM)** chips. These programs are loaded, or **booted,** automatically when the computer is switched on. ROM programs may include routines for checking the operational condition of

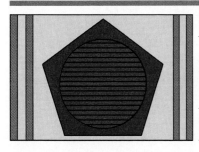

PHOTO ESSAY

HARDWARE

More and More for Less and Less

End users input data from their desks.

▥ THE INPUT-PROCESS-OUTPUT/STORE CYCLE

The processing of data, or any computational activity, involves four fundamental functions. Information is **input** to the computer, it is **processed,** results are **output,** and data are **stored** in machine-readable form. Computer equipment can be classified according to these four primary functions.

Input equipment transforms information from a physical (often human-readable) form into data in a machine-readable form. **Processing equipment** transforms data into desired results. **Output equipment** transforms results from an electronic form into a physical or human-readable form. Finally, **storage equipment** saves data, in some machine-readable form, for subsequent processing. The difference between storage and input and output is functional rather than physical. Storage equipment also performs input and output functions, and often the same equipment is used for all three functions. However, the difference is that storage equipment does not translate between machine-readable and human-readable forms. Rather, it saves the data in magnetic, optical, or other machine-readable form.

As the following pages illustrate, there exists an incredible variety of equipment, most of which serves the same function. Why? Equipment — hardware and software — varies in performance (speed, capacity, and quality) and cost. Every year sees the rise of new technological innovations that improve performance or reduce costs, or both. When selecting computer equipment, the purchaser needs to know the system's immediate and future requirements in order to select sufficient (but not excessive) speed, capacity, and quality.

This modem is used to transmit data from the customer's computer via telephone to a typesetter.

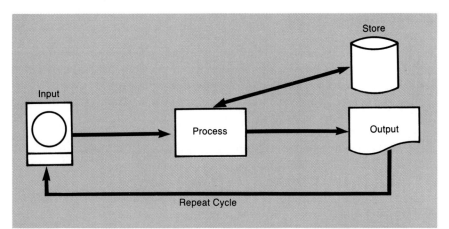

The input, process, output/store cycle.

Processing by a popular (Spectrum) minicomputer.

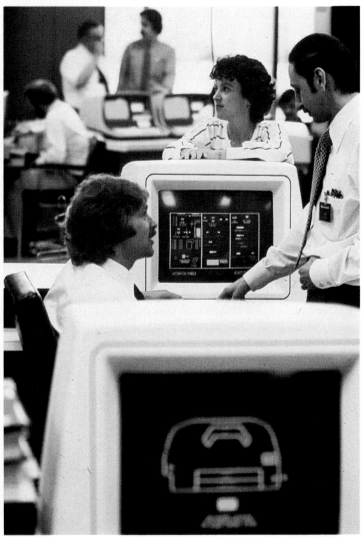

Output is viewed by a user as he enters data.

Keyboard data entry allows businesspeople to record information readily and quickly.

Today's banks utilize online data entry for accurate and current information.

▦ KEYBOARD INPUT

Keyboard input hardware requires a person to key in the data. Generally, the keyboard is similar to that of a typewriter. A video-display tube (VDT) is usually used for displaying data.

Keyboard hardware can be online or offline. If it is **online,** the keyboard is connected directly to a computer. Data flows from the keyboard device straight to the processing computer. If it is **offline,** the keyboard device ultimately produces a magnetic tape or disk. The tape or disk is later read by a tape or disk unit that is connected to the processing computer.

Most keyboard terminals contain a microprocessor. In less expensive terminals a simple microprocessor is used in order to reduce the cost of the terminal. However, a **smart** or **intelligent** terminal contains a powerful microprocessor that allows it to perform some of the functions of the processing computer. In addition to reducing the processing computer's workload, an intelligent terminal reduces the amount of communication required between the terminal and the processing computer.

Another type of keyboard operator is the **end-user** operator. An end user does not generally spend all the time keying data. Rather, keying data is only part of the end user's job. A bank teller using an online terminal is an example of an end-user operator. Although end users employ computer equipment in their jobs, they are generally not assigned to the data-processing department. Rather, end users work for another part of an organization. Bank tellers report to the head teller, not to the manager of data processing.

End users input data from their desks.

Key-to-disk data entry.

Production data-entry personnel are
employed by companies with continual
data-entry needs.

Many organizations prefer end-user data entry. The end users feel
that they have greater control when they do their own data entry. They
must also live with their own mistakes, and, consequently, some
companies find that the accuracy of data is higher when it is entered
by end users.

Data entry via keyboards is very error prone. A production data-
entry operator may key in hundreds of documents in a single day.
Unfortunately, accurate computer processing requires accurate input
data. Therefore, procedures to verify the accuracy of data input are
crucial. For example, such procedures might involve manually counting the number of documents processed and comparing this count
with a computer-calculated count, or adding, by hand, the amounts of
all orders and comparing this sum to a computer-generated sum.

Data entry using a light pen.

The HP Touchscreen II personal
computer helps automate offices by
providing ready, quick, and accurate
access to data stored in minicomputers.

▦ NON-KEY INPUT

Keyboard input devices are slow for some applications. A variety of
other, special-purpose devices have therefore been developed.

Terminals have a **cursor** that show the user's position on the screen.
The cursor might be a blinking underscore, a highlighted square, or
some other, similar character. Moving the cursor around the screen
takes time. Most terminals have special keys for up/down, left/right
movement, but even with these keys cursor movement can be slow and
cumbersome. A **mouse** is a hand-held device for moving the cursor
quickly. The user moves the mouse around on a level surface, and the
cursor moves correspondingly. Moving the mouse left causes the cursor
to move left, moving it back (away from the user) causes the cursor to
move up the screen, and so forth.

A **light pen** is another device that reduces cursor movement and
keystrokes. A user with a light pen simply points the pen to the desired
spot on a screen and pushes a button. The terminal senses where the
light pen is located and responds accordingly. Light pens are often
used to select options from a menu on a screen. The user points the pen
to the menu item desired. With some terminals, the user can actually
use the light pen to draw on the screen.

UPC (Uniform Product Code) **bar codes** are used on grocery products. The bar pattern corresponds to an item number. The sensing
device sends the number to a computer for processing. UPC codes save
time not only for the clerk, but also for the people who would otherwise mark prices on the items. Furthermore, the grocery store can
change prices with minimal effort.

Digitizers sense marks on a document and convert those marks into digital data (whole numbers). For example, digitizers are used in the medical profession for storing X-ray pictures magnetically.

Paper strip scanners are used to input specially encoded files from paper. Some of these devices can also encode and write a file on paper. These devices are inexpensive and use technology similar to that used for UPC bar codes. A personal computer user can, for example, read in a properly encoded program published in a computer magazine, or transfer files between two computers by writing the encoded file to paper using one computer and reading it into another.

Optical character recognition devices are able to read a limited set of standard typefonts and translate the characters into machine-readable form. Some stores use them instead of UPC bar codes for reading prices on items being purchased—an advantage in that the customer and the machine see the same price. These devices are also used to input typewritten documents into a computer for updating, translating, or electronic mailing.

Computer designers and engineers have had only limited success with devices that recognize handwritten characters, because of the complexity of this problem. Usually, recognition is limited to a few characters such as digits. For example, a zip-code recognition device can save the postal service hours of labor.

Speech recognition devices translate spoken words into machine-readable form. A recognition device is **speaker independent** if it can understand words spoken by any speaker. A **speaker dependent** recognition device understands words spoken by one person only and must be trained by that person. Training involves having the intended user repeat several times each word in the device's vocabulary. The recognition device stores important characteristics of the speech sounds for later comparison.

Speaker-independent recognition devices can usually recognize only a few words (yes and no, and digits), as they must accommodate a variety of speaker's voices and accents. Speaker-dependent recognition devices are more widely used because they can recognize larger vocabularies (up to several hundred words) with greater reliability. The organization that coordinates organ-transplant donations in North America employs such a system.

Speech recognition devices are used by all manner of workers whose hands are not free to enter data, such as product inspectors, the handicapped, and researchers viewing objects under a microscope. Speech recognition devices are also employed for computer telephone polling, whose limited response requirements allow speaker-independent recognition devices to be used.

A scanner uses a low-grade laser to sense UPC barcodes in this grocery store.

The 'mouse' controls the movement of a cursor on the screen.

PROCESSING, HARDWARE, AND ENVIRONMENTS

Processing equipment includes the central processing unit (CPU) and main memory. There are three common types of CPUs: those used in microcomputers, minicomputers, and mainframes. The characteristics of the three types of processors are summarized in the chart at the end of this essay.

Main memory consists of thousands of on/off devices. Each on/off device represents one **binary digit** or **bit. A byte** is a group of bits that represents a single character, such as A or 7. Most computers have 8 bits per byte. In processing, the size of main memory is usually stated in bytes—for example, 256K bytes for a microcomputer. Although people often say that 256K equals 256,000, the letter K actually represents 1024. Thus, a 256-byte memory actually has 262,144 bytes. Common memory sizes are 256K, 512K, 1024K, and multiples of 1024K in the microcomputer area.

The distinction between the physical characteristics of microcomputers, minicomputers, and mainframes has almost disappeared due to advancing technology. Smaller minicomputers and microcomputers have become indistinguishable as have large minicomputers and mainframes. Networks of microcomputers with shared access to data storage and output services are beginning to take over minicomputer and mainframe applications.

The characteristics that define applications and environments also no longer fit neatly into the microcomputer, minicomputer, and mainframe categories, except in the general sense of small, medium, and large. The most important characteristics of a computer system are

Processing inside a microcomputer occurs within one small hardware unit.

A microcomputer environment — this Macintosh computer sits on a desk top.

DEC's micro VAX provides minicomputer power in a small space.

A designer at a Sun Microsystem terminal.

whether it runs applications in an online, interactive mode or in batch mode, what sort of environment it resides in, and its processing power. The number of simultaneous users that an interactive system can accommodate is another important characteristic. This depends both on the processing power of the system as well as the software programs that run on it.

A user of an interactive system enters data and receives an immediate response from the system. A single-user system has one user and a multi-user system can have multiple users ranging from a handful to thousands. Clearly, the larger the number of simultaneous interactive users of a system, the more powerful the system must be. An airline reservation system that handles thousands of terminals requires the power of a mainframe computer. Business applications that require a few users, such as order entry, general ledger, inventory control, and the like typically use a minicomputer. Most single-user systems used

The Digital Equipment VAX 8600—a minicomputer with mainframe power continues to blur the definition between hardware types.

as personal assistants for word processing, electronic spreadsheets, personal databases, and educational programs are based on microcomputers.

An interactive computer system can be composed of a network of microcomputers that can share output and storage equipment. The cost of storage and output equipment, called **servers,** is amortized over all of the users of the system. A database server allows users on different microcomputers connected to the network access to the same data. A print server allows multiple users to share one, usually high-quality, printer. Unlike minicomputer and mainframe systems, the failure of one microprocessor affects only one user rather than the entire system. Also, the processing power of such a system can be incrementally increased by adding a single microcomputer. A popular use of a network of micros is in the area of computer-assisted design and manufacturing (CAD/CAM). The microcomputer network provides each user with the large amount of processing power required for interactive graphics while maintaining the minicomputer's advantages of centralized databases and shared output devices such as expensive, color printer-plotters.

Another type of interactive system is a specialized controller that receives information from and exerts control over other devices, such as temperature sensors and controllers, rather than users. These types of systems are based either on microcomputer, minicomputer, or mainframe applications, depending on the power and memory requirements of the task at hand. For example, both minicomputers and microcomputers are used to monitor and control power-plant operations, and both types are used to control circuit switching in the telephone system.

In batch mode, a large amount of information that has been entered offline is fed to a computer and processed without user interaction.

Most batch jobs are massive and require mainframe computers. Billing for credit cards and policy processing for insurance companies are business applications that run in batch mode on mainframe computers. Many science applications such as weather simulation and forecasting, or aircraft simulation, require large mainframes running in batch mode.

Microcomputers, usually desk-top computers, do not require a special environment and are typically run by their owner-user. Microcomputers used as specialized controllers and servers can be found in laboratories and equipment closets. Some minicomputers require a special air-conditioned environment, or contain sensitive data and are therefore kept in computer rooms, usually with controlled access. Other minicomputers are located in a user's work area, laboratories, and equipment closets, depending on their function. Most mainframes require very specialized environments with air-conditioning, raised floors, while some even require water supplies for water-cooled CPUs. Mainframes and related equipment are typically run by a highly trained operations staff in a formal and controlled operating environment. The workload of the computer is controlled by a preauthorized schedule.

The terminals for any computer system can be located near the computers, or thousands of miles away. External terminal users often access computers via dial-up phone lines. Because anyone can theoretically dial up the computer, prohibiting access to these machines by unauthorized users has become a major security problem. At the very least, access to these computers is usually controlled by passwords, which users must enter in order to use the machine. However, passwords are not that powerful a security measure. Where security is essential, either no external terminal access is provided, or special procedures are used to identify the caller. An example of this is a dial-up computer, which allows the caller to indicate who he or she is and where the call is coming from. The computer then hangs up, verifies the validity of the caller and the calling number, and calls the user back.

Processor and memory technology is constantly changing. Memory is becoming less expensive and smaller (1 megabyte is now available on a single chip). Processors, especially microprocessors, are becoming more powerful and less costly, and new concepts are developing every year. For example, an important new concept in processor design involves RISC (Reduced Instruction Set Computers) machines. The idea is that a processor will have fewer, or at least simpler, instructions, and therefore will execute them more quickly. The number of instructions needed to perform a given function, such as adding two numbers, may actually increase, but because the new instructions are so simple they can be executed more quickly than the few, complex instructions they are replacing. The commercial viability of this approach has not yet been determined, but most high-technology processor manufacturers have a RISC project in development and some have RISC-based products already on the market.

A CRAY II is an example of the ultimate mainframe environment.

An electronic publishing system can proceed from an idea to its representation in final copy in one sitting.

Line printers produce output at very high speeds.

▦ OUTPUT

Output equipment transforms results from electronic into physical form. One common output device is the CRT screen. CRTs are used both to display data being input and to display results.

Printers are a common output device. **Line printers** print a line at a time. **Serial printers** print only a single character at a time. **Full-character printers** print a complete letter the way a typewriter does. **Dot-matrix printers** print letters composed of small dots. Impact printers use hammers to transfer ink (either dots or characters) from a ribbon to the paper, as in a typewriter. Nonimpact printers use other, quieter techniques; **ink-jet printers** spray ink onto the paper, and **laser printers** fuse toner onto paper using a xerographic process like that of a copy machine.

How should a company choose among all of these alternatives? The answer again depends on the company's requirements. Speed and print quality are the most important characteristics, but cost and noise level should also be considered. For example, line printers are faster than serial printers, but the quality of print is not as good. Letter-quality output can be produced either by slow, full-character impact printers or by fast, dot-matrix laser or ink-jet printers. Impact dot-matrix printers are slower and produce less attractive output, but they are also less expensive. New technologies are constantly presenting new printer products with improved cost-performance characteristics.

Some companies store information on microfilm and microfiche rather than on paper, which is bulky and expensive. The procedure for transferring information from the computer to microfilm or microfiche requires a special-purpose microphotography device. The computer produces a magnetic tape containing the desired information. This tape is mounted onto the microphotography device which photographs the reports onto microfilm or microfiche. These devices are very expensive so many companies instead use a service bureau for microphotography. They send the magnetic tape to the service bureau and in turn receive the microfilm or microfiche back.

A more recent alternative to microfilm and microfiche for long-term storage is the **optical disk.** For example, banks use optical disks because they are highly reliable and the information can be retrieved by computer when needed. This is not true of microfilm and microfiche, which require humans to retrieve information. (This technology is also discussed in the section on storage.)

Voice output is emerging as a form of computer output. In its simplest form, a prerecorded message can be selected and played. Often the prerecorded message has been digitized (converted into digital signals) and compressed to simplify the storage and playback requirements. Examples are automobiles that instruct drivers to turn off their lights or inform them that their fuel level is low.

More sophisticated voice-output devices employ **text-to-speech** technology. This technology automatically translates text into spoken words. This procedure is more costly but it doesn't require that all phrases to be spoken be programmed in advance. This technology might be used by an executive to have a document "read" by a computer over the telephone.

Today's fastest printers use laser technology to print over a hundred pages a minute.

This Xerox plotter is the world's first narrow-format electrostatic color plotter.

The Hewlett-Packard Company's LaserJet 500 PLUS printer with its two, 250-sheet input bins, can print documents on more than one size and type of paper. More importantly, it's quiet!

Magnetic tapes provide an inexpensive and secure method of storing data in this tape library.

ⅢⅢ STORAGE

Some data must be stored because it is needed more than once. For example, for a payroll system employee name, address, pay rate, and other data are needed every pay period. Such data cannot be left in the computer's main memory for several reasons. First, main memory is very expensive and, for the largest computers, is limited to 32 million bytes (which may sound large, but even small companies need more than that). Furthermore, main memory is volatile. When the power is shut off, the contents of main memory are lost. Thus, computers need **secondary storage (memory)** that is less expensive and larger than main memory, as well as nonvolatile.

There are two fundamental types of secondary-storage equipment. Sequential devices allow only sequential access to the data. For example, to access the 50th record in a file or magnetic tape, the first 49 records must first be read. Furthermore, additions can only be made to the end of a sequential file, or wherever a large enough record was deleted.

Magnetic tape is the most common sequential-storage device. A variety of tape devices are available. The most common device uses tape that is similar to stereo tape but is ½-inch wide. Some microcomputer systems do use stereo tape, however. Tape is inexpensive; a 2400-foot reel of ½-inch tape can be purchased for $15. Because tape is cheap, it is often used for backup storage. Data that resides on other types of secondary storage is often off-loaded onto tape until it is needed.

The second type of secondary storage is direct-access storage, which is suitable for disks. Direct-access data can be accessed in any order on a disk. The 50th record can be obtained directly, without having to plough through the first 49 records.

There are several types of direct-access disk devices. All of them have a circular recording surface mounted on a spindle. The surfaces rotate under read/write heads. Data is recorded to or read from concentric circles called **tracks.** Hard or floppy magnetic disks are the most commonly used type of direct-access storage devices.

A most promising alternative to magnetic-disk storage is optical-disk storage. Optical disks are more permanent than magnetic disks and hold far greater amounts of data (up to a gigabyte per side). It isn't currently possible to erase optical disks. Once a track has been used it can't be reused (whereas magnetic disk space can be erased and reused repeatedly). However, the enormous amount of storage available on an optical disk makes it feasible to simply continue to write more and more on the same disk.

Compact disks are becoming popular for distributing information. In the future there will be cost-effective technology for writing information onto these disks as well.

The manufacturing of a disk surface takes place in a clean and controlled environment.

A 3½-inch floppy disk is inserted into a disk drive.

A COMPARISON BETWEEN MICRO, MINI, AND MAINFRAME COMPUTERS

	MICRO	MINI	MAIN
Main Memory (1000 bytes)	32–20000	2000–8000	8000–32000
Instruction Speed (millions per second)	.2–4	.5–5	5–100
Disk Storage (bytes)	.2–20 million	up to 1 billion	up to 20 billion
Cost	$500–$15,000	$50,000–$250,000	$500,000–$10 million +
Notes	Usually single-user Often used in network with shared storage and output devices Minimum vendor support	Single- or multi-user Often sold by OEMs	Multi-user Sold by vendor Extensive support

QUESTIONS

1. Name and describe the four fundamental functions of processing data.
2. Describe the difference between online and offline data entry.
3. Describe the difference between production data entry and end-user data entry.
4. What steps can be taken to compensate for the error-prone nature of data entry?
5. Explain the use of **cursor**, **mouse**, and **light pen**.
6. Describe two keyboard data-entry devices.
7. Describe two non-key data-entry devices.
8. Distinguish between the hardware characteristics of microcomputers, minicomputers, and mainframes.
9. Distinguish between the processing environments of microcomputers, minicomputers, and mainframes.
10. Explain the difference between:
    a. Line and serial printers
    b. Full-character and dot-matrix printers
    c. Impact and nonimpact printers.
11. Describe the two fundamental types of storage hardware.
12. What is a mass-storage system?

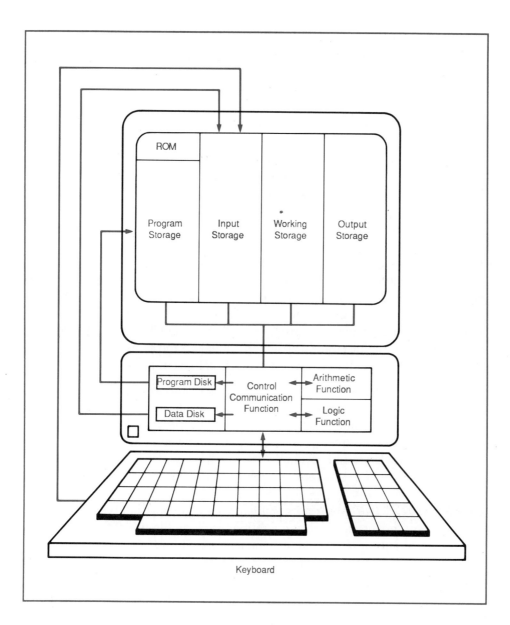

ROM

Program Storage

Input Storage

Working Storage

Output Storage

Program Disk

Control Communication Function

Arithmetic Function

Data Disk

Logic Function

Keyboard

Figure 5-1.

Main memory is divided into four functional sectors. Program instructions are routed to program storage, and selected and interpreted within the control unit. Based upon these instructions, data from input storage are manipulated and routed through working and output storage as needed.

hardware components and certain system software routines, as well as a routine for automatic loading of the operating system from disk. ROM programs also may allocate available memory into the four functional areas of program, input, working, and output storage.

Input storage.   The input storage area holds data for processing. Data items may be entered through the keyboard by operators or read from disk. Data held in main memory are accessed significantly faster than data residing in disk files. For this reason, memory capacity is a factor in determining system performance. That is, the more data that can be held in memory at one time, the faster that data can be accessed. The input storage section might hold an entire data file or a subset of the file structured to the available memory space.

Working storage.   Working storage holds data on an interim basis as required to support processing. The two-state nature of computer hardware dictates that processing take place incrementally, or as sequences of simple actions. Remember that the most complex computer arithmetic is broken down into a series of simple additions. Under most program designs, a single data value might be affected by multiple program instructions. Further, the same data value might change many times before a desired result is achieved.

Working storage has designated areas set up by the operating system to hold and to keep available needed inputs (such as program instructions and data items) and interim results (such as subtotals, factors, etc.). In larger or older systems, these functions sometimes are performed by separate, special hardware devices called *registers* and accumulators. The term, register, is so prevalent that it sometimes is used to indicate temporary holding areas within memory.

Output storage.   The output storage area of main memory holds small amounts of data ready for distribution to operations such as file update, printing, and other types of output. As a rule, mechanical operations take longer to execute than electronic functions. Most output operations involve movements of mechanical parts, such as read/write heads, printing mechanisms, etc. The processor can execute many operations while a printer or disk unit, with its own control structures, is completing one output instruction. The output storage area ensures that a steady stream of data is available to output equipment.

Buses.   From the above sections, it should be obvious that the capacities of the processor and main memory are significant factors for determining processing performance. The ability to transfer data and processing instructions between these components also affects performance. The hardware device in microcomputers that carries out these transfer operations is known as a ***bus.***

Figure 5-2.

The internals of a microcomputer consist of circuit boards that fit into racks that establish connections with a communications bus.

A bus can be thought of as a set of parallel wires. Each wire carries a single bit value—0 or 1. Remember: computers speak a two-state language, called binary notation. To maximize processing efficiency, bus capacities should complement the operational capabilities of the processor and main memory. The bus and other internals of a computer are shown in Figure 5-2. The **width,** or number of parallel connectors, of the bus determines the amount of data that can be transferred between the processor and main memory in one operation. If the capacity of the bus is less than the bit orientation of the processor and main memory, a resulting bottleneck may reduce processing performance.

1. Enter INVOICE program to PROGRAM area of main memory.

2. Create memory area for item record; with spaces for all fields.

3. Create register and accumulator areas in working storage.

4. Read transaction record for item.

5. Read master record for item; based on record key (item number).

6. Move item record to working storage.

7. Multiply quantity value by price value and write answer into EXTENSION field and INVOICEAMOUNT accumulator.

8. Move item record to output memory area.

9. Move item record to invoice record on disk.

10. Print item record to invoice document.

Figure 5-3.

Computer processing involves repeated, simple tasks. These processing steps, when executed, produce a single line item for an invoice report.

PROCESSING

In many respects, the interaction between main memory and the processor parallels the information processing cycle of functions: input, output, processing, and storage. Under the direction of the control function, data are input to the processor, transformed or combined with other data to add meaning for users, and output back to main memory. Many ***iterations,*** or repetitions, of this cycle usually are required to perform even relatively simple processing tasks.

Figure 5-3 lists processing steps for producing a ***line-item*** in an invoicing application. A line-item describes a single product sale on an invoice, and includes the product description, packaging unit, units sold, unit price, and extended price for the product. Figure 5-4 illustrates an invoice document produced as an output for the invoicing application. The highlighted area in the figure is the line-item described Figure 5-3.

Keep in mind that, collectively, the figures are meant only to present an overview of a processing operation. In addition, the processing steps described are generic. Actual ***program code,*** or instructions written in computer language, is lengthier and written in a format specific to the programming language.

The first step in this process is to enter the INVOICE program to the program storage area of main memory. From program storage, program instructions are

```
                          INVOICE
                       Acme Stationers
                     12345 Gratiot Avenue
                  Warren, Massachusetts  04569




    SOLD TO:  JOE'S MARKET              DATE: 11/23/87
              593 Atlantic Boulevard
              Tenafly, New Jersey  34423

    QTY    UNIT  NUMBER  DESCRIPTION    UNIT PRICE   EXTENSION

    3      box   4852B   Pens           $  16.50     $  49.50




                                       TAX    $    2.67
                                              --------
                                       TOTAL  $   52.17
```

Figure 5-4.

Invoices include line items, customer identification data, and other information to support transactions.

read and interpreted in control circuits—and processing is directed accordingly. An initial operation described by the program is to create space in memory for source data. That is, the input storage area is defined. In addition, a working storage area also is created, as well as areas within working storage set aside for registers and accumulators.

After needed register and accumulator areas are established, the **transaction record** for the item is read into the input storage area. A transaction record contains information describing a specific transaction. In this example, the transaction record describes a vendor, Acme Stationers, a buyer, Joe's Market, a product identifier (number), and the number of items purchased. See Figure 5-5.

The product number is used as a **record key.** A record key is a unique identifier for a record and is used to access that record within a larger collection of records, or **file.** In this example, the operator inputs fields for product number and units sold. The system searches the product master file for an item record that describes Item #4852B. The item record contains data items that identify the product as pens, the unit of sale as boxes, and the price as $16.50 per box. The

```
      FILE:   INVOICE                          RECORD NO.   14
      -------------------------------------------------------------

         SOLDTO     JOES MARKET
         DATE       11/23/87
         ITEM       4852B
         QTY        3
         UNIT       BOX
         DESCRIP    PENS
         UNPRICE    16.50
         XTENSION   49.50


      Use UP/DOWN cursor keys to scroll
      Press RETURN to display next record
      Or enter record number and press RETURN >
```

Figure 5-5.

Data describing transactions often are entered directly on microcomputer terminals.

item, or product description, record for this example is shown in Figure 5-6. Other items typically contained in product description records include applicable taxes, discount structures, and physical specifications.

In most business systems, the product master file is contained in some type of external storage medium. Once the appropriate record is located, it is loaded into the input storage area of main memory. From input storage, the item record is moved into working storage. This move provides access for the calculating operations that follow. The **extended price,** or price for the total amount of pens purchased, is derived by multiplying units purchased by unit price. The result of this operation is written into the EXTENSION field and the INVOICE-AMOUNT accumulator. This accumulator keeps a running subtotal of the total value of the transaction described on the invoice.

When all fields in the line-item have been filled with appropriate data items, the processing cycle now moves to output operations. The item record—now containing a data item for extended price—is moved to the output memory area. This record is moved to (and combined with) the invoice record created previously on disk. Each line item is added to the invoice record as it is processed. In addition, the item record from the output storage of main memory is printed on the invoice document.

```
    FILE: ITEM                              RECORD NO.   45
    -----------------------------------------------------------------

        ITEMNO      4852B
        DESCRIP     PENS
        UNIT        BOX
        UNPRICE     16.50
        TAX         Y
        DICOUNT     Y
        SPECS       BOX=12 DOZEN PENS




    Use UP/DOWN cursor keys to scroll
    Press RETURN to display next record
    Or enter record number and press RETURN >
```

Figure 5-6.

Under an invoicing application, product numbers can be set up as record keys and used to retrieve descriptions of ordered products.

Operating Sequences

In an invoicing application, as well as many other business applications, much of the input by which processing is directed comes directly from users. That is, user responses to prompts ultimately control many of the processing selections implemented by the control function. In addition, users are required to turn computers on and off, load programs, and perform many other vital operations. For this reason, Figure 5-7 presents a list of steps, much like the processing steps described above. This new figure, however, presents operational steps for implementing and using a microcomputer application—and includes user operations as well.

Notice again the number of processing steps involved in creating and printing the handful of data items on the invoice document in Figure 5-4. This number is multiplied many times when these processing steps are converted into program code. This may seem like a large number of steps for limited results—and it is. However, all these steps are performed in fractions of a second—and the accuracy and consistency of results virtually is guaranteed. Thus, the harnessing of computer power for this application probably is warranted.

The above example illustrates a common thread in the application of computers to virtually any type of problem. The benefits provided by computers, in

Figure 5-7.

Operational steps for implementing applications involve supplying power, inserting diskettes, and entering data and commands.

OPERATING SEQUENCE FOR MICROCOMPUTERS

1. Insert o/s disk into drive.
2. Turn on power switch.
3. Read startup and checkup instructions from ROM into control unit. Execute automatically.
4. Read operating system into memory.
5. Prompt for application program entry or auto-execute application program loading.
6. Load application program into appropriate memory sector.
7. Display menu or prompt for selection of application program module and/or data entry.
8. Load data for application.
9. Acquire application program instructions one at a time.
10. Move instructions and data items into working storage, following a sequence of control commands.
11. Get instructions and data from working storage and present to circuits for processing of arithmetic or logic functions.
12. Write interim results to working storage or, if appropriate, final results to output storage.
13. Store or print.
14. Update files as necessary.
15. Return control to operating system for startup of new application or termination of use.

most cases, center around time savings and increased accuracy (or decreased chances of human error). Processing tasks are broken down into laborious sequences of simple subtasks, but the smaller tasks are executed at ultra-high speeds. For business managers, decision making pertaining to microcomputers and the application of microcomputers to business operations often is enhanced by understanding how maximum performance is achieved. Peformance factors are the subject of the section that follows.

Performance and Architecture

In effect, processing performance is determined by a number of factors, described as follows:

- The capacity of main memory determines the amount of data and programs that can be held at one time. The content of main memory is accessible quickly, compared with mechanical access operations involving external storage devices.

- The bit orientation of microprocessors and buses determines the amount of data that can be transferred at one time. During processing, data and programs are transferred continually between main memory and the processor. A machine featuring a 16-bit processor—common in post-IBM standard microcomputers—and buses should execute instructions twice as fast as an 8-bit machine—the pre-IBM standard—because of increased transfer volumes for data and processing instructions.

- The cycle rate of the computer's **internal clock** determines the speed with which transfer operations are executed. The internal clock generates regular electrical pulses which trigger or synchronize operations. Internal clocks are not the same as time clocks that are built into many microcomputers. For microcomputers, internal clock speeds range from 4 to 16 **megahertz,** or millions of cycles per second.

The above discussions of performance factors refer to single-processor designs, also called **von Neumann architecture.** A von Neumann processor—named after its designer, John von Neumann—executes instructions one after another, in sequence. Improvements in processing performance, then, should be possible by linking multiple processors to execute instructions simultaneously. Some machines, called **array processors,** implement **parallel processing** by installing a series of processor chips on a single board. See Figure 5-8.

Many experts believe that multiple-processor computers signal the next generation of computer technology. Although full-scale parallel processing is still in developmental stages, related technologies have been implemented to improve performance.

The design, or **architecture,** of many microcomputers includes one or more **co-processors** for performing specialized tasks. Co-processors execute specialized or time-consuming operations, freeing the main processor to perform other tasks. Many microcomputers are equipped with a **math co-processor,** for executing the complex calculations required to support many database and spreadsheet applications.

As another example, a **graphics co-processor** has been installed as standard equipment in many types of microcomputers. The graphics co-processor handles the geometric conversions required to plot and display graphics on a screen or to produce graphic output. As program instructions call for conversion operations, they are transferred to the co-processor. The primary processor continues to execute program instructions sequentially. The co-processor interrupts the primary processor upon completion of its operations, the results of which are incorporated into the overall processing scheme. Processing also is interrupted

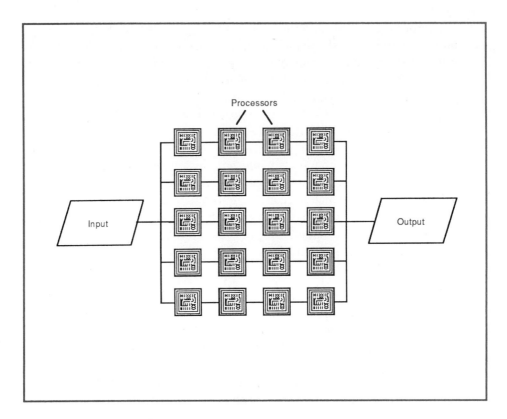

Figure 5-8.

Significant increases in computer performance may be achieved under architectures that feature multiple processors.

if the primary processor requires data from the co-processor. Even with these interruptions, co-processors provide increases in processing speed.

Understanding the capabilities of the CPU can enhance your present and future experiences with microcomputers. Any investment in microcomputer systems generally must be justified by its ability to meet human needs. In general, the greater your understanding of operations, the more effective are your abilities to derive results with microcomputer tools. The section that follows describes output devices, and completes the function-oriented view of hardware begun in the previous chapter. The importance of output devices stems from their role as the final link between computers and people.

OUTPUT DEVICES

Outputs are results of processing delivered in a human-readable form. Literally hundreds of makes, models, and types of equipment are used to generate computer outputs—and the list grows almost daily. Outputs may be displayed on terminal screens, produced on paper or film, converted into audio signals, or generated as communication signals.

In business organizations, ***hard-copy,*** or paper, documents are used far more than any other type of output. Documents usually consist of alphanumeric data (letters, numbers, and special characters) or graphics (pictures). In addition, documents may involve different levels of quality requirements, depending on the need to be filled. For any requirement, however, an appropriate output device is available.

Printers and Plotters

Computer printers can be classified according to the quality of outputs they produce. Printed outputs fall within two general categories—draft quality and letter quality—that are determined by the ***resolution***, or clarity, of output images on documents. User requirements generally determine the choice of printer within any microcomputer system.

Draft-quality printers usually are unsuitable for producing business letters to customers. Most business letters should be clear and easy to read, since they represent an organization and its commitment to quality. However, draft-quality outputs usually are obtained at much lower costs than with letter-quality devices. Therefore, lower resolution outputs may meet requirements for producing inventory listings, internal financial worksheets, and internal memos. Draft- and letter-quality devices are discussed in a section that follows.

User requirements for output devices also include timeliness and volume capacity of productions. In decision making processes, all these factors are weighed against cost considerations.

The sections that follow present an overview of the most common devices used to produce document outputs from microcomputer systems. Emphasis is placed upon the type and quality of documents each device produces. Keep in mind that configuring microcomputer work stations involves evaluating these specifications against business requirements. The most common output devices used with microcomputers include:

- Dot-matrix printers
- Letter-quality printers
- Laser printers
- Plotters.

Dot-matrix printers.   Dot-matrix printers are the most widely used type of ***character printer*** for microcomputer systems. A character printer generates output one character at a time, one after another. Character printers range in speed from 15 to more than 600 characters per second.

```
He preaches well that

lives well,

quoth Sancho,

that's all the divinity

I understand.



From Don Quixote

Miguel De Cervantes
```

Dot-matrix printers get their name from the way they form characters. Each character is composed of an arrangement of tiny dots within a rectangular matrix. The higher the number of dots in the matrix, the greater the resolution of printed characters. In addition, an advantage of dot-matrix printers is that the formats of characters can be changed easily. Different type styles, or *fonts,* and different sizes of each font can be produced. The formats for these fonts usually are stored on diskettes or ROM chips inside the printer. See Figure 5-9.

Most dot-matrix printers are *impact printers.* That is, a printing mechanism strikes an inked ribbon and leaves impressions on paper. The printing mechanism consists of a series of wires arranged in a matrix. The wires are connected separately to the print controller. Wires can be energized selectively to form individual characters.

Dot-matrix printers produce draft-quality documents. They generally are used to prepare working versions of documents or memos and other documents that are slated for internal circulation only. Some newer printers produce *near letter-quality* text. That is, the densities and patterns of characters approach the quality of text produced by ball-element typewriters.

In addition, many dot-matrix printers are able to produce graphics. These printers operate in a *dot-addressable mode.* This means that each wire, or dot, in the matrix is set to print (or not print) according to the shapes to be printed.

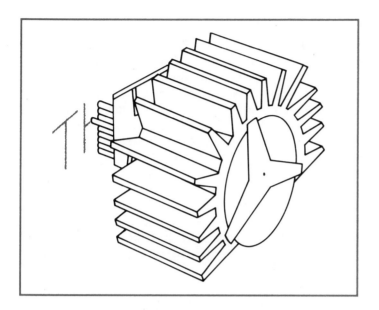

Figure 5-10.

Dot-matrix printers form characters as patterns of dots. The zig-zag surface of the mechanism is designed to dissipate heat.

The printing mechanism moves across and down the page, line by line, and prints dots in patterns that compose a picture. Printers of this type also may alternate between character and graphic modes to produce labeled charts, graphs, and diagrams. Some dot-matrix printers even offer color printing. A multicolored ribbon is included with such devices and combinations of ribbon colors produce a variety of output effects.

Other types of dot-matrix printers include **ink-jet printers** and **thermal printers.** Both form characters as arrangements of dots. An ink-jet printer is a **nonimpact printer** that sprays droplets of ink instead of striking a ribbon. A thermal printer uses a pin mechanism, but does not use a ribbon to make character impressions. Instead, the printing mechanism is heated and dots are burned onto heat-sensitive paper. See Figure 5-10.

Letter-quality printers.   Most letter-quality printers (the most notable exception is the laser printer, discussed below) use printing mechanisms that contain a full set of characters. Each character is struck against the ribbon and the impression of the character is left on paper. The resolution and readability of documents produced by these devices duplicates the quality of documents produced on single-element electric typewriters. See Figure 5-11.

The most popular type of letter-quality printer uses a typing element called a daisy wheel. The character set of a daisy wheel printer is arranged at the ends of spoke-like plastic or metal strips that extend outward from a central hub. As the wheel spins, the desired characters are struck by a hammer and impacted against the ribbon.

> This document was produced on a letter-quality printer. The print quality of the document resembles that produced by a single-element electric typewriter. The printer that produced this document is known as a daisy wheel printer. It is so named because of the typing element that is used to imprint characters on the page. An example of a daisy wheel print element is shown in Figure 5-12.
>
> Letter-quality printers are more preferable than dot-matrix printers for producing certain types of business documents, including letters and reports. Documents produced on letter-quality printers are more readable than documents produced on dot-matrix printers.

Figure 5-11.

Characters formed with letter-quality printers are clearly defined and easy to read.

Daisy wheel character sets with different fonts are removable and interchangeable—providing some of the flexibility of dot-matrix printers. Some printers of this type even support character sets for foreign languages or specialized character sets, such as symbols for engineering or mathematical formulas.

One of the drawbacks to daisy wheel printers is speed—daisy wheel printers operate at speeds that range from 14 to 55 characters per second. In addition, the impacts of hammer on paper create a lot of noise, and special enclosures usually are required for these and other impact printers, such as **thimble printers.** The operation of thimble printers is similar to that of daisy wheel printers. The basic difference lies in the arrangement of characters. Whereas the characters of daisy wheel printers extend outward like the petals of a daisy, the characters of a thimble printer point upward. The print mechanism spins around the hammer to position the proper character for imprinting. (See Figure 5-12.)

Laser printers. A laser printer operates much like a xerographic copier. A laser is a beam of highly concentrated, focused light. The laser traces characters onto a drum that becomes sensitive to light under an electrostatic charge. The characters on the drum are magnetized temporarily and attract pigmented particles of plastic, known as **toner,** and microscopic steel pellets, called **developer.** The developer enhances the attraction of toner to the drum. Then, the toner is fused,

Figure 5-12.

The daisy-wheel printer derives its name from the shape of the print mechanism. The wheel spins to position characters that are struck against an inked ribbon to produce an image on paper.

or melted, onto paper that is passed across the surface of the drum. The drum then is demagnetized and the developer falls off and is reused.

Laser printers are classified as ***page printers*** because they produce an entire page at one time. Speeds of laser printers are faster than any other type of printer. Relatively inexpensive ($2,000 to $7,000) laser printers, designed primarily to be used with microcomputers, may reach speeds of 8 to 15 pages per minute. The cost of laser printers is expected to decrease in the future.

Laser printers form characters within dot matrices of roughly 300 by 300 dots per inch. As the technology develops, it is expected that laser printers will be able to produce near-typeset quality documents (1,200 by 1,200 to 2,500 by 2,500 dots per inch). This high resolution results in high quality outputs, emulating that of offset printing. Font changes may be controlled by ROM programs by interchangeable disks or cartridges built into the devices. As an alternative, character sets may be handled by the microcomputer and transferred, or ***downloaded,*** to the printer. In effect, a virtually unlimited number of type sizes and styles can be produced with laser printers.

Laser printers also can produce both text and graphics on a single page—when the system is equipped with special page-oriented software. These capabilities have been instrumental in the development of ***desktop publishing.*** A desktop publishing system consists of a computer, page layout software, and a typeset

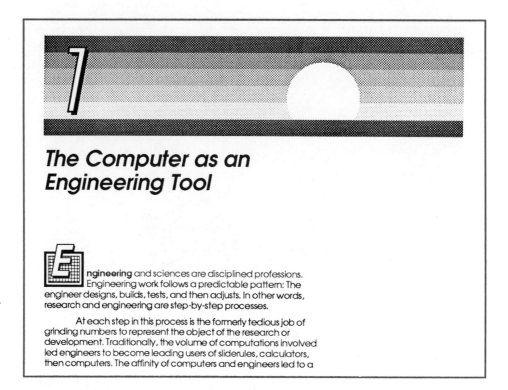

Figure 5-13.

With desktop publishing capabilities, text and graphics can be integrated, and document pages can be formatted and produced as high-resolution outputs.

quality output device. Figure 5-13 presents an output display from a desktop publishing system.

With current technology, the images produced by a laser printer are slightly less than typeset quality. However, desktop publishing systems minimize manual composition procedures traditionally required to produce typeset documents. Laser printers also cost a small fraction of the price of typesetters. The lower quality of laser outputs is offset by the speed and comparatively low cost of laser printers. If full typeset quality is needed, microcomputers with page makeup software can be connected directly to electronic typesetters. Laser printers and desktop publishing are discussed in greater depth in a later chapter.

Plotters. A plotter uses a pen-like device, called a *stylus,* to produce actual line drawings—often in multiple colors. Of course, the movement of the stylus is controlled by digitized instructions from a computer. Figure 5-14 presents a graphic output produced by a plotter. Figure 5-15 shows the stylus mechanism of a plotter.

Two common types of plotters are *flat-bed plotters* and *drum plotters.* Both types of plotters operate in similar fashion. A stylus is attached to a holder on some type of tracking device. With flat-bed plotters, the drawing surface remains

Figure 5-14.

Producing graphic images of this type may require special output devices, such as plotters.

stationary and the stylus can be moved in two directions, back and forth and up and down across the surface. Precise, two-dimensional line drawings can be produced. Color changes require changing the stylus. On a drum plotter, the stylus moves only left and right across a surface. However, the paper or film is mounted on a drum and rotated beneath the stylus to achieve the second dimension.

Plotters are low-speed, low-volume devices. However, plotted outputs have seen significant use in the production of presentation-quality graphics. Charts and graphs—either on paper or film—project a professional business image to an audience. In addition, graphics are more easily understood than volumes of statistics or numeric data from which they are produced. Business graphics are discussed further in a later chapter.

MODEMS FOR MICROCOMPUTERS

Another important hardware device "falls between the cracks" of the information processing cycle. In the previous chapter, displays are described as input/output devices because of their role in both functions. Another type of device, the **modem,** can be described in the same way. Modems are used to establish a link over communication lines for transferring data between two computers. At one end of a communication link, a modem is required to initiate the connection. That is, a modem handles the output of encoded data for transmission to another computer. At the other end of the link, another modem is required to handle the receiving of this data. Therefore, a modem functions as an output device at the sending machine, and as an input device at the receiving machine.

Sending and receiving data between computers is called **data communication.** Most data communication operations involve signals carried over telephone lines. Computer systems, however, produce signals that are incompatible with the signals handled by telephone systems, as well as most other communication systems. Modems, then, also perform the conversions required to overcome this incompatibility.

Computers produce binary, or two-state signals, that correspond to the 1s and 0s of binary notation under which data are represented. Binary signals also may be called **digital** signals, describing the patterns of 1s and 0s through which data are represented.

Communication systems, on the other hand, are set up to carry *analog* signals. Analog signals consist of continuous sounds, or tones. Analog signals are encoded by varying the volume, pitch, or wave patterns to emulate binary notation.

To initiate a data communication link, then, the output signal from the sending microcomputer must be converted to analog. This process is known as modulation. At the receiving end, the analog signal must be reconverted back into a digital signal for input to a computer. This process is called demodulation. The term, modem, is an abbreviation of these two conversions.

Types of Modems

There are three general types of modems for connecting microcomputers into communication lines. An *acoustic coupler* plugs into a computer and connects to a standard telephone. The handset of the telephone is inserted into a pair of rubber cups. Carrier signals are produced and received through the mouthpiece and earpiece of the telephone handset.

A *direct connect* modem connects a computer to a telephone without requiring use of the handset. Instead, transmission wires are connected directly from the computer into a modem. Otherwise, the operation of this type of modem is identical to acoustic couplers.

A *smart modem* is built on a circuit board that resides within the computer. A telephone jack connects directly to the microcomputer. The name is derived from the software-driven nature of smart modems. Smart modems are capable of dialing telephone numbers automatically, keeping a directory of numbers called, and other services.

Data communication with microcomputers is the subject of a later chapter. For present purposes, keep in mind that microcomputers equipped with modems can transfer data between virtually any two points in the world that have telephone service. These capabilities have spurred development of entirely new methods for handling data and configuring information systems. For example, information services, for a subscription fee, provide access to an extensive list of databases. By paying this fee, a microcomputer user can access stock quotes, airline schedules, software, dating services, and so on.

Consider also the New York Stock Exchange. In the 1950s, the NYSE experienced trading volumes of 10 to 20 million shares daily. In the 1980s, daily volumes have surpassed 200 million shares on several occasions. NYSE transactions are conducted between the exchange and a worldwide network of stockbrokers. To achieve such trading volumes, transactions must be supported through data communication.

Microcomputers and Networks

Data communication also has given rise to a new type of information system. Information systems can be configured with several microcomputers linked over communication lines to each other or to a central minicomputer or mainframe. These systems are known as **networks.** A network allows computers to share data and information resources. Microcomputer-based networks vary in complexity. The simplicity or complexity depends on the type of communication service supported and the geographic distribution of terminals.

Remember the discussion in an earlier chapter of the flow of a transaction throughout an organization. The flow, or path, of the transaction is defined by transaction data, often contained on transaction documents. Data and information flow through an organization in the same manner as transactions. However, the data may not be handled within the same building or area at which transactions are executed. Computer networks can be established to handle data flow to and from remote sites.

For example, a manufacturing organization might implement a network of microcomputer terminals, or work stations. A terminal in the order department would be used to enter incoming orders. This terminal can be used to access inventory files from the inventory function to determine that sufficient quantities of the ordered products are available. If so, order data can be transferred over communication lines to another terminal in the warehouse. The order is assembled from these data. The warehouse terminal, in turn, sends destination information to the shipping department. An invoice can be produced at any point within this network, depending upon the requirements of the organization.

A later chapter of this text presents a comprehensive discussion of data communication, modems, networks and related topics. For present purposes, the important point is that data can be shared and transferred by different computers, even computers far away. Further, microcomputers can establish links with larger, mainframe computers as well. The chapter that follows discusses an application package that also deals with microcomputers applied to communicate data, in this case written (or printed) words, or text. This application is known as word processing.

KEY TERMS

central processing unit (CPU)	extended price	letter-quality printer
processor	internal clock	thimble printer
microprocessor	megahertz	laser printer
main memory	architecture	toner
primary storage	von Neumann architecture	developer
adder	array processor	page printer
accumulator	parallel processing	download
condition test	co-processor	desktop publishing
control function	math co-processor	plotter
peripheral device	graphics co-processor	stylus
read-only memory (ROM)	hard-copy	flat-bed plotter
boot	resolution	drum plotter
register	dot-matrix printer	modem
bus	character printer	data communications
width	font	digital
iteration	impact printer	analog
line-item	near letter quality	acoustic coupler
program code	dot-addressable mode	direct connect
transaction record	ink-jet printer	smart modem
record key	thermal printer	network
file	nonimpact printer	

DEFINITIONS

Instructions: Define each term according to its use in this chapter.

1. peripheral device
2. primary storage
3. impact printer
4. desktop publishing system
5. architecture
6. transaction record
7. iteration
8. network

T R U E / F A L S E

Instructions: On a separate sheet, write T for true and F for false for each statement.

1. Computer logic refers to a computer's ability to add and subtract values.

2. Registers contain start-up routines stored on ROM disks.

3. Actual computing is performed by the central processing unit.

4. An array processor represents an improvement in design over von Neumann architecture.

5. A smart modem provides capabilities for dialing telephone numbers directly and keeping a directory of numbers called.

6. Data held in main memory and data residing on disk files can be accessed in virtually the same amount of time.

7. With current technology, laser printers can produce images slightly better than typeset quality.

8. Processing performance hinges on bus capability as well as processor and memory capacity.

9. Control function circuits act as a "traffic cop" in directing signals passing through the processor and main memory.

10. A flat-bed plotter uses a stylus to produce line drawings, whereas a drum plotter utilizes a xerographic process.

11. Computer networks that cover large geographic distances are known as relay-dependent systems.

12. On an invoice document, a line-item includes such elements as product description, units sold, and extended price.

13. A math co-processor enables a computer to perform the conversions necessary to produce graphic outputs.

14. The CPU performs all of these vital functions: arithmetic, logic, control, and primary storage.

15. For typical microcomputer applications, the user is seldom free to direct processing by responding to prompts.

Instructions: On a separate sheet of paper, answer each question in one or two brief sentences.

1. What are the differences in quality among documents produced on dot-matrix, daisy-wheel, and laser printers?

2. How does von Neumann architecture differ from that of an array processor?

3. Describe, in simple terms, computer arithmetic operations.

4. Name the two parts of the CPU and describe how they interact during the processing cycle.

5. What output devices can produce documents with both text and graphics? What devices are used only for graphics production?

6. What function do modems perform to facilitate data communication?

R E S E A R C H   P R O J E C T

Imagine you own a small business that is about to purchase a computer for invoicing and record-keeping. Obtain sales literature on at least three brands of microcomputers. Compare them on the basis of such criteria as memory size, register size, processing speed, and bus width. Choose the system you prefer for your application and explain why. Further, state what type of output device will best meet your needs.

Microcomputer Software: Word Processors

II

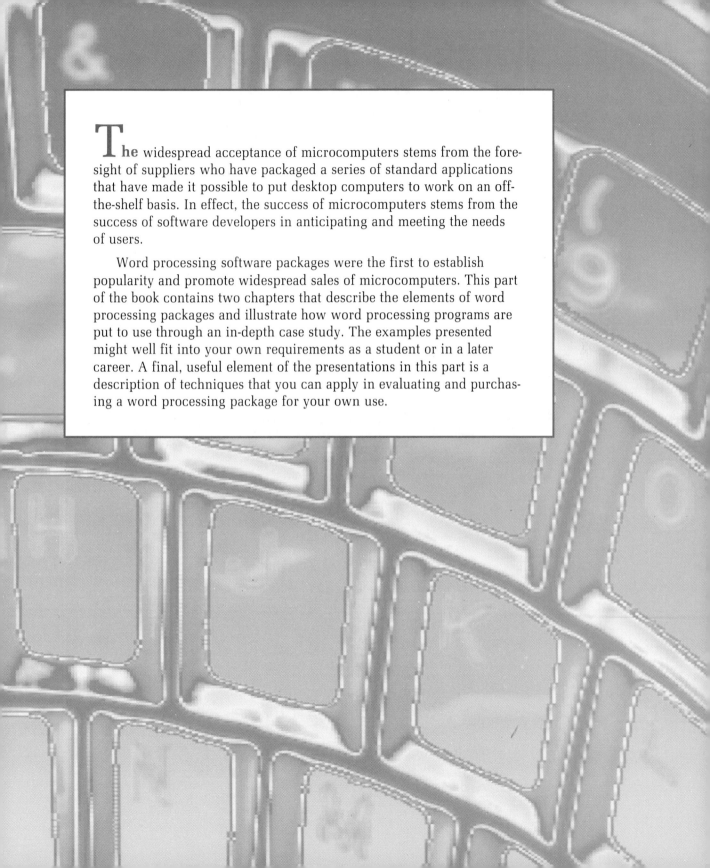

The widespread acceptance of microcomputers stems from the foresight of suppliers who have packaged a series of standard applications that have made it possible to put desktop computers to work on an off-the-shelf basis. In effect, the success of microcomputers stems from the success of software developers in anticipating and meeting the needs of users.

Word processing software packages were the first to establish popularity and promote widespread sales of microcomputers. This part of the book contains two chapters that describe the elements of word processing packages and illustrate how word processing programs are put to use through an in-depth case study. The examples presented might well fit into your own requirements as a student or in a later career. A final, useful element of the presentations in this part is a description of techniques that you can apply in evaluating and purchasing a word processing package for your own use.

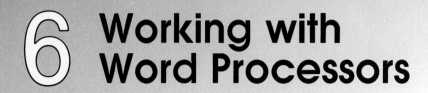

6 Working with Word Processors

COMMUNICATION: A BUSINESS REQUIREMENT

Efficient communication is a necessity for business survival.

HANDLING TEXT: SPECIAL REQUIREMENTS

Text and data files present different requirements and challenges in the storing and retrieval of computer-maintained files. Data files are uniform, or structured; text files are unpredictable, or unstructured.

WORD PROCESSING FUNCTIONS

A system of word processing is implemented in a series of steps, which range from creating a file to printing a finished document.

Create a File

The first step in document creation is to set up a file, a place on the disk where the document will be stored.

Key the Document

Entering a document involves use of a keyboard to record text in memory.

Save the Document

To preserve a document for future revision and printing, the text must be saved in external storage.

Edit the Document

Documents are edited to correct mistakes and to ensure the desired message is being communicated. Only corrections need be entered; retyping of accurate text is eliminated.

Print the Document

Documents are printed directly from text stored on disk.

ELECTRONIC EDITING

Computerized word processing streamlines the editing process. Executives can gain direct control over document creation.

Case Scenario: Delinquent Account

A case study shows how word processing can be used for effective business communication. In this case, the flexibility of word processing makes it possible to take special care with the wording of a collection letter.

Mail-Merge: Power Typing

Word processing can be used to mass produce individually typed and personalized form letters.

COMMUNICATION: A BUSINESS REQUIREMENT

In business, a problem can be defined loosely as a situation that presents requirements to be met or that requires corrective action. In this sense, all businesses face the problem of communicating effectively. Without effective mechanisms for communication, most businesses would fail. A business needs to convey messages—at a minimum, descriptions of products and/or services for sale—to the customers upon whom the organization depends for its continuing existence.

Communication refers to the exchange of ideas, thoughts, or information between two or more people. A sales letter, for example, conveys a message intended to induce potential customers to consider purchasing a product or service. The sales message, then, should attract the reader's attention, create a desire for a specific product or service, and motivate the reader to respond—either with a purchase or an expressed interest in the product or service. See Figure 6-1.

Effective communication is important for businesses for several reasons. Businesses need to cultivate and maintain relationships with customers, other businesses, and the public. These relationships are supported by communication: either spoken or written. Spoken language is the most common form of business communication. However, the role of written words, or **text,** cannot be overlooked. Consider some examples:

- Internal memos often are circulated to departments by managers. These memos convey messages of encouragement, warning, policy statements, and so on. For instance, a manager might circulate to all employees a memo that describes new procedures for recording work hours. The importance of these messages dictates that they be presented as effectively as possible. Wording of the messages should be clear and to the point. The document itself should be clean and readable. A sloppy, poorly written document is less likely to be taken seriously than one that is clearly understandable and presented professionally.

- Business letters emphasize the importance of written communication. Letters to outsiders represent the organization. Business letters may be sent to potential customers, clients, or people "on the street" whose collective opinion may add up to good or ill will for the company. The receiver of a business letter may base his or her opinion of the entire organization on that single letter. For these reasons, business letters should be of the highest quality possible—both in content and appearance.

- Manuals are textual documents that describe operations and/or procedures. For example, most computer manufacturers and software developers include one or more operations manuals with their products. Many organizations

```
September 22, 1987


Miss Cynthia Hathaway
5317 Borland Road
San Diego, CA  92723

Dear Miss Hathaway:

It was with great excitement that we read of your recent engagement.
Please accept our heartiest congratulations!

The Howard House Bridal Salon provides a free consultation service for
brides to be.  We invite you to join us for tea and croissants, any
Saturday morning at 10 a.m., to see our shop.  We carry an exquisite
selection of wedding gowns.  In addition, since we specialize in bridal
parties, we have gowns and accessories for bridesmaids, flower girls--and
we pay special attention to moms.  We also carry a full line of tuxedos
for purchase or rent.

We hope to see you next Saturday.  While you are here, we will explain our
layaway plan.

Sincerely,


John David Howard
```

Figure 6-1.

The message conveyed by a sales letter should create interest in a product or service, as well as an image of the selling company.

produce training manuals as reference guides to policies and procedures for employees.

- Price lists are collections of information describing products, prices, discount structures, and applicable taxes for products and/or services sold by an organization. Price lists may require frequent updating, depending upon the type and nature of the organization.

- Catalogs contain detailed descriptions of products and/or services sold by an organization. Catalogs might include information concerning product performance, components, guarantees, and so on. Like price lists, catalogs must be kept current. In medium- to large-sized organizations, updating catalogs—and price lists—may involve extensive text processing systems.

- In many organizations, engineering specifications are produced and maintained. Engineering specifications are exact and specialized descriptions of parts or components. The dimensions of machinery parts, for example, may be presented in terms of millimeters. Other descriptions might involve the ability of certain materials to withstand heat. Documents of this type must be kept current and accurate. To achieve this level of specialization, intensive editing may be involved in the production of engineering specifications.

These forms of communication largely are conveyed through written, or printed, words, or text. The use of computers to create and handle text is an application known as ***word processing.*** Word processing applications now seem natural for computers. However, some important obstacles had to be cleared before this application became practical. An understanding of this development should enhance your overall knowledge of computerized word processing. The section that follows presents a brief overview of the evolution of word processing packages.

HANDLING TEXT: SPECIAL REQUIREMENTS

Business documents can be classified by the type of information they present: data or text. In this sense, data refers to data items of fixed length and format. Text lends itself to neither fixed length nor fixed format. Both types of information make up files that are handled under different methods in microcomputer systems.

Consider the haphazard nature of the use of words for human communication. Words are collections of letters. Collections of printed words form sentences and paragraphs, each individual and unpredictable in terms of computer storage requirements.

Data files are relatively uniform and predictable. For example, a data file might be comprised of order entry records. Data elements within these records, such as customer identification numbers, item numbers, prices, taxes, and so on, all are of predictable and uniform length. Overall file sizes are multiples of record size, plus an allowance for expansion. The field and record structure of data files can be accommodated by the track and sector divisions of disk devices. In short, data storage needs are predictable and can be met efficiently.

Now, think of a letter or memo as a document file. There is no way to predict the size of a text file, since its constituent data items (words) are subject to the individual style of the writer and to rules of grammar. That is, words are grouped into sentences and paragraphs by a writer, and there are many correct ways of conveying a single message. These characteristics present special storage requirements.

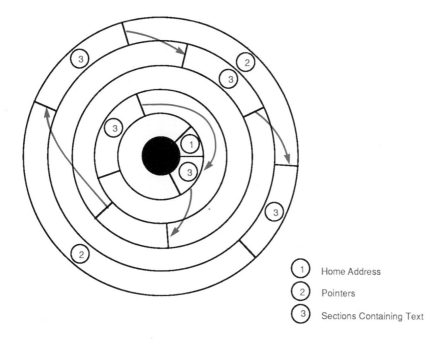

1 Home Address

2 Pointers

3 Sections Containing Text

Figure 6-2.

Text files are stored on diskettes in multiple sectors, chained together under a system of pointers.

To illustrate, consider again the document creation process. Text documents usually are produced through a series of working versions, or **drafts.** Drafts are revised, corrected, and changed until the final version is accepted. Business managers, and other users of word processors, may have several documents in draft stages at the same time. Storage of text files requires capabilities for handling files of unpredictable length. Further, once it is created, each file may vary in length each time it is processed.

Random access systems that use floppy disks provide the required storage capabilities. Random access refers to storage schemes that provide direct access to specific storage locations, regardless of sequence. Under random access systems, text files are written to disks that are divided into tracks and sectors in the same way as for storage of data files. (See Figure 6-2.) As sectors are filled, remaining text is written to the next available sector. However, the next available sector is not always next in sequence. Other files may have been created since the previous access of the original file.

To compensate for gaps in file sequences, a text file can be written to nonsequential sectors, **chained** together under program control. Chained files are referenced by **pointers** that link constituent sectors. Access operations proceed from one sector to the next as if they were part of a continuous string, or chain.

Suppose a business manager is working on a letter. The text file for the letter occupies two printed pages, roughly 5,000 characters to be stored. Suppose the letter is written on a microcomputer system that designates 512 characters per storage sector. Obviously, the file will occupy a considerable number of sectors and tracks. The system establishes a reference to the address of the first sector, called the **home address** of the document. As sectors are filled with text, the system inserts pointers at the ends of sectors. These pointers indicate the address of the next sector on which the file is written.

In effect, pointers are part of a referencing scheme for text files. Pointers are interpreted by the operating system; the operating system directs the read/write head to follow pointers to chained sectors until an entire file is accessed. Under random access schemes, then, additional portions of text created during editing are written to available disk sectors and referenced by pointers. Subsequent access operations are directed from sector to sector regardless of their physical disk locations.

Chaining of text files to multiple locations results in relatively inefficient use of storage media. However, diskettes are so inexpensive that these inefficiencies are insignificant.

The remainder of this chapter focuses on solving problems, or meeting situational requirements, with microcomputers and word processing software. The initial discussion that follows centers around the basic functions through which word processing is implemented.

WORD PROCESSING FUNCTIONS

The first chapter explains that the success of microcomputers results partly from their capability to implement a modular approach to applications. This concept holds for microcomputer systems configured for word processing. That is, word processing can be broken down into a series of modules, or organized steps, which include:

- Create a file.
- Key the document.
- Save (store) the document.
- Edit the document.
- Print the document.

```
A>dir b:

 Volume in drive B has no label
 Directory of  B:\

C8        DOC    45568   8-14-86    9:23a
C5        DOC    69632  10-10-86    3:59p
C9NEW     DOC     3584   1-01-80   12:05a
C9        DOC    82944   1-01-80   12:06a
INVOICE   DOC     3072   8-04-86   12:47p
UPDATE    DOC     3584   1-01-80    3:17a
C6        DOC    36864   8-06-86   10:20a
C7        DOC    49664   8-15-86   12:46p
C13       DOC    45568   1-01-80   12:14a
DBCONCPT DOC     8192   1-01-80    6:57a
       10 File(s)     11264 bytes free

A>
```

Figure 6-3.

A disk directory contains file names, as well as information about the sizes of files, time and date of creation or edit, and available storage.

Create a File

In word processing systems, an initial task involves creating a file, or establishing a storage area, for the document. Usually, this procedure is executed interactively. A menu selection is made, and the system prompts the user for a file name, usually any combination of eight characters that begins with a letter. File names are entered into a disk **directory.** The directory is a reference file for documents stored on disk. For the user, directory entries contain information relating names of files, dates of last edit, type of file, and file size. See Figure 6-3. For the system, the directory indicates storage locations for each file. The system uses a home address to direct read/write operations to the physical starting point of a disk file. Successive sectors are chained and accessed by pointers imbedded within files.

Key the Document

Once a file is created, the document can be input through keyboard entries—a procedure often called **keying** the document. Keying documents on a word processing system resembles typing operations. Keystrokes are input to computer memory and echoed on display screens. Displayed entries can be viewed and corrected in main memory before hard copies or storage files are produced.

Word processors invariably provide a **word wrap** capability. This feature eliminates the need to enter **hard returns** at the end of each line. A hard return corresponds to a carriage return at the end of each line entered on a typewriter. Word wrap moves words that are too big to fit at the end of a line down and left, to the beginning of the next line. Hard returns are needed only to designate paragraph endings or to insert blank lines into a document.

Most systems also provide a set of **formatting commands.** These commands establish a layout of the document on the screen, and subsequently, on a printed page. That is, line length, margin parameters, page length, headings, and footnotes can be established by keyboard-entered commands.

Many systems also support text **justification** as part of the format command set. This function is used to align left and right margins, as is done in this book. Text is arranged so that both margins are straight and parallel. Most systems also contain a feature for centering single headings.

Save the Document

Keying a document creates a version that exists only in main memory. Storage in main memory is volatile, or temporary. If the machine loses power for any reason, content of main memory is lost. Documents to be stored for later editing or reuse must be written to external storage. All word processing packages provide some method for storing documents.

Saving a file refers to the transfer of a document from main memory to external storage, usually a diskette. The SAVE command initiates file writing operations. An initial word processing task, discussed above, involves creating a storage area for a file. After the file is keyed into memory, the SAVE function is executed, and the file is written to the storage area designated for that file.

Most word processing manuals advise operators to save, or update, documents frequently during work sessions. Frequent saves reduce the chance and magnitude of work losses in the event of power or equipment failures.

Edit the Document

A document is **edited** to locate and correct errors in spelling and grammar, and to ensure that the text conveys the meaning intended. The editing process usually involves several iterations of correction and/or rewriting before a final version of the document is produced.

The edit process is streamlined by word processing capabilities. A document is brought into main memory, and viewed on a display screen. Simple changes usually require only a few keystrokes. For example, suppose an operator keys

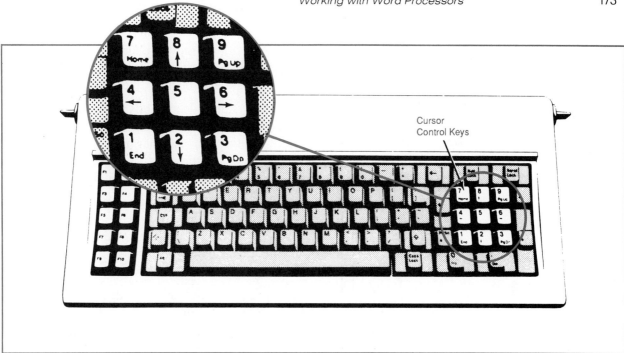

Cursor
Control Keys

Figure 6-4.

Cursor movement keys are used to position the cursor and to scroll through displayed files.

"sistems" instead of "systems." The correction is made simply by positioning the cursor over the incorrect letter (i) and pressing the key for the correct letter (y).

Other edit operations are more complex, and may involve moving, copying, deleting, or adding large portions, or ***blocks,*** of text. Word processors typically include sets of commands that simplify these operations as well. For example, common functions included within the command set of word processors include:

- Scroll
- Move and copy
- Insert and delete
- Search and replace.

Scroll.   The scroll function is used to move a text file up or down or side to side for review. This function allows a user to view desired portions of text files. Further, users must be able to position the cursor so that corrections can be entered. Most microcomputer keyboards designate certain keys as ***cursor movement keys.*** These keys are labeled with arrows pointing up, down, left, and right. See Figure 6-4.

To move the cursor up, down, left, or right, a user simply presses the appropriate key. Cursor movement proceeds one character at a time for left and right moves, and line by line for up and down moves. Users also have the option of holding keys down to execute repetitive moves. However, for large-scale scrolling or cursor movement, other methods may be available.

For example, most word processors provide methods for moving the cursor directly to left and right margins. Consider MultiMate, a popular word processor for the IBM PC, as an example. In this package, margin moves are executed by pressing the alternate key (ALT) and a function key (F3 for left margin, F4 for right margin) simultaneously.

Another standard scrolling feature involves moving the cursor to the beginning or end of a display. For the IBM PC, individual keys are designated for this purpose. Pressing the Home key, for instance, moves the cursor to the top left corner of a screen of text. Pressing the End key moves the cursor to the end of a screen of text.

Other standard scrolling functions include screen, or page, moves. The IBM PC designates individual keys for these functions too. The PgUp (Page Up) key causes an entire portion of text to be moved down, and the preceding screenful of text to be displayed. The PgDn (Page Down) key initiates a full-screen move in the opposite direction.

Methods for executing standard functions differ according to maker and type of machine and word processing package. For example, in some systems, including those made by Apple for the Macintosh microcomputer, standard scrolling functions are executed using a pointing device, called a mouse. Cursor positioning is directed by mouse movement across a surface. Further, *scroll bars* are displayed along the right side and bottom of the screen. By moving the mouse to point to relative positions along these bars, the user directs the cursor to other locations in the file. *Scroll arrows* allow the user to scroll continuously left, right, up, or down. See Figure 6-5.

The mouse-controlled scrolling functions described above are implemented with *file-oriented* packages. File-oriented packages save documents in their entirety. In turn, entire files are brought into memory for editing, printing, and other operations. Documents created by these packages are *paginated,* or divided into pages, either by the user or by the system during printing operations. A potential drawback to these systems, however, is that the size of files is controlled by the size of available memory.

Many word processing packages, such as MultiMate, are *page-oriented.* Page-oriented packages differ from file-oriented packages in that files are saved, and loaded into memory, one page at a time. With page-oriented packages, file pages usually reflect the page divisions of the hard-copy document. Most packages of this type provide an option for moving directly to specific pages within

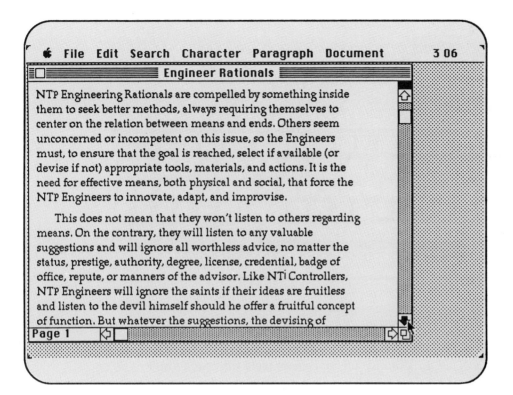

NTP Engineering Rationals are compelled by something inside them to seek better methods, always requiring themselves to center on the relation between means and ends. Others seem unconcerned or incompetent on this issue, so the Engineers must, to ensure that the goal is reached, select if available (or devise if not) appropriate tools, materials, and actions. It is the need for effective means, both physical and social, that force the NTP Engineers to innovate, adapt, and improvise.

This does not mean that they won't listen to others regarding means. On the contrary, they will listen to any valuable suggestions and will ignore all worthless advice, no matter the status, prestige, authority, degree, license, credential, badge of office, repute, or manners of the advisor. Like NTi Controllers, NTP Engineers will ignore the saints if their ideas are fruitless and listen to the devil himself should he offer a fruitful concept of function. But whatever the suggestions, the devising of

Figure 6-5.

Under mouse-oriented systems, scroll operations are directed by selecting appropriate scroll bars and scroll arrows.

the file. To illustrate, the GOTO ("go to") function is executed in MultiMate by pressing the function key F1. The user then is prompted to enter the number of the page to which he or she wishes to move. The system then accesses that page and brings it into memory. As an alternative, the Home or End keys also can be pressed as a prompt response, to move to the first or last page in the file. Mouse-oriented systems may include this feature as an option.

Move and copy.   To be understood, the message within a document should follow a logical order. To achieve this, the editing process often requires rearranging text. That is, users often need to enhance readability by moving words, sentences, and/or paragraphs to other locations. In manual systems, this process might involve cutting and pasting portions of hard copies. Of course, a presentable final version would have to be retyped.

Word processing systems allow users to "cut and paste" a displayed document electronically—with a few simple commands. Initially, the portion of text to be moved or copied must be defined. For example, in the WordStar program, the keys CONTROL, K, and B are pressed to designate, or **delimit,** the beginning of a block to be handled. The keys CONTROL, K, and K delimit the end of the block. Then, the cursor is moved to the location at which the block is to be moved

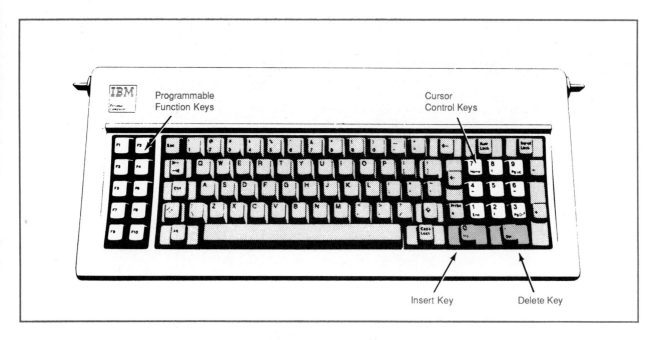

Programmable Function Keys

Cursor Control Keys

Insert Key

Delete Key

Figure 6-6.

Most microcomputer keyboards include special keys dedicated to insert and delete functions.

or copied. Finally, simple commands, such as CONTROL, K, and C for copy or CONTROL, K, and V for move, complete the operation.

Insert and Delete.   Many word processing systems dedicate individual keys to the insert and delete functions. These keys, shown in Figure 6-6, are pressed to initiate their respective operations—adding or removing text.

The *insert* function is used to add text. The execution of insert commands varies, however. With all packages, an insert begins when the cursor is moved to the point at which the insert is to begin. In some packages, an insert command causes existing text after the cursor to drop off the screen. Then, additions are keyed by the user. Upon completion, the remaining text is brought up to the end of the inserted portion. With other packages, displayed text moves to the right to accommodate insertions as characters are keyed.

The *delete* function refers to the removal of text. Delete operations are executed differently, depending on the amount of text to be removed. For large portions, many systems provide delimiting routines, such as those used for move and copy operations. A block of text is defined, or delimited. Then, the delete key is pressed and the delimited block is erased from memory. The term, delete, means to wipe out or destroy. Deleted text is just that—gone, with few exceptions.

The delete capability represents a significant danger of computerized word processing. In manual systems, typists cannot wipe out an entire document with a few incorrect keystrokes; word processing operators can. For this reason, word processing manuals stress the importance of caution in executing delete functions.

Search and Replace. Another important word processing feature is the **search** function. In this sense, a search refers to the ability of a system to locate specified **character strings** within files. A character string is a specific sequence of letters, numbers, or symbols.

To illustrate, suppose you are working with a lengthy text document about the life of Abraham Lincoln. You wish to check specific references to the Gettysburg Address. One method for executing this operation would be to scroll through the document, either line by line or page by page, visually checking for references to this topic. Increased efficiency, however, may be realized by implementing the search function. Function keys are pressed, and the targeted string is entered in response to a prompt display.

In this case, you may choose the string "Gettysburg" as the search target. In effect, you instruct the system to scroll through the document automatically and hold the cursor at the beginning of each occurrence of the targeted string. The search can be reactivated by pressing appropriate function keys again.

The **search and replace** function allows operators to find and change every occurrence of a particular character string. Depending upon the package, many search and replace operations can be started from any point within the file and may proceed toward the beginning or end of the file.

Suppose, for example, you have keyed a 20-page report about a famous (though fictitious) historian, named Bernard Duke. Before you print the report, you bring the file into memory and scroll through the text. You discover a recurring error: Duke often occurs as "Suke," probably due to the proximity of the "d" and "s" keys on the keyboard. Using the search and replace command, you can instruct the system to search for every occurrence of the incorrect character string (Suke) and replace it with the correct string (Duke).

Two replace options are available with most packages. One option is called a **global search and replace.** As in the above example, a global operation finds and corrects every occurrence of the designated string from the starting point to the end of the text.

The second option is called a **discretionary search and replace.** The operator is given a choice of replacing occurrences selectively. That is, at each occurrence of the specified string, a prompt is displayed that gives the user a choice to replace that string or to move to the next string. For instance, suppose you are editing a document in which the author occasionally uses the spelling "there" in place of "their." The mistake does not occur in each instance of "there." You

A major advantage

of word processing applications involves computer-driven printing operations.

can use a discretionary replace to fix only the erroneous usage. With either option, however, the system implements changes automatically.

Print the Document

A major advantage of word processing, then, is the ability to manipulate text electronically. Documents can be edited in memory, then stored on inexpensive diskettes. However, the most significant advantage may be the ability to print documents automatically. That is, the content of a document can be sent from main memory to a printer for output—virtually eliminating the occurrence of human typing errors.

In addition, word processing systems allow users to control printing operations with two types of commands:

- Operating commands
- Format commands.

Operating commands. *Operating commands* instruct the printer to start or stop printing. These commands act as an on/off switch for the user. Some word processors include a feature for using the printer as a typewriter. That is, the printer is instructed to imprint individual characters or lines as keystrokes are made on the keyboard.

Format commands. *Format commands* are used to establish page layouts for documents. These commands specify parameters such as page length, line width, margin formats, paragraph indents, and so on. Format commands also can set up **headers** or **footers** on each page. A header is a line or block of text printed across the top of each page of a document. A footer is a similar notation printed at the bottom of the page. Format commands also may instruct the printer to number pages and to place page numbers in designated locations.

Special software routines may be required to establish compatible transfers of files from computer to printer. These routines are called **printer action tables** or **printer drivers** and usually are part of application package software.

The functions described here can be applied to a wide range of document production requirements. The sections that follow present scenarios describing word processing operations that are carried out regularly in business organizations.

ELECTRONIC EDITING

Computerized word processing streamlines the edit process. Consider the scenario that follows. This scenario presents a business executive composing a collection letter to one of the organization's clients.

Case Scenario: Delinquent Account

Lou Bishop is the manager of collections at the fictional company, Big Time, Inc., referred to throughout this text. Bishop is sitting in front of his personal computer, composing a collection letter to a client, from Marlin Industries, who has not paid an outstanding invoice. Previous letters from Bishop stated that "unless the matter is resolved, it will be turned over to our attorney." The attorney advised Bishop to send one more letter.

Bishop turns on his machine, loads the operating system and word processor, and selects the menu selection for CREATE A FILE. A prompt is displayed that requests a file name. Bishop names the document COLLECT. See Figure 6-7.

After the file name has been entered and recorded by the system, Bishop is ready to begin composing the collection letter. Bishop wants to create a specific

```
                         CREATE A FILE

             Enter the Name of the New Document

        Drive:  C              Document :  Collect

    Approximately 00052736 characters [00021 Page(s)] available on C:
    ADDRESS  CHAPTER3  DOCUMENT  FIGURE5   FIGURE6   REPORT    LETTER
    LETTERA  LETTERB  REPORT1   REPORT2   REPORT3   SUMMARY




                Press return to continue, PgDn to switch drives
       Press Ctrl Home for default directory, Ctrl End for next directory
```

Figure 6-7.

The CREATE A FILE function of word processors is used to name a document file and to establish a storage area for the file.

Figure 6-8.

A first draft created under word processing techniques is displayed on a terminal screen for editing.

```
    Dear Mr. Fisher

    Our letter of June 28, speled out our intentions.  If your overdue
    account of @45.55 was not paid in 8 days (yesterday), we would be
    forced to turn the matter over to our attorneys.

    That's exactly what we did.  Our attorneys, however, advised us to
    give you one more opportunity to settle the score.  We disagreed, but
    went along anyway.  Attorneys have a nack for getting their way,
    don't they.

    We had already said "No more Mr. Nice Guy," but out attorneys talked
    us out of it.

    Well, you can bet this is our final letter, your last chance to keep
    from meeting our atorneys.  (Actually, they're a fine bunch of folks,
    extremely compitent.)  Please send us a check in reply.

    Sincerely



    Lou Bishop
    Vice-President
    Big Time, Inc.
    djs/jd
```

```
July 7, 1987

Mr. Ronald Fisher
Marlin Industries
2358 Seascape Lane
Boston, Ma.  83930

Dear Mr. Fisher:

Our letter of June 28, speled out our intentions.  If your overdue
account of @45.55 was not paid in 8 days (yesterday), we would be
forced to turn the matter over to our attorneys.

That's exactly what we did.  Our attorneys, however, advised us to
give you one more opportunity to settle the score.  We disagreed, but
went along anyway.  Attorneys have a knack for getting their way,
don't they?

We had already said "No more Mr. Nice Guy," but out attorneys talked
us out of it.

Well, you can bet this is our final letter, your last chance to keep
from meeting our atorneys.  (Actually, they're a fine bunch of folks,
extremely compitent.)  Please send us a check in reply.

Sincerely,



Lou Bishop
Vice-President
Big Time, Inc.
djs/jd
```

Figure 6-9.

Document editing involves finding and correcting errors or in-
consistencies in spelling,
grammar, and meaning.

tone for this letter, one that is polite, yet firm, and conveys a message of impend-
ing action if the account is not paid promptly. The first draft of the letter he composes is shown in Figure 6-8.

Bishop believes that editing is best applied to hard-copy documents. He
prints out the initial draft, and edits the letter manually. This may seem like a
waste of time and some inefficiencies are apparent. The point to remember,
however, is that microcomputers are tools, and tools should be applicable to the
needs and desires of users. The user should not be forced to make fundamental
changes in work habits to accommodate tools.

Figure 6-9 presents the edited version of the letter. Notice Bishop's handwritten corrections. These corrections must be entered into the text file. Bishop
selects the menu option for EDIT AN EXISTING FILE, and the file is read into
memory and displayed on the terminal screen. Bishop can scroll through it to
enter his corrections. Of course, Bishop could have chosen to enter these corrections without first producing a hard copy.

```
DOCUMENT: figsix10                    |PAGE:   3|LINE:   1|COL:   1|   MOVE WHAT?
|1..».....».....»..............................................................«
Our letter of June 28, speled out our intentions.  If your overdue
account of $45.55 was not paid in 8 days (yesterday), we would be
forced to turn the matter over to our attorneys.«
«
That's exactly what we did.  Our attorneys, however, advised us to
give you one more opportunity to settle the score.  We disagreed, but
went along anyway.  Attorneys have a nack for getting their way,
don't they.«
«
We had already said, "No more Mr. Nice Guy," but our attorneys talked
us out of it.«
«
Well, you can bet this is our final letter, your last chance to keep
from meeting our atorneys.  (Actually, they're a fine bunch of folks,
extremely compitent.)  Please send us a check in reply.«
«
Sincerely«
«
«
«
Lou Bishop«
Vice-President«
  N:ü
```

Figure 6-10.

To execute a MOVE operation, the user must indicate a portion of text to be moved.

Notice that Bishop wants to move the entire third paragraph to the beginning of the letter body. To execute this correction, Bishop presses function keys to initiate a MOVE operation. Bishop moves the cursor to the beginning of the third paragraph. He then presses the RETURN key twice, to move the cursor to the second hard return.

Portions of text usually can be delimited for MOVES or other block operations in this way. The operation is initiated, usually, by pressing function keys. The beginning point of the block is the cursor position at the time the MOVE is initiated. Pressing keys moves the cursor to the next occurrence of that character. This includes carriage and punctuation marks. To delimit the entire paragraph, Bishop simply presses the return key.

Figure 6-10 presents the display screen at this point in the operation. Notice the third paragraph is highlighted. The prompt in the upper right corner reads MOVE WHAT? When Bishop has specified a block of text, he presses the MOVE function key again. A succeeding prompt reads TO WHERE? Bishop moves the cursor to the location at which the paragraph is to appear, hits the function key for MOVE once again, and the paragraph is moved.

```
July 7, 1987                      Big Time, Inc.
                                  225 Hourglass Lane
                                  Milwaukee, WI 45987

Mr. Ronald Fisher
Marlin Industries
2358 Seascape Lane
Boston, MA  03930

Dear Mr. Fisher:

We had already said "No more Mr. Nice Guy," but our attorneys talked
us out of it.

Our letter of June 28, spelled out our intentions.  If your overdue
account of $45.55 was not paid in 8 days (yesterday), we would be
forced to turn the matter over to our attorneys.

That's exactly what we did.  Our attorneys, however, advised us to
give you one more opportunity to settle the score.  We disagreed, but
went along anyway.  Attorneys have a knack for getting their way,
don't they?

Well, you can bet this is our final letter, your last chance to keep
from meeting our attorneys.  (Actually, they're a fine bunch of
folks, extremely competent.)  Please send us a check in reply.

Sincerely,



Lou Bishop
Vice-President
Big Time, Inc.
djs/jd
```

Figure 6-11.

The finished document should be free of errors and presented neatly on the page.

Bishop then corrects the minor spelling and grammar errors indicated by the manual edit. For most errors, the cursor is positioned at the incorrect character and the correct character is typed over it. In other instances, characters are missing. Bishop shifts into INSERT mode to add spaces for characters as needed. Figure 6-11 presents a copy of the corrected letter.

The entire edit operation is completed within a few minutes. A letter this short probably might be retyped in the same time. However, if the typist makes an error, the document may have to be retyped again. As documents increase in length, the time savings and convenience of word processing capabilities also increase. In addition, word processing packages provide other capabilities that many systems cannot. One of those capabilities, mail-merge, is the subject of the scenario that follows.

Mail-Merge: Power Typing

Suppose Bishop receives a favorable response to the collection letter he mailed to Marlin Industries. Bishop might assume that the message conveyed by his letter meets his needs, and he decides to send the letter to all customers whose accounts are seriously delinquent. Bishop targets 32 customers whose accounts are overdue more than 60 days, and who have been sent preliminary collection notices.

In other words, Bishop needs to produce 32 **form letters,** or documents with the same message addressed to multiple customers. This means that the inside addresses and salutations are different for each letter, while the body of the letter remains the same. Further, the letters must be as neat and professional in appearance as if they were created individually.

Most word processing packages provide capabilities for meeting these requirements efficiently, without requiring separate document-creation operations. This capability is called **mail-merge,** or **power typing.** Mail merge involves setting up two types of files, a **primary file** and a **secondary file.**

The primary file contains the part of the letter that stays the same—in this case, the body of the collection letter. The secondary file consists of **variables,** or entries that are to change with each letter. Figure 6-12 illustrates the screens that Bishop uses to implement the mail merge. Notice that the primary file designates entry areas for the variables held in the secondary file.

When both files have been created and saved, the print operation can begin. Given appropriate instructions, the system locates, brings into main memory, and sends the primary file and a set of variables for each letter to the printer. That is, customer names, addresses, salutations, and outstanding balances are inserted into the appropriate place in 32 different letters. Each letter is printed individually and automatically, under system control.

Further, each letter is printed accurately; the incidence of typing error is eliminated. Mail merge also provides capabilities to print addresses from secondary files onto envelopes or mailing labels. In other cases, prompts can be set up for printing at certain locations within documents. When print operations reach these locations, users are requested to key in needed information.

In summary, word processing systems broke many barriers of resistance to microcomputers in business organizations. The time and cost savings realized through word processor capabilities, such as screen editing and mail-merge, convinced many business managers to buy microcomputers.

Figure 6-12.

In a mail-merge application, the primary file (top) includes designations for inserts of variables. The secondary file (bottom) contains actual entries for these variables.

```
DOCUMENT: COLLECT              |PAGE:   3|LINE:   1|COL:   1|
|1..»....»....»...............................................«
«
«
├date┤«
«
├title┤ ├first name┤ ├last name┤«
├company┤«
├address┤«
«
«
Dear ├title┤ ├last name┤«
«
We had already said, "No more Mr. Nice Guy," but our attorneys talked us
out of it.«
«
Our letter of ├date b┤, spelled out our intentions.  If your overdue
account of ├amount┤ was not paid in 8 days (yesterday), we would be forced
to turn the matter over to our attorneys.«
«
That's exactly what we did.  Our attorneys, however, advised us to give
you one more opportunity to settle the score.  We disagreed, but went
along anyway.  Attorneys have a knack for getting their way, don't they?«
«
```

```
DOCUMENT: addrsses             |PAGE:   1|LINE:   1|COL:   1|
|1..»....»....»...............................................«
├title┤«
Mr.┤«
├first name┤«
Ronald┤«
├last name┤«
Fisher┤«
├company┤«
Marlin Industries┤«
├address┤«
2358 Seascape Lane«
Boston, MA 03930«
«
├title┤«
Mr.┤«
├first name┤«
David┤«
├last name┤«
Langley┤«
├company┤«
Redundant Industries┤«
├address┤«
38477 Halloreen Street«
 N:Ü
```

Microcomputer-based

word processing systems are replacing most traditional methods for producing documents.

COURTESY OF DATA GENERAL
CORPORATION

Word processors, like electronic spreadsheet packages, are application programs. In a basic sense, application packages are relatively straightforward and understandable. Interactive execution makes it possible to obtain results from many programs without reading a manual. For these applications, a minimally skilled operator usually can work through directories, help screens, and menus until desired results are achieved.

However, in any field, the difference between an ordinary worker and a skilled professional is knowledge. For example, carpenters can build cabinets without knowing what type of wood they are using. On the other hand, a master carpenter incorporates a knowledge of the characteristics of different types of wood and chooses material carefully to match each project.

The same holds true with computers—especially microcomputers. Knowledge of the file-handling methods of an application package can enhance the productivity of the operator. At another level, knowledge of the software environment within which applications are run can augment professional computer skills. This environment is established by a set of "housekeeping" programs known as **system software**, the subject of the chapter that follows.

KEY TERMS

text
word processing
draft
random access system
chaining
pointers
home address
directory
keying
word wrap
hard return
formatting command
justification
saving
editing
block

scroll
cursor movement keys
scroll bar
scroll arrow
file oriented
pagination
page-oriented
move and copy
delimit
insert
delete
search
character string
search and replace
global search and replace
discretionary search and replace

operating commands
format commands
headers
footers
printer action table
printer driver
form letter
mail-merge
power typing
primary file
secondary file
variable
system software

DEFINITIONS

Instructions: On a separate sheet, define each term according to its use in this chapter.

1. word processing
2. home address
3. directory
4. text justification
5. scroll
6. paginated
7. character string
8. footer

T R U E / F A L S E

Instructions: For each statement, write T for true or F for false on a separate sheet.

1. Word processing does away with the need to retype entire documents each time a change is made.

2. Random access systems allow direct access to specific files or records within files regardless of where they are located in memory or storage.

3. On a word processing system, the term "word wrap" refers to the number of words that can be "wrapped up" in a specific document.

4. Format commands let an operator establish the layout of the document on the printed page.

5. In a page-oriented system, the text is saved on disk and loaded into memory one page at a time.

6. Word processing systems allow a user to rearrange text and data electronically within a displayed document.

7. With word processing, a file that is deleted accidentally can be recovered easily.

8. Word processing software can be used to find specific words in a document automatically.

9. Word processing software can be used to replace one word in text with another.

10. Word processing software can be used to find and correct grammatical errors in a document.

11. A word processing document stored for more than one month begins to disintegrate and must be checked carefully for spelling errors before being printed.

12. With word processing, a form letter may be created and typed "personally" numerous times, with a different name and address automatically inserted each time.

13. A secretary or other human being must be present each time a word processor types a letter to correct any mistakes it makes.

14. As documents increase in length, the time savings and convenience of word processing capabilities also increase.

15. Word processing capabilities played a major role in building acceptance for microcomputers in business organizations.

SHORT ANSWER QUESTIONS

Instructions: On a separate sheet of paper, answer each question in one or two brief sentences.

1. Why are different methods needed for handling text and data files in computers?

2. How does a computer store and keep track of a text file that is too big to fit in a single sector of disk storage?

3. How does a word processor streamline writing and editing of text?

4. Describe a situation in which the search command of a word processor might save you time and improve the quality of your document.

5. Name and describe the types of files that have to be created and used to send out "personalized" form letters.

6. What is an application package?

RESEARCH PROJECT

1. Talk to friends or family members and collect a variety of "personalized" form letters from sales organizations, political candidates, charities, groups advocating social or legal action, etc. Try to get several different versions of the same form letter. Identify and explain differences in the letters. If there are no differences, describe changes that could be made. Then compare methods for producing copies of the form letter, including printing, individual typing, using an office copier and inserting names and addresses on a typewriter, or word processing on a computer. Find out about and compare costs. Discuss the differences in effectiveness of the identified methods. That is, which kind of letter would be read by recipients and which would be likely to produce the best results? Explain your answers.

2. Assume you are working on a project to raise money for a new soccer team in your school. You are to solicit contributions from throughout the community. Your specific job is to supervise a direct-mail appeal in which letters are sent to leaders of the business community. Compare at least three alternate methods of appeal. Which is best? Why?

7 Solving Problems With Word Processors

ROLE OF WORD PROCESSORS

Word processing packages adapt microcomputers for creating and producing text documents.

STANDARD WORD PROCESSING FUNCTIONS

All word processing packages must be able to perform certain functions. These basic capabilities are generic, or common to almost all word processing packages.

Create

Place a file name on a disk file and provide space for recording text.

Save

Write a document from main memory to a disk file.

Recall

Read a document from disk into main memory.

Print

Send a document from memory to a printer for document generation.

Scroll

Turn pages electronically; move text up or down, left or right, to expose unseen portions of a document on a display screen.

Move and Copy

Relocate and reproduce defined blocks of text.

Insert and Delete

Add and remove text from a document.

Search and Replace

Instruct the system to find specified character strings, with options for substituting other strings.

Merge

Insert multiple variables into designated locations of documents for the production of form letters.

ADVANCED WORD PROCESSING FEATURES

Many word processors provide sophisticated tools for increasing the efficiency of document production and the quality of outputs.

Keyboard Macros

Sequences of keystrokes can be recorded and executed as a single entry.

Spell Check

Spelling errors are reported by comparing text with a dictionary file.

Thesaurus

On-line access is provided to word definitions and lists of synonyms.

Style Checkers

Common writing weaknesses are flagged and changes suggested.

Doing Word Processing

Common word processing functions are incorporated into an iterative process of document creation and production. These standard procedures can be used for any word processing operations.

CASE SCENARIO: PETERSEN COMMUNICATIONS

A microcomputer system configured to create and produce text can enhance the effectiveness and efficiency of an organization's written communication.

Case Example: Press Release

A press release is an announcement distributed for publication. These documents are subject to many reviews and, therefore, benefit from use of word processing capabilities.

First Draft

Draft and revision are basic to the process for creation of quality documents.

The MERGE Operation

Organizations with extensive mailing lists and document distribution requirements can profit from the automatic file merging capabilities of word processing software.

Document Output

To output documents under merge operations, the computer switches between files to find needed text content.

CASE SCENARIO: MOM'S VIDEO MARKET

Needs are identified for improving the efficiency of document production and of text quality.

Problem Identification

In the case scenario, the scope of evaluation of word processing packages is narrowed by a decision to purchase a menu-driven, rather than command-driven, package.

Merge Printing: An Initial Requirement

Generating backorder notices provides a starting point for defining specifications.

Boilerplate Text Modules

Standard messages can be used for generation of business notices such as notices about backorders or product receipts.

REQUIREMENTS SPECIFICATION

Capabilities specified for producing mass mailings.

Microcomputer work stations

have become mainstays for word processing services in organizations.

COURTESY OF AES DATA, INC.

ROLE OF WORD PROCESSORS

Federal Express fills 60 jet airplanes daily with some 60,000 small parcels for overnight delivery. Most of these parcels contain business documents. Even parcels containing products or other items usually include a cover letter. This means that about 10 million documents are transferred each week by this single carrier. Federal Express carries about 37 percent of total overnight parcel volume. Therefore, production of urgent documents by organizations throughout the country approaches 1 billion annually. This volume, bear in mind, represents a small fraction of total document production. The great majority of letters and other text items are carried in regular mails and in internal company mails.

Documents contain information in the form of written (or printed) words, or text. The above figures point out the magnitude of document production and exchange among organizations. Most businesses have requirements for creating text documents and records. Not surprisingly, then, many businesses meet these requirements with computerized tools known as **word processors.**

The term, word processor, refers to application packages that provide capabilities for applying the power of computers to the creation and handling of text. Under computerized techniques, documents are keyed into main memory, much like a typing operation. Keystrokes are *echoed,* or displayed simultaneously, on terminal screens. Operators can correct errors simply by rekeying incorrect entries.

Word processors also include electronic functions such as INSERT, DELETE, MOVE, and COPY that can streamline the editing of documents held in memory. Operations that previously required cut-and-paste operations with normal typing techniques now can be executed electronically, again a matter of keystrokes. From main memory, documents can be written to disk files. Text files can be sent back to memory for further revisions or routed to a printer for accurate transcription.

At each step in the document creation process, electronic capabilities effectively reduce the occurrences of human error. In addition, the advantages of word processing techniques often translate into improved document quality. Given the volume of documents sent throughout the modern world—with both private and governmental carriers—word processors play a key role in business organizations.

STANDARD WORD PROCESSING FUNCTIONS

Word processing packages provide common features that can be evaluated generically to provide a basis for understanding the pros and cons of individual packages. Virtually all word processing packages contain several standard functions, which include:

- CREATE
- SAVE
- RECALL
- PRINT
- SCROLL
- MOVE and COPY
- INSERT and DELETE
- SEARCH and REPLACE
- MERGE

Create

CREATE often is called a housekeeping function of word processors. This function sets up and manages text files in which documents are stored. CREATE commands instruct the system to set up a storage area on disk for a file. The system then prompts the user to enter a name for the file. The system also records the disk address of the first portion of the file. Succeeding portions are chained to this initial portion and are referenced by pointers within the file.

Save

The SAVE command instructs the system to write a file from computer memory to a designated disk file. This function creates a reusable, semi-permanent

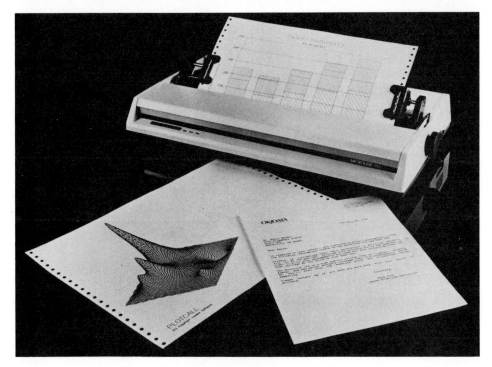

High speed,

high quality printing is a key to effective word processing. Text and graphic documents are generated automatically. Top photo shows a daisy-wheel printer; bottom is a matrix unit.

TOP PHOTO COURTESY OF AES DATA, INC. BOTTOM PHOTO COURTESY OF OKIDATA, AN OKI AMERICA COMPANY

copy of the file. Frequent use of SAVE operations protects against text losses due to power failures, user error, and other accidents.

Recall

The RECALL, or RETRIEVE, command is executed to read a file from disk storage into main memory. This function permits the revision and/or reuse of text files that have been saved on disks.

Print

The PRINT function is used to create hard copies of text files. The content of a text file is sent to some type of printer for output. Two categories of printing commands are provided with word processors: operating commands and formatting commands. Operating commands act as switches, instructing printing devices to start or stop printing. Formatting commands are system instructions for page length, margin positions, page numbering, header and footer inclusion, and so on.

Scroll

SCROLL commands are used to move through files in main memory. By executing SCROLL commands, users can move to left or right margins on a line, or move through a file line by line and page by page. See Figure 7-1. In addition, a GOTO command can be used to proceed to specific pages of a document.

Move and Copy

MOVE and COPY functions are editing commands used to rearrange portions, or **blocks,** of text. The MOVE command changes the position of a designated block of text. The COPY command duplicates a block of text in another position. Blocks are designated, or marked with delimiters, according to procedures specified by individual packages. See Figure 7-2. Delimiters often are used to delete blocks of text as well.

Insert and Delete

Document editing procedures often require the ability to add or remove text. INSERT and DELETE commands provide these capabilities. The INSERT command is used to add text to a document. A keystroke command shifts the system into the insert mode, creating extra space beginning at the location of the cursor. Additional text is keyed into the document. Finally, the system is instructed to reposition the entire document around the inserted text portion.

Figure 7-1.

```
DOCUMENT: figseven1              |PAGE:   1|LINE:   2|COL:   1|
|2.....».».....»...............................................«
«
«
ʰ2«
MEMO«
ʰ5«
«
«
November 24, 1987«
«
«
TO:    »Albert King«
       »Harold Land«
       »Robert Johnson«
«
FROM: »John Bonds«
RE:    »Reviews of remaining manuscript«
«
«
To meet deadlines, it is necessary to apply pressure on one and
all:«
«
From here on, manuscript segments will have to be turned around
 N:ü
```

SCROLL commands are used to move through document files. Notice the line numbers displayed at the top of each of these screens.

```
DOCUMENT: figseven1              |PAGE:   1|LINE:  40|COL:   1|
To meet deadlines, it is necessary to apply pressure on one and
all:«
«
From here on, manuscript segments will have to be turned around
in a maximum of 72 hours after receipt--by overnight mail.  The
enclosed packagè can wait until December 3 because of the
holiday.  But, there is little time to waste--the typeset pages
have to be out of here before the end of December.«
«
The situation is complicated by the decision to kill about a
quarter of the book, which was already in type.  However, if we
all pitch in, we might even allow time for a few carols and
some cheer around December 25.«
«
«
Regards.....«
```

```
DOCUMENT: figseven1                |PAGE:  1|LINE:  20|COL:  37| COPY WHAT?
To meet deadlines, it is necessary to apply pressure on one and
all:《
《
From here on, manuscript segments will have to be turned around in
a maximum of 72 hours after receipt--by overnight mail.  The
enclosed package can wait until December 3 because of the holiday.
But, there is little time to waste--the typeset pages have to be
out of here before the end of December.《
《
†The situation is complicated by the decision to kill about a
quarter of the book, which was already in type.  However, if we all
pitch in, we might even allow time for a few carols and some cheer
around December 25.《
†《
《
《
Regards........《
```

Figure 7-2.

COPY commands are used to designate a portion of text for duplication. Then, the cursor is positioned to indicate the location of the copied text.

The DELETE command removes unwanted text. Deletions may be executed one character at a time. Most systems provide a dedicated key for this purpose, usually labeled DEL. As an alternative, blocks of text can be removed. The DELETE mode is entered through keystroke commands, a block of text is delimited (see MOVE and COPY above), and the block removed with additional keystrokes. Remaining text is repositioned to fill space previously occupied by the deleted block. See Figures 7-3 and 7-4.

Search and Replace

SEARCH and REPLACE commands provide capabilities for locating and changing specific character strings. A character string is a specific sequence of letters, numbers, and/or special characters. For example, in composing a document, a writer might use an abbreviation such as N.Y. Before the final version is produced, the same writer could execute a search for every occurrence of the character string, N.Y., and replace each with another character string, New York.

SEARCH and REPLACE commands typically involve an initial command, and then a series of prompts and responses. The system is shifted into search mode with a keystroke command. Once the search mode is entered, the user is

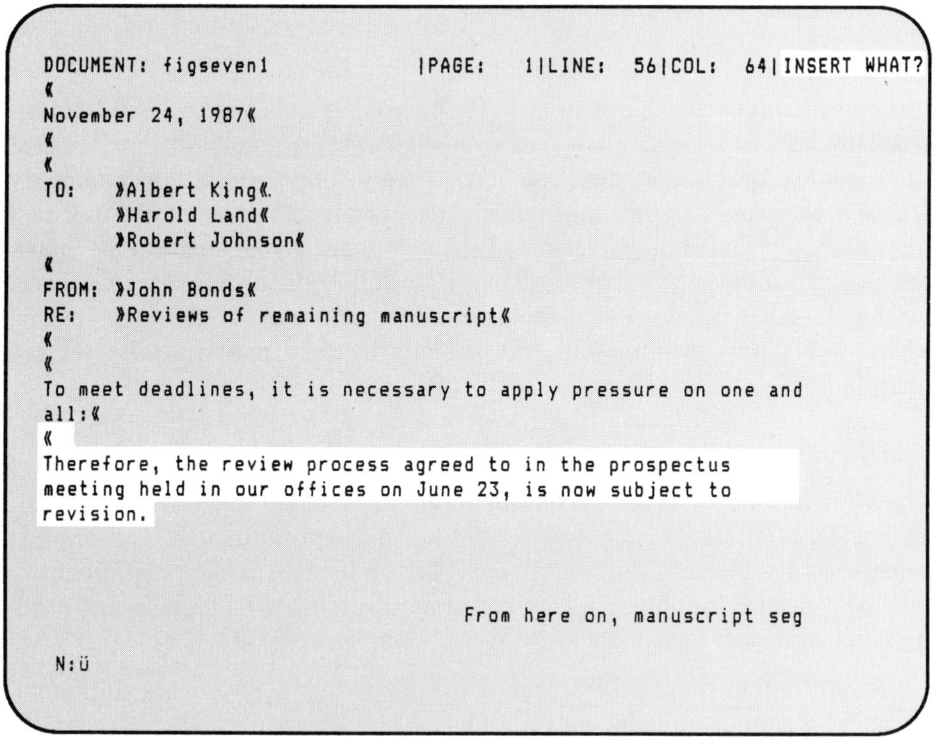

```
DOCUMENT: figseven1            |PAGE:    1|LINE:  56|COL:  64|INSERT WHAT?
«
November 24, 1987«
«
«
TO:    »Albert King«.
       »Harold Land«
       »Robert Johnson«
«
FROM: »John Bonds«
RE:    »Reviews of remaining manuscript«
«
«
To meet deadlines, it is necessary to apply pressure on one and
all:«
«
Therefore, the review process agreed to in the prospectus
meeting held in our offices on June 23, is now subject to
revision.



                                 From here on, manuscript seg

  N:ü
```

Figure 7-3.

Many word processing packages implement insert operations by dropping text to the bottom of the screen, creating a space into which additional text can be keyed.

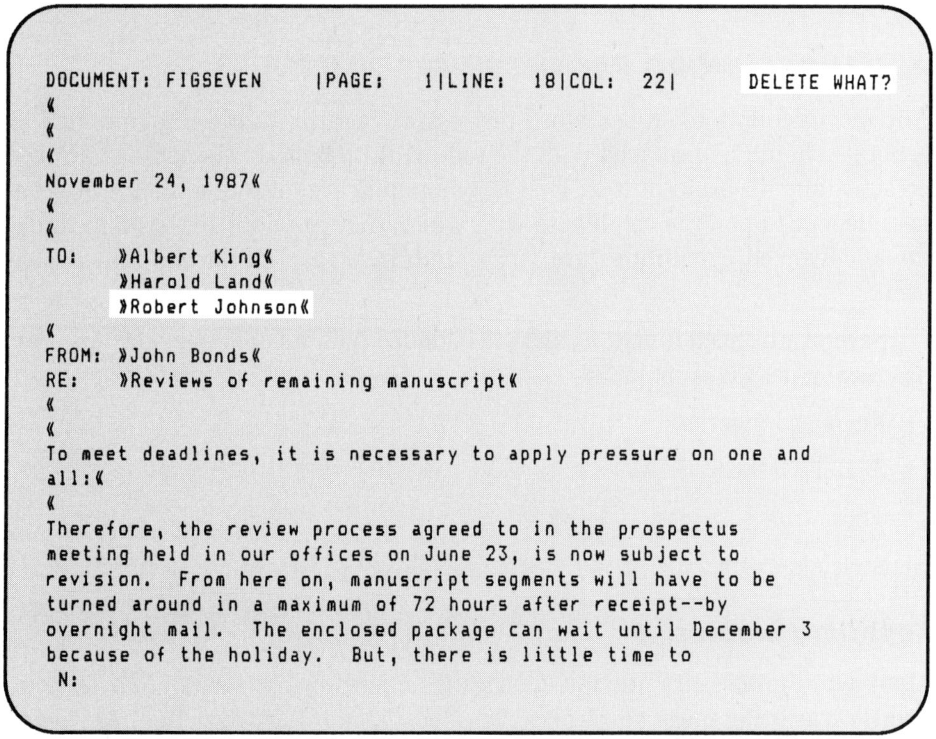

Figure 7-4.

Blocks of text to be deleted are highlighted, or delimited, as in move and copy operations.

```
DOCUMENT: FIGSEVEN       |PAGE:    1|LINE:  18|COL:  22|       DELETE WHAT?
«
«
«
November 24, 1987«
«
«
TO:    »Albert King«
       »Harold Land«
       »Robert Johnson«
«
FROM: »John Bonds«
RE:    »Reviews of remaining manuscript«
«
«
To meet deadlines, it is necessary to apply pressure on one and
all:«
«
Therefore, the review process agreed to in the prospectus
meeting held in our offices on June 23, is now subject to
revision.  From here on, manuscript segments will have to be
turned around in a maximum of 72 hours after receipt--by
overnight mail.  The enclosed package can wait until December 3
because of the holiday.  But, there is little time to
  N:
```

prompted to enter the character string to be used as a search target. With most word processors, several options are available for replacing the string. The user can execute repeated searches, changing strings as required. Or, a ***discretionary search and replace*** can be implemented. For this type of operation, the user supplies a target string and a replacement string. For each occurrence of the target, the user is prompted whether to replace it or not. A ***global search and replace,*** on the other hand, locates and replaces every occurrence of the target string. Figure 7-5 shows examples of the prompts used in a search and replace operation.

Merge

The MERGE function is used to produce large quantities of repetitive documents, such as ***form letters.*** Form letters are produced to send the same, or nearly the same, message to many different people. To produce form letters efficiently, a method is needed for entering the body, or message, of the letter once, and headings and addresses repeatedly. Most word processors provide these capabilities.

In addition to standard features, word processors may provide additional, advanced document creation and editing features. The applicability of these features depends, to a great extent, upon the requirements and skill levels of users. Advanced word processing features are discussed in the section that follows.

ADVANCED WORD PROCESSING FEATURES

Any discussion of advanced word processing features—indeed, computers in general—should be prefaced with the following statement: Computer power is no substitute for brain power. That is, computers are tools, and their effectiveness depends upon the astuteness with which they are applied. In many situations, advanced capabilities are more hindrance than assistance for capable users.

Several advanced functions that are included with relative frequency in word processing packages include:

- Keyboard macros
- SPELL CHECK
- Thesaurus
- Style checkers.

Keyboard Macros

Many word processors provide capabilities for recording series of keystrokes, and for executing these keystrokes repeatedly under user direction. ***Keyboard***

```
DOCUMENT: temp4              |PAGE:  20|LINE:  36|COL:  78|      SEARCH MODE
|2..».....».....».................................................................«
All or most of these application requirements exist in thousands of
businesses.  These busines needs, cumulatively, have created a market for
standard application software.  Developers of these application packages profit
from the ability to sell products to many businesses.  Individual businesses
profit because it costs less to buy a standard package thean to custom-develop
each application.«
    »This principle applies as well to standard processing routines within
application programs.  For example, many applications require that data be
sorted.  Suppose a university student is taking five classes.  Instructors for
all classes--including the five in which the above-mentioned student is
enrolled--turn in grade reports for all students.  Thus, the university
collects data items that identify students, and other data items that reflect
class enrollment and student grades.«
    »In a major university with thousands of classes and students, this
collection of records can be massive.  Transcript reports--which consist of
identification data combined with grade records for individual students--must
be made available upon request.  Given a computer with sufficient capacity and
SEARCH FOR:  capabilties



    N:ü
```

```
DOCUMENT: temp4              |PAGE:  20|LINE:  36|COL:  79|     REPLACE MODE
|2..».....».....».................................................................«
All or most of these application requirements exist in thousands of
businesses.  These busines needs, cumulatively, have created a market for
standard application software.  Developers of these application packages profit
from the ability to sell products to many businesses.  Individual businesses
profit because it costs less to buy a standard package thean to custom-develop
each application.«
    »This principle applies as well to standard processing routines within
application programs.  For example, many applications require that data be
sorted.  Suppose a university student is taking five classes.  Instructors for
all classes--including the five in which the above-mentioned student is
enrolled--turn in grade reports for all students.  Thus, the university
collects data items that identify students, and other data items that reflect
class enrollment and student grades.«
    »In a major university with thousands of classes and students, this
collection of records can be massive.  Transcript reports--which consist of
identification data combined with grade records for individual students--must
be made available upon request.  Given a computer with sufficient capacity and
REPLACE WITH: capabilities



    N:ü
```

Figure 7-5.

In a search and replace operation, a user enters a character string to be used as a search target (top). Then, the user enters a string that is to be used to replace the target string (bottom).

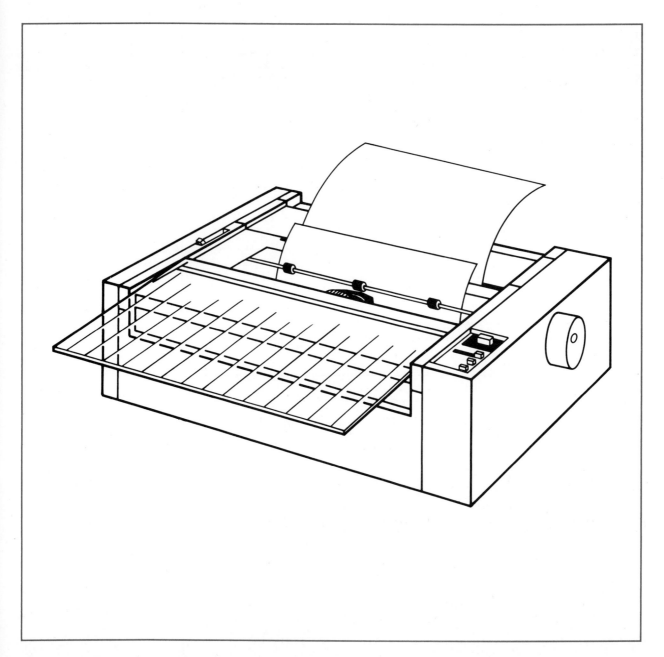

Form letter production

*can be expedited through use of
printers that handle and print on
regular stationery.*

macros can be used to perform a standard, repetitious task by recording the
sequence of keystrokes that are needed to execute the task. In effect, a keyboard
macro is a program of keystrokes. Setting up keyboard macros involves entering a command, a name for the procedure, entering keystrokes for performing
the task, then exiting macro mode with another command.

```
                            MEMO
   DATE:
   TO:
   FROM:  YOUR NAME
```

Figure 7-6.

Keyboard macros can be used to set up memo headings, or to perform any series of frequently used keystrokes.

For example, suppose you are a business executive who frequently produces memos in the course of your work. The same format is used in all memos. A keyboard macro could be set up to enter the heading MEMO, labels for DATE: and TO: entries, and a final heading entry, FROM: YOUR NAME. For every memo you produce, then, the entire heading (shown in Figure 7-6) can be entered by executing the macro procedure.

Setting up the keyboard macro is a simple procedure. A document file is created and named. Then, the macro file must be set up. For example, under MultiMate, a popular word processor for the IBM PC, a macro file, called a key procedure file, is set up by pressing the Control and F5 keys simultaneously. Then, a prompt is displayed requesting a user entry to name the key procedure file. See Figure 7-7.

Notice the key procedure file in this example has been named MEMO. At this point, pressing the F10 key instructs the system to begin building the keyboard macro. A highlighted character, B, is displayed at the bottom right of the screen. A record of all keystrokes is accumulated in main memory. Remember, a keyboard macro is a sequence of keystrokes. The keystrokes you enter to create the memo heading are held, then written to disk when you again use the key procedure command, Control and F5.

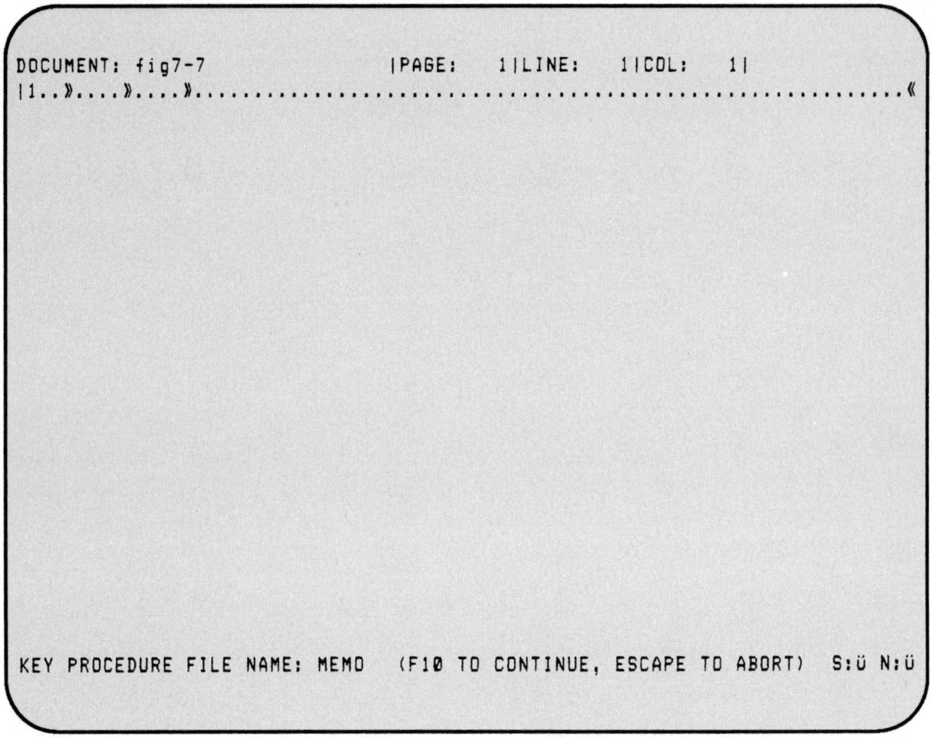

```
DOCUMENT: fig7-7                    |PAGE:   1|LINE:   1|COL:   1|
|1..»....»....».................................................«
```

KEY PROCEDURE FILE NAME: MEMO   (F10 TO CONTINUE, ESCAPE TO ABORT) S:ü N:ü

Figure 7-7.

Keyboard macros are built and executed through use of names designated by users.

The key procedure file then is written to disk. The macro file can be called up at any time with another command, Control and F8, and the file name. Keystrokes recorded in macro files are executed in sequence, as if they were being entered by the user.

Spell Check

Many word processing packages include dictionary files and processing routines that check automatically for spelling errors. The SPELL CHECK command instructs the system to compare each word in the document with dictionary file entries. When differences are found, disputed words are *flagged,* or highlighted, in some way. The user then decides whether disputed words should be corrected. It should be pointed out, however, that most spell checkers cannot make distinctions between words like "reed" and "read," and since both are valid words, errors of this type are not detected.

Spell checkers may also allow users to make entries into the dictionary file. Users can enter proper names, technical words, and unusual terms used frequently. This feature prevents situations in which names and special terms are marked repeatedly as misspelled. See Figure 7-8.

```
DOCUMENT: SPELLCHEK          |PAGE:  1|LINE: 20|COL: 39|
|2..》.....》....》................................................《
    》This scenario illustrates a primary consideration for designers of large
systems and microcomputer work stations.  That is, as users become more skilled
and familiar with computers, they demand more and better capabilities.  In
effect, the overall evolution has been driven by this cycle:  demands arise,
capabilities are developed, demands are met, capabilities are applied,
additional demands arise, increased capabilities are developed, and so on.《
    》Similarly, the evolution of microcomputers has been driven by this cycle.
In fact, the ability to configure work stations according to application
requirements has accelerated this evolution--to a point where microcomputer
systems are viewed as vital tools for manging businesses.《
    》In their role as management tools, most microcomputer systems have
provisions for supporting flexible file organization schemes.  For example, the
operating system software in most systems (described in the chapter that
follows) automatically creates directories and identifies home addresses for
                     Please enter desired function
         0)    Add this word to the Custom Dictionary
         1)    Ignore this place mark and find the next mark
         2)    Clear this place mark and find the next mark
         3)    List possible correct spellings
         4)    Type replacement spelling
         5)    Delete a word from the Custom Dictionary
         Esc)  End Spell Edit and resume Document Edit
  N:ü
```

Figure 7-8.

In a spell check operation, challenged words are flagged and the user is given a list of editing options.

Thesaurus

A ***thesaurus*** is a collection, or book, of words and their synonyms. A synonym is one of two or more words that have the same, or nearly the same, meaning. Some word processors provide thesaurus files that can be accessed during document creation. That is, any word within a document can be looked up in the thesaurus file. If the thesaurus contains an entry for that word, the meaning and a list of synonyms is displayed. The user then has a choice of replacing the word or returning to the document. See Figure 7-9.

Style Checkers

Style checking programs often are advertised as being capable of improving a user's writing style. These packages search for common writing weaknesses and make suggestions for changes. For example, many books about writing stress the importance of using active verbs. Passive verbs, it is believed, are ineffective for writing with impact. A sentence written in the passive voice reads: "The proposal is under consideration by the committee." Under a style checking routine, a prompt is displayed suggesting that the sentence be changed to read: "The committee is considering the proposal." In this example, the second sentence is

```
DOCUMENT: SPELLCHEK            |PAGE:  1|LINE: 14|COL:  29|
|2..》....》....》........................................................《
   》This scenario illustrates a primary consideration for designers of large
systems and microcomputer work stations.  That is, as users become more skilled
and familiar with computers, they demand more and better capabilities.  In
effect, the overall evolution has been driven by this cycle: demands arise,
capabilities are developed, demands are met, capabilities are applied,
additional demands arise, increased capabilities are developed, and so on.《
   》Similarly, the evolution of microcomputers has been driven by this cycle.
In fact, the ability to configure work stations according to application
requirements has accelerated this evolution--to a point where microcomputer
systems are viewed as vital tools for manging businesses.《
                              THESAURUS
                              evolution


    noun:  progressive advance from a lower or simpler to a higher or more
    complex form


    1) development         4) growth              7) unfolding
    2) evolvement          5) progress
    3) flowering           6) progression



Enter Number for Replacement,  ESC - Exit Thesaurus,  Alt T - Look Up New Word.
   N:ü
```

Figure 7-9.

A thesaurus entry includes a definition of and several synonyms for a designated word. Notice the editing options displayed at the bottom of the screen.

arguably more concise. However, the English language adheres to no hard and fast rules for usage. Style checkers should be used with this fact in mind.

Doing Word Processing

Just as common word processing functions can be identified among many word processing packages, common steps are involved in applying word processors to create documents. As a general rule, the process of creating documents with microcomputers involves five steps:

- Create a file.
- Key the document.
- Save the document.
- Edit the document.
- Print the document.

Create a File.   Before a document is produced as a hard copy, a file for that document must be created. Creating a file involves setting aside a storage location (under system control), and assigning a name for the file. A typical entry screen for creating a file with a word processor is provided in the previous chapter, in Figure 6-7.

Key the Document.   Once a file is created, the actual work of entering text, or word content, can begin. As documents are keyed, keystrokes are echoed on the display screen. The user is able to view the results of keying operations and to make corrections and/or additions as needed. Most word processors also provide a ***word wrap*** feature. As documents are keyed, words that do not fit at the end of a line are shifted automatically down and left, to the beginning of the next line. However, the user can enter ***hard returns*** as needed at the end of paragraphs and to add blank lines to the document. See Figure 7-10.

Save the Document.   After text has been entered, a copy of the document is written to external storage. In this form, it is available for further editing or additions, or for printing. Documents are written to file spaces designated during the first step, Create a File.

Edit the Document.   In business organizations, documents typically are revised four to seven times before final versions are produced. Word processors effectively eliminate the necessity to re-key a complete document at each revision. Only changes need be made. Documents can be read into main memory, and edited using functions described in the above section. Printing is a separate operation.

Print the Document.   The printing of documents is the final step in document creation under word processing techniques. Once an acceptable, final version is produced, it can be sent to a printing device. Under system control, document printing is virtually error free. Further, word processors provide special capabilities for formatting printed documents. Users can choose to ***justify*** right margins. That is, words are spaced to create straight margins on both sides of the page, as in this book. Other commands can create ***boldface*** type. Boldface—a type treatment in which character imprints are darker than normal—is created simply by instructing the printer to strike characters twice. In addition, printing commands usually are provided by which users can produce type of different sizes, or even of different ***fonts,*** or type styles.

Word processors can provide advantages for virtually any type of document creation or text handling operation. To repeat, computerized techniques can improve document quality, streamline revision/rewrite processes, and maximize the efficiency of volume document production procedures. To illustrate, the remainder of this chapter presents an evaluation of word processing packages in the context of case examples.

```
DOCUMENT: chap1                    |PAGE:   1|LINE:   5|COL:  80|
|1..>....>....>.........................................................(
(
;1/SMALL COMPUTERS, BIG IMPACT/1/(
The early space missions of the late 1950s and early 1960s were supported by
the largest computer systems available at the time.  Behemoth computers
occupied multiple rooms, occasionally entire buildings.  These systems, regarde
```

```
DOCUMENT: chap1                    |PAGE:   1|LINE:   6|COL:   9|
|1..>....>....>.........................................................(
(
;1/SMALL COMPUTERS, BIG IMPACT/1/(
The early space missions of the late 1950s and early 1960s were supported by
the largest computer systems available at the time.  Behemoth computers
occupied multiple rooms, occasionally entire buildings.  These systems,
regarded
```

Figure 7-10.

Word wrap eliminates the need to enter a hard return (a press of the return key) at the end of each line of text. At top, text entry approaches the end of a line. At bottom, the word is transferred to the next line.

CASE SCENARIO: PETERSEN COMMUNICATIONS

Petersen Communications is a public relations firm that specializes in dealing with print media, such as newspaper releases, trade releases, promotional mailings, and so on. Petersen's services require tailoring a client organization's message to a specific audience or medium. The owner, Donald P. Petersen, is a professional writer.

Petersen's philosophy is simple: Effective communication supported by efficient production. As a professional, Petersen knows that communication involves sender and receiver. For this reason, Petersen establishes a two-part organizational operating guideline. First, the message must be comprehensible to the intended audience. Second, the message must be presented to the audience in a timely manner.

Petersen makes extensive use of computerized tools to implement this policy. Petersen Communications has developed a microcomputer-based system that is configured for creating and producing documents. The components of this system include:

- A microcomputer
- A word processing package

- A dot-matrix printer
- A laser printer
- Storage media.

As stated previously, system components can be classified according to the functions they perform. Information processing functions include input, processing, output, and storage. In this example, input, processing, and storage components are incorporated within the microcomputer terminal. Input takes place through a keyboard, processing is executed within the central processing unit, and storage is on disk drives built into the computer.

Output from Petersen's system is through one of two printers. A dot-matrix printer is used to produce drafts of documents during editing stages. The laser printer outputs near typeset quality documents that are used as finished product. Laser printers and their applications are discussed in a later chapter dealing with desktop publishing.

To illustrate the capabilities of this system, consider the following examples. Petersen's clients regularly hire him to distribute messages, or releases, about product introductions, personnel changes, and promotional or related events. The releases are mailed to different parties depending upon their nature and target audience. That is, a release describing the technical specifications of a hardware device would be mailed to trade publications. A release describing a large donation to charity would be mailed to general-interest publications, such as newspapers. Business organizations use trade and newspaper releases to publicize their products (see example below).

Generating and maintaining mailing lists are integral to Petersen's operation. To illustrate, consider the example that follows.

Case Example: Press Release

A computer manufacturer, ACME Corporation, has installed a microcomputer-driven manufacturing system in a local sailmaking business, Competent Sailmakers, Inc. To generate publicity for both organizations, ACME has hired Petersen to send press releases to newspapers within a 500-mile radius.

As stated previously, the system at Petersen Communications provides all capabilities required for performing this task efficiently. To begin, Petersen composes a rough draft of the release on a microcomputer screen. After an initial edit, Petersen prints the release and gives it to his administrative assistant for another editing pass. The first page of the release Petersen composes is presented in Figure 7-11.

First Draft

This initial version now undergoes several revision/review cycles. The administrative assistant indicates and corrects errors in spelling and grammar. Then, the release is reviewed again by Petersen. Petersen looks for uncaught errors, as well as discrepancies in meaning and content. Then, the release is sent to a representative of ACME Corporation for suggestions for further changes and final approval. Figures 7-12 and 7-13 illustrate the changes and revisions required to bring the release to mailable quality.

Consider also the changes prescribed for initial versions. These changes are executed efficiently and conveniently with standard word processing functions, such as insert, delete, copy, move, and so on. Once the final version is produced, MERGE capabilities are implemented to complete the operation.

The MERGE Operation

Petersen maintains several mailing lists as floppy disk files. Mailing lists are tailored to specific audiences, such as trade journals and newspapers, or may include customer lists from client organizations. Petersen has selected a word processing package that handles files in the ASCII format. This feature makes it possible to accept client customer lists, also in ASCII, in the form of storage files. That is, ASCII files are compatible with Petersen's system; no conversion or manual entry operations are required. The mailing list for the ACME case example is a collection of listings for newspapers in the area. Each record contains data elements such as newspaper name, address, and the editor responsible for technical or business articles.

MERGE operations require two types of files: the primary file and the secondary file. The primary file contains the portion of a document that remains the same. The secondary file contains **variables,** or data elements inserted into primary documents to personalize them. For this example, then, the primary file contains the press release described above. The secondary file contains the newspaper listings. A screen display of the secondary file is presented in Figure 7-14.

Notice that the press release is addressed to no specific person. The release is written as a news story. Entries from the secondary file, however, are needed to address envelopes. There are many ways to use secondary files to streamline the addressing process. Petersen accomplishes this task by using sheets of blank mailing labels that can be fed through a printer. Addresses are printed on the labels, which then can be affixed manually to envelopes.

```
CONTACT:
Bill Maloney
Competent Sailmakers, Inc.
(598) 555-2984

Harriet LeDuke
ACME Corporation
(333) 555-4392


        "A NEW TACK FOR SAILMAKERS"


    MARBLEHEAD, Mass. ... Designers are splicing old skills with new

technology at Competent Sailmakers, Inc., (CSI).

    The specifications of more than 100 sail, boat, and rig designs are

stored on computer diskettes.  Designers use an ACME XL personal computer

to manipulate traditional sail dimensions--clew height, luff

perpendiculars, headboard, leach, and luff.

    Approximately 100 designers, stitchers, and cutters work in a

cavernous "loft" on the outskirts of Marblehead, Mass.  Scissors, splines,

and sewing machines coexist with a laser sail cutting machine and ACME

personal computers.

    "Personal computers are replacing loft batons and pencils," said Frank

Elder, a CSI sail designer.

    "Using a special mouse-driven, three-dimensional graphics program on

microcomputers, we can make instant modifications to sail designs.  This

improves our efficiency."

                        - MORE -
```

Figure 7-11.

The first draft of the press release is printed to facilitate the editing process.

```
DOCUMENT: press          |PAGE:   1|LINE:  20|COL:  44|       MOVE WHAT?
|1..».....».....».............................................«
«
«
«
    »    »    »CONTACT:«
    »    »    »Bill Maloney«
    »    »    »Competent Sailmakers, Inc.«
    »    »    »(598) 555-2984«
«
    »    »    »Harriet LeDuke«
    »    »    »ACME Corporation«
    »    »    »(333) 555-4392«
«
    »    »"A NEW TACK FOR SAILMAKERS"«
«
    »MARBLEHEAD, Mass. ... Designers are splicing old skills with new
technology at Competent Sailmakers, Inc. (CSI).«
    »The specifications of more than 100 sail, boat, and rig designs are
stored on computer diskettes.  Designers use an ACME XL personal computer
to manipulate traditional sail dimensions--clew height, luff
perpendiculars, headboard, leach, and luff.«
    »Approximately 100 designers, stitchers, and cutters work in a
cavernous "loft" on the outskirts of Marblehead, Mass.  Scissors, splines,
    N:ü
```

```
DOCUMENT: press          |PAGE:   1|LINE:  30|COL:  33|       TO WHERE?
to manipulate traditional sail dimensions--clew height, luff
perpendiculars, headboard, leach, and luff.«
    »Approximately 100 designers, stitchers, and cutters work in a
cavernous "loft" on the outskirts of Marblehead, Mass.  Scissors, splines,
and sewing machines coexist with a laser sail cutting machine and ACME
personal computers.«
    »"Personal computrers are replacing loft batons and pencils," said
Frank Elder, a CSI sail designer.«
    »"Using a special mouse-driven, three-dimensional graphics program on
the mcirocomputers, we can make instant modifications to sail designs.
This improves our efficiency."«
                         é- MORE -«




    N:ü
```

```
DOCUMENT: MERGE              |PAGE:   1|LINE:   1|COL:   1|
⊦title⊦《
Mr. ⊦《
⊦first name⊦《
Henry⊦《
⊦last name⊦《
Andersen⊦《
⊦address⊦《
24395 Bellingham《
Tacoma, WA  92332⊦《
⊦credit limit⊦《
$2,500.00⊦《
《
⊦title⊦《
Miss⊦《
⊦first name⊦《
Jane⊦《
⊦last name⊦《
Hathaway⊦《
⊦address⊦《
352 Canon Drive《
Beverly Hills, CA. 91439⊦《
⊦credit limit⊦《
$5,000.00⊦《
 N:ü
```

Figure 7-14.

Variable entries to be inserted into a form letter are collected in a secondary file, as shown.

To include variable data entries within a primary document, similar procedures are required. Petersen often writes promotional letters for his clients and coordinates mass mailings of these letters. For example, consider the promotional letter in Figure 7-15. This letter describes a pre-approved line of credit from a local bank. The bank has a list of potential customers with excellent credit ratings to whom the offer is made.

Notice that spaces for customer address have been included in this letter. In addition, another variable is set up for credit limits offered to customers. To complete the merge, a secondary file must be created.

The secondary file is created by clerks working for the client bank. These clerks key customer names, addresses, and credit amounts into files, as shown in Figure 7-16.

Document Output

During the print operation, the program stops at each variable code (codes will vary with application program) in the primary file. At each variable, the program derives the appropriate entry from the secondary file, inserts it into the document, then continues printing. After documents are completed, variables are derived from the next succeeding record of the secondary file. This process continues until a document has been printed for each listing in the secondary file.

214

```
DOCUMENT: MERGE                    |PAGE:   1|LINE:   1|COL:   1|
|1..》.·..》....》................................................《
《
《
《
《
August 11, 1987《
《
《
├title┤ ├first name┤ ├last name┤《
├address┤《
├city/state┤《
《
Dear ├title┤ ├last name┤:《
《
As a special service to you, one of our most favored customers, we
have established a pre-approved line of credit in the amount of
├credit┤.  To take advantage of this offer, read the enclosed
brochure, fill out the application, and bring it into your nearest
City Bank office.  As always, it is our privilege to serve you.《
《
Sincerely,《
```

Figure 7-15.

Form letters are used by many organizations for many purposes. In this example, a pre-approved letter establishing consumer credit is targeted for specific customers.

Figure 7-16.

The secondary file in this scenario contains names and addresses of customers who qualify for pre-approved lines of credit.

```
DOCUMENT: VARIABLS                 |PAGE:   1|LINE:   1|COL:   1|
|1......》..........》..........》................》....................》.....《
《
《
《
《
《
        》FIRST    》LAST《
TITLE   NAME      NAME       ADDRESS              CITY/STATE              CREDIT《
========================================================================《
Mr.    》Henry    》Andersen  》190 Palatine Dr.   》San Marino, CA 91301  》$2,000《
Mrs.   》Mei-Ling 》Chung     》8951 Vagabond St.  》Montebello, CA 91320  》$1,500《
Ms.    》Margaret 》Hillman   》1496 Las Lunas     》Pasadena, CA 90731    》$2,000《
Mr.    》Tyrone   》Jackson   》478 Washington     》Pasadena, CA 90732    》$1,500《
Mr.    》Roberto  》Rodriquez 》2435 Borland Rd.   》Los Angeles, CA 90045 》$1,500《
Mr.    》Steve    》Sansone   》731 Rollin St.     》San Gabriel, CA 91654 》$2,000《
Ms.    》Evelyn   》Yamamoto  》826 Hermosa Dr.    》Alhambra, CA 91701    》$1,500《
Mr.    》William  》Malhotra  》1023 Berkeley St.  》Los Angeles, CA 90032 》$1,500《
```

For the Petersen example, the secondary file is used to create mailing labels for envelopes.

CASE SCENARIO: MOM'S VIDEO MARKET

Another client of Petersen Communications is a video cassette rental and sales organization known as Mom's Video Market. The owner of Mom's, Christine Beeman, currently is using a microcomputer system for transaction processing and for developing plans and budgets. (These applications are discussed in later chapters.) Beeman studies Petersen's system as a step toward selecting and implementing a word processing package.

Beeman knows that the quality of the documents she produces has begun to suffer, probably due to rapid and significant growth. For example, Mom's sends notices to members with reservations for cassettes, notifying them that the cassette is expected to be available shortly. These notices, under current procedures, are typed by one of several employees at the end of each business day.

Beeman observes that, probably due to time and volume demands, notices have been sent with spelling and transcription errors. Beeman feels that this conveys a negative image to her customers. Further, Beeman wants to implement promotional mailings to customers, and would like to increase her capabilities to personalize these letters. In short, Beeman wishes to apply microcomputer capabilities to produce documents.

Problem Identification

Beeman's wish stems from three problem areas that she has identified, which include:

- Document creation procedures are error-prone.
- Some documents are subject to frequent change and revision.
- Existing capabilities and procedures for creating volume mailings are inadequate.

Beeman knows that word processors provide capabilities for solving these problems, and already has made a decision to purchase a package. She also knows that many packages exist that can meet her requirements. However, Beeman narrows the scope of her evaluation by making an initial decision concerning the type of word processor she will purchase.

Word processors can be classified in two general categories: command-driven and menu-driven. Both types of packages offer standard functions (discussed above) but differ in manner of executing functions. Command-driven packages provide a series of keystroke commands for implementing functions such as COPY, MOVE, INSERT, DELETE, and others. Users of these packages are required to learn a series of separate commands for executing each function. Menu-driven packages provide a series of menus and prompts that list processing options and request entries as needed.

Regardless of package chosen, Beeman knows that it will be used by several employees on a regular basis. Therefore, she wants a package that will require as little training as possible. For this reason, Beeman decides to concentrate her evaluations on menu-driven packages.

Merge Printing: An Initial Requirement

In many respects, the heart of Beeman's business is the existing transaction processing system. The development of the transaction processing system is discussed in a later chapter. For present purposes, keep in mind that the transaction processing system involves a database, or a collection of files organized for multiple applications.

One of the outputs of transaction processing is a backorder report. The backorder report, in effect, is a waiting list of customers and the titles of video cassettes for which all copies are out on rental. If a customer wants to rent a tape for which no copies are available, a record of the request is entered into the backorder file. The backorder file includes customer numbers and product numbers, organized according to sequences of requests. As tapes are returned, a report is produced that lists the tape and the next customer on the list. Customers are notified by mail that the tape they have requested is available.

Boilerplate Text Modules

The backorder message is simple and subject to few or no changes. Thus, one method for producing backorder notices is to create a **boilerplate** file. In this sense, the boilerplate is the part of a document that never changes. That is, the body and closing portions of the letter can be saved. For each notice, the boilerplate is retrieved and the date, customer name and address, and cassette title are added under control of the INSERT function. Figure 7-17 presents a boilerplate for the backorder notices.

The boilerplate method may meet Beeman's requirements sufficiently for present purposes. However, Beeman knows that as volume increases, additional capabilities may be needed. One way to increase volume production efficiency is to derive the variable data elements for backorder notices directly from database files. Then, the system could be instructed to print as many notices as needed, and to insert variables from the backorder report. In effect, the notices could be created with only supervisory input from operators.

```
DOCUMENT: BOILERPL              |PAGE:   1|LINE:   1|COL:   1|
|1..».....».....».......................................................«
«
«
«
«
«
(ENTER DATE)«
«
«
Dear (CUSTOMER NAME):«
«
You are on our waiting list for the video cassette, (ENTER TITLE).
We expect to have that cassette available for rental on (ENTER
DATE).  As per our membership agreement, we will hold that tape for
you for two days.  Thank you for doing business with Mom's.«
«
Sincerely,«
«
«
«
Christine Beeman«
```

Figure 7-17.

The boilerplate method involves the creation of a file that contains all but variable entries. Names, titles, headings, and other entries are inserted as needed.

The capability to derive data elements from database files, then, is a highly desirable option. To implement this capability, the format of the database and the format of word processing files must match. At this point, because database files already have been created, package evaluations should be targeted toward a package that saves files in the same format as the database, or that is capable of performing necessary conversions.

The capability to insert variables into a standard document format is known as mail-merge. Beeman plans to use merge techniques to produce promotional mailings as well as backorder notices. Promotional mailings will consist of mass-produced, "personalized" letters mailed to all customers. Because she has not produced large volume mailings as yet, Beeman arranges to study operations at Petersen Communications.

REQUIREMENTS SPECIFICATION

In a general sense, defining procedures and requirements for a microcomputer application is a type of *system specification.* This term usually is applied to a collection of documents produced in conjunction with systems development projects. For systems projects, specifications include detailed descriptions of the problem to be solved, an overall description of processing, and the data elements and files that will make up the system.

Figure 7-18.

A well-defined statement of a problem and requirements for solution facilitates package selection.

REQUIREMENTS SPECIFICATION

Problem Definition: Select a word processing package that can run on existing microcomputer equipment and that can be purchased and installed for less than $500.

Package should provide standard editing functions: CREATE, ENTER, SAVE, INSERT, DELETE, MOVE, COPY, and PRINT.

Package should include MERGE capability for producing mass mailings of promotional material. In addition, it is highly desirable that the package accept records from customer files in transaction processing database as inputs.

Package should be simple enough to use so that any qualified employee can master production of backorder notices in two working days or less.

It should be possible to handle production of backorder notices in two working hours or less.

While there are significant differences between specifying an application package and an information system (discussed in a later chapter) the idea remains the same. Tools are meant to meet needs; therefore, a comprehensive specification of requirements aids selection of software packages.

Beeman focuses her initial specification on the backorder notice. She knows now that the capabilities for producing the backorder notice can be applied to create her promotional mailings. For present purposes, however, Beeman concentrates her efforts on the backorder notice.

Both the primary and secondary files for the backorder notice application exist currently as paper documents and as files within the transaction processing database. Initial considerations, then, will center on the capacities of application packages for handling customer files. In addition, Beeman wants to be able to use the customer and backorder files directly as secondary MERGE files. The specification of these two requirements, in effect, probably will be the strongest decision factor. That is, the combination of these two requirements—and the earlier specification of a menu-driven package—probably will limit her choices to a manageable number of packages. This is exactly why requirements are specified. Once the number of packages is narrowed, Beeman can evaluate each one in terms of editing functions provided, and ease of use. The final specification that Beeman produces is shown in Figure 7-18.

Beeman studies the system at Petersen Communication to enhance her knowledge of word processing and mail-merge techniques. This is an accepted method for analyzing requirements for computer-based tools. Both scenarios—Petersen Communications and Mom's Video Market—are described further in later chapters to enhance your understanding of database systems, electronic spreadsheets, and other applications. The two chapters that follow present a comprehensive discussion of database concepts and applications.

KEY TERMS

word processors
echo
CREATE
SAVE
RECALL
PRINT
SCROLL
MOVE
COPY
INSERT
DELETE
SEARCH
REPLACE
MERGE
block
discretionary search and replace

global search and replace
form letter
keyboard macro
SPELL CHECK
flag
thesaurus
style checker
word wrap
hard return
justify
boldface
font
variable
boilerplate
system specification

DEFINITIONS

Instructions: On a separate sheet, define each term according to its use in this chapter.

1. echo

2. keyboard macro

3. global search and replace

4. flag

5. hard return

6. font

7. boldface

8. boilerplate text

T R U E / F A L S E

Instructions: For each statement, write T for true or F for false on a separate sheet.

1. Search and replace commands provide capabilities for locating two or more different character strings, and switching them.

2. The mail/merge function is used to produce large quantities of repetitive documents, such as form letters.

3. When it comes to performing highly complex mathematical functions, computers are slower than humans.

4. Many word processing systems can check both spelling and punctuation.

5. It is possible to add words to many word processor dictionaries.

6. A thesaurus is a collection, or book, of words and their synonyms, antonyms, and homonyms.

7. Under the word wrap feature, words that do not fit at the end of the line are shifted automatically down and left, to the beginning of the next line.

8. A boilerplate file is used to simplify the coding of cooking instructions in recipes.

9. In a general sense, defining procedures and requirements for a microcomputer application is a type of system specification.

10. Under a command driven word processing system, instructions are entered through use of menus.

11. Creating a file involves setting aside a storage location (under system control), and assigning a name to the file.

12. The SAVE command instructs the system to write a file from computer memory to a designated disk file.

13. The process of printing a hard copy of a document automatically erases the document from the computer's external storage system.

14. The DELETE command takes unwanted text and moves it into a storage file, where it is kept until it is needed for another document.

15. In business organizations, documents typically are revised four to seven times before final versions are produced.

S H O R T   A N S W E R   Q U E S T I O N S

Instructions: On a separate sheet of paper, answer each question in one or
two brief sentences.

1. Give two examples of how the "search and replace" function could be
   used to improve speed and accuracy in word processing.

2. Name and explain the two categories of printing commands provided with
   word processors.

3. What is a keyboard macro and how is it used?

4. What is the major problem inherent in any spelling checker?

5. Why is it important to save a document on a regular basis?

6. What advantages does word processing provide for virtually any type of
   text handling or document creation?

R E S E A R C H   P R O J E C T

Create a form letter. Write a form letter that could be sent to five different
friends or family members of different ages and with different interests. First
write a general letter. Then write a number of inserts that could go in two or
three different versions of the letters. Show the changes that would have to be
made in each letter to "personalize" it. Explain the purpose of each insert
and its intended impact on the recipient.

Microcomputer Software: Databases

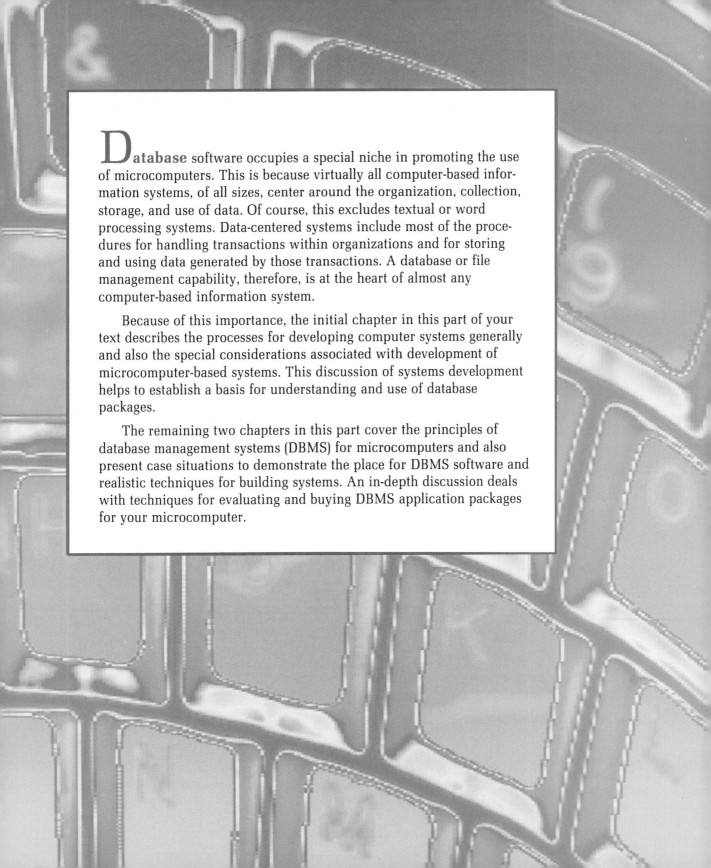

Database software occupies a special niche in promoting the use of microcomputers. This is because virtually all computer-based information systems, of all sizes, center around the organization, collection, storage, and use of data. Of course, this excludes textual or word processing systems. Data-centered systems include most of the procedures for handling transactions within organizations and for storing and using data generated by those transactions. A database or file management capability, therefore, is at the heart of almost any computer-based information system.

Because of this importance, the initial chapter in this part of your text describes the processes for developing computer systems generally and also the special considerations associated with development of microcomputer-based systems. This discussion of systems development helps to establish a basis for understanding and use of database packages.

The remaining two chapters in this part cover the principles of database management systems (DBMS) for microcomputers and also present case situations to demonstrate the place for DBMS software and realistic techniques for building systems. An in-depth discussion deals with techniques for evaluating and buying DBMS application packages for your microcomputer.

8 Microcomputer Systems Development

SCOPE

Microcomputers have impacted virtually every business area and function. Organizations that wish to use microcomputers should develop standard procedures for selecting and implementing application packages.

SYSTEMS DEVELOPMENT

Developing and implementing a mainframe system can require millions of dollars and years of effort. As a result, some type of formal project structure usually is necessary.

THE SYSTEMS DEVELOPMENT LIFE CYCLE

A structured, phased systems development plan usually is called a systems development life cycle (SDLC). An example is reviewed that breaks the systems development process into five phases: investigation, analysis and general design, detailed design and implementation, installation, and review.

Investigation

The investigation identifies and develops solutions for the problems to be solved.

Analysis and General Design

A system solution is designed from the user's perspective.

Detailed Design and Implementation

Programs are designed, written, tested, debugged, and documented; operational procedures are developed and documented.

Installation

The system is put into operation.

Review

The results of the development project are evaluated to see if the new system meets specified design, functional, and operational requirements.

THE ENTREPRENEURIAL APPROACH

Since the cost of a microcomputer is within the range of authorized expenses for many middle managers, people at this level can build individual microcomputer systems to meet their requirements.

Prototyping

Under the entrepreneurial approach, trial-and-fit techniques can be applied to systems development.

SYSTEMS DEVELOPMENT FOR MICROCOMPUTERS

Development of microcomputer systems must comply with individual needs of users and also must establish compatibility with practices and standards that apply throughout an organization.

The Decision Making Process

Rather than requiring major development projects, creation of microcomputer systems can be achieved through an orderly procedure for decision making. This involves stating the need, identifying possible alternatives, evaluating the alternatives, and selecting the best solution.

BUILDING INFORMATION RESOURCES WITH MICROCOMPUTER TOOLS

Five basic concepts are common to most methodologies used to build information resources: define desired results, specify and create files, process transactions against files, generate specified outputs, and provide for protection and backup of information resources.

DEFINE DESIRED RESULTS

Many business operations begin to build information systems by defining expected results, or outputs.

SPECIFY AND CREATE FILES

Defining output requirements provides a basis for describing the data needed to produce these outputs. These data must come from files, which are defined at this point.

Data Modeling

Data modeling is a procedure for creating data files or databases that reflect the operations and status of an organization. Data modeling techniques can be applied to the package selection process.

Building Files

Data files are created and loaded with data elements.

PROCESS TRANSACTIONS AGAINST FILES

Data are entered and processed to determine that files can handle transactions and can support the system under development.

GENERATE SPECIFIED OUTPUTS

The system is instructed to retrieve needed data elements and to include them on specified reports.

Report Specification

Report specification is used to name a report, enter headings, and specify character types. A query language can be used for selecting fields from database files to be printed within a report.

PROVIDE FOR PROTECTION AND BACKUP OF INFORMATION RESOURCES

The data files and programs that are critical to the operation of the system and the continuity of the company should be copied and stored in protected facilities. Backup and restart procedures should be established to restore service following emergency interruption or destruction of files.

Security and Privacy

Access to a database should be provided only to those who need it, and be limited to needed data elements.

SCOPE

Microcomputers perform many roles in organizations. By their very presence, microcomputers have impacted virtually every business area and function—including systems development practices. This chapter discusses the development of information systems in which microcomputers are the primary processing component. Emphasis also is given to systems implementation under database management techniques. This emphasis stems from the complimentary nature of systems requirements and DBMS capabilities. As a point of contrast, the initial discussion focuses on larger, mainframe-based systems development procedures.

SYSTEMS DEVELOPMENT

For mainframe systems, implementation projects can involve expenditures of millions of dollars and years of effort. Such systems also may require construction of new facilities to house equipment and data stores. For systems projects of this magnitude, the capital budgeting mechanisms of an organization usually come into play. For most organizations, capital expenditures involve tools, machinery, facilities, land, and other items that contribute to the production and distribution of goods and/or services. Large computer information systems involve expenses that fall within this defined range.

Because of the magnitude of expenditures, some type of formal, structured approach to the development of large systems is required. Usually, technical personnel and users are appointed to a project team to perform development activities. The overall task then is broken down into a series of smaller activities. At the completion of each sub-task, or phase, the project team presents design or development results to a steering committee for review and disposition. The steering committee either recommends the project be modified, or gives its approval for the team to proceed to the next phase. In addition, the steering committee can cancel the project at any point. In this way, serious overruns, typical in early systems projects, are contained or avoided effectively.

THE SYSTEMS DEVELOPMENT LIFE CYCLE

To provide control, development projects often are executed under a formal methodology. The purpose of this methodology is to break down a large-scale project into discrete, manageable phases, and to maintain control of the implementation of each phase. Development methodologies may vary among business organizations. However, for discussion purposes, a common set of phases, with common requirements and functions in each, can be identified. In this text, the methodology is called the *Systems Development Life Cycle (SDLC)* and consists of five phases:

- Investigation

- Analysis and general design

- Detailed design and implementation

- Installation

- Review.

A diagram of the SDLC is presented in Figure 8-1.

Investigation

The purpose of the investigation phase is to identify and define the problem to be solved. Initial activities are directed toward isolating the problem, its causes, and the impact of the situation throughout the organization. A decision is made regarding the feasibility of remedying the situation with a computer information

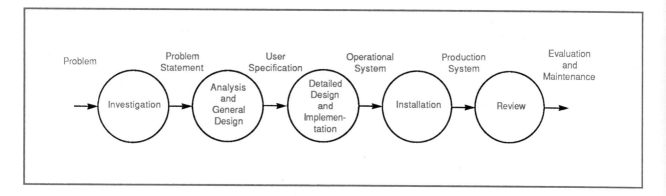

system. To support this decision, a problem statement is produced, solution objectives are defined, and tentative budgets and schedules are established.

Analysis and General Design

The analysis and general design phase builds upon the problem statement and solution objectives produced during the initial investigation. Activities reflect an increased level of attention to detail. The system solution is designed from the perspective of users—usually based upon user interviews and written inputs. Alternative solutions are generated and described, and a preferred alternative is chosen for implementation (subject to steering committee approval). Required hardware components are described and initial schedules and budgets for their acquisition are produced. An end product of this phase is a document called a **user specification.** This document outlines benefits and requirements from the user viewpoint. Upon acceptance, the user specification becomes the basis for designing of programs and procedures to implement the system.

Detailed Design and Implementation

During this phase, the user specification is used to develop a technical solution to identified needs. Program specifications for implementing the solution are produced. Programs themselves are designed, written, tested, debugged, and documented. Computer operations procedures are developed and documented. Equipment is purchased and installed as needed. User and computer center personnel are trained. The entire system is tested and brought to a point of readiness for actual, day-to-day operation.

Installation

During the installation phase, the system is put into regular operation by users. Computer professionals remain in the background, restricting their role to troubleshooting and special assistance.

Figure 8-1.

The Systems Development Life Cycle (SDLC) provides a structured methodology for designing and installing computer-based information systems.

Extensive planning and care are required to manage the cutover from existing systems and procedures to new ones. One major activity centers around setting up the files needed by the new system. For large systems, loading data into files may require several hundred hours of effort. Projects of this magnitude require careful planning for installation. In many situations, it is necessary to run existing systems in parallel through one or more complete cycles. Conversion methods for microcomputer systems are discussed in a later section of this chapter.

Regardless of installation method, once a system is running, it is subject to review and, if needed, modification.

Review

Upon completion of a development project, a management review is conducted by the project team. The review serves dual purposes. The system is reviewed to determine its success or failure in meeting the objectives described during the investigation phase. In addition, the project itself is reviewed to evaluate development procedures. Findings can be applied to future projects.

Throughout typical projects, activities are monitored by the steering committee. Project teams usually prepare formal results summaries at the end of each development phase for presentation to the committee. Approval is required before the project can proceed to the next phase. The review phase runs concurrently with other phases throughout the systems development life cycle. These controls are dictated by the nature of the expenditures involved in large, mainframe-based systems. Without effective monitoring mechanisms, systems projects of this type can exceed budgets substantially and/or lose sight of solution requirements. In effect, a truly elegant system may fail, or succeed only partially, to meet the defined requirements.

THE ENTREPRENEURIAL APPROACH

In supporting transaction processing, microcomputers certainly contribute to the production and distribution of goods and services. However, capital budgeting processes usually are not required to implement microcomputer systems. Most middle managers or executives can implement individual microcomputer-based information systems without justifying the expenditures to a steering committee. The cost of microcomputer equipment is within a range of expenses that many middle managers and executives can commit to with a signature. In this environment, systems design and installation may be reduced to a series of relatively simple decisions for selecting and purchasing equipment and application software packages.

In effect, managers and executives have the means for building individual microcomputer systems to support their tasks. This approach, often called the **entrepreneurial approach,** may provide significant advantages. Because of the flexibility and manageability of microcomputers, personnel involved in this process are able to focus on solutions to business problems or needs. The abundance of application packages also makes it possible to implement systems with a minimum of technical assistance. Systems of this type can be "personalized" to support the functions and roles of individual managers or executives.

Prototyping

Under the entrepreneurial approach, trial-and-fit techniques can be applied to systems development. An executive can sit down at a microcomputer terminal and design output reports using a word processor or spreadsheet package. If these outputs meet with user approval, advanced **fourth-generation** tools can be used to build a system that supports the production of these outputs. (Fourth-generation tools are discussed further in the next chapter.)

If the sample outputs are rejected by users, or if modifications are suggested, the executive can go "back to the drawing board," or, in this case, the terminal screen. Modifications are made on screen and brought again to users until approval is gained. This development method, known as **prototyping,** provides quick, effective solutions for many requirements and situations. The prototype system can be run through several processing cycles on a trial basis. User response, collected during the test period, can be used to "fine tune" the system before it is brought into regular operation. The system can be fine-tuned as it is being developed.

Entrepreneurial systems ideally should be compatible with and integrated into the information processing scheme of the overall organization. If personalized systems are allowed to proliferate unchecked within an organization, incompatibilities may create a form of anarchy. In a worst case, microcomputers used unwisely or maliciously may alter the overall files of an organization and render these files unreliable. Or, individual systems may be at cross purposes with corporate objectives. To realize management values, microcomputer systems must be coordinated with corporate systems. For these reasons, system development projects for microcomputers may benefit from structured methodologies.

SYSTEMS DEVELOPMENT FOR MICROCOMPUTERS

The entrepreneurial approach is reinforced by the increased sophistication of users. In current organizational environments, even entry-level users possess fundamental skills and knowledge of computers gained from prior educational or professional experience. In most organizations, decision makers have had little choice but to adjust to this new situation.

Users also must be aware of the overall organizational conditions under which systems operate. This may seem a straightforward achievement. Corporate goals and strategies usually are documented. However, environmental factors, also called **corporate culture,** should be given appropriate consideration.

Corporate culture consists largely of intangibles that are said to establish the "personality" of a company. Every organization presents a different image, and tends to have characteristics that set it apart, or **differentiate** it, from others—even others of the same size or within the same industry. Although corporate culture is difficult to define specifically, it is comprised of overall management philosophies, goals, and policies. These beliefs may be stated formally or may be an informal attitude of "the way we do things around here."

Environmental factors may be categorized as business requirements. Remember: systems are built to meet requirements. An implicit requirement of any development project is to further the goals and to comply with the policies of the host organization.

The point is that, while microcomputer systems may be installed under a "shopping list" approach, selection decisions should be made with the overall requirements of the business in mind. Because of this impact, and possible ramifications, decision factors should be analyzed and evaluated thoroughly. Many organizations find it useful to take a formal or semi-formal approach to decision making.

The Decision Making Process

Decision making can be broken down into a series of small, individual tasks, and organized so that all pertinent factors are considered. In addition, a decision making model of this type can be applied to many business functions—including the SDLC or methodologies for developing entrepreneurial systems, discussed later in this chapter. Figure 8-2 presents a diagram of a typical decision making concept, or model. For microcomputer systems, this model can serve, in effect, as a scaled-down substitute for the SDLC project methodology.

The decision making model establishes the steps, or phases, that follow:

- Decision statement
- Alternatives
- Evaluation of alternatives
- Selection
- Implementation
- Review and evaluation.

To repeat, this model may be applied in any type of decision situation. The model may be a tool within an SDLC project. Or, the decision making approach may be used to guide full-scale selection and implementation of a microcomputer system.

The model also identifies *feedback loops* between decision making stages. *Feedback* is a response to procedures or conditions used for quality control or corrective action. Thus, a feedback loop is repeated until satisfactory results are achieved.

For example, a decision statement (described below) may lack sufficient clarity of purpose. This shortcoming should be identified by feedback before the process moves to further steps. Another decision statement then is produced and additional feedback is received. This loop may be repeated several times, until clear, suitable content is established. This type of refinement occurs at each stage in the decision process.

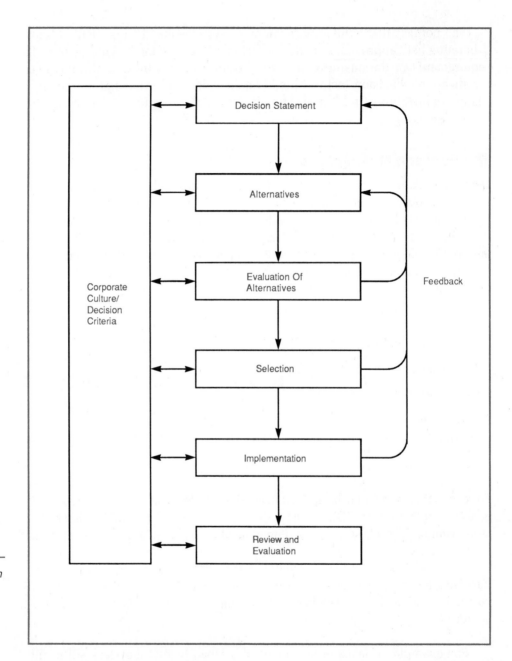

Figure 8-2.

Effectively applied, this decision making model ensures that a reasonable number of alternatives are generated and evaluated, and that a workable course of action is chosen.

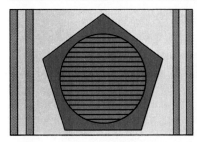

MICROCOMPUTERS

How To Become a Smart Shopper

Word-processing requirements in law offices typically originate with dictation. Documents often call for the inclusion of standard legal elements.

Which microcomputer should I buy? What do I need to buy to go with it? How do I choose software? What kind of printer do I need?

People buy microcomputers for many reasons. Some want to manage personal business accounts, some want to keep up with stock prices, some want to manage small business records, and on and on. For most, a microcomputer is a major purchase. Although computer hardware is continually decreasing in price, and may indeed be the least expensive component, other costs such as software, training, other computer devices, and supplies are financial considerations. And, as if it were not difficult enough just to decide when to buy a microcomputer, there are dozens of options available for most components.

So how do you decide what to buy?

There is a process for developing a system, regardless of the application. The process has four basic steps:

1. Define your requirements
2. Identify and evaluate your alternatives
3. Select the alternative that is best for you
4. Install, use, and evaluate the system.

To demonstrate this systematic process, consider a hypothetical case involving the initial purchase of a microcomputer system.

Searching for suitable microcomputer hardware and word-processing legal software requires first selecting several sample documents produced regularly by the law firm.

Typing legal transcripts and inserts is both tedious and error prone. Making an insert into a legal document means that the whole document has to be retyped from scratch.

As a basis for selecting a microcomputer, a series of requirements is established and listed. This list, in effect, becomes a shopping and selection guide.

A computer dealer should be able to understand and recommend workable solutions for business problems.

▥ STEP ONE: DEFINE YOUR REQUIREMENTS

Chris Peterson is a legal assistant in a small law firm. She learned to use word processing, spreadsheet, and database microcomputer software at school. However, she now works in an office that prepares all documents manually with an electric typewriter.

In addition, Chris handles some of the firm's legal research. In visiting local libraries, she has learned about legal database systems that hold promise for her firm. She understands that, if she had a microcomputer workstation, she could use these same resources.

Lynn Allen, the attorney for whom Chris works, is aware that it is taking a considerable amount of overtime for the young and growing firm to keep up with the work volume. Lynn and Chris decided to attend a seminar on the use of microcomputers in a legal practice sponsored by the local bar association. They also shared articles about microcomputer applications from professional journals and business publications. After visiting several other law firms that were successfully using microcomputers, Lynn and Chris decided that their own office could benefit from a microcomputer system.

Chris and Lynn gave a lot of thought to their requirements for a microcomputer system. They listed the requirements needed for the present and foreseeable future:

Evaluate the computer store while waiting for help from a salesperson. The initial approach and questions by the salesperson can be important indicators of the quality of a store's service and expertise.

A. A WORD-PROCESSING REQUIREMENT

1. The system must be able to process and store documents up to 100 pages in length
2. Since legal documents often use standard forms and text passages, the system must be able to move sections of text from one file to another
3. The system should allow the user to create subject listings of contents for each document, and have the ability to search for specific listings throughout all documents.

B. A SPREADSHEET REQUIREMENT

1. There must be an ability to create numerical documents and to move them into the word-processing documents.

C. A MAILING-LIST REQUIREMENT

1. To meet the need for legal notifications, the system must have the capability for building and maintaining mailing lists, and for using those lists to generate multiple copies of letters and briefs to different people.

D. A HARDWARE REQUIREMENT

1. Because of the firm's extensive legal text library, the system should have a lot of memory
2. The system should be able to utilize online legal databases.

E. A PRINTING REQUIREMENT

1. The printer should produce attractive, readable, high-quality legal documents
2. The printer must be able to "feed" stationery, and to address envelopes.

F. A "BACK-UP" REQUIREMENT

1. The system should allow for the easy creation and storage of all documents produced on it.

G. A BUDGET REQUIREMENT

1. The total purchase price should be in the range of $7000 to $9000.

Software selection is the key element in the purchase of a microcomputer. The software will determine the features and capabilities required of the microcomputer itself.

In addition to listing their requirements, Lynn and Chris selected several sample documents of the type produced regularly by the firm. Chris agreed to visit several microcomputer stores to evaluate the software and hardware that would best meet their requirements. She also was to prepare sample documents and print them out on the system of her choice.

▥ STEP TWO: IDENTIFY AND EVALUATE ALTERNATIVES

Prepared with the requirements checklist, Chris faced the first challenge: Where to buy? After visiting four stores she realized that there are major variations in the types of hardware, software, service, and sales support available from store to store.

Chris decided to go back and ask several of the law firms visited earlier how they'd selected a store. After getting quite a few tips, she came up with a list of guidelines for narrowing down her options.

Choosing a Microcomputer Store

Here are some tips for choosing a store:

- Look for stores that attract business people; avoid stores that look as though they are havens for hobbyists or technical experts.
- Look for stores that carry a limited number of hardware brands. If a store carries a large number, be suspicious about their ability to install and service what they sell.
- Look for stores that are authorized to do warranty work. If you buy from an unauthorized dealer, you may not be eligible for equipment warranty coverage.
- Evaluate the sales staff carefully. Beware of salespeople who attempt to sell you equipment before asking about your specific needs. Also avoid those who make heavy use of computer jargon. A qualified salesperson will take the time to find the software and hardware that will best meet your needs.
- Find out the kinds of training available to you from the store. Also find out what kinds of support will be available for any software packages you purchase. Be sure that the store will meet your own needs.
- Ask the store for names of other customers for whom they have installed hardware and software.
- Ask for a formal proposal. Review it carefully to make sure that it covers all of your requirements and is within the established price range.

In shopping for a microcomputer, you should resist the temptation of rushing headlong into keyboarding and instead establish some realistic requirements first, such as your precise needs and some specifications for the computer.

▥ STEP 3: SELECT THE ALTERNATIVE THAT IS BEST FOR YOU

Chris visited a total of six computer stores, then chose the one she felt would give her the best help and support. She recalled how the salesperson at the one store listened to her requirements, and then asked her numerous questions about the business. How many briefs do you handle each week? How long are they? How many clients does each attorney have at a time? Which word processors did you work with in school? After about 45 minutes, the salesperson suggested that Chris prepare documents on two word-processing packages and one spreadsheet package available in the store.

All packages were useable on several brands of computer. Chris asked to try out the packages on a couple of them. The salesperson

Selecting a microcomputer should begin with a serious, detailed review of the work to be done and the conditions under which the system will be used.

An initial understanding of the work to be done will dictate the selection of application software packages to be reviewed and tested.

loaded the software, showed Chris how to run it, then left her to work on the sample documents. Chris experimented with the packages on both machines. She liked all of the packages, but one of the computers felt more comfortable. Chris picked up the literature on the hardware and the software, and went back to the office to share her findings with Lynn and the other attorneys. Chris learned that microcomputer software can fall into several categories.

Choosing Microcomputer Software

Here are some tips on choosing microcomputer software:

- Word-processing software should be considered by any user with a need to prepare typewritten materials. The ability to easily edit documents can result in significant productivity gains. Also consider the need to send multiple copies of the identical letter to different people — a mailing list capability.
- Spreadsheets should be selected by people who work with columns and rows of numbers. The spreadsheet should easily recalculate all affected totals when a single number is changed. Determine if you need to reproduce or compare numerical totals graphically.

- Database programs allow you to store, sort, and retrieve large amounts of data from many sources.
- Integrated software usually takes word-processing, spreadsheet, and database functions, and permits interchange between the different functions. Additional features of graphics and other communication between user and computer are common.
- Utility software takes care of the miscellaneous tasks that you may need. Included are easy recovery of files, productivity packages, and fancy printing.
- CAD (Computer-Aided Design) is the computer replacement for the draftsperson's table. Mechanical and architectural drawings can be created easily with this type of software.
- Communications software allows one microcomputer to share information with another. Communications may be through a local area network or over phone lines to any other computer.
- Graphics software continues to be an exciting part of computing. Graphics software exists that creates maps or builds business graphics. Desktop publishing combines the features of word processing with the graphics capabilities available to produce camera-ready page images.

To get you started reviewing application software packages, the salesperson will typically demonstrate the equipment and the features of the software.

The following week, Chris returned to the computer store. She selected the word-processing and spreadsheet packages. Then she told the salesperson she was now ready to talk about hardware. Reviewing Chris' requirements, the salesperson suggested several options. All of them, he said, would meet those requirements.

Several of the systems requirements were dictated by the software Chris had chosen. For instance, the word processor required 256K of memory and a 20 megabyte hard disk for data storage. Still other requirements were dictated by taste, such as Chris' preference for the amber monitor over the green one.

The salesperson encouraged Chris to pay special attention to the printers. There were so many to choose from, each one offering a unique combination of features and benefits.

Printers

Here are ways to tell the differences between one printer and another:

• The technology used to print characters:
  dot-matrix printers print dots in a pattern that looks like a letter
  impact printers strike a print element such as a Selectric ball against

Hands-on practice is an important part of the process of evaluating your potential microcomputer system.

As part of the hands-on practice session, Lynn captures portions of test documents brought along for this purpose.

an inked ribbon and transfer the character to the paper
laser printers use a photographic process somewhat similar to that used in photocopiers.
- The quality of output:
  letter quality
  near letter quality
  draft quality.
- The width of paper the printer will accept:
  eight-inch width for standard correspondence
  up to fourteen inches wide for financial reports.
- The method of "feeding" the paper: some printers have sprockets that feed paper continuously.
- The speed of the printer — which is stated in characters per second.
- The ability to print envelopes.

The salesperson made his recommendations to Chris, also listing a few alternatives. Interestingly, the total price was below $7000, which more than met the budget requirements. He specifically suggested the following:

- A word-processing program that included a calculating function for relatively simple arithmetic calculations, as well as mailing and indexing functions

Detailed attention to the features and capabilities of printers is an important part of system configuration.

As part of the system selection process, the system's requirements in the form of supplies — including diskettes, ribbons, and paper — are studied.

- A spreadsheet program that would let data be transferred to the word-processing program
- A microcomputer with 512K of memory, to allow for processing of the longer documents
- A 20-megabyte hard disk for the storage of many lengthy documents
- A letter-quality dot-matrix printer
- A communications program with a built-in modem for online research
- A service contract
- Software upgrades (new releases) for six months
- A supply of diskettes for backups for the disk.

Chris and Lynn reviewed the proposal, and concluded that it met the requirements list initially developed for the system.

Chris returned to the store, finalized the purchase, and began to prepare a place in the office for the system. New furniture was ordered, and new procedures for training and computer useage were developed. Procedures for taking good care of the new system were also discussed and developed.

Back at the office, preliminary decisions about system configuration and components are reviewed in detail. A final visit to and another demonstration at the computer store are also planned.

Microcomputer Care

Here are some tips for taking good care of a computer system:

- A computer system should be exposed to no more of a harsh environment than you are. The temperature should be between 64 and 80 degrees, and covers should be used to keep dust from the machine.
- Diskette heads should be cleaned regularly with proper equipment.
- Practice good habits of handling diskettes. Never touch the exposed part of the magnetic medium, as your fingers can leave traces of oil that cause data loss. Insert the diskette carefully into the computer — never force it. Never bend the diskette. Avoid magnetic fields such as those found around monitors or radios. Always replace the diskette in a protective jacket.
- Consider a protection device to give you uninterrupted power. A loss or a surge of power could damage your computer and cause a loss of data.
- Clean your computer case with mild soap and water. Clean the screen with a glass-cleaning substance.

An important step that precedes equipment installation is attendance at a class held in the computer store. Instruction should cover the specific hardware and software to be used.

▥ STEP FOUR: INSTALL THE SYSTEM

As soon as the equipment arrived, a store representative came to the office to assemble and test the system, go over the documentation manuals with Chris, and answer any questions. He also spent time going over the store's liberal service policy with her again, which impressed her a lot.

Six months later, Chris realized that the microcomputer system was loaded with work — unable to take on growing volumes. To increase capacity, it was obvious that the existing system would have to be expanded either through a new work station or through additions to the existing equipment. By this time, everyone in the office knew what to do: The staff met to discuss and specify the new requirements.

Thus, the cycle repeats itself. The systems development process reviewed in this insert is usable whenever information processing needs arise. For your further use, the process is described in greater depth in another chapter.

The microcomputer system is ready for installation.

A microcomputer can be put to productive use in a short time.

Your Insurance: Good Service

Computer service may be provided by several sources. A dealer may have someone on staff capable of running simple diagnostic routines and replacing malfunctioning parts. This person should also be able to deal with problems such as memory failures, diskette drive replacement, and power supply replacement.

How do you evaluate your dealer's service personnel? Ask about their previous training. Manufacturers often certify technicians for training on their product. Make sure your dealer has a spare parts kit on hand. At a minimum, your dealer should always have a stock of replacement parts.

The service you get often depends on whether you have a service contract. A service contract is a type of insurance policy on your computer equipment. Some contracts cover all parts and labor in the event of a failure. Others provide "loaner equipment." Still others provide on-site service or 24-hour phone service.

A second method of service is provided by large, nationwide service organizations. These organizations are usually based in major cities. Because they are typically large they are equipped with many repair people. Still, make sure that they are familiar with your particular equipment before signing an agreement.

A third and final source of equipment and repairs is the manufacturer itself. This source is rarely appropriate for complete systems, and tends to be more expensive.

QUESTIONS

1. What are the four steps in the system development process?
2. Does the list of requirements developed by Chris and Lynn seem adequate? What can you add to the list?
3. What measures can be used in evaluating microcomputer stores?
4. Can you think of other ways in which Chris could have researched the use of microcomputers in legal offices?
5. Was it important that Chris take sample documents along to the microcomputer store? How should Chris react if the store refuses to let her prepare the documents on demonstration hardware and software?
6. Why is it important to select proper software programs before hardware is investigated?
7. Develop your own list of procedures for staff training and daily use of the microcomputer system to be installed in the legal offices.

Decision statement.   A ***decision statement*** is a proposed solution to an identified problem. That is, the outcome, or results, being sought are described in the decision statement. A typical decision statement might read:

> *Determine the feasibility of performing order entry directly into microcomputer terminals and integrating this function with master files of customer accounts so that invoices for orders may be generated on a next-morning basis.*

In other words, a decision statement describes the terms of a successful project. Notice that the decision statement also presents quantitative criteria, in this case a specification that invoices be available the morning following order receipt. The decision statement also should give an indication of the scope of the project. Scope identifies the operational areas affected by decision execution. In the above example, scope is indicated by the phrase "performing order entry directly into microcomputer terminals." This means that alternative solutions (described below) must be implementable on microcomputers. In addition, the alternatives generated should focus on the order entry and invoicing applications.

Alternatives.   The input for this step is the decision statement. The purpose of this step is to investigate the problem and to identify a reasonable number of alternative solutions. Alternatives are described in enough detail for comparison with the decision statement and with other alternatives. This step also may involve one or more feedback loops if the original decision statement is found unworkable and requires modification.

Evaluation of alternatives.   Evaluation of alternatives involves gathering and comparing data about the options identified in the previous step. Two tools commonly used to facilitate evaluations are decision tables and cost/benefit analyses. ***Decision tables*** present quantitative ratings on how well each alternative meets the established requirements.

Cost/benefit analysis may be implemented during any step in the decision making process. This type of evaluation involves the assignment of measurable values to the costs and potential benefits of each alternative. Both elements are compared to determine if benefits exceed costs. An alternative for which benefits exceed costs is said to be justified. Benefits may be difficult to quantify. For example, benefits may be based upon user estimates of labor reductions, or total benefits may be expressed as numeric values assigned by appropriate managers. The results of cost/benefit analyses may be presented as a decision table, as shown in Figure 8-3.

	1986	1987	1988	1989	1990
PROPOSED SYSTEM: Developmental and Operating Costs					
Hardware/Software	80,000	40,000	20,000	22,000	25,500
Personnel	140,000	80,000	75,000	65,000	60,000
Training	20,000	10,000	2,000	2,000	1,000
Supplies	7,500	5,000	5,300	5,600	5,900
Overhead	10,500	5,500	5,700	5,900	6,100
Total Costs	$258,000	140,500	108,000	100,500	98,000
EXISTING SYSTEM					
Total Operating Costs	$135,500	150,500	165,000	185,500	206,500
BENEFITS	$ -122,000	10,000	57,000	85,000	108,500

Figure 8-3.

A cost/benefit analysis is a tool for applying quantitative values to decision making criteria.

Evaluation of alternatives also involves the identification of potential negative consequences for each option. In effect, this process may be described as attempting to see "both sides of the coin." Negative consequences are examined to ensure objectivity on the part of decision makers. Negative consequences usually are based upon speculation, centering around possible adverse effects of new systems on the work habits and job satisfaction of operators.

Selection.   Alternative evaluations are subjected to review and feedback from users and other personnel. After an appropriate number of feedback loops, the most desirable alternative is selected for implementation. Often, a chosen alternative is not the one that has the most favorable cost/benefit ratio. Decision making tools are used merely to determine the overall impact of a course of action. Final selection power lies with the appropriate manager or other decision maker.

Implementation.   Once an alternative has been selected, a project can move to the implementation stage. Implementation refers to the actual, physical execution of a decision. In this case, implementation refers to converting procedures and equipment from an existing to a new system. Typically, system implementation involves many operations which include: purchasing and installing required equipment and/or resources; training users and other affected personnel; modifying programs or software packages; and configuring system components to reflect identified requirements.

Several implementation methods may be used. These methods include the following:

- *Phased conversion* involves installing a new system in stages. That is, the order entry application might be converted first, followed by the receiving application, then inventory control, then accounting, and so on. In this way, system implementation proceeds in a controllable, logical progression.

- *Parallel conversion* involves implementing a new system, and running it simultaneously with the existing system for a specified "changeover" period. The idea behind this method is to have "something to fall back on" until users are comfortable with new machines and methods.

- *Immediate conversion* often is dictated by the nature of the business or system being installed. For example, accounting systems, by nature, are replaced at the ends of reporting periods. The old system is used to complete processing for a specific period, then the new system immediately begins processing for the succeeding period.

Review and evaluation.   Upon implementation, a new system is evaluated against the original decision statement. Recall that the example decision statement (presented above) states that invoices be produced by the morning following order entry. If the system produces invoices that meet all other requirements, but that are not available until the following afternoon, the system has failed to meet established goals.

Feedback from this step serves dual purposes. The system may be refined further on the basis of feedback following evaluation. In addition, evaluation results may serve to build skills that can be applied by decision makers to future development projects.

The decision making model is a method for organizing the decision process. This model can be applied to any area of systems development. Earlier chapters present overviews of factors involved in configuring collections of hardware components into a work station. Evaluation and feedback techniques can be used to determine needs and to guide the purchase of required components.

If an organization uses separate files for single applications, most of the work of systems development would be finished at this point. Individual files would be built for all applications (invoicing, accounting, spreadsheets, etc.). Files would be updated each time an application is run. These files could be built with minimal attention to referencing or indexing schemes. However, building a system around coordinated information resources requires that files be structured to allow integrated access and updating of files among applications.

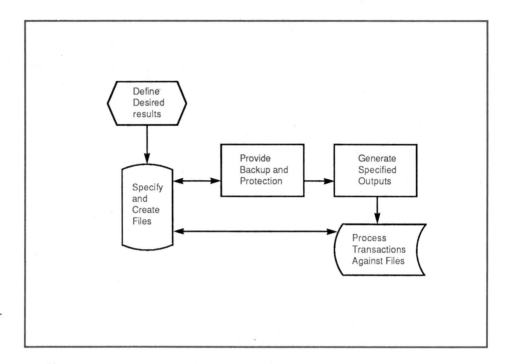

Systems development

procedures for microcomputers
resemble this model.

BUILDING INFORMATION RESOURCES
WITH MICROCOMPUTER TOOLS

The development of systems of information resources proceeds from the "top down," or from results forward. Initial activities involve describing outputs required to support processing. Then, a pool of data is built from which information is derived to produce the outputs. The data pool, a collection of files, must be structured to allow access, retrieval, and updating according to the requirements of multiple applications.

In effect, this methodology involves the creation of a ***database.*** A database is a collection of files organized to support multiple applications. For this type of system, it becomes vital that development projects adhere to a formal methodology. Methodologies vary among different business organizations, but basic concepts and common functions can be identified. The functional stages of this type of development project include:

- Define desired results.

- Specify and create files.

- Process transactions against files.

- Generate specified outputs.

- Provide for protection and backup of information resources.

Each of these steps involves a number of decisions. Therefore, the process is enhanced by the application of the decision making techniques described in the above section. Evaluations should be conducted and feedback collected and analyzed for each step.

DEFINE DESIRED RESULTS

Many business operations begin with consideration of results. Recall that prototyping (discussed above) involves the generation of sample outputs as an initial development activity. In systems terminology, results are outputs. For microcomputer systems that support transaction processing, the most common form of output is hard copy documents or reports.

Consider again the fictional clock manufacturing company, Big Time, Inc., discussed in an earlier chapter. Suppose the inventory manager, Mary Stewart, has been appointed to oversee development of a system for automating transaction processing in that company. Stewart begins by defining desired results, or system end products.

Stewart decides to begin system definition activities with accounts receivable reports. Her reasoning for this decision is relatively straightforward. Stewart knows that Big Time does not want to implement a large-scale, interactive system at the outset. If such a system were being implemented, system definition probably would focus on invoices. In effect, invoices represent the ultimate destination of a transaction path, and a logical beginning point for a top-down system definition.

In this case, however, invoices will be written manually or on typewriters as customers call or mail order information. Invoices will be source documents that, initially, will support a system for maintaining information on customer payments—accounts receivable. However, Stewart recognizes that it is necessary within any system to encompass plans for manual, as well as machine-processing procedures and results. At this point, invoices are critical to the system because they are the source of data for this report.

The accounts receivable report is to be comprised of selected data items from invoice files. The report is to describe customer order activities during the reporting period. Order activities are described on invoice documents and recorded in invoice files. Thus, the report will include a customer number for each customer who places an order during the period. In addition, the report will present detail information about customer orders. Other data items on the report, then, will include invoice numbers, invoice amounts, and invoice due dates. Finally, a total amount due for each customer record will be generated by the system.

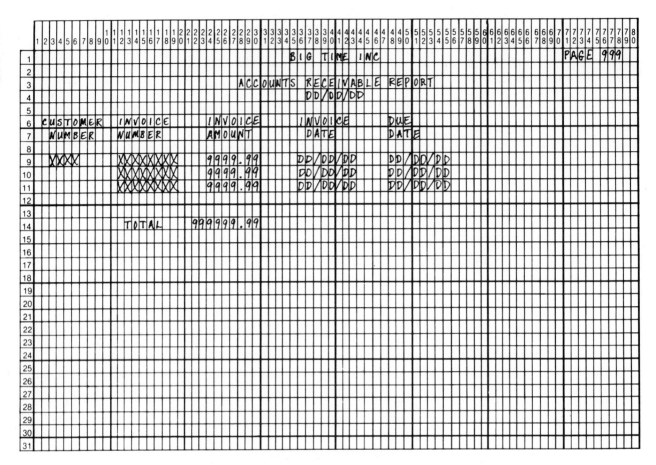

Figure 8-4.

A report specification form describes requirements for data elements that are to be output by the system.

Stewart documents the layout, or **format,** of the report on a special form, shown in Figure 8-4. The form presents a notation scheme common to data and file definition activities. Specific types of data characters (alphanumeric, numbers, logical) are indicated by entries on the form. Alphanumeric characters are indicated by the letter "C," and numeric characters within date fields are indicated by the letter "D." Numeric characters are indicated by the number "9." The number of characters in each field is indicated by the number of characters in the format layout. Fields representing dollar amounts provide for inclusion (or exclusion) of decimal amounts.

SPECIFY AND CREATE FILES

By producing the report layout specifications, Stewart has begun to identify and define the data files from which outputs will be derived. It stands to reason that data fields within file records should match the format of the report. To illustrate, notice that the customer number field on the report layout contains four spaces

MULTIPLE LAYOUT FORM

1.	CUST NO	INVOICE NO	INVOICE AMT	INVOICE DATE	DUE DATE	NOT USED

9 9 9 9 9|9 9 9 9 9 9 9 9|9 9 9 9 9 9 9 9 9|9 9 9 9 9 9|9 9 9 9 9|9 9 9 9 9 9 9 9 9 9 9 9 9 9 9 9 9 9 9 9 9 9 9 9 9 9 9 9 9 9 9 9 9 9 9 9 9 9 9
1 2 3 4 5 6 7 8 9 10 11 12 13 14 15 16 17 18 19 20 21 22 23 24 25 26 27 28 29 30 31 32 33 34 35 36 37 38 39 40 41 42 43 44 45 46 47 48 49 50 51 52 53 54 55 56 57 58 59 60 61 62 63 64 65 66 67 68 69 70

2.

9 9 9 9 9 9 9 9 9 9 9 9 9 9 9 9 9 9 9 9 9 9 9 9 9 9 9 9 9 9 9 9 9 9 9 9 9 9 9 9 9 9 9 9 9 9 9 9 9 9 9 9 9 9 9 9 9 9 9 9 9 9 9 9 9 9 9 9 9 9
1 2 3 4 5 6 7 8 9 10 11 12 13 14 15 16 17 18 19 20 21 22 23 24 25 26 27 28 29 30 31 32 33 34 35 36 37 38 39 40 41 42 43 44 45 46 47 48 49 50 51 52 53 54 55 56 57 58 59 60 61 62 63 64 65 66 67 68 69 70

3

9 9 9 9 9 9 9 9 9 9 9 9 9 9 9 9 9 9 9 9 9 9 9 9 9 9 9 9 9 9 9 9 9 9 9 9 9 9 9 9 9 9 9 9 9 9 9 9 9 9 9 9 9 9 9 9 9 9 9 9 9 9 9 9 9 9 9 9 9 9

Figure 8-5.

A file specification describes and defines the data elements that make up records within a specific file.

for numeric characters. It would be unworkable and self-defeating, then, to design a customer master record that specifies a six-space, alphanumeric customer number.

In effect, determining system requirements by specifying reports is an effective method for building system files. That is, a **data model** can be defined—and used to build the system or to evaluate and select a database package.

Data Modeling

A data model is a set of descriptions and definitions that identifies the logical structure of files. The logical structure is used to establish access paths for support of applications. By installing this structure, users are able to compile data from several sources to implement applications. After outputs have been defined (such as accounts receivable reports, purchase orders, and others), Stewart shifts her attention to the building of files. Ideally, Stewart would like to purchase a software package that meets her needs without requiring additions or modifications. She finds that data modeling techniques can be applied to the package selection process.

To begin, Stewart produces a File Specification form for the accounts receivable files, as shown in Figure 8-5. In effect, this form describes a single record within the file. Each field is named, character type specified, width (number of characters) established, and number of decimal positions for numeric fields indicated. Notice that, even though notation methods are different, character types and numbers of characters within fields match those described on the report layout form presented in Figure 8-4.

Stewart also produces specifications for files such as product descriptions, inventory stock records, and others. Those specifications are omitted here for the sake of brevity.

The accounts receivable file.   The accounts receivable file contains records that represent each purchase until it is paid. Recall that, for many transactions, especially those between two businesses, delivery is separate from payment. An account receivable represents the exchange value of a transaction until it is completed. The accounts receivable file, then, reflects the status of each customer account. This file will be updated periodically to reflect new invoices or payments. Information within this file also will indicate the currency or delinquency of specific accounts.

The main identifying fields for this file are CUSTNO (customer number) and INVNO (invoice number). These fields can be used as sort values for the file. Stewart can sort the accounts receivable file first by invoice number, then again by customer number. The report then is produced with both customer and invoice numbers in sequence.

Notice also that the CUSTNO field is the only identifying field for records. It is not necessary to maintain redundant data, such as customer addresses and product descriptions, in the accounts receivable file. The interrelation of key elements, or *record keys,* is part of the logical structure implemented by database systems. This interrelation provides a reference through which the system can access master records as required for updating, or to produce invoice reports, billing statements, and other outputs.

The integration of files establishes a highly efficient processing environment, and provides for application processing support from multiple sources (files). For example, the INVAMT field can be used to ensure that proper payments are received. As another example, an exception reporting routine based on use of the DUEDATE field easily can be generated. When accounts become delinquent—as indicated by a comparison of DUEDATE with current date— exception items are reported, and collection procedures initiated. These applications also make use of customer identification data, such as customer address and/or telephone number from other master files.

Stewart produces specifications for every file in the system. Then, she uses these specifications as a "shopping list" with which to select an application package that provides required features. The specifications in this example probably require capabilities provided by database management systems (DBMS).

For example, the package must be capable of accommodating designations for primary and secondary record keys. The selection process may involve extensive research, evaluation, and testing of multiple packages. Selection criteria include capabilities for manipulating files—and records and data elements within files—as required. For present purposes, however, assume that Stewart selects and purchases a package that meets the above-mentioned requirements.

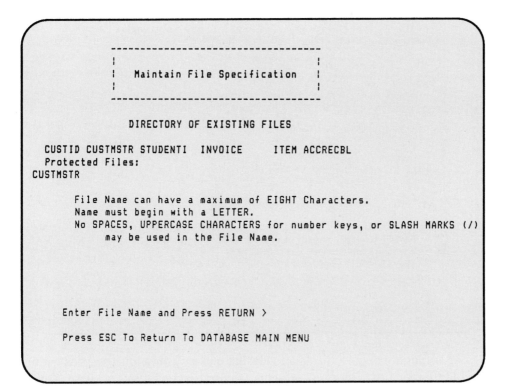

```
        ----------------------------------------
        :                                      :
        :     Maintain File Specification      :
        :                                      :
        ----------------------------------------

               DIRECTORY OF EXISTING FILES

   CUSTID CUSTMSTR STUDENTI  INVOICE      ITEM ACCRECBL
   Protected Files:
   CUSTMSTR

        File Name can have a maximum of EIGHT Characters.
        Name must begin with a LETTER.
        No SPACES, UPPERCASE CHARACTERS for number keys, or SLASH MARKS (/)
            may be used in the File Name.




     Enter File Name and Press RETURN >

     Press ESC To Return To DATABASE MAIN MENU
```

Figure 8-6.

To build files, the user first must give them names. In this example, the package is set up to create a new file for entered names that have not been used for existing files.

NOTE: For this discussion, and to reinforce your learning experience, the development scenario that follows uses functions and illustrations from the LEARNware software package that accompanies this text. These examples are used to provide you with an understanding of development concepts. The LEARNware package is not intended to support actual business operations. However, the concepts and functions illustrated here are applicable to actual business systems featuring any number of commercial packages.

Building Files

To this point, then, Stewart has defined file specifications and selected a software package. For present purposes, assume that Stewart indeed has selected a database package. The next step is to build the actual files. The specifications produced previously facilitate this process. Most database packages provide entry screens to facilitate the creation of files, as shown in Figure 8-6.

First, the file is given a name—entered into the appropriate field on the screen. File names identify the file and are used to access the file. Most users prefer names that refer to file function. Thus, the customer master file for the case scenario is called, CUSTMSTR.

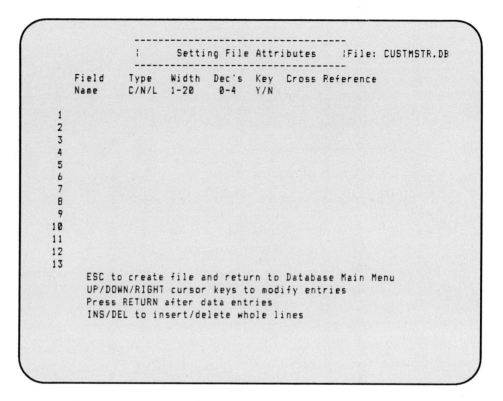

```
          ------------------------------------
          ¦      Setting File Attributes    ¦File: CUSTMSTR.DB
          ------------------------------------
    Field   Type   Width   Dec's   Key  Cross Reference
    Name    C/N/L  1-20    0-4     Y/N

 1
 2
 3
 4
 5
 6
 7
 8
 9
10
11
12
13

    ESC to create file and return to Database Main Menu
    UP/DOWN/RIGHT cursor keys to modify entries
    Press RETURN after data entries
    INS/DEL to insert/delete whole lines
```

Figure 8-7.

File formats, or the collective attributes of component records, are determined by user-supplied specifications.

After files are named, the data fields that make up individual records within the file are specified. Figure 8-7 presents an entry screen for this purpose. Notice that menu entries for this function parallel the File Specifications form in the above section. In effect, the fields, or attributes, specified on this screen determine the layout of file records. All records in a file have identical formats, including field names, sizes, and character types.

Stewart identifies the record format to be used in this file simply by keying in appropriate information within spaces for menu entries. See Figure 8-8. Thus, each field is named and specified through entries about data characters, field width, and decimal positions (for numeric fields). Another type of data character, known as logic characters, can be entered into the menu field designated "Record Key." A logic character entry answers a yes-or-no question about the record or field.

In the menu illustration, a "Y" (yes) or "N" (no) entry designates whether the field being specified will be used as a record key. Remember: the indexing structure of a database provides for referencing of individual data items.

Theoretically, each item in every file could be treated as a record key. This type of indexing, however, may be superfluous to application requirements. Further, key elements should be limited to fields that identify a record uniquely, such as customer number or customer name. For example, it is not likely that a user would need to locate a customer master record on the basis of the value within

```
            ------------------------------------------
            !      Setting File Attributes     !File: CUSTMSTR.DB
            ------------------------------------------
     Field     Type   Width  Dec's  Key  Cross Reference
     Name      C/N/L  1-20   0-4    Y/N

  1  CUSTNO    C        4            Y
  2  CUSTNAME  C       20            Y
  3  STADDR    C       14            N
  4  CITY      C        8            N
  5  STATE     C        2            N
  6  ZIP       C        5            N
  7  CRLIM     N        8      2     N
  8  ACTBAL    N       10      2     N
  9
 10
 11
 12
 13
       ESC to create file and return to Database Main Menu
       UP/DOWN/RIGHT cursor keys to modify entries
       Press RETURN after data entries
       INS/DEL to insert/delete whole lines
```

Figure 8-8.

*Building files involves specifica-
tions of field names, data types,
field widths, decimal places, and
record keys.*

the field for outstanding balance. In the event this need is encountered by a user,
most database packages provide query capabilities with which this type of
retrieval could be executed. The selection of fields as record keys should be based
upon application requirements and unique record identification.

Loading data.   Implementation of new systems can require patience and effort.
File specification and creation, in effect, is at the heart of any system. With these
procedures, files are built and the logical relationships that are utilized for access operations are established. Recall from previous discussions that it is the
access structure of a database that gives these packages the flexibility and power
to support businesses as resources.

At this point, the design aspect of building a transaction-processing system
is nearly finished. In a strict sense, processing procedures are built into the database package Stewart selects. For most database packages, users are provided a
set of manipulation/query commands with which they can access and retrieve
data elements needed to support applications. Processing specification is discussed in the section that follows.

At this point, then, files have been specified and directories created. All that
is needed is to **load** the database, or to enter data elements into appropriate
records within the files. For Stewart, this operation is relatively straightforward.
The physical entry operation is directed by processing menus. Operators simply

```
        ----------------------------------------
        !        ENTERing Data Records        !        Record No.  1
        ----------------------------------------        CUSTMSTR.DB
    Field    /Data/Field/No. of/       VALUE ENTRY
    Name     /Type/Width/Decim./

    CUSTNO     C      4            1001
    CUSTNAME   C     20            AAA DRUGSTORE
    STADDR     C     14            123 BAKER
    CITY       C      8            MESA
    STATE      C      2            AZ
    ZIP        C      5            87342
    CRLIM      N      8      2      500.00
    ACTBAL     N     10      2       345.50
            ESC to update record in file
            TAB key to duplicate previous entry
            UP/DOWN cursor keys to modify entries -- Press RETURN after data entries
```

Figure 8-9.

The formats of entered records must conform to file specifications. Errors detected during entry are corrected easily.

follow screen formats for keying data, validating entries, and saving files to disk. Figure 8-9 shows a completed entry screen for the first record in the CUSTMSTR file.

However, suppose Big Time, Inc., has 10,000 customer records to load into the system. Suppose further that an entry operator can capture and validate 35 records an hour. Under these conditions, setting up files and loading the database can involve months of staff hours. Stewart may choose to hire temporary operators for the data entry session. As an alternative, she may offer overtime to existing operators. In either case, this procedure will involve significant labor expenditures, and careful evaluations by the project leader.

PROCESS TRANSACTIONS AGAINST FILES

Processing refers to manipulations upon data to provide meaningful outputs. In a sense, the very act of establishing storage files provides meaning. That is, organizing records into files, such as the customer master file, provides meaning for the business. Such files represent sources of income.

Continuing the example, file structures for the Big Time, Inc., system are designed as a processing environment within which transaction data can be processed. These applications can be executed through a set of **manipulation/ query commands** provided by DBMS packages. These commands provide standard processing routines for executing inquiries and other operations without extensive consideration of computer procedures.

Command **syntax** may vary depending upon packages. In this sense, syntax refers to the arrangement of and structures for processing commands. Syntax may vary among packages, but commonalities can be identified. For example, files may be updated, or transactions posted to master records, with the UP-DATE command.

To execute an UPDATE command, a few specifications must be included. For example, the system must be directed to the appropriate transaction and master files. In addition, the affected data items are designated, and the type of posting operation specified. Posting operations usually include ADD, SUB-TRACT, and REPLACE. That is, a user can add, subtract, or replace the value of a transaction item and a corresponding item in the master file. To illustrate, a typical UPDATE command might read:

Update CUSTMSTR from OPEN-ITEM, Add AMT to ACTBAL

This statement describes an update operation through which current customer balances are increased to reflect incoming orders. The OPEN-ITEM file contains records of transaction activity. Within this file, orders for purchases and/or payments made are described in terms of customer number, amount of purchase, invoice number, date, payments made, and payment due dates. The UPDATE command instructs the system to add the value of AMT in the OPEN-ITEM file to the CUSTMSTR field, ACTBAL. This operation is executed to reflect ongoing transactions within overall customer balances.

Of course, this UPDATE procedure applies only to customers who have placed orders. Therefore, the system updates only those records that are common to both files—as indicated by common **key** fields, or CUSTNO figures. This update procedure is diagrammed in Figure 8-10.

Several UPDATE actions may be derived from an open-item file. For example, items within the AMTPD field (none are shown in the above example) reflect payments made on outstanding invoices. These values are updated to the ACTBAL field in the CUSTMSTR file. However, payments are subtracted from current balances, rather than being added as in the preceding example.

Thus far, the system-implementation discussion has centered around the specification and creation of files and the posting of transactions. That is, a file structure has been created and procedures implemented for maintaining the resources

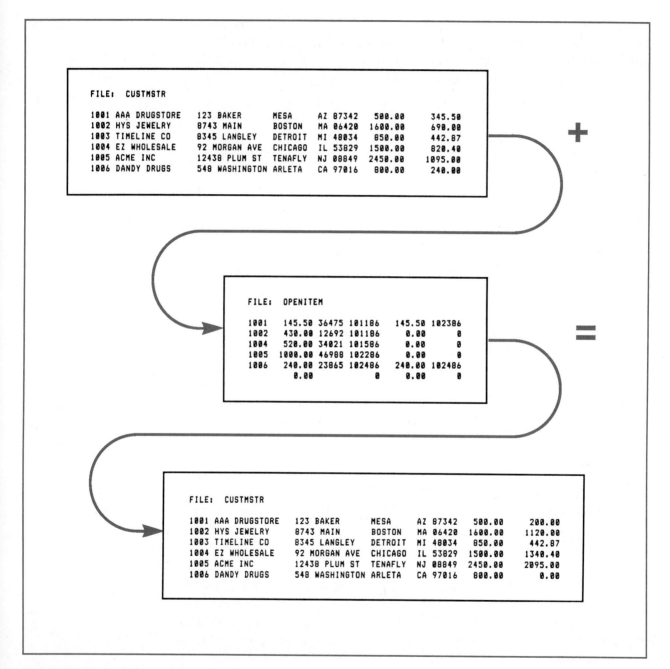

Figure 8-10.

Master files are updated to reflect the effects of current transaction activities.

within it. The next step involves the delivery of results to users, or the generation of specified outputs.

GENERATE SPECIFIED OUTPUTS

Outputs are the results of information systems delivered in a human-readable
form. Systems are set up to deliver results. Many systems projects define outputs
as an initial, design-related activity. Earlier in this chapter, an invoice specification was drawn up as a target for system outputs.

Invoice reports produced by the system, then, should conform to these
specifications. With many DBMS packages, these specifications are entered into
the system using entry screens similar to those used for file specifications. That
is, the system is given instructions describing the physical arrangement, or format, of the report and of the data elements it contains. This kind of feature allows
users to design their own report formats.

As an alternative, many packages include standard formats for standard
reports, such as transaction listings and financial statements. Many packages
provide standard formats for complete sets of business or accounting reports.
These formats may be used "as is" or modified according to individual requirements. For present purposes, the section that follows covers report specification
procedures. In this way, you can get an overall view of the process and procedures involved.

Report Specification

Report specifications are used to name a report, enter headings, and specify
character types. The report name also is used to designate a file that holds the
data from which a report is derived. These files may be database files, such
as master files, or auxiliary files created through use of manipulation/query
commands.

For example, to produce a list of past-due accounts, the system is instructed
to retrieve the customer identification and overdue balance fields from the customer master file. Further instructions initiate a PRINT operation for producing
the hard-copy report.

Regardless of report formatting capabilities, most DBMS packages provide
some feature for performing inquiries into file content. That is, capabilities are
included for listing and displaying records according to user requirements. A
query language is a set of **high-level commands** for retrieving selected and varied
data elements from a database. High-level commands resemble natural English

```
            INVOICE REGISTER                              OCTOBER 23, 1987
    =======================================================================

    INVNO    CUSTNO      TAX        AMT        CREDLIM        CURBAL
    -----------------------------------------------------------------------
    82737    1001        3.50      28.25        500.00        465.33
    87422    1001        5.10      44.80        500.00        465.33
    90312    1001        1.24       9.80        500.00        465.33
    48395    1003        4.90      42.70        850.00        238.90
    56231    1003        2.50      17.90        850.00        238.90
    81246    1005        6.45      48.40       2460.00       1456.90

                TOTALS  23.69     191.85
```

Figure 8-11.

In most transaction processing systems, summary reports are generated periodically to reflect business conditions and to support management decision making.

statements. For example, a user may wish to execute a query by entering a high-level command that reads:

FIND ALL CUSTOMER ACCOUNTS WITH BALANCES OF MORE THAN $5,000. DISPLAY NAMES, ADDRESSES, AND OUTSTANDING BALANCES FOR EACH ACCOUNT.

A query language can be used for selecting fields to be printed within reports. Query languages implement the compilation of required data, which then can be formatted and output according to requirements.

For example, a report file might be comprised of product numbers of an invoice file, product descriptions from the product master, and customer addresses from a customer master. Collectively, this data might provide information relating buying habits to geographic areas.

As a further example, Figure 8-11 presents a daily summary report that is used to support the invoicing activities described throughout this chapter.

Notice that the entries in this report are taken from multiple files. Invoice numbers (INVNO) and purchase amounts (AMT) are taken from the Accounts Receivable Open-Item File. Tax information (TAX) originates in an invoice file. The credit (CRLIM) and outstanding balance (ACTBAL) fields are derived from the customer master. All these entries are related by the remaining report field, the customer identification number (CUSTNO).

An invoice register summarizes periodic, daily in this case, order activities. Information on these reports describes commitments by customers to purchase goods or services. The important fields in this report are found on the totals line. These totals present the accumulated value of incoming orders each day. Incoming orders also trigger an accounts receivable to represent transaction value. The two totals, then, for invoice amount and for accounts receivable, should match, or *balance.*

In this case, however, both totals, since they have been derived by the system, may be inaccurate. An external source of control, such as a calculator total kept during order entry, may be valuable for maintaining the *integrity* of the data files. Integrity refers to the quality, accuracy, reliability, and timeliness of data. An information system, in essence, is the keeper of valuable business resources. The system should provide capabilities for safeguarding the quality and utility of data. These considerations, as well as system security factors, are discussed in the section that follows.

PROVIDE FOR PROTECTION AND BACKUP OF INFORMATION RESOURCES

To repeat an earlier point, integrity is achieved through controls written into transaction processing designs. That is, a system design should provide for a number of internal, or built-in, control mechanisms. (Again, these controls might be a standard feature of the selected package.) A sequence of processing steps must be completed before file content reflects an actual transaction, such as a payment, order, bank deposit, and so on. Integrity controls may be applied throughout this process. Controls common to many packages include the following:

- *Validity checks* are executed to ensure that data entries conform to file specifications, such as character type, value range, field width, and so on.

- *Transaction completion controls* involve monitoring the transaction to be sure that alterations for all identified portions of a database are executed.

- *Recovery* procedures restore a database that has been damaged. Recovery procedures, in simple terms, involve the re-posting of a *transaction log* against a *backup* version of the system.

A transaction log is a running journal of all transactions, recorded sequentially, or in their order of occurrence, and stored separately. A backup version of the system is created each time the system is updated. That is, a copy of the entire system is made as it exists prior to transaction processing activities.

Under these precautionary methods, the system can be rebuilt if storage files are destroyed. Transactions recorded on the log are processed on the backup copy of the system, as though they were newly input at the time of backup. This is known as a *roll forward* operation.

Maintaining backups is an important requirement. Figure 8-12 shows a three-disk backup method that is recommended by many software vendors. Creating

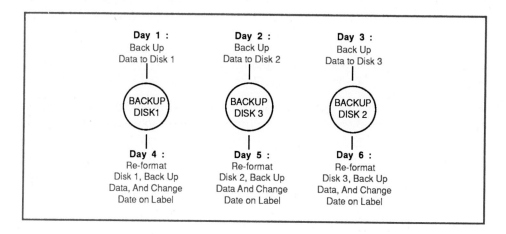

Figure 8-12.

A good method of maintaining
backup disks is to use three
disks in rotation, as shown
here.

backups of files stored on hard disks is crucial to maintaining system operations. The best way to back up hard disk files is on special tape cassettes, though floppy disks also may be used.

Security and Privacy

Security refers to limiting access to data objects according to needs. An order entry operator, for example, might not need to see the invoice register summary reports described above. Privacy implies the right of individuals or organizations to restrict the dissemination of information about themselves.

Security and privacy measures may be as simple as locking doors to rooms in which systems are housed. On another level, suppose order entry is performed on the same microcomputer system as the one used by a manager to produce summary reports. The manager needs a method for restricting access to summary report routines.

This type of control often is implemented through use of **passwords.** A password is a character string that must be entered into a system for achieving access to certain portions of the database. Password entry can be set up as a requirement for producing summary reports or for accessing certain data elements. For example, in a transaction processing system, an order entry operator may be able to access credit limit fields within customer records. But, the same operator may not be authorized to change the value of credit limits. Passwords, then, support authorization schemes.

In summary, transaction-processing systems present many and varied requirements. These requirements are met with great success by information systems built and supported by microcomputer tools. These systems present an almost unlimited degree of flexibility for manipulating data to support organizations. One of the most advanced transaction-processing tools for the microcomputer, called a database management system, has been discussed briefly in this chapter. Database tools also are the subjects of the two chapters that follow.

KEY TERMS

Systems Development Life Cycle (SDLC)

user specification

entrepreneurial approach

fourth generation

prototyping

corporate culture

differentiate

feedback loop

feedback

decision statement

decision table

cost/benefit analysis

phased conversion

parallel conversion

immediate conversion

database

format

data model

record key

load

manipulation/query command

syntax

key

query language

high-level command

balance

integrity

validity check

transaction completion control

recovery

transaction log

backup

roll forward

security

password

DEFINITIONS

Instructions: On a separate sheet, define each term according to its use in this chapter.

1. user specification

2. feedback

3. data model

4. load

5. manipulation/query commands

6. syntax

7. decision statement

8. integrity

T R U E / F A L S E

Instructions: For each statement, write T for true and F for false on a separate sheet.

1. The decision making process can be broken down into a series of small, individual tasks, and organized so that all pertinent factors are considered.

2. "Corporate culture" refers to the criteria used by people who determine the sophistication levels of a proposed microcomputer system.

3. Since a microcomputer system operates independently of other computers, it is not necessary to make sure that data files can be shared with other company computer systems.

4. A decision statement describes a proposed solution to an identified problem.

5. "Parallel conversion" refers to running two similar systems on identical jobs to see which one functions better to help decide which one to implement.

6. In systems terminology, results are called outputs.

7. A data model describes physical devices or processing through graphic outputs.

8. The decision making model is a method for organizing the decision making process.

9. An accounts receivable file contains records that represent each purchase until it is paid.

10. Most database packages provide menus or entry screens to facilitate the creation of files.

11. Posting operations usually involve adding, subtracting and replacing data items.

12. A transaction log is a standard term used by many hardware and lumber stores to keep track of the amount of wood sold.

13. Many software vendors recommend using a three-disk backup system.

14. To perform a cost/benefit analysis of systems, it always is wisest to go with the least expensive system.

15. File integration establishes a highly efficient processing environment— and provides support for multiple applications.

SHORT   ANSWER   QUESTIONS

Instructions: On a separate sheet of paper, answer each question in one or
two brief sentences.

1. Why is "evaluation" the last step in the six-step decision making model?

2. Why is file specification a particularly important step in the creation of a
database?

3. What is the purpose of a validity check?

4. What is a recovery procedure and what is its purpose?

5. What criteria should be applied to evaluate entrepreneurial benefits of a
microcomputer system?

6. In normal system design planning, how many times should you plan on
having a feedback loop repeated?

RESEARCH   PROJECT

Create, on paper, a toy manufacturing company that employs more than 50
people and conducts a great deal of mail-order sales to people in the U.S.,
Canada, Mexico, and France. The company also sells to department stores
and has its own retail outlet next to its plant. What specific capabilities
would a computer system need to deal with the exchange values of foreign
currencies so that sales figures from one country could be compared with
those in another country?

9 Working with Databases

MODELING WITH DATA

Modeling reality with information is a basic human activity. Illustrations include discoveries (Columbus deciding the world is round) and inventions (the airplane).

Nature of a Data Model

A data model represents the operation and status of an organization through information.

DATA AS AN ASSET

When a database exists, its contents become assets of the organization in much the same way as money, buildings, or equipment.

Evolution of Data Uses

Early computers did not store data files internally. Individual data items were entered, processed, then output. Files were external and were not directly accessible. As computers gained the ability to store and use files, additional uses were found for available information.

Transition From Files to Databases

The proliferation of files to support individual applications led to duplication of data content and to recognition of the value of being able to combine and interrelate records from different files. Databases evolved to meet this perceived value.

DATA MODELS

Many different approaches have been devised to aid the creation of data models, which serve as the foundations for databases.

Hierarchical Model

This model, also called a tree structure, organizes data items in a top-down order, according to established relationships. All access begins at top-level items and proceeds downward.

Network Model

A network model uses a structure similar to that of the hierarchical model, except that access is possible at multiple levels. Also, data items can have both top-down and bottom-up relationships within a network structure.

Relational Model

A relation is a traditional-type file that consists of records and fields. A database is formed by supporting access to multiple files through central index files.

THE DATABASE MANAGEMENT SYSTEM

A database management system (DBMS) uses multiple programs to provide software support and control over the use of a database.

Logical and Physical Database Design

The schema, or organization plan, represents the structure of data from the viewpoint of the user. In turn, the schema interacts with software elements of the DBMS to control the physical organization and structure of data.

DBMS Functions and Capabilities

Most DBMS packages include a series of commands that can be used to access and process data items. Together, these commands usually are called a query language.

FOURTH-GENERATION LANGUAGES

Complete application systems can be developed from database resources if 4GL capabilities are added to a DBMS. In effect, a 4GL makes it possible to link query commands and automate system execution. These methods are said to make computers more "user friendly."

USING DATABASE AND 4GL SYSTEMS

The availability of a database emphasizes the collection of information that models an organization. Once a database exists, systems development is simplified because it no longer is necessary to build files specifically to support individual applications.

SPECIAL
BELOW PUBLISHER PRICES

Stored data files

model an organization and its activities. In this photo, books and other items are represented by data elements and records in product files maintained by the business.

MODELING WITH DATA

Modeling is part of the human experience—the use of information, images, or reduced-size structures to represent ideas, objects, organizations, or even dreams.

- Columbus interpreted information derived from astrologers and from his own observations of ships at sea. From this information, he modeled a world that was round rather than flat.

- The Wright Brothers modeled flying machines through computations dealing with natural forces, such as wind and gravity. They drew pictures and developed physical models of aircraft to come. From their modeling grew an aerospace industry with transportation capabilities that have led others to dream in terms of worldwide economic models and societies.

- Architects model buildings not yet constructed through plans, drawings, and scaled-down structures of their planned projects.

- Business executives model the performance of their organizations by using accounting-type figures to project results of planned operations. For this type of modeling, special types of computer software have come to the forefront. One kind of software package used for business modeling is the spreadsheet, discussed elsewhere in this text. This chapter deals with a major technique for representing an organization in terms of the data it generates and accumulates. The tools are **databases**, and the software that makes them available is the **database management system (DBMS).**

Nature of a Data Model

A data model uses information or images to represent an organization and/or its operations. At a simple level, you take part in a modeling process each time you make a purchase. Think about what happens when, for example, you buy a record album or tape at a stereo store. You take possession of a record, which you exchange for money. This is the physical transaction. The modeling occurs when the salesperson writes an invoice or produces a receipt when your transaction is processed by a cash register.

The handwritten invoice or the cash register receipt is a **transaction document** that models the sale. From your vantage point, the data model substitutes a receipt for the money you spent. If the merchandise is faulty, the receipt that models the transaction will be the basis for receiving replacement items or a refund of your money.

The store develops a different model that adapts the same information to its own needs. For management of the store, the information on the sale becomes part of income. Income information is compared with the cost of buying the record and of running the business—expenses. The difference between income and expense is profit, one of the underlying reasons the store exists. In addition, the store will use information from the transaction model to manage its inventory model. That is, the store maintains a data model with records on each product stocked and sold. When your sales transaction impacts this model, the quantity on hand for the item you bought is reduced. When enough items are sold, the model tells store management that it is time to order additional copies of the record.

Data models, then, represent operations and values of an organization. The cumulative set of information that reflects the status and needs of an organization is a database.

DATA AS AN ASSET

When a database exists, it becomes far easier to ask a computer to deliver information about status and operations than to gather the information physically. Suppose, for example, that the stereo store at which you bought your record is part of a chain. A dozen stores each might stock 30,000 different items, in differing quantities. If an executive at the home office needed information on inventories of a given item, one way to collect data would be to call all 12 stores and ask the managers to count the quantity on hand.

However, if a database-oriented computer system were used to keep track of product inventories, the information could be secured in a few seconds with a simple keyboard entry. Multiply this by 30,000 and you get just a small part of the picture of the total power of databases as tools for monitoring status and making decisions about business operations.

Evolution of Data Uses

At their beginning, computers were not seen as tools for data management. Rather, the idea was to process one item of data at a time, carry the processing to its conclusion, then output one item of data for every input. The program was housed in computer memory. Data items were not. For example, in processing a payroll, the computer would accept an input of an employee's pay rate and store this amount temporarily. In the meantime, the computer would output the pay rate item to a new file kept on punched cards or magnetic tape. Then the figure for hours worked would be entered. The computer would multiply rate by hours worked and output an amount for gross pay. The output records with gross pay amounts would then be grouped with items on payroll deductions and the process would be repeated.

Under methods such as this, information was fragmented. It was hard for managers to get an overview of their business status from masses of detailed, specialized files. As a further drawback, the files that were assembled were external to the computer. There was no way to search for and assemble information to model business status or operations.

Even with the limited capabilities of card or tape storage systems, managers began to recognize, during the 1950s, that accumulations of data represented a major benefit of computer use. For example, transaction data could be processed to develop files that modeled the status of inventories. Development of computer-produced reports on inventory status might lag days, or even a week, behind the transactions from which data items were captured. Nonetheless, managers did recognize that information derived from computer systems could increase efficiency and reduce costs. By today's standards, efforts of the 1950s appear cumbersome. Since data files were external to processing-oriented systems, files had to be built, item-by-item before meaningful outputs could be generated.

The big breakthrough—one of the most important in the history of business computing—came with the introduction of random access disk storage. The first system to make files of data available for on-line processing through disk storage

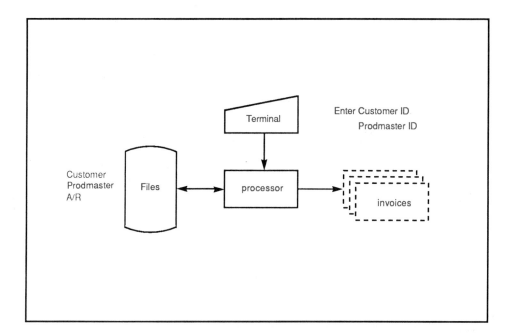

Random access

capabilities made it possible to integrate computer processing into business transactions.

was the IBM 305 RAMAC (for RAndoM ACcess). This device, which included a computer and a stack of rotating disks, could store, retrieve, process, and update records for files and programs with a capacity of up to 3.5 million characters of data. In 1959, this capacity seemed to provide an infinity of opportunity. Today, this is less than 10 percent of the storage capacity of some microcomputer systems with hard disks.

With the introduction of disk files, direct, on-line transaction processing on computers became possible. The RAMAC file housed multiple files, typically for customer and product information. Special programs were written that accessed multiple files separately in response to entries by the computer operator. The operator, for example, would enter a customer name or number from information received over the telephone or from written source documents. The computer would respond by finding the customer's record and entering the data on the heading of an invoice form. Then the operator would enter a product number and quantity sold. The computer would retrieve a description of the product and its price, and would calculate the value of each item sold. At the same time, inventory records would be updated. If an item was out of stock, a special message was generated.

Disk capabilities brought computers into the mainstream of company operations. Previously, computer processing and information reporting had taken place only after transactions were history. With the introduction of random access disk capabilities, it became possible to integrate computers directly into transaction processing operations. For example, a company that sold automotive parts to garages and service stations could have a computer terminal right on its service counter. As requests for items were received, computer entries were made. If a part was out of stock, information could be relayed to customers immediately. Computer information files were current within split seconds after transactions were completed.

In effect, the computer knew about the status of inventory items—and about the potential need for reordering supplies—before company managers did. Managers recognized the value of the information in these computer-maintained files. Accordingly, programs were developed to cause the computers to print out lists of inventory items with stock levels indicating a need to reorder. Also, reports were printed containing information on customers whose accounts were past due.

Reports of this type were derived through use of comparison capabilities of computers. For example, in inventory records, managers might set up a field for the stock level at which items should be reordered. When report programs were activated, these reorder levels were compared with values for stock on hand. If the values in the reorder fields were equal to or less than the inventory levels, items were included on the report directed to management. Records with stock-level conditions that differed from normal were identified as ***exception*** items. The reports were said to implement capabilities for ***management by exception.*** That is, managers could concentrate their attention on the exception items that represented perhaps 2 or 5 percent of inventory records. The computer made it unnecessary for managers to become involved in the 95 or 98 percent of items that fell into the range of normal conditions.

Systems that implemented capabilities for management by exception became known as ***management information systems (MIS).*** In turn, the advent of MIS reflected the fact that managers had recognized that the major value of computers had shifted from emphasis on processing speed to a reliance on the value of data maintained by computer systems with random access capabilities.

Transition From Files to Databases

On-line files changed the way managers thought about their computers. Files associated with management information systems came to be known as ***information resources.*** Information was recognized as being similar to other critical resources, such as money, equipment, buildings, and inventory. Further, with the advent of the information resources concept, there was an interest in developing the ability to relate records from different files. For example, payroll figures

The IBM 305 RAMAC

was the first computer to provide capabilities for building files of data and making them available for processing through disk storage.

could be used to help develop accurate information on manufacturing costs. Purchasing information on raw materials also could help management to compute and understand manufacturing costs.

Bringing together diverse sets of records to support analysis triggered a search for ways in which computers could coordinate the handling of files on multiple operations. The approach that emerged to meet this need was the construction of data models.

DATA MODELS

Once the potential for using data to model and predict behavior of organizations was discovered, computer use was ready for a new, expanding era. Computer professionals set out to design models that could be used to implement databases. Many methods evolved. These fall into three broad groups:

- Hierarchical
- Network
- Relational.

Within the scope of databases and their uses, a model is the method used to organize data items for storage and retrieval. You can think of the model as a foundation upon which a database is built. That is, the model organizes the data

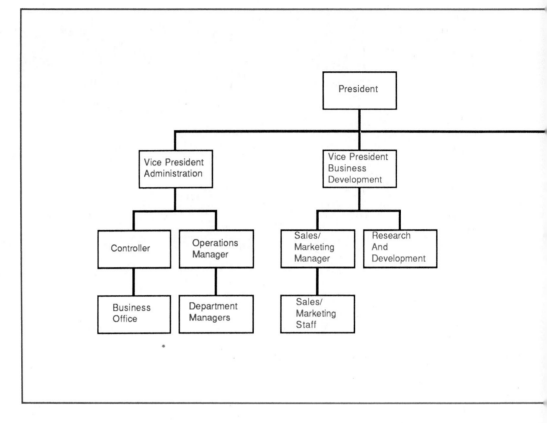

Figure 9-1.

An organization chart illustrates the hierarchy of responsibility and authority delegated by management to other key personnel.

logically, or according to needs of users. In turn, database software structures built on top of the model manage the use of data physically, according to instructions from users. The type of model used, in effect, establishes the character and usage patterns for a database.

Hierarchical Model

A **hierarchy** is an organizational model that applies control from the top downward. For example, a hierarchy exists in the structure for the assignment of responsibility and authority within a company. Such a structure typically is modeled through use of an **organization chart** like the one in Figure 9-1. As indicated, the chairman of the board of directors typically is at the highest level of an organization chart. This kind of illustration models the fact that the chairman is responsible for everything that happens in the company—and has authority to direct all actions and decisions on behalf of the company.

In a large organization, a single individual cannot cope with all of this responsibility and authority. So, authority and responsibility are assigned, or delegated, to persons at lower levels. The relationships between the top level and

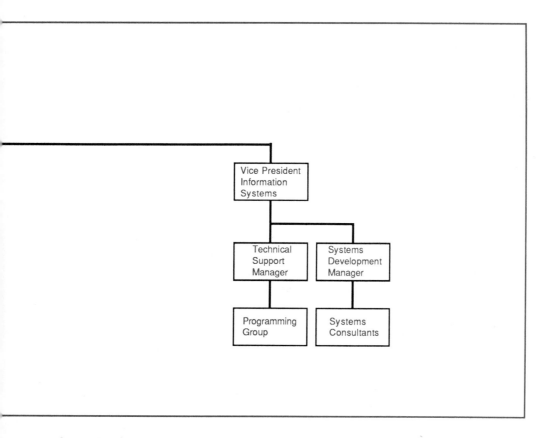

lower levels of an organization are shown by connecting lines that illustrate the assignment of responsibility and authority. People at the top of the organization delegate portions of their responsibility and authority to lower levels.

A **hierarchical data model,** diagrammed in Figure 9-2, follows the same principles as an organization chart. Data items are organized for storage and access on a top-down basis—in a number of levels. At the top level is a leading item that identifies a group of data records. Within a hierarchical model, the records are known as **nodes.** This term is borrowed from methods of describing communication networks. In a communication sense, a node is a point at which signals are received and relayed. Nodes within a hierarchical data model store data records and make them available.

The topmost unit of information is called a **root node.** The term, root, reflects the fact that a hierarchy also is called a **tree structure.** The source of the **branches** within a tree structure is a central point, or root. Branches, in turn, connect nodes at different levels with one another. High-level nodes are called **parents** and those at lower levels are identified as **children.**

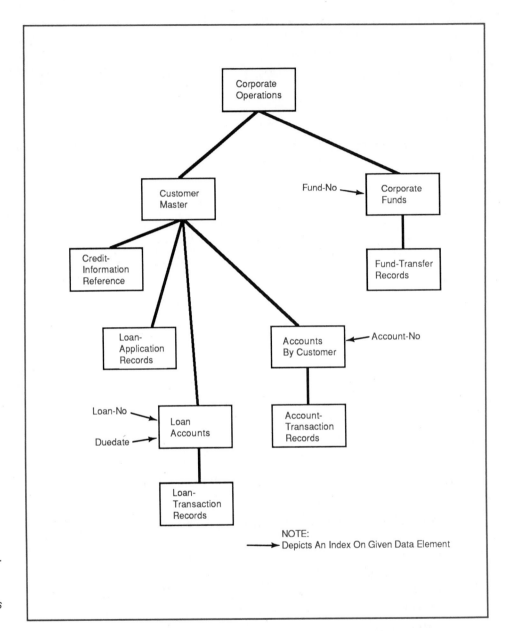

Figure 9-2.

Within hierarchical databases, data are organized into levels according to logical relationships among data elements.

Because connections between nodes are fixed by the modeling technique, access to information in a hierarchical model can be extremely rapid. However, relationships of data items are fixed and, therefore, hierarchical models tend to be inflexible as compared with other designs.

Hierarchical models are in wide use on mainframe database systems. This is partly because the hierarchical model was introduced first as database software was developed. Another factor, however, is that a hierarchical model tends to match the data structures within hierarchically organized companies.

Network Model

Network models were developed to meet the demands of users who wanted more flexibility than was available through single-entry methods of hierarchical models. Similar principles of data relationships apply for network and hierarchical models. However, as shown in Figure 9-3, a network model does not follow a tree structure. Instead, multiple relationships can exist among nodes at all levels. Also, it is possible to initiate inquiries at any point within a network-structured database.

Relational Model

As demands for database capabilities increased, special concerns arose among organizations that already had extensive information resources in files that supported individual applications. Users were not anxious to restructure all of their files to meet demands of hierarchical or network models. They preferred to find a way that would make it possible to work within the traditional file structures with which they already were familiar. The **relational model** was designed to meet the demands of this category of user. DBMS software built upon relational models also is the most popular approach in the design of database packages that run on microcomputers.

A relational model is made up of one or more traditional-type files that consist of records and fields. That is, each file in a relational database consists of a collection of records. Each record is structured in the same format, in terms of number and length of fields, as every other record. Files that make up a relational database often are described as **two-dimensional tables.** This means that a file can be represented as a series of columns and rows, as illustrated in Figure 9-4. In this format, columns represent fields and rows are records.

A set of two-dimensional files becomes a database because of capabilities that make it possible to cross-reference data items from multiple files. This means that it is possible to draw data items from multiple files. These items are organized into new files that are, in turn, used to generate transaction documents and/or

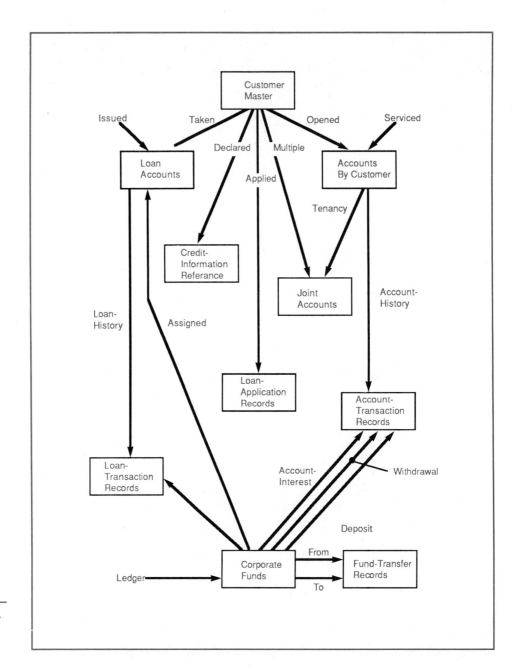

Figure 9-3.

The network model provides for
multiple, interlevel relationships
among database nodes.

PRODNO	PRODNAME	ONHAND	REORDER	COST	PRICE
12458	WIDGET	364	169	22.34	43.87
12459	WOOZIE	750	422	11.40	24.55
12460	WACKLE	452	208	32.19	62.31
12461	WINTOE	60	18	187.44	429.60
12462	WIFFIE	264	154	2.45	5.11

Figure 9-4.

Files can be represented as two-dimensional tables, or series of columns and rows.

reports. Cross-referencing is supported by sets of tables that index records within the files, as illustrated in Figure 9-5.

To use a relational database, the software refers first to one or more indexes that identify the needed item and its location. The software then directs the computer to the storage location for the needed record. In this way, DBMS packages that use relational models make it possible for users to have traditional files as well as database capabilities for storing and using multiple files for individual applications. To produce an invoice under a system supported by a database, for example, the computer gathers sets of records to form a working transaction file with invoicing data. At the same time, the computer prints transaction information onto an invoice document. Files within the database are updated as entries are processed.

Efficiency is enhanced by database techniques because indexing makes it possible to eliminate or minimize duplication of data items. When traditional systems development methods are used, as described in the previous chapter, data items tend to be duplicated within files for each application they support. Under database techniques, duplication of data items is not required because the indexes can find and use data items from any file within a relational database.

THE DATABASE MANAGEMENT SYSTEM

To create and apply a database, people use a series of software tools that make up a DBMS. For a microcomputer, these elements usually involve one or more diskettes from which the software is loaded and one or more manuals for instruction and reference. Before data can be entered, a format must be established on a data disk to accommodate its content. This means that, for each file, the user must think about and specify a **data structure.**

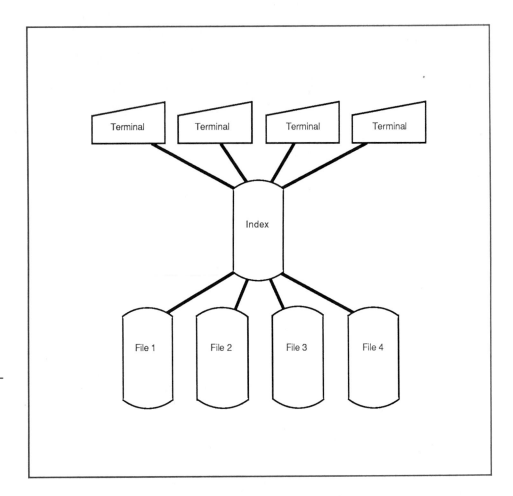

Figure 9-5.

A relational database includes an index file that cross references identifying fields within files. Under this organization scheme, data can be drawn from multiple files, by multiple users.

A data structure is a design of the format for records that make up a file. The user must name each field to be included in the record format. Other specifications needed for fields include width, type of data (numeric, character, date, etc.), number of decimal positions (for numeric fields only), and indication of whether each field is to be used as a record key. These dimensions of a data structure are described further and illustrated in the chapter that follows. Part of the process of data structure design includes identifying and minimizing **data redundancies,** or multiple occurrences of data items within files.

When a data structure has been designed, its specifications are entered into a special screen provided as a standard tool in virtually all microcomputer DBMS packages. Screens used for specification of file formats are illustrated elsewhere. These specification entries within a database create a format or layout known as a **schema.** The schema is recorded within the DBMS software as a basis for creating a framework for data storage and as a guide to data retrieval operations.

Logical and Physical Database Design

The schema represents the structure of data within a file from the "view" of the user. This means, in turn, that the schema describes data items as they relate to a model of the business. The schema is used, in turn, as a basis for designing and implementing data processing applications through use of database resources. Data organization schemes that reflect the user viewpoint are referred to as *logical data structures.* In this sense, logical organization conforms to usage patterns.

The schema also serves another key role. These organization specifications are used by other software elements within a DBMS to establish a *physical data structure.* The physical design that supports a database manages the storage areas on which data are recorded. Typically, a physical data structure determines where each element of data will be recorded on a disk file. Physical storage schemes are established and monitored automatically by DBMS software.

One purpose of a DBMS is to free the user from the need to worry about the allocation and maintenance of physical file facilities. By communicating with the system through a schema, the user is able to step back and concentrate upon designing and implementing applications that use computing power. There is no need for concern with the physical characteristics or storage schemes within computer system devices.

DBMS Functions and Capabilities

The DBMS package also provides screen formats to guide the entry of data and the completion of additions or changes to files. Beyond the "housekeeping" capabilities required to load data into and modify file content, a series of commands is needed to access and manipulate data. These access and manipulation capabilities are the real keys to use of databases as management tools. (Management applications of microcomputers are covered in Chapter 17.) Together, the commands that make possible the handling and retrieval of data are called a *query language.* Each DBMS package provides slightly different sets of query commands or varies the names given to these commands. For your guidance, however, the commands identified and described below form a generic set. Most of these capabilities will be available on most systems.

ENTER.   This function is used to load data into a file through entries to a format, or schema. When the schema is created, a blank file with no data content exists. The ENTER function then displays the established format and provides spaces for the keying in of entries. Each ENTER function creates a new record within the formatted file. Most systems are designed so that you have a chance to review entries before they are written to disk. At this point, accuracy should be checked. Any necessary changes can be made before the data are loaded into the file. On a signal from the operator, the entries are written to disk and become part of the database.

EDIT.   This function is used to change records that already are part of a file. The system displays all fields in a selected record. Changes can be recorded in separate entry areas. Any entered changes are substituted for the existing fields.

SORT.   This function arranges records within a single file in sequence. The SORT function operates upon one field in each record of an identified file. The program checks the values of this field and places the records in ascending order (lowest to highest; A to Z, 1 to 9) or descending order (highest to lowest; Z to A, 9 to 1). Sorting typically is used to arrange records in desired order for a report to management.

INDEX.   This function creates an index used to find records within a file. Each index contains a series of records used as a basis for finding records within database files. Index entries note a key field value and the physical location within a database file for each data record.

SELECT.   This command causes the system to review content of a file within a database. Field values are presented to the SELECT function. On the basis of these values, records are copied from an existing file into a new, working file that can be used for further processing. An example of a SELECT operation would be to search for and list all unpaid invoices with dates that were more than 90 days old. The SELECT function copies complete records, or rows, into a working file, leaving the existing file undisturbed.

PROJECT.   The PROJECT function is similar to SELECT, except that selection and copying are done for columns of data items, rather than rows. That is, the PROJECT function makes it possible to copy entire columns of data into a new, working file.

JOIN.   This function guides the creating of new, composite files. One or more columns from an identified file may be positioned side by side with one or more columns from a second file. A new, working file is created. The JOIN function can play a key role in use of databases for management analysis. For example, sales figures can be extracted from one file and associated with customer records from another.

UNION.   A UNION command is similar to a JOIN function, except that rows are combined, rather than columns. One or more rows from a file may be appended to one or more rows from another file. An example of the value of this function can be seen in the ability to combine customer identification information with records showing amounts owed by individual customers.

RETRIEVE. This command causes the system to read the content from a file stored on disk and display the data records on the microcomputer screen. This command is valuable for computer operators and managers who have to review the content of files stored under the control of a database.

PRINT. This command also causes the computer to read the content from a file. However, instead of being displayed on a screen, the records are printed on paper in a format that reflects the organization plan of the schema. That is, each record is printed as a row, with fields presented in a series of columns.

REPORT. This function also triggers the printing of content from one or more files within a database. The difference between the PRINT and REPORT functions is that REPORT makes it possible to select and format the outputs to conform to the needs of users. In other words, REPORT makes it possible to reorganize data, while PRINT simply reproduces the file format.

FOURTH-GENERATION LANGUAGES

As features are added to make data more accessible and easier to use, computers are said to become more **user friendly.** This term indicates that computers are adapted for use by nontechnical people, who need less guidance and direct help from computer specialists.

When a database has been implemented with a DBMS package, a logical next step is for users to develop their own processing systems. System development without traditional programming has been accomplished through extensions of DBMS software identified as **fourth-generation languages (4GL).** Recall that a DBMS usually has a query language, a set of commands for data access and for database maintenance. A query language can provide enough capability to implement systems directly, simply by executing a series of commands to organize and use data. Procedures can be developed under which keyboard entries create files, capture data, and create outputs that meet management needs. However, use of a query language requires human execution of the commands, in sequence. The idea works. But the process is much like using a hand-held calculator, rather than a programmed computer, to perform numeric processing. A program-controlled computer generally is more efficient.

A 4GL, in simple terms, provides an additional series of commands that automate execution of query commands. Under fourth-generation methods, sets of commands are linked to form a working program. The command set, in most instances, corresponds with common business applications. For example, a 4GL might provide a standard procedure, with menus and prompt screens, that can be used to build a file of transactions. Another 4GL function would make it possible for users to specify edit procedures that validate the content of transaction records. Still another feature would control the updating of master files through use of transaction files. Together, these procedures would automate file maintenance, eliminating the need to change records individually as transactions occur. Of course, 4GL methods also include functions that control the creation of displays and reports from databases.

With 4GL methods, which still are being developed and refined, it becomes possible to assemble complete systems around the content and capabilities of a DBMS. The need to design and write special programs, a requirement of third-generation methods, is sidestepped. The time required to create and implement a system is reduced drastically. A user's control of his or her information resources also is enhanced.

USING DATABASE AND 4GL SYSTEMS

The availability of a database and 4GL software changes the way data resources are viewed within a computer-using organization. Under a traditional file-oriented approach, data resources are assembled and organized to support each individual application. Under this outlook, data resources are regarded as requirements to support computer processing. Processing design and implementation are the keys to computer use.

Under a database-oriented view, the focus is upon assembling data that reflect the operations of an organization and the information needs of its management. Data are in place as established resources. Therefore, it is not necessary to create data files to support processing. Rather, 4GL methods can become a means of accessing and using existing resources.

When a database exists, it is not necessary to write detailed programs to access, process, and output data content. Rather, query language and 4GL commands can be used to collect, manipulate, and access data to meet dynamic information needs with flexible tools. Managers can extract and organize data on demand rather than having to pay for, then await development of, special programs.

Databases, in short, are tools that, by modeling operations and status, assist in the management of the organizations they represent. The chapter that follows presents dramatic examples of how database resources can be applied to the solution of problems and the management of organizations.

K E Y   T E R M S

database	tree structure	EDIT
database management system	branch	SORT
(DBMS)	parent	INDEX
transaction document	child	SELECT
exception	network model	PROJECT
management by exception	relational model	JOIN
management information system	two-dimensional table	UNION
(MIS)	data structure	RETRIEVE
information resources	data redundancy	PRINT
hierarchy	schema	REPORT
organization chart	logical data structure	user friendly
hierarchical data model	physical data structure	fourth-generation language (4GL)
node	query language	
root note	ENTER	

D E F I N I T I O N S

Instructions: On a separate sheet, define each term according to its use in this chapter.

1. exception

2. hierarchy

3. schema

4. management information system

5. node

6. data structure

7. query language

8. fourth-generation language (4GL)

T R U E / F A L S E

Instructions: For each statement, write T for true and F for false on a separate sheet.

1. An information model establishes a visual picture of an organization.

2. A database management system (DBMS) consists of a set of programs for building and using a database.

3. A data model represents the operation and status of an organization through use of information.

4. A database eliminates the need for application program packages.

5. A schema is a plan for the organization of data within a database.

6. Every application file requires a schema.

7. Data redundancy is necessary to keep track of information items within a database.

8. Most DBMS packages contain a set of query language commands for listing and displaying file contents according to applications requirements.

9. The term, tree structure, is used to describe a relational database.

10. Branches are used to link data within hierarchical databases.

11. In systems terminology, a relation is a three-dimensional table made up of columns, rows, and records.

12. A hierarchical data model resembles an organization chart for a company.

13. Under a database-oriented view, the focus is upon assembling data that reflect the operation of an organization and the information needs of its management.

14. Because connections between nodes are fixed by the modeling technique, access to information in a hierarchical model can be rather slow.

15. A fourth-generation language is designed to enable computers to understand and operate from human speech.

S H O R T   A N S W E R   Q U E S T I O N S

Instructions: On a separate sheet of paper, answer each question in one or two brief sentences.

1. How do business executives model a company's performance?

2. How did early computers handle data items?

3. The IBM 305 RAMAC was a major breakthrough in 1959. How much data was it capable of storing, and how does that capacity compare to today's capabilities?

4. What led to the development of the data model?

5. How does the type of model used establish the character and usage pattern for a database?

6. Give a short definition of a database.

R E S E A R C H   P R O J E C T

Think about the data items required by a school or college to keep track of students and their coursework. List and describe the data items needed for files on students, faculty, course offerings, and grades.

10 Solving Problems with Databases

ANALYZING REQUIREMENTS

Goals must be known and requirements defined before a database management system is initiated.

DEFINING APPLICATIONS

Before selecting any application package, determine and describe the data needed as output from the application.

CASE SCENARIO: MOM'S VIDEO MARKET

A scenario presents the creation of a database-oriented system for a video cassette rental business.

THE SYSTEM SPECIFICATION

To implement a new microcomputer system, there should be a clear, complete list of specifications that can be presented to prospective suppliers as a basis for proposals.

Problem Definition

A problem definition is a document that describes the results to be attained.

System Flow Description

A system flow description provides a simple, annotated system flowchart as a basis for translating the definition statement into a series of events and elements that provide the beginning of a computer solution.

Data Structure Definition

The data structure definition names each field within a record and identifies the types and number of characters to be included.

Input Description

The best way to specify inputs is to provide copies or layouts of source documents.

Processing Description

The processing description is a list of the processing functions that will be applied to file or input records to produce either updated files or outputs.

Output Description

Outputs are defined through samples of the displays or documents to be produced. Often, these are generated through use of a word processor.

Test Data

It is an accepted practice to provide a set of data to be processed as a means of determining whether a system will do the job for which it is intended. Test data should require execution of all input, processing, output, and storage functions of a system.

SPECIFICATION PREPARATION

To prepare a set of specifications, the users review their operations to gather all the information needed.

Information Needs

The amount of information needed by any system is the amount required to get the desired job done in the specified way.

Describing Inputs

The input documents for the video store scenario are identified; these documents determine the data items to be handled by the system.

Specifying Processing Requirements

The processing description identifies the links that must be established among files to generate desired outputs.

Defining Output Reports

The output description should be clear enough to serve as the basis for accepting a completed system; three reports are identified in the scenario as output requirements for the system.

Defining File Structures

All data items required by Mom's Video Market system are identified within three primary files.

A system specification is outlined that corresponds with the requirements of the video store scenario.

Once it has been designed and implemented, a system specification becomes a method for dealing with the potential suppliers of microcomputers and software.

ANALYZING REQUIREMENTS

In any field, tools should meet the requirements of the people who use them. A professional golfer, for example, uses tools—such as golf clubs and golf balls. Most professional golfers know exactly what equipment they need. They probably have a favorite brand of golf balls. They know whether they need right- or left-handed clubs. Further, they have special preferences for the length, weight, and flexibility of their clubs.

Golf clubs are tools for playing golf, just as computers and software packages are tools for doing business. A golfer's performance probably will suffer if he or she has to adapt to fit different equipment. Similarly, business performance may falter if established methods and procedures are changed to fit an inappropriate system or software package. This situation can be avoided, however, if requirements are defined *before* tools are purchased.

DEFINING APPLICATIONS

In developing applications for microcomputers, acquiring an existing software package usually is less costly and quicker than writing new programs. The software market has developed to a level that makes it possible to assume that a package is available for any information-handling task. The variety of packages is so

great that a major challenge for users lies in evaluating alternatives and selecting the features and/or packages that best meet their needs.

Making an informed purchase decision, then, requires analysis and evaluation of application requirements. By definition, the data resources that make up a database ***model*** the organization. Therefore, a good starting point for selecting application packages is to determine and describe the data needed to support applications.

If a database models an organization, data items are the building blocks with which the model is built. To model an organization with data, it is necessary to know how data are used by the organization. Decision makers need to answer questions that include:

- What type of decisions are to be made?
- What commitments must be made to maintain operations?
- What purchases will be required?
- What is to be sold?
- Who are the customers?
- How will performance be measured?

Collectively, the answers to these questions describe the information that will model the business and the processing that will support its activities. These answers are a basis for creating data resources and for manipulating them to produce desired results. In this case, the result desired initially is a functional information system.

The scenario that follows describes the creation of a database-oriented system for a video cassette rental business. For the sake of discussion, the business presented is in its pre-opening stages. Thus, the project begins with considerations of data and procedures. In reality, systems are installed in existing, functioning organizations; data and procedures considerations are dictated by those already in place.

At the end of this chapter, there is a table showing features and capabilities of a number of commercial database packages. A business manager might use a similar table to support the decision making process involved in purchasing an application package. For present purposes, the table is a logical extension of the application development scenario presented in this chapter. Effective microcomputer systems development projects often begin with definitions of requirements, followed by evaluations of the capabilities of available packages against those requirements.

CASE SCENARIO: MOM'S VIDEO MARKET

Chapter 7 presents a scenario about developing a word processing application for a video rental business, Mom's Video Market. In this chapter, you will see how the owner, Christine Beeman, started the video store with the development and acquisition of a *database management system (DBMS)* to support business operations.

Because Beeman's business started from scratch, no data resources existed. Beeman had little choice but to design and build files and applications before she opened the store. In other words, Beeman built data resources that modeled the business, and then used the specifications for that model to select a DBMS package.

Although system needs were defined before a purchase decision was made, Beeman knew that the package would be a database management system. Beeman felt that DBMS packages provide the capabilities to cross-reference files for application execution.

Beeman was confident that a commercial package existed that would meet her needs. She knew that defining system requirements provided a basis for evaluating packages, making the right purchase, then implementing a system that would provide the results she wanted. Following procedures set up with the help of information gleaned from management courses and from discussions with her accountant, Beeman set out to create a system specification. The plan would be to provide copies of the specification to prospective vendors and to buy the system that provided the best projected results.

THE SYSTEM SPECIFICATION: MOM'S VIDEO MARKET

Despite the fact that microcomputers are sold in thousands of stores, each system installed by every user usually is unique in some way. Thousands of combinations of hardware features can be configured, depending upon the make and/or model of computer, memory size, storage devices and capacities, monitors, keyboards, and other features. Thousands of additional options can be created through selection and implementation of software packages, or combinations of packages.

Beeman recalls being told that building a computer system has a lot in common with constructing a building. A modern building has certain standard parts and must meet structural codes. There must be a foundation, power, plumbing, and often standard clearances between floors and ceilings. To deal with contractors on building construction projects, specific plans and specifications are needed. To build a computer system, the user who really wants to solve problems or meet needs should prepare clear, complete specifications. These specifications should be documents that can be presented to prospective suppliers as a basis for proposals.

System specification documents can and do vary according to the values and working preferences of the people who prepare them. However, certain common denominators can be identified that should be spelled out as a preparation for developing any system. The elements and content of such a specification are outlined in the discussion below. These materials are geared specifically for guidance of prospective customers for microcomputer equipment that will use standard software packages. Elements of a *system specification* include:

- Problem definition
- System flow description
- Data structure definition
- Input description
- Processing description
- Output description
- Test data.

A complete system specification for the Mom's Video Market sales analysis system is presented near the end of this chapter in Figure 10-13. The presentations that follow begin by establishing the information requirements for preparation of a system specification. Then, a series of descriptions take you on a "walk-through" of the Mom's operations, during which information is gathered for the creation of a specification document.

Problem Definition

A **problem definition** is a description of results to be attained. The description should be complete enough to cover all expectations. Any constraints or special requirements also should be clarified.

For example, a restaurant operator trying to implement a payroll system might specify a necessity to meet government regulations on the reporting of tips and on-job meals consumed by servers.

In the video store example, the inventory control system might specify a requirement for detailed printouts, to be available immediately, to reflect exactly what tapes have been ordered from distributors. This list would be used to check in tapes as orders are received. Employees would be instructed not to sign for any items that were not ordered and delivered.

Each of these problems translates into different file, input, processing, and output requirements. The prospective user's responsibility is to state his or her business needs in terms that computer professionals can understand. Without this basis for communication, computer systems simply do not go together.

An effective problem definition statement presents these business requirements in a paragraph or two, perhaps up to one page. This definition statement then becomes a framework for the further detailing provided in the remaining parts of a system specification.

System Flow Description

This section of the specification provides a simple, annotated **system flowchart** as a basis for translating the definition statement into a series of events and elements that provide the beginning of a computer solution. To illustrate, Figure 10-1 is a system flowchart for the videotape receiving situation described above.

Data Structure Definition

The **data structure definition** identifies the types and numbers of characters to be included in all the fields that make up individual records. Each required

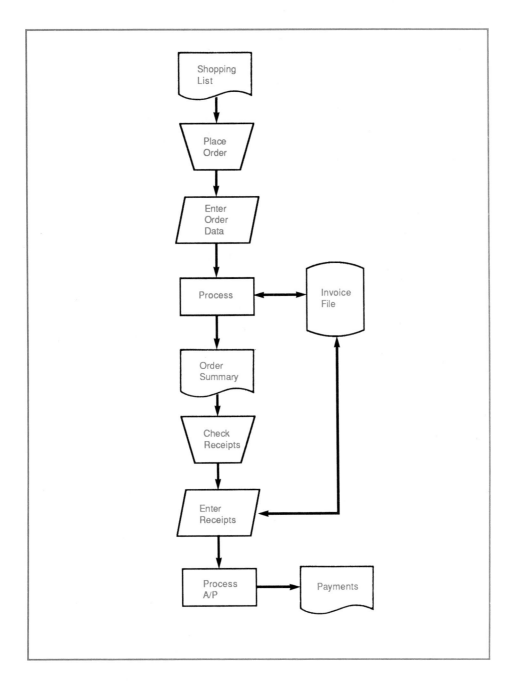

Figure 10-1.

A system flowchart describes the events and elements that make up the problem solution.

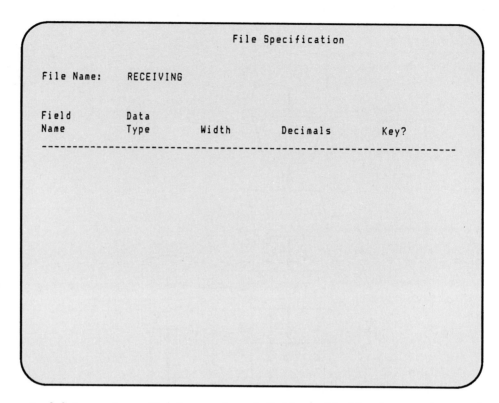

File Specification

File Name: RECEIVING

Field   Data
Name   Type   Width   Decimals   Key?

Figure 10-2.

A data definition table provides input fields for descriptions of the data elements that make up records. A format is established easily through a display created with a word processing package.

set of data can be outlined on a ***data definition table*** like the one shown in Figure 10-2.

A data definition table is prepared to identify each item, or field, in every set of data that will be needed to support the system. A simple way to complete data definitions is to set up a working form within a word processing program. In this way, entries can be made and modified as needs are reviewed.

In this illustration, a NAME field is assigned that identifies each data item uniquely. That is, no two data items can have the same name, though the same item may be used as a key in multiple files, as is demonstrated below in the Mom's case. Because of the abundance of available packages that run in a Disk Operating System (DOS) environment, Beeman applies naming standards that comply with this operating system. (Operating systems are discussed in Chapter 13.) Field names may contain up to eight characters or numbers and must start with a letter. Uppercase characters for the numeric keys may not be used. Specific instructions for naming fields should be included in the documentation for each package. At the specification stage, be aware that names must be short and that names must be unique within each record. Adjustments of format can be made later, when the system is implemented.

DATA TYPE entries establish processing controls. The user indicates whether each field contains character (C), number (N), date (D), or logic (L) entries. Character entries refer to alphanumeric data. If an N is entered, the field will contain only numbers, such as prices, with significant value. The system will apply calculations only to items within these fields. Date entries must be identified because special formatting controls are applied for these items. Typically, the format for a date entry is DD/DD/DD to indicate year, month, and day. A logic field is one used to implement a computer selection. Entries can be Y for yes and N for no. This type of entry can be used to control processing when data are accessed.

The *field width specification* establishes the number of data columns to be provided. These measures can be adjusted if necessary during implementation. At this point, providing field width information establishes the amount of storage capacity a record will require. For numeric fields, the number of DECIMAL PLACES is specified for formatting purposes. Many systems provide an entry type for dollar amounts, and automatically establish two decimal places for these fields.

Within every computer-processed file, at least one field per record must be identified as the *key,* the item that identifies the record uniquely and separately from all others. As an example, a social security number often is used in files with records on people. For inventory files, product number often is the key. Some systems allow the use of multiple record keys; others permit only one. This is why it is a good idea to identify the number of keys needed at an early point.

To complete a data structure definition, the prospective user simply lists each data item in a record to be created and describes its format. This format structure then will be recorded in a blank file by the computer. The user can call upon this format to load data into a file in preparation for using an application. As an example, Figure 10-3 shows a format that could be created for a receiving record at a videotape store. Along with identification of data items and their characteristics, a specification also should estimate the number of records to be included in each file. This is an important factor in evaluating software packages and in specifying hardware.

Input Description

The best way to specify inputs is to provide copies or layouts of source documents. In the above example, the source documents might be standard order forms, copies of vendor invoices, and the receiving report. Other source documents that might be used to specify input for Mom's include copies of the rental agreements used in the store, copies of bank charge slips, and copies of membership card applications.

```
                              File Specification



        File name:  RECEIVING



        Field        Data

        Name         Type      Width        Decimals       Key?

        ------------------------------------------------------------------


        Vendor       C          15            0             Y

        RecDate      N           6            0             N

        ItemNo       C           5            0             Y

        Title        C          15            0             Y

        Qty          N           3            0             N

        Unitprice    N           5            2             N

        Extension    N           6            2             N
```

Figure 10-3.

It is a good practice to print copies of file specifications and to review them with users. This specification represents a typical printout.

Processing Description

In simple terms, the user should list the processing functions that will be applied to file or input records to produce either updated files or outputs. To determine the price for an ordered item, for example, the user simply might indicate:

$$COST = UNPRICE * QTY$$

Assume that the fields described in the above statement (COST, UNPRICE, and QTY) have been specified and created. This statement presents a processing requirement: Multiply unit price by quantity to derive a purchase cost.

Output Description

Outputs are defined most readily by using a word processor. Reports and other outputs can be laid out on screen or report layouts can be printed. Both methods depict formats for presenting information on output documents. These methods are discussed later in this chapter.

Test Data

The purpose of a system specification is to provide the basis for accepting the best proposal for a system. It is accepted practice to provide a set of data to be processed as a means of determining whether the system will do the job for which it is intended.

For this purpose, a set of **test data** can be assembled that exercises a full range of input, processing, output, and storage capabilities for the system. The test data also should contain erroneous and/or unacceptable items. The idea is to present both valid and invalid data items. If the test data set is designed properly, the valid transactions will test a system to its full capabilities and the invalid items will make sure that the system can deal with entries that require rejection.

To illustrate, suppose a system specifies a set of product numbers ranging from 100 through 999. Transactions would be presented with item values of 99, 100, 999, and 1,000. In this way, the data provide a means for discovering whether the system can handle its full range of specified values and also whether it can deal with and recover from presentation of invalid data items.

SPECIFICATION PREPARATION: MOM'S VIDEO MARKET

To prepare a set of specifications, the user reviews his or her operations to gather information needed. The narratives that follow trace Beeman's activities in gathering information to be incorporated in a system specification for Mom's Video Market.

Information Needs

A business is shaped by management decisions. Management decides what kinds of transactions are to be conducted with what portion of the market. For example, Beeman knows that most of the transactions for her business will be rentals. Therefore, her system definition activities begin with another question:

What is needed, in terms of data, to execute a rental transaction?

To execute a rental transaction, an organization needs a product, a customer, a rental agreement, a payment, and a **deposit.** A deposit refers to secured value for the product during the rental period. In the event the product is lost or destroyed by the customer, the renting organization retains the deposit in exchange. As a convenience to customers, most rental businesses accept credit card charges for deposits. Customers simply sign a credit card voucher for the secured value. This voucher is destroyed if terms of the rental agreement are met satisfactorily.

One of Beeman's first concerns, then, involves customers. Accepting credit cards is a method for securing deposits and also a convenience to customers. Customers who use credit cards do not have to make cash deposits. Beeman also wishes to encourage return business. She implements a membership system under which customers who purchase annual memberships are entitled to discounts on all sales and rentals. As a further service, a security agreement (including a signed credit card voucher) eliminates the need to fill out and sign credit card vouchers for each rental. Once a membership agreement is on file, customers need only present their membership card and sign a rental agreement to rent cassettes. Members also will be entitled to receive a monthly newsletter and to make reservations for certain video cassettes over the telephone.

The basic transaction, then, goes as follows: a customer makes a deposit and signs a rental agreement. Mom's collects a rental fee and agrees to hold the deposit for a specific period in exchange for use of the video cassette.

In any business information system transactions are represented by data. The answer to the above question provides a starting point for describing system specifications.

Describing Inputs

In Beeman's system, the initial creation of transaction data is performed on rental agreements. These documents will contain source data from which will stem file creation, update execution, and report generation procedures. That is, data from rental agreements will be found in master files, transaction entries to files, and activity reports. To meet requirements, then, an application package must be able to accept and handle data items described on these documents without error. A sample rental agreement is illustrated in Figure 10-4.

Other inputs come from membership applications filled out by customers and from charge slips for bank credit cards. The bank charge slip is a standard form. An example of a membership application is provided in Figure 10-5.

In general, DBMS packages provide two types of input procedures: **menu-driven** and **command-driven.** Users interact with menu-driven packages through menus. Lists of processing choices are displayed and users simply make selections to direct processing. In command-driven packages, users must learn a set of commands to direct processing.

MOM's Video Market

9624 Gresham Blvd
Los Angeles, CA 90028

VIDEO HOME PREVIEW AGREEMENT

NAME_____CUSTOMER NO._____
ADDRESS_____
CITY_____STATE_____ZIP_____
PHONE_____
CREDIT CARD #_____DEPOSIT_____

PRODUCT NO.　　　　　　　TITLE　　　　　　　　PRICE
_____　　_____　　_____
_____　　_____　　_____
_____　　_____　　_____
_____　　_____　　_____
　　　　　　　　　　　　　　　　TOTAL_____

I, the undersigned, do hereby accept the above listed vedeotape(s) for the purpose of viewing same in my home, and acknowledge that they are in good working condition. I authorize MOM's Video Market to charge the full retail purchase price of the above videotape(s) if they are not returned within seven (7) days by submitting a sales draft against my credit card account and authorizing its payment without my signature. After payment, the videotape(s) become my property. I also authorize MOM's Video Market to charge my credit card account for damage and late fees of said videotape(s). By signing this draft, I agree to its terms.

It is understood that FEDERAL LAW PROHIBITS THE REPRODUCTION OF ALL COPYRIGHTED VIDEOTAPES.

RENT DATE_____DUE DATE_____

SIGNATURE_____

Figure 10-4.

A rental agreement contains data items that describe a rental transaction. The document is designed for ease of reference for data capture on the store's microcomputer.

At this point, input procedures need not be specified in terms of command-driven or menu-driven. What is stated, however, is a quantitative criterion for ease of use. Input procedures must be easy enough for qualified employees to master in two days or less.

Notice that the solution is beginning to take shape. The rental agreement and other source documents determine data items that must be handled by the system.

Specifying Processing Requirements

The processing specifications for this system refer to the relationships, or links, that must be established among files to produce desired outputs. In addition, processing involves specific functions through which outputs are produced. A

MOM's Video Market

MEMBERSHIP APPLICATION

Lifetime ☐   1 Year ☐

NAME_____

ADDRESS_____

CITY_____ZIP_____

PHONE_____

SOCIAL SECURITY #_____

BANK_____

VISA#_____

MC #_____

AE #_____

EMPLOYER_____

ADDRESS_____PHONE_____

RULES

Tapes are to be paid for when they are rented.

Do not leave your tapes on the counter unattended.

Tapes not rewound will be 50 cents each.

New movies are to be returned by 7:00 p.m. on the day specified in the rental agreement, older movies by 8:00 p.m. EXCEPTION: when rented on Sunday, tapes are due before 6:00 p.m. Tuesday.

If tapes are returned after these times on the day they are due a $1.00 charge will be paid on each tape.

Any tape brought in after closing on the day that it is due is considered one day late!

SIGNATURE_____

Figure 10-5.

A membership application contains data items that will be input to a customer identification master file.

package must provide these functions and be capable of establishing specified links.

As an example, for member customers, rental agreements identify customers only by customer number. Once customer identification files (discussed below) are in place, there must be some way to obtain addresses, phone numbers, and/or credit information to support rental transactions. However, having customers, especially members, write in identification information on every rental agreement would be inconvenient and inefficient.

A backorder report requires specialized capabilities for handling date fields. The system will need an internal calendar. Then, date entries can be compared with current date, and a message displayed if discrepancies occur. Most packages provide this capability. For the package Beeman will ultimately select, this capability is mandatory.

In addition, the business in this scenario presents special requirements for handling video cassette titles. Beeman knows that the product file in her system will be extensive—consisting, perhaps, of several thousand records. To include titles within each record would require a great deal of storage space. For most processing tasks, a product number identifies video cassettes sufficiently. Thus, Beeman wants to create an **index** file of product titles and numbers. Most of the needs for product titles will come in response to customer inquiries. With an index in place, clerks can search according to index files.

The index file, however, must be related to the product file. Suppose additional copies of a specific title are needed. The product number applies only to Beeman's system; a vendor probably accepts orders based upon title. Thus, a purchasing clerk must be able to relate product number to title and vice versa. Finally, a clerk could not be expected to call a customer with an overdue rental and inquire about tape number T3242-04. There must be some capability to interrelate and cross-reference files.

Note, incidentally, that the review of processing definitions involves identification of file requirements. This is to be expected, since much of the data content to be processed comes from stored files. Under Beeman's approach, she has elected to track input, processing, and output requirements and to identify file structures later, just prior to preparation of the specification document.

Defining Output Reports

Beeman has figured that an average cost for video cassettes is $30. The investment recovery time for a cassette, in her estimate, is 15 rentals. That is, Beeman receives an average of $2 each time a cassette is rented, and after 15 rentals, the average purchase cost is recovered. Accordingly, Beeman wants a report that identifies titles that are not moving fast enough to recover their costs. Her goal is to produce a report, monthly, that lists all titles that have not rented more than 15 times in the past three months.

Slow mover report.   Beeman has estimated the recovery rate on cassettes for several reasons. A formula based on the recovery rate will be applied at the end of each reporting period to activity entries within the activity field labeled PREVPER, for previous period, in the product master file. The slow mover report will be generated by applying to this field the formula:

PREVPER < 16

This report indicates which cassettes are not paying for themselves in three months or less. These cassettes will be the first to be discounted or removed if

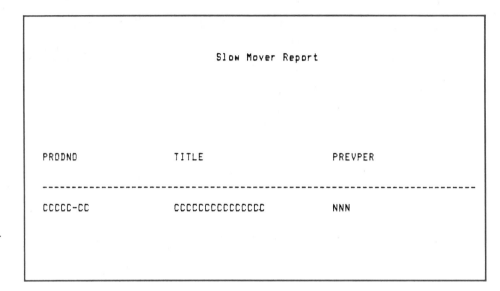

```
                            Slow Mover Report




        PRODNO                 TITLE                     PREVPER

        ------------------------------------------------------------------

        CCCCC-CC               CCCCCCCCCCCCCCC            NNN
```

Figure 10-6.

Producing a layout for output reports, such as the slow mover report illustrated here, provides a basis for identifying, formatting, and building storage files.

shelf space is needed. Figure 10-6 provides a copy of the format for the SLOW MOVERS report. At this point, the format and content of this and other reports only reflect Beeman's preliminary ideas for output requirements.

Backorder report.   Beeman also wants to design a mechanism for maintaining waiting lists and for reserving cassettes. What is needed is a report of out-of-stock situations. An out-of-stock situation occurs when a customer requests a tape for which all copies are rented. When this situation occurs, the customer is asked whether he or she wants to be put on a waiting list. For members, this service is available for telephone requests.

In this system, the waiting list is to take the form of the backorder report file. This file is simply a collection of product numbers and customer numbers. The customer number field repeats for every customer who requests a specific tape. For each cassette, represented by product number, customer numbers are maintained sequentially. Entry sequence, therefore, will reflect the sequence in which requests are received.

The backorder file, in effect, is a list of customers waiting for specific tapes. Then, when these tapes become available—having been returned from previous rentals—customers on the waiting list are notified by telephone. Record sequences in this file reflect the order of requests. In this way, distribution of back-ordered tapes is on a ''first come, first served'' basis.

The backorder file also is used for entry of reservations made by members. If a reservation is made for a cassette, the backorder file is browsed. If a back-order record exists for a requested title, the customer's identification number is

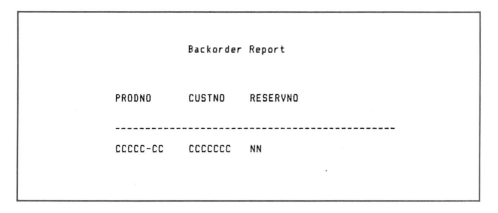

```
                    Backorder Report


        PRODNO        CUSTNO     RESERVNO

        ---------------------------------------------

        CCCCC-CC      CCCCCCC    NN
```

Figure 10-7.

The backorder report includes customer numbers and product numbers for handling reservations or out-of-stock situations.

entered at the next available position. As requests are filled, customers move up the list. The customer whose number appears first in the record, then, is given first privilege to rent the tape he or she requests.

Beeman has two options for implementing this application: She may provide terminals for clerks, who then can search the file in main memory. Or, the backorder file can be printed daily.

In addition, Beeman wants to set up an exception reporting routine for tapes with heavy demand. The exception report is to be triggered by four (or more) out-of-stock listings for one tape in a single week. Beeman will use these reports to support decision making involving the purchase of additional copies.

To produce this exception report, the system must be capable of maintaining a count of the number of records in the backorder file. Beeman would prefer a DBMS package that provides a built-in feature for counting records in files. As an alternative, a record count may be achieved with most packages by establishing a separate field for record number—and comparing values in that field with given parameters (dates) through a SELECT operation.

Based on the requirements discussed above, Beeman designs a rough format for the BACKORDER report, shown in Figure 10-7.

Overdue report. Another reporting requirement involves cassettes that have not been returned by due dates specified in rental agreements. In effect, a report is needed to identify transactions that are deviating from terms specified in rental agreements. This report is needed for two reasons:

- Customers who hold cassettes longer than the time for which they have paid are liable for additional charges.

- After a certain grace period, specified in rental agreements, customers who still have not returned cassettes may forfeit deposits.

```
                           Overdue Report


     PRODNO      TITLE                  DUEDATE           CUSTNO

     -----------------------------------------------------------

     CCCCC-CC    CCCCCCCCCCCCC          NN/NN/NN          CCCCCCC


                 CUSTNAME               ADDRESS           PHONE

                 CCCCCCCCCCCCCCCCCCC    CCCCCCCCCCCCCC    CCC-CCCC
```

Figure 10-8.

Data included on overdue reports identify customers who are late in returning rented cassettes.

The rental agreement is to be represented by data items within the rental file. A field representing due dates for rentals will specify end of rental periods. The overdue report, then, will consist of records in which the DUEDATE field is less than the current date. To produce the report, a SELECT operation may be executed. A command might be entered in a form similar to the one below.

SELECT DUEDATE < (User enters current date)

Executing this command creates a separate file, consisting of the customer number, product number, rental charge paid, and due date of overdue rentals. This file supports procedures that Beeman has developed for contacting customers holding overdue cassettes. For example, the OVERDUE file can be cross-referenced with the customer file, specifically to access customer addresses and telephone numbers. Then, letters or telephone calls can be directed to these customers before deposits are forfeited.

Beeman outlines the format and content of the OVERDUE report, as shown in Figure 10-8.

Defining File Structures

Between the requirements that have been stipulated for outputs and inputs, Beeman feels she is ready to prepare specifications for the files to be created. Working on the files in this way, she feels, gives her a chance to monitor the incidence of repetition of data elements. She keeps in mind that she wants to eliminate redundant occurrences of non-key items within her database.

Customer file. Beeman already has established some key requirements for the customer file. She will need to be able to distinguish between three categories of customers: members, non-members, and non-members on file. Members pay an annual fee in exchange for discounts and special services. A non-member on file has not paid a membership fee, but signs a credit agreement to make rental procedures convenient. Non-member records are maintained as a measure of business performance and for analyzing customer purchase patterns.

Categories of customer records are to be indicated by entries (MEM, NON, NMF) within a record field labeled STAT for status. Other fields are to be included for a customer number, customer name, address, telephone number, a credit card number, a credit card expiration date, a membership expiration date, and two activity fields. The customer file is to be referenced by two key fields, the customer number and customer name. Customer numbers are derived from the first letter of the last name and the fifth through tenth characters of the credit card number.

Activity fields are included to provide a measure of customer activity. The first activity field is to hold data representing the number of rentals by customers during the current year. The second activity field represents the number of rentals by customers during the previous year. A data definition table for this file is presented in Figure 10-9.

To execute a rental transaction, however, additional data are needed. Beeman's interest in the transaction involves the video cassette. Data are needed that reflect the video cassettes that are to be rented and/or sold. These data will make up the product file.

Product file. To execute the rental transaction, a customer file (specified above) represents the renter's part in the transaction. That is, Beeman has defined the data items that are to represent needed customer records. She now must do the same for the products to be rented.

To specify the product file, Beeman first needs to identify products, or video cassettes. The product file will be referenced by product number. The product number is to consist of seven alphanumeric characters. The first character is a designation of the market segment toward which the tape is targeted. The first character classifies tapes into categories such as: humor, kids, drama, thrillers, classics, fitness, and adult. (See Figure 10-10.)

The last two characters of the product number reflect a copy number for the specific title. That is, product number T3242-04 is the fourth copy of a particular cassette. Beeman knows that, for many popular titles, several copies are needed.

```
                 -------------------------------------
                  |      Setting File Attributes     |File: CUSTOMER.DB
                 -------------------------------------
        Field     Type   Width   Dec's  Key   Cross Reference
        Name      C/N/L  1-20    0-4    Y/N

   1    CUSTNO    C        7             Y
   2    STAT      C        3             N
   3    EXPDATE   N        6       0     N
   4    CUSTNAME  C       15             Y
   5    ADDRESS   C       15             N
   6    PHONE     C        7             N
   7    CRCARD    C       16             N
   8    CCXDATE   N        6       0     N
   9    CURRPER   N        3       0     N
  10    PREVPER   N        3       0     N
  11
  12
  13

        ESC to create file and return to Database Main Menu
        UP/DOWN/RIGHT cursor keys to modify entries
        Press RETURN after data entries
        INS/DEL to insert/delete whole lines
```

Figure 10-9.

The customer master file includes fields for customer status (STAT), as well as two activity fields, current year (CURRPER) and previous year (PREVPER).

Figure 10-10.

The product number in this scenario includes a copy number and a category designation for each item.

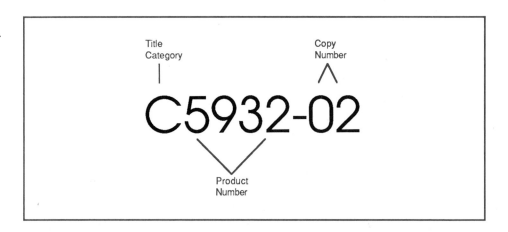

The file specification for the product file is shown in Figure 10-11. This file contains two activity fields, designated as current period (CURRPER) and previous period (PREVPER). Beeman wants to monitor closely the "movement" of video cassettes and will establish a three-month reporting period for products. Reports and reporting procedures for product activity are discussed later in this chapter.

```
          --------------------------------------
          :          Setting File Attributes     :File: PRODUCT.DB
          --------------------------------------
     Field       Type   Width   Dec's   Key   Cross Reference
     Name        C/N/L  1-20    0-4     Y/N

 1   PRODNO      C        7              Y
 2   TITLE       C       15              Y
 3   CURRPER     N        3       0      N
 4   PREVPER     N        3       0      N
 5   PRODCOST    N        5       2      N
 6   RENTCHRG    N        4       2      N
 7
 8
 9
10
11
12
13
     ESC to create file and return to Database Main Menu
     UP/DOWN/RIGHT cursor keys to modify entries
     Press RETURN after data entries
     INS/DEL to insert/delete whole lines
```

Figure 10-11.

Specifications for the Product file include both descriptions and activity summaries.

The product file described here and the customer file described earlier represent sources for transaction processing information. In addition, Beeman determines that she needs access to information about tapes currently being rented.

Rental file. To this point, system definition activities have focused upon file requirements for executing rental transactions. In effect, the product and customer files represent the parties and products involved in this type of exchange. Data representation of transactions also must include exchange value. In this system, the exchange value of rentals is reflected in a set of records that make up a rental file.

The rental file, in this case, is similar in purpose to the accounts receivable file discussed in an earlier chapter. Recall that an accounts receivable file was created for the Big Time, Inc., scenario. An account receivable is a representation of money owed to a selling organization. In most businesses, delivery is separate from payment. In this case, delivery and payment are simultaneous, but transactions are not completed until rented products have been returned. Thus, the rental file in this system contains data that represent deposits until cassettes are returned.

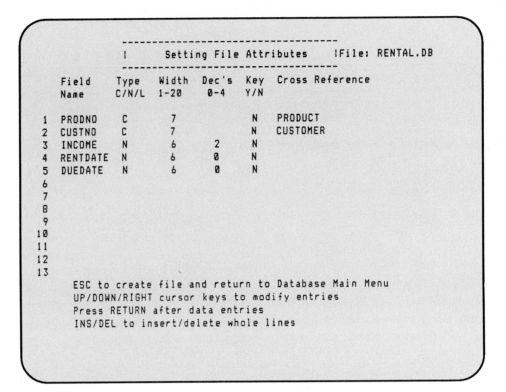

```
                    ---------------------------------------------
                    !    Setting File Attributes    !File: RENTAL.DB
                    ---------------------------------------------
         Field      Type   Width   Dec's   Key   Cross Reference
         Name       C/N/L  1-20    0-4     Y/N

    1    PRODNO     C        7              N     PRODUCT
    2    CUSTNO     C        7              N     CUSTOMER
    3    INCOME     N        6       2      N
    4    RENTDATE   N        6       0      N
    5    DUEDATE    N        6       0      N
    6
    7
    8
    9
   10
   11
   12
   13
         ESC to create file and return to Database Main Menu
         UP/DOWN/RIGHT cursor keys to modify entries
         Press RETURN after data entries
         INS/DEL to insert/delete whole lines
```

Figure 10-12.

Records within the Rental file record contract and revenue information. Entries are validated through reference to master files for product number and customer number fields.

The rental file is a collection of dynamic records. The purpose of this file is to create a temporary record of income from the transaction and the exchange value (deposit for cassette) until the transaction is completed. In this system, the rental file is to be based upon data from source documents—rental agreements—created manually by clerks. Beeman's decision to create these documents manually, rather than through interactive computerized techniques, stems from the requirement for customer signature. In addition, for two of three customer categories, clerks need not write addresses and other identifying information. A customer number serves as a sufficient identifier.

Beeman designs rental agreement forms with detachable portions, or stubs, at the bottom. These stubs will be retained by customers as deposit receipts. The same receipts will be returned with cassettes and used as input for updating the rental file.

The customer number and product number for each tape is written on the deposit receipt. Upon completion of rental agreements, these data items are used to locate the appropriate record within the rental file. Those records then are deleted.

The rental file is to be set up with PRODNO and CUSTNO fields. Both fields will be used to access the rental file during various posting and reporting operations. Other fields within the file include the cost of the rental (INCOME), the rental date (RENTDATE), and the return date (DUEDATE). The data definition table for the rental file is presented in Figure 10-12.

At this point in the scenario, Beeman has established the requirements for her system. Once a package is purchased, system implementation involves creating files and entering data. In making the purchase decision, Beeman considers many packages. The evaluation of multiple packages should be simplified by the system specification she will produce. Bringing together the information she has gathered, Beeman prepares the system specification shown in Figure 10-13.

THE MOM'S SPECIFICATION

A system specification should stand on its own and speak for itself. However, in carrying forward the Mom's case, a few elements of the accompanying specification should be noted.

In the problem statement, notice the references to specific time periods and dollar amounts. These details are needed to determine whether an installed system actually meets requirements. Beeman makes it clear that she intends for the system to pay for itself through operating efficiencies. The ability of employees to master the system quickly is important, as is the working time to be devoted to the system. Since these will affect her decision on whether to buy a system and which system to buy, it is important to communicate these guidelines to prospective vendors.

The flowchart communicates the processing sequence clearly. To interpret the content of the flowchart, refer to Figure 10-14, which contains a set of flowcharting symbols and identifies their meanings. As an alternative, a step-by-step description of processing and control steps could have been provided. Flowcharting, however, is a widely accepted method of computer systems documentation and design.

Note that the information media gathered in Beeman's survey can be used, directly, as part of the system specification. The specification indicates that input source documents and file definition tables are attached as references for use with the specification.

The output section indicates a desire to produce control break reports. A control break occurs when the system recognizes a change in keys as it processes a sequence of records. When a key value changes, the system prints a subtotal for all records that have been identified by the same key.

The subtotals within control break reports can be valuable. For example, suppose Beeman decides to produce a report on revenue from rentals. She would like to have figures on revenue for each title and for the store as a whole. To do this, she would sort the product file by product number. The system then could be instructed to use the product number as a control break. In this way, after the last record for a title is listed, the system would print a subtotal. The finished

System Specification

System I.D.. Mom's Video Market--Sales Analysis

Designer: C. Beeman

Problem Definition Statement

Devise a system that can run on an inexpensive microcomputer to accept data from transaction documents as source inputs, and to provide outputs that report rental activity for individual video cassettes, status of customer rentals, and establish waiting lists to handle backorders and reservations.

This application is to be implemented on a microcomputer system not to exceed $6,000.

The final system should be simple enough to use so that any qualified employee can master its operation in two working days or less.

It should be possible to handle all updating and output operations in four working hours per day or less.

The system should pay for itself through benefits to the business in nine months or less and should have an operational life of two years before major revisions are required.

System Flow Description

The attached flowchart summarizes the flow of information and control through the proposed system.

Data Structure Definition

The attached data definition tables represent the content of three master files to be included in the initial implementation of the system. [See Figures 10-9, 10-11, and 10-12.]

In addition, the DBMS software must be able to establish a directory, or index, to control references to all files. The system should have the capability to extract content from multiple files to support a single transaction processing application.

Customer file must accommodate 1,400 records. Product file must have room for 2,000 records. Rental file must accommodate 500 records.

Figure 10-13.

Page 2 of 3.

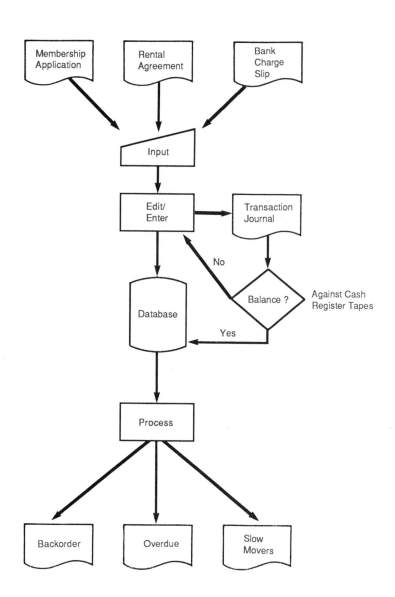

304

Input Description
Inputs will be derived from rental agreements, membership applications, and bank credit card transaction slips. Copies of these documents are attached. [See Figures 10-4 and 10-5.]

Processing Description
Requirements include:

* System must be capable of inserting current dates into transactions.
* Software must support on-line updating of files to reflect transactions.
* Query language command requirements include SELECT, PROJECT, UNION, JOIN, PRINT, DISPLAY, SORT, COMPUTE, and REPORT.
* The DBMS must support creation, addition, modification, and deletion of records.
* The capability to modify formats of existing file structures is highly desirable.

Output Description
Report formatting capabilities should include ability to specify two levels of titles and two levels of column headings. Report should be capable of presenting up to two levels of control breaks, plus grand totals.

Test Data
Test data will be provided on a series of about 12 each of the three types of transaction documents described above. The documents will contain an assortment of valid and invalid data items. Valid items will have values at the upper and lower limits of the record formats involved. The system will be expected to accept or reject entries on an interactive basis, both for the creation of files and for the posting of transaction data to existing files.

Figure 10-13.
_____

Page 3 of 3.

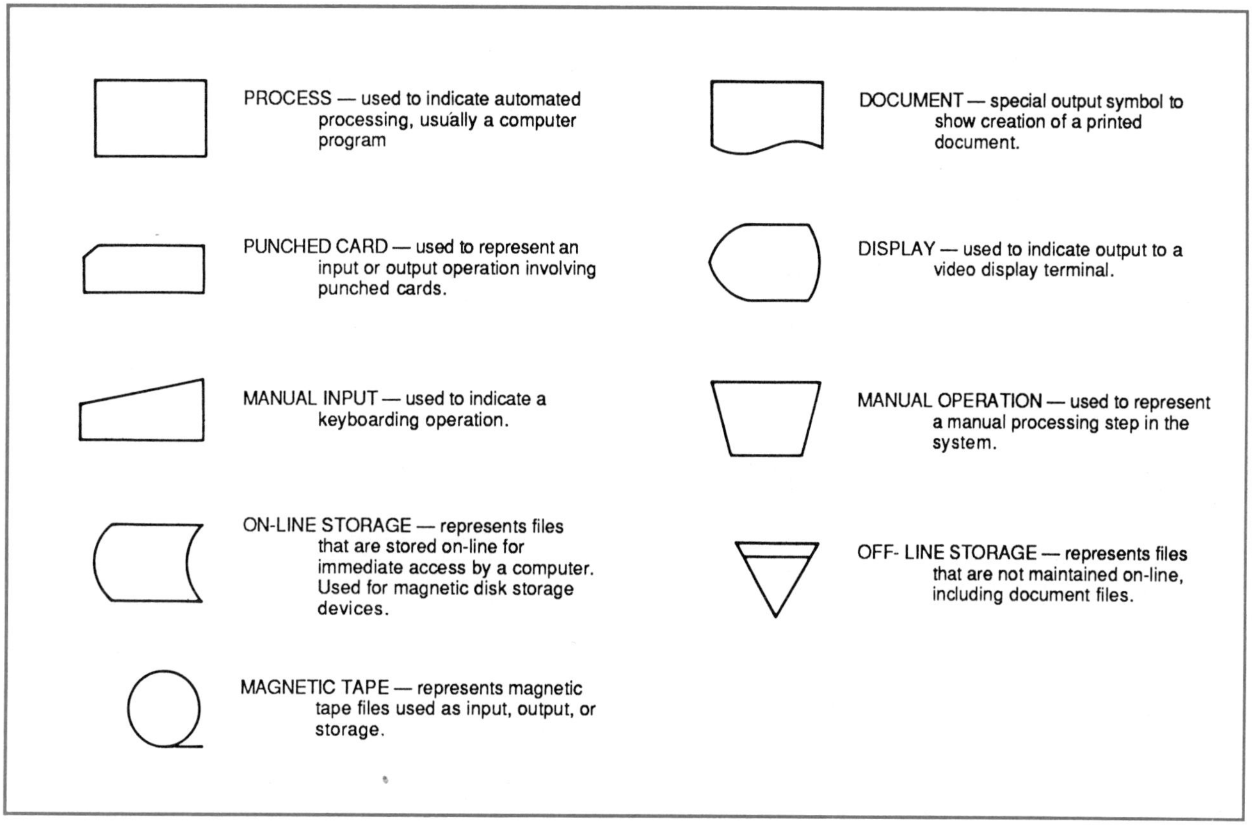

PROCESS — used to indicate automated processing, usually a computer program

DOCUMENT — special output symbol to show creation of a printed document.

PUNCHED CARD — used to represent an input or output operation involving punched cards.

DISPLAY — used to indicate output to a video display terminal.

MANUAL INPUT — used to indicate a keyboarding operation.

MANUAL OPERATION — used to represent a manual processing step in the system.

ON-LINE STORAGE — represents files that are stored on-line for immediate access by a computer. Used for magnetic disk storage devices.

OFF- LINE STORAGE — represents files that are not maintained on-line, including document files.

MAGNETIC TAPE — represents magnetic tape files used as input, output, or storage.

report would show numbers of rentals and revenues for each title and for the company as a whole.

Figure 10-14.

Flowcharts use a limited number of graphic symbols to represent information handling functions.

USING THE SYSTEM SPECIFICATION

A completed system specification becomes a method for dealing with the marketplace. Just as important, preparation of the specification has provided the discipline necessary to help Beeman focus clearly on the needs of her own business and on the management methods that are most appropriate for achieving her goals.

To enter the marketplace for a satisfactory computer system, Beeman would distribute copies of the specifications to qualified computer stores, systems integration specialists, consultants, microcomputer maintenance organizations, and others who might be able to meet her needs. She can specify deadlines for receipt of proposals from these vendors. Then she can use her own specifications and test data to find out which combination of hardware, software, and procedures does her job best.

	DBASE III	PC FOCUS	PFS FILE	R:BASE 5000	TIM IV
Version Number	1.1	1.0	B.00	1.0	4.02
Relational: (Fully, Partially, or Not)	F	N	N	F	P
Memory Required	256K	512K	128K	256K	128K
Disks Required	2	HD	1	2	2
Documentation Error Message Explanation	—	•	•	•	—
Index	•	•	•	•	•
Tutorial	•	•	•	•	•
Specifications Number of Separate Files (Disk Cap.)	D/C	D/C	LTD/REC	40	D/C
Maximum Characters/Field	4,000	255	1,679	1,530	60
Maximum Fields/Record	128	255	3,200	400	40
Maximum Records/File	UNLTD.	UNLTD.	1,100	UNLTD.	32,767
Maximum Record Size (BYTES)	4,000	4,096	4,095	1,530	2,400
Number Files Open at Once	10		1	40	1
Entry/Edit Variable Field Lengths	•		•	•	—
Edit Fields After Record is Entered	•	•	•	•	•
Simulates Paper Forms on Screen	•	•	•	•	•
Calculated Fields	•		•	•	•
Data Checking Table Look-up	•	—	—	•	•
Data Validation	•	—	—	•	—
Range Checking	—	—	—	•	—
Default Entries	•	—	•	•	—

	DBASE III	PC FOCUS	PFS FILE	R:BASE 5000	TIM IV
Data Types Floating Point	•	•	—	•	—
Different Date Formats	•	•	—	•	•
Dollar Fields	•	•	—	•	•
Sorting Ascending	•		•	•	•
Descending	•		—	•	•
Auto Indexing	•	•	—	•	•
Number of Sort Keys Allowed	7	32	1	400	16
Reporting Customized Report Format	•	•	!	•	•
Multifile Access	•	•	—	•	•
Reports Wider than 80 Columns	—		•	•	•
Query Language	•	•	—	•	•
Auto Page Numbering	•		!	•	•
Auto Page Breaks	•		!	•	•
Total Average Counts	TAC		!TAC	TAC	TA
Print Numbers with Commas	•		!	•	•
Headers/Footers	•		—	•	H(only)
Built-in Quick Report	•	•	—	•	•
Mailing Labels	•		•	•	•
Other Procedural Language	•	•	—	•	—
Graphics Capability	—	•	—	—	—
Utilizes Color	•	—	•	•	•
Function Keys	•	•	•	•	•

	DBASE III	PC FOCUS	PFS FILE	R:BASE 5000	TIM IV
IBM AT Compatible	•	•	•	•	•
Copy Protected	•	•	•	—	—
Password Security	—	•	—	•	•
Command and/or Menu Driven	CM	CM	M	CM	M
Help Screens	•	•	•	•	•
Data Dictionary	•	•	—	•	•
Warranty Period	90		90	30	90

! With add-on report package
Languages
 1 French
 2 German
 3 Spanish
 4 Japanese
 5 Norwegian, Finnish and/or Dutch
 6 Dutch and/or Swedish
 • •Brochures available in foreign language

1

KEY TERMS

model

database management system (DBMS)

system specification

problem definition

system flow description

system flowchart

data structure definition

data definition table

field width specification

key

input description

processing description

output description

test data

deposit

menu-driven

command-driven

index

DEFINITIONS

Instructions: On a separate sheet, define each term according to its use in this chapter.

1. system specification

2. system flowchart

3. data definition table

4. field width specification

5. key

6. data structure definition

7. deposit

8. index

T R U E / F A L S E

Instructions: For each statement, write T for true and F for false on a separate sheet

1. Writing a new program for a specific application is usually cheaper than trying to find an existing software package that will meet the requirements for the job.

2. If a database actually does model an organization, the model is built from the information that represents the operation and status of the business.

3. Effective microcomputer system development projects often begin with definitions of requirements, followed by evaluations of the capabilities of available packages against those requirements.

4. By definition, a DBMS package does not provide the capabilities to cross-reference files for application execution.

5. Constructing a computer system has much in common with constructing a building.

6. A system specification includes problem and data structure definitions, descriptions of system flow, input, processing, and output, as well as test data.

7. Prospective system users are responsible for explaining their business needs in terms that systems designers can understand.

8. The data structure definition states exactly where data will appear on the computer screen.

9. The field width specification states how wide the computer screen must be to display all the data needed by the system.

10. In any computer-processed file, at least one field per record must be selected as the key, the item that identifies the record uniquely and separately from all others.

11. A business is shaped by management decisions.

12. In any business information system, transactions are represented by data.

13. In general, DBMS packages provide two types of input procedures: menu-driven and command-driven.

14. Only invalid data items should be used for test data.

15. In a business system, the data representations of transactions do not need to include the exchange value.

SHORT ANSWER QUESTIONS

Instructions: On a separate sheet of paper, answer each question in one or two brief sentences.

1. How can standardized systems solve unique problems?

2. What should a problem definition include?

3. How is a problem definition statement used?

4. What is a simple way to set up a data definition table?

5. What sort of test data should be provided, and why?

6. What is the major difference between menu-driven and command-driven systems?

RESEARCH PROJECT

Expand Mom's Video Market operations by creating a home pickup and delivery service. Prepare a business plan outlining all aspects of the new service. It should deal with the overall region within which deliveries will be made; whether there should be clearly defined areas within the region; established routes and timetables for pickups and deliveries; the charges—if any— for the service to both members and non-members; etc. Once you have established exactly what the expanded service will consist of, show the changes and additions that will have to be made to the database and data fields to integrate them with the rest of the system.

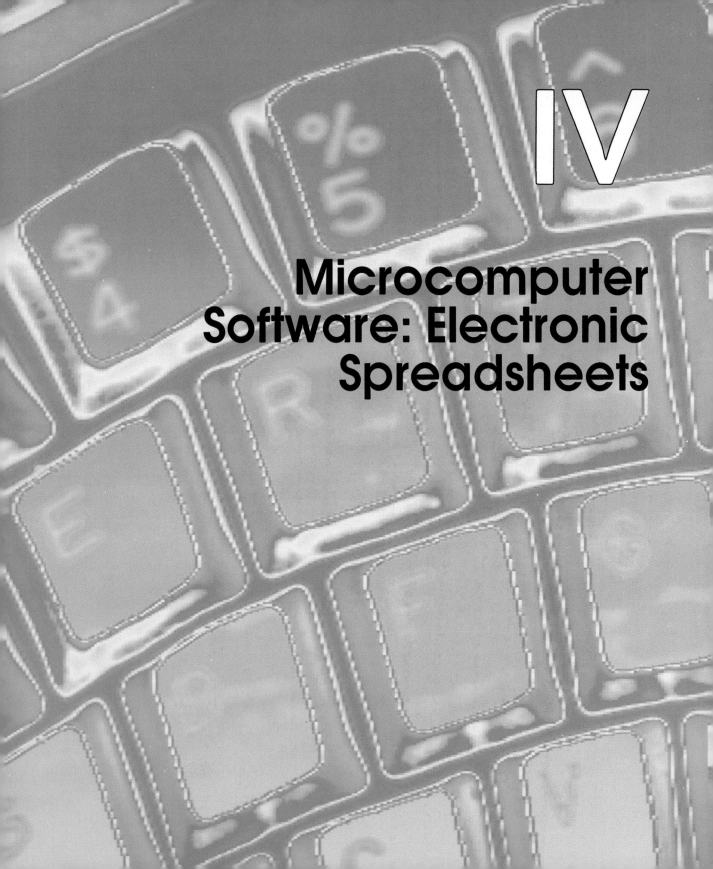

IV

Microcomputer Software: Electronic Spreadsheets

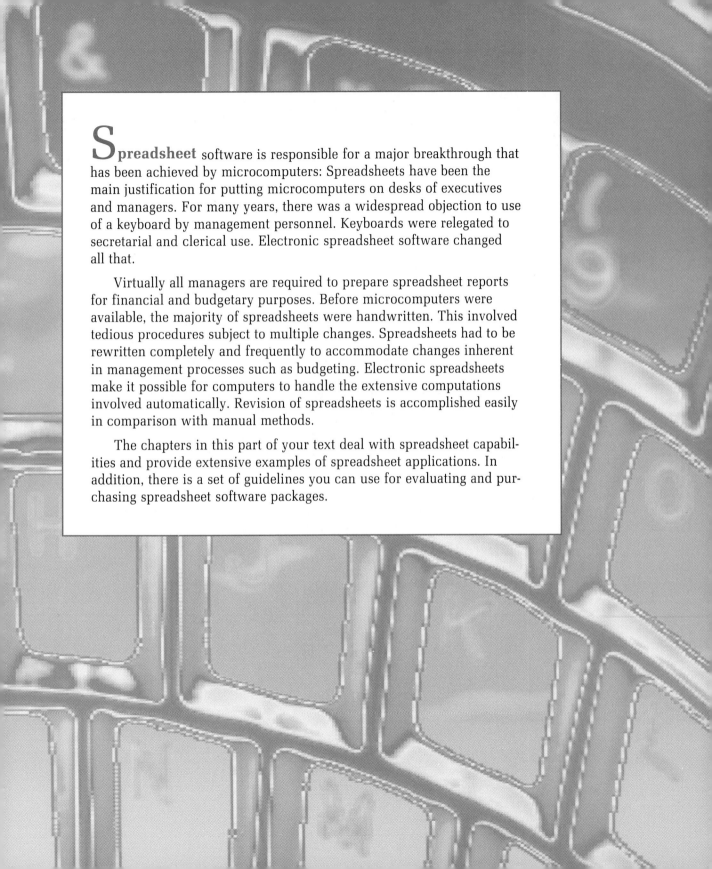

Spreadsheet software is responsible for a major breakthrough that has been achieved by microcomputers: Spreadsheets have been the main justification for putting microcomputers on desks of executives and managers. For many years, there was a widespread objection to use of a keyboard by management personnel. Keyboards were relegated to secretarial and clerical use. Electronic spreadsheet software changed all that.

Virtually all managers are required to prepare spreadsheet reports for financial and budgetary purposes. Before microcomputers were available, the majority of spreadsheets were handwritten. This involved tedious procedures subject to multiple changes. Spreadsheets had to be rewritten completely and frequently to accommodate changes inherent in management processes such as budgeting. Electronic spreadsheets make it possible for computers to handle the extensive computations involved automatically. Revision of spreadsheets is accomplished easily in comparison with manual methods.

The chapters in this part of your text deal with spreadsheet capabilities and provide extensive examples of spreadsheet applications. In addition, there is a set of guidelines you can use for evaluating and purchasing spreadsheet software packages.

11 Working With Spreadsheets

KEY IDEAS

MODELING TOOLS

Models represent the operations and status of an organization. Microcomputers are important tools for implementing models.

Spreadsheets for Problem Solving

Spreadsheets, also called worksheets, are tools for presenting operating or financial information in a comparative format to help in identifying and solving problems.

ADMINISTRATIVE APPLICATIONS

Management uses data provided by electronic spreadsheets to formulate and produce plans that guide, or direct, the organization.

PLANNING TOOLS: BUDGETS AND FORECASTS

Budgets are plans for receiving and spending money. Forecasts are targets that establish an organization's goals.

THE ROLE OF SPREADSHEETS WITHIN ORGANIZATIONS

Information from spreadsheets guides managers in decision making on the basis of analysis of financial and/or numeric data.

"What if . . . ?" Analysis

"What if . . . ?" analysis is a method of presenting an assumption or estimate, through use of spreadsheets, as a basis for projecting business performance.

FEATURES OF SPREADSHEET PACKAGES

An electronic spreadsheet package is a tool for entering data and mathematical formulas, then letting the computer perform calculations automatically. Revision of entries is simplified.

Formulas

A formula describes the calculation to be performed, and is entered into or identified with the cell in which results are to be displayed.

Functions

Most electronic spreadsheets feature built-in formulas, called functions, which represent standard calculations that are used frequently.

Templates

A template is a standard configuration included with a spreadsheet package. A template can be used as a tool for specifying the number and capacity of columns and rows.

SPREADSHEET COMMANDS

Spreadsheet packages provide a wide range of commands and capabilities for entering and manipulating data, formatting worksheets, and generating results or output.

Move and Copy

The move and copy commands make it easy for the user to rearrange spreadsheet content.

Add and Delete

The add and delete commands let a user add or erase portions of a spreadsheet.

Scrolling and Windowing

Spreadsheets often are formatted into more rows and columns than can be displayed at one time on a microcomputer screen. Scrolling and windowing let the user see the needed portions of the screen at any time.

Report Writing

Report writing modules within spreadsheet packages produce hard-copy outputs of spreadsheet displays.

Graphics

Graphics are pictorial representations of numeric data. Many spreadsheet packages have program modules that convert numeric data automatically to produce graphic outputs.

File Import

The file loading, or file import, feature is used to enter data automatically into spreadsheet cells from external sources, usually database files.

MODELING TOOLS

As tools, microcomputers are applied to do work. In business situations, work efforts are directed to solve problems, or to meet situational requirements.

Problem solving in business—as well as in life in general—often involves generating and evaluating alternative solutions. Alternative solutions usually can be described quantitatively, as collections of data items. Problem situations also can be represented, or *modeled,* as quantitative data.

Modeling provides capabilities for evaluating solutions before action or commitment. That is, data representing alternative solutions can be applied to the model of the problem, and results can be derived, or projected. Repeating this process for each alternative provides an overall look at the problem and possible solutions. This type of evaluation is enhanced by presentations of data items in comparative formats.

Spreadsheets for Problem Solving

Norman Stratton has a problem, although it's a problem he doesn't mind having. He needs to save money during the months of June, July, and August to cover his expenses at a local university for the fall semester. Stratton has been offered two summer jobs. The first involves driving a forklift in a warehouse. The second position is as a clerk in a retail market. In short, Stratton needs to make a decision: Which job offer should he accept?

Stratton's first inclination is to take the job that pays the higher wage. After some thought, however, he realizes that other factors, such as *expenses,* will

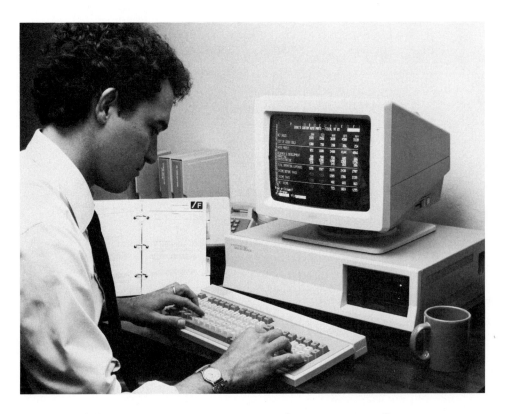

Electronic spreadsheet

software has become a major management tool.

COURTESY OF FUJITSU
MICROELECTRONICS, INC.

affect his ability to save money. Expenses refer to amounts of money spent to support an activity. Stratton realizes that a close look at all the factors will enhance his decision making capabilities.

The warehouse job pays a higher wage. Stratton figures his take-home pay (after taxes have been withheld) will be roughly $650 per month. This job is a considerable distance from his home, however, and Stratton figures car expenses will come to roughly $95 per month. In addition, to work this job, Stratton is required to purchase a pair of steel-toed safety shoes, which cost $40.

The retail clerk position pays less, an estimated $580 per month take-home pay. However, the market is close to home. Stratton figures he can take the bus to work, reducing transportation expenses to $15 monthly for a student bus pass. Further, the second position requires no special clothing.

Stratton has tried to evaluate the merits and drawbacks of both positions mentally—with little success. He realizes that he needs to evaluate both positions carefully. Stratton takes a sheet of paper and divides it into rows and columns. Then, by labeling the rows and columns, he creates a **worksheet.** A worksheet is a tool for presenting data items in a comparative format. The worksheet that Stratton produces is shown in Figure 11-1.

INCOME/EXPENSE SUMMARY

	JUNE	JULY	AUGUST	TOTAL	
INCOME					
Warehouse Job					
Take-home Pay					
TOTAL					
EXPENSES					
Transportation					
Clothing					
TOTAL					
POTENTIAL SAVINGS					
INCOME					
Retail Job					
Take-home Pay					
TOTAL					
EXPENSES					
Transportation					
Clothing					
TOTAL					
POTENTIAL SAVINGS					

Figure 11-1.

Data for inclusion in spreadsheets should be organized initially on a worksheet.

Stratton arranges the entry positions of his worksheet to facilitate the evaluations he needs to make. He labels the columns by month—June, July, and August. Then, he designates rows as income, expenses, and expected savings for both jobs. Entries at the intersections of rows and columns are to reflect those factors for a month (indicated by column label). Finally, he fills in the worksheet with the data items that he is comparing to make his decision. The completed worksheet is shown in Figure 11-2.

The worksheet presents a surprising conclusion: The retail clerk job offers greater potential for saving money—even though it pays less than the warehouse job.

The evaluation that Stratton performs in support of his decision making activities is repeated every day in the management of organizations. The majority of

INCOME/EXPENSE SUMMARY

	JUNE	JULY	AUGUST	TOTAL
INCOME				
Warehouse Job				
Take-home Pay	650.00	650.00	650.00	1950.00
TOTAL				1950.00
EXPENSES				
Transportation	95.00	95.00	95.00	285.00
Clothing	40.00	0.00	0.00	40.00
TOTAL				325.00
POTENTIAL SAVINGS				1625.00
INCOME				
Retail Job				
Take-home Pay	580.00	580.00	580.00	1740.00
TOTAL				1740.00
EXPENSES				
Transportation	15.00	15.00	15.00	45.00
Clothing	0.00	0.00	0.00	0.00
TOTAL				45.00
POTENTIAL SAVINGS				1695.00

standard management functions involves this kind of evaluation. Worksheets like those shown in figure 11-2, also known as **spreadsheets,** have been used in businesses for over a century. **Electronic spreadsheets** are powerful, problem-solving application packages that, in many ways, put microcomputers on the business map—or at least on countless business desktops. Electronic spreadsheet packages provide capabilities for generating and formatting worksheets in computer memory, and for entering and manipulating data within worksheets.

Figure 11-2.

Manual methods of spreadsheet preparation were tedious and time-consuming.

ADMINISTRATIVE APPLICATIONS

To understand the impact of electronic spreadsheets in organizations, it may be helpful to consider the role of business managers. At the administrative level, middle managers and other executives are responsible for making decisions and producing plans that guide, or direct, the organization. In effect, administrative personnel are plotting the route and driving the vehicle toward the organization's future.

Traditionally, managerial functions fall into five categories, which include:

- *Planning* involves the setting of short- and long-term goals and objectives and selecting methods for achieving them.

- *Organizing* refers to the relating of people, activities, and resources into a coordinated system for producing results.

- *Staffing* includes recruiting, training, promoting, and/or terminating personnel.

- *Directing* involves motivating and guiding subordinates to apply their efforts in achieving company goals or objectives.

- *Controlling* involves evaluating actual performance, comparing it with expectations, and taking corrective action, if needed.

In a general sense, the thrust of managerial activities involves planning—the setting of goals and objectives. Once plans are in place, management functions center around implementing them, and solving problems that impede successful implementation. In effect, managers attempt to direct and coordinate the activities of the entire organization to meet established goals and objectives. In this sense, managerial functions can be summarized with the saying "Plan your work and work your plan."

To implement this concept, managers need tools for comparing planned with actual performance. The remainder of this chapter reviews methods under which electronic spreadsheets are used for this purpose.

PLANNING TOOLS: BUDGETS AND FORECASTS

Managers use many tools to fulfill their responsibilities. Budgets and forecasts are such tools.

Virtually any manager responsible for spending money also is responsible for producing some type of *budget.* A budget is a document that presents estimates of income and expenditures for a given period of time. A budget may be specialized—reflecting a discrete business function or area—or may be general. In addition, a budget may be short-term (covering one year or less) or long-term.

Regardless of the manager's responsibilities, a budget plays an important role in the management of any business. Each budget, in effect, is a plan for making or spending money. Information within budgets predicts performance (income

```
        SpreadSheet File: ELEVEN3


              January Performance Report

                           BUDGET      ACTUAL

        INCOME
          Dealer Sales       7912.35     8532.84
          Direct Sales       3457.60     3925.52
          Will Call Sales    2443.18     1124.33

        TOTAL INCOME        13813.13    13582.69

        EXPENSES
          Labor              4717.50     4511.25
          Materials          2511.13     2629.97
          Plant Costs        1132.48     1324.22
          Overhead           3196.74     2942.20

        TOTAL EXPENSES      11557.85    11407.64

        PROFIT               2255.28     2175.05
```

Figure 11-3.

Managers can monitor operations and make decisions on the basis of reports presenting budgeted performance, actual performance, and the amount of deviation between the two to monitor and control organizational activities.

and expenditures) for the business. At the end of each budgeting period, performance is evaluated by comparing planned and actual results. Figure 11-3 shows a typical budget statement. Notice the column-and-row arrangement of this statement. This arrangement implements a spreadsheet format.

Notice the sales figures in the column labeled "Budget." Expected revenues from sales on the budget statement are derived from a sales ***forecast.*** A forecast is a projection of a future business condition or event. Forecasts are the starting point for the budgeting process. That is, budgets present predictions of future income and estimated resources for producing that income. Budget predictions, or forecasts, are based on historical data and on the analysis and evaluation of that data by a manager or other decision maker.

Past performance is indicated by summaries of historical data. These summaries, called ***trends,*** identify patterns of business conditions over a period of time. For example, suppose Big Time, Inc., the fictional clock manufacturing company, posted the sales figures shown in Figure 11-4 for the previous five years.

By evaluating these data, you can see that sales for this company have increased steadily during this period. This trend may have been caused by added salespersons, advertising campaigns, or any combination of a myriad of market factors. Trends often are presented as graphic representations, known as ***trend***

```
SpreadSheet File... BRKDOWN

                Big Time, Inc.
           Five Year Sales Breakdown

                1983     1984     1985     1986     1987
Territory A   345822   356233   369153   388212   402184
Territory B   112398   117933   120745   122985   125893
Territory C    79822    88135    84288    87255    89127
TOTAL SALES   538042   562301   574186   598452   617204
```

Figure 11-4.

Historical data presented on spreadsheet reports indicate trends for organizational activities.

lines, shown in Figure 11-5. Trend lines, and other types of business graphics, are discussed in a later section of this chapter.

A trend line is an effective tool for evaluating past performance. This performance can be extended, or ***extrapolated,*** to project future performance. This is a simple type of projection, involving a straightforward extension of the trend line. See Figure 11-6.

For example, an average percentage of growth for these years might be calculated and the same percentage applied to future years. Management may be satisfied with maintaining this average—or might call for further increases because of market factors such as reduced costs of components, increased production, and so on. Conversely, percentages might be projected at lower or downward levels to reflect adverse economic conditions.

Budgets and forecasts are tools used by managers to evaluate decisions and plans. An additional degree of accuracy can be achieved by comparing plans with actual performance—as a means of determining needs for and courses of corrective action. Spreadsheets become particularly valuable for this type of evaluation.

THE ROLE OF SPREADSHEETS WITHIN ORGANIZATIONS

In the opening section of this chapter, a student evaluates data to support decision-making activities. Data evaluation in support of managerial decision making usually involves analysis of financial and/or numeric data. A longstanding method used to compare numerical data is the spreadsheet. A spreadsheet is a wide sheet of paper divided into vertical columns and horizontal rows— defined by ruled lines. Under manual systems, columns and rows provide space for entry of descriptions and numbers, typically dollar amounts.

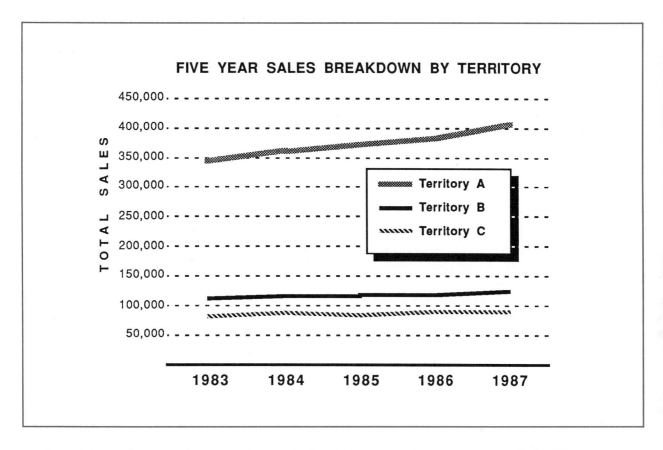

FIVE YEAR SALES BREAKDOWN BY TERRITORY

Figure 11-5.

Line graphs convert spreadsheet data into graphic trend lines that compare results over time periods.

Spreadsheets, for example, are used extensively within accounting systems. Most accounting systems produce documents that present income and expense figures for periods of two to five years. This type of document is illustrated in Figure 11-7. Notice that each column provides numeric data for a given item of income, expense, or *equity.* Equity refers to the actual monetary value of a business and is calculated as the value of assets less the value of liabilities.

The columns in the figure are designated by year. Items of income and expense are assigned rows. Values for each year are entered into the *cell,* or entry position, at the intersections of rows and columns. The resulting spreadsheet presents a view of the financial status of the company for each of the previous years.

For this type of application, a spreadsheet provides a functional presentation format. In addition, producing the spreadsheet by hand presents little difficulty. Historic data are fixed, or not subject to frequent change.

Developing budgets and/or forecasts, however, is a dynamic process, subject to frequent and extensive revisions and adjustments. For example, consider the

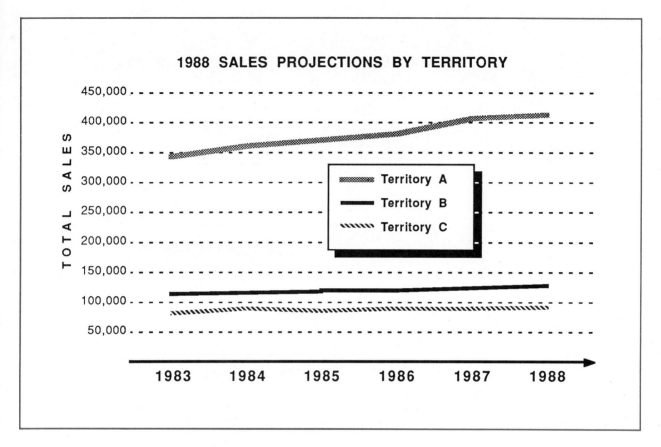

Figure 11-6.

Trend lines may be extended, or projected, to represent expectations or projections for future performance.

above illustration of the sales trend at Big Time, Inc. Recall that sales increased by a specific percentage rate for each of five previous years.

Now suppose that the board of directors at Big Time has a plan that calls for a sales increase of 12 percent for the next year. In this case, administrative managers must produce budgets and forecasts that reflect this plan.

This type of budget development becomes a trial-and-fit process. Managers can achieve the desired increase in a number of ways. For example, an increase in production can lead to increased revenues. As an alternative, reducing the price of certain products may produce desired results. It also is realistic to expect to execute a combination of actions. That is, budget figures and projections probably will be manipulated repeatedly until the desired results are reflected by forecast entries. These figures can be applied to other factors to project the overall effect of the action on the organization. For example, price reductions may induce increased sales, but may cause a reduction in profits as well. Managers often try several different approaches until the budget conforms to organizational plans.

INCOME/EXPENSE SUMMARY	YEAR 1	YEAR 2	YEAR 3	YEAR 4	
INCOME					
Direct Sales	260000	305000	355000	400500	
Mail-Order Sales	80000	92000	111600	120000	
TOTAL	340000	397000	466600	520500	
EXPENSES					
Personnel	130000	140000	160000	190000	
Advertising	11000	12400	15000	20700	
Supplies	15200	17700	18400	24300	
Rent/Utilities	17000	18200	20000	22200	
TOTAL	173200	188300	213400	257200	
EQUITY	35000	43000	50500	60000	

In such situations, manual spreadsheets are ineffective for dealing with dynamic budget development. For example, suppose a spreadsheet has 500 entry positions (5 columns × 100 rows). For manual spreadsheets, the trial-and-fit process described above can deteriorate quickly into a sloppy sheet of erasures and crossouts. Changes or recalculations in one cell may affect cells throughout the spreadsheet.

Suppose the managers at Big Time are able to reduce the cost of a clock motor by $500 per thousand units. This new entry will change figures for total costs, costs of goods sold, gross profits, net profits, and other pertinent data items. Suppose also that the same managers find that, by purchasing additional volumes, costs of the same part can be reduced even further. Again, the entire spreadsheet might have to be redone manually. Original values are erased and recalculated, and results are changed also. The spreadsheet becomes sloppy in appearance. The entire spreadsheet may have to be recopied for professional presentation.

"What if . . . ?" Analyses

The scenario above describes simple changes made to a relatively small number of entries. Consider how difficulties increase for spreadsheets involving many more rows and columns. This section discusses electronic spreadsheet packages and the advantages of these packages over manual methods.

Figure 11-7.

Standard business reports frequently are formatted as spreadsheets.

325

Analyses to support

*plans and decisions can benefit
from graphic outputs generated
by spreadsheet software.*

COURTESY OF HONEYWELL, INC.

Electronic spreadsheets are among the most popular types of program sold for microcomputers—and have been instrumental in bringing microcomputers onto business desktops. Electronic spreadsheets originally evolved as standalone packages. That is, the spreadsheet packages were designed to operate independently, with no interaction or data transfers from files created by other packages. However, consider the function of spreadsheets: to present data from many sources in a comparative format. This function is applicable for decision making activities in virtually every area of business. A business is an integrated system of people, equipment, and functions. Spreadsheets are an ideal format for the outputs of many types of database processing. In fact, most database packages include a spreadsheet program as part of their overall "tool kit."

For example, development and evaluation of budgets often involve historic data. The access methods designed into a database system make it possible to load a spreadsheet with historic data produced by other applications. "Actual" performance figures can be derived from financial reporting applications. These figures can be presented alongside projected figures and manipulated electronically. Managers can ask virtually endless sets of "What if . . . ?" questions in support of budgeting and/or forecasting processes.

The purpose of a "What if . . . ?" question is to present an assumption or estimation as a basis for projecting business performance. Managers ask these questions to implement a trial-and-fit approach to preparation of budgets or forecasts. Examples of "What if . . . ?" questions include: What if costs of raw materials increase by 20 percent? What if sales of Product Y increase by 12 percent and sales of Product X decrease by 22 percent? What if employee wages increase by 7 percent?

Managers deal with these questions by altering values and functions within spreadsheet cells. Recalculations are performed by the computer and displayed on terminal screens. This process can be repeated until desired values are achieved. Erasures and crossouts are eliminated. In fact, several versions of a spreadsheet can be saved on disk or printed as outputs for comparison. Common types of entries and functions of spreadsheet packages are described in the section that follows.

FEATURES OF SPREADSHEET PACKAGES

An electronic spreadsheet package is set up to handle four types of cell entries:

- *Heading* entries appear at the top of the form.

- *Labels* identify data entries within individual cells, rows, and columns.

- A *numeric value* represents financial or statistical data to be processed.

- A *formula* is a calculation performed to derive the value of a particular cell. A formula may be applied to keyed data or entries within other cells. For example, a column of sales figures can be totaled by entering a formula into the bottom cell of the column. Changes in any column cell will be reflected in the total. *Functions* are standard formulas, such as for generating sums, averages, percentages, and so on, included with spreadsheet packages.

In addition to cell entry, an electronic spreadsheet includes many features that enhance processing capabilities. These features and functions are described below.

Formulas

Probably the greatest advantage of electronic spreadsheets over manual methods is the ability to perform calculations—and recalculations—automatically. This feature allows an operator to reconfigure an entire spreadsheet neatly, quickly, and easily. The calculating function of spreadsheets is set up by formulas entered into spreadsheet cells.

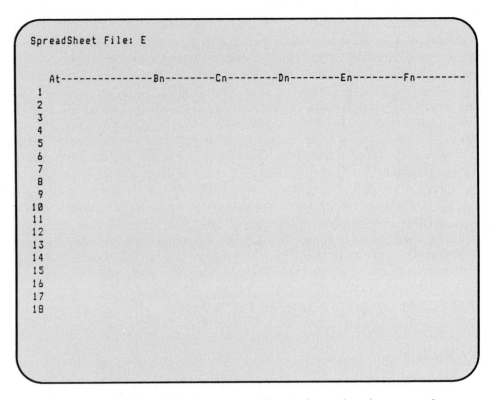

```
SpreadSheet File: E


    At--------------Bn---------Cn---------Dn---------En---------Fn--------
   1
   2
   3
   4
   5
   6
   7
   8
   9
  10
  11
  12
  13
  14
  15
  16
  17
  18
```

Figure 11-8.

In electronic spreadsheets, columns are identified by letters, rows by numbers.

A formula describes the calculation to be performed and is entered into or identified with the cell in which results are to be displayed. Data items and formulas are entered into spreadsheet cells in one of two ways. The first method is to position the cursor at a desired cell and key entries, which then are echoed in that cell.

In other spreadsheet packages, cell entries are introduced with a slightly different method. A **data entry area** is provided at the top or bottom of the screen. Formulas or data are keyed into the data entry area and reflected in the identified cell.

Regardless of entry method, formulas can be used extensively to support budgeting and forecasting. Formula entries usually resemble arithmetic notation, with cell designations substituted for numbers. For example, consider the formula:

D4 – D5

This indicates that the entry for cell D5 is to be subtracted from the value of D4. In spreadsheets, columns are labeled alphabetically, and rows are labeled numerically (See Figure 11-8). Thus, the cell, A1, is at the top left corner of virtually every spreadsheet. Other arithmetic operations are indicated by symbols such as (+) for addition, (∗) for multiplication, and (/) for division.

Functions

To simplify this process even further, most spreadsheets feature built-in formulas, called functions. Functions represent standard calculations that are used frequently in spreadsheets. Functions have special names that reflect their use and that indicate type of calculation. The three most popular functions are:

- @SUM, to add numbers within a range of cells. The @ symbol to the left differentiates the function from a cell heading. To obtain a total for the range of values in cells B2 through B22, the function, @SUM(B2..B22), is entered into the cell in which the total is to be entered. See Figure 11-9.
- @COUNT, to tally the number of entries within a range of cells.
- @AVG, to calculate an average value for the entries within a range of cells.

Templates

A **template** is a spreadsheet configuration set up to receive data entries. A template is a tool for specifying the number and capacity of columns and rows in a spreadsheet. For example, standard formats may be provided for analyzing income and expenses, forecasting trends, preparing financial statements, establishing budgets, and so on. This feature simplifies processing. A user displays a standard or tailored format, enters data into appropriate cells, and initiates processing with a simple command. The user does not have to spend time designing formats or entering standard formulas.

SPREADSHEET COMMANDS

Spreadsheet packages provide a wide range of commands and capabilities for entering and manipulating data, formatting worksheets, and generating results or outputs. In addition to the features discussed above, most packages provide a command structure for executing standard operations. In general, the commands and operations provided by most packages include:

- Move and copy
- Add and delete
- Scrolling and windowing
- Report writing
- Graphics.

Figure 11-9.

Formulas can be entered into spreadsheet cells (top) to gener- ate column totals (bottom) or other calculations.

```
SpreadSheet: ELEVNINE                          Press ESC to quit
Create Format Enter Sum Save Print Retrieve Insert Remove Copy Move Prot Delete
Enter headings, formulae, and data into a spreadsheet
   At-----------------Bn------------Cn------------Dn-------------En-------------
1                        EXPENSE   SUMMARY
2
3                       January       February      March
4
5 Operating Expenses
6    Salaries           3456.33       3532.89       3298.45
7    Advertising         542.45        389.70        421.67
8    Rent                860.00        860.00        860.00
9    Utilities           112.45        108.55        106.44
10   Materials           322.45        318.45        320.22
11   Equipment           112.34        120.99        134.66
12   Depreciation         56.80         55.43         52.76
13   Insurance           208.99        208.99        208.99
14
15 Total Expenses     @SUM(B6..B13) @SUM(C6..C13) @SUM(D6..D13)
16
```

```
SpreadSheet: ELEVNINE                          Press ESC to quit
Create Format Enter Sum Save Print Retrieve Insert Remove Copy Move Prot Delete
Calculate values for formulae in active spreadsheet and display
   At-----------------Bn------------Cn------------Dn-------------En-------------
1                        EXPENSE   SUMMARY
2
3                       January       February      March
4
5 Operating Expenses
6    Salaries           3456.33       3532.89       3298.45
7    Advertising         542.45        389.70        421.67
8    Rent                860.00        860.00        860.00
9    Utilities           112.45        108.55        106.44
10   Materials           322.45        318.45        320.22
11   Equipment           112.34        120.99        134.66
12   Depreciation         56.80         55.43         52.76
13   Insurance           208.99        208.99        208.99
14
15 Total Expenses       5671.81       5595.00       5403.19
16
```

Move and Copy

Spreadsheet packages are designed to be expanded or contracted easily. The *move* and *copy* commands make it easy for the user to rearrange spreadsheets. As the names imply, these functions are used to move and/or copy portions of a worksheet, or *ranges* of cells, from one location to another. Information can be positioned to enhance analyses or presentations. For many packages, relationships among cells established by formulas are reconfigured automatically by the software.

Add and Delete

The *add* and *delete* commands also enhance the flexibility of spreadsheet packages. Portions of a spreadsheet can be added or erased according to user requirements and commands. Again, relationships among cells are preserved under program control.

Scrolling and Windowing

Spreadsheets often are formatted into more rows and columns than can be displayed on a microcomputer screen at one time. Most screens can accommodate roughly 24 rows of 80 characters each. Typically, this means the displayed area of a spreadsheet will contain six or eight columns and 20 rows. *Scrolling* refers to moving a spreadsheet vertically or horizontally until a desired portion is displayed.

In other situations, *windowing* provides a similar capability. A *window* is a separate display frame typically superimposed over a portion of the display already appearing on the screen. Many spreadsheet packages allow two or more windows of the worksheet to be displayed simultaneously.

Report Writing

Report writing operations produce hard copy outputs of spreadsheet displays. Portions of or an entire spreadsheet can be routed to a printer for output. Some packages include options for copying selected parts of spreadsheets to a word processing program. In this way, spreadsheet tables can appear within printed reports.

Graphics

Graphics are pictorial representations of numeric data. Recall the earlier discussion in this chapter of trend lines. The purpose of graphics is to simplify a large volume of numeric data as a pictorial representation. Many people understand

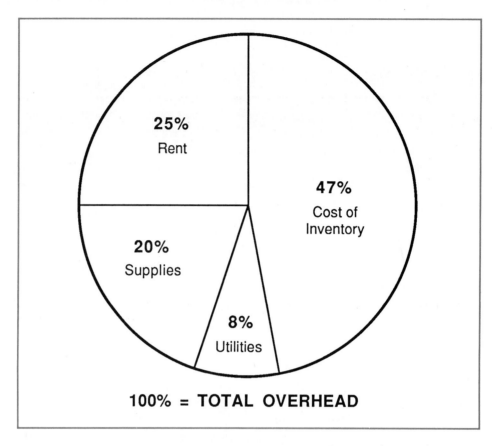

25%
Rent

47%
Cost of
Inventory

20%
Supplies

8%
Utilities

100% = TOTAL OVERHEAD

Figure 11-10.

Data representing portions of a whole entity can be represented effectively as a pie chart.

pictures more easily than collections of numbers. For example, Figure 11-10 presents a type of graphic, called a ***pie chart***, that is based on spreadsheet figures for a company's expenses. A pie chart is used to show the relations of component parts to a whole. Thus, the individual expenditures in the figure are related to overall overhead, just as if they were all pieces of the same pie.

In addition to trend lines and pie charts, a third type of graphic, known as a ***bar chart,*** often is used to present numbers as a picture. A bar chart, also called a ***histogram,*** is illustrated in Figure 11-11. A bar chart uses vertical or horizontal bars to represent numeric values. Comparisons of numeric values are reflected by varying lengths of the bars.

Most spreadsheet packages include processing routines by which tables can be converted and presented as graphic outputs. Special printers or plotters may be required to produce graphics, and a wide variety of devices and outputs is available. For example, some displays or printers can produce graphics in different colors for emphasis.

Other packages make use of standalone graphics routines. With these packages, data are read by and ***imported*** into graphics programs. This feature is discussed in the next section.

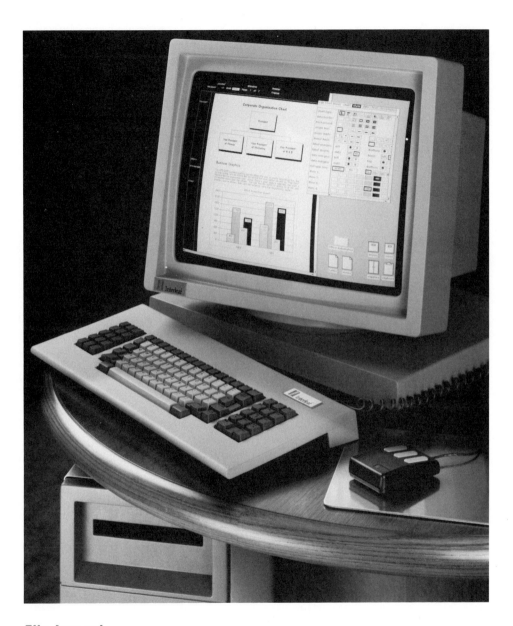

File import

capabilities often are implemented with the aid of integrated software packages.
COURTESY OF INTERLEAF, INC.

File Import

The file loading, or **file import,** feature is used to enter data into spreadsheet cells from data files. Thus, sales data maintained within company files can be selected and entered into a table automatically. This feature effectively eliminates the need to rekey data items each time they are presented in a spreadsheet format. In fact, using templates and the file loading feature, a user conceivably could format and load a spreadsheet with data by using only program commands.

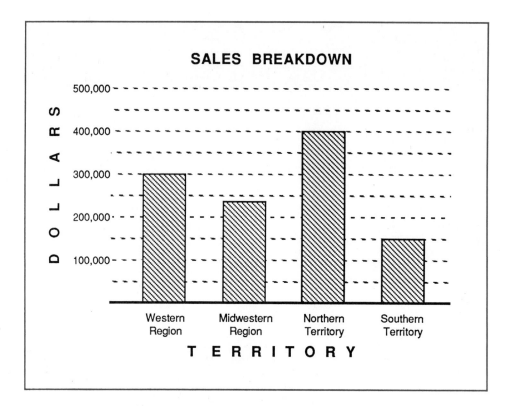

Figure 11-11.

Numeric values for comparisons are presented on a bar chart (histogram) as lines or bars of varying lengths.

The return on investment provided by spreadsheet packages is substantiated easily. There is a saying in business: Time is money. The costs of electronic spreadsheets are covered by time savings over manual methods. Electronic techniques have eliminated the tedious, time-consuming tasks of erasing and recalculating entries. In the process, the appearance and utility of spreadsheets within businesses have improved. The chapter that follows presents the concepts discussed here in the context of a case scenario.

K E Y   T E R M S

modeled	extrapolation	copy
expenses	equity	range
worksheet	cell	add
spreadsheet	heading	delete
electronic spreadsheet	label	scroll
planning	numeric value	windowing
organizing	formula	window
staffing	function	report writing
directing	data entry area	pie chart
controlling	@SUM	bar chart
budget	@COUNT	histogram
forecast	@AVG	imported
trend	template	file import
trend line	move	

D E F I N I T I O N S

Instructions: On a separate sheet, define each term according to its use in this chapter.

1. spreadsheet

2. electronic spreadsheet

3. budget

4. forecast

5. extrapolation

6. equity

7. cell

8. formula

T R U E / F A L S E

Instructions: For each statement, write T for true and F for false on a separate sheet.

1. A worksheet is the document on which a work order is based.

2. Spreadsheets have been used in business for more than a century.

3. In general terms, the main job of managers involves planning—the setting of goals and objectives.

4. A budget is a record of how much money was taken in and how it was spent.

5. Equity is the actual monetary value of a business, and is calculated as the value of the assets less the value of the liabilities.

6. Electronic spreadsheets are among the most popular types of microcomputer programs sold today.

7. Budgets often are based on historic data.

8. Mathematical formulas may be applied to keyed data or entries within the cells of a spreadsheet.

9. The asterisk (*) is the computer symbol for subtraction.

10. The slash (/) is the symbol for division.

11. Standard formats are available for analyzing income and expenses, forecasting trends, preparing financial statements, establishing budgets, etc.

12. "Window" is another term for your computer screen.

13. "Histogram" is another term for bar chart.

14. The file import feature allows the user to produce hard-copy outputs of spreadsheet displays.

15. Most spreadsheet packages include processing routines with which tables can be converted and presented as graphic outputs.

SHORT ANSWER QUESTIONS

Instructions: On a separate sheet of paper, answer each question in one or two brief sentences.

1. What is the difference between planning and organizing?

2. Give a short, one-sentence summary of the management function.

3. What is the purpose of a "What if . . . ?" question?

4. What is probably the greatest advantage of an electronic spreadsheet over a manual spreadsheet?

5. As a rule, how are spreadsheets labeled, and how would the top left cell be identified in most spreadsheets?

6. Why is the ability to scroll and use windows important with electronic spreadsheets?

RESEARCH PROJECT

Create a spreadsheet that will help you plan your budget for the next six months. Enter all your anticipated income and expenses.

12 Electronic Spreadsheets

KEY IDEAS

EVALUATING PERFORMANCE THROUGH RESULTS

Everyone is evaluated on the basis of results produced. Athletes are evaluated through statistics such as batting averages. Businesses and managers are evaluated on the basis of financial results, expressed most usefully on spreadsheets.

Monitoring Performance

The monitoring, or tracking, of past results guides present and future decisions.

CASE SCENARIO: INCOME/EXPENSE SUMMARY

In the case presented, data elements from cash register tapes and check registers are used to prepare statements of income and expenses.

BUILDING ELECTRONIC SPREADSHEETS

An electronic spreadsheet is comprised of headings, column labels, format (columns and rows), data items, computation formulas, and totals.

Formatting Electronic Spreadsheets

Entering headings and labels is the logical way to begin formatting, or laying out, an electronic spreadsheet.

Entering Spreadsheet Data

To enter data into an electronic spreadsheet, the operator usually switches to the ENTER mode. This allows the cursor to be moved to specific cell positions at which entries are to be placed.

Using Spreadsheets for Planning

Spreadsheets can be used to develop strategic, tactical, and operational plans.

CASE EXAMPLE: BUDGETS

In the case presented, the budget reflects the expectations and standards established by an operational plan.

Projecting Sales

Spreadsheet information on past sales figures can be used to predict future sales volumes.

CASE SCENARIO: MOM'S VIDEO MARKET

In the case presented, various ways in which an electronic spreadsheet's capabilities can be applied to a specific business are reviewed.

Defining Requirements

You should know what you want a spreadsheet program to do before you go out and choose one.

Generating Reports

To design a spreadsheet, you have to begin by determining what you want the final report to look like.

GRAPHICS: THE BIGGER PICTURE

In terms of spreadsheets, graphics are used to distill large volumes of data into easy-to-understand illustrations.

Bar Charts

Bar charts, also called histograms, are used to represent data values as bars or lines of different lengths.

Pie Charts

Pie charts are used to show relationships among the component parts of an organization or endeavor.

Trend Lines

Trend lines, or line graphs, show the relative up and down movements of data values.

Using Spreadsheet Graphics

Most spreadsheet packages include integrated graphics capabilities that can be used to provide a "picture" of the patterns and relationships among data elements.

CASE SCENARIO: GENERATING GRAPHICS FROM SPREADSHEET DATA

An example of how graphic outputs are designed and generated is provided using the Lotus 1-2-3 software package.

EVALUATING PERFORMANCE THROUGH RESULTS

Everybody is subject to some type of standard. That is, everybody performs some kind of work that is evaluated by some quantitative criteria (set of numbers). In professional sports, evaluations usually involve statistics (collections of quantitative data). For example, gymnastic performances are evaluated by judges, who look for artistic as well as athletic merit, and assign numeric values, or scores, to performances. One measure of performance in baseball is a batting average. Batting averages are derived by dividing the number of hits a player makes by the number of official times at bat.

Monitoring Performance

Part of any manager's job is to monitor performance. Monitoring performance involves generating, comparing, and evaluating pertinent data. Continuing the example of baseball performance, suppose a manager is preparing for an upcoming game in which the opposing pitcher is an outstanding left-hander. Statistics indicate that right-handed batters, on the average, hit more effectively than left-handed batters against left-handed pitchers. The manager might decide to juggle personnel for that game to include as many right-handed batters as reasonable.

Baseball managers often make decisions on the basis of accumulated, historical data maintained by the team or an outside organization. Overall statistics can be compiled and/or refined to meet the needs of specific games or situations. Transaction data, in effect, are the statistics of business.

An earlier chapter points out that the status of a business changes with every transaction. Every transaction involves an exchange of value. A company that completes a sales transaction has less product and more money than before the transaction. The sum of an organization's transactions, then, is an indication of the organization's financial condition, or status. Monitoring business performance involves determinations and evaluations of financial status.

Business managers rely heavily upon analysis of transaction data for monitoring the performance of organizations. Historic data describe results of actions in past situations, providing information that can be applied to support decision making under current conditions. As an example, consider a ***summary of income and expenses.***

A summary report of income and expenses presents total profits or losses realized by a business during a reporting period. In simple terms, a business makes a profit when revenues (income) exceed expenses. A loss situation occurs when expenses are greater than revenues. Income/expense summaries are generated throughout organizations to determine the profit/loss standing of an organization as a whole or of functions and departments within the overall organization.

Business managers monitor performance to gain an idea of current status. This knowledge is applied to decision making that determines future goals and directions of a business. In short, managers calculate exactly "where we are now" before they decide "where will we go." Financial reporting plays an integral role in this process. In the section that follows, a case scenario of this type of financial reporting is presented.

CASE SCENARIO: INCOME/EXPENSE SUMMARY

Spreadsheets present data in formats that facilitate comparison. Remember: a spreadsheet is a configuration of rows, columns, and cells (entry positions at row/column intersections). The spreadsheet format is ideal for presenting summary reports of income and expenses, described above.

To illustrate, consider the case example of Mom's Video Market, introduced in earlier chapters. For businesses of this size, income/expense summaries typically are submitted periodically to banks with which credit lines have been established, and to accountants as source documents from which tax returns are prepared.

At Mom's Video Market, the data elements from which income/expense summaries are prepared are accumulated on cash register tapes and check registers.

```
                    CA   $      6.37
                    CA   $      3.44
                    CR   $    12.55
                    MS   $      2.37

                    CA   $ 438.97   X
                    CR   $ 311.22   X
                    MS   $ 127.41   X

                TTL      $ 980.97   Z

                    **THANK YOU**
```

Figure 12-1.

Transaction data in the form of cash register entries are summarized, or totaled, at the end of each business day.

Cash register tapes are journals, or listings, of data items that represent money put into or taken out of the register. Different types of entries are designated by different keys on the register. For example, a rental charge of $6.37 that is paid with cash will be represented on the register tape as:

CA $ 6.37

A credit rental for the same amount would be recorded as:

CR $ 6.37

Miscellaneous revenues, such as sales of recorded cassettes, blank cassettes, carrying cases, and other items are indicated by another notation, shown here:

MS $ 6.37

At the end of each business day, Beeman balances, or **zeros,** her register. This operation generates daily totals and sets the register back to zero. Subtotals for each entry category also are generated as part of this operation. Subtotals and totals also are recorded on the register tape. Figure 12-1 presents a register tape that reflects the results of a zeroing operation.

The X and Z designations to the right of the entries in Figure 12-1 refer to subtotals and totals, respectively. On this day, Beeman's total receipts, including cash rentals, credit rentals, and miscellaneous sales, should total $980.97.

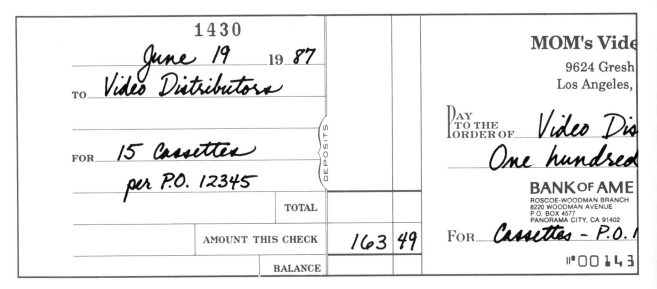

1430

June 19   19 87

TO Video Distributors

FOR 15 Cassettes
     per P.O. 12345

DEPOSITS

TOTAL

AMOUNT THIS CHECK   163 | 49

BALANCE

MOM's Vide

9624 Gresh
Los Angeles,

PAY
TO THE
ORDER OF   Video Di

One hundred

BANK OF AME
ROSCOE-WOODMAN BRANCH
8220 WOODMAN AVENUE
P.O. BOX 4577
PANORAMA CITY, CA 91402

FOR Cassettes - P.O.

⑈00143

Beeman keeps register tapes in an archive file and records daily subtotals and totals in a ledger. Ledger entries contain data items from which income/expense summaries are derived. At the end of each quarter, Beeman uses a calculator to obtain totals for revenue categories. Expense entries are recorded in a check register. Each time Beeman writes a check on the company account, she enters the amount, the payee, and a short code that indicates the type of expense for which the check is written. A portion of Beeman's check register is illustrated in Figure 12-2.

Beeman divides expenses into five categories: product costs, overhead (including rent), credit fees, payroll expenses, and miscellaneous expenses. Product costs refer to purchases of video cassettes and other items that are to be offered for sale or rental. Overhead expenses include rent, utilities, equipment, and any expenditures that are applied to the physical facility. Credit fees are charged to businesses that accept credit cards for purchases or rentals. Payroll expenses are wages paid to clerks and other employees.

Beeman enters income and expense figures into a spreadsheet format, as shown in Figure 12-3.

Produced quarterly, worksheets like the one in Figure 12-3 create a historical record of business activities. For example, the current worksheet can be compared with the previous year's summary. Increases or decreases in income or expenses can be pinpointed to specific categories. Problem areas readily become apparent and managers can direct their attention to these areas.

Suppose, for example, a quick examination of figures for both years indicates that the PRODUCTCOST figure has doubled, while the NET PROFIT figure has

Figure 12-2.

Expense transactions are represented by data items created manually in the check register.

	1st QTR	2nd QTR	3rd QTR	4th QTR	YEAR END
MOM's Video Market					
Income/Expense Statement					
INCOME					
Credit Revenue	13756.80	11908.75	14750.75	17985.55	58401.65
Cash Revenue	9234.80	8034.40	11893.50	14894.33	44057.03
Other Revenue	548.90	590.80	450.60	780.50	2370.80
TOTAL INCOME	23540.50	20533.75	27094.85	33660.38	104829.48
EXPENSE					
Product Cost	655.70	805.40	785.40	1080.60	3327.10
Overhead	7220.35	6145.80	5359.50	9465.75	28191.40
Credit Fees	540.55	490.70	675.90	784.30	2491.45
Payroll	2787.50	2754.30	2824.50	3495.70	11862.00
Miscellaneous	743.88	940.55	853.90	790.55	3328.88
TOTAL EXPENSE	11947.98	11136.75	10499.20	15616.90	49200.83
PROFIT					55628.65

Figure 12-3

Beeman's income/expense summary breaks income and expense summaries into functional categories.

increased by only 10 percent. Closer evaluation reveals that purchase prices (Product Cost) have gone up dramatically. Based upon this evidence, Beeman may decide to raise the rental charge for certain tapes. As an alternative, she may look for vendors with lower prices. Or, she may decide to do nothing, as long as an acceptable profit margin is maintained.

Regardless of outcome, this example points out an important aspect of business management. Monitoring and controlling business performance involves compiling transaction data in formats that reflect performance areas under evaluation. Spreadsheets provide an ideal format for this type of evaluation. Further, electronic spreadsheet packages enhance evaluations with capabilities for electronic entry, formatting, editing, and computation of spreadsheet data. Electronic spreadsheet capabilities are discussed in the section that follows.

BUILDING ELECTRONIC SPREADSHEETS

Electronic spreadsheets are computerized versions of manual worksheets, such as the one described above. Electronic and manual spreadsheets share many characteristics. For example, both types of spreadsheets provide column-and-row layouts, and allow users to make entries at intersections, or cells. Electronic spreadsheets, however, exhibit marked differences in the way they are built and handled. The major differences that separate electronic from manual spreadsheets include:

- Electronic spreadsheets appear on the display screens of microcomputer terminals rather than on ruled paper pads.

- Electronic spreadsheets displayed on terminal screens are held in main memory. In main memory, spreadsheet entries and formats can be revised, manipulated, and edited extensively, *before* a hard copy is produced.

- For electronic spreadsheets, data entry is performed through a keyboard, rather than with a pencil or other writing instrument.

- Electronic spreadsheet software develops all needed totals automatically.

- Electronic spreadsheet packages provide capabilities for calculating cell entries by performing arithmetic functions upon values within cells. These computations are specified by user-designated formulas and functions.

- Electronic spreadsheets can be written to external storage for further use and/or revision.

- Outputs of electronic spreadsheets are produced on computer printers, eliminating transcription errors.

The section that follows presents step-by-step procedures for building an electronic spreadsheet.

Formatting Electronic Spreadsheets

The first task in building an electronic spreadsheet is to devise the overall layout, or format. Spreadsheet layouts refer to designations for column and row entries. The four types of entries that can be made within spreadsheet cells include headings, labels, numbers, and formulas or functions. Headings are titles and identifications that apply to the complete content of the spreadsheets. Labels identify the entries within individual rows and columns.

Entering headings and labels represents a logical starting point for creating the overall spreadsheet layout. Figure 12-4 presents a display screen in which headings and labels for a typical income/expense report have been entered.

```
SpreadSheet: INCEXPSM                        Press ESC to quit
Create Format Enter Sum Save Print Retrieve Insert Remove Copy Move Prot Delete
Enter headings, formulae, and data into a spreadsheet
   At--------------Bc--------Cc--------Dc--------Ec--------Fc--------
  1                        MOM'S VIDEO MARKET
  2                        INCOME/EXPENSE STATEMENT
  3
  4
  5    INCOME
  6
  7 Credit Revenue
  8 Cash Revenue
  9 Other Revenue
 10
 11    TOTAL INCOME
 12
 13    EXPENSE
 14
 15 Product Cost
 16 Overhead
 17 Credit Fees
 18 Payroll
 19 Miscellaneous
 20
```

Figure 12-4.

Spreadsheet formats can be presented on terminal screens for easy viewing and revision.

Entering headings and labels gives the user an idea of the sizes and types of entries the spreadsheet will hold. As a second step in creating a spreadsheet layout, entries are specified in terms of size (number of character spaces) and data type. Figure 12-5 presents a typical entry screen for specifying spreadsheet formats. Notice the parallels between these cell specifications and data structure definitions for a database application.

In this example, four entry types are provided: numeric (N), text (T), currency (C), and percentage (P). Numeric entries refer to numbers and include designations of decimal places as needed. Text entries are included to specify labels and headings. Currency entries automatically establish a decimal point and two decimal places for the columns. Percentage fields set up three digits for a percentage, a decimal point, one decimal place, and two additional spaces for readability. Percentage cells, then, contain seven character spaces. For other entries, the user must specify the number of characters in every column.

In doing this, sufficient character positioning should be provided to allow for space between columns. Spacing should allow for the possibility that cells containing totals may require more character spaces than the accumulated items.

```
        ---------------------------------------
        :      FORMAT SPREADSHEET       :  FILE NAME: INCEXPSM
        ---------------------------------------
             Data Type      Width      No./Decs.
             (n/t/c/p)      (1-25)      (0-9)
Column A         t            17
       B         c            10          2
       C         c            10          2
       D         c            10          2
       E         c            10          2
       F         c            10          2
       G
       H
       I
       J
       K
       L
       M
       N

   Use UP/DOWN/RIGHT cursor keys; Press RETURN after data entry
   INSERT, REMOVE, COPY, and MOVE are on SpreadSheet Command Line
   ESC to return to SpreadSheet Command Line
```

Figure 12-5.

Many spreadsheet packages provide entry screens for format specifications that resemble the data definition tables of database packages.

Entering Spreadsheet Data

Once the initial layout has been created, an electronic spreadsheet is developed by entering data and formulas into cell positions. To perform this operation, the user shifts the program into the ENTER mode. This action usually involves selecting the ENTER option from the processing menu, typically displayed at the top or bottom of the spreadsheet display. In the ENTER mode, the cursor is moved to cell positions at which entries are to be placed. In some systems, entries are keyed into these positions. In others, entries are made in a special area of the screen and transferred to identified locations. Then, pressing the RETURN key causes the system to record the entry and move to the next cell position. See Figure 12-6.

Entry procedures for formulas or functions are identical to those for data entries. For example, suppose a user wanted to derive a total as the last entry in a certain column. This total can be derived simply by entering a formula and by including the ***range*** of cells to which the formula is applied. A range is a group of consecutive cells, such as in a column or row. In Figure 12-7, a formula for deriving a total from a range of cells is illustrated (using the LEARNware spreadsheet package).

Figure 12-6.

The ENTER function is implemented to input formulas or data values into spreadsheet cells. The cursor moves from the command line (top) to the actual worksheet (bottom) when the ENTER option is selected.

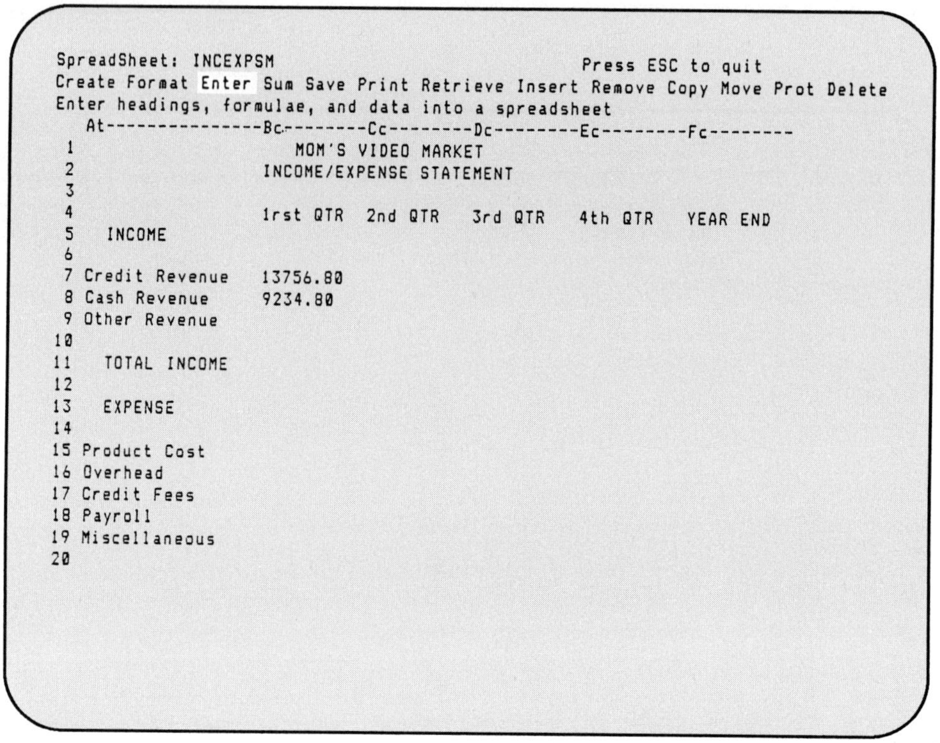

```
SpreadSheet: INCEXPSM                        Press ESC to quit
Create Format Enter Sum Save Print Retrieve Insert Remove Copy Move Prot Delete
Enter headings, formulae, and data into a spreadsheet
  At--------------Bc--------Cc--------Dc--------Ec---------Fc--------
 1                        MOM'S VIDEO MARKET
 2                        INCOME/EXPENSE STATEMENT
 3
 4                        1rst QTR  2nd QTR   3rd QTR   4th QTR   YEAR END
 5    INCOME
 6
 7 Credit Revenue    13756.80
 8 Cash Revenue       9234.80
 9 Other Revenue
10
11   TOTAL INCOME
12
13   EXPENSE
14
15 Product Cost
16 Overhead
17 Credit Fees
18 Payroll
19 Miscellaneous
20
```

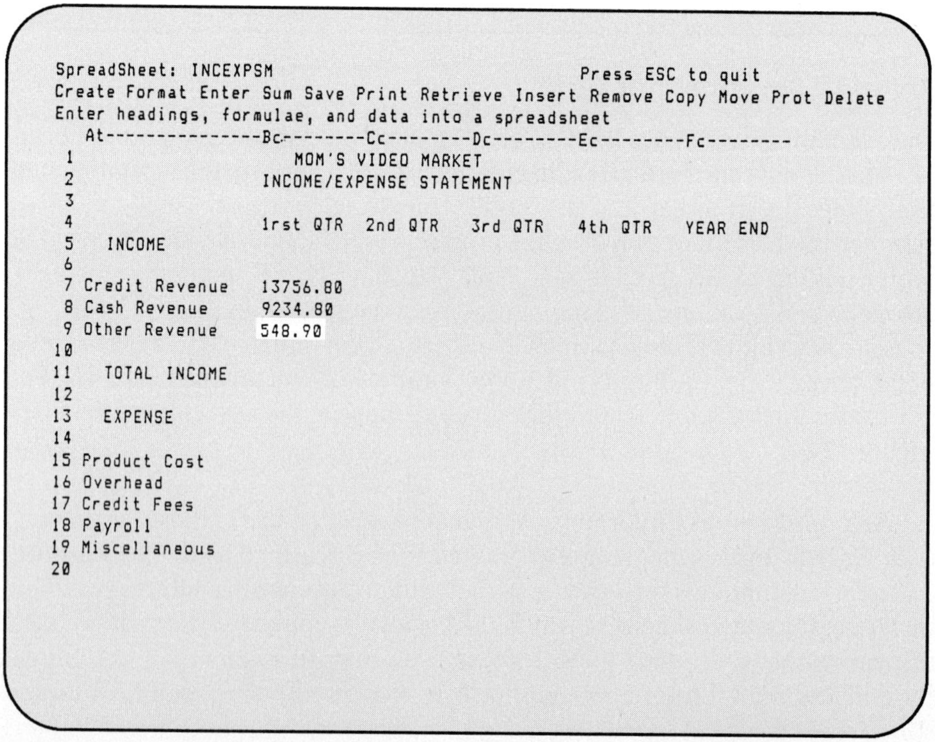

```
SpreadSheet: INCEXPSM                        Press ESC to quit
Create Format Enter Sum Save Print Retrieve Insert Remove Copy Move Prot Delete
Enter headings, formulae, and data into a spreadsheet
  At--------------Bc--------Cc--------Dc--------Ec---------Fc--------
 1                        MOM'S VIDEO MARKET
 2                        INCOME/EXPENSE STATEMENT
 3
 4                        1rst QTR  2nd QTR   3rd QTR   4th QTR   YEAR END
 5    INCOME
 6
 7 Credit Revenue    13756.80
 8 Cash Revenue       9234.80
 9 Other Revenue       548.90
10
11   TOTAL INCOME
12
13   EXPENSE
14
15 Product Cost
16 Overhead
17 Credit Fees
18 Payroll
19 Miscellaneous
20
```

```
 SpreadSheet: INCEXPSM                        Press ESC to quit
 Create Format Enter Sum Save Print Retrieve Insert Remove Copy Move Prot Delete
 Enter headings, formulae, and data into a spreadsheet
    At--------------Bc--------Cc--------Dc--------Ec--------Fc--------
  1                    MOM'S VIDEO MARKET
  2                    INCOME/EXPENSE STATEMENT
  3
  4                 1rst QTR  2nd QTR  3rd QTR  4th QTR   YEAR END
  5    INCOME
  6
  7 Credit Revenue  13756.80  11908.55 14750.75 17985.55  B7@E7
  8 Cash Revenue     9234.80   8034.40 11893.50 14894.33  B8@E8
  9 Other Revenue     548.90    590.80   450.60   780.50  B9@E9
 10
 11   TOTAL INCOME  B7@B9     C7@C9    D7@D9    E7@E9     F7@F9
 12
 13   EXPENSE
 14
 15 Product Cost     655.70    805.40   785.40  1080.60   B15@E15
 16 Overhead        7220.35   6145.80  5359.50  9465.75   B16@E16
 17 Credit Fees      540.55    490.70   675.90   784.30   B17@E17
 18 Payroll         2787.50   2754.30  2824.50  3495.70   B18@E18
 19 Miscellaneous    743.88    940.55   853.90   790.55   B19@E19
 20
```

Figure 12-7.

The formula, B7@B9, is entered
to generate a figure for total
first-quarter income in cell B11.

As noted, some packages use a ***data entry area*** at the top or bottom of spread-sheet displays. For these packages, keystrokes are echoed initially in the entry area. The ***current cell,*** or the cell in which the cursor is positioned, holds the entry—which may result from calculation—upon execution, usually initiated by pressing the RETURN key. See Figure 12-8.

Electronic spreadsheet functions.   ENTER is a standard function for spreadsheet packages. Other standard functions, which typically appear on the processing menu at the top or bottom of spreadsheet displays, include the following:

- The FORMAT function, described above, sets up data types and sizes for column entries.

- The INSERT function is used to place additional rows or columns within an existing spreadsheet. In turn, the existing spreadsheet is reformatted to make room for new rows or columns.

- The DELETE function is used to remove columns or rows from existing spreadsheets—and reformats the spreadsheet to reflect changes.

```
       A          B          C          D          E          F          G
    --------------------------------------------------------------------------------
 1                                  Bob's Toolshop
 2                                  Income Worksheet
 3
 4                                  July       August    September   (October)
 5
 6   Gross Sales                    59,374     54,752     57,194     57,107
 7   Cost of Goods Sold             22,805     23,961     21,562     22,776
 8   Gross Profits on Sales         36,569     30,791     35,632     34,331
 9
10   Operating Expenses:
11       Salaries                    4,156      4,156      3,920      4,077
12       Advertising                   650        325        400        458
13       Rent                        1,100      1,100      1,100      1,100
14       Utilities                     750        807        793        783
15       Depreciation                  460        460        460        460
16   Total Expenses                  7,116      6,848      6,673      6,878
17
18   Net Income before Taxes        29,453     23,943     28,959     27,453
19
20
    ================================================================================
    Format   Insert   Delete   Move   Copy   Edit   File   Print   Erase   Quit
    D18: (D8-D16)
```

Figure 12-8.

With many spreadsheet packages, a data entry area above or below the spreadsheet is provided for input of data values or formulas.

- The MOVE function permits a row, column, or range of cells to be relocated as needed. Formulas within cells of affected entries are adjusted to reflect new locations.

- The COPY command duplicates rows, columns, or ranges in other locations. As with the MOVE command, COPY operations involve adjusting formulas to new locations.

- The FILE, or SAVE, command writes a spreadsheet from main memory to external storage.

- The PRINT command creates a hard copy of a spreadsheet.

- The QUIT command is used to exit the spreadsheet program and return control to the operating system.

Collectively, the capabilities mentioned above comprise a powerful tool for compiling, comparing, and analyzing data. Capabilities for deriving cell entries through calculations described by formulas provide much of the attraction of electronic spreadsheets. Electronic spreadsheet packages free users from the need for tedious—often frustrating—manual entries and computations. Users concentrate on data content and relationships among entries rather than on performing often complicated calculations. In addition, electronic spreadsheets can be revised and recalculated extensively and repeatedly—without requiring repetition of entry and format procedures.

These capabilities have been instrumental in the acceptance of the electronic spreadsheet as a management tool. The power of spreadsheet tools becomes even more apparent for planning applications.

Using Spreadsheets for Planning

In the opening section of this chapter, a point is made that everybody is subject to some kind of performance evaluation. Evaluations are based upon established standards or expectations. In many businesses, the standards by which managers are evaluated are plans. Management performance, then, involves a need for anticipating and planning for different stages in future and developing events. Plans generally are broken down into three categories, which include:

- Strategic
- Tactical
- Operational.

Strategic planning.   *Strategic* plans describe long-range goals (generally five to seven years) for a business. Strategic plans are set at the highest management levels, and provide guidelines for both tactical and operational planning decisions. At this level, plans are general in nature, describing goals in terms of desired growth, size, product mix, market percentages, and so on.

Tactical planning.   *Tactical* plans usually cover one to three years. Tactical plans describe strategic goals in terms of intermediate stages. For example, a strategic plan might dictate the introduction of a new product. The tactical plan would break this goal down into phases for research, purchasing and installing equipment, manufacture, and marketing of the new product. Tactical plans also might present estimates of expenditures needed for implementation.

Operational planning.   *Operational* plans are short-term in scope, usually spanning one to six months. Operational plans usually are directed toward specific departments or managers, and deal with the day-to-day realities of meeting general goals. At this level, plans describe procedures for implementing objectives described at higher levels. Because of their short-term nature, operational plans also might describe reactions to previous experiences, such as an adjustment of staff levels if payroll expenses reach unacceptable levels.

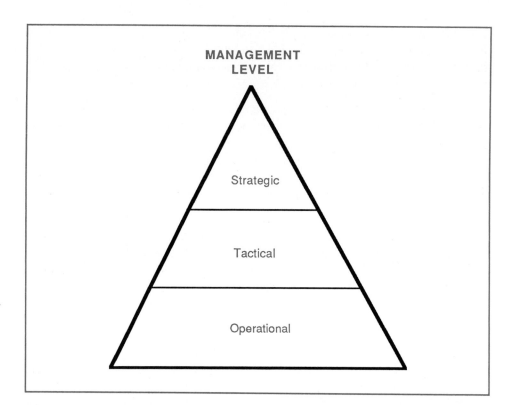

**MANAGEMENT
LEVEL**

Strategic

Tactical

Operational

Figure 12-9.

Planning is implemented at three organizational levels. Requirements for volumes of data increase at lower levels, as indicated by the broad base at the bottom of the pyramid.

Planning structures often are represented by a pyramid, as shown in Figure 12-9. The more detailed the planning, the more specific the data required. At tactical and operational levels, data reflecting expenditures to implement plans often are compiled and presented as a spreadsheet report called a ***budget.***

CASE EXAMPLE: BUDGETS

A budget is a plan for receiving and spending money. In addition, budgets are mechanisms for "scoring" performance. Budgets reflect the expectations and standards set up by strategic plans. Actual performance, then, can be monitored and evaluated by comparisons with budget targets. Budgets also may describe varying levels of detail, and may be developed for the overall organization or individual departments, functions, managers, plant sites, product lines, and so on.

Budget development often involves status reports and projections. Status reports give managers an idea of current conditions. These reports are extended to represent future actions. Budgets, then, describe expected results—in terms of revenue and expenses—of these actions.

For example, suppose a business realizes a 10 percent increase in sales for each of four previous years. From this data, managers might project an increase

```
            A              B          C          D          E          F
       ==================================================================
   1.
   2.                            Sales Projection Report
   3.
   4.                   1984         1985       1986       1987      1988  (Proj)
   5.
   6.  Sales  (Units)    500          550        605        666       733
   7.
   8.                                                                    .
   9.
  10.
```

Figure 12-10.

Printouts from spreadsheet software reflect screen formats.

of 10 percent for sales in the coming year. A 10 percent increase in sales means that income will increase, and that production—and production costs—may have to be increased. Analyses and projections such as these also are facilitated under spreadsheet techniques.

Projecting Sales

To illustrate, Figure 12-10 presents a spreadsheet report for the sales projection example described above. Notice the relationships among figures for succeeding years.

These relationships can be expressed mathematically. That is, dividing the 1985 sales figure by the figure for 1984 produces a quotient of 1.10 (550/500 = 1.10), indicating a 10 percent increase (1.10 = 1 + .10) in sales. Applying the same calculation to figures for succeeding years produces the results that follow:

1986 Increase = 605/550 = 1.10
1987 Increase = 666/605 = 1.10.

To produce the projected figure for 1988, then, the figure for 1987 can be multiplied by the factor derived from an analysis of previous years. That is, the figure for 1987 is multiplied by 1.10, as shown below.

1988 Projection = 666 × 1.10 = 733.

The projected sales figure, 733 units, becomes a standard against which sales for the coming year will be measured. Further, to implement this goal, managers must make expenditures for production, advertising, staff levels, and other related factors. These expenditures, along with the expected revenues from sales, will be described in a budget document. The budget represents a detailed breakdown of expected performance. Comparisons of actual performance to budget projections, at any stage in the budget period, can indicate specific areas of success and failure.

In effect, just as baseball managers depend upon statistics tailored to specific situations to prepare teams for upcoming games, business managers depend upon skilled analyses of transaction data to prepare their organizations for future activities. Electronic spreadsheets are tools that provide managers with enhanced capabilities for status reporting and planning.

'What if . . . ?' analyses.   It should be stressed that the above example is an extreme simplification. In the real world, sales figures rarely increase (or decrease) uniformly from year to year. Rather, sales figures may increase by a certain percentage one year, decrease by another percentage the next year, and stay the same the year after. To achieve targeted performance, then, planning and budgeting mechanisms need to stay abreast of changing conditions.

Business planning and budgeting involve many factors. In the above example, product cost figures might be subtracted from sales revenues to determine **gross profits.** Or, sales figures might be broken down by individual products, of which there may be hundreds, by time periods, sales areas, store locations, and so on. The point is that spreadsheets enhance data analyses, and that electronic spreadsheets provide further enhancements.

In an actual business situation, the calculations and analyses of data can become rather complex. Further, planning and budgeting managers usually rely on a "What if . . . ?" approach to development.

Typically, managers evaluate historical data and ask a series of questions such as: What if sales decrease by 3 percent? What if the introduction of a competing product forces us to reduce prices for product X? What if a recession reduces discretionary income in our area by an average of $500 per household?

"What if . . . ?" analyses usually are iterative, or repeated, processes that incorporate factors derived from managers' experience, assumptions, and speculation. Presenting analysis results on spreadsheets often requires repeated moving and recalculating of entries. Electronic spreadsheets provide significant benefits to managers in supporting this type of analysis.

To illustrate, the section that follows returns to the case example of Mom's Video Market to discuss the purchase and implementation of an electronic spreadsheet application.

In essence, a spreadsheet package is a tool for comparing data, a tool that is used to manipulate resources to achieve results. The format of spreadsheet tools is flexible and can be changed repeatedly to meet requirements. In fact, the power of spreadsheet packages is enhanced by their ability to handle continuously changing formats. A spreadsheet package, however, still involves an expenditure—an expenditure that is wasted if the tool (package) doesn't do the intended job. While a tool is not a system, a systematic approach to the selection and purchase of any tool can provide many benefits.

Spreadsheet packages

are complete tools ready for application to requirements defined by people.

CASE SCENARIO: MOM'S VIDEO MARKET

Based upon her evaluations, Christine Beeman generally is satisfied with the performance of Mom's Video Market. Beeman already has designed and installed a database-oriented sales analysis system that is producing desired results. Both the customer and product files are growing steadily.

As her business grows, Beeman realizes that electronic spreadsheet capabilities can be applied in many areas. For example, she has been using manual techniques to produce income/expense summaries. In doing so, she identifies an attention-grabbing increase in product costs. Beeman realizes through this experience that, as the numbers of records and transactions increase, the potential for losses also increases—unless her analytical capabilities can keep pace. Therefore, Beeman makes a decision to enhance her reporting capabilities with an electronic spreadsheet package.

After an initial investigation, Beeman decides that the first requirement for package selection is that it must run on existing equipment. The microcomputer already in place (purchased for the sales analysis system) is available for periods of three to four hours in the morning and evening.

Beeman also discovers that—as is the case with most types of packages—hundreds of products exist that potentially can meet her needs. In short, Beeman is faced again with an abundance of choices and a need to evaluate and select from these choices systematically.

Defining Requirements

Beeman knows she first needs to understand exactly what she wants to do before she can implement a spreadsheet application effectively. Beeman decides to focus her initial activities on creating spreadsheet layouts, or formats. A spreadsheet layout designates column sizes, column and row headings, and formulas for calculated cell entries. Creating layouts is roughly equivalent to defining the data content of files for a database. By creating spreadsheet layouts, Beeman specifies data elements that will make up spreadsheet reports, as well as functions and capabilities required of the package. Beeman will incorporate these layouts into an abridged specification document that she can use to solicit proposals from potential vendors.

Beeman creates layouts for three spreadsheet reports:

- The income/expense summary, previously created manually, is the first report required.

- The *cost/profit analysis* breaks down product cost and revenue from products by individual cassettes, with subtotals generated for each title category.

- The activity report is an offshoot of the gross profit report. This spreadsheet presents data concerning number of rentals for title categories, and generates a percentage of total business for each category. In addition, corresponding figures for the previous year are presented for comparison.

Spreadsheets are tools for presenting and comparing data, and are adaptable to many situations. Viewed in this light, it might be tempting to purchase a package with as many features, functions, and, thus, as much flexibility as possible. This approach, however, easily leads to overkill in terms of both functions and capabilities. A package might be purchased that, because of its extensive capabilities, is difficult to learn and operate, and involves unnecessary expense as well.

To avoid these problems, Beeman studies and specifies requirements beforehand. The layouts that she creates as a means of defining requirements are discussed in the sections that follow.

Spreadsheet formulas. A spreadsheet formula is a mathematical operation described in a special way, according to the command structure of the application package that is used. Each formula applies to two values, or **operands.** Operand is a term that identifies a value used within mathematical operations. In spreadsheet formulas, operands are identified by their column and row positions. A cell is identified by the letter identifying the column and the number designating the row. Thus, the cell in the fourth row of the second column from the left is B4.

The functions to be performed are indicated by symbols placed between the operands:

- A plus sign (+) indicates an addition operation.

- A hyphen (−) is used for subtraction.

- An asterisk (∗) identifies a multiplication.

- A slash (/) is used as the sign for division.

- Another symbol, such as @, may be used to identify a range of cells to be totaled. When a range total is indicated, the computer will add and total all values in the group.

Each formula is entered into the cell in which the answer is to be carried within the spreadsheet.

Generating Reports

Designing layouts for output reports provides a basis for formatting spreadsheets. Spreadsheet entries will conform to the specifications described on these layouts. Keep this in mind as you read the sections that follow.

```
SpreadSheet: INCEXPSM                          Press ESC to quit
Create Format Enter Sum Save Print Retrieve Insert Remove Copy Move Prot
Retrieve a spreadsheet previously Saved in a disk file
   At--------------Bc--------Cc--------Dc--------Ec--------Fc--------
 1                     MOM'S VIDEO MARKET
 2                     INCOME/EXPENSE STATEMENT
 3
 4                   1rst QTR  2nd QTR  3rd QTR  4th QTR  YEAR END
 5    INCOME
 6  Credit Revenue                                       B6@E6
 7  Cash Revenue                                         B7@E7
 8  Other Revenue                                        B8@E8
 9    TOTAL INCOME  B6@B8    C6@C8    D6@D8    E6@E8    F6@F8
10
11    EXPENSE
12  Product Cost                                         B12@E12
13  Overhead                                             B13@E13
14  Credit Fees                                          B14@E14
15  Payroll                                              B15@E15
16  Miscellaneous                                        B16@E16
17    TOTAL EXPENSE B12@B16   C12@C16  D12@D16  E12@E16  F12@F16
18
19    NET PROFIT    B9-B17   C9-C17   D9-D17   E9-E17   F9-F17
20
```

Figure 12-11.

Once an overall format has been established, spreadsheet preparation typically involves entering headings, labels, and formulas.

Income/expense summary. Data elements for the income/expense summary are first recorded on cash register tapes and, subsequently, in the sales journal maintained by Beeman. Other entries come from the checkbook register. In effect, the work of creating a layout for this spreadsheet has been done already. Beeman simply uses the layout created for the manual report. This layout is presented in Figure 12-11.

Notice the entries in cells in the YEAREND column, in the TOTAL INCOME and EXPENSE rows, and in the NET PROFIT cell. These are the formulas through which entries in these positions will be derived. These formulas represent capabilities that will translate into requirements during package evaluations.

Formulas also will be used for projections and analyses. To illustrate, Figure 12-12 presents the income/expense report layout with additional entry positions for DIFFERENCES. These additional cells will indicate how much each entry category has increased or decreased since the last quarter. These numbers may be positive or negative. The package selected must be able to handle both types of numbers.

```
SpreadSheet: INCEXPSM                        Press ESC to quit
Create Format Enter Sum Save Print Retrieve Insert Remove Copy Move Prot
Remove a row or column from the spreadsheet
   At--------------Bc--------Cc--------Dc--------Ec--------Fc--------
   1                    MOM'S VIDEO MARKET
   2                    INCOME/EXPENSE STATEMENT
   3
   4              1rst QTR  2nd QTR  3rd QTR  4th QTR   YEAR END
   5   INCOME
   6 Credit Revenue                                    B6@E6
   7 Cash Revenue                                      B7@E7
   8 Other Revenue                                     B8@E8
   9    TOTAL INCOME  B6@B8    C6@C8    D6@D8    E6@E8   F6@F8
  10
  11   EXPENSE
  12 Product Cost                                      B12@E12
  13 Overhead                                          B13@E13
  14 Credit Fees                                       B14@E14
  15 Payroll                                           B15@E15
  16 Miscellaneous                                     B16@E16
  17    TOTAL EXPENSE B12@B16  C12@C16  D12@D16  E12@E16 F12@F16
  18
  19    PROFIT       B9-B17   C9-C17   D9-D17   E9-E17  F9-F17
  20 Differences              C19-B19  D19-C19  E19-D19
```

Figure 12-12.

Beeman adds a row, labeled "Differences", to indicate profit differences from one quarter to the next.

Beeman can apply this analysis to planning and budgeting activities. For example, Beeman might set a planning goal such as: Increase net profits by 10 percent. There are many ways to achieve this goal. Beeman might decide to increase advertising expenditures, or to purchase additional products. Of course, these actions must result in a revenue increase that is equivalent to the increase in expenses plus a 10 percent revenue increase.

On the other hand, net profits can be increased by reducing expenses. For example, Beeman might decide to promote cash sales to reduce credit card fees, or to implement a campaign of turning off unnecessary lights, heating ducts, and cutting back on staff time. Notice that all these courses of action will affect the worksheet entries. By controlling the operations that produce these entries, Beeman can derive a reasonable plan for meeting her goal. Then, the worksheet that describes her plan is used as a budget, a plan for spending and receiving money. At the end of each quarter, Beeman can compare actual performance with expected performance, as described in the budget. Serious deviations require corrective action or, perhaps, a reworking of the plan.

For example, consider again the quarterly differences for expenses and revenue. These figures show that, for the second quarter, expenses increase by

```
Product Number        C1234-01
Title                 Gone With the Wind
Current Period        $  33.00
Previous Period        106.00
Product Cost         __61.36
Product Profit        $  77.64
```

Figure 12-13.

Some of the entries for the cost/profit analysis can be derived from database references to product records.

$196.75 and revenues decrease by $3,006.75. Reviewing the figures, Beeman realizes that she can achieve her goal, a 10 percent net increase, by reducing expenses and increasing total revenues, both by 5 percent, during that quarter. Beeman speculates that the reduction in revenues is because the second quarter traditionally is when people take vacations. For this reason, she feels justified in cutting back staff hours to achieve the desired reduction. Further, to stimulate sales during this quarter, Beeman initiates a sales incentive. For every 10 cassettes rented by a single customer during the second quarter, the customer earns one free rental. This should motivate additional rentals.

Cost/profit analysis.   The next worksheet that Beeman wishes to prepare involves breakdowns of product profitability according to title categories. Title categories are designated by PRODNO fields within product records in a database file. Further data items for this worksheet, such as number of rentals, and revenue by quarters, and product cost figures, will be derived from the product file. This presents two considerations for Beeman.

First, most of the work of layout creation for this worksheet has been done already. That is, field widths from the database files will provide an indication of spreadsheet cell width. Beeman consults the data definition table for the product file, shown in Figure 12-13.

There are differences, however, between designations of field widths for physical storage and of cell widths on documents. Physical storage is "read" by computers; documents must be readable to humans. For this reason, Beeman must add two spaces to field widths to compensate for margins between cells. Without these spaces, spreadsheet entries would run together continuously, and would be hard to read. Further, a numeric field with two decimal places translates into another additional space on a spreadsheet, the additional space used to hold the decimal point. As part of her requirements specification, Beeman drafts a sample of the format she visualizes. This format is shown in Figure 12-14.

Notice the rows labeled SUBTOTAL in the layout. Entries within these rows will represent quarterly indications of the performance of specific product categories. In setting up this worksheet, Beeman has created another powerful

```
At-------Bn-------Cn-------Dn-------En-------Fn-------Gn-----Hn------
 1
 2                    Sales/Analysis Report
 3
 4 PRODUCT  REVNUE   REVNUE   REVNUE   REVNUE   REVENUE  PRDCT  GROSS
 5 NUMBER   QRTR1    QRTR2    QRTR3    QRTR4    YEAR     COST   PROFIT
 6
 7                                              B7@E7           F7-G7
 8                                              B8@E8           F8-G8
 9                                              B9@E9           F9-G9
10                                              B10@E10         F10-G10
11                                              B11@E11         F11-G11
12 SUBTOTAL B7@B11   C7@C11   D7@D11   E7@E11   F7@F11   G7@G11 F12-G12
13
14                                              B14@E14         F14-G14
15                                              B15@E15         F15-G15
16                                              B16@E16         F16-G16
17                                              B17@E17         F17-G17
18                                              B18@E18         F18-G18
19 SUBTOTAL B14@B18  C14@C18  D14@D18  E14@E18  F14@F18  G14@G18F19-G19
20
```

Figure 12-14.

A spreadsheet can be developed to compare revenues and costs by product. The result is a profit analysis for each product.

tool for analyzing her business—specifically her customers. Titles are categorized according to general market segments toward which they are targeted. The largest selling category should indicate the largest market segment with which Beeman is dealing. Beeman will use this information to set prices, design advertising campaigns, sales promotions, and so on. Beeman also decides to produce a related worksheet, an activity report.

Rental activity report. The final spreadsheet that Beeman designs is related to the cost/profit analysis, but deals with activity, or numbers of rentals, by tape category. Profitability is an indirect measure of activity, but profitability depends upon cost of product as well as rental charge. In this analysis, Beeman wants to analyze rental activity exclusively. That is, the activity report is to describe the amount of rental activity, by category, and the percentage of total activity each category represents.

Data elements for this spreadsheet also will be derived from the product file in the database created for the sales analysis system. That is, a monthly total will be derived for each category using the CURPD field in the product file. Then, these entries will be related to entries in other cells for current year-to-date, and to the percent total of yearly activity. In addition, the same entry headings will be designated for the previous year.

Figure 12-15.

Spreadsheet programs can be used to analyze revenue according to market segment. Display at top has formulas in place. Bottom display shows computed results.

```
SpreadSheet File: ACTREP


   At--------Bn------Cn------Dn------Ep-----Fn------------Gn------Hp-----
 1                          MOM'S VIDEO MARKET
 2                          ACTIVITY REPORT
 3
 4                                              PREVIOUS YEAR'S FIGURES
 5 TITLE      YEAR    THIS    YEAR    PER-         THIS    YEAR    PER-
 6 CATEGORY   TODATE  MONTH   TODATE  CENTAGE      MONTH   TODATE  CENTAGE
 7
 8 Adult                      B8+C8   D8/D16                       G8/G16
 9 Children                   B9+C9   D9/D16                       G9/G16
10 Drama                      B10+C10 D10/D16                      G10/G16
11 Fitness                    B11+C11 D11/D16                      G11/G16
12 Humor                      B12+C12 D12/D16                      G12/G16
13 Kids                       B13+C13 D13/D16                      G13/G16
14 Thriller                   B14+C14 D14/D16                      G14/G16
15
16   TOTALS  B8@B15  C8@C15  D8@D15  E8@E15     F8@F15  G8@G15  H8@H15
17
```

```
SpreadSheet File: ACTREP


                        MOM'S VIDEO MARKET
                        ACTIVITY REPORT

                                            PREVIOUS YEAR'S FIGURES
    TITLE      YEAR    THIS    YEAR    PER-      THIS    YEAR    PER-
    CATEGORY   TODATE  MONTH   TODATE  CENTAGE   MONTH   TODATE  CENTAGE

    Adult      15428   6437    21865   42.4      5576    11287   38.3
    Children   10539   4537    15076   29.2      4976    13827   46.9
    Drama       4589    479     5068    9.8      4687      427    1.4
    Fitness      210     15      225    0.4       124        3    0.0
    Humor       2789    312     3101    6.0       473     3298   11.2
    Kids        4609    458     5067    9.8      4875      502    1.7
    Thriller    1095     99     1194    2.3      1287      122    0.4

     TOTALS   39259   12337   51596 9990.0     21998   29466 9990.0
```

```
PROBLEM DEFINITION FOR SPREADSHEET SELECTION

Implement an electronic spreadsheet package that can run on
the existing microcomputer and can support the analyses and
reporting activities illustrated in attached layouts.
     Package should be capable of producing spreadsheets on
terminal screen and as printed outputs.
     Package should include standard data manipulation
functions: Join, Erase, Delete, Insert, Move, as well as
capabilities for performing arithmetic operations upon entries
within columns and rows.
     Package should be able to accept keyboard inputs of data
items.  The ability to pull selected items from database files
is highly desirable.
     A menu capability for defining spreadsheet formats must be
included.
     Package should be capable of handling data elements and
formats specified in attached layouts.
     Layouts are to serve as test data.  Selection decision
will be based upon "walkthroughs" of report production from
these layouts.
```

Figure 12-16.

Beeman's investigation of system requirements leads to a comprehensive problem definition.

Figure 12-15 presents the activity report layout. A finished version of the report is included. Consider the information that can be derived from the finished report. In effect, the report indicates many of the buying habits of Beeman's customers. The inclusion of previous year figures shows which categories—and customer groups—are increasing or decreasing in activity. From this information, Beeman forms marketing strategies. She may decide, for example, to sell off tapes in slow-moving categories at a discount. The title categories that exhibit intense activity might be featured in advertising or promotional campaigns.

The creation of layouts for these three applications—income/expense summary, cost/profit analysis, and rental activity report—provides a basis for selecting an application package. These layouts are the basis of the specification she uses to support her purchase decision. The specification parallels the system specification Beeman developed to implement the sales analysis system. The specification for the spreadsheet application is presented in Figure 12-16.

```
            A              B            C            D            E            F
 1   ============================================================================
 2   SAMPLE DATA
 3   ============================================================================
 4
 5                    Product V     Product W    Product X    Product Y    Product Z
 6                    ----------    ----------   ----------   ----------   ----------
 7   Unit Price           10.95        11.95        14.95         6.95        21.95
 8   Unit Sales           22,300       15,300       20,700      128,900       6,500
 9   Dollar Sales       $244,185     $182,835     $309,465     $895,855     $142,675
10
11   Unit Cost             5.47         6.02         7.35         3.20        11.40
12   Costs of Goods     $121,981      $92,106     $152,145     $412,480      $74,100
13                    ----------    ----------   ----------   ----------   ----------
14   Gross Margin       $122,204      $90,729     $157,320     $483,375      $68,575
```

Figure 12-17.

This spreadsheet printout presents revenue and cost figures for individual products.

Notice that the problem definition excludes any requirement for graphics capabilities. Although Beeman sees no immediate need for graphics capabilities, she realizes that many leading spreadsheet packages include graphics. For this reason, it is highly likely that the package that best meets her requirements will include graphics. The generation of graphics from spreadsheet data is discussed in the section that follows.

GRAPHICS: THE BIGGER PICTURE

An old saying can be paraphrased to read "One picture is worth a thousand data items." That is, graphics are based upon the principle of distilling large volumes of data to promote meaning and understanding. As an example, consider the spreadsheet in Figure 12-17.

This spreadsheet presents a breakdown of product costs, units sold, sales revenues, and gross profit margins for products labeled V through Z. The relationships among these data items are many and varied. To illustrate, consider the relationships among total dollar sales, costs of goods sold, and gross margins for each product. In the spreadsheet, these relationships are represented by a collection of data items that includes figures for dollar sales, costs of goods sold, and gross margin for all products. These relationships may not be discernible to people unfamiliar with spreadsheet formats.

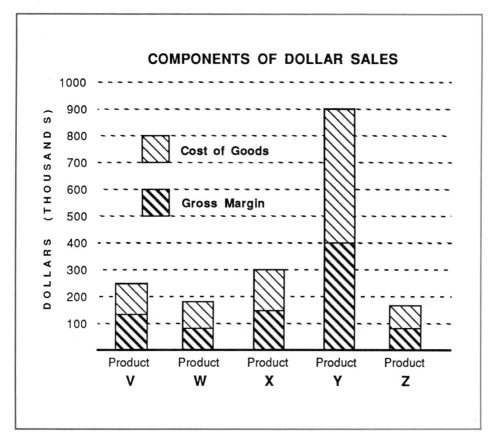

COMPONENTS OF DOLLAR SALES

Figure 12-18.

Data representing dollar sales and costs of goods may be presented as a stacked bar chart.

As an alternative, consider the graphic in Figure 12-18. The total sales amount for each product is represented by the entire bar. In turn, each bar includes segments representing gross margin and cost of goods sold. The relationships among these factors become readily apparent in this type of graphic, known as a **stacked bar chart.** A stacked bar chart is one of several standard types of graphics included with many spreadsheet packages. These standard graphics include:

- Bar charts
- Pie charts
- Trend line graphs.

Bar Charts

Bar charts, also called **histograms,** represent data values as lengths of bars. See Figure 12-19. Multiple comparisons, or breakdowns of overall figures, can be set up for comparison in stacked bar charts, described above.

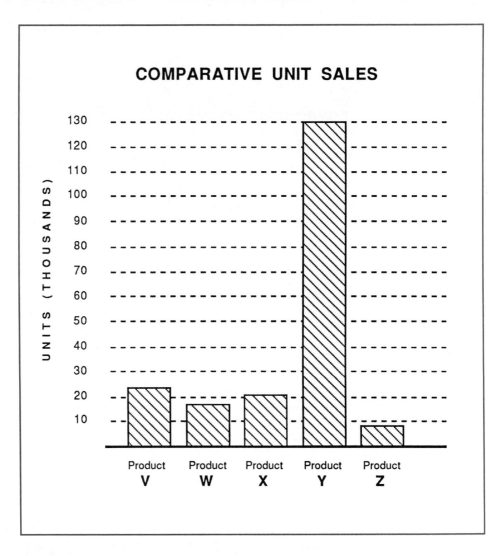

Figure 12-19.

Bar charts facilitate comparisons of data values.

Pie Charts

Pie charts are used to show the relationship of component parts to a whole. For example, individual categories of expense items can be related to overall operating expenses. See Figure 12-20.

Trend Lines

Trend lines, or **line graphs,** show the relative up and down movements of data values, such as for income or expense, during a certain time period. Figure 12-21 presents trend lines for sales, costs, and profits across a period of several months. Notice that the trend lines are extended into a future period. Trend lines are used in this way to make projections. The trend line simply is extended to a point in time represented on the graph. The value at which the line intersects with the point in time is the projected value.

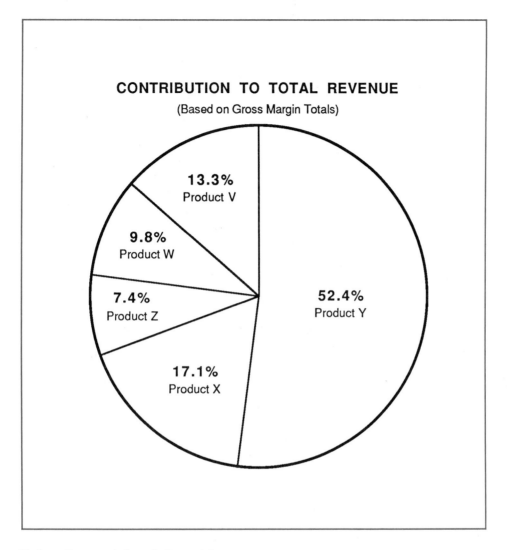

CONTRIBUTION TO TOTAL REVENUE
(Based on Gross Margin Totals)

13.3%
Product V

9.8%
Product W

7.4%
Product Z

17.1%
Product X

52.4%
Product Y

Figure 12-20.

A pie chart illustrates the relationships of parts to a whole value.

Using Spreadsheet Graphics

Many spreadsheet packages include integrated graphics capabilities. That is, data from spreadsheets can be read into programs for generating graphs on screen displays. To produce hard copies, a separate print program may be required.

Business graphics usually are used in one of two ways. Produced as screen displays, they provide a "picture" of patterns and relationships among data elements in a spreadsheet. Thus, a graphic might be used to enhance evaluations, such as those described above. In addition, graphics often are used in formal presentations. Managers and other business professionals who make these presentations usually want extensive flexibility in terms of type sizes and styles for headings, and for graph types. There are many ways of producing presentation-quality graphics. For example, a properly equipped system can create multicolored graphic outputs on color video displays or special printers. Or,

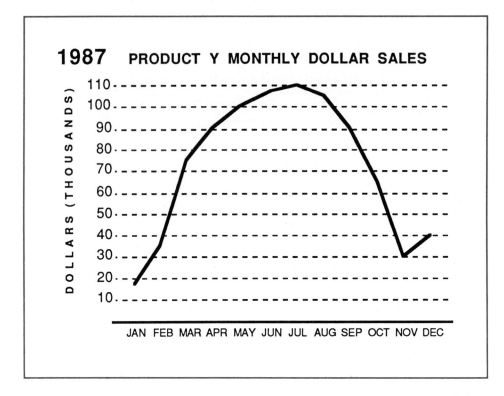

1987 PRODUCT Y MONTHLY DOLLAR SALES

Figure 12-21.

Trend lines like this one are effective tools for tracking and displaying data about performance over time, or trends.

photographs of screen displays can be taken and developed as projection slides. Regardless of method for producing outputs, however, generation of business graphics from spreadsheet data usually is executed under certain common techniques.

These types of considerations would go into a problem definition for an application under which graphics are required.

CASE SCENARIO: GENERATING GRAPHICS FROM SPREADSHEET DATA

Spreadsheet packages with graphics capabilities usually include a graphics option on the main menu. The examples in this section are taken from a popular spreadsheet package, Lotus 1-2-3. Suppose you are using this package and want to create a line graph from the spreadsheet display shown in Figure 12-22.

Notice the GRAPH option on the main menu at the top of the display. Selecting this option shifts the system into the graphics mode. In this mode, the program displays a subsequent menu for creating and formatting graphs. The first selection that must be made concerns the type of graph you wish to create. Again, notice that executing these decisions simply involves choosing selections from menus that proceed through logical steps to complete the task. Thus, the TYPE and LINE options are selected consecutively from menu displays.

```
       A           B          C          D          E          F
 1  =============================================================================
 2                          INCOME/EXPENSE SUMMARY
 3  =============================================================================
 4
 5                  1RST QRTR  2ND QRTR   3RD QRTR   4RTH QRTR  YEAR END
 6                  ---------  ---------  ---------  ---------  ---------
 7  INCOME
 8    Credit        13756.80   11908.55   14750.75   17985.55   58401.65
 9    Cash           9234.80    8034.40   11893.50   14894.33   44057.03
10    Other           548.90     590.80     450.60     780.50    2370.80
11  TOTAL           23540.50   20533.75   27904.85   33660.38  104829.48
12
13  EXPENSES
14    Product cost    655.70     805.40     785.40    1080.60    3327.10
15    Overhead       7220.35    6145.80    5359.50    9465.75   28191.40
16    Credit fees     540.55     490.70     675.90     784.30    2491.45
17    Payroll        2787.50    2754.30    2824.50    3495.70   11862.00
18    Misc            743.80     940.55     853.90     790.55    3328.88
19  TOTAL           11947.98   11136.75   10499.20   15616.90   49200.83
```

Figure 12-22.

An income/expense report usually presents data for several reporting periods.

At this point, the system is ready to accept data for use in creating the graph. The ABCDEF option on the graph menu allows you to include up to six ranges on a graph. In this example, two trend lines—one each for income and expense figures—are to be included. Selecting the A option causes a prompt to be displayed requesting a range of values. On the spreadsheet, income figures appear in the range of cells, B4 through B9. Thus, the entry "B4..B9" is keyed in response to the prompt. For 1-2-3, a range is specified with two periods (..). The second trend line is created by selecting the B option from the main menu and specifying the range of values for expense figures (C4..C9).

The final step in generating the graph is to enter VIEW from the graph menu. Selecting this option causes the system to convert the format and data information you have entered into the appropriate graph—provided your system is equipped with graphics capability. Without this capability, the graph still can be sent to an appropriate printer. Assuming that you do have this capability, the line graph now is displayed on your terminal screen.

To complete the graph, titles, labels and other information must be included. The graph menu includes an option for this procedure, labeled TITLES. Selecting this option causes the system to display a prompt screen that gives you the choices that follow:

FIRST   SECOND   X-AXIS   Y-AXIS.

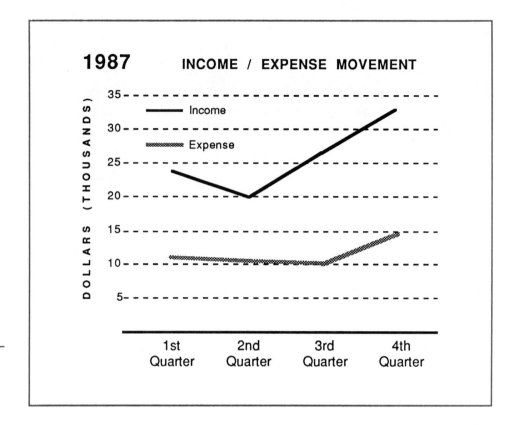

Figure 12-23.

The trend line derived from the income/expense report in the previous figure is presented here.

The FIRST and SECOND options are used to enter two lines of heading for the overall graph. In this example, one line of heading identifies the graph sufficiently. The FIRST option is selected, a prompt is displayed requesting a title entry. The title, Income/Expense Movement, is entered for this example. The SECOND option might be used to identify the year represented by the graph. The X-AXIS and Y-AXIS options are selected to label the horizontal and vertical axes, respectively, of the graph. The 1-2-3 package provides an option for specifying the content of spreadsheet cells as labels. The entries, QUARTERS and DOLLARS (THOUSANDS), can be keyed or the cells in which they are held can be specified in response to appropriate prompts.

The final task is to label the two trend lines in the graph. This is done by selecting the OPTIONS and then LEGENDS selections from processing menus. At this point, different symbols and labels can be assigned to the income and expense trend lines. Once this information has been specified, the graphic should be understandable. The final graphic, produced as a result of the operations described above, should resemble the one presented in Figure 12-23.

Other options provided by the 1-2-3 package include capabilities for manipulating the scale, or the graduated measure of axes, to meet requirements for output, such as paper size. Line graphs can be output as continuous lines, series of scattered points, combinations of lines and symbols, and so on.

K E Y   T E R M S

summary of income and
   expenses

zero

range

data entry area

current cell

strategic planning

tactical planning

operational planning

budget

gross profits

cost/profit analysis

operand

stacked bar chart

bar chart

histogram

pie chart

trend line

line graph

D E F I N I T I O N S

Instructions: On a separate sheet, define each term according to its use in
this chapter.

1. summary of income and expenses

2. current cell

3. strategic plan

4. tactical plan

5. operational plan

6. cost/profit analysis

7. operand

8. trend line

T R U E / F A L S E

Instructions: For each statement, write T for true or F for false on a separate sheet.

1. The cost/profit analysis—also known as the cost of making a profit—is a study that tells a business how much money it must spend before it can generate enough income to show a profit.

2. Business statistics are based on transaction data.

3. Spreadsheets present data in formats that make comparison unnecessary.

4. In a standard spreadsheet, the cell in the fourth row of the second column from the left is 4B.

5. Designing layouts for output reports provides a basis for formatting spreadsheets.

6. "Zeroing" a cash register is another term for balancing it.

7. Electronic spreadsheet packages provide capabilities for calculating cell entries by performing arithmetic functions upon values within cells.

8. The first step in building an electronic spreadsheet is laying out all the numeric data in ascending order and the labels and headings in alphabetical order.

9. Entry procedures for formulas or functions are made from a different section of the keyboard than is used for making data entries.

10. In a standard spreadsheet program, the FORMAT function sets up data types and sizes for column entries.

11. Presenting analysis results on spreadsheets often requires repeated moving and recalculating of entries.

12. A trend line is the line that divides the pieces of a pie chart.

13. A histogram is an old or "historic" bar chart.

14. Pie charts are used to show relationships among the component parts of a whole.

15. Graphics capabilities are usually an expensive add-on to the final price of any spreadsheet package.

S H O R T   A N S W E R   Q U E S T I O N S

Instructions: On a separate sheet of paper, answer each question in one or two brief sentences.

1. What is a spreadsheet?

2. What is the first step in preparing a spreadsheet, and why is it the first step?

3. Why is the spreadsheet an ideal format for presenting summary reports of income and expenses?

4. How can a spreadsheet help you "score" business performance?

5. What, in general terms, is the main difference between a strategic plan and a tactical plan?

6. How does the use of formulas and functions enhance the flexibility of electronic spreadsheets?

R E S E A R C H   P R O J E C T

On paper, design the rows, columns, headings, labels, and formulas you would need to create a spreadsheet showing your academic and/or economic performances over the past three years. Use these figures to project an achievable goal for next year, and develop the operational plans necessary to meet it.

V
More Microcomputer Software

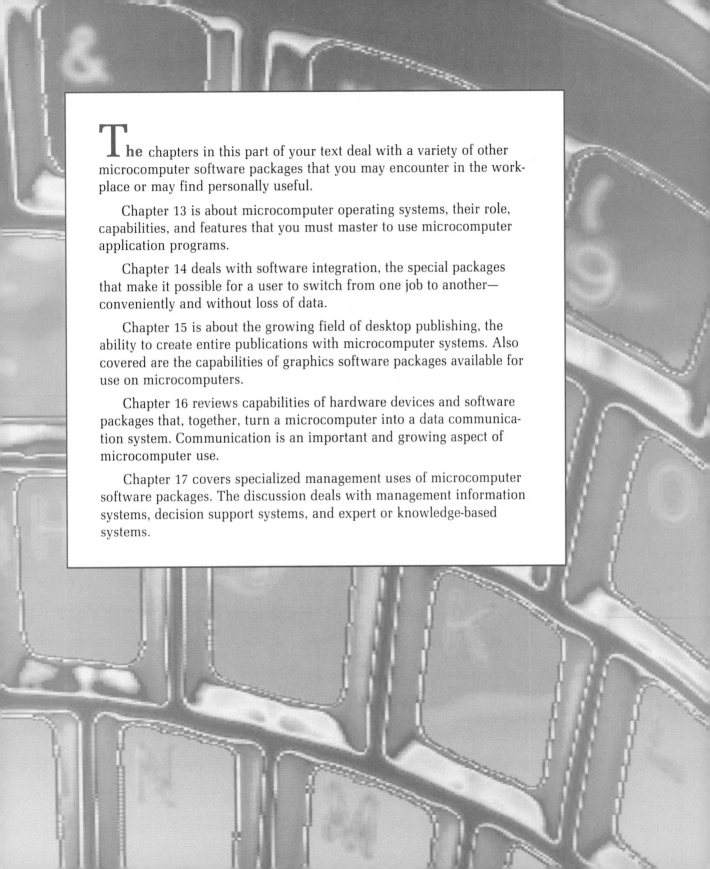

The chapters in this part of your text deal with a variety of other microcomputer software packages that you may encounter in the workplace or may find personally useful.

Chapter 13 is about microcomputer operating systems, their role, capabilities, and features that you must master to use microcomputer application programs.

Chapter 14 deals with software integration, the special packages that make it possible for a user to switch from one job to another—conveniently and without loss of data.

Chapter 15 is about the growing field of desktop publishing, the ability to create entire publications with microcomputer systems. Also covered are the capabilities of graphics software packages available for use on microcomputers.

Chapter 16 reviews capabilities of hardware devices and software packages that, together, turn a microcomputer into a data communication system. Communication is an important and growing aspect of microcomputer use.

Chapter 17 covers specialized management uses of microcomputer software packages. The discussion deals with management information systems, decision support systems, and expert or knowledge-based systems.

13 Microcomputer System Software

SOFTWARE DEVELOPMENTS

The development of packaged software systems for computers is a relatively recent trend.

DISK OPERATING SYSTEM (DOS)

The Disk Operating System (DOS) does just what its name implies: it operates the computer system and is stored on disk.

Disk Handler

Part of DOS, the disk handler is a basic segment of the operating system that maintains a directory of files stored on disk devices.

Peripheral Controller

The peripheral controller is a DOS subprogram that interacts with the keyboard, display screen, communications devices and other peripherals.

Command Interpreter

The command interpreter is a DOS subprogram that contains routines for copying, deleting, renaming, and erasing files. In addition, it usually handles tasks related to loading programs.

CP/M

CP/M stands for Control Program for Microprocessors, which was developed in 1975 to establish a processing environment for the eight-bit processor used for most of the original microcomputers.

SOFTWARE DEVELOPMENTS

Computers are programmed to perform specific tasks. Even the most generic operations—such as formatting storage areas, executing calculations, or producing outputs—are based on instructions written by programmers. The development of packaged software for standard applications is a relatively recent development for computers.

In the past, application programming required specialized knowledge of memory circuits and binary coding, as well as processing specifications. Programs were written in binary notation, strings of 0 and 1 entries. In effect, computers were programmed on a bit-by-bit basis, and every individual operation was specified. For example, to retrieve a single data element, the computer required instructions that described the specific data element, its external storage location, and the memory address into which it was to be put.

As software evolved, generic processing functions, such as establishing directories and formatting disks, were written to establish processing environments into which other programs could be incorporated. Programs could be written as collections of subsystems, or modules, that interacted with the generic functions of *system software.* System software refers to programs that control and monitor hardware operations and other software routines.

377

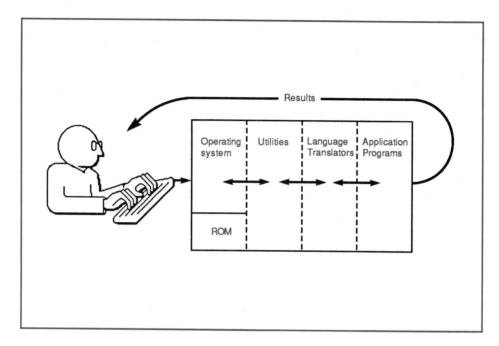

Results

| Operating system | Utilities | Language Translators | Application Programs |

ROM

Figure 13-1.

Microcomputer software translates user requirements into machine commands through a series of program levels.

In another development, translator programs converted high-level, or English-like, statements, into executable machine-language instructions. The configuration of systems moved from a programming-intensive process to a process that focused on the logic of problem solutions. Systems could be built as layers, or levels, of software. At high levels (close to users), processing instructions consist of user responses to prompts. Prompts are displayed by application programs. Application programs interact with lower-level (close to hardware) system software routines to implement processing. The relationships among software levels are diagrammed in Figure 13-1.

Of course, the evolution of software was highly complex—much more so than the brief treatment given here. The point is that throughout this process, common processing functions were identified at all levels. For example, virtually any information system requires the creation of files, and the writing of data and information to files. Directories must be created to identify files and to locate those files for access operations. In addition, some systems establish reference schemes, such as indexes, within file structures that are set up and maintained under software control.

One of the results of identifying common software functions is the application software package, discussed in previous chapters. For microcomputer systems, the writing of program code to execute standard business applications is extremely rare. Software has evolved to a point at which systems can be built, level by level, with programming components purchased "off the shelf." As stated in earlier chapters, knowledge of the internal workings of these components is not a prerequisite for computer use. However, professionalism implies a supporting body of knowledge.

Thus, computer users—at any level of proficiency—can benefit from an understanding of the nature of software and of the functions and services that are provided at each level. This chapter discusses the software component that establishes a processing environment for microcomputer-based application packages—system software.

A computer cannot run most application programs until an ***operating system*** is loaded into memory. An operating system is a set of programs that monitors and operates computer hardware and other software routines. An operating system is the major element of system software.

Just as application packages meet common business requirements, operating systems were developed to perform common system functions. Common functions include the following processes:

- Control interaction between hardware components, such as the keyboard, processor, display, disk drives, and printers.

- Allocate storage space and monitor files.

- Generate signals for data communication and for the operation of printers, plotters, and other peripheral devices.

- Supervise use and execution of application software.

- Accept programming language instructions written by people and transform these instructions into machine language that can be accepted and processed by computers.

In effect, an operating system gives the user control of a microcomputer system. However, each operating system provides control, in the form of services and functions, in a different way. The section that follows discusses the most common operating systems used for microcomputers. Each discussion includes examples of the commands and methods used to execute the functions mentioned above.

DISK OPERATING SYSTEM (DOS)

The ***disk operating system (DOS)*** was developed for the IBM PC, a popular business tool. DOS is sold through two vendors, IBM and Microsoft. The IBM version, known as PC-DOS, usually is purchased with an IBM microcomputer. However, since the introduction of the IBM PC, many manufacturers offer machines that are compatible with IBM systems. For these types of computers, called PC compatibles, an equivalent version of DOS is available. This version, called MS-DOS, derives its name from Microsoft, the company that markets it. For discussion purposes, and because the two versions are functionally identical, the term, DOS, is used comprehensively here.

The largest number of computers sold for business use are IBM PCs or PC compatibles. In turn, the largest number of software packages available are designed to run in a DOS environment. This fact is of great importance to business users. In effect, the greatest flexibility is afforded by a PC or compatible system operating in a DOS environment.

DOS consists of four fundamental sections, which include:

- Disk handler

- Peripheral controller

- Command interpreter

- Utilities

Disk Handler

As stated previously, a basic function of operating systems is the maintenance of file directories stored on disk devices. Because of the fundamental nature of this function, the DOS disk handler subprogram is stored in a **hidden file,** or **system file.** This type of file requires special handling before it can be accessed and/or manipulated by a user. In addition, this file is not listed in regular directory displays.

In PC-DOS systems, the **disk handler file** is labeled IBMDOS.COM. The format of this file name is typical of the way operating systems label files. Notice the name consists of a string of characters, a period (.), and three more characters. The first string of characters is unique to that file. In effect, the file is identified by this initial string. The period separates the identifier from its **suffix.** A suffix designates a specific type of file. Many operating systems use the ".COM" suffix to describe files that contain command routines.

The disk handler executes commands for creating and maintaining disk directories. In addition, the disk handler locates files for reading and/or writing operations and performs other built-in file-handling functions.

Peripheral Controller

The **peripheral controller** interacts with the keyboard, display screen, communication devices, and other peripherals. This subprogram is located in another hidden file, called IBMBIO.COM in PC-based systems. The characters, BIO, in this label are an acronym for basic input/output, and refer to the interaction of software and equipment. Many systems control peripherals through a combination of system software routines and read-only memory (ROM).

The peripheral controller performs many basic functions. Keyboard entries are converted into machine-language notations and echoed on the display screen. In addition, this subprogram generates error messages when peripherals do not function properly. For example, a message such as "PRINTER NEEDS ATTEN-TION" might be generated because a transfer of information to a printer cannot be completed.

Command Interpreter

The **command interpreter** contains several common functions. This subprogram usually is stored as a file labeled, COMMAND.COM. This file is accessible to users and may be modified with relative ease. In general, this file contains routines for copying, deleting, renaming, and erasing files. The commands within this file also handle tasks related to loading programs. For this reason, the command interpreter must be loaded before applications are run.

Batch files.   The command interpreter is responsible for handling **batch files** set up by users. That is, a routine is included by which a series of keyboard commands can be stored as a file. Then, the commands can be executed in their order of entry. For example, when DOS is booted, or loaded, a ROM operation is initiated to search for a file labeled, AUTOEXEC.BAT. In this context, the ".BAT" suffix designates a batch file.

If the AUTOEXEC.BAT file is located, the computer automatically executes the resident commands. This file is set up and used to save users the time of loading individual files. For example, a writer might set up an AUTOEXEC.BAT file to load the operating system, display time and date, and load a word processor—simply by inserting the disk and turning the system on. This type of batch file frees business executives and other users from the necessity of learning special commands to start programs.

In effect, batch files are instruction sets built by users from standard operating system commands. To enhance this capability, the command interpreter contains internal commands—such as GOTO, IF/IF NOT, PAUSE, and REM—that allow users to set up interactive routines and/or specialized batch operations.

Housekeeping commands.   The term, **housekeeping commands**, describes a set of routines internal to the command interpreter. That is, loading the operating

```
A>DIR

   Volume in drive A has no label
   Directory of  A:\

   COMMAND  COM    17792   10-20-83   12:00p
   AUTOEXEC BAT       83    3-17-86    3:03p
   WP       EXE   153344    4-16-84    4:19p
   WPMSG    TXT    12813    3-15-84    5:26p
   WPHELP   TXT    40378    2-21-84    4:07p
   WPSYSD   SYS      407    1-01-80   12:02a
   EPSONFX  PAT     1920   11-03-83    5:12p
   WPQUE    SYS      900   12-04-86    3:24p
   FORMAT   COM     6912   10-20-83   12:00p
   SETCLOCK COM      853    9-19-82
   ASTCLOCK COM      813    9-18-82
   CHKDSK   COM     6400   10-20-83   12:00p
   DISKCOPY COM     2576   10-20-83   12:00p
   DISKCOMP COM     2188   10-20-83   12:00p
   COMP     COM     2534   10-20-83   12:00p
   RECOVERY EXE    28032    5-15-83    3:50p
          16 File(s)      54272 bytes free

A>
```

Figure 13-2.

A DOS directory display presents a listing of file names and sizes, as well as date and time of last access.

system automatically loads the command interpreter. Then, housekeeping commands can be executed without the necessity of locating and accessing these subprograms on disk. The DOS housekeeping commands used most commonly in business applications include:

- The COPY command is used to copy stored files from one device to another. The most common application for this function is to create backup copies of files for storage on separate disks.

- The DIR command is used to display the contents of a directory, the size in bytes of each file, and the date and time each file was created or last changed. See Figure 13-2.

- The DEL or ERASE command is used to delete, or erase, files.

- The TIME command is used to display the time of day. A DATE command also is included in most DOS systems.

This list, by no means complete, is meant to give you an idea of the types of command module functions. Other internal functions can be found in an appropriate DOS manual. The command interpreter also controls the execution of utility programs, discussed below.

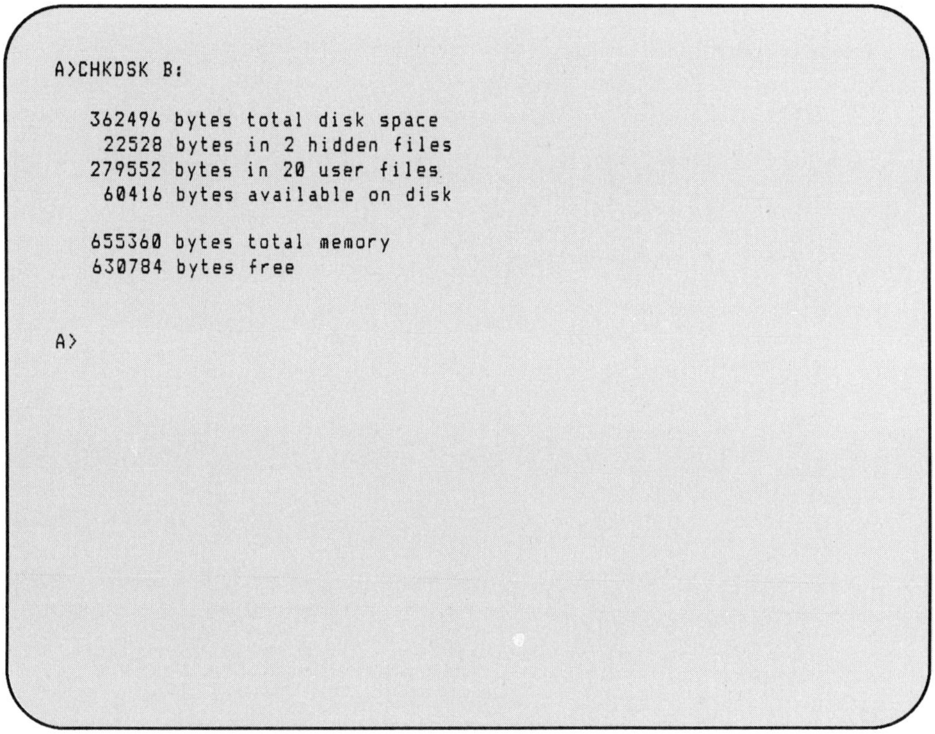

```
A>CHKDSK B:

    362496 bytes total disk space
     22528 bytes in 2 hidden files
    279552 bytes in 20 user files
     60416 bytes available on disk

    655360 bytes total memory
    630784 bytes free


A>
```

Figure 13-3.

The CHKDSK utility presents a summary of physical space allocation on a specified disk and in main memory.

Utilities. A *utility program* also performs standard system functions. Utility programs are stored externally, or on disk. Thus, the command interpreter finds and executes utilities in response to user (or application program) requests—provided the appropriate disk is accessible (inserted into a disk drive).

The execution of most DOS utilities is interactive—and therefore, easily performed by users. For example, to format a disk, a user keys the command, FORMAT, when the "A>" prompt is displayed. Then, a series of prompts instructs the user to insert a disk to be formatted into the proper disk drive and to strike a key when formatting should begin. This type of processing is described as *user friendly,* and is one factor in the widespread acceptance of DOS.

Users may access several utility programs commonly found in DOS:

- The DISKCOPY utility is used to make an exact copy of an entire diskette. This command is useful for making backup copies of disks.

- The CHKDSK utility is used to check the filled and free space on a disk. Executing this routine generates a screen display like the one in Figure 13-3. This utility also provides options by which capabilities are provided to correct errors in file directories. These options are discussed in DOS manuals, which should be consulted before the CHKDSK option is executed.

```
A>format b:
Insert new diskette for drive B:
and strike any key when ready

Formatting...Format complete

    362496 bytes total disk space
     46080 bytes in bad sectors
    316416 bytes available on disk

Format another (Y/N)?
```

Figure 13-4.

A FORMAT operation prepares a diskette for recording. Message displays indicate the amount of readable and unreadable sectors (if any) on the formatted diskette.

- The COMP utility is used to compare the content of one file, or set of files, with another. Thus, the COMP utility could be run after a COPY procedure to ensure that the original and backup versions of a file are identical.

- The FORMAT utility is used to prepare a disk for recording in a DOS format. As part of this utility, the tracks of a disk are analyzed to locate defective areas. This procedure often is called ***initializing*** a disk. Formatting a disk erases all data on the disk, or at least all directory entries for the disk. Therefore, the FORMAT utility should be used with caution. See Figure 13-4.

- The MODE utility is used to set the mode of operation on a printer, monitor, or communications device. That is, this utility sets parameters of data transfer to match those of receiving devices. This utility is discussed further in later chapters.

- The RECOVER utility provides capabilities for recovering files from disks that contain defective sectors. For example, suppose a data file has developed a single bad sector. Under normal access procedures, an error message is displayed and no portion of the file can be accessed. With the RECOVER utility, all sectors except the bad one can be recovered. In addition, if a directory has been damaged, it may appear that the entire disk has been lost. The

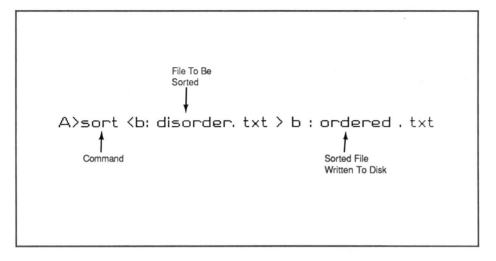

File To Be
Sorted

A>sort <b: disorder. txt > b : ordered . txt

Command

Sorted File
Written To Disk

Figure 13-5.

*The command structure for a
SORT operation includes specifications of the file to be sorted
and a name for the sorted file.*

RECOVER utility bypasses the defective directory and accesses files on the
disk.

- The SORT utility is used to arrange data in a specified order, usually the
  order in which characters appear in the ASCII table. See Figure 13-5.

Programming utilities. Most business users will never need to write or edit
program code to run applications. Thus, programming utilities may be of little
interest. However, DOS provides three utilities by which users can write, edit,
and debug many levels of program code. Remember: the power of microcomputers stems from the ability to tailor the configuration of systems to application
requirements. The programming utilities merely extend this capability.

The three programming utilities included with DOS systems include:

- The EDLIN utility is a type of program known as a ***line editor.*** A line editor
  is used to create and edit text or batch files, line by line. Thus, EDLIN can
  be used to create and edit ***source programs,*** or programs written in human-
  readable programming languages. In addition, EDLIN can be used to insert,
  delete, change, or display lines of text. EDLIN also provides limited search
  and replace capabilities. Files created or edited with EDLIN can be saved to
  disk for reuse or further changes.

- The LINK.EXE utility is a professional programming tool used mainly by
  programmers. In essence, the LINK utility combines, or links, separately
  produced modules of object programs. This utility also provides other options for specialized situations.

- The DEBUG.COM utility is an extensive programming tool. This utility is an
  interactive, machine-language program debugger. That is, capabilities are

provided for debugging, or correcting errors, within machine-language programs. These capabilities are enhanced by provisions to access any location on a disk file or any memory address. The DEBUG utility included in later versions (2.0 and above) of DOS also features an ASSEMBLE command. This command can be used to write short, **assembly language** programs. An assembly language, or **assembler,** is a program that converts alphanumeric statements into machine language instructions on a one-to-one basis. This is the only assembly capability included with most DOS systems.

The above discussion of DOS functions presents an overview of this common operating system. In addition, Microsoft and IBM continually improve and update this operating system. For example, as updates have been added, DOS has gained capabilities to accommodate hard disks and increases in floppy disk capacities, to support additional peripheral devices, to set communications protocols, and other options.

There is a saying in the computer field: As hardware goes, so goes software. This refers to software developments responding to increasing hardware capabilities. This pattern is expected to continue—with new application packages, operating systems, and utilities continually being developed to reflect the increasing sophistication of hardware.

For example, DOS was developed, in part, to take advantage of a hardware development, the 16-bit processor. Recall the discussion in an earlier chapter on processor capacities. A 16-bit processor is able to handle two eight-bit bytes of data at one time. Before 16-bit processors were adapted, most microcomputers used eight-bit configurations and used an operating system known as CP/M, which is the subject of the next section.

CP/M

The acronym, CP/M, stands for **Control Program for Microprocessors.** CP/M was developed in 1975 by Dr. Gary Kidall, to establish a processing environment for the Intel 8008 processing chip. This chip was an eight-bit processor used for most of the original personal computers—such as those produced by Apple, DEC, Tandy, Wang, Vector, and many other companies.

By offering a standard operating system for nonstandard equipment, CP/M was a marvel of its time. During the era of eight-bit systems, CP/M was as prevalent in personal computers as DOS is today. DOS was developed, and soon proliferated, in response to the introduction of 16-bit machines. CP/M has been updated since to operate in a 16-bit environment. However, CP/M represents a small percentage of the operating systems used for microcomputers today—and its use is limited effectively to programming applications.

CP/M consists of component parts that are roughly equivalent to the four sections of DOS:

- The BIOS (Basic Input/Output System) is similar in function to the IBM-BIO.COM in DOS. This is the component that controls peripheral devices, such as keyboards, displays, communications, and storage devices. Like DOS, the BIOS builds upon similar capabilities of a ROM chip.

- The BDOS (Basic Disk Operating System) is the disk handling function of CP/M. The BDOS coincides with the IBMDOS.COM section of DOS.

- The CCP, or Console Command Processor, is the internal command set of CP/M systems. The CCP is the equivalent of COMMAND.COM in DOS. CP/M provides most of the same capabilities as DOS. CP/M differs from DOS in that DOS operations executed with special function keys are initiated in CP/M through use of commands that utilize standard alphabet keys. For instance, the command, UD, might be used to update files. In addition, the CCP controls the execution of external, or disk-resident, utilities.

In terms of features and functions, then, CP/M does not differ significantly from DOS. The biggest difference is the command structure orientation—16 bits for DOS, and 8 bits for CP/M. Thus, CP/M runs slower and handles less data or instruction content at one time. The user-accessible area of main memory in a microcomputer is an exponential multiple (or mathematical power) of the number of bits in its instruction format. So, 16-bit instructions can address many times more main memory than eight-bit instructions.

This factor, combined with the overwhelming abundance of software packages designed to run in DOS environments, tilts the scale away from CP/M. However, many modern microcomputers are being made with 32-bit processors. In effect, DOS may one day face obsolescence because of this development. It remains to be seen whether DOS will be upgraded to a 32-bit mode, or whether a new operating system will prevail. One such system, designed for machines with larger capacities, is known as Unix.

UNIX

The **Unix operating system** was developed originally at Bell Laboratories for use with minicomputers. Many different versions of Unix are available for microcomputers (Venix, Xenix, etc.) from many different vendors. However, the term, Unix, is used inclusively in this discussion.

Unix is a multiuser, multitasking operating system. A **multiuser** system is one in which several users run applications on the same processor. **Multitasking** refers to the ability of a single user to execute several applications at the same time. A Unix system can support multiple functions or users without compromising speed or accuracy. That is, in a system with more than one user, each user operates as if he or she "owns" the processor. The same holds for a multitasking system. Multiple applications are executed as if no other programs are present.

In effect, Unix uses the CPU with increased efficiency. Most of the time a user is operating a microcomputer—especially during interactive processing routines—the CPU is idle, waiting for keystrokes or commands. In a Unix system, these gaps are filled with additional processing tasks.

This capability is at the heart of Unix systems. Unix is built as layers of software. The **kernel** interfaces directly to the computer's CPU. The kernel drives peripheral input/output devices and also contains the memory management unit. The memory management unit protects programs from other executing programs and provides independent processing for each program or user.

Surrounding the kernel is the **shell,** which performs many roles. First, the shell acts as the command interpreter, reading user entries and responding to them as required. The shell also provides piping and filtering capabilities, functions that have been incorporated into later versions of DOS.

Piping refers to the ability to designate the output of one program as input for another. As a simple example, consider the MORE utility. This utility allows outputs to be displayed one screen at a time, a helpful capability for displays of long files, or directories.

Suppose you wanted to view a directory of 99 files. Simply executing the DIR command causes the directory to be displayed rapidly, and most listings fly off the screen before they can be read. A **pipe command,** however, could be entered as follows:

DIR¦MORE

The "¦" symbol indicates that a pipe is being established. After entering the command, a full screen of listings is displayed with a "-MORE-" prompt at the bottom. Pressing any key displays the next screen, and so on until the end of the directory.

The MORE command is a **filter command,** and implements a **filtering** routine. That is, data for output are passed through a software routine to modify the format of the output. For example, suppose you wanted to display the same directory in alphabetic order. This can be done in a Unix system (or later versions of DOS) with an additional filter command, such as SORT. The SORT command

arranges a file in ascending or descending order of the ASCII data representation scheme. In this case, the command would be entered:

DIR¦SORT¦MORE

In this example, the directory is piped into a SORT filter, then piped again into the MORE filter. A temporary disk file is created by the system to hold the output data until they are needed. Then, the directory is displayed one screen at a time, and in alphabetic order.

The Unix shell also contains a flexible command language. This function provides great flexibility for writing user programs. In effect, Unix is equipped with a resident programming language.

Around the shell are various utilities and workbenches. A **workbench** is a collection of software tools designed for a specific purpose. For example, a text processing workbench, commonly included with Unix, includes a spelling checker, a page formatting routine, line and screen editors, and other features. Most Unix systems also include a workbench designed to increase a programmer's productivity.

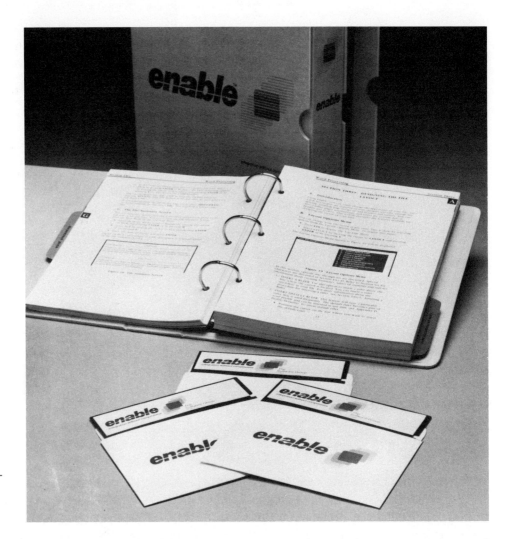

Integrated software

*packages rely heavily on oper-
ating system capabilities.*

COURTESY OF THE SOFTWARE GROUP

With most operating systems, workbenches and utilities can be removed and/or inserted easily to configure systems to individual requirements. Unix provides additional flexibility in that the kernel, or processor interface, can be modified to run on different processing chips. This allows the Unix operating system to be **transportable,** or moved easily to different equipment.

When Unix originally became available for microcomputers, many experts felt that it would soon replace DOS as the de facto standard for business systems. Unix does offer many advantages, specifically flexibility. However, the business market has invested heavily in DOS systems and in DOS-related applications. Thus, the future of Unix may hinge upon its ability to run DOS applications. Many Unix vendors are incorporating this capability into updated versions.

COMPILERS AND INTERPRETERS

Another level of support is provided by a subset of system software known as translator programs. Translator programs accept high-level commands and convert them into machine instructions. The purpose of translator programs is to allow programmers to focus on the logic of the solution to a problem, rather than on computer procedures that implement a solution.

An assembler, covered in the section above on the DOS operating system, is a type of translator program. In comparison with other translators, the capabilities of assemblers to translate high-level instructions are limited. An assembler accepts symbolic instructions, usually in the form of alphanumeric characters. Conversions are executed on a one-to-one basis, or one character command is translated into a single machine instruction. Consider this simple operation:

$$A = B + C.$$

Using an assembler, this operation would require a series of instructions. First, the computer would be instructed to retrieve the data element, B, which is placed by the system into a memory register. Then, the data element, C, would be retrieved, requiring another instruction. The next instruction would execute the addition operation. Finally, an instruction would be required to place the results of the operation into another register.

The commands used to perform this operation are understood relatively easily. For example, the characters (A and B) representing data elements are written as they would appear in English. Remember: a computer handles characters as bytes, or groups of one and zero values, that correspond with internal circuitry.

Assembly programmers, however, must be knowledgeable about computer procedures and must consider these procedures at every step of program development. In the above example, the programmer gives the computer exact memory addresses of locations in which to place data elements awaiting processing. In addition, another memory location is specified for processing results. As programs grow in size and complexity, this preoccupation with physical procedures can detract from logical considerations, such as problem requirements and solutions.

Fortunately, translator programs with increased capabilities are available. Programmers using these programs can focus on nonprocedural requirements. In effect, a program is designed according to the logic of the operation and is written in high-level statements. Then, a special translator program converts the high-level statements, or **source program,** into an executable **object program** comprised of machine-language instructions.

The two types of translator programs that provide this level of service are known as:

- Compilers
- Interpreters.

Compilers

In effect, a **compiler** performs a function similar to that of an assembler. Source statements written in a high-level language are converted by a compiler into machine-language instructions. The difference, to borrow a phrase from the first chapter, is a matter of scale.

A compiler generates code for multiple processing steps from a single source instruction. Consider again the above example involving the source statement:

$$A = B + C$$

With a compiler, this entry would be converted into multiple machine-language instructions that execute the required data retrievals, memory assignments, and calculations. In other words, compiler-based programming is problem oriented. The compiler allocates memory and controls input and output. Programmers are freed from extensive considerations of operational details and can focus on logical solutions to problems or processing situations.

A compiler can be thought of as a program that writes programs. That is, a set of source statements is written as input to the compiler program. Processing results in a machine-language object program. The object program then is loaded directly into the computer for processing. The object program also can be saved for further use. Revisions are made to source code.

Interpreters

An **interpreter** can be thought of as an interactive compiler. Source statements are converted into multiple instructions written in machine code. However, an interpreter works interactively. Each source statement is translated into machine language and executed while the program is running. In other words, program statements are compiled and executed in one step. This method has both disadvantages and advantages.

The main disadvantage is that the overall execution of programs is slower under interpreter methods. Source statements are entered directly, converted into machine instructions, and then executed. The extra step required to perform translations increases processing time.

Advantages are realized for program development activities. Because source statements are compiled individually, errors can be caught and located directly. Additions and changes to programs can be made and tested quickly. Program development often involves extensive testing and debugging, or error correction. An interpreter can streamline this process. In addition, under some translator software, operational programs written in interpreter languages can be compiled into an executable object program.

The BASIC language.   The most common interpreter language is called *BASIC*. The name is derived from an acronym meaning Beginner's All-purpose Symbolic Instruction Code. BASIC was developed by professors John Kemeny and Thomas Kurtz at Dartmouth College as a tool for teaching computer-based problem solving.

BASIC is a general-purpose programming language. That is, BASIC combines the data handling and formatting capabilities required for both business and scientific, or mathematical, applications. The BASIC language is easy to learn and contains a powerful and versatile command set. These features are desirable for personal computers and for microcomputers in business. In fact, BASIC is the most common language for application development on microcomputers. Virtually all microcomputers now being delivered and installed for business applications are supported by some version of BASIC.

Program development, regardless of programming language, consists of common functions. These commonalities are indicated by the list and descriptions of the following BASIC commands:

- The READ command inputs a record into memory and assigns positions for data elements within the record.

- The LET command assigns a value to a storage area, or position. This command is used to initialize a storage position or to store results of a calculation.

- The IF command is used to test the value of a storage position to see if it matches stated conditions.

- The PRINT command prints a heading or a line of data on an output report.

- The DATA command defines records to be processed.

- The REM command is used to add remarks or explanations for program operators or authors.

- The END command tells the computer to end processing and shows the physical end of the source code.

Notice that the operands for these commands resemble the operations they implement. This feature makes it easy for nonexpert users to write and run BASIC programs. With these types of commands, the work of program development focuses largely upon understanding what is to be done, and structuring the commands into a format understandable to the computer.

In summary, translator programs were developed originally in the 1950s for use with large, centralized systems. Before these developments, programs were written as series of binary statements. Each binary instruction, data object, interim result, and final output was allocated to a specific memory location. Systems programmers were viewed as technological wizards who could communicate with computers using hieroglyphic-like codes.

As translator programs were developed, an increased level of service was provided to computer users. Although this increased support was provided mainly to programmers, the computer moved closer to nontechnical users. In other words, the evolutionary process had taken a giant step.

Operating systems provided a level of service to nontechnical users that parallels the service provided to programmers by translator programs. Operating systems perform the "housekeeping" chores, such as memory management, binary translations, and peripheral interactions, that previously had stymied nontechnical users. In effect, operating systems freed users from concerns over hardware details. Computers became accessible to any user with basic skills and an understanding of problems to be solved.

The evolution continues today, as is evidenced by the hundreds of hardware and software products introduced each year. As computers have evolved, they have become smaller, more powerful, and less expensive. For businesses, though, one fact remains constant: Computers are tools for meeting business needs and solving business problems. The evolution of computers has reached a point at which even the smallest of businesses may realize benefits from implementing computer-based information systems.

However, a computer system is more than a collection of programs and devices. Similarly, configuring a system involves more than purchasing components. The creation of computer information systems for businesses involves the evaluation and analysis of problems and requirements. Developing and implementing microcomputer-based information systems is discussed in the chapter that follows.

KEY TERMS

system software

operating system

Disk Operating System (DOS)

hidden file

system file

disk handler file

suffix

peripheral controller

command interpreter

batch files

housekeeping commands

utility program

user friendly

initializing

line editor

source program

assembly language

assembler

Control Program for
   Microprocessors (CP/M)

Unix operating system

multiuser

multitasking

kernel

shell

piping

pipe command

filter command

filtering

workbench

transportable

source program

object program

compiler

interpreter

BASIC

DEFINITIONS

Instructions: On a separate sheet, define each term according to its use in this chapter.

1. operating system

2. suffix

3. batch files

4. initializing

5. assembler

6. multitasking

7. workbench

8. BASIC

T R U E / F A L S E

Instructions: For each statement, write T for true or F for false on a separate sheet.

1. As software evolved, generic processing functions, such as establishing directories, were written to establish processing environments into which other programs could be incorporated.

2. Software and computer developers created translator programs to convert computer instructions and manuals into foreign languages to improve export sales.

3. Most microcomputer software systems available today are designed to run under DOS systems.

4. In the IBM PC, the "disk handler file" is named IBMDOS.COM.

5. The ".COM" suffix on a file means it is a "communications" file.

6. Housekeeping commands describe a set of routines internal to the command interpreter.

7. Most business users eventually have to learn how to write or edit programs to run applications.

8. CP/M systems are faster and handle more memory than DOS.

9. In a multiuser Unix system, each user must learn to share time on the computer according to mutually agreed upon schedules.

10. As programs grow in size and complexity, a preoccupation with the physical procedures can detract from logical considerations, such as problem requirements and solutions. The operating system serves users by handling these functions.

11. A compiler can be thought of as a program that writes programs.

12. BASIC is an acronym for Beginner's All-purpose Symbolic Instruction Code.

13. In the 1950s, systems programmers were viewed as technological wizards who could communicate with computers using machine-language codes.

14. In programming, source program refers to machine-language instructions executable by a computer.

15. The CHKDSK utility is used to check on the filled and free space on disk.

S H O R T A N S W E R Q U E S T I O N S

Instructions: On a separate sheet of paper, answer each question in one or two brief sentences.

1. What purposes do directories serve?

2. What is the difference between MS-DOS and PC-DOS?

3. Explain the statement: "As hardware goes, so goes software."

4. What is the purpose of a translator program?

5. Why has DOS surpassed CP/M on the market?

6. In BASIC, what do the READ and LET commands instruct a computer to do?

R E S E A R C H P R O J E C T

Identify and describe three ways in which DOS functions support the use of user application program packages.

14 Software Integration

NEED FOR SOFTWARE INTEGRATION

Software integration techniques were developed because users often need to make use of more than one application package at a time.

FILE TRANSFER SOFTWARE

Software integration is based on the ability to share and transfer data among different applications.

INTEGRATED SOFTWARE PACKAGES

Integrated software packages provide capabilities for moving quickly among different applications.

Navigating Menus

In combining applications, windowing techniques are used to display different pull-down menus.

Integrated Accounting Packages

Accounting software is set up to process transactions and to prepare general ledger and financial status reports.

Working With Accounting Packages

Accounting packages focus on accounting-specific goals and objectives; however, the implementation and installation of accounting systems generally follows the functional stages in developing database systems.

SYSTEM INTEGRATORS

System integrators enhance system software capabilities by providing capabilities for opening programs without leaving the current program and for moving data among programs easily.

DESKTOP MANAGERS

Desktop managers are personal productivity packages that encompass the functions of tools normally found on executive desktops, such as telephone directories, calculators, and notepads.

NEED FOR SOFTWARE INTEGRATION

Results required by computer users often extend beyond the capabilities of individual application software packages. For example, a businessperson who is writing a report needs to do more than enter and edit text. He or she often needs tabular presentations of spreadsheet figures, or graphs derived from spreadsheets. In addition, a manager preparing a market analysis with a spreadsheet package needs to do more than enter numbers and formulas. Market analyses often include written comments or acknowledgments of information sources. In the course of creating a market report, the businessperson may receive telephone calls. He or she suddenly may need quick access to notes made at a recent meeting, a customer record, invoice documents, or the phone number of an associate.

All these application processes may be created and handled with the same microcomputer. However, under traditional techniques, data created under a specific program can be accessed only while that program is in active use. To access data used in another application, the user must leave the program he or she is currently operating and load the other program. This operation can require tedious disk switching operations, and, in effect, the user also must "switch" to the command syntax of a different program.

Software integration, in this sense, refers to capabilities for sharing data among applications. Software integration can be achieved with a variety of software tools, including the following:

- *File transfer software* converts files from a format produced by one program into a format that can be used in another program.

- *Integrated software packages* combine multiple applications into a single, unified package.

- *System integrators* build an interfacing structure through which selected applications can be run more or less simultaneously.

- *Desktop managers* combine several personal productivity functions that can be called up while other programs are in use.

FILE TRANSFER SOFTWARE

The sharing and transferring of data among applications is at the heart of software integration. The ability to combine files, application programs, and system operations can increase user productivity. For example, many users first encounter needs for data transfer when the output of a graphics program is needed for inclusion in some type of text document. See Figure 14-1. That is, initial data transfer requirements often involve moving spreadsheet data into a word processing format.

This type of operation often can be executed with capabilities inherent in operating systems, combined with features of spreadsheet and word processing programs. This method also may be applied to database files. Recall that the ASCII format is a standard method for data representation. For this reason, most printers accept data in the ASCII format. To print any type of file, output must be sent to a printer in this format.

Print operations can be sent to disk storage as well. That is, rather than print a hard copy of a spreadsheet or other file, the file can be "printed," or sent—in ASCII format—to external storage.

Many word processing packages store files in the ASCII format. These packages read the ASCII spreadsheet file as if it were a text document. In this case, the spreadsheet file can be appended, or added, to the text file of the report, formatted or edited as needed, and output as a single document.

Other word processors, however, store files in unique formats. For these packages, other options are available. One option involves printing the text file to disk in ASCII format. Then, the two ASCII files, one for the spreadsheet and one for text, are combined and printed under control of the operating system. This transfer method may be effective under limited circumstances, and may

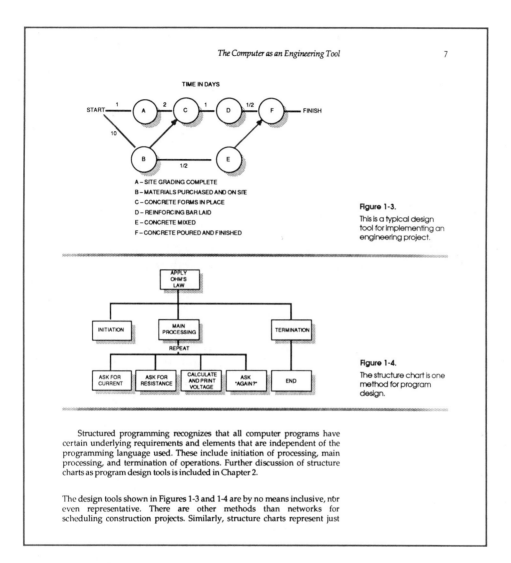

The Computer as an Engineering Tool   7

TIME IN DAYS

A – SITE GRADING COMPLETE
B – MATERIALS PURCHASED AND ON SITE
C – CONCRETE FORMS IN PLACE
D – REINFORCING BAR LAID
E – CONCRETE MIXED
F – CONCRETE POURED AND FINISHED

Figure 1-3.
This is a typical design tool for implementing an engineering project.

Figure 1-4.
The structure chart is one method for program design.

Structured programming recognizes that all computer programs have certain underlying requirements and elements that are independent of the programming language used. These include initiation of processing, main processing, and termination of operations. Further discussion of structure charts as program design tools is included in Chapter 2.

The design tools shown in Figures 1-3 and 1-4 are by no means inclusive, nor even representative. There are other methods than networks for scheduling construction projects. Similarly, structure charts represent just

Figure 14-1.

Integrated software makes it possible to combine graphics and text in a single sequence, as is necessary for computer-related books.

present drawbacks. First, transfer under this method can be time-consuming and inefficient. In addition, printing under control of the operating system usually provides only limited formatting capabilities.

As another option, many word processors contain functions for converting files from standard formats, such as ASCII, into the format of the word processor. Conversion functions, or utilities, provide capabilities for relatively efficient file transfer into word processor formats. Still another option involves purchase of a file transfer software package.

File transfer software reads a file in a format created by one program and converts it into a format that can be read and manipulated by another program.

File transfer software exists for virtually any conversion need. The operation of these programs usually is straightforward, and is directed through relatively simple menu and prompt responses.

Many packages even provide capabilities for transferring files between different makes of microcomputers. For example, the MacLink package provides capabilities for transferring data between IBM PC and Apple Macintosh microcomputers. Figure 14-2 illustrates the extent of conversion types possible with the MacLink package.

Conversion programs provide many advantages, as well as some disadvantages, for microcomputer users. At face value, the ability to transfer files among programs should increase a user's production. The main drawback involves transfers of graphic files. This problem is due largely to a lack of standard formats among software systems for storing graphics. With the advent of desktop publishing (discussed in a later chapter), however, standards should be forthcoming.

INTEGRATED SOFTWARE PACKAGES

For most users, a complete range of requirements can be met by some combination of five common application packages: word processing, spreadsheets, database, graphics, and communications. For this reason, many manufacturers have developed products that combine several or all five applications as single packages.

Integrated packages provide capabilities for moving quickly among applications. Data and text are transferable among programs. This capability effectively eliminates redundant data entry operations. In addition, all applications are executed with common commands and/or command structures. Users need not learn different commands for each application. For example, electronic spreadsheets and word processors usually include MOVE and COPY functions. In an integrated package, commands for executing these functions involve identical or similar keystrokes regardless of which program is being run.

Many integrated packages also provide capabilities for running two or more applications simultaneously. During processing, program messages and/or processing results are displayed in **windows,** a portion of a screen dedicated to a single purpose. Integrated packages usually allow multiple window displays. For example, a word processing document can be displayed in one window, while a spreadsheet can be displayed in another window. Many packages also make it possible to combine data from different applications for processing and output. That is, spreadsheet data can be transferred to a graphics program and converted to graphics. In fact, the first program to integrate applications, Lotus 1-2-3, combined spreadsheet and graphics on outputs. As another example,

CHOICES FOR FILE TRANSFERS "TO PC"	
File "Contains"	File "Becomes" Choices
MacWrite file	Wordstar file Multimate file DCA (IBM Revisable) Text
Word (CONVERT format)	Word (PC format)
Multiplan (SYLK format)	Lotus (WKS or WRK format) Multiplan (SYLK format) DIF (DIF format)
Excel (WKS format)	Lotus (WKS or WRK format)
Jazz (Lotus format)	Lotus (WKS or WRK format)
DIF (DIF format)	DIF (DIF format) Lotus (WKS or WRK format) Multiplan (SYLK format)
Binary file (Mac format)	Binary file (Mac format)
Binary file	Binary file Binary file (Mac format)
Text	Text

CHOICES FOR FILE TRANSFERS "FROM PC"	
File "Contains"	File "Becomes" Choices
WordStar	MacWrite file
MultiMate	MacWrite file
DCA (IBM Revisable)	MacWrite file
Word (PC format)	Word (CONVERT format)
Lotus (WKS or WRK format)	Multiplan (SYLK format) DIF (DIF format) Excel (WKS format) Jazz (Lotus format)
Multiplan (SYLK format)	Multiplan (SYLK format) DIF (DIF format)
DIF (DIF format)	DIF (DIF format) Multiplan (SYLK format)
Binary file (Mac format)	Binary file (Mac format)
Binary file	Binary file Binary file (Mac format)
Text	MacWrite file Text

Figure 14-2.

Conversion packages provide software routines for moving files between IBM PCs and Apple Macintoshes.

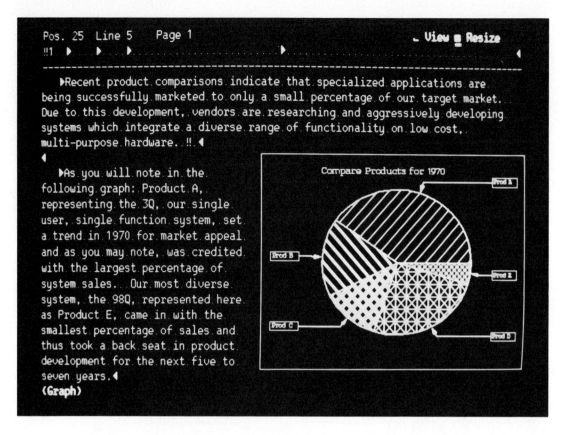

Pos. 25   Line 5   Page 1   View ■ Resize
!!1   ▶   ▶   ▶ . . . . ▶ . . . . ◀

▶Recent.product.comparisons.indicate.that.specialized.applications.are.
being.successfully.marketed.to.only.a.small.percentage.of.our.target.market..
Due.to.this.development,.vendors.are.researching.and.aggressively.developing.
systems.which.integrate.a.diverse.range.of.functionality.on.low.cost,.
multi-purpose.hardware..!!.◀

▶As.you.will.note.in.the.
following.graph:.Product.A,.
representing.the.3Q,.our.single.
user,.single.function.system,.set.
a.trend.in.1970.for.market.appeal.
and.as.you.may.note,.was.credited.
with.the.largest.percentage.of.
system.sales...Our.most.diverse.
system,.the.98Q,.represented.here.
as.Product.E,.came.in.with.the.
smallest.percentage.of.sales.and.
thus.took.a.back.seat.in.product.
development.for.the.next.five.to.
seven.years.◀
(Graph)

Compare Products for 1970

Figure 14-3.

Integrated packages provide
capabilities for displaying graphics and text on the same
screen, and for producing outputs in the same format.
COURTESY OF WANG LABORATORIES,
INC.

spreadsheet data and/or graphics can be moved into text reports created with word processors. See Figure 14-3.

Depending on the individual package, operations in more than one application may be executed simultaneously. That is, a word processing document may be printed at the same time that a database file is sorted or a spreadsheet is recalculated. The display in Figure 14-4 shows the packages available on an integrated software system.

Navigating Menus

Access to the multiple capabilities of integrated packages typically is through use of related menus organized into a series of access levels. To illustrate, consider the use of the version of Microsoft Word for the Apple Macintosh. This package combines a popular word processor with a capability to format text into a variety of typesetting fonts. Illustrations created under spreadsheet or graphics software also can be "imported" into typeset files.

To initiate use of the Word package, the user is presented with a **menu bar** that lists available functions or services across the top of the screen. As an example, one of the menu bar options is EDIT. This is a generalized function that

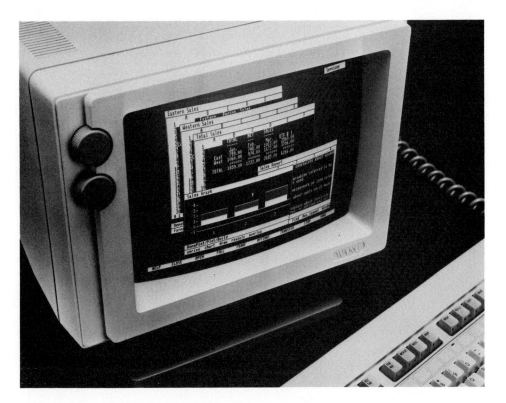

Figure 14-4.

*Integrated software display
shows the software packages
and files available to a user.*
COURTESY OF WANG LABORATORIES,
INC.

will require additional definition by the user to the system. As one instance, the system will need to know whether the editing will be done in a new file or in an existing file stored on disk.

To make this first level of choice, selection of a menu-bar item leads to presentation of a ***pull-down menu***. This is a list of options that appears directly below the menu-bar item that is selected. Figure 14-5 shows the selection of the EDIT function on the menu bar and the accompanying, pull-down menu used in this case, to indicate that an existing file is to be edited.

Selection of the option for editing an existing file causes the system to display a submenu like the one shown in Figure 14-6. Included in this submenu is a listing of all available files. The user scrolls through the list of file names and selects the one to be edited. When this file name is highlighted, the user moves the cursor to a selection option and tells the system it is OK to retrieve and display the identified file.

Integrated Accounting Packages

Accounting software is set up to process transactions and to provide capabilities for analyzing the results of transaction processing. Transaction processing is one

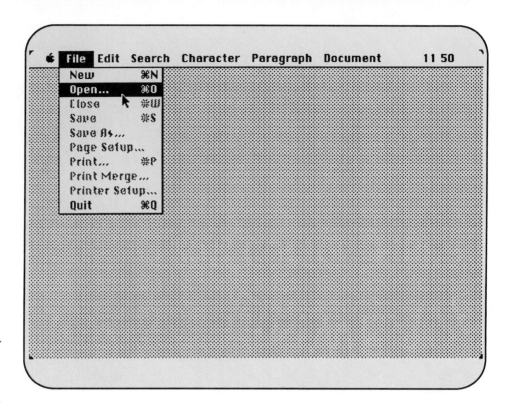

Figure 14-5.

Pull-down menus supplement menu-bar listings to provide a first level of user selection.

Figure 14-6.

Submenus request further detailing of user function selections.

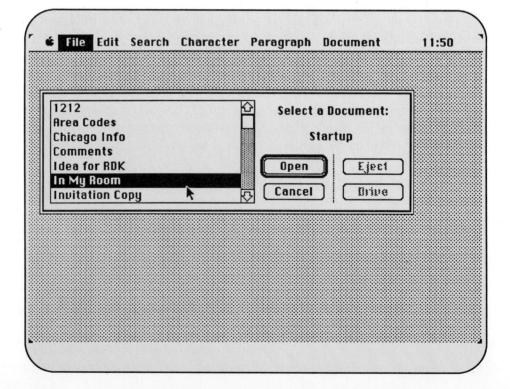

of the first areas in which software integration has been implemented effectively. Recall that, in an earlier chapter, interrelationships among functions in a transaction processing system are discussed. Transaction processing packages that are integrated functionally are described here as accounting packages.

Data created in one area or function of any system often are processed at other component stages. In an accounting system, for example, data about incoming orders are created as part of the order entry function. Order data describe customers, purchases, and prices. The same data are used to create the invoice documents that request payment from customers, and then to set up accounts receivable representing order values until invoices are paid. In such systems, data files take on value as assets, because they often represent money due, received, or spent by an organization.

In an earlier chapter, functional relationships among transaction data are said to create a transaction path through the organization. In effect, this "path" is defined by the movement of data through the file structures used by transactions. Because data are inherently interrelated, transaction processing lends itself to organization as a database. Databases consist of files organized for multiple applications.

Database organization schemes are at the heart of many integrated accounting packages. Many packages are developed as series of modules. Organizations can purchase modules as needs arise—or as a phased conversion to computer techniques is implemented. For most packages, modular routines correspond with the transaction processing functions discussed in a previous chapter:

- *Order entry, invoicing,* and *accounts receivable* routines set up accounts, or records, of debts owed to an organization. These routines provide capabilities for entering data on customer orders, for producing invoices that request payment for ordered goods or services, and for adjusting account balances as payments are received.

- *Accounts payable* routines set up other accounts representing money owed by an organization to vendors. Outputs of these routines can take the form of checks for payment of monies owed.

- *Payroll* routines handle transactions between employers and employees.

- *Inventory control* routines are tied into the order entry function. These applications monitor product inventory levels to control restocking.

- *General ledger* routines form the management reporting and analysis portion of an integrated accounting package. General ledger records are organized according to a *chart of accounts.* The chart of accounts categorizes transactions generally as income or expenses, then breaks these categories into further details. The chart of accounts becomes the basis for reports that establish the financial status of the company.

General ledger routines also are set up to produce summary reports of transaction activities, known as *financial statements.* Three types of financial statements generally are created: income statements, balance sheets, and statements of changes in financial condition. Income statements summarize income and expenses. Balance sheets describe—in terms of *assets, liabilities,* and *equity*—the overall worth of a company. A statement of changes presents a picture of the movement of financial resources during a reporting period.

Many systems also include a word processing module or word processing capabilities as part of the overall package. These capabilities are included so that output reports can be combined with text summaries or explanations. Word processing capabilities also provide advanced functions for formatting any type of printed output.

Working With Accounting Packages

The implementation or installation of accounting systems with integrated packages, because of their database orientation, roughly follows guidelines first described in an earlier chapter. Recall the functional stages in developing database systems:

- Define desired results.
- Specify and create files.
- Process transactions against files.
- Generate specified outputs.

However, because the scope of these systems has been narrowed to accounting-specific goals and objectives, many decisions have been made and written into package procedures. Keep this in mind as you read the sections that follow.

Define desired results.   Many system development projects begin with specifications of results, most commonly hard-copy outputs. For accounting packages, much of this work already has been done. That is, outputs are defined according to guidelines generally known as "generally accepted accounting principles."

While the principles under which accounting packages are set up may be more or less standard, most organizations tend to be unique and present unique requirements. Thus, accounting packages usually provide capabilities for formatting outputs to meet individual requirements.

Specify and create files.   To paraphrase a previous point, the attraction of accounting packages is that many, even most, developmental tasks are installed as package components. Recall that specifying and creating files involves naming and describing data fields. Field names and descriptions, known as *data definitions,* comprise part of the indexing scheme under which the database is organized. Accounting packages, again, define data according to common or standard requirements. Rather than name and define data fields, a user need only approve or edit the definitions built into the package. These definitions are used to compile entry screens, through which files are created.

Process transactions against files.   In a database environment, processing maintains files and derives information from existing files to create specified reports. Just as the specification of reports and files largely is built into package procedures, processing specifications also are included. It almost becomes redundant to state that accounting packages are set up to perform standard processing operations. That is, standard reports are derived through procedures already written. Again, accounting packages necessarily must provide capabilities for individual processing against files.

Data definitions built into accounting packages—or specified individually by users—form the basis for the posting of transactions. That is, data entered through order entry screens trigger the creation of an account receivable and, in turn, an invoice output. The invoice entries, in turn, modify the general ledger database, as do entries for payroll, accounts payable, and other transactions. In an integrated accounting system, files are maintained as by-products of transaction processing.

Generate specified outputs.   For an integrated accounting package, outputs are dictated by laws and professional standards. Therefore, most of the outputs are designed into packages as standard components. To illustrate, a typical income statement is shown in Figure 14-7.

An earlier chapter attributes the success of microcomputers to the development of application packages. Application packages, including integrated accounting packages, take advantage of commonalities among business operations. However, packages must provide some amount of flexibility. Users should not have to change or redesign existing procedures to work with a software tool. In turn, many users might not wish to change existing software tools to achieve integration. For these users, software tools known as system integrators, discussed in the section that follows, might provide effective solutions.

```
                    Wanda's Restaurant Supply House

Run Date: 08/23/87


               June 1987      June 1986     YTD 1987        YTD 1986
INCOME
      ------------------------------------------------------------------
Grocery        $83,482.93     $79,374.22    $984,298.33     $883,232.22
Meats          $11,289.33     $14,232.33    $184,520.74     $157,320.28
Dairy          $22,984.10     $24,873.93    $258,284.23     $304,872.32
Produce        $18,329.33     $16,824.20    $248,528.47     $228,375.92
Frozen Foods   $31,842.88     $29,472.84    $329,462.88     $318,428.28
Condiments     $12,984.22     $10,324.48    $153,823.82     $119,823.84
Paper Goods     $8,428.74      $6,087.34     $96,263.85      $78,185.34
Soft Goods      $5,620.64      $5,319.47     $58,453.97      $49,762.99
Stationery      $2,843.09      $1,952.22     $29,653.97      $27,482.85

      ------------------------------------------------------------------
Gross Income  $197,805.26    $188,461.03  $2,343,290.26   $2,167,484.04
      ==================================================================

EXPENSES
      ------------------------------------------------------------------
Costs of Goods $83,753.93     $79,284.34    $996,231.49     $851,285.35
Payroll        $28,482.27     $27,932.46    $345,681.39     $359,835.26
Rent            $3,573.39      $3,462.95     $35,654.18      $37,408.45
Utilities         $489.23        $524.83     $58,248.24      $61,283.28
Equipment         $264.98      $1,832.94      $1,966.43       $4,283.28
Advertising       $832.74        $793.64      $2,387.64       $2,793.62
Administration    $384.29        $857.25      $2,793.75       $9,732.98
Insurance       $2,483.83      $4,287.47     $11,468.96      $65,843.44
Depreciation      $387.52        $403.74      $1,583.85       $1,646.98

      ------------------------------------------------------------------
Total Expenses $120,652.18   $119,379.62  $1,456,015.93   $1,394,112.64
      ==================================================================

NET INCOME      $77,153.08     $69,081.41    $887,274.33     $773,371.40
```

Figure 14-7.

Integrated accounting packages usually include routines for producing standard business reports, such as this income-expense statement.

SYSTEM INTEGRATORS

Suppose you work in a decision making capacity for a major corporation. You have come to rely on your microcomputer for generating all text documents, and for evaluating and analyzing budget projections. Further, you often make report presentations and use graphics to back up your recommendations. Up to now, you have been using a word processing package for documents, an electronic spreadsheet package for evaluations and analyses, and a graphics package for graphics. The standalone nature of these packages requires a great deal of moving in and out of application programs. Further, transferring data among programs with operating system methods (described earlier in this chapter) has become tedious and inefficient.

You realize that you could streamline your operations by purchasing and installing an integrated software package. However, you aren't motivated to learn an entire, new command structure for a new package. In addition, you are generally satisfied with the performance and features of your existing packages. In short, your requirements are simple: You want to use the packages you already have like an integrated software package.

This is the premise behind system integrators. In effect, system integrators, such as IBM's TopView, Apple's Switcher, and Microsoft's Windows, enhance system software capabilities.

Consider what happens under conventional methods when you move from one program to another. First you close the program you are in and return to the level of the operating system. Then, you instruct the operating system to load another program. To move back to the first program, you must again go through the operating system.

System integrators provide capabilities for opening programs without leaving the current program and for moving data among programs easily. Different programs use different methods to accomplish similar objectives.

For example, Windows uses a system of screen display segments for integrating programs. Windowing is used by many integrated software packages, as discussed above. A spreadsheet window can be superimposed upon a word processing display, and manipulations upon spreadsheet data executed. Similarly, data from the spreadsheet can be moved to the text document with relative ease.

Apple's Switcher uses memory partitions instead of windows. Different programs are loaded into different memory partitions. Thus, displays cannot be viewed simultaneously. However, moving from one program to another requires only a few keystrokes, or a click of a mouse, and is accomplished in a few seconds. See Figure 14-8.

Figure 14-8.

The Switcher package provides capabilities for moving quickly from one application package (top) to another (bottom).

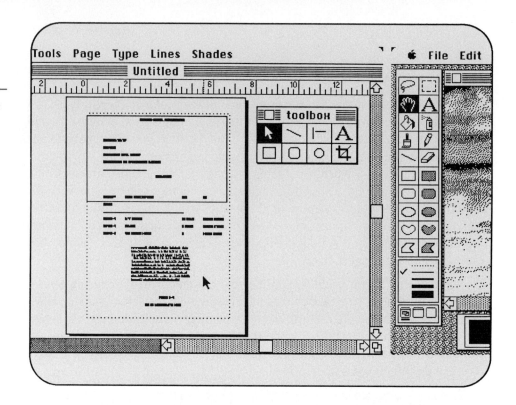

System integrators may provide a "best of both worlds" solution to data transfer bottlenecks. However, system integrators are designed to handle specific packages. Achieving compatibility might require additional utilities, especially for DOS-specific programs such as MultiMate and Lotus 1-2-3. In addition, system integrators require extensive computer memory—which means that application execution may become slow, and that working storage for data files may be limited.

A common feature of both integrated software packages and system integrators is a feature known as a desktop manager. Desktop managers also can be purchased as individual packages, and are discussed in the section that follows.

DESKTOP MANAGERS

Desktop managers are often referred to as personal productivity tools. Regardless of package, desktop managers usually operate under windowing techniques and encompass functions of tools normally found on executive desktops, such as telephone directories, calculators, and notepads.

Figure 14-9 illustrates a window display for a popular desktop manager, called SideKick. The SideKick main menu appears within the window. Notice

```
DOCUMENT: COLLECT              |PAGE:   2|LINE:   9|COL:   1|
Marlin Industries«
2358 Seascape Lane«
Boston, MA 03930«
«
Dear Mr. Fisher:«
«
We had already said, "No morer  SideKick Main Menu   ¡attorneys talked us
out of it.«                   |                     |
«                             | F1    Help          |
Our letter of June 28, spelle| F2    NotePad       |f your overdue
account of $45.55 was not pai| F3    Calculator    | we would be forced
to turn the matter over to ou| F4    caLendar      |
«                             | F5    Dialer        |
That's exactly what we did.  | F6    Ascii-table   |advised us to qive
you one more opportunity to s| F7    Setup         |agreed, but went
along anyway.  Attorneys have| Esc   exit          |ir way, don't they?«
«                             L_____J
Well, you can bet this is our final letter, your last chance to keep from
meeting our attorneys.  (Actually, they're a fine bunch of folks,
extremely competent.)  Please send us a check in reply.«
«
Sincerely,«
«
--move bar. Select by pressing a highlighted letter, a function key, or <-┘
```

Figure 14-9.

SideKick routines are designed to replace common desktop accessories, such as calendars, calculators, notebooks, phone directories, and so on. This is the main menu that serves as a user starting point.

```
DOCUMENT: COLLECT             .|PAGE:   2|LIN┌─────────────────────────────────┐
Marlin Industries«                 |  ┌────────────────────────────┐  |
2358 Seascape Lane«                |  |                     0.0000  |  |
Boston, MA 03930«                  |  | Dec                         |  |
«                                  |  └────────────────────────────┘  |
Dear Mr. Fisher:«                  |─ Hex ─┬─ Mem ─┬─ Numeric ─|
«                                  |       |   R C | = 7 8 9 - |
We had already said, "No more Mr. Nice Guy," | A  B  | M + - |           |
out of it.«                        | F5 F6 |   * / | / 4 5 6 |
«                                  | C  D  ├ Modes ┤           |
Our letter of June 28, spelled out our intent| F7 F8 | Dec     | * 1 2 3 + |
account of $45.55 was not paid in 8 days (yes| E  F  | Bin     |           |
to turn the matter over to our attorneys.«   | F9 F10| Hex     | Ø   .     |
«.                                 |───────┴──────┴───────────|
That's exactly what we did.  Our attorneys, h| And  Or  Xor | C  CE |
you one more opportunity to settle the score.└──────────────────────────┘
along anyway.  Attorneys have a knack for getting their way, don't they?«
«
Well, you can bet this is our final letter, your last chance to keep from
meeting our attorneys.  (Actually, they're a fine bunch of folks,
extremely competent.)  Please send us a check in reply.«
«
Sincerely,«
«
 F1-help  P-program key with displayed number Esc-exit          NumLock
```

Figure 14-10.

SideKick routines reside in main memory; users can call up calendars, calculators (as in this display), notebooks, phone directories, or other features without leaving the current program.

the list of options a user has—while he or she is in another program. A telephone directory can be accessed, and if the system is equipped with a modem, phone numbers can be dialed automatically. A notepad can be called up and short notes posted to another window, or file. In the same way, entries can be made to an appointment calender that can be consulted quickly. A calculator display, shown in Figure 14-10, provides all the capabilities of a hand-held electronic calculator. The ASCII table option displays a table of ASCII references needed for many types of programming tasks. The SETUP option is used to customize the configuration of SideKick files.

Data files created for SideKick, such as telephone directories or important notes, can be saved to disk and accessed repeatedly. Further, SideKick makes it possible to move data into and out of windows and programs. For example, a writer composing a document could import a bulleted list of important points, and consult that list as he or she explains the main points described in the list.

A desktop manager, then, "personalizes" a microcomputer system for its user. In addition, the microcomputer begins to reflect the working habits of the user. The chapter that follows discusses an application, known as desktop publishing, that makes extensive use of the integration techniques discussed here.

K E Y   T E R M S

software integration	pull-down menu	general ledger
file transfer software	order entry	chart of accounts
integrated software package	invoicing	financial statements
system integrator	accounts receivable	assets
desktop manager	accounts payable	liabilities
window	payroll	equity
menu bar	inventory control	data definition

D E F I N I T I O N S

Instructions: On a separate sheet, define each term according to its use in this chapter.

1. file transfer software

2. integrated software package

3. system integrators

4. desktop managers

5. window

6. software integration

7. accounts payable

8. inventory control

T R U E / F A L S E

Instructions: For each statement, write T for true or F for false on a separate sheet.

1. File transfer software allows the user to move a file from one program or system to another, without having to convert the format of the file.

2. System integrators build an interfacing structure through which selected applications can be run at exactly the same time.

3. Desktop managers are personal computers small enough to fit on top of a desk.

4. Word processing, spreadsheets, databases, graphics, and communications are five of the most common application packages available today.

5. Transaction processing is one of the first areas in which software integration has been implemented effectively.

6. The chart of accounts categorizes transactions generally as income or expenses, then breaks these categories down into further details.

7. Accounting packages usually provide capabilities for formatting outputs to meet individual requirements.

8. For an integrated accounting package, outputs are dictated by laws and professional standards.

9. Very few word processing packages store files in the ASCII format.

10. In an integrated system, users still have to learn different commands for each application.

11. A menu bar is the bar across the top of a keyboard where a template can be attached explaining the use of the various function keys.

12. The idea behind any type of software package is to produce results.

13. Database organization schemes are the heart of many integrated accounting packages.

14. Data definitions are the labels put at the top of columns in spreadsheets.

15. It is helpful in implementing an accounting package to specify and create files before defining desired results.

S H O R T   A N S W E R   Q U E S T I O N S

Instructions: On a separate sheet of paper, answer each question in one or two brief sentences.

1. How does a desktop manager personalize a microcomputer system?

2. What is the purpose of software integration?

3. How does software integration increase user efficiency?

4. Which type of application is the most difficult to use with conversion programs? Why?

5. What role do windows play in integrated systems?

6. How does the implementation of accounting packages resemble the development of a database system?

R E S E A R C H   P R O J E C T

What functions would a desktop manager have to perform to make your life as a student easier? Identify features and explain advantages to you.

15 Desktop Publishing and Microcomputer Graphics

REQUIREMENTS AND SOLUTIONS

The type of printing used for a document should be guided by its purpose, intended audience, and budget, as well as available technology.

PUBLISHING TECHNOLOGY

Publishing technology began in the 1450s, and continues to develop with new and better ways to automate typesetting and printing.

COMPUTERS IN TYPESETTING

Computers can actually generate a variety of typefaces and also control the elements of type size, spacing, and format.

DESKTOP PUBLISHING SYSTEMS

Desktop publishing systems incorporate extensive typesetting and document design capabilities within microcomputer systems and laser printing devices.

MICROCOMPUTER

The microcomputers that drive desktop publishing applications usually require large amounts of main memory and external storage.

EXTERNAL STORAGE

An external hard-disk drive is a virtual necessity for a desktop publishing system.

PERIPHERALS

Desktop publishing systems are configured from standard microcomputer components and a laser printer.

Laser Printer

Laser printers provide capabilities for producing near-typeset quality images of graphics and text.

Other Peripherals

A mouse, graphics tablet, and scanner are other peripherals used frequently in desktop publishing systems.

PAGE DESCRIPTION SOFTWARE

Capabilities for bringing text and graphics together and for organizing them as finished outputs are provided by two types of page description software: code-oriented and WYSIWYG.

Page Description Capabilities

Page description programs provide capabilities for formatting the elements involved in designing pages for output.

DESKTOP PUBLISHING: HOW IT WORKS

Desktop publishing systems are based upon the ability to integrate text and graphics on high-quality outputs.

Bit Mapping

Bit mapping relies on plotted locations of bits for representing text and graphics.

Vector Algorithms

Vector algorithms apply mathematical formulas to generate lines and shapes.

Publishing capabilities

---

can be set up on desktops.
COURTESY OF INTERLEAF, INC.

REQUIREMENTS AND SOLUTIONS

At the Boeing Corporation, it often is said that total documentation for a 747 weighs more than the plane itself. While this claim may be exaggerated, it illustrates the enormous amounts of information that are produced as printed documents by large organizations. These demands are present, on different scales, in organizations of any size.

Requirements for document quality vary according to how and why documents are used, and their target audiences. For example, sales pamphlets and brochures should be high enough in quality to match the image management wishes to project for an organization and its products. Parts specifications, such as may be found at aerospace companies, are used "in-house." These documents need not be of the same quality as sales brochures, but it is important that they be legible and understandable. These documents also must be updated regularly.

The point is that requirements exist for publishing systems that fall within a quality range between full-scale typesetting (discussed below) and typewriter or letter- or draft-type computer-driven printer outputs. Desktop publishing systems meet these requirements.

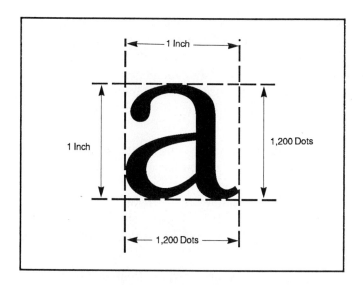

Figure 15-1.

The term, typeset quality, refers to documents produced with resolutions of at least 1,200 by 1,200 dots per inch.

In a strict sense, **publishing** refers to the production of "publication-quality" outputs. This level of quality traditionally is delivered only by typesetting systems with resolution capabilities at or above 1,200 by 1,200 dots per inch. Characters are formed as patterns of dots within a matrix, as shown in Figure 15-1. The matrix is divided into 1,200 vertical and 1,200 horizontal dot positions, for a total of 144,000 dot positions. The more dots, the higher the **resolution,** or readability and appearance, of characters.

Microcomputers driving laser printers produce outputs up to 300 by 300 dots per inch. The difference in quality is acceptable to most untrained eyes. This difference, in many cases, can be offset by savings in time and money spent on production.

In essence, a parallel exists between desktop publishing systems and word processing packages. The potential cost and time savings provided by word processors were instrumental in their acceptance. Desktop publishing systems promise—and can deliver—equally significant savings.

Many of the terms used today in publishing systems stem from precursor technologies. To introduce these terms in perspective, the section that follows presents a brief overview of publishing technology.

PUBLISHING TECHNOLOGY

Since the 1450s, publishing technologies have been developed to automate the printing of words and pictures, or text and graphics, on paper. The first major development in publishing, aside from the invention of paper and ink, was the invention of metal movable type in the 1450s.

About that time, Johann Gutenberg molded pieces of metal with raised letters, numbers, and symbols on their faces. These pieces of metal, type, could be assembled into text. The assemblies of type, in turn, were placed on the bed of a wine press. Ink was applied to the face of the type. Paper was placed over the type, and the press was used to apply pressure. Character images were transferred from the press to the paper, and multiple copies of the assembled type could be produced.

The printing press, as it came to be known, provided capabilities for printing one page at a time. Each printing required another application of ink, and changing text required manual positioning of character forms. However, the ability to derive multiple images from a single assembly of type was a vast improvement over previous methods, which required that all documents be handwritten. By the end of the fifteenth century, more than 10 million printed images had been generated.

In the 1880s, more than four hundred years later, the **linotype** process was invented. Linotype machines assemble type molds to form text. The molds are assembled under keyboard control. Then, a complete line of type is molded in a single operation. Typed lines are used for single publications only. Then, they are remelted and used to produce new type. This eliminated the need to replace individual pieces of type in storage cases for reuse. Also, the use of a keyboard speeded the assembly of text in typeset form.

Linotype reigned supreme for 70 years or so, but had its drawbacks. Linotype characters were made of lead, and 50 or 60 pounds of this metal might be required to **set** type for a single newspaper page.

During the 1950s, **phototypesetting** came into use. Under phototypesetting techniques, images of type characters are projected onto photo-sensitive film or paper. These media are exposed, or developed, and processed chemically. The finished product is a clear, sharp picture of a body of text. Many phototypesetting outputs are long strips, or **galleys,** of text that are cut and pasted into page arrangements.

Phototypesetting techniques provide many advantages over previous technologies in terms of image quality and production speed. Another advantage stems from the ease with which phototypesetting can be adapted to computer capabilities. Part of the process of typesetting involves spacing letters and words and arranging, or **formatting,** text on paper. Computers provide electronic capabilities for performing formatting functions. Text can be arranged on pages—a process known as **layout**—displayed on computer screens. Actual production is not initiated until a satisfactory layout has been created electronically. Regardless of technology, layout involves professional knowledge and skills, which are discussed in the section that follows.

COMPUTERS IN TYPESETTING

A central tenet of this book is that computer capabilities enhance human skills; computers do not, and cannot, replace human skills. Think of a surgeon. The invention of an advanced scalpel may enable a surgeon to perform more efficiently or effectively, but it will not enable a carpenter to perform surgery on humans.

The point is that **typesetting** is a professional skill, and like any skill, requires knowledge and practice before proficiency is achieved. In this sense, typesetting refers to converting printed words into publication-quality outputs. Publication quality encompasses many intangibles, such as readability, aesthetics—in short, the ability to "please the eye." The section that follows discusses some of the elements involved in achieving this level of quality.

Published outputs take many forms. An obvious example of a published output is this book. In addition, you probably come across other forms of published outputs daily, such as newspapers, magazines, newsletters, catalogs, order forms, employment applications, and so on. Production of virtually all of these outputs involves some kind of typesetting.

To illustrate, consider the decisions and operations required for a single page of publication-quality output. One of the first tasks in any form of communication is to consider the audience. It may be helpful to begin by asking a series of questions that include:

- Who will receive the message?
- How can the message be presented most effectively to this audience?

The answers to these questions provide a basis for designing a page that communicates the message effectively. For example, an evaluation of your audience leads to a number of decisions that determine the appearance of the page. Initially, decisions center around text elements. Later, graphic elements come into play. Decisions and capabilities involved with handling graphics are discussed later in this chapter. Factors pertinent to text design include:

- Typeface
- Type size
- Spacing
- Format.

Typeface.   The term, typeface, refers to the style, or character set, in which text is produced. Figure 15-2 illustrates a primary distinction among typefaces. Typefaces are characterized by the presence or absence of **serifs,** or cross lines at the

SERIF TYPE — This group of faces, patterned by letter forms used in classical Roman inscriptions, looks better in mass than when examined letter by letter. The letters are extremely readable because they are open, wide and round, with pointed serifs that make a pleasing contrast between the heavy and light strokes.

SANS SERIF TYPE — This comparatively new type enjoys great popularity today because of its simplicity of design. The letters have no serifs, and with few exceptions are optically evenly weighted. Sans serif types are widely used for display composition and headlines, as well as captions.

Figure 15-2.

Serif typefaces include cross lines, or serifs, at the ends of letter strokes for emphasis. Characters in sans serif typefaces have no serifs.

ends of letter strokes. Serifs may add emphasis to letters and induce the eye to flow across a page. ***Sans serif*** typefaces, without serifs, may be used to create striking headings or to vary the look of a page.

Type size. Under most publishing systems, character sets are variable. That is, the same style of type may be made larger or smaller to match design goals. Type size, under traditional typesetting systems, is measured as ***points*** and ***picas.*** There are 72 points to an inch; a point represents roughly 1/72 of an inch. A pica is twelve points, or one-sixth of an inch. Points generally refer to the height of type characters. Picas usually describe width, but can describe height. Figure 15-3 presents an illustration of type size measurement.

Spacing. The spacing of letters, words, and lines contributes greatly to readability. Different systems may handle letter spacing in different ways. For example, most typewriters and word processing systems provide an equal space regardless of character. Under this spacing scheme, called ***monospacing,*** an "i" takes up the same space as a "w." Monospacing often results in uneven spacing, and readability may suffer. ***Proportional spacing*** assigns letter spaces according to letter format. Under proportional spacing, an "i" takes up less space than a "w".

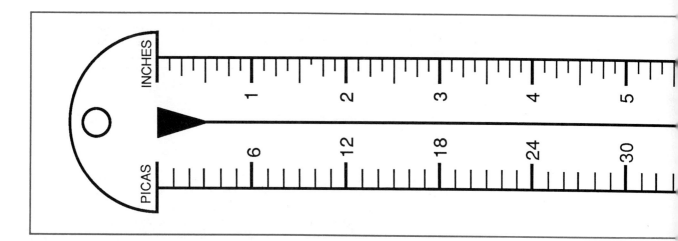

Kerning refers to capabilities for varying letter spaces to fit adjoining letters. Letters may present sides that are round (O, b, C), flat (L, N, F), angular (A, V, w), or with white spaces (T,L). Using kerning techniques, characters run together smoothly, and distracting gaps are eliminated.

Format. The arrangement of text and graphic images on a page or document is known as a **format.** Page formatting, also called page layout, involves positioning page elements for maximum effect. An initial formatting consideration involves the number of columns of text and the length of text lines. An extensive line length may be more difficult to read than a shorter one. This is because the reader's eye experiences more difficulty in moving between lines as formats become wider. One reason for splitting text on a page into multiple columns is to facilitate reader eye movement. Other considerations for designing page formats include the following elements:

- **Margins,** or border spaces, can be varied four ways. See Figure 15-4. **Justified** text fills a line completely; both left and right margins of this text are justified. **Flush left,** or **flush left, ragged right** text is justified along the left margin only. Justified text requires capabilities for splitting words with hyphens at line ends. Justification without hyphenation results in distorted word spacing. **Flush right** refers to text that is justified along the right margin only. This technique may be effective for short pieces but is not recommended for long blocks of text. **Centered,** or **ragged center** text is spaced evenly along the middle point of a column or line.

- **Indents** refer to variations in margins for specific purposes. Notice that the first line of most paragraphs in this text are indented right. Indent capabilities are important for formatting pages that include different elements, such as the bulleted list in this section. See Figure 15-5.

"Four score and seven years ago our fathers brought forth, upon this continent, a new nation, conceived in Liberty, and dedicated to the proposition that all men are created equal."

Flush Left (Rag Right)

"Four score and seven years ago our fathers brought forth, upon this continent, a new nation, conceived in Liberty, and dedicated to the proposition that all men are created equal."

Justified

"Four score and seven years ago our fathers brought forth, upon this continent, a new nation, conceived in Liberty, and dedicated to the proposition that all men are created equal."

Centered

"Four score and seven years ago our fathers brought forth, upon this continent, a new nation, conceived in Liberty, and dedicated to the proposition that all men are created equal."

Flush Right (Rag Left)

Figure 15-4.

Justification and centering of text can add to the "professional" appearance of a document.

Figure 15-5.

Documents may be formatted with indents and other treatments to add emphasis to specific text portions.

line length may be more difficult to read than a shorter one. This is because the reader's eye experiences more difficulty in moving between lines as formats become wider. One reason for splitting text on a page into multiple columns is to facilitate reader eye movement. Other considerations for designing page formats include the following elements:

- *Margins,* or border spaces, can be varied four ways. See Figure 15-4. *Justified* text fills a line completely; both left and right margins of this text are justified. *Flush left,* or *flush left, ragged right* text is justified along the left margin only. Justified text requires capabilities for splitting words with hyphens at line ends. Justification without hyphenation results in distorted word spacing. *Flush right* refers to text that is justified along the right margin only. This technique may be effective for short pieces but is not recommended for long blocks of text. *Centered,* or *ragged center* text is spaced evenly along the middle point of a column or line.

- *Indents* refer to variations in margins for specific purposes. Notice that the first line of most paragraphs in this text are indented right. Indent capabilities are important for formatting pages that include different elements, such as the bulleted list in this section. See Figure 15-5.

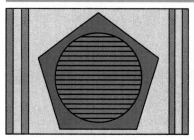

BUSINESS COMPUTER GRAPHICS

Persuasive Power at Your Fingertips

A picture is worth a thousand words, but why? Some experts believe that there are fundamental differences between the way the human brain processes words and the way it processes pictures. Words are processed one at a time. Visual images, on the other hand, seem to be processes in parallel. Many separate brain circuits processed different parts of the visual image simultaneously. Consequently, humans are able to assimilate more data graphically than they can reading words or tables of data.

"Not only can graphics applications save corporate time and money, but they are also another step toward converting data processing into a strategic and competitive weapon."

Alan Paller, AUI Data Graphics

▦ WHY GRAPHICS?

Every picture tells a story, but some pictures tell it better than others. Hence, the art of computer graphics — the professional polish of sharp, lively images that allow your audience to focus on the important aspects of your presentation.

Computer Graphics has quickly become one of the fastest growing fields in the computer applications industry. Why? Several reasons, among them lower hardware and software costs and advances in computer graphics technology.

Another significant reason for the growing demand for and popularity of graphics is that people today are more visually oriented than in the past. Not only are they attracted to colorful graphics; they expect them.

Graphics: Yet another computer application that can offer companies improved sales effectiveness and satisfied customers.

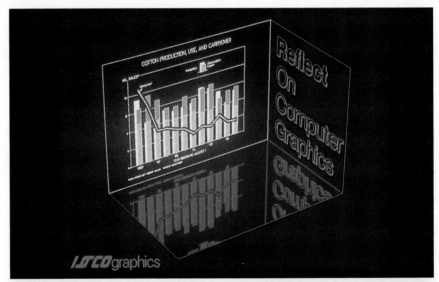

Business graphics would be worthless if they did not satisfy a need. Obviously they do.

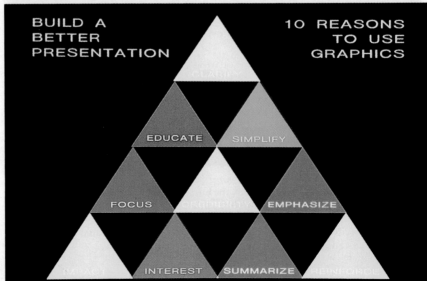

▦ GRAPHICS: A TREND

Research done by a magazine, Personal Computing, found that almost half of their subscribers already use a microcomputer for presentation graphics. Within the next year, an additional 36% plan to begin using microcomputer graphics.

The amount of dollars spent on computer graphics over the past few years reflects this trend.

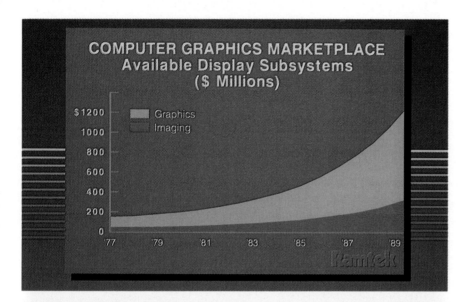

The business graphics marketplace is booming. Graphics hardware and software are becoming more and more sophisticated, providing more options as to how you display information.

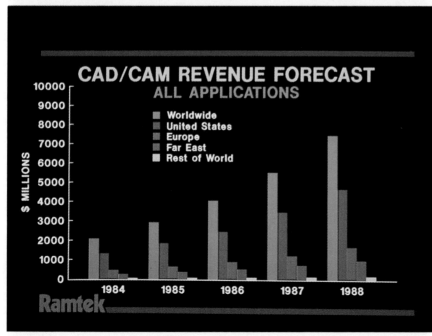

While computer-aided design/-computer-aided manufacturing (CAD/CAM) still represents the largest segment of the computer graphics industry, the emergence of business graphics has helped to move the technology into the commercial sphere.

▥ HARDWARE: WHAT'S REQUIRED FOR YOUR MICROCOMPUTER?

The capacity to generate and display graphics is a prerequisite for using presentation software.

Once you have a microcomputer, the minimum hardware includes:

- Monitor (color is best)
- Enough RAM for the program and any special data storage
- Input devices, such as the keyboard or joystick
- Printers, from dot matrix to color plotter
- On-line storage devices
- A graphics board or addition, depending on the microcomputer

Several sources of presentation hardware.

HARDWARE

Color Digital Imager   Bell and Howell, 411 Amapola Ave., Torrance, CA 90501; (213) 320–5700

Datacom 35   Photographic Sciences Corp., PO Box 338, Webster, NY 14580; (716) 265–1600

HI PC Pens Plotters   Houston Instrument, 8500 Cameron Road, Austin, TX 78753; (800) 531–5205

HP Graphics Plotters, LaserJet   Hewlett-Packard Corp., 16399 W. Bernardo Drive, San Diego, CA 92127; (800) 367–4772

IBM Color Printer, Color Jetprinter   IBM Corp., PO Box 1328, 1000 N.W. 51 St., Boca Raton, FL 33432; (800) 447–4700

Matrix PCR   Matrix Instruments, Inc., 1 Ramland Road, Orangeburg, NY 10962; (914) 365–0190

Polaroid Palette   Polaroid Corp., 575 Technology Square, Cambridge, MA 02139; (800) 225–1618

VideoShow   General Parametrics Corp., 1250 Ninth St., Berkeley, CA 94710; (800) 556–1234

Videoscope, Multiscan projectors   Sony Corp. of America, Sony Drive, Park Ridge, NJ 07656; (201) 930–6432

More and more for less and less. That trend applies to graphics software as well as graphics hardware.

▥ SOFTWARE: WHAT'S MOST IMPORTANT?

Once you've had experience developing and using business graphics, you'll become a more critical user. You'll become especially sensitive to the capabilities of graphics software to make your presentations more effective.

SOFTWARE

Chart-Master, Sign-Master, Map-Master   Decision Resources, Inc., 25 Sylvan Road South, Westport, CT 06880; (203) 222-1974

ExecuVision, Concorde   Visual Communications Network, Inc., 238 Main St., Cambridge, MA 02142; (617) 497–4000

GEM Graph, WordChart   Digital Research, Inc., 60 Garden Court, PO Box DRI, Monterey, CA 93942; (800) 443–4200

Graphwriter, Freelance   Graphic Communications, Inc., 200 Fifth Ave., Waltham, MA 02254; (617) 890–8778

Harvard Presentation Graphics, PFS:Graph   Software Publishing Corp., 1901 Landings Drive, Mountain View, CA 94043; (415) 962–8910

Inset   American Programmers Guild, Ltd., 12 Mill Plain Road, Danbury, CT 06811; (203) 794–0396

Microsoft Chart   Microsoft Corp., 16011 N.E. 36th Way, Box 97017, Redmond WA 98073; (206) 882–8088

PC Storyboard   IBM Corp., PO Box 1328 1000, N.W. 51 St., Boca Raton, FL 33432; (800) 447–4700

Show Partner   Brightbill-Roberts & Co., 120 E. Washington St., Suite 421, Syracuse, NY 13202; (315) 474–3400

Several sources of presentation software.

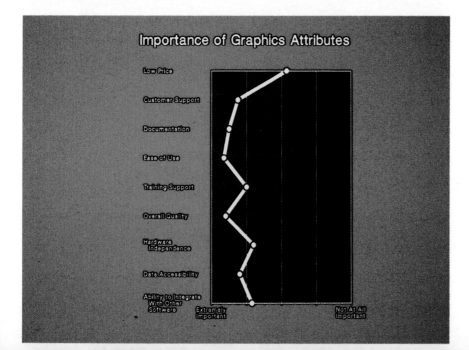

Quality and easy of use rank as the most important graphics software attributes, according to users.

▦ RUNNING THE SOFTWARE: THE EASY PART

With the appropriate software and hardware, your microcomputer will let you prepare a professional-looking presentation — from start to finish — in one sitting.

No longer does this user have to create an image in his head.

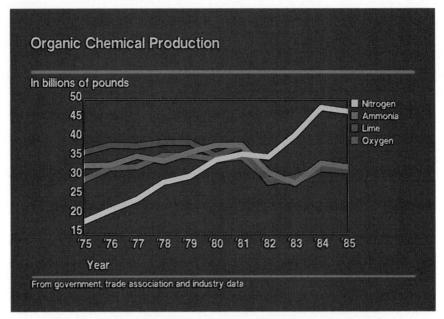

Adding color helps get the point across more effectively than black and white.

This experienced user of business computer graphics says that the process of developing graphics forces him to present his information more succinctly.

Artistic talent isn't a necessary prerequisite, either. Let's say you want to create a graph in Lotus 1-2-3. Basically, these are the steps you would follow:

1. Title your graph and the categories of your data or information
2. Enter your data or information
3. Select the kind of graph you want the program to create
4. Name the data range to be shown on the graph
5. Decide how to use the X and Y axes
6. Choose your colors (if you have a color monitor). . . .

And poof! The computer does the drawing for you. Often it's that simple.

This user doesn't have a printer. She prefers to photograph her graphics while they are displayed on the screen. She uses the resulting prints and slides in visual presentations.

Some spreadsheet programs, such as Lotus, include graphing programs. This integrated feature makes it easy for this user to take information or data directly from his electronic spreadsheet and put it into a graph.

Even though graphs do not supply all the details of the raw data, they make it easier for this user to recognize trends and conditions.

▥ APPLYING COLOR FOR IMPACT: HELPFUL HINTS

Andrew Corn, Admaster, Inc., a design and production agency, suggests the following elements of design in creating a presentation:

- Maintain good contrast such as dark text and brightly colored graphics set against a light background.
- Choose appropriate colors — yellow, blue, and green are usually good choices.
- Fill charts with bright, solid colors. They're pleasing to the eye and easy to distinguish.
- Spare the colors, don't spoil the picture. More than five colors in one graphic will overshadow the message.
- Accentuate with color — bright color to emphasize, darker or lighter colors to anchor the remaining pieces.
- Adapt color to your environment. Factors like lighting and audience size should influence your use of color.

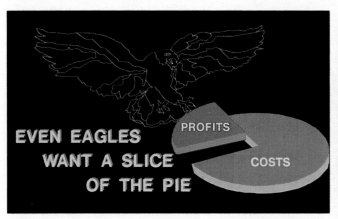

Company logos can be displayed on the screen to help viewers associate a company name with its products.

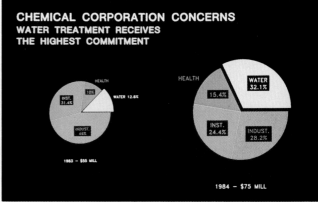

The pie chart is popular and widely used for simple business applications.

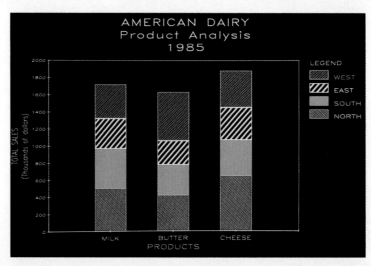

Bar charts are commonly used to illustrate business data.

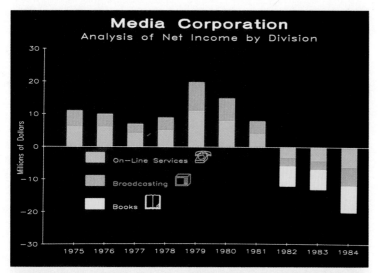

Bar charts may be stacked one on top of the other to summarize the income of several divisions.

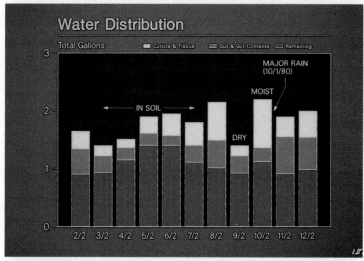

This bar chart illustrates the impact of contrast; that is, the use of light text and of brightly colored graphics set against a dark background.

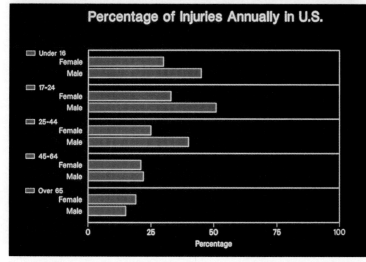

Bar charts can be drawn horizontally or vertically. The selection of this format is useful for a change of pace to get, or retain, the viewer's attention.

▥ KNOWING WHAT YOU WANT TO SAY: THE CHALLENGE

But slick isn't everything. Once you've learned how, putting your chosen medium to work for you is the easy part.

What makes some graphs effective, valuable, and memorable when so many are unnecessary or misleading? What is your challenge?

Line graphs are excellent for displaying financial and daily, weekly, monthly, quarterly, and yearly data. It is also possible to plot more than a single relationship on the same chart for purposes of comparison.

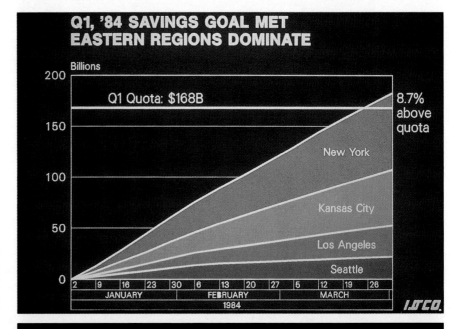

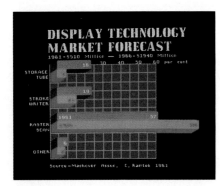

Three-dimensional graphics are far less common than bar graphs or pie charts. Most users aren't willing to spend more for the required hardware and software. But for some users the benefits outweigh the costs.

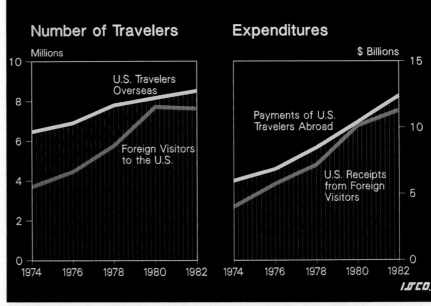

Filling in spaces with color can dramatize and add meaning to the presentation of data.

Above all, it's how well you know your audience and the information you want to communicate.

Computers can generate vast quantities of data, but more data is not necessarily better for your reader. Concepts can confuse and numbers can numb without the instant translation that pictures can relate.

Again, the art of computer graphics is to focus the viewer's attention, to communicate, to persuade.

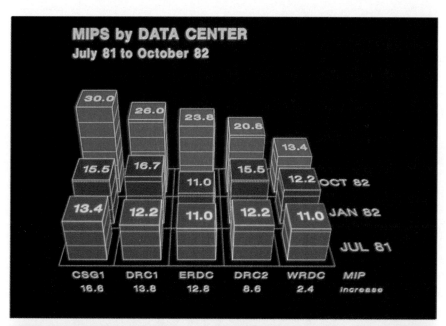

This three-dimensional graphic provides an interesting presentation of a bar chart.

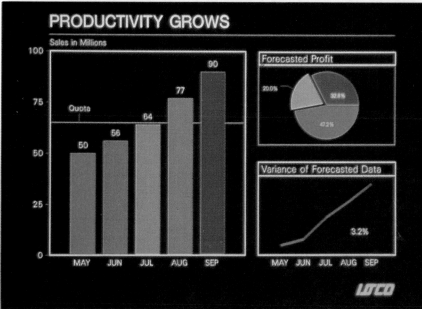

Pie, line, and bar charts may be designed to illustrate the same information. However, bar charts can incorporate the widest range of variables through the use of colors and different shadings.

Using different types of charts in one presentation gives the viewer several perspectives from which to analyze the data.

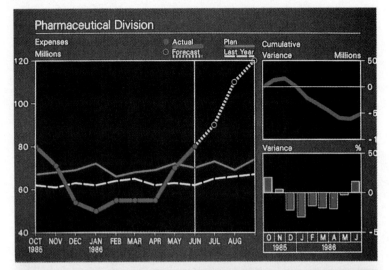

Bar and line charts can be combined to give both the big picture and the detailed picture simultaneously.

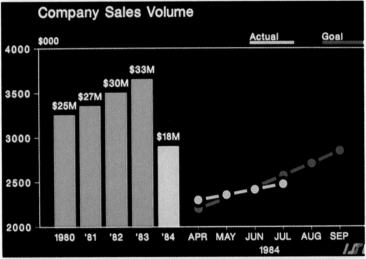

This combination of charts gives managers immediate access to key performance indicators, allowing them to reinforce outstanding performance quickly and to anticipate weak performance before it becomes critical.

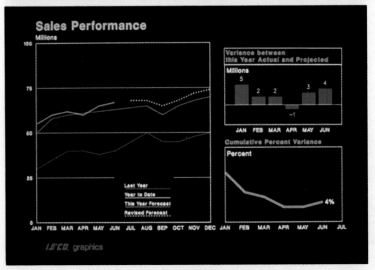

▨ HOW TO BE PERSUASIVE

Microcomputer graphics are a tool for the professional to use in accomplishing business objectives. Common objectives of business graphics are:

- To evaluate past relationships between variables
- To project expected relationships for decision-making
- To monitor ongoing business operations
- To find and demonstrate trends and deviations
- To communicate information to a targeted individual or group
- To sell your ideas — and yourself!

First, what point do you want to make? Answering this question will be your biggest challenge. To do so, you must first gain an understanding of the essential ingredients of a persuasive presentation: your audience and the information you want to communicate.

Once you've answered this question, then and only then are you ready to select the data and graph type that will best illustrate your point.

According to a recent University of Minnesota/3M study, presentations using visual aids were found to be 43% more persuasive than unaided presentations.

Graphics is likely to be the key communication aid of the next decade.

A recent study from the Wharton School of Business demonstrated that those who used graphics in their presentation enjoyed shorter meetings, and that they also achieved consensus quicker than those who did not use graphics.

Commercial art and photography shops offer you an alternative to enlarging an image yourself.

▥ TYPICAL BUSINESS APPLICATIONS

The number of applications of computer systems continues to grow.

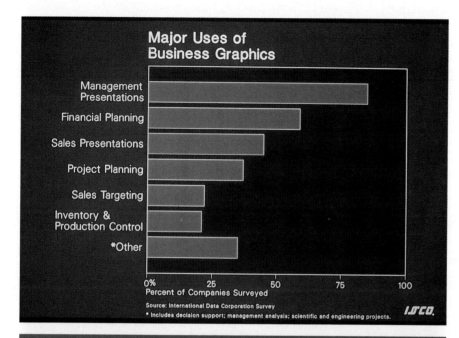

Uses of business computer graphics are not only increasing but spreading into all areas of business. Still, graphics are used primarily for management presentations and summaries.

3M is just one of the many companies that now prepares and delivers "on-call" graphics.

3M has an alternative for users who would rather not, or who can't afford to, purchase a computer system and develop their own graphics: graphics by phone — 24 hours a day, seven days a week.

Here's how it works:

1. Choose a format from the more than 100 displayed in their format guide

2. Relay your choice to 3M with a keyboard of any microcomputer that has telephone communication capability

3. Within two days your 35mm slide, overhead transparency, or full color print will arrive.

▥ WHAT'S AHEAD?

In the midst of the changes, the measure of an effective business graphic remains constant. The important consideration is whether or not actions will result from the graphic, whether decisions will be made on the basis of it.

Computer graphics stands at a crossroads: It can either be supported as a personal tool for presentations or as a strategic resource for decision-making. Many successful organizations have discovered that their strongest approach combines and supports both these aspects of computer graphics.

QUESTIONS

1. What are two of the many reasons the use of computer graphics is increasing in the business world?

2. What are the minimum hardware requirements for a microcomputer graphics system?

3. Name three attributes of microcomputer graphics considered important by users.

4. Identify three guidelines to be considered in the use of color graphics.

5. Describe three business objectives that can profit from the use of business computer graphics.

6. What are three important considerations in creating presentation graphics?

7. What is the greatest challenge in creating effective computer graphics?

- Special effects often draw attention to section headings or other elements. Special effects are achieved by altering character widths, heights, and/or **baselines,** the lower horizontal alignment levels upon which text is positioned. Special effects also encompass mathematical or engineering symbols, superscripts, subscripts, and so on.

Under conventional phototypesetting techniques, columns of type on special phototypesetting paper are cut and pasted in place on paper boards. These boards then are photographed to create printing plates. Systems supported by large computers make it possible to compose pages electronically on display screens instead of boards, and to create printing plates directly from computer files.

As stated previously, desktop publishing refers to microcomputer-based systems that provide all—or many—of the capabilities described above. Some experts believe that desktop publishing represents a potential "new wave" in the microcomputer revolution. Desktop publishing systems are discussed in the section that follows.

DESKTOP PUBLISHING SYSTEMS

In most cases, desktop publishing systems can be configured with hardware and software "off the shelf," and implemented for an investment of roughly $10,000. For text documents, desktop publishing systems may reduce production time by 40 percent and production cost by 50 percent over traditional typesetting and cut-and-paste composition techniques. For line illustrations, the time and money spent on preparation may be reduced by 25 to 30 percent. Another key advantage of desktop publishing lies in the flexibility of microcomputer-based systems. Under traditional techniques, last minute changes or corrections might require a two-day delay, compared with less than a half hour for desktop publishing systems.

The components of a desktop publishing system include:

- Microcomputer
- External storage
- Peripherals (including a laser printer)
- Page description software.

MICROCOMPUTER

The systems that drive desktop publishing applications usually require large amounts of main memory and external storage. This requirement stems from two factors. First, software components are memory intensive. That is, publishing programs must generate graphics, handle free-form drawings (both types of graphics are discussed below), provide different character sets, manipulate the size of typefaces, and handle special effects. Second, the handling of graphics requires large amounts of memory and storage. To illustrate, a page of type composed under typesetting programs requires 15 or 20 times more memory or storage than a page of text captured under a word processing program.

Recall that the more data and programs that can be held in main memory, the quicker an application runs. In desktop publishing systems, main memory is a significant consideration. A popular machine for these systems, the Apple Macintosh Plus, contains a full megabyte of main memory. IBM PCs and PC compatibles usually must be upgraded to 512K or 640K of main memory to handle publishing tasks efficiently.

EXTERNAL STORAGE

An external hard-disk drive is a virtual necessity for a desktop publishing system. At present, there is no other practical way to accommodate all of the software and graphic storage needed to support desktop publishing. Most desktop publishing systems are configured with hard-disk storage capacities of 20 megabytes or more.

PERIPHERALS

With few exceptions, desktop publishing systems are configured from standard microcomputer components. As is the case with any type of systems development, application requirements should dictate hardware and software selections. That is, systems are configured to meet the specifications of outputs and operating preferences. One output device used in most desktop publishing systems is a laser printer.

Laser Printer

Systems are developed to produce outputs. Desktop publishing applications were developed concurrently with laser printers. Laser printers provide capabilities for producing near-typeset quality images of graphics and text. Recall that image quality, or clarity, is expressed in terms of its resolution.

Laser printer technology resembles xerographic duplicating machines, or copiers. A revolving drum holds a positive electrical charge. A laser, an intense beam of focused light, neutralizes this charge when it passes over the drum. The laser produces images on the drum by reversing the positive charge on image areas. White spaces retain positive charges. The drum rolls through **toner**—positively charged, pigmented powder—which is attracted to negatively charged image areas.

Toner then is transferred from drum to paper. Paper is given a negative charge as it enters the printer. As the paper passes over the drum, the toner image, attracted by the negative charge, is transferred. Heat is applied to **fuse**, or melt, the toner into the paper. Rapid cooling fixes the image onto the paper and a high-resolution output is produced.

As desktop publishing technology has evolved, laser printers have advanced significantly. For example, the resolution of laser printer outputs is higher than most output devices for microcomputers. Laser printers produce outputs with resolutions of 300 by 300 dots per inch, and this figure should increase under the pressures of demands and competition.

Laser printers that support desktop publishing require capabilities that go beyond the needs of conventional, character output devices. Large memory capacities must be built into laser printers used for desktop publishing. For example, the LaserWriter by Apple features a **page-description language** called Postscript. Postscript enhances the capability of laser printers to process signals representing graphics and text. Postscript occupies 1/2 megabyte of read-only memory (ROM) within the control unit of the LaserWriter. The LaserWriter Plus, an upgraded version, contains 1.5 megabytes of random-access memory (RAM) and a microprocessor. In effect, the LaserWriter, as well as many laser printers in its class, houses its own microcomputer to support the extensive demands of graphics software.

Other Peripherals

To repeat a previous point, desktop publishing systems can be configured largely from standard microcomputer components, according to requirements. In addition to a laser printer and a high-capacity external storage device, other peripherals commonly used to make up these systems include:

- Mouse
- Graphics tablet
- Scanner.

Mouse.   A **mouse** is a hand-held box connected by a wire to a computer. Within the mouse is a protruding roller. When the mouse is moved over a flat surface, corresponding movement is transferred to a cursor on the display screen. This makes it possible to write or draw on the screen with a mouse. However, the most important use of a mouse is for rapid cursor movement and selections from menus. The mouse is moved until the cursor is positioned over a description or *icon* (graphic image) for a menu choice. The operator presses a button on the top of the mouse and the selection is activated. Desktop publishing software typically is organized under a multilevel structure. Initial selections are made from a *menu bar* that displays the names of key functions across the top of the screen. When a function is selected, a supporting submenu extends downward from the top of the screen. These *pull-down menus* are used to select detail operations to be performed.

Graphics tablet.   A *graphics tablet* provides a flat surface from which drawn or handwritten images can be input to a computer. The tablet contains a series of electrically sensitive points that transmit signals when touched. An artist moves a pen-like device called a *stylus* across the face of the tablet. Corresponding lines of the image appear on the video screen of the microcomputer.

Scanner.   A *scanner* uses a laser beam to read and input graphic data. A laser beam is passed back and forth over documents in a scan, a pattern that covers the entire image. At closely spaced points along the scan lines, the laser beam senses the density, or degree of darkness, of the image. These signals are stored in the computer and used to reproduce the image within desktop publishing systems. Scanning can be done with devices that use moving laser beams or by video cameras.

PAGE DESCRIPTION SOFTWARE

The software component of desktop publishing systems may consist of one or more programs. For example, text portions of output documents usually must be keyed initially with a word processor. Graphics might be generated from data created with an electronic spreadsheet package. Or, free-form graphics might be produced with some type of "paint" package. The creation and handling of both types of graphics are discussed later in this chapter.

Under most desktop publishing systems, data from several programs might go into a final page of output. The text and graphics that make up an output page must be collected and arranged into a single file for output. *Page description programs* provide capabilities for bringing text and graphics together and for organizing them as finished outputs.

Two basic types of page description programs are available. The first is called *code-oriented* software. This name stems from format instructions that are entered within documents. These programs produce output designs in much the same way many word processing programs handle printing enhancements. Figure 15-6 shows a document coded for output under a typical code-oriented

```
\SM2800\SF03\SL130\LI0300FUNKHOUSER  SOFTWARE[
BUSINESS  REPORT[
\LI0400\SF02PUBLICATIONS  DEPARTMENT[
\SF011986 was an extremely productive year for Funkhouser
Software's Publications Department.[
\LI0106\IN0200,0200\HA0200
\HI0+Fifteen technical manuals were written and released to
support new product releases.[
\HI0+A company-wide internal documentation system was
developed and implemented.[
\HI0+The establishment of a technical reference library was
completed.[
\IN0000,0000\LI0200
In addition, the cost per page was reduced significantly through
the use of a software package that produces typeset quality
output using an in-house laser printer.[\IX
```

SM2800.............Set a line measure of 28 picas.

SF03................Set typeface 03, Times Roman 10-point bold.

SL130...............Set a line leading of 13 points.

LI0400..............Lead immediately 4 picas down the page.

IN0200,0200 ......Used to indent 2 picas on the left margin and 2 picas on the right margin, to make the three informational lines stand out from the rest of the text.

HA200..............Used to set a hanging indent, where only the first line is full width and all other lines are indented the specified amount.

HI...................Used to begin the hanging indent that was previously defined.

+....................EM Space, used as fixed space to keep all the first letters of the

[....................Quad (Flush) Line Left is used to end a line flush left

IN0000,0000....... Used to end indented text and return to full measure.

IX ....Cancel all indents including hanging indent. This code could have been used in place of the indent zeros; then it would not have been necessary here.

program. The drawback to code-oriented programs is that a user cannot see the finished product on the display screen. Code-oriented programs typically require less capacity in terms of storage and memory than their counterpart, WYSIWYG programs.

WYSIWYG is an acronym that stands for "what you see is what you get." WYSIWYG packages provide capabilities for producing exact screen images of outputs. In this way, users can see the results of their page designs before hard-copy outputs are produced. Figure 15-7 presents a screen display of a page designed under a WYSIWYG program.

Page Description Capabilities

Page description programs also provide capabilities for designing pages for output. That is, these programs usually feature a "tool kit" of functions for formatting the elements that make up finished pages. Tools are selected, under most programs, from levels of pull-down menus. Consider the menu structure of PageMaker, a popular page description package, presented in Figure 15-8.

The display in Figure 15-8 represents a **desktop** that corresponds roughly with an application **main menu.** Operations begin with this display. Users then navigate through the various levels of menus, finding and selecting the processing options, or tools, they need. Each entry along the menu bar of this display represents a pull-down menu. To select any of these options, the cursor is directed to the desired selection and the mouse is "clicked." This means that the button on the mouse is pushed to execute these operations. Throughout this chapter, the phrase, clicking the mouse, is used to describe the finding, selecting, and executing of menu selections. For example, clicking the mouse on any of the entries in the menu bar causes a set of processing options to be "pulled down" and displayed. Selections from these options are made by clicking the mouse again.

The selection of many of these options results in the display of a **dialog box.** A dialog box is used to make selections. As the name implies, however, users can make selections interactively. For example, the dialog box shown in Figure 15-9 provides entry areas for specifying the number of columns and the space between columns on a document. These entries are performed through the keyboard.

Under most page description programs, working sessions are executed through iterations of this process. The cursor is navigated through menu structures using a mouse as a pointing device. Menu options are chosen as needed, often resulting in succeeding selections or keyboard entries.

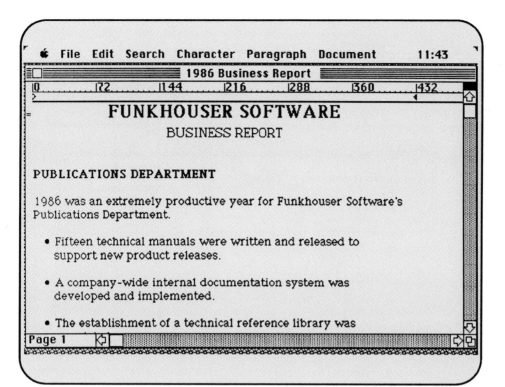

Figure 15-7.

WYSIWYG packages provide capabilities for producing exact screen images of output documents.

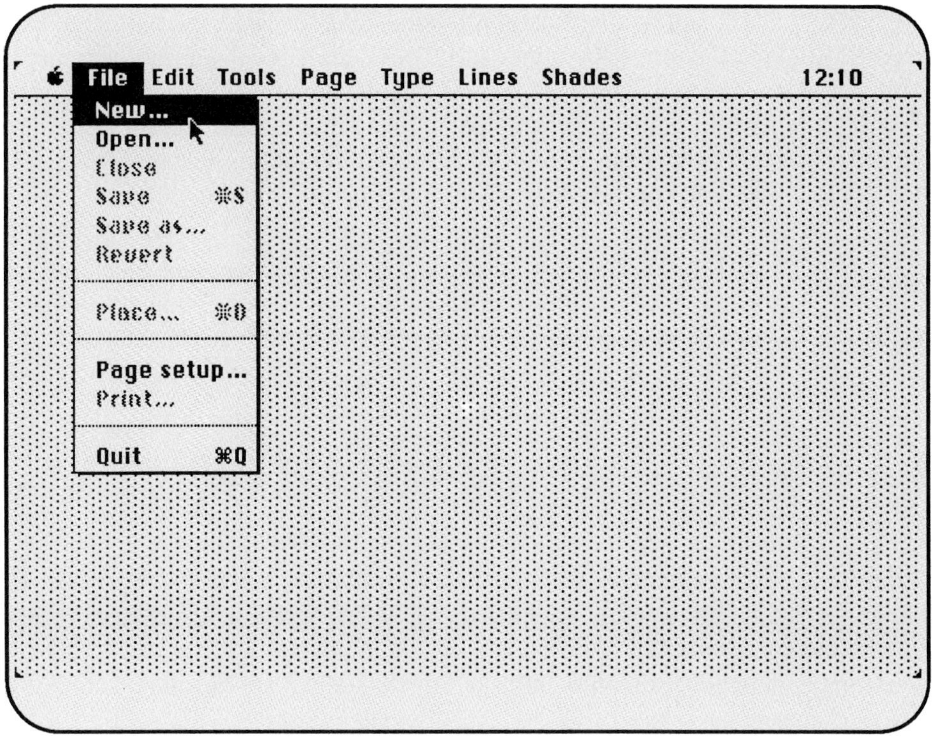

Figure 15-8.

This display presents the main menu, or desktop, for the PageMaker program.

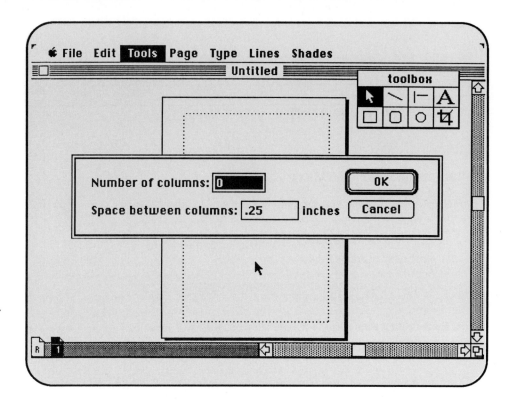

Figure 15-9.

A dialog box provides an area where the system can prompt for needed information or instructions and the user can respond.

The mouse can be used to *scroll* through documents as well. The cursor is directed to the horizontal or vertical *scroll bars* along the right and bottom of the desktop. Clicking the mouse on either scroll bar causes the displayed document to be moved up, down, left, or right, as indicated by arrows. In this way, text and graphics are brought onto a displayed page, formatted, saved, and output. This process is presented as a case example in a later section of this chapter. The point is that menu selections present "tools" for creating high-quality output images.

The tools, or capabilities, can be classified by the document elements to which they are applied. Under these classifications, page description capabilities include:

- Text

- Graphics

Text.   Text can be brought in, or imported, from files created in other programs. File import capabilities, involving both text and graphic files, are subject to the formats and compatibilities of the page description packages. Most packages provide transfer capabilities with popular word processing, spreadsheet, and database packages.

Figure 15-10.

Portions of images can be lassoed and moved as needed.

Once in the page description program, the character style, or typeface, in which text appears can be changed. Most programs of this type provide several typefaces. The size of type also can be manipulated. Many packages also provide options for expressing type measurements in inches, millimeters, and/or points and picas. Further, different treatments, such as italics and boldface, can be applied to text.

Graphics. Graphics also can be imported from files created in other programs, depending upon the specifications of the package. Graphics, or portions of graphics, then can be moved and placed on a page. These operations may involve use of **lassos,** or boxes. See Figure 15-10. Using these tools, portions of graphics are selected by drawing a circle around them with a mouse, then moved and placed as needed.

The presentation of graphics often can be enhanced by boxes or lines. Pictures then are offset from text, and seem to float in space on the page. In addition, graphics can be cropped, or sized, to fit within overall page designs. A variety of treatments can be applied to graphics as well. For example, most packages provide different types of screens, and densities for each screen type, that can be used to fill in backgrounds or other image portions. Depending upon the specifications of the package, images often can be manipulated to fit the aims of page designs. That is, graphics can be moved left, right, up, down, or even rotated 360 degrees.

Page description capabilities implement the design schemes of users. An understanding of these capabilities may be enhanced by a description of microcomputer methods for handling text and graphics. This description is presented in the section that follows. A later section in this chapter presents a case example that illustrates the production of finished outputs under these systems.

DESKTOP PUBLISHING: HOW IT WORKS

In a simple sense, the attraction of desktop publishing systems is based upon capabilities for integrating text and graphics on high-quality outputs. To provide these capabilities, desktop publishing systems implement two basic techniques for handling text and graphic data, which include:

* Bit mapping
* Vector algorithms.

Bit Mapping

Bit mapping relies on plotted locations of bits for representing text and graphics. As the name implies, the system divides an image area, the screen, into vertical and horizontal, or X and Y, axes. The screen, then, is divided into ***coordinates,*** similar to those used on maps and line graphs. Bits are plotted according to locations along the resulting ***grid.*** Bit locations then are assigned ON or OFF values to form images.

For handling graphic images, for example, bit locations are plotted within the screen display area. See Figure 15-11. Scanners use bit mapping techniques. An optical reading device scans a page, line by line. Each line is divided into a series of read locations by the scanner. For each location, the presence of black (image) or white (space) is converted to an ON or OFF signal. Images are built as bit patterns along a screen grid.

Many desktop publishing systems also use bit mapping techniques for storing different typefaces. A plotted grid representing each character is stored in a ***lookup table*** and accessed as needed. Suppose the system is instructed to display or print the letter "Z" in a typeface called Palatino. The system accesses the lookup table for that typeface, then uses the coordinates for the letter "Z" to plot the letter on the screen.

Suppose further, though, that the system is instructed to display the same character in italics. Italic images, in most cases, are generated mathematically.

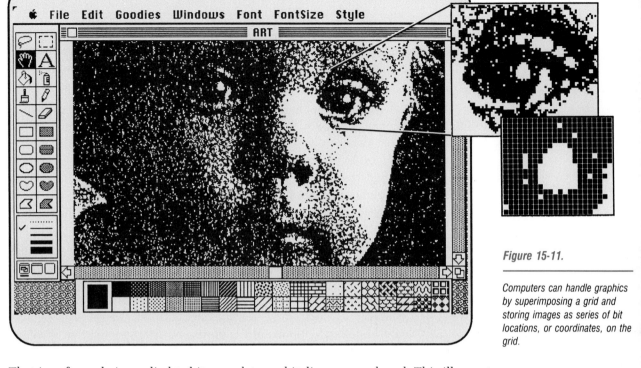

Figure 15-11.

Computers can handle graphics by superimposing a grid and storing images as series of bit locations, or coordinates, on the grid.

That is, a formula is applied to bit map data and italics are produced. This illustrates one drawback of bit mapping techniques. Bit maps require large amounts of memory, and may not provide all the treatments required under most desktop publishing systems.

Another drawback is that the bit maps are hardware dependent. A bit map resolution of 72 by 72 **bpi (bits per inch),** may limit outputs to that figure—regardless of output device capabilities. In other words, the 72 bpi map is reproduced exactly, even on laser printers capable of 300 by 300 bpi.

This situation can be alleviated by multiplying, under program control, the density of bit maps by a whole number. Suppose, for example, that an output device has a resolution capability of 288 by 288 bpi. Bit map density can be multiplied by a factor of 4 (under system control) and outputs produced at the higher resolution. This solution works best when the ratio between output capabilities and bit map resolutions is a whole number. Uneven ratios produce unpredictable and unacceptable output images.

Vector Algorithms

The **vector algorithm** method for handling text and graphic images involves complicated mathematics beyond the scope of this chapter—even this book. An **algorithm** is a list of steps for performing a specific task. In effect, an algorithm is a formula for achieving results.

Under the vector algorithm method, points are established on a screen and images are defined mathematically, according to algorithms. Steps within algorithms define individual lines, or shapes, that are combined to form an overall image.

The vector algorithm method provides several advantages over bit mapping. Images are generated rapidly. The system does not have to scan and plot images bit by bit. Algorithms occupy less storage space than bit maps, which is another reason why images are produced faster under this method. In addition, the vector algorithm method is object oriented, rather than hardware dependent. This means that the generation of images is based upon a description (algorithm) of the image, rather than on a specific representation (bit map) of the image.

In summary, the capabilities provided by desktop publishing systems can be applied to an enormous range of requirements. To implement these systems effectively, however, knowledge and skills from other professional fields may be needed. This is true because desktop publishing systems represent a merger between two technologies, computing and publishing. In the chapter that follows, another "dual-technology" application is discussed. This application involves microcomputers used to communicate over distances.

K E Y   T E R M S

publishing	margins	stylus
resolution	justified	scanner
linotype	flush left	page description program
set	flush left, ragged right	code-oriented
phototypesetting	flush right	WYSIWYG
galleys	centered	desktop
formatting	ragged center	main menu
layout	indents	dialog box
typesetting	baseline	scroll
serif	toner	scroll bar
sans serif	fuse	lasso
point	page-description language	coordinates
pica	mouse	grid
monospacing	icon	lookup table
proportional spacing	menu bar	bpi (bits per inch)
kerning	pull-down menu	vector algorithm
format	graphics tablet	algorithm

D E F I N I T I O N S

Instructions: On a separate sheet, define each term according to its use in this chapter.

1. phototypesetting

2. layout

3. typesetting

4. serifs

5. sans serif

6. monospacing

7. WYSIWYG

8. mouse

T R U E / F A L S E

Instructions: For each statement, write T for true or F for false on a separate sheet.

1. Publishing develops messages and images that deliver information and entertainment to people.

2. There is no difference in quality between laser printing and printing presses.

3. Typesetting once required professional skill, but computers have made that skill unnecessary.

4. Four factors important to text design are typeface, type size, spacing, and format.

5. The term "typeface" refers to the kinds of type used by designers to create pictures out of words and letters.

6. There are 72 points, or 12 picas, to an inch.

7. Long, horizontal lines of type are easier to read than short ones.

8. A page of type composed under a typesetting program requires less computer memory than the same amount of text captured under most word processing programs.

9. A graphics tablet is a device on which computer graphics are output.

10. A scanner is a computer security device used with code-oriented programs to identify the operator.

11. Clicking the mouse turns your computer on or off.

12. Kerning refers to varying letter spaces to eliminate distracting gaps between adjoining letters.

13. Algorithms occupy more computer storage space than bit maps.

14. With justified text, left and right margins are ragged.

15. Laser printer technology resembles xerographic duplicating machines (copiers).

S H O R T A N S W E R Q U E S T I O N S

Instructions: On a separate sheet of paper, answer each question in one or two brief sentences.

1. What was the first major breakthrough in publishing technology, and why was it important?

2. What are the two most important decisions in developing any communications strategy?

3. What is the difference between picas and points?

4. How are pages prepared with conventional phototypesetting methods?

5. How are pages prepared with computerized typesetting?

6. What savings are possible with desktop publishing?

R E S E A R C H P R O J E C T

Select three or four different types of publications (magazine, newspaper, book, catalog, newsletter, etc.) and study them. Describe techniques used to lay out type and images for reader appeal. Then, explain how these layout techniques enhance or detract from the purposes of each publication.

16 Microcomputer Communication

KEY IDEAS

THE MICROCOMPUTER AS COMMUNICATOR

Microcomputers have evolved into important communication tools for exchange of data and transmission of textual information.

EXCHANGING SIGNALS

A modem performs the signal conversions necessary to link microcomputers to telephone lines.

Modulation and Demodulation

Microcomputers and telephone networks have signal processing standards that are basically incompatible. Modems perform the code translations needed to enable computers to communicate over telephone lines.

Modems for Microcomputers

Three types of modems are used with microcomputers: acoustic couplers, direct connect devices, and smart modems.

MAKING A CONNECTION

Once a microcomputer is equipped with a modem, it can be used to communicate with other modem-equipped computers.

Baud Rate

The speed at which data transmissions are carried out is called the baud rate.

Data Bits

Data characters are encoded for transmission in ASCII format, and may consist of either seven or eight data bits each, depending upon the ASCII format used.

Parity

Parity checking is a method for detecting transmission errors.

Stop Bits

Stop bits are added to identify the end of a data character transmission.

DATA COMMUNICATIONS FOR ORGANIZATIONS

Data communication techniques enhance capabilities for distributing processing and sharing resources within organizations.

Local Area Networks

Three main topologies are used for implementing local area networks: bus, ring, and star.

Local Area Network Software

To ensure security for data resources, and to prevent simultaneous accessing of files, control measures for most local area networks (LANs) are provided by communications software.

ELECTRONIC MAIL

With electronic mail, you can send and receive private messages through your telecommunications system.

BULLETIN BOARDS

Electronic bulletin boards use large-capacity storage devices set up as mailboxes shared by groups of users.

INFORMATION SERVICES

For a fee, private information services will allow access to their databases and provide special services to callers.

THE MICROCOMPUTER AS COMMUNICATOR

In general, technology is demand-driven. To keep pace with demands, technologies are developed that provide increased capabilities, usually at less cost to the user. This situation usually signals further demand and still more developments. As a result, new technologies have been invented, existing technologies have been merged, and tools have taken on new roles.

Microcomputers, for example, have evolved into communication tools, as well as information-handling tools. Most microcomputers can be adapted to link with telephone systems and can send and receive data to and from virtually anywhere in the world. To implement this capability, a microcomputer must be equipped with a special hardware device, called a ***modem,*** and a communication program. A modem acts as a link between microcomputers and telephone systems. Then, a compatible transmission must be established. In effect, the specifications of sending and receiving machines must be compatible to handle identical signals. Establishing a connection is a relatively simple task, and usually is performed with help from interactive software.

A microcomputer can be equipped for communication for roughly $500. The returns on this investment, however, can be substantial. An entire industry has sprung up around this capability. Microcomputer users now can plug into a whole new world of information-related services. For example, stock quotations, airline schedules, software, dating services, news, and banking services—to name just a few—are provided to users with microcomputers equipped as communication terminals. At the organizational level, several microcomputers can be linked to form networks for sharing data and information. Many organizations also provide a central database of information and services that can be accessed from remote locations by authorized personnel.

EXCHANGING SIGNALS

A modem equips a microcomputer for communication. A modem performs the signal conversions needed to link microcomputers with telephone systems. The term, modem, is derived from two types of conversions, modulation and demodulation. ***Modulation*** refers to conversions of digital signals, handled by computers, to analog signals, handled by telephone systems. ***Demodulation,*** the reverse of modulation, involves analog-to-digital signal conversions. Both types of conversions are discussed below.

Modulation and Demodulation

Microcomputers and telephone lines handle different signals. Microcomputers represent data as ***digital signals.*** Microcomputers handle data as bits and bytes,

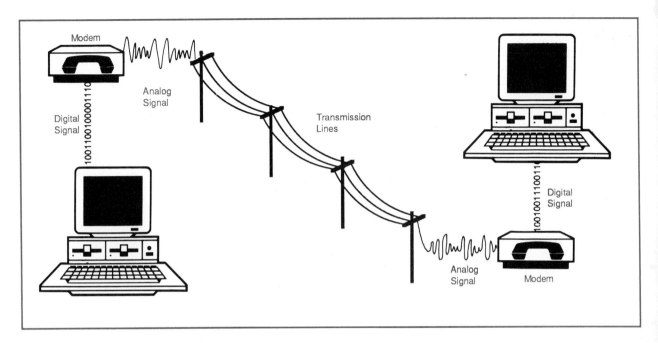

consisting of patterns of 1 and 0 symbols. Transmission of digital signals is accomplished through a series of on or off signals.

Most telephone and/or voice communication systems handle **analog signals.** Analog signals are transmitted as continuous tones. Therefore, data communication requires that on/off (digital) signals be converted into wave signals at the sending end. At the receiving end, analog signals must be converted back into digital mode. This process is illustrated in Figure 16-1.

The wave signals exchanged by modems are called **carrier signals.** Modems convert, or **encode,** digital signals in one of three ways:

- **Frequency modulation (FM)** encodes signals by varying the frequency, or oscillations, of a signal per specified period. Higher frequencies are designated as one bits, lower frequencies indicate zero bits.

- **Amplitude modulation (AM)** involves variations in the magnitude, or voltage level, of a signal representing zero and one bit values. High levels of amplitude, or signal volume, represent one bits, low levels represent zero bits.

- **Phase modulation (PM)** uses wave position to encode data. Wave signals move up and down in relation to a central reference along the wave pattern. Bit values are assigned to high and low positions along the waveform. Above the central point, a value of 1 is indicated. Below the central reference, a 0 value is indicated.

Figure 16-1.

Telecommunication connections between microcomputers require carrier circuits and signal conversions at both sending and receiving terminals.

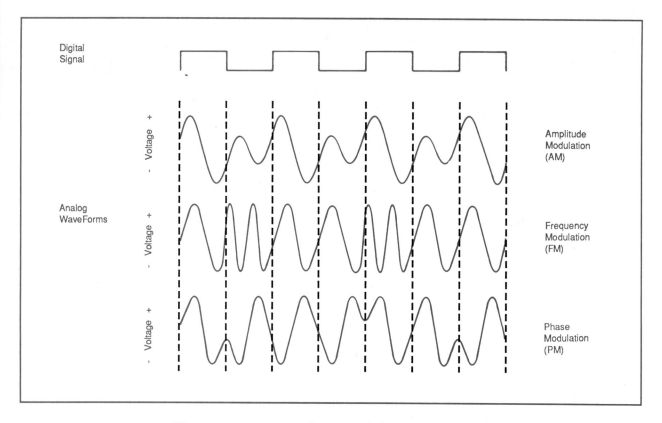

Figure 16-2.

Communication signals (digital and analog) and patterns for encoding data for transfer are presented in these diagrams.

Figure 16-2 presents a diagram of the three types of analog wave forms generated by modems. The most important consideration in establishing a communication link, however, is that both modems are instructed to handle the same signal, at the same time. Establishing links is discussed later in this chapter. Different types of modems are discussed in the section that follows.

Modems for Microcomputers

In an earlier chapter, three types of modems are discussed. *Acoustic couplers* connect microcomputers to communication systems through telephone handsets. The mouthpiece and earpiece of a telephone handset fit into special receptacles in the modem. Output signals converted by the modem are sent out directly through the mouthpiece, and received at the other end through an earpiece.

A *direct connect modem* is linked directly into a telephone. The handset is not needed to establish a connection. Rather, transmission signals are routed from the modem directly into telephone circuits. Direct connect modems are unaffected by environmental noise that may affect the transmission performance of acoustic couplers.

Smart modems. A point is made throughout this text that, as technology evolves, increased capabilities usually are available at reduced costs. Modems have evolved in this way. The **smart modem** has become the tool of choice for most microcomputer users. Smart modems are direct-connect modems; most smart modems plug directly into the expansion slots of microcomputer processors. The "smart" in these modems stems from their abilities to use processing and memory capabilities from their host microcomputers.

Smart modems provide many desirable features. For example, smart modems—in conjunction with accompanying software—usually provide capabilities for creating and maintaining an on-line telephone directory. Telephone numbers can be dialed automatically, in response to keyboard input. In addition, most smart modems can be set to answer incoming calls automatically. The modem detects incoming transmissions, answers the phone, sets up a communication link, then disconnects the phone when the transmission is completed. Considerations for establishing a compatible transmission are discussed in the section that follows.

MAKING A CONNECTION

Once a microcomputer is equipped with a modem, it can be used to communicate with other modem-equipped computers. Transmissions conform to accepted standards in most cases. For example, most data transmissions are encoded in ASCII format. Most communication-oriented software packages use or can convert files to ASCII code. Connections can be made with microcomputers equipped with different makes or types of modems, as long as signals are compatible. Data communication even makes it possible, in many cases, to exchange data between different makes of microcomputers.

Establishing a compatible transmission involves the modulation/demodulation conversions described above. In addition, within microcomputer systems, data bits are transferred in parallel mode—as complete bytes—among system components. Telephone lines handle data serially, a single bit at a time. The difference between serial and parallel transmission is depicted in Figure 16-3. Data sent over communication lines must be output through a serial port. A **port** is a hardware connection for input or output. (Most microcomputers come equipped with a serial port, as well as one or more parallel ports.)

Another important consideration involves the transmission orientation of communication channels. Communication lines may be set up to handle one-way or two-way transmissions. If sending and receiving terminals exchange information in one direction at a time, the transmission is called **half-duplex. Full-duplex** channels permit simultaneous, two-way signal transmission. A telephone conversation is a full-duplex transmission. You can tell a connection is full duplex

Figure 16-3.

Under parallel transmissions, data are sent over communication lines as whole bytes; under serial transmissions, data transfer occurs one bit at a time.

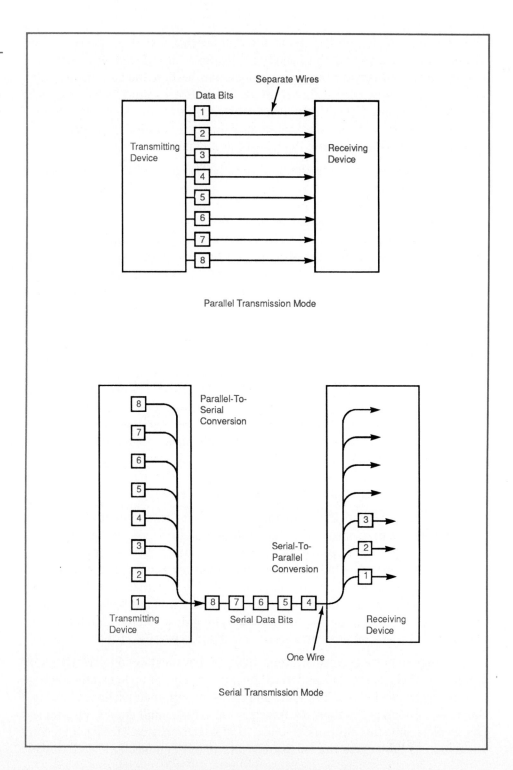

if both parties can talk at once. To set up data communication links, it may be necessary to set modem switches for full-duplex or half-duplex transmission.

Other factors that are involved in microcomputer-based communication include the following:

- Baud rate
- Data bits
- Parity
- Stop bits.

Together, these factors represent the ***protocol,*** or bit orientation, of a data transmission and usually are controlled by setting internal or external switches in the modem itself. Most communication software packages, however, provide capabilities for setting these switches.

Baud Rate

The speed at which data transmissions are carried is called the ***baud rate.*** This rate refers to the number of times per second that a carrier signal changes its state. Remember, carrier signals fluctuate in amplitude, frequency, or phase to represent bit values. A 1200 baud modem, then, is capable of sending data at an approximate rate of 1200 bits per second. Many modems can be set at different speeds, according to needs.

Baud rate can be an important consideration. Telephone calls cost money. Faster transmissions take less time, and may save money (especially over long distances). Standard telephone lines usually handle speeds of 110, 300, 1200, and 2400 baud. Telephone lines have been developed that can handle 9600 baud transmissions for specially equipped microcomputers, and new developments (and faster rates) can be expected.

Data Bits

Data transmissions, to repeat, are encoded in ASCII format. Two ASCII character sets may be used. ASCII-7 is made up of seven-bit characters, or bytes. For example, the letter "D" is encoded 1000100 in ASCII-7, which includes 128 possible characters. ASCII-8 characters are comprised of eight bits. The additional bit provides for a parity checking capability, as described below. The setting for data bits, then, is "7" or "8," depending upon coding format.

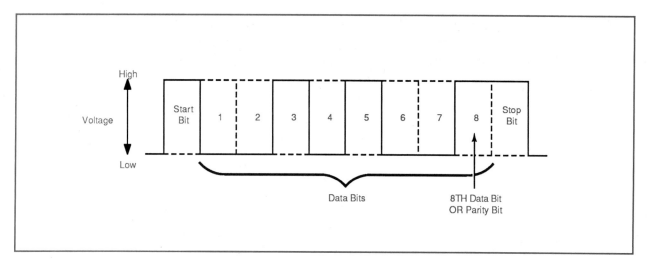

Figure 16-4.

A packet of bits for transmission usually includes a start bit, seven or eight data bits, and one or two stop bits.

Parity

Parity checking is a method for detecting errors of transmission. This method involves adding a **parity bit** to each represented data character. That is, a separate bit is added to each byte of data. For each character, or byte, the system checks for either an even or an odd number of bits with a 1 value. The parity bit is given a 1 or 0 value to establish an odd or even count. For example, suppose the parity setting is even. For all bytes with an odd number of 1 bits, the parity bit is given a 1 value. All bytes transmitted, then, will have an even number of 1 bits. For bytes with an even number of 1 bits, the parity bit takes a 0 value. With the parity setting even, bytes that come across with an odd number of 1 bits trigger an error message or other error procedures.

Stop Bits

The final setting involves **stop bits.** Stop bits are added to identify the end of a data character transmission. One, two, or no stop bits may be added to the end of each character. Most transmission setups also include a single **start bit** at the beginning of each character. Because the value of a start bit is always zero, there is no setting for this bit.

A complete character for transmission, then, usually involves a packet of approximately 10 bits: a start bit, seven or eight data bits, and one or two stop bits. Figure 16-4 illustrates the order and composition of a transmission packet.

For microcomputer systems equipped with smart modems, the bit orientation, or protocol, for a transmission is set under program control. With other types of modems, protocol settings might be established with external switches. Regardless of modem type, protocol settings must be identical for both terminals, sending and receiving, to complete a transmission. Data communication can be applied at two levels: within the overall processing schemes of organizations, and to enhance the personal capabilities of individuals. Both levels of application are discussed in sections that follow.

DATA COMMUNICATION FOR ORGANIZATIONS

Organizations create and handle data across functional and geographic lines. Data items created for an order entry function are used by invoicing applications, inventory, accounts receivable, and so on. In other organizations, data are created at remote sites, or points of transaction. A point is made earlier in this text that microcomputers provide capabilities for distributed processing. Distributed processing, in simple terms, means that tools are placed in the hands of people performing work. Data communication techniques enhance capabilities for distributed processing.

Within organizations, microcomputers can be linked in arrangements known as **networks** to share data and information. Networks also provide capabilities for making the most efficient use of equipment. Expensive or infrequently used peripherals, such as laser printers or high-capacity storage devices, might be shared as needed by several terminals within a network.

In other organizations (with different requirements), microcomputer terminals might be linked to minicomputers or mainframes. Under this arrangement, users are provided access to many or all of the resources maintained by the larger machines. These networks make use of **uploading** and **downloading.** Uploading refers to capabilities for sending data from remote terminals to the minicomputer or mainframe, for using remote terminals to manipulate data maintained on larger machines. Downloading is the reverse of this process; files or processing capabilities are transferred from the central computer to microcomputer terminals. These operations may involve special data-handling techniques to support transfers among different machines. The important point, for this discussion, is that data communication techniques provide virtually limitless opportunities for sharing data resources.

Local Area Networks

Networks literally may connect terminals across oceans and continents. The simplicity or complexity of networks, in other words, depends on the extent of distribution and communication needed. Microcomputers often are linked directly

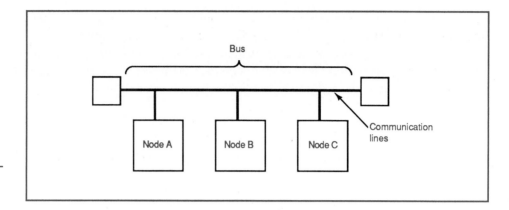

Figure 16-5.

This diagram shows a network configured under bus topology.

by dedicated cable connections used exclusively for computing equipment in a limited area, such as within a single building or several buildings nearby, such as on a college campus. This kind of microcomputer network is known as a **local area network (LAN).**

The configuration of devices making up a network is called its architecture, or **topology.** This term refers to the way data transmissions flow throughout the network, rather than the physical arrangement of devices. Three main topologies are used for implementing LANs:

- A **bus topology** connects all devices, or **nodes,** to a central cable, or bus. All signal exchanges are sent over the bus. In a bus network, each node has access to all other nodes at all times. There is no central, controlling node. Figure 16-5 presents a diagram of a network configured under bus topology.

- A **ring topology** is similar to a bus topology in that there is no central, controlling device. In a ring network, nodes are connected to form a large circle. Signal exchanges are transferred from node to node until destination nodes are reached. However, if any node becomes inoperative, the entire network may be shut down. Figure 16-6 presents a diagram of a ring network.

- A **star topology** connects all devices to a central, controlling computer, as shown in Figure 16-7. All signal exchanges are sent first to the controlling device, or **host,** then routed to the appropriate destination node. Thus, if the host device becomes inoperative, the network is shut down for repairs. Equipment failures in outlying nodes do not affect the network as a whole.

All networks, regardless of topology, risk errors caused by simultaneous signal transmissions over the same channel. Most networks are implemented with some type of control mechanism to prevent these errors. At a minimum, channels are

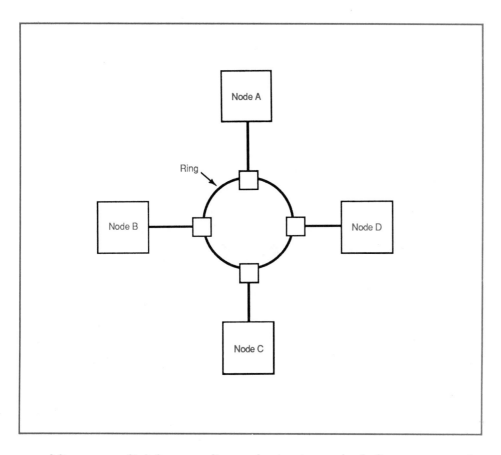

Figure 16-6.

This diagram presents the topology of a ring network.

tested for an open link from sending to destination nodes before any transmission occurs. As another control mechanism, priority schemes might be built into these control systems. That is, nodes are assigned priorities, usually according to the overall processing priorities of the organization. Transmission channels are allocated to comply with this priority scheme.

Local Area Network Software

For most LANs, control mechanisms are set up by software. For example, in the illustration given above, testing for an open channel can be handled automatically by the software after a user has indicated that a transmission is ready to be sent.

Operating systems and application programs for network microcomputers may require adaptation. Most programs are designed to be run on standalone machines—terminals not linked to any others. Storage files can be retrieved, edited, and saved as needed. In a network, two or more users might need to work on the same file at the same time. Operating systems and/or application programs

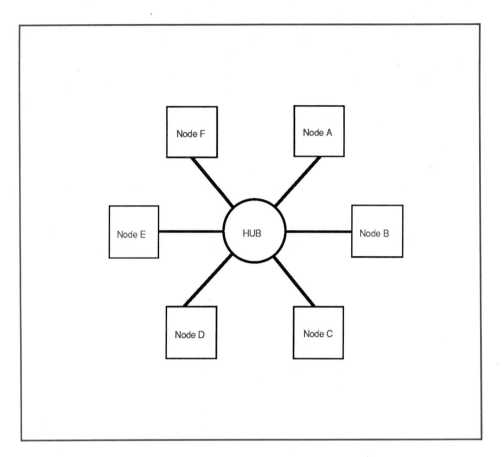

Figure 16-7.

All nodes in a star network are connected to a central, controlling communication switch.

must be designed to prevent simultaneous accessing of files. If multiple users access the same record, control over content and procedures for change is lost. To prevent this, files must be "locked" as soon as they are accessed. When a user saves or quits the file, it is "unlocked," and made available to other users in the network.

Software for network terminals also must establish control measures to ensure privacy and security for data resources. Any time processing is distributed, methods must be set up to prevent the accessing and altering of files by unauthorized users. For most networks, security measures involve passwords and authorization levels. The principles of these methods are discussed in an earlier chapter.

Networks can extend the range of support provided to organizations by microcomputers. At another level, electronic mail can enhance the effectiveness of organizational personnel, as well as individual users. Electronic mail is discussed in the section that follows.

ELECTRONIC MAIL

Within electronic mail systems, **electronic mailboxes,** or spaces within computer-maintained files for receiving messages, are assigned to users. Messages addressed to specific users can be sent directly to appropriate mailboxes. Messages are received automatically. Users check their mailboxes for messages on a regular basis.

To illustrate, Manager A, in Pittsburgh, might initiate a communication and deposit a message in Manager B's mailbox, in Detroit. The next time Manager B checks for messages, the presence of the message from Manager A is indicated. Some systems are set up to generate message indicators each time the system is accessed.

Many large organizations use electronic mail techniques in message-forwarding systems for their personnel. By itself, the telephone has limits to its message exchanging capabilities—even though telephone systems now span the globe. A major difficulty lies in finding the right person, when that person has time to talk. Scheduling problems often degenerate into a game of "telephone tag," in which two frustrated parties with conflicting schedules repeatedly try—and fail—to contact each other. A letter or memo sent through regular mails might resolve this situation, but may take a day or two to reach its destination. Electronic mail provides a solution to these problems. In effect, electronic mail provides the speed of the telephone and the insured message delivery of postal systems.

Another advantage of this type of system (and of others discussed below), is that messages may be "addressed" to one or more specific mailboxes. For example, a manager might address a congratulatory message to a specific salesperson. The same manager, in another situation, might post a meeting notice for the entire sales staff. Messages are addressed to specific recipients through codes imbedded within message files. If needed, recipients can transfer message files to storage or output devices at remote terminals.

Electronic mail services are available in many forms. For example, many subscription services are offered by commercial carriers, such as MCI, Western Union, ITT, GTE, The Source, CompuServe, and many more. Many of these services, such as The Source and CompuServe, are provided in conjunction with bulletin boards and information services. These subjects are discussed in sections that follow.

BULLETIN BOARDS

An **electronic bulletin board** can be thought of as a large-capacity mailbox shared by a group of users. Messages posted to bulletin boards are shared by any user accessing the board.

Communication services

available to microcomputer
users include database and electronic mail services.
COURTESY OF TELECOM CANADA

As large-scale information exchange services, bulletin boards often are set
up for special interest groups or organizations. User groups for specific makes
of microcomputers often exchange operating hints, upgrade tips, and other information over bulletin boards. As another example, a bulletin board might be
set up for people interested in French-style cooking. Recipes can be posted on
the bulletin board and shared by all users.

Many bulletin boards are set up with electronic mailboxes available for
private message exchanges. In the example of the French cooking bulletin board,
mailboxes might be provided so that recipes, or other messages, can be exchanged privately.

Bulletin boards also can be an excellent source for free and inexpensive software. Many bulletin boards provide collections of **public-domain programs** that
can be copied by users. These programs usually are written by individuals and
made available to any user who accesses the bulletin board. The developer of the
software may ask for minimal, voluntary payments from users. Virtually any application covered by commercial packages also can be found in some type of
public-domain form.

Bulletin boards are set up and maintained on some type of computer. Depending upon the size of the board, and the number of users, microcomputers may provide enough capacities to handle incoming calls and message exchanges. After the initial setup, most of this work is performed by the computer without human intervention. For convenience, though, most bulletin boards include a telephone number that can be called for personal help from a **system operator (Sysop),** a person skilled in the workings of the system.

Many bulletin boards are too large to run on microcomputers, although virtually all boards are designed to be accessed by microcomputers. The services offered and capacities needed by some boards require that they be set up on minicomputers or mainframes. This is also the case with many information services, discussed in the section that follows.

INFORMATION SERVICES

Information service organizations maintain files for public access and provide special services to callers. Because these services add to conventional communication capabilities, the companies are said to provide **value added** capabilities. Subscribers pay fees for the services they use. Information services provide information on virtually any subject: personal finance, business, entertainment, education, health, and more. As an overview of some of these services, the three most popular information services are described below:

- **CompuServe Information Service** carries stories and features from newspapers, wire services, and organizational profiles; financial news; electronic banking and funds transfer; airline scheduling and reservation services; movie, theatre, book, and restaurant reviews; medical and health information; electronic games; mail service and shopping; on-line encyclopedias; personal computing software; and many other features and software.

  In effect, a subscriber of CompuServe (and other services like it) can perform research for a presentation; make airline reservations to a distant city where the presentation will be given; transfer funds among bank accounts to pay for the flight; send messages to arrange for an airport pickup, check reviews of restaurants in that city; and even consult weather reports to help pack appropriate clothing for the trip—all with a single communication.

- **The Source** is a general-purpose service. The Source provides many of the same types of information as CompuServe, such as news stories, electronic mail, classified ads, financial information, entertainment reviews, and financial services.

- ***Dow-Jones News/Retrieval Service*** provides business- and financial-oriented services to users. These services include stock market quotations, profiles of business organizations, financial news and forecasts, as well as general news stories and services.

Literally thousands of other information services exist today, serving both general- and special-interest markets. For example, the PR Wire is a news service geared toward professionals in the public relations field. PR agencies or individuals subscribing to this service can send press releases to newspapers and magazines across the country.

The services available are diverse, and are available for a minimal investment. All that is needed is a microcomputer equipped with a modem—and a telephone. Once this hardware is installed, establishing communications is a matter of navigating (selecting in logical sequence) the menu structures of communication software and the services themselves.

Such applications are changing the way people look at and use information. Expanded access to information implies extended uses to which information can be put. Extended use, or application, makes for increased effectiveness in homes, schools, and workplaces. The chapter that follows also discusses microcomputer applications that enhance personal capabilities—especially for decision makers and managers within organizations. These applications include management information systems (MIS), decision support systems (DSS), and expert systems.

KEY TERMS

modem
modulation
demodulation
digital signal
analog signal
carrier signal
encode
frequency modulation (FM)
amplitude modulation (AM)
phase modulation (PM)
acoustic coupler
direct connect modem
smart modem
port

half-duplex
full-duplex
protocol
baud rate
parity checking
parity bit
stop bit
start bit
network
upload
download
local area network (LAN)
topology
bus topology

node
ring topology
star topology
host
electronic mailbox
electronic bulletin board
public-domain program
system operator (Sysop)
value added
CompuServe Information Service
The Source
Dow-Jones News/Retrieval
   Service

DEFINITIONS

Instructions: On a separate sheet, define each term according to its use in this chapter.

1. modem

2. frequency modulation

3. amplitude modulation

4. phase modulation

5. port

6. baud rate

7. public-domain programs

8. Sysop

T R U E / F A L S E

Instructions: For each statement, write T for true or F for false on a separate sheet.

1. Microcomputers represent data as digital signals, bits and bytes consisting of patterns of 1 and 0 symbols or on/off signals.

2. Telephones handle analog signals, signals which are transmitted as continuous tones.

3. The wave signals exchanged by modems are called carrier signals.

4. To change an FM signal into an AM signal, you must double the phase modulation vibration.

5. Once an acoustic coupler has been connected directly, it becomes a smart modem.

6. Computer ports are called ports because the first early computers with input/output hardware connection slots were used by the U.S. Navy, and they just happened to be on the port side.

7. Standard telephone lines usually handle speeds of 110, 300, 1200, and 2400 baud.

8. There are six bits in an ASCII byte.

9. A complete character for transmission usually involves a packet of 10 bits; a start bit, seven or eight data bits, and one or two stop bits.

10. In simple terms, distributed processing means that tools are placed in the hands of the people performing the work.

11. Software for network terminals must establish control measures to insure privacy and security for data devices.

12. No matter which commercial electronic mail carrier you use, you still have to use U.S. postage stamps.

13. A Sysop is an electronic mailman.

14. Information service organizations are said to provide value added capabilities.

15. Many phones now come with built-in modems.

S H O R T A N S W E R Q U E S T I O N S

Instructions: On a separate sheet of paper, answer each question in one or two brief sentences.

1. How must signals be changed to achieve data communication?

2. Why are smart modems more desirable than acoustic couplers or direct connect modems?

3. Identify and describe the three main topologies used within local area networks.

4. Describe the control functions performed by local area network software.

5. What is meant by transmission protocol?

6. What is the difference between uploading and downloading?

R E S E A R C H P R O J E C T

Compile a list of information services and bulletin boards that offer specific special-interest databases or services that would appeal to you and your family or friends. Use your school or public library as an information source.

17 Microcomputers and Management Applications

EXECUTIVES AND MICROCOMPUTERS

Microcomputers and easy-to-use software have made it feasible for executives to gain direct control of the information resources that have become critical to effective management.

The Breakthrough: Spreadsheet Software

Hands-on use of microcomputers by executives has been tied to the development of software tools such as spreadsheet packages.

Microcomputer Values for Managers

Microcomputer capabilities have placed control of information resources onto managers' desks. These capabilities have promoted independent, individual analysis and decision making, or a spirit of entrepreneurship.

THE ART OF MANAGING

Management styles and techniques vary, and should match the purpose and philosophy that have gone into creating and building a company.

Required Skills

Managers must be able to promote understanding and interaction among people and to reach and implement effective decisions.

Role of Microcomputers

Managers use microcomputers for direct support in performing their basic responsibilities: planning, monitoring and directing operations, problem solving, and decision making.

IMPLEMENTING MANAGEMENT PROGRAMS

In many organizations, the assignment of management responsibilities is divided into three levels.

Top Management

Top managers, or executives, establish the framework within which planning and decision making take place. This is done by formulating strategies and strategic plans.

Middle Management

Middle management usually controls and monitors actual operations.

Operating Management

Operating managers oversee the processing of transactions and the internal operations that support transactions.

INFORMATION SYSTEMS FOR MANAGERS

All managers need specific types of information.

Transaction Processing Systems

One of a microcomputer's greatest strengths is its ability to support transaction processing.

Management Information Systems (MIS)

Management information systems make use of accumulated data to monitor business operations.

Decision Support Systems (DSS)

In building a decision support systems (DSS), an executive develops the resources to call up information from a wide variety of databases maintained by industry groups, government agencies, etc., as well as from internal information resources.

Expert Systems

An expert system captures and applies the processes by which human specialists analyze and solve problems.

EXECUTIVES AND MICROCOMPUTERS

The microcomputer is pictured frequently as the focal point of a new, exciting presence in business organizations—the executive work station. Traditionally, high-level managers and executives have been pictured in plush surroundings, distributing the real work of running an organization to subordinates. Through the first decades of computer growth in business, the likelihood of involving executives in the use of keyboards was thought to be somewhere between highly improbable and definitely impossible.

That was before the microcomputer. Today, a work station that includes its own microcomputer has become something of a status symbol for the modern, forward-looking executive.

The reason: Microcomputers and accompanying, easy-to-use software have made it feasible for executives to gain direct control of the information resources that have become critical to effective management. Today, an executive with just a few hours of training and experience with a microcomputer can, literally, tap into a world of information resources that can make a direct contribution to job performance.

The Breakthrough: Spreadsheet Software

In the overall world of business, acceptance of microcomputers has been tied to a series of software innovations that have made computing power easy to master and have, in turn, made people more productive. The initial impact, which occurred during the mid- and late-1970s, was achieved by word processing software. During this time period, business organizations were spending increasing amounts on machines designed to make written communication faster and easier. When word processing packages were introduced, it was clear that microcomputers could perform better, at less cost, in generating business documents. Millions of microcomputers moved from growing numbers of factories to secretarial and clerical desks for use in text and word processing applications.

Some executives became intrigued with and involved in the use of word processing applications on microcomputers. With their own microcomputers, executives could edit document drafts prepared by secretaries. Or, in a reversal of roles, a number of executives undertook to draft letters and other documents, leaving editing and finalizing of documents to secretaries. This is identified as role reversal because, traditionally, executives edited drafts prepared by secretaries from dictation. With microcomputers in the picture, the responsibilities of and opportunities for office workers were altered.

At the management level, however, the mass appeal of microcomputers came with the introduction of electronic spreadsheet capabilities. For a century or more, spreadsheets have been a generally unpopular necessity of life for managers. The term, spreadsheet, tended to be synonymous with detail and tedium. As you know from earlier chapters, traditional spreadsheet preparation meant the detailed entry of rows and columns of numbers onto ruled sheets. The problem was considered to be unavoidable. The great majority of managers, in the great majority of companies, have budget-preparation responsibilities.

Electronic spreadsheet techniques eased the strains of budget preparation. These capabilities endeared microcomputers to harried executives and led to a newfound acceptance of keyboarding at top organizational levels. Microcomputers rapidly became fixtures within executive work stations.

Microcomputer Values for Managers

All microcomputer executive work stations are not created equal. Each executive has individual expectations and requirements. Each executive may choose to apply different software packages and implement different applications. The possibilities are too great for in-depth review. However, there are two broad categories of microcomputer configuration that are worth noting:

* Managers may seek independent, or "standalone," processing capabilities used to support fulfillment of their personal responsibilities. This approach, which encourages managers to operate on their own, sometimes is described as promoting **internal entrepreneurship.** That is, managers can use their own computers to support and explore decisions within their own sphere of responsibility. As long as applications of the microcomputer are internal to the department or function—and do not require integration with corporate information bases—this approach can work. However, if a system is used to produce information that will be consolidated with corporate-level reports, even independent work stations should be set up for compatibility with corporate information systems. In terms of equipment, a typical standalone work station will include its own disk files, processor, keyboard, monitor, and some printing capability. Today, a majority of microcomputers delivered for executive use have hard-disk capabilities.

* Departments or entire organizations may interconnect executive microcomputers through a local area network (LAN). This makes it possible for members of a department to interchange or reference files created by others. For example, department heads can review drafts of correspondence or spreadsheet reports. In many instances, LANs link microcomputers to central, mainframe systems. This makes it possible for individual users to **download** records and files from the main system for personal use. Also, in applications

that involve consolidation of data from departments on an organizationwide basis, individuals can **upload** files created on microcomputers into the corporate system.

The value of microcomputer capabilities in business organizations lies in support for the management functions that shape and direct an entire organization. At this level, microcomputers are tools that are applied directly to meeting the responsibilities and challenges of management. Therefore, a full appreciation of the role and value of microcomputers as management tools requires an understanding of the missions and responsibilities of managers.

THE ART OF MANAGING

Broadly, managers are responsible for running companies and for the results produced by those organizations. Management styles and techniques, therefore, vary among companies, each of which is individual and has its own identity. The idea is that the methods of any manager must match the purpose and philosophy that have gone into creating and building a company.

A company's management needs, in turn, are defined by its reason for existence and the end results that are targeted. This is significant because the flexibility of microcomputers has played a key role in building their popularity as management tools. As has been established in this text, one of the real values of microcomputers lies in their ability to handle, capture data from, and analyze business transactions. In turn, any company can be described as an organization that has been formed to conduct specific kinds of transactions associated with the delivery of products and services to specific markets or types of customers. In other words, a company exists to conduct certain types of transactions with specific customers.

Given this overall reason for being, a company is managed through a series of relationships that make it possible to achieve its basic purpose. Relationships extend over the full range of operations for a business. External relationships center around contacts with and services to clients or customers. Each client or customer encounters only a small part of the staff of an organization, perhaps sales or service personnel. These people, in turn, form a chain of relationships that extends into and through the entire company. Salespeople are supported by service personnel who, in turn, depend upon employees who purchase supplies, develop paychecks, and ship orders to customers. Others perform any of literally thousands of tasks that can be required in a modern business. A key management challenge lies in forming, nurturing, and maintaining the relationships essential to a company's existence.

In this context, transactions implement business relationships. Success of a company lies in identifying and building the relationships associated with the handling of transactions. Managers identify the targets for external relationships and forge the support structures that make these relationships possible.

Required Skills

In the operation of a business, management responsibilities are said to involve planning, organizing, monitoring, and controlling. Common denominators of these responsibilities include the following:

- Managers must understand and be able to promote effective, productive interactions among people.

- Managers must be expert in the skills of identifying and solving problems and making decisions.

A company—any company—is a complex entity. The conduct of business rarely is totally smooth. Management skills are required for situations in which difficulties arise in the carrying out of plans that are supposed to direct a business along a pathway to success. Accidents happen. Orders are cancelled. Competitors make unexpected moves. Infinite numbers of conditions can interrupt the flow of relationships required within a well-managed, successful company. Therefore, the real challenges of management lie in development and application of skills for problem solving and decision making.

Role of Microcomputers

Skillful problem solving and decision making require the ability to find and use information. Because microcomputers have put extensive information processing and analysis capabilities on desktops, these devices have become major management tools. Specific areas in which microcomputers are used to implement management responsibilities include:

* Planning

* Monitoring and directing business operations

* Problem solving and decision making.

Planning.   One oversimplified description of an effective system of management is: "Plan your work, then work your plan." Though there is more to management, the advice does have merit. Plans are needed to establish the framework within which businesses operate. Plans identify the customers and markets to be served, the goals toward which a business will strive, and the way in which a business will be organized to reach its goals.

In part, plans reflect the experiences and the ambitions of people who run a company. But plans are more than a wish list. The targets envisioned by leaders must be evaluated to determine if they are attainable. If so, further analysis is needed to provide for the resources that will be necessary to move toward identified goals.

Monitoring and Directing.   Plans become targets. Strategic plans are supplemented with tactical plans that cover one to three years. These tactical plans establish targets for intermediate-range operations. In effect, a plan predicts what a company should achieve in a given time period. Monitoring uses *feedback* reports that compare actual achievements with plans. Operations are adjusted and decisions are made on the basis of this feedback. The directing function of management is carried out through decisions based on operational feedback.

Problem solving and decision making.   People and their interactions with one another are known to be unpredictable. Since people are involved in the conduct of a business, results rarely match corresponding plans. When things do not go as expected, a problem results. Managers at all levels are expected to analyze and solve problems. To do this, they must make and implement decisions.

In fulfilling all of these responsibilities—planning, monitoring, directing, problem solving, and decision making—managers have come to rely heavily on the microcomputers that have placed information system capabilities on their desktops.

IMPLEMENTING MANAGEMENT PROGRAMS

In many organizations, the assignment of management responsibilities is structured at three levels and according to three time frames. Planning and other responsibilities are delegated to different levels of the organization:

- Top management
- Middle management
- Operating management.

Top Management

Top managers, or executives, establish the framework within which planning and decision making take place. Business leaders at this level are responsible primarily for **strategic planning,** which guides the business toward its long-range goals. Strategic planning generally is considered to encompass views of the organization within time spans ranging from three to seven years.

The framework for strategic planning—and for planning at all other levels—consists of philosophies that guide management and operations and business strategies. Companies guide their actions according to philosophies in much the same way that people do. Top management applies a set of basic beliefs in making decisions and in committing actions by a company. Part of management responsibility lies in communicating these basic beliefs to employees and the public. These beliefs are reflected in such diverse areas as employee benefits, product warranties, and the investment of profits for the building of the company or for ownership in other businesses.

A strategy, in turn, consists of a set of policies and programs that follow through on a philosophy. Strategies determine the products or services offered, the markets or customers targeted for sale of those products or services, and the methods used in marketing and delivery. Part of strategy also involves the structuring of a company to "differentiate" it from its competitors. This is a vital part of marketing and operational directions. Think of competing companies with which you are familiar. As an example, consider the fast-food field. Some companies specialize in hamburgers, others in chicken, and still others try to do both. Advertising for one company in this field stresses clean, comfortable, convenient

470

Information for managers

is readily available with desktop convenience through use of microcomputers. Decision making and operational monitoring are supported.

COURTESY OF HAYES MICROCOMPUTER PRODUCTS, INC.

places to eat. Another stresses charcoal broiling of hamburgers, while a third promotes the idea of having hamburgers cooked to order. These are just a few, simple ways in which managers meet their challenges for building company identity, or image, for customers.

A strategy, then, is a position that a company holds. A strategy encompasses what a company is, what it sells, to whom it sells, and how it is structured. Philosophies and strategies, as indicated, are frameworks for planning. The plans, organization structures, and operations that implement these philosophies and strategies are divided into different time frames.

Top management is concerned primarily with long-term planning. The plans that result are known as strategic plans. This is because, given their time frame, long-range plans establish the most permanent commitments of the organization. Long-range plans, like statements of strategy, tend to deal with markets to be served, products to be developed and offered, and with meeting requirements for resources. To illustrate, top managers would be concerned with whether an organization should move into new geographic regions, whether new factories or warehouses are needed, and whether a company should diversify by buying other businesses or creating new products.

Simply stated, top managers make decisions about what their companies will look like in five to seven years. These decisions require imagination and analysis, activities enhanced greatly if microcomputers are available and used to best advantage. Databases containing market information can, for example, help managers to look at prospects for products or services in the light of economic and market trends. In almost any field, projections will exist in some external, public database about assumed demand and sales levels for a decade or more into the future. A sophisticated manager can incorporate this kind of information into a database, then manipulate the figures on the basis of assumptions. For example, a conservative manager may decide to cut industry projections by one-third to see if prospects still look good at this reduced level. Once the data are included in a database, such computations are simple.

Another major tool for top managers is the use of spreadsheet software for long-range projections. Spreadsheets can be used to model the effects of decisions on the operating results of a company. Different assumptions, such as different levels of growth or even decline, can be expressed as percentages of impact on future income and expense. In effect, a manager asks "What if . . . ?" questions that reflect operational or economic assumptions. The hypothetical conditions then are tested through development of spreadsheets that reflect financial conditions as though the projections really developed. Assumptions can be optimistic or pessimistic, positive or negative. Usually, managers like to look at a variety of possibilities for both favorable and unfavorable results. Then, if the unfavorable conditions still justify investments or commitments, decisions are guided accordingly.

When development of projections and forecasts was done on mainframe computers, special programming often was necessary. Delays could result. Or, if the costs were great enough, managers used approximations instead of complete projections. With microcomputers, managers have convenience and thoroughness. Consequences of decisions can be evaluated as extensively as necessary, until the decision makers are comfortable in making a commitment.

Plans and commitments at top levels then are passed along to and provide a framework for management activities at lower levels, as illustrated in Figure 17-1. Note that this illustration uses a pyramid shape. This serves to illustrate that the number of people involved in management is greater at low levels, smaller at high levels.

Middle Management

The main responsibilities of top managers lie in the areas of policy formation, strategy setting, and planning. Planning, remember, is one of the key functions

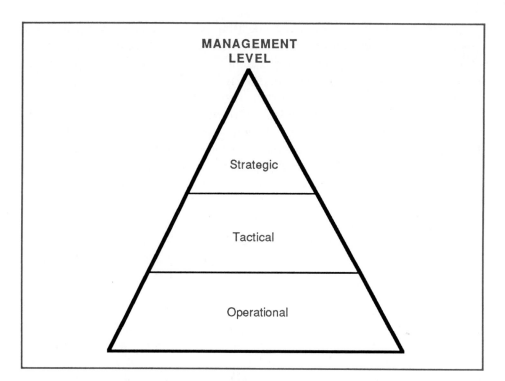

MANAGEMENT LEVEL

Strategic

Tactical

Operational

Figure 17-1.

Management and planning responsibilities tend to be structured at three levels, as shown. The pyramid diagram indicates that more people are employed and more information is needed at lower levels.

of management. Another key management function, controlling of operations, usually is delegated to middle managers. Control responsibilities involve the implementation of plans at higher levels and the review and correction of conditions that result from feedback reports from lower-level managers.

Middle management outlooks and techniques have been impacted dramatically by the availability of microcomputers. The information models that reflect operations and status of organizations are reviewed and acted upon by middle managers. Middle management decisions adjust company operations to the realities pictured in computer-produced reports. For example, through computer displays or outputs, middle managers may discover that some inventory items are understocked while others are overstocked. Some departments may have insufficient numbers of employees while others are overstaffed. Middle managers set standards for and reach decisions on the basis of summarized status reports generated by computers.

To illustrate, a middle manager in a manufacturing company may be in charge of parts inventories. These are stocks of parts that are assembled into finished products. Decisions made by this manager determine whether and how efficiently the factory can operate. If the stockroom runs out of certain parts, production of a key product may have to be shut down. On the other hand, if decisions by this manager lead to overstocking, the company may be tying up too much ***capital,*** or invested funds, in inventories. To avoid these problems, a manager may specify stock levels at which items should be treated as ***exceptions.*** An exception is any item that requires attention from a decision maker. A computer system can be programmed to flag exceptions automatically and to generate reports on exceptions for manager review. At any given time, more than 90 percent of the parts for which this manager is responsible may reflect normal levels and conditions. There is no need to waste the time of a manager reviewing these items in a database. Rather, the availability of a microcomputer linked into a corporate system can help this manager to identify the small percentage of items that represent exceptions and require attention. Management information systems, discussed later in this chapter, have been developed largely as tools for the control-oriented decisions made by middle managers.

Operating Management

Operating managers oversee the processing of transactions and the internal operations that support transactions. In some organizations, these managers are identified as ***first line supervisors.*** The jobs involved can include departmental supervisors in factories, office managers, managers of individual sales departments in department stores, and managers of individual units within fast-food chains.

As information users, these people work at levels of extreme detail. For example, all of the sales at a department store or a supermarket usually are entered into cash registers. Operating managers in this organization would be responsible for checking and balancing the entries in the registers and for making sure that the computed totals match the value of cash, checks, or credit card vouchers turned in by salespeople. In a factory, a supervisor would be responsible for counting the parts used and products produced—and for validating the input of these values to a computer system. Other operating managers process and generate transaction documents in the form of shipping orders, invoices, and merchandise receiving reports.

Information system outputs for operating managers must be highly detailed. Typically, for instance, an operating manager would receive reports that present the full content of detail files within computer systems. Middle managers would receive summaries of these reports, possibly at a departmental or product level. Top managers would receive outputs that are summarized even further, perhaps at the division level.

Figure 17-2 represents both the levels of management described above and their information requirements. Typically, except for word processors or special terminals, higher volumes of data are required at lower levels of management. This

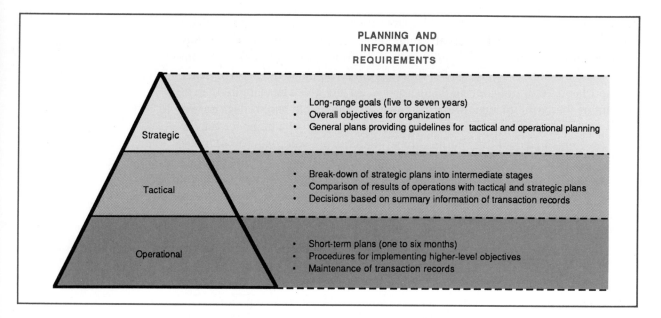

**PLANNING AND
INFORMATION
REQUIREMENTS**

Strategic
- Long-range goals (five to seven years)
- Overall objectives for organization
- General plans providing guidelines for tactical and operational planning

Tactical
- Break-down of strategic plans into intermediate stages
- Comparison of results of operations with tactical and strategic plans
- Decisions based on summary information of transaction records

Operational
- Short-term plans (one to six months)
- Procedures for implementing higher-level objectives
- Maintenance of transaction records

Figure 17-2.

Information requirements for supporting planning and decision making differ at top, middle, and operating management levels.

means that at higher levels, there are reductions in volume and also in detailed analysis of data. These are just some of the reasons why microcomputers have come to be regarded as valuable personal tools for middle and top managers.

INFORMATION SYSTEMS FOR MANAGERS

Within the context of this discussion, all managers can be viewed as information users. As shown, differing types of information, reflecting different types and degrees of detail, are needed at different management levels. Information systems that serve managers fall into four general categories:

- Transaction processing systems
- Management information systems (MIS)
- Decision support systems (DSS)
- Expert systems.

Transaction Processing Systems

Capabilities for **transaction processing** are among the outstanding strengths of microcomputers. Many microcomputers have been installed specifically to process invoices and other transaction documents. In this area, the microcomputer serves as a replacement for previous methods for generating transaction documents. Some of these were manually operated systems under which transaction entries were duplicated on accounting journals as clerical personnel wrote invoices. Perhaps the most common technique for generating transaction documents was the electromechanical bookkeeping machine. This machine operated electrical counters to accumulate totals for transaction documents and accounting journals as entries were made on typewriter-like keyboards.

When large computers were introduced, many business organizations discontinued manual or electromechanical processing of transactions. Instead, source documents with transaction information were brought to central computer facilities. As described earlier, this led to a situation in which ownership and custody of information were centralized in mammoth computer centers. Operational managers responsible for handling transactions tended to feel that they had lost control of the tools needed to carry out their work assignments. These managers were frustrated because they lost possession of actual documents and records reflecting their dealings with customers or with other internal business units.

As data communication became feasible, a major trend evolved for decentralization, or distribution, of computing capabilities. This trend got a strong start through the use of on-line terminals. However, the trend escalated rapidly as low-cost microcomputers with their own processing and data storage capabilities came into widespread use. With microcomputers at the points where transactions occur, operational managers can collect and use files to control their own operations. These managers are in better control of the functions they are responsible for directing. At the same time, it is possible to upload data from microcomputers for consolidation into companywide databases. Under this approach, managers who require consolidated information can be served by large, central computers, while operational groups can support and manage their own functions.

As required, operational managers can generate the documents and build the files needed for local control of day-to-day functions. Operations may include the issuing of invoices, the generation of accounting reports, or the preparation of work orders in a factory. In a small company, all transaction processing and accounting systems can be operated on a microcomputer—perhaps the same equipment that is used for writing letters and developing spreadsheets to summarize accounting data.

Management Information Systems (MIS)

Transaction processing builds files. Files, in turn, can be summarized to meet needs of middle- and top-level managers. Use of accumulated data to monitor business operations is the basis for **management information systems (MIS)**. One of the first—and still one of the clearest—examples of management information systems can be seen in inventory control applications.

As described earlier, inventory files are accessed and updated as part of transaction processing systems. Each time an item is sold, purchased, or received, the processing of transaction information changes the content of fields within the record for that item. The information about sales volumes and stock levels for the item, in turn, are used as guidelines for a number of decisions by middle managers. For example, if the inventory supports a retail store, sales information helps managers decide where and how to display the merchandise. Items with consumer appeal generally are placed in prominent positions. Also, faster selling items are given more display space.

Several data items within an inventory record affect purchasing decisions. One is the number of units in stock. Logically, a manager wants to order when stocks are low and before the item is sold out. The placement of the order should allow time for the supplier to make deliveries before stocks run out. To control this process, a manager relies on analysis of information. One important item of information is the "lead time" between the placement of an order and receipt of merchandise. Another is the rate at which the item is selling.

To illustrate, consider an item such as a portable vacuum cleaner sold in the housewares section of a department store. Assume that the time required to write an order, mail it, receive a shipment, and replenish stock in the department is about three weeks. If sales average 20 units a week, the store needs a stock of at least 60 units on hand when orders are placed. In most stores, an allowance is made for delays by planning for some extra units, called "safety stock." For protection against out-of-stock situations, the store might decide to stock 80 units. Each time an order is placed, the rate of sale would be rechecked and a decision would be made about how many units to buy.

The procedure is fairly simple if only a few items are stocked. However, a major department store might maintain 1 million "stock keeping units (SKUs)" for which inventories must be monitored and orders placed. There just isn't time, even if the store has a number of middle managers who buy merchandise, to keep track of all these items on a regular basis. This is where management information systems are applied. One MIS method is to set up a field in each record for "reorder quantity." In the case of the portable vacuum cleaner, this might be the safety stock volume, 80 units.

When each transaction is processed, the program causes the computer to compare the reorder quantity with the stock on hand. If the stock on hand is equal to or lower than the reorder quantity, the record is identified for inclusion in an "open-to-buy" report. These open-to-buy records are called exception reports. Under **management by exception (MBE)** techniques, the computer focuses management attention on items that require attention. The manager can assume that non-exception items do not need attention. At any given time, a small percentage of stock records will qualify as exception items. This means that managers can focus attention on problems and need not worry about the great majority of items with normal status situations.

At higher levels, computer files can accumulate and analyze information that models the operation of entire stores or even of a large chain of stores. Computer-generated summaries can report on sales, expenses, and profits for departments, stores, warehouses, or other "business units." The attention of top-level managers can be directed by such reports to business units for which performance is lower than expected.

The ability of computers to accumulate and analyze information leads to management and organizational efficiency. Initially, management information system capabilities were implemented on large computers. Gradually, microcomputers have assumed a major role in the MIS area. One obvious opportunity has occurred for smaller companies. Microcomputers now have the capabilities needed to provide MIS-type monitoring and reporting on smaller organizations. Still another important MIS application for microcomputers has been at departmental or other business unit levels in large organizations. Managers can use microcomputers linked to mainframe systems through local area networks or telephone service. Managers can derive information that relates to their individual operations. Then, they can use their microcomputers to implement exception reporting programs on collections of data that apply to their specific requirements.

Managers who use microcomputers and suitable off-the-shelf software can deal with information analysis requirements as they arise. This creates both a flexibility and a responsiveness that generally are out of reach for companies using large computers only. For large computers, systems design and program development requirements lead to delays of months, even years, before MIS reporting capabilities can be implemented. The effect of microcomputers, then, has been to extend MIS capabilities and to make them more economical.

Decision Support Systems (DSS)

Decision support systems (DSS) are logical developments from MIS capabilities in much the same way as MIS systems grew from transaction processing. Use of DSS capabilities appeals especially to top-level managers. This is because the kinds of decisions made at top-management levels require organization and analysis of data beyond the conventional capabilities of an MIS. Consider that an MIS usually is applied to files developed from transaction processing. This means that the majority of information analyzed by an MIS is historic; the transactions that provide data already have happened.

Many high-level management decisions require analysis of information that must be accumulated from outside the scope of transaction processing. For example, a manager may be considering introduction of a new product line. Some MIS information on sales, expenses, and profits for existing products may be of value. However, it also may be necessary to secure marketing information from industry or government sources. Economic reports also may be of value. Some of these outside sources can be accessed through the communication capabilities of microcomputers. The executive can call up information from a variety of information pools maintained by industry groups and government agencies.

Some top-level decisions also may require accumulation of special information files. For example, suppose a manager is considering three possible locations for a new factory. Information would have to be assembled about land and construction costs, transportation rates, and wage levels in each of the regions considered.

For reasons such as this, many managers have used microcomputers to assemble information that models serious, costly decisions. The most common tool for implementing a DSS is a microcomputer database package with extensive query language capabilities. The need is for a system that can accommodate a number of files that may be relatively small but require extensive selection and retrieval capabilities.

For example, the manager looking for a factory location may want a database that encompasses less than 50 building lots. However, there would have to be capacity to consider and compare a wide variety of costs and other factors. Database items might deal with local tax rates, highway access, distance from rail lines, distance from airports, configurations that provide parking, local zoning laws, and many other factors. In effect, the manager must be able to define special needs and to find software that is both flexible enough and simple enough to support creative analysis of information.

DBMS programs designed for microcomputers are doing this job for large numbers of managers. In addition, managers facing decisions with financial consequences frequently use spreadsheet packages to model results of multiple decision alternatives. In effect, spreadsheet packages make it possible to look ahead to financial consequences of a variety of different choices.

Expert Systems

One piece of advice often given to people who are about to take their first look at expert systems is to forget everything they have learned about computer programs and data processing systems. This advice usually is intended at least partly as a joke. Obviously, in looking at advanced techniques, any knowledge you have will be to your advantage. At the same time, however, it is true that the principles applied to implement expert systems are different from those used for traditional programming or database management. Keep this factor of differences in mind as you read the descriptions that follow.

Expert systems get their name from the fact that they try to model the procedures and techniques of human experts. At this time, computers do not even come close to replicating the full scope of human thought processes. However, as discussed earlier in this book, problem solving does lend itself to a series of orderly steps. Modeling techniques attempt to capture and apply the processes rather than attempt to replicate human thought.

Possibly the most common use of expert systems involves medical monitoring and diagnosis. As one example, computers are used by doctors to aid diagnoses for certain types of diseases. To develop such systems, input is accumulated from human experts, doctors with experience in diagnosing the conditions under study. The human experts are asked how they go about testing to determine the presence of the disease. Typically, this leads to a listing of certain bodily conditions and symptoms. Once symptoms are identified, the expert might proceed to describe relationships among the independent symptoms. For example, many diseases may have high temperatures as symptoms. In some situations, the temperatures may be accompanied by sweating; in others, by dry skin or thirst.

In effect, all of the available knowledge about a disease is assembled into a special kind of database that contains descriptions and/or identifying symptoms for a given disease. To apply the database, symptoms for a patient being diagnosed are entered and compared with the statements reflecting the procedures followed by a human expert. The computer applies its limited logic capabilities under control of human specialists. Given the symptoms for a patient, for example, the computer may identify some matching conditions and others that are not present. Under some programs, the computer can ask if missing symptoms are present in the patient. When the additional information is entered, the comparison continues. In the end, however, the computer responds to questions reflecting one disease or condition at a time. Responses are of a binary nature. Asked if a disease probably is present, the computer will provide only a true or false answer. Even if the computer suggests the presence of a disease, further checking by qualified doctors still is necessary.

As indicated by this example, computers are limited to basic capabilities of computation and comparison. However, skilled application of these capabilities can make important contributions to human analyses and decisions. In the instance of medical diagnosis, for example, the computer can make many thousands of comparisons and logic tests in a few minutes. Even the most knowledgeable people might require days or weeks to sift through the same body of information.

Other names and trends. The term, expert systems, is used commonly to designate techniques under which the computer tests for conditions described in statements included in a special-purpose file. The file often is called a ***knowledge base*** to distinguish the type of content involved from a traditional database. For this reason, the terms ***knowledge systems*** or ***knowledge-based systems*** often are used for the techniques identified above as expert systems.

The term ***logic systems*** also is used to describe similar techniques. This usage stems from the fact that the methods used are rooted in mathematical principles known as logic, or logic programming.

Other terms include ***artificial intelligence*** and ***fifth-generation language.*** References to artificial intelligence stem from the attempts, described above, to capture and reproduce some of the processes involved in human reasoning within computer programs. The fifth-generation language designation is used by people who have identified four earlier periods, or generations, in the development of computer software. These begin with machine language and carry through to assembly language, compilers, and program generators or non-procedural languages that mark fourth-generation methods.

Regardless of the names used, the trend toward knowledge systems is undeniable. New microcomputer software products are being introduced at a rapid rate. Extensive sales already have been recorded for the most popular of these programs, PROLOG (PROgramming in LOGic). At this writing, logic programming techniques are being used extensively for operations analysis applications. The most prominent single application problem lies in design and operation of robots for manufacturing operations.

Packaged programs have begun to appear for such areas as medical analysis and analysis of geological data to support decisions about drilling for oil wells. The chemical and oil refining fields also have made wide use of knowledge-based applications.

For all of these applications, and for many to follow, the implication is both clear and important. The microcomputer has been recognized as a vehicle for extending the imagination and creative vision of humans. This relationship between people and microcomputers undoubtedly will grow and will assume new dimensions. However, one characteristic can be expected to remain constant: Microcomputers encourage and support people and expand human capabilities. But the challenges and the opportunities belong to people.

K E Y   T E R M S

internal entrepreneurship

download

upload

feedback

strategic planning

capital

exception

first line supervisor

transaction processing system

management information system
   (MIS)

management by exception (MBE)

decision support system (DSS)

expert system

knowledge base

knowledge system

knowledge-based system

logic system

artificial intelligence

fifth-generation language

D E F I N I T I O N S

Instructions: On a separate sheet, define each term according to its use in this chapter.

1. internal entrepreneurship

2. download

3. upload

4. exception

5. management information system (MIS)

6. management by exception (MBE)

7. feedback

8. strategic planning

T R U E / F A L S E

Instructions: For each statement, write T for true or F for false on a separate sheet.

1. In a reversal of roles, more and more executives do the first drafts of letters and memos and let their secretaries edit them.

2. A company's management needs are defined by its reason for existence and the results that are targeted.

3. The flexibility of microcomputers has played a key role in building their popularity as management tools.

4. Thanks to computers, managers no longer have to be expert in the skills of identifying and solving problems and making decisions.

5. Managers must understand and be able to promote effective, productive interactions among people.

6. Spreadsheets can be used to model the effects of decisions on the operating results of a company.

7. Under management by exception (MBE) techniques, exceptional managers are promoted to even greater responsibilities.

8. Expert systems get their name from the fact that using them makes you an expert.

9. Problem solving lends itself to a series of orderly steps.

10. Computers are limited to basic capabilities of computation and comparison.

11. The higher up the management ladder people are, the less outside information they need to make sound business decisions.

12. Artificial intelligence is what computers can bestow on the unwise manager.

13. Knowledge-based system is another name for a management information system.

14. First line supervisors require more detailed information than top management.

15. Management techniques that are effective at one company are guaranteed to be effective at another company of similar size dealing in a similar product.

S H O R T   A N S W E R   Q U E S T I O N S

Instructions: On a separate sheet of paper, answer each question in one or two brief sentences.

1. What are the challenges faced by managers?

2. How can computer systems help doctors to diagnose illnesses?

3. What single type of microcomputer application package has had the greatest effect on business managers? Why?

4. Describe the kinds of information required by an MIS and a DSS.

5. What is a business?

6. What is a computer?

R E S E A R C H   P R O J E C T

Identify and describe the management levels present in your school. Cover responsibilities at each level and describe relationships among levels.

Glossary

A

account payable   The balance due to a creditor on a current account.

account receivable   The balance due from a debtor on a current account.

accumulator   A memory area used to build running totals for use within a program.

acoustic coupler   A signal input/output unit within a type of modem that connects microcomputers into standard communication lines.

adder   Special circuitry that performs arithmetic—addition, subtraction, multiplication, and division.

aged trial balance   A report that shows the amounts owed by customers according to payment due dates.

algorithm   A list of steps, or formulas, for performing a specific task or achieving results.

alphanumeric field   A data field that will accept letter and numeral entries.

American Standard Code for Information Interchange (ASCII)   A coding scheme used for presentation of data within the communications industry and on some microcomputers.

amplitude modulation (AM)   A method of modulating the volume of a signal in response to input information.

analog   A type of communication carrier signal that applies continuous tones, or electrical values, for transmission. Analog signals carry radio broadcasts and most telephone conversations.

anode   A metal plate that picks up electrons from an emitter to complete or close a circuit.

application program   A computer program that follows an algorithm to solve some phase of an identified user problem, or perform a specific task.

architecture   The logic structure of a computer system.

array processor   A machine that links multiple processors to execute instructions simultaneously.

artificial intelligence   Techniques for applying stimuli to a database for automatic computer reaction or decision making in carefully defined situations. Examples include robotic devices used for automated manufacturing.

assembler language   A programming language in which alphanumeric codes are used to represent computer instructions and addresses. Also called assembly language and assembler. An assembler is a low-level language that requires a separate instruction for each execution by the computer.

asset   An item that represents a value of an organization. An example is money in the bank.

B

backup   Copies of stored data, files, hardware, and software, that are located in a separate, secure storage area for protection against loss or destruction of data or programs.

balance   The accounting term for totals of two accounts that must match as a verification of accuracy.

balance sheet   A report that describes the worth of a business.

bar chart   A graphic chart that represents data values in lengths of bars. Also called a histogram.

bar code   Data expressed as a series of bars and spaces printed in a small field on a tag or product label. Used for capture of product identification fields by optical code reading equipment.

barter system   A mercantile system in which one commodity is exchanged for another, each commodity having approximately equal value.

baseline   The lower horizontal rule upon which text is positioned.

batch file   A file that contains a series of data items organized for processing as a group.

binary   A numbering system for computers that is based on sets, or values, of two.

binary number system   *See* binary.

bit (Binary digIT)   The value represented in one position of a binary number. May have a value of 0 or 1.

block   A large portion of text. A group of data organized for efficient processing.

boilerplate   A standard, repeated part of a text document.

boldface   A type of print that is darker than normal impressions. Created by instructing a printer to strike a character twice.

boot   To load an operating system (DOS) into a computer's memory.

bpi (bits per inch)   A measure of data recording density, the number of characters recorded in a linear pattern on one inch of magnetic tape.

branch   An alternate path from a decision point toward an action, as represented within a decision tree or network data structure diagram. Also a choice of processing options by a SELECT function that responds to a condition of data handled within a program.

budget   A plan for receiving and spending money.

buffer   A memory device that stores data temporarily during processing or data transfer operations.

bus   A high speed connector capable of handling one or more bytes of data through parallel circuits.

bus topology   A topology that connects all devices to a central cable, or bus.

byte   A group of bits representing a number, letter, or other character. Most commonly, a byte consists of eight data bits and one parity bit, or check bit.

C

calculate   To apply arithmetic operations (addition, subtraction, multiplication, and division) to data items.

capital   Assets that add to the long-term net worth of a corporation.

capture   To record information in a specific pattern using a given set of symbols or values. *See also* record.

carrier signals   The wave signals that carry voice and data signals over communication channels.

cathode ray tube (CRT)   A video display used for computer input and output. A component of a user terminal.

cell   A modular, convenient unit of storage.

center   The ability of a computer to center a string of characters on a text line.

central processing unit (CPU)   Portion of a computer's processor containing the control unit and the arithmetic logic unit.

chain   A system of storing records that links records in lists or groups for retrieval and use.

character   The smallest unit of data that can be presented to a program; a letter, numeral, or special symbol.

character printer   An output device that prints documents one character at a time under control of a computer.

character reader   An input device that reads images of text which are then input to memory and echoed on a display screen. *See also* scanner.

character string   A sequence of letters, numbers, or symbols.

chart of accounts   A list that separates and organizes the effects of transactions to reflect their impact upon the financial condition of the company.

child   One of two or more lower-level nodes in a tree data structure connected by a branch to a higher-level node.

classify   To put records with similar characteristics into the same category.

code   The source instructions that the computer will follow in compiling a program to process an application.

code-oriented software   A type of page description program that includes format instructions in the documents.

command interpreter   A subprogram within a language compiler, or query language, that contains the instructions necessary to interpret program statements and translate them for execution.

compact disk   A secondary storage device that uses laser-recorded coding under methods similar to those employed in entertainment recordings. *See also* optical disk.

compact disk read-only memory (CDROM)   A description of a process that uses compact disks to record permanent program files as a supplement to computer memory. *See also* optical disk.

compare   The basis of computer logic, which is the ability of a computer to compare two data items and to direct processing on the basis of the results.

compiler   A program that translates source code instructions into machine language commands.

condition test   A test that determines whether a user-defined descriptive term is true for a value or set of values that apply to the data item under consideration.

control function   A computer "traffic cop" that sends appropriate data items through processing circuits and main memory.

control key   A key on a computer keyboard which signals a shift in operating mode.

controls   One or more components responsible for interpreting and carrying out manually initiated instructions.

coordinates   Any set of numbers used in specifying the location of a point on a line, surface, or in a space.

co-processor   A sub-processor that executes specialized or time-consuming operations, freeing the main processor to perform higher-priority tasks.

corporate culture   The intangible qualities and characteristics that give a corporation its personality and set it apart from other corporations in the same industry.

current cell   The cell on a spreadsheet display in which the cursor is positioned.

cursor   A highlighted line or block on a display screen that marks the location at which the next keystroke or input entry will appear.

cursor movement keys   Designated keys used to move the cursor up, down, left, and right on the computer screen.

custodian   Within an information processing system, the person or function entrusted with the possession of data.

D

database   A collection of files organized to support multiple applications.

database management system (DBMS)   A software system that incorporates a plan of structure and management that controls the accumulation and use of data.

data capture   Procedures for recording and encoding data into a system through keyboarding or other methods.

data communication The transmission of data between two or more physical sites through use of public and/or private communication channels or lines.

data element Basic unit of data that has a specific meaning for the system in which it is used.

data entry Converting or transcribing source data into a form acceptable for computer processing.

data item A string of characters, letters, numbers, and/or punctuation marks, that represents names, addresses, prices, etc. Also called an item.

data model A set of descriptions and definitions that identify the logical structure of files.

data structure The techniques used in any organization to represent, store, and retrieve data. Term encompasses both physical storage, such as data items, records, and files, and logical organization methods.

decision statement A proposed solution to an identified problem.

decision support system (DSS) Type of computer information system that assists management in formulating policies and plans by projecting the likely consequences of decisions.

dedicated A unit of equipment designed and built to run specific systems or applications.

delete The function that removes characters, words, lines, or whole sections of text.

delimit To mark the starting and closing points of the portion of text that is to be copied, moved, or deleted.

demand Occurs when a worker or manager requires a product or service to perform a job.

demodulation The conversion of information structured in ASCII binary analog code into a digital signal for use by a computer communications system.

deposit A secured dollar amount for a product, usually a percentage of the total value.

desktop manager Software used to integrate productivity functions such as telephone directories, applications, and calculators. This software usually operates under windowing techniques.

desktop publishing A computer system that consists of a computer, page layout software, and a typeset quality output device (printer). Used to produce nearly professional printed text and documents.

developer The microscopic steel pellets used in xerographic printers.

dialog box A type of graphic menu used to make format or layout selections and specifications for text.

digital Reference to a device or process that can encode information in the form of on-and-off or high-and-low pulses.

diode An electronic device that performs binary, or two-state, switching.

direct connect A type of modem that connects a computer to a telephone without requiring use of a handset.

direct data entry The combination of data capture and data entry performed simultaneously on a microcomputer through a keyboard.

directory A reference file for documents stored on disk.

discretionary search and replace A function that allows the user to search and replace character string occurrences selectively.

disk A round, flat, magnetically coated platter on which data can be recorded and accessed randomly.

disk drive A data storage device that houses magnetic disks and implements the reading and writing of data to and from these disks.

disk operating system (DOS) Operating system in which primary processing routines reside in memory, but auxiliary routines remain on disk. *See also* operating system.

distributed system   A computer system in which the central computer facility is linked to remote or outlying work stations.

document   To record a business transaction. Also, an original or official paper relied on as the basis, proof, or support for an agreement or transaction. *See also* record.

dot-addressable mode   In printers that can produce graphic images, each wire, or dot, in the matrix is set to print, or not to print, according to the shapes to be produced.

download   To transfer data and/or programs from a mainframe computer to a microcomputer.

draft   A preliminary version of a document subject to changes, revisions, and corrections.

driving force   The motivation, underlying purpose, or mission of a business.

drum plotter   Graphic device using a round drum to hold the paper on which lines are drawn under computer control.

E

echo   Description for the screen display of characters or images in response to entries from a keyboard or other device.

edit   To make changes, additions, and corrections in text, and to make sure that the text conveys the intended meaning.

electronic bulletin board   An electronic device used to store announcements, messages, or news items. This board can be accessed by many users and the information on the board can be used by anyone.

electronic mailbox   A space within computer-maintained files for initiating and receiving messages.

electronic publishing   Computer systems that give users the ability to format document pages integrate text and graphics on the same page.

electronic spreadsheet   A computer-based method for organizing and presenting financial or other comparative data.

electronic tablet   A device with a touch sensitive surface on which images are created and/or moved on the display screen when pressure is applied with a pen-like device. *See also* touch screen.

emitter   A filament that is heated to cause emission of electrons.

encode   A process for recording information in a specific pattern through use of a given set of symbols or values.

entrepreneurial approach   A policy for use of microcomputers under which managers/users are permitted latitude to develop their own applications to promote success of their own business units.

equity   The worth of a business after the value of the liabilities have been subtracted from the value of the assets.

erasable programmable read-only memory (EPROM)   A write-protected memory chip that can have its circuit logic erased and reprogrammed.

exception   Any item that requires attention from a decision maker. Also, a case or situation to which a rule does not apply.

exchange of value   Occurs when an organization supplies a good or provides a service in exchange for something that has value.

Extended Binary Coded Decimal Interchange Code (EBCDIC)   A standard coding system for representing data in an eight-bit byte format.

extended price   The gross amount charged for merchandise. Derived by multiplying the unit price by the number of units ordered.

external storage   A method for storing data on peripheral devices external to, but accessible by, a computer.

F

feedback   A response to procedures or conditions used for quality control or corrective action.

feedback loop   Repetition of the feedback process until planned results are achieved.

field A basic, processing-oriented unit of data formed by a set of characters in a predetermined format; usually combined with other fields of data to form a record.

fifth-generation language Reference to software techniques that permit users to address computers through use of terms natural to their own speech or discipline. The computer processes sets of facts and rules stated by the user to search for and report on relationships. Fifth-generation languages apply mathematical principles known as logic or logic programming.

filament A glowing wire through which electricity flows and gives off electrons when voltage is applied.

file A collection of data records with related content.

file-oriented packages Word processing packages that load files into memory one page at a time.

file transfer software Software that converts files from a format produced by one program into a format that can be used in another program.

filtering A routine used to modify the byte format of output.

financial statement A set of documents that consolidates the detailed account listings of a general ledger to reflect the financial condition of the company.

first generation Refers to the computers that were developed during the 1950s and used vacuum tubes as switching devices.

first line supervisor An operations manager who oversees the processing of transactions and the internal operations that support transactions.

fixed asset Items of value such as land and buildings that do not realize a cash value immediately.

fixed-length Refers to a file organization or device in which all records are of equal length.

flag To highlight a word or data item for recognition by a processing program.

flatbed plotter Graphic output device that uses a flat area to hold the paper on which lines are drawn under computer control.

flush left Describes text that is justified or aligned along the left side.

flush left, ragged right Text is justified or aligned along the left margin and unjustified at the right margin.

flush right Describes text that is justified along the right margin.

font A set of characters, numbers, and symbols designed to present a unique appearance.

forecast To project or estimate future results, decisions, or actions.

format commands Commands that specify text parameters such as page length, line width, margins, and paragraph indents.

formatting The use of commands to establish a layout of the document on a display screen, and subsequently, on a printed page.

form letter Documents with the same message addressed to multiple customers.

fourth-generation language A nonprocedural programming language such as those used in application generators or as supplements to database management systems.

fourth-generation tools Command structures or functions incorporated within fourth-generation languages.

frequency modulation (FM) Communication technique in which the frequency of a carrier or signal is varied in response to input information.

front-end processor A computer that is dedicated to communication and peripheral operation functions to free a larger system for high processing productivity.

full-duplex A type of transmission that permits simultaneous two-way signal communication.

function keys Keys on a computer keyboard that are assigned standard processing operations such as copying, changing format lines, and searching.

fuse To combine or blend thoroughly by using heat; used to fix xerographic images.

G

galley Output form for typesetting. A long strip of text that is cut up and used to arrange pages.

gap A space used to separate data records and blocks for input and processing control.

gates Electronic switching devices that perform processing operations.

general ledger A set of accounting records used to allocate income and expense to accounts that represent business segments. A general ledger accounting package is part of a financial management and reporting system.

gigabyte One billion bytes.

global search and replace A search and replace operation that applies to all occurrences of a target string within a document or file. *See also* search and replace.

graphic A displayed image; may be produced through digitizing of analog signals.

graphic board A computer board that uses micro-chips to translate geometric information into display images.

graphic co-processor A co-processor that handles the geometric conversions required to plot and display graphics on a screen or to produce graphic output. *See also* co-processor.

grid A pattern of uniformly placed horizontal and perpendicular lines.

gross profit The sum total of all incomes for a business.

H

half-duplex A transmission method in which sending and receiving terminals exchange information in one direction at a time.

hard copy Computer output printed on paper.

hard disk Storage medium consisting of a rigid metal platter coated with a metallic-oxide substance upon which data are recorded as patterns of magnetic spots.

hard return A fixed return recorded within a stored file, as distinct from a temporary "soft return" used for line endings to implement word wrap.

hardware An inclusive term identifying all computer equipment.

heading Information at the top of a page or column that defines and/or describes the information printed below. *See also* label.

hierarchical data model A method of structuring data items according to a top-down relationship.

hierarchy A top-down, multilevel organizational scheme in which components of problems, systems, or programs are layered in a top-to-bottom, general-to-detailed fashion. *See also* tree.

high-level command A program command that resembles an English statement.

histogram *See* bar chart.

home address The starting point for each track on a disk.

host A central computer in a multiprocessing system or communication network.

hyphen A punctuation mark used to divide or compound words, word elements, or numbers.

I

icon A symbol that represents a processing option.

identification field A field interspersed between data records on a magnetic disk track that is used to identify the size of the next data record.

immediate conversion An implementation method that converts from one system to another between the end of one cycle of a process and the beginning of the next cycle.

impact printer Printing device that creates impressions by striking a ribbon that transfers images to paper.

indent Increased margin space, usually five spaces at the beginning of a paragraph in body text.

index A file or list of names, numbers, subjects or other data organized in an alphabetical or numerical fashion. Used primarily for reference purposes.

information processing cycle A recurring series of the information processing functions: input, processing, output, and storage (IPOS).

information processing system Collection of components (people, data, hardware, programs, and procedures) that interact to process data and deliver meaningful information.

information resources Files and documents that are necessary to the continuing existence of an organization.

ink jet printer A nonimpact printing device that sprays microscopic ink particles onto paper to form characters.

input A method for converting data into a computer-readable format and entering the data for processing.

input device Any device that allows data to be entered into a computer system.

insert The function used to add words, lines, paragraphs, and pages to text.

integrated circuit (IC) A miniaturized complex of electronic components and their connections manufactured on a small slice of semiconductor material.

integrated software package Software that supports coordinated access to multiple applications through a single, unified package.

integrity Refers to the quality, accuracy, reliability, and timeliness of data.

interactive processing Service carried out through a continuing dialog between a user and the computer. A user communicates through keyboard entries, and the system communicates by displaying either a prompt or a menu.

internal clock A timing device that controls the frequency of a computer's processing cycles.

internal entrepreneurship A management concept in which managers use independent or standalone workstations to support and explore decisions within their own sphere of responsibility. *See also* entrepreneurial approach.

inventory control A function or procedure set up to establish and maintain appropriate stock levels.

invoice A document that represents, or models, a sales transaction by detailing the products or services sold and demanding payment.

item *See* data item.

iteration Repetition. A process is repeated for successive items, until a predefined condition is sensed and the repetition ends.

J

justification A word processing function used to align left and right margins, the text is arranged so that both margins are straight and parallel.

K

kernel An element of software within the Unix operating system that interfaces the functional programs with the central processing unit of the computer.

kerning A term derived from typesetting terminology (kern) to minimize space between letters.

key Access control field that uniquely identifies a record or classifies it as a member of a category of records within a file.

keyboard A typewriter-styled input device on which data entries are converted into computer-readable data ready to be processed.

keying Typing on a computer keyboard. The keystrokes are input to computer memory and echoed on a display screen.

knowledge-based system An alternate term used to describe applications of artificial intelligence or fifth-generation software techniques. *See also* artificial intelligence, fifth-generation language.

L

label   Name that identifies entries that appear within the column or row of a spreadsheet. *See also* heading.

large-scale computer   A computer that can handle massive file and transaction volumes. *See also* mainframe.

·e-scale integration (LSI)   Fabrication of large ·umbers of components or control circuits on integrated circuit (IC) chips.

lasso   A method of selecting and moving portions of graphics or text. This is usually done with a mouse.

layout   The process of arranging, or designing, pages of text either manually or electronically to be "pleasing to the eye."

liability   Amount owed, such as unpaid taxes, loans, or accounts payable.

light pen   An input device, resembling a pen, that allows users to manipulate data on the face of CRT screens. Used chiefly for engineering and design applications.

line editor   A program utility used to create and edit text files line by line.

line item   Product description, including price, on a merchandise invoice.

Linotype   A keyboard-operated typesetting machine that produces one line of type at a time.

liquid asset   Money and certain securities that can be spent easily.

load   To enter data elements into the appropriate records within files.

local area network (LAN)   An interconnected group of microcomputers that serves a limited area; can include shared peripherals and a link to a mainframe system.

logical data structure   A model indicating the content of files. Also, a data organization scheme that reflects the user's viewpoint.

logic field   A field that will accept condition entries (Yes/No, True/False) used for option selection.

logic gate   A switching device designed to perform basic transformations on electronic signals that represent encoded data.

logic operations   The ability of a computer to compare data items and determine whether a given (base) item is equal to, greater than, or less than an item presented for comparison. The result of the comparison must guide selection of processing alternatives.

logic system   A group of interconnected logic elements that act in combination to perform relatively complex operations.

lookup table   A software device that provides menu-type access to functions or processing options.

M

mail merge   A word processing technique that merges information from a list of names and addresses into a standardized letter, making each letter appear to be an original document.

mainframe   A large, central computer; includes the central processor, main memory, arithmetic-logic unit, and often an operator console. The term is usually applied only to medium- and large-scale computer systems.

main memory   Device connected to the computer processor unit that supports the handling of data by the control or arithmetic-logic units. Used for temporary storage of data and programs during program execution.

main menu   A directory to other menus and programs.

management by exception (MBE)   A system under which a computer monitors status information and generates reports on items that, on the basis of condition tests, require management attention.

management information system (MIS) Type of computer information system that provides meaningful summarization of data to support organizational management control functions and highlights exception conditions requiring attention or corrective action. Implements management by exception.

man-hours A measure of time worked; used in project planning and reporting.

manipulation/query commands Computer commands that provide standard processing routines for executing inquiries and other operations involving content of a database.

margin The space around (to the left and right, above and below) the text portion of a document.

master file A file which contains information that reflects the current and past history of business activities.

math co-processor A co-processor that executes the complex calculations required to support many database and spreadsheet applications.

medium of exchange Something commonly accepted in exchange for goods and services and recognized as representing a standard value.

medium-scale integration (MSI) Integrated circuit with intermediate numbers of components that function as simple, self-contained logic systems.

megahertz (MHz) One million hertz (cycles per second).

memory cell A single storage element of a memory; when combined with associated circuits, it is used for inserting and removing one bit of information.

memory chip The chips used in main memory to store data and programs temporarily to support processing operations.

menu A list of options from which a user makes selections to direct processing.

menu bar A display on a single line of a screen that shows processing choices.

microchip Miniaturized circuitry and electronic components integrated on a small silicon base.

microprocessor A microchip containing the circuitry and components for arithmetic, logic, and control operations of a microcomputer.

model A simulation of an organization's policies and procedures. Used to determine the current status or condition of the business.

modem From MODulator-DEModulator, a device that translates analog code into digital code, and digital into analog, allowing computers to utilize telephone lines for direct communication.

modulation The conversion of digital signals into analog signals so that computers can communicate with other electronic devices.

monitor A display device used in almost all computer systems, large and small. *See also* cathode ray tube (CRT) and video display terminal (VDT).

monochrome monitor A monitor which displays text and graphics in only one color.

monospacing Allowing an equal amount of space for each letter, regardless of the size of the letter.

motherboard A main circuit board on which processing and memory chips are housed.

mouse A cursor-control device that resembles a small box on two wheels. As the box is rolled on a flat surface, wheel positions signal the computer to move the cursor on the display screen in direct proportion to the movement of the mouse.

multitasking Refers to the ability of a user to execute several applications at the same time.

N

nanosecond One billionth of a second.

navigate In a database system, to follow a sequence of selections to access functions or data.

near letter-quality Refers to the densities and patterns of characters in a printer which approach the quality of text produced by ball-element typewriters.

network Graphic flow diagram relating a sequence of activities; used in project evaluation and review technique (PERT) and critical path method (CPM). Also, a system in which communication is possible from one location to one or more remote locations. In data communications, the linking of computers and peripheral devices across distances is through use of communication lines.

network model   A technique for organizing data for storage and access under database management software. A network model provides structured access paths to data nodes and also permits entry into the database for searches at any level. *See also* hierarchical data model.

node   A switching point within a communications network. Often controls the transmission of data between a host computer and a cluster of terminals or smaller computers. *See also* root node, tree.

nonimpact printer   A printing device that causes images to be imprinted without actual contact between print mechanism and paper. *See* ink jet printer, thermal printer.

O

object program   The machine-language program generated by a compiler which translates a source program.

off-line   Refers to equipment or programs not under the control of the central processing unit.

operands   Values used within mathematical operations.

operating commands   Commands that instruct a printer or other peripheral device to stop or start functioning.

operating system   The sets of programs and other software routines that monitor and operate the computer hardware to facilitate its use. A form of system software.

operational plan   Plans that deal with the day-to-day realities of meeting goals.

operations manual   Describes the commands and actions for operating hardware devices or running application programs.

optical disk   A secondary storage device that uses rotating disks encoded and read from patterns burned into the surface by a laser beam. Optical disk storage has extremely high capacity but, at this writing, functions on a read-only basis. (Once data are encoded, they cannot be changed.) *See also* compact disk.

order entry   Procedures for capturing data on incoming orders that are recorded and entered into the transaction processing system.

organization chart   A graphic description of the structure of an organization and its chain of authority.

output   The results of computer processing, delivered in a form and format—and on a schedule—that makes the end products usable by people.

owner   In data security, an individual who is responsible for creating, monitoring, and establishing rules of access for data records.

P

page description language   A software feature that enhances the capability of laser printers to convert signals representing graphics and text into output.

page description program   A program that provides the capabilities for bringing text and graphics together and for converting them into finished outputs.

page-oriented packages   Word processing packages in which files usually reflect the page divisions of the hard-copy document.

page printer   A printer that can produce an entire page at one time.

paginate   To divide text into pages.

parallel conversion   An implementation method used to change from one computer system to another. This involves installing the new system and running it simultaneously with the old system so users can become accustomed to the new system.

parallel processing   The processing of more than one program at a time through more than one active processor.

parent A higher-level node within a tree or network data structure that points to two or more lower-level, child nodes.

parity bit The channel or position in a data recording pattern used for automatic checking of the validity of a character. The parity bit is used to check that the appropriate number of bits, odd or even, is present in each byte. Also called the check bit.

parity checking A technique for counting the number of 1 bits in a byte for presence of an odd or even total to check the accuracy of transmitted or processed data.

password A character string that must be entered into a system to achieve access to restricted areas of a database.

perfect To complete a transaction at the time of occurrence.

peripheral An auxiliary device attached to or used in conjunction with a computer. Peripherals include input, output, storage, and other hardware units.

phased conversion An implementation method used to change from an existing computer system to a new one. This involves installing the new system in phases to maintain a controllable and logical progression.

phase modulation (PM) A method of encoding data for transmission by assigning zero and one values to the upper and lower crests of a wave signal.

phototypesetting The composition of text directly on film or photosensitive paper for reproduction.

physical data structure Format definition and planned structure for the retention and access of data items on secondary storage devices, such as disk files.

pica A unit of measure used in typesetting that is 1/6 (one-sixth) of an inch long.

picking order A document used to assemble or gather merchandise for shipment.

pie chart A circular graphic chart cut up like a pie to show relationships between component parts to a whole.

piping Refers to the ability to designate the output of one program as input for another program.

pixel A video and computer graphics term that indicates a separate light or dark picture element.

plotter A computer-driven graphic output device that creates line drawings on paper by guiding a pen-like stylus.

point A unit of measure in typesetting that is 1/72 (one seventy-second) of an inch long. Twelve points make a pica.

pointer A reference item that links constituent sectors of data on a disk.

point of transaction The location where a business transaction occurs. For example, the cash register at a store. *See also* source.

port A hardware connection for input or output.

post To use data items or other information to update files.

power typing The use of electronic devices for high-production, usually repetitive, typing operations.

primary file In a match/merge operation, the part of a letter that remains the same.

primary storage *See* main memory.

printer A computer-driven device that produces and delivers hardcopy outputs of computer processed information.

printer action table A routine that establishes compatible transfer of files from computer to printer. Also called printer driver.

processing The manipulation of data to change or add to its meaning. This function is based on the arithmetic capability which executes calculations, and the logic capability which directs processing through simple comparisons of two values.

processing unit The device that executes arithmetic and logic operations and controls the transfer of data to and from other system devices. Also called processor.

program A set of instructions that causes a computer to perform a series of steps without human intervention so as to solve a problem or meet a need by delivering specific results.

program code Instructions written in a computer language.

programmable read-only memory (PROM) Computer memory chips that can be programmed permanently, by burning the circuits in patterns, to carry out a predefined process.

prompt A displayed request for user input.

proportional spacing A typesetting method that assigns space to letters according to their size.

protocol Informal set of rules that governs the exchange of data transmission between processing systems.

prototype A first full-scale, and usually functional, form of a new type or design of a product or system.

public-domain program Software offered for low, voluntary payments to users of computer bulletin boards.

pull-down menu A function-selection technique under which users select options from a menu bar, a series of master choices listed horizontally at the top of the screen. When a menu-bar selection is made, a submenu of functions "drops down" from the corresponding position on the menu bar. This is the "pull-down menu."

purchase order A transaction document that orders goods or services.

Q

query language An instruction set used within a database management system to locate and retrieve selected information.

queue A line of tasks waiting to be processed.

R

ragged center *See* center.

range The limits of a series, or the difference between the least and greatest values of attributes, sequences, or variables.

read-only memory (ROM) Memory chips with preprogrammed circuits for storing often-used software, such as language translators and other system software. *See also* programmable read-only memory (PROM).

record A collection of data fields relating to a single entity, such as a person or a business transaction. A number of records with related content make up a file. Also called a logical record. Also, to set down in writing or furnish written evidence of something.

record key A data item that is unique to a record and is used to identify and locate the record within a file.

recovery A control procedure that will restore a damaged database by using a transaction log and a backup version of the system.

register *See* accumulator.

relational model Consists of one or more traditional-type files that are made up of records and fields and controlled through a computer-maintained index.

reorder level An inventory control system feature that indicates when merchandise needs to be restocked.

requisition A transaction document that describes a need and requests that a required good or service be purchased.

resolution Refers to the density of pixels in a display matrix. The higher the density, the more clear and sharp the screen image. At lesser density, the screen image is poor and difficult to read.

resource Anything that is manipulated or applied to obtain results.

ring topology   In data communication, a circular, decentralized distributed-processing system in which messages are passed continuously around the circuit.

roll forward   Refers to the ability to rebuild damaged or destroyed storage files by processing transaction records on the backup copy of the system as if they were newly input.

root node   The highest level superordinate node in a tree data structure.

S

sans serif   Without serif. *See* serif.

save   To write data from memory to a disk for storage.

scanner   A reading device that translates bar codes and other visual images into input data.

schema   A format or layout that provides specifications of a data structure.

scroll   A control function that moves data or text across a computer screen continuously in one direction at a time; left, right, up, or down.

scroll arrow   A function that allows the user to scroll continuously left, right, up, and down.

scroll bar   A word processing function that allows a cursor to move to another location in a file. Usually used in conjunction with a mouse.

search   To locate a specific character string.

search and replace   The function that allows the user to find and replace every occurrence of a particular character string with another character string.

secondary file   In mail/merge, the entries that change with each form letter, such as name, address, and phone number.

sector   An area of storage on a disk that occupies a portion of a track. Sectors can be addressed directly by computers.

security   Protection against unauthorized access, use, disclosure, modification, or destruction of data.

semiconductor   A material with properties that are between those of a conductor and an insulator.

serial   Refers to the method in which data are transmitted and received or stored. In this method, data are sent or received in a sequential order, one bit after another, or stored in the order in which they are captured.

serif   Any of the short lines stemming from, and at an angle to, the upper and lower ends of the strokes of a letter.

shell   The outline of a program that contains basic or frequently used routines.

shipping order   A document used to authorize the shipment and delivery of specified merchandise.

smart modem   A type of modem that is built on a circuit board, resides within a computer, and interacts with system and application software.

software   Computer operating systems and application programs, together with the operating procedures for their use.

software integration   The ability to share programs to produce coordinated results.

solid-state device   Any element that can control an electrical current without moving parts, heated filaments, or vacuum gaps.

sort   To arrange data items in a desired sequence.

source   A point of origin or procurement.

source document   A form used for initial recording of data to be input to a computer or system.

spreadsheet   A means for representing numeric data in comparative formats.

stacked bar chart   A graphic chart that breaks down overall figures and sets them up for comparison.

standalone   A device, such as a personal computer system, that is fully integrated to provide a user with autonomous processing capabilities.

start bit   A bit that is always zero (it has no setting) used at the beginning of each character in data transmission.

star topology   A centralized, distributed data processing system in which the central processor acts as the control point in logging and monitoring information transmission.

statement of changes in financial condition   A report that compares financial status information for a current period with the same figures for an earlier period. A standard element of corporate financial reports.

storage   Reference to the ability to record data on peripheral devices for access by a computer.

storage media   The disks or tapes used to store data and information.

store   To keep and maintain information for future use.

strategic plan   A plan that sets long-term goals for an organization.

stylus   A pen-like device used in plotters to produce line drawings, controlled by digitized instructions from a computer. Also a device used for graphic input.

subsystem   A secondary or subordinate system within a large system.

summarize   To reduce the volume of data items while enhancing and defining their meaning through use of totals and subtotals for groups of items.

summary of income and expense   A type of financial statement that develops a total for profits or losses realized by a business during the reporting period.

syntax   The structure and usage rules of a programming language.

system   A set of interrelated, interacting components (people, data, equipment, programs, and procedures) that function together as an entity to achieve specific results.

system file   A disk operating system file that is not found in a regular directory and requires special handling before it can be accessed by users. Also called a hidden file.

system integrators   A software tool that enhances software capabilities, provides for opening programs without leaving the current program, and for moving data among programs.

system operator (Sysop)   A person skilled in the workings of a particular computer or communications system.

systems development life cycle (SDLC)   Organized, structured methodology for developing, implementing, and installing a new or revised computer information system.

system software   Programs and other processing routines that activate and control the computer hardware to facilitate its use. *See also* operating system.

system specification   A statement or document defining the procedures and requirements for a microcomputer application.

T

tactical plan   A plan that describes strategic goals for an organization or development of a new product in terms of intermediate stages.

terms of payment   A document indicating when and how a buyer is asked to pay for goods or services received.

text   The written or printed words that make up a document.

text processing   The creation and handling of documents with computer tools. *See also* word processing.

thermal printer   A nonimpact printing device that develops images through exposure of special paper to heat.

thimble printer   A printer that is similar to a daisy wheel printer, except that the characters in the thimble printer point upward, and the print mechanism spins around the hammer to position the proper character for imprinting.

token A segment of a message to be transmitted over a network.

toner The pigmented particles of plastic used in xerographic printers.

topology The configuration of devices that make up a network. Also called architecture.

touch-screen A device for inputting data directly through touch contact with specially sensitized locations on the face of a video display screen.

track A concentric, circular recording path around the hub of a disk.

training manual A document that orients people to a new information system, or makes the transition from a manual system to computerized operations smooth.

transaction A basic act of doing business. The exchange of value for goods or services received.

transaction document Any document that is used to record transaction data. Also known as a source document.

transaction file A file that contains the accumulation of data items from individual transactions.

transaction flow The path documents take within the internal procedures and exchanges of an organization.

transaction log A running journal of all transactions recorded in their order of occurrence and stored separately.

transaction processing Refers to collecting and maintaining transaction data and manipulating that data to produce information about the status of the organization.

transaction record A collection of data fields that contains information describing a specific transaction.

transistor A three element (emitter, base, and collector) semiconductor electronic device used in electronic circuits.

tree A graphic data structure in which there is no more than one edge connecting any two nodes. *See also* hierarchy.

trend line Line graphs that show the relative up-and-down movements of data values during a certain time period.

two-dimensional table A graphic table that represents a series of columns and rows.

typeset To capture in type.

U

unit price The amount charged for a single unit of a specific product.

universal product code (UPC) Bar code used extensively in supermarkets and other retail outlets for optical sensing of product identification.

update To modify a file or document so that it contains and reflects the most current data and information.

upload Refers to the capability to transfer data maintained by a microcomputer to a mainframe.

user Any person or organization served by an information system.

user friendly Refers to a type of software that allows users to do processing with relative ease.

user specification A document that outlines the benefits and requirements of a system from the user viewpoint.

utility A software program within an operating system that performs repetitive, basic functions such as sorting data, merging and copying files, and producing reports.

V

validity check A computer control that is executed to ensure that data entries conform to file specifications.

value added A description of a computer service center that provides more than straightforward communication. Typical added values include special-industry application programs and text or statistical databases.

variable   Data values that change for a series of records within a data stream. Example: transaction data items.

vector algorithm   A mathematical method for handling graphics. With this method, points are established on a screen, and images are defined mathematically, according to algorithms.

vendor   A seller of merchandise or services.

very large-scale integration (VLSI)   Refers to the fabrication methods that produce integrated circuit (IC) chips with hundreds of thousands of components.

video display terminal (VDT)   Visual display device, also called a computer monitor. *See also* cathode ray tube (CRT).

voice recognition   A means of input in which computers are programmed to accept spoken commands and/or spoken responses to initiate direct processing.

von Neumann architecture   Computer processing structure named after its designer, John von Neumann, that contains a single processor, which executes instructions one after another, in sequence.

W

wafer   A thin semiconductor slice of silicon or germanium with parallel faces on which microcircuits can be formed.

width   Refers to the number of bits a bus can carry at one time.

Winchester drive   Fixed-disk peripheral storage device of high memory capacity that is plug-compatible with microcomputers.

window   A display frame within an overall monitor screen that represents the status of an application package other than the one in use.

word processing   The use of computers to capture and edit text and to produce finished documents.

word wrap   A word processing function that will move a word that is too big to fit at the end of one line down and left to the beginning of the next line.

workbench   A collection of tools designed for specific purposes.

working capital   Financial resources available for company operations or projects.

WYSIWYG   The acronym for the sentence "What You See Is What You Get." It refers to displayed output being identical to printed output.

Index

Page numbers in *italics* refer to figures in the text.

APPLICATION
SOFTWARE
TUTORIAL

APPLICATION SOFTWARE TUTORIAL

Keiko M. Pitter

MITCHELL PUBLISHING, INC.
INNOVATORS IN COMPUTER EDUCATION
915 River Street
Santa Cruz, California 95060

Dedication to Quality Publishing: All employees of Mitchell Publishing, Inc.
Sponsoring Editor: Erika Berg
Director of Product Development: Raleigh Wilson
Production Management: i/e inc.
Interior Design: Gary Palmatier
Printing: R. R. Donnelly and Sons Company

Disclaimer: This book and the accompanying magnetic disk are designed
to help you improve your computer use. However, the authors and
publishers assume no responsibility whatsoever for the uses made of this
material or for decisions based on its use, and make no warranties, either
expressed or implied, regarding the contents of this book or any
accompanying magnetic disks, its merchantability, or its fitness for any
particular purpose.

Neither the publishers nor anyone else who has been involved in the
creation, production, or delivery of this product shall be liable for any
direct, incidental, or consequential damages, such as, but not limited to,
loss of anticipated profits or benefits resulting from its use or from any
breach of any warranty. Some states do not allow the exclusion or
limitation of direct, incidental, or consequential damages, so the above
limitation may not apply to you. No dealer, company, or person is
authorized to alter this disclaimer. Any representation to the contrary
will not bind the publisher or the author.

dBase III PLUS is a registered trademark of Ashton-Tate.
WordPerfect is a registered trademark of WordPerfect Corporation.
SuperCalc3 is a registered trademark of Computer Associates.
IBM is a registered trademark of International Business Machines Corporation.

MATERIALS AND REQUIREMENTS FOR USE OF THIS PACKAGE

This **Application Software Tutorial** consists of this manual and software diskettes for the following commercial application packages:

- WordPerfect (one diskette)
- SuperCalc 3 (one diskette)
- dBASE III PLUS (two diskettes).

To use the software, you will need an IBM PC (or compatible) microcomputer with at least 256 K of memory and two disk drives. You also should have a printer available to output documents you will create in completing assignments included in this manual.

Before you start using the software, you also should have a formatted diskette of your own. This diskette is to be used to record and store the data that you generate as you complete the assignments in this manual.

Be sure that you have all of the provided diskettes and your own data diskette ready for use before you begin assignments involving use of a microcomputer.

Contents

WORDPERFECT

SUPERCALC 3

Preface

This manual was first published in 1984 as *Using Microcomputers: An IBM PC Lab Manual.* It was designed for use in the lab of a microcomputer applications course or as a supplement in an introductory computer course. It presented several then-popular software programs spanning applications of word processing (WordStar), spreadsheet (VisiCalc and LOTUS 1-2-3), and file management (PFS:File), in a manner that reduced greatly the need for instructor intervention to assist students.

As time passes, however, some interesting phenomena occur in Computerdom. For one thing, software comes and goes. VisiCalc has become a thing of the past, whereas dBASE is gaining popularity. Then, there is always the problem of a software vendor coming out with a newer version of software, called an upgrade. The second edition of this manual, *Using IBM Micro - computers: Second Edition,* published in 1986, took these factors into consideration and featured WordStar, dBASE III Plus, and LOTUS 1-2-3 Release 2.

My goal always has been to teach some of the more popular software packages in their latest versions so that a student may gain a marketable skill. Thus, in this newest version of the manual, WordPerfect 4.2 is used for word processing, SuperCalc3 for spreadsheet, and dBASE III Plus for file management. The manual also takes advantage of educational versions of these software packages that are made available through the efforts of Mitchell Publishing, Inc. These educational versions of commercial software are not tutorials. They are the actual working copies of the software that may be limited in certain capabilities, such as in the number of pages a document may produce.

MANUAL DESIGN

The manual answers most questions asked by students in a manner which is neither technical nor too elementary. It uses many screen displays and is written so that students either are told or shown, at every step, what response to expect from the computer and what entries to make next. Wherever possible, the reason for the response or the entry is given. Intermittently, PRACTICE TIME exercises are given to test the student's understanding of the material. The solutions for these are not given. If a student cannot do any one of the exercises, he/she should review the material given immediately before the exercise.

SPECIAL FEATURES

The strengths of this book include:

- It contains keystroke-by-keystroke instructions.
- It is written for the beginner.
- It is practical—covering the most popular software packages.
- Its modular format is adjustable to any course.
- It is a complete package, including software disks students can keep.
- It is well illustrated.
- It includes interesting applications.
- It is flexible—it can be a supplement or core text.

SOFTWARE REQUIREMENTS

For the first module in the manual, each student needs a disk containing DOS (Disk Operating System) and a scratch disk. A scratch disk is a disk that either is blank or contains information no longer needed.

Three software packages are covered in this manual: Module 2 discusses WordPerfect 4.2 for word processing; Module 3 discusses SuperCalc3 for electronic spreadsheet; and Module 4 discusses dBASE III Plus, a powerful relational database management system. For each module, the student needs the accompanying disks that contain the educational versions of the software and at least one scratch disk that has been formatted, with the exception that SuperCalc3 does not require a scratch disk.

HARDWARE REQUIREMENTS

The hardware configuration required is an IBM PC with 256K bytes of RAM memory (384K if you are using dBASE III Plus with DOS version 3.0 or higher). Also required are a monochrome or color monitor, two floppy disk drives, and either a printer or access to an IBM PC with a printer.

LAB SESSION STRUCTURE

Everyone using the manual should go through Module 1 first. Its purpose is to acquaint the student with the microcomputer and give him/her confidence in the use. After that, it is up to each individual (or instructor) to decide which modules to study, and in what order. Each module is completely independent of the others. Each consists of three lab lessons, projects for students to do on their own, and a summary of commands (appendices).

ACKNOWLEDGEMENTS

I extend much gratitude to the staff at Mitchell Publishing, Inc., particularly Erika Berg and Raleigh Wilson, for encouraging me and trusting me with this project. Also, Benedict Kruse of i/e, inc., deserves much credit for being so understanding and patient. As always, I thank my husband, Richard, and my friend and assistant, Darlene Fiecoat, for checking the accuracy of the text. Above all, Santa Claus should be good to my children, Greg and Jackie, who put up with the mother who never had time.

Keiko Pitter
Reno, Nevada

December, 1986

Introduction

ORIENTATION

You walk into a computer store and the salesperson says, "Sit down and try it." You wave your hand and walk away.

You are at a computer demonstration and you are asked to come up and press some keys. You shake your head. You are envious as you watch other people work with computers. You know that computers are here to stay. You know that one of these days you have to learn how to use one. Yet, you won't even try.

Why?

Are you afraid of making a fool of yourself? Do you think people will laugh if you admit that you are actually afraid of computers?

Do you think you don't have what it takes to work with a computer?

Welcome to the club. You are one of many such people. The way to get over these fears is to use a computer, personally. You will soon realize that a computer is just a machine—like the washing machine and microwave oven. Whereas the washing machine only washes and the microwave oven only emits microwaves, the function of a computer can be changed.

You can change a computer's function by putting in a new set of instructions, called a **program** or **software,** and connecting appropriate attachments, called **peripherals.** With word processing software and a printer, the computer becomes a word processor; with video game software and possibly a joystick, it becomes a video machine; and with graphics software and a graphics printer, it becomes a machine with which you can draw.

1

Just as you cannot operate the microwave oven with the operating instructions, or **commands,** for the washing machine, you cannot, in general, use the commands of one software system to operate another. Each program comes with its own, often unique, set of commands; you need to learn what they are and what they do. It does not take a super, electronics-oriented mind to learn how to use a computer. Think about it—you don't have to understand how an engine works to drive a car or how xerography works to make photocopies.

One skill that may help, however, is typing. A lot of information is entered into a computer by typing on a keyboard. If you have to spend time hunting and pecking for keys, you will not have time to think about the commands you are entering. One of the advantages of using a computer is its speed, and if you cannot type, you are not making full use of this advantage.

As you proceed with the lessons, you might remember that there is no one correct way of using software to derive the end product. The commands must be used correctly, of course, just as in driving a car: you have to step on the accelerator to go and the brake to stop. The object in driving a car is to get from one place to another safely. You may take one route while someone else takes another, and one route may be shorter or faster than the other; but in the end, they both get you to where you are going. You cannot say that one is wrong. Using software to accomplish a task works the same way. As you become proficient, you will recognize the more efficient methods. In the meantime, if the method you use accomplishes the objective, it is acceptable.

This manual assumes that you have had very little or no previous exposure to computers. It starts by showing you what makes up a computer, that is, its **hardware** components, and what their functions are. It guides you as you turn the computer on for the very first time and helps you familiarize yourself with the IBM PC keyboard, which is remarkably similar to a typewriter keyboard. New computer terms are explained as they are introduced—throughout the text.

The manual then covers three popular software programs. These programs, provided in their educational versions, are for applications of word processing (WordPerfect 4.2), spreadsheet (SuperCalc3), and file management (dBASE III Plus).

Lesson 1
Components of the IBM PC

GETTING STARTED

As you sit in front of the IBM PC computer, you will see pieces of equipment, known as hardware, in front of you, as shown in the accompanying illustration.

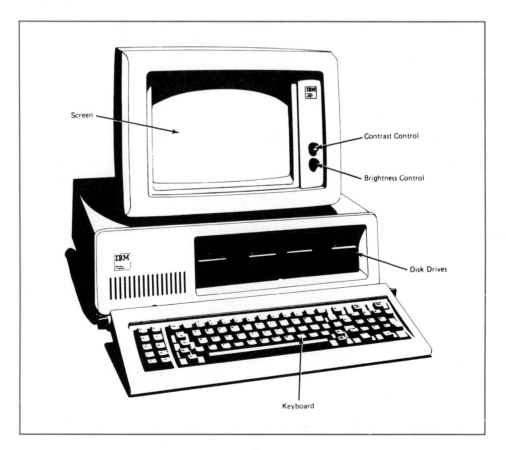

Screen

Contrast Control

Brightness Control

Disk Drives

Keyboard

The screen is the **monitor,** or **CRT (cathode-ray tube).** It is similar to a television set at home. Under the monitor is a box that contains the computer. On the front of the computer are one or two disk drives. The typewriter-like keyboard is attached to the box by a coiled cable. There may or may not be a printer attached to the IBM PC.

FUNCTION OF A COMPUTER

The function of a computer is to process **data** and produce a result. Data include any raw facts you enter into the computer for processing. The result of processing is the processed data, or information presented in a format (or medium) that can be used by people, computers, or other machines.

This means a computer system not only **processes** data, but also must provide ways for data to be entered, **input,** and for the results to be produced, **output.**

PROCESSING COMPONENT

The component of the IBM PC that processes data is inside the computer case. The inside of the computer case contains circuit boards that are similar in appearance to those in the accompanying photograph. A number of options are available for the IBM PC, so the way your computer is configured may not be identical to that in the photograph.

MPU

What you see most are little black rectangular boxes arranged over several boards. The large board on the bottom is the **motherboard,** which connects all the individual pieces electronically. The black rectangular boxes are called **integrated circuits,** or **chips.**

One of the larger chips on the motherboard is the **microprocessing unit,** or the **MPU.** In the IBM PC, this is an 8088 chip. The number refers to the design of a specific make and model of chip. Other microcomputers use different chips: for example, the Radio Shack TRS-80 uses the Z80, and the Apple IIe uses the 6502. Inside the MPU is all the circuitry needed to do the addition, subtraction, comparison, and other functions that a computer performs. It is the unit that performs actual computing.

Storage: RAM, ROM

A computer also needs a place to store information while data are processed. That place is called **main memory.** The main memory is on chips. The **random access memory,** or **RAM,** also is located on the motherboard. RAM stores what you enter into the computer as well as the intermediate results of processing. The memory stores both programs and data.

RAM is volatile, meaning its contents are erased when the power is turned off. The IBM PC RAM ranges from approximately 128,000 characters, or 128K **bytes,** to 512K bytes or more. A character is a single letter, digit, or special symbol. A byte is a computer-system format for encoding characters.

Read only memory, or **ROM,** is another kind of memory. A ROM chip comes already loaded with the information that the computer needs to perform some of the Disk Operating System commands. The information on ROM is not volatile; you can use the information, but you cannot erase or change the stored data.

For a program to be **executed** (processed) on a computer, its instructions must be brought into the main memory. Any data to be processed also must be brought into the main memory first. The MPU fetches both instructions of a program and data to be processed from the main memory as needed.

Expansion Slots

At the back, left of the motherboard are five **expansion slots.** Your monitor and your printer, if you have one, are connected to boards in these slots. These boards are called **interface** boards. They allow the IBM PC to be connected, or interfaced, to peripherals (devices that perform support functions).

Power Switch

On the back, right side of the computer is the power switch. On the back panel, there are places to plug in the power cord, a keyboard connection, and places to plug the interface boards into various peripherals.

Output Components

The information produced by the computer must be delivered on a medium that a person, a computer, or other machines can use. The medium that can be used by noncomputer machines is not discussed here.

Printer and Monitor. When a person uses the output, it must be in a readable format. The output can be printed on paper or displayed on the screen. The devices that provide outputs for people, then, are the printer and the monitor.

Disk Drive. When outputs are to be used by a computer, data must be in a computer-readable format. The medium used most commonly is a **disk,** (also called **diskettes, floppy disks,** or **floppies**). Disks are discussed in more detail later.

Another reason why information should be put on an output medium is that the main memory, the RAM, is volatile. When the machine is turned off, the information is erased. RAM provides temporary storage. If you want to save the information for later use or for historical purposes, you have to put it somewhere more permanent. If you put the information on paper, you can re-enter it later as needed. If you record output on a disk, the information can be entered later directly into the computer's memory from a disk drive. A disk is a permanent storage medium, one form of **auxiliary memory.**

The way in which the information is put on an output device depends on the software being used and is discussed in each application module.

Input Components

The last item is the input. There must be a way to input data to the computer.

Keyboard. You can enter data through a keyboard. As you type the information on the keyboard, the corresponding characters are displayed on the monitor. For some information you enter, you must press the ENTER (or RETURN) key to have the computer process the typed data; for other information the separate entry function is unnecessary. The entry method depends on the software you are using.

Disk Drive. If the information you want to process is on a disk, you use a disk drive for input. The use of disks and the disk drive are explained later.

SUMMARY

Microcomputer components include:

- **Computer**

    Keyboard

    Random Access Memory (RAM)

    Read Only Memory (ROM)

    Power Supply

    Peripheral Interfaces or Expansion Boards

    Microprocessor

- **Disk Drive(s)**
- **Monitor**
- **Printer**

Lesson 2

The Keyboard

GETTING ACQUAINTED

To see how the keyboard works, you must first turn on your IBM PC. In this way, you can see how the characters you type on the keyboard are displayed on the screen. The computer messages are explained later in this module, so don't worry about what they mean.

Make sure that you have a DOS disk, and just follow these steps. A DOS disk is either the IBM Disk Operating System disk (DOS System disk) or a disk that has DOS placed on it.

1. Turn the monitor switch ON. The monitor switch is usually located to the right of the screen. Its exact location and the type of switch depends on the model. Some models do not have a separate monitor switch. The monitor is turned on with the computer.

2. Make sure the computer is OFF.

3. Lift the door for drive A (the drive on your left or on top). If there is a disk in the slot, remove it carefully and put it away.

4. Remove the DOS disk from its envelope and insert it into drive A, oval-cutout end first, label side up. Be careful not to bend or force the disk. If you feel any resistance, pull the disk back out slowly and try again.

5. Close the drive door.

6. Turn the computer switch ON. The power switch is located outside the computer case, at the right, rear.

   ◻ It takes about 15 seconds for anything to happen. The IBM PC goes through a diagnostic routine each time it is turned on. Be patient.

   ◻ The red light on the disk drive lights up and the disk drive starts to operate.

   ◻ The following message appears on the screen:

```
Current date is Tue 1-01-1980
Enter new date (mm-dd-yy):
```

7. Usually, you will enter the date. For now, you will press the ENTER key to leave the date unchanged. Press the ENTER key.

   ◻ The ENTER key is the gray, down-left arrow key between the main keyboard and the numeric keyboard on the right. The ENTER key is referred to as the RETURN key in some software.

   ◻ The following message appears on the screen:

```
Current time is 0:00:41.24
Enter new time:
```

   ◻ Again, usually you will enter the new time. However, this time, you will again press the ENTER key to accept the current time.

8. Press ENTER. The screen displays a message similar to the following:

```
The IBM Personal Computer DOS
Version 3.10 (C)Copyright International Business
              Machines Corp 1981, 1985
(C)Copyright Microsoft Corp 1981, 1985

A>
```

This is the IBM PC DOS copyright notice. **A>** is the DOS prompt. A prompt is a message from the computer to an operator that requests a response or entry. This prompt indicates that drive A is the logged drive. More information about disk drives is presented later in this module.

   ◻ The flashing underscore character to the right of the prompt is the cursor. The cursor shows the position on the screen where your entries are made.

9. Remove the disk from the drive and place it in its protective cover.

KEYBOARD FEATURES

The next illustration shows the IBM PC keyboard. You might notice how similar it is to a typewriter keyboard. The purpose of the keyboard is to send characters to the computer. Which of these characters are recognized or what each is used for depends on the software that is being used at the time.

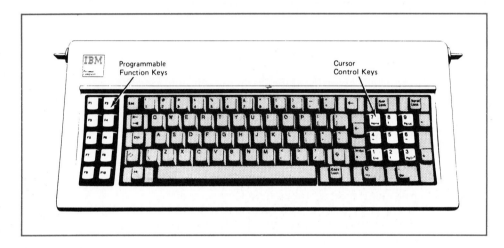

Characters

The keyboard can generate 256 characters. Not all of these characters are visible, and many have special meanings. The **character set** of an IBM PC includes 26 lowercase letters, 26 uppercase letters, 10 numerals, and 34 special characters. The uppercase letters can be generated by holding down one of the keys with the broad up arrows (a SHIFT key) while you press the key or by pressing the key marked **Caps Lock** (the CAPS LOCK key) once and then pressing the keys. Some of the special characters require that you hold down the SHIFT key even if the CAPS LOCK key has been pressed. These are the characters that appear on the upper half of a key. For example, the key with a semicolon, ;, has a colon, :, on the upper half. To type a semicolon, you just press the key. But, to type a colon, you must hold the SHIFT key down while you press the key. CAPS LOCK is a toggle key. The first time you press it, it shifts the keyboard into uppercase mode. The second time, all letters are lowercase (unless the SHIFT key is pressed).

Space Bar

The long bar at the bottom of the keyboard is the space bar. This can be used to place blank spaces between characters.

Strike a few keys to get a feel for the keyboard. In fact, as you read the manual, try different things. You will notice that as you type characters, the characters appear on the screen and the cursor moves to the right along the typing line.

As you press the keys, the computer might respond with the error message: **Bad command or file name.** The computer is indicating that DOS, the software that is running in the computer right now, does not recognize what you typed. Ignore this message for the time being.

ENTER

The ENTER key is the down, LEFT ARROW key located between the main keyboard and the numeric keyboard. It does not necessarily have the same function as on a typewriter keyboard. Its use depends on the software.

Pressing ENTER might cause the cursor to move to the beginning of the next line. In that case, the ENTER is being used to indicate the end of a line or is being used as a cursor movement key. This use is similar to the use of a carriage return on a typewriter.

Pressing ENTER might indicate the end of a command (or an instruction). In this role, ENTER signals the computer to accept the line just typed. Until ENTER is pressed, the computer does not recognize the line.

Some software does not require that the ENTER key be pressed after a command. In fact, SuperCalc, WordPerfect, and dBASE III Plus often do not require that you press anything at all. You must pay particular attention to these rules as you study this manual.

Control Characters

There are 32 control characters that can be entered into the computer. These are formed by holding down the key marked **Ctrl** (the CTRL key) and pressing a character key (shown as CTRL/character or ^character). Use of control characters may or may not display any images on the monitor screen. But these commands have specific functions, which are defined by each software system.

Function Keys

To the left of the main keyboard are 10 function keys, marked F1 to F10. Some software uses the function keys as shortcuts for entering certain commands. For example, WordPerfect makes extensive use of function keys, both by themselves and in conjunction with other keys.

ALT

The key marked **Alt,** located to the left of the space bar, is the **Alternate** key. It is another key whose function depends on the software. In WordPerfect, for example, it is used in conjunction with the function keys to enter commands.

Numeric Keyboard

To the right of the main keyboard is the numeric keyboard, about which you should know several important things.

For the numerals or the period to be entered, the **SHIFT** key must be held down or the **NUM LOCK** key must be pressed. NUM LOCK is a toggle key, like the CAPS LOCK key. Once you press the NUM LOCK key, the characters that appear on the upper half of the numeric keyboard are entered. If the NUM LOCK key is pressed for the second time, the characters on the bottom half of the numeric keyboard are entered.

On the lower half of the 8, 6, 4, and 2 keys are short arrows. In lower case mode, these may be used for **cursor movement** if the software in use supports these functions. That is, when one of the arrow keys is pressed, the cursor moves one position in the direction of the arrow.

On the lower half of the 7 key is **Home.** The HOME key also may be a cursor move key. Under control of some software, pressing the HOME key sends the cursor to the top, right corner of the screen.

On the 1, 3, and 9 keys are the labels **End, PgDn,** and **PgUp,** respectively. These keys may have special cursor moves defined by a software package.

ESC

At the upper, left corner of the main keyboard is the escape key, marked Esc (the ESC key). Its function, again, depends on the software.

TAB

The **TAB** key (which has two arrows pointing opposite directions) is found just below the ESC key. Under WordPerfect, for example, the TAB key is used in the same way as the TAB key on the typewriter. That is, pressing this key sends the cursor to the next tab setting.

PrtSc

The key marked **PrtSc** (for **Print Screen**) on the upper half is found just below the ENTER key. To get a printout of the current screen display, you hold down the SHIFT key and press PrtSC (provided that you have a printer attached to your computer, of course). In some software, however, the SHIFT/PrtSc feature is disabled.

Backspace

The key with the arrow pointing left, found just above the ENTER key, is the **BACKSPACE** key. It may be used to move the cursor to the left one position, or to erase the character to the left of the cursor.

INS, DEL

Two wide keys found at the bottom of the numeric keyboard are the INS and DEL key. **INS, or Insert,** is a toggle key. Sometimes, as you insert characters in the middle of a pre-typed line, the characters to the right of the cursor move over to let you insert the new characters. If you were to press the INS key, the characters you type replace the characters already there. If you were to press the INS key for the second time, the characters you type are inserted once more. The third time, they overstrike, and so on.

The **DEL** key is used by some software to delete the character at the cursor position.

The **Scroll Lock** key at the top right corner of the keyboard is not discussed.

DIFFERENCES FROM A TYPEWRITER

There are some distinct differences between a computer keyboard and that of an ordinary typewriter.

Character Wrap

On a typewriter, you must press the carriage return at the end of each line. On a computer, if you keep on typing past the right edge of the screen, the next character will appear on the next line down. This feature is called **character wrap.** It allows you to enter lines that are longer than the width of the screen, which is 80 characters.

Auto-Repeat

Another difference from a typewriter is the auto-repeat feature. If you press a key and hold it down, the character it generates starts to repeat.

Keys to Watch Out For

Some characters must be used precisely. On a typewriter, you can substitute one character for another if it looks similar. On a computer, you must type the exact key, since each key generates a unique signal to the computer. Specifically:

Lowercase letter L and number 1. If you want the number, use the key for number 1, which is just above the letter Q.

Letter O (oh) and number 0 (zero). Again, if you want the number, use the number key.

Single quote. Use the one on the key with the double quote. The one on the key with the tilde (~) should not be used.

Blank space. Use the space bar. There are other keys that generate a blank space on the screen, but those mean something different to the computer.

LEARN TO USE THE SOFTWARE

Each key generates a unique signal to the computer. The function of each key and its recognition by the computer depends on the software being used. Even the method used to correct your typing errors depends on the software being used. You should be getting the idea that, beyond turning it on, learning how to use a computer means learning how to use specific software.

BRIEF COMPARISONS

Since your computer was turned on earlier with the DOS disk in the disk drive, the commands the computer recognizes right now are DOS commands. As you prepare to use other software, a good starting point is to compare how some of the keys are used in DOS with the use of these keys in other software.

HOME	DOS does not recognize the HOME key.
	In WordPerfect, pressing the HOME key twice and the UP ARROW key moves the cursor to the beginning of the document. In SuperCalc, HOME sends the cursor to cell A1.
DEL	The DEL key is not recognized by DOS.
	WordPerfect uses the DEL key to erase the character at the cursor position. In SuperCalc, the DELETE key is used to erase characters.
Correction	Type in some characters. If you want to change what you entered, press the BACKSPACE key to go back, and then retype.

In WordPerfect, the DEL key is used to erase the character at the cursor position. The BACKSPACE key is used to erase the character to the left of the cursor. In SuperCalc, the DELETE key is used to erase characters.

Clearing Screen   In DOS, typing CLS and pressing the ENTER key clears the screen and sends the cursor to the top, left corner of the screen.

In WordPerfect, you erase the screen by pressing the Exit key, the F7 function key, then answering N to the question asking if you want to exit WordPerfect. In SuperCalc, you can clear your workspace by entering /ZY followed by ENTER.

Function Keys   In DOS, the F1 through F6 function keys have various editing uses.

Each software package has special uses for the various function keys.

Don't be frustrated or intimidated. If you type in the command for the wrong software, the computer usually responds with an error message indicating that it doesn't recognize what you typed. These errors do not harm the computer. And, most often, they do not affect whatever it is you are trying to accomplish by using the computer. The worst that can happen is that you might have to turn the computer off and start over.

At this time, you will end your lesson.

1. If you have not already done so, remove the disk from the drive and replace it in its protective envelope.

2. Turn OFF two switches: one for the computer and one for the monitor. The order in which you turn off the computer and monitor is not important.

Lesson 3

Disks and the Disk Drive

DISK CONTROLLER CARD

For this part of the manual, you need the DOS System disk and a **scratch** disk. A scratch disk is a blank disk or one whose content you no longer need. Formatting instructions are presented later in this lesson.

The IBM PC comes with one or more installed disk drives. Each disk drive must be connected to a disk interface board, otherwise known as the **disk controller card.** The disk controller card, in turn, is inserted into one of the expansion slots in the computer. If there is only one drive, it is known as drive A. If there are two drives, they are drives A and B.

IDENTIFYING DISK DRIVE

To select a disk drive for use under DOS, you give the letter of the drive followed by a colon. Drive A is referred to as **A:** or **a:,** for example.

DISK

The disks used with the IBM PC disk drives are 5-1/4-inch floppies. In this manual, floppy disks are referred to simply as **disks.** The accompanying illustration shows the parts of a disk.

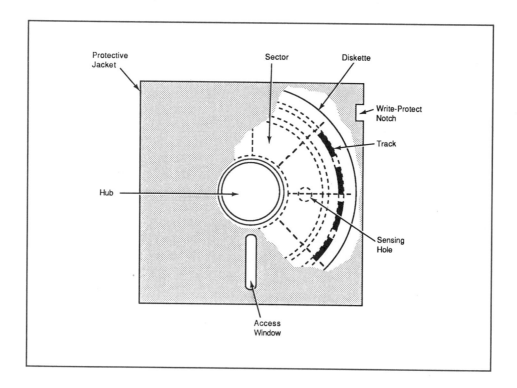

A disk stores data as magnetic spots on a circular piece of mylar that has an oxide coating. The disk is inside a protective jacket that should never be opened. In fact, you should never touch the surface of the disk. The oil from fingerprints, dust, smoke particles, or hair can damage the oxide coating and cause loss of information. The information is written on and read from the disk through the oval opening on the jacket. This opening is known as the **access window**.

Write-Protect Notch

There is a small notch on the side, known as the **write-protect notch.** If you cover the write-protect notch, the disk is protected from being written over or changed. When you purchase disks, metallic tabs are provided for this purpose. The computer can read the information from the disk even when the notch is covered. To write, however, you must uncover the write-protect notch.

Tracks, Sectors

Information is stored on disk along concentric recording positions known as **tracks.** The number of tracks recorded on a disk depends on the disk drive being used. A common number is 40, numbered from 0 to 39.

For convenience, each track is subdivided into storage areas called **sectors.** Each track and sector can be identified by number. Data items are accessed directly from the disk by identifying the track and sector numbers. The track and sector information is needed for retrieving data from a disk and is kept on the directory that controls the reading and writing of data on a disk.

Soft Sector, Hard Sector

On the disk surface, there is a small hole known as the **sensing hole,** which can be used to show the location of the first sector. As the disk spins inside the jacket, the sensing hole lines up with the little round opening on the jacket once every turn. Every time that happens, the disk drive can tell it has reached the beginning of the first sector. This type of disk, with just one sensing hole, is known as a **soft-sector** disk (as opposed to a **hard-sector** disk, which has sensing holes for every sector).

TERMS USED TO SPECIFY DISKS

The terms you should know if you are to purchase disks include:

Single-sided (SS) or double-sided (DS). Information can be stored only on one side of the disk (single) or on both sides (double).

Single-density (SD) or double-density (DD). Double density disks have a higher quality of recording surface, and can hold a greater density of data.

Soft-sector (SS) or hard-sector (HS). There is just one sensing hole on the disk (soft) or multiple holes (hard).

Reinforced hub (RH). There is reinforcement along the opening, or **hub.** This is optional, but it does help the disk to last longer.

You should consult the disk drive reference manual concerning the disk specifications for your computer. For IBM PC disk drives, you use either single or double sided disks, double density, soft sector, and optional reinforced hub.

CARE AND HANDLING OF DISKS

You must use care in handling disks. They are extremely fragile. Here are some suggestions for their care and handling:

- Always keep the disk in its envelope when it is not in use.

- Do not touch the surface of the disk or wipe the surface with rags or tissue paper.

- Do not let disks collect dust.

- Keep disks out of the sun and away from other sources of heat that can cause them to warp and/or lose data.

- Keep disks at least two feet away from magnetic fields, such as those generated by electrical motors, radios, television sets, tape recorders, and other devices. A strong magnetic field may erase information from a disk.

- When you write on a label already attached to the disk, use only a felt-tipped pen. Never use any sort of instrument with a sharp point.

- Store disks in a vertical position.

- Never bend disks or attach paper clips to them.

- Never open the drive door or remove a disk while the drive is running, that is, while the red light is on in front of the disk drive. If you do, you can damage your disk.

- Remove disks **before** you turn OFF the computer.

Because the disks are so fragile, you may want to create a backup for any information you store on a disk. That is, keep a second disk with the same information on it. This practice is discussed later.

DISK OPERATING SYSTEM

The computer program that controls information transfer between the computer and the disk drives is known as the **disk operating system,** or **DOS.** Some software provides its own set of instructions for interfacing with the disk drives, but most IBM PC software must be installed before it can be used. Installation involves transferring some programs from one disk to another. Each software package has step-by-step instructions on how to perform the installation.

BOOTING UP

To use the A drive, you have to load DOS into the computer. This process is known as **booting up.** Again, boot up the computer with the DOS System disk. You did this earlier in studying the keyboard.

1. If your monitor has a separate control, turn it ON. The computer should still be OFF.

2. Place the DOS System disk in drive A and close the drive door.

3. Turn the computer ON. The following message appears on the screen after a few seconds.

> Current date is Tue 1-01-1980
> Enter new date (mm-dd-yy):

> ¤ The computer offers you a chance to reset its internal calendar, which begins at 1-01-80 when the computer is booted up. The calendar format is month-day-year, with the numbers separated by hyphens. On September 29, 1987, for example, you can enter 9-29-87.

7. Enter the date, as shown above. Then, press the ENTER key. Another message appears on the screen:

> Current time is 0:00:41.24
> Enter new time:

> ¤ The computer offers you a chance to reset its internal clock, which started when it was booted up. The time format , using a 24-hour clock, is hours:minutes:seconds with the numbers separated by colons. If you want to set the clock at 2:35 p.m., you enter 14:35.

8. Enter the time, as shown above. Then press the ENTER key. The following message appears on the screen:

> The IBM Personal Computer DOS
> Version 3.10 (C)Copyright International Business
>   Machines Corp 1981, 1985
> (C)Copyright Microsoft Corp 1981, 1985

You may have a slightly different message, depending on the version of DOS you are using.

> ¤ Finally, the prompt appears. The prompt is the A> below the copyright message.

You have just done a **cold start.** A cold start involves turning the computer ON to let the disk boot up automatically.

You can reboot the computer when it is ON without turning the power switch off. This is done by holding down the CTRL and ALT keys while you press the DELETE key. This is called a **warm start,** since the computer already is on and warmed up.

DEFAULT DISK DRIVE

The prompt consists of two characters. Right now, the first character is an **A.** The second character is always a **>.** The purpose of the first character is to indicate the **default** disk drive, the drive the computer will use unless it is instructed otherwise. When you give a command, it may require the computer to get a file from the disk. If you want the computer to get a file from a disk in a drive other than the default drive, you must indicate the drive to be used. This will become clearer in the next section.

DOS COMMANDS

You should become familiar with some of the commands in DOS and how to specify disk drives. Even though each software system has its own way of doing things, much of the software for the IBM PC uses some of the DOS commands. Also, there are times when you want to prepare a disk to store data, examine the contents of a disk, or transfer files (for creating backup, for example), without going into any application software.

Some DOS commands are **internal** and others are **external.** Internal commands are transferred to memory when DOS is booted. This means that, once you load DOS by booting, you do not need to have the DOS disk in a drive to carry out these commands. External commands are on a disk as files. Therefore, the disk containing the command files (generally the DOS System disk) must be in a disk drive for the command to be carried out. The following commands are discussed briefly in this manual:

Internal Commands

DIR	Displays a directory with the names of all the files on the disk in the disk drive.
COPY	Copies a file.
ERASE	Erases a specified filename.
RENAME	Renames a file.

External command

FORMAT	Formats a disk.

An internal command can be issued by simply typing the proper entry. For an external command, you must specify which drive contains the System disk. If the drive that contains the System disk is the default drive, you may omit the drive specification. For example, you can use the DIR command simply by typing **DIR.** However, if the System disk is in drive B and the default drive is A, you must type B:FORMAT to issue the FORMAT command.

CHANGE DEFAULT DRIVE

Try some of these commands. As a starter, learn how to change the default drive:

1. Type **B:** and press ENTER to change the default disk drive from A to B.

   ¤ The prompt now reads **B>.** The prompt always indicates the default drive setting.

2. To change the default back to A, simply type A: and press ENTER.

FORMAT

Next, you need to know how to prepare a disk for use. When you buy blank disks, there is nothing on them. A disk must be **formatted** before you can record information on it. To format a disk means to prepare it to store information.

In WordPerfect and dBASE III Plus, you will need to have a formatted disk to store data. However, in SuperCalc lessons in this manual, you will be storing your data on the same disk that holds the software. There is no need to have a separate data disk. However, you may want to create a backup, or a second copy, of your data files on a separate data disk, just in case.

Some software provides instructions on how to format a disk from within the command set for that package. Other software packages require that your data disk already be formatted. The following is the procedure of formatting a disk in DOS with the FORMAT command.

1. Insert the DOS System disk in drive A. Make sure that the default drive is A.

   The FORMAT command is an external command. You must specify the drive on which the file that contains the FORMAT command can be found. Since the DOS System disk is in drive A and the default drive is A, you can just type FORMAT. Had the System disk been in drive B (with default still being A), you would have had to type B:FORMAT. On the other hand, if the default was B and the System disk was in A, you would have had to type A:FORMAT.

   As part of the FORMAT command, you also have to specify the disk drive in which you intend to insert the disk to be formatted. If it is to be in drive A, you type FORMAT A:, and if it is to be found in drive B, you type

FORMAT B:. If you do not specify this, the computer assumes that the new disk is in the default drive.

2. Type **FORMAT B:** and press the ENTER (or RETURN) key. The command can be typed in uppercase or lowercase, but there must be a space before the B. The screen displays the message:

```
Insert new diskette for drive B
and strike ENTER when ready
```

3. Insert a scratch disk in drive B. A scratch disk is either a blank disk or one whose contents you no longer need. You can reformat a disk that already contains information. However, when you do, the existing information is lost. Therefore, you must make sure that you no longer need the information on a disk before you reformat it.

4. Press ENTER to begin formatting. When the formatting is complete, the screen message shown may look as follows:

```
Formatting...Format  complete

362496  bytes  total  disk  space
362496  bytes  available  on  disk

Format  another  (Y/N)?
```

   □ DOS specifies that the disk is formatted for a total of 362496 bytes, or characters, and that all 362496 bytes are available for storing information. The program is ready to format another disk, if it is instructed to do so. You are to enter **Y** or **N**, depending on whether you want another disk formatted.

5. Enter **N** if you do not want to format any more disks and press ENTER.

6. Leave the newly formatted disk in drive B.

   □ The disk in drive B is formatted and ready for use. You cannot boot the computer with it, since it does not contain DOS, but it is ready to hold your data.

   □ To format a disk that can be used to boot the computer, you must use system parameter (/S) with the format command. That is, you type FORMAT B: /S. The disk formatted this way still does not contain external command files. Consult the DOS manual for details.

DIR COMMAND

To see what files are on a disk, use the DIR command. DIR is an internal command. You can issue it at any time after you have booted the computer. Again, you can specify the drive in which the disk to be examined is located. If none is specified, the default drive is assumed.

7. With drive A as the default, type DIR and press ENTER. The directory for the disk in drive A is displayed. If it is the DOS System disk, a display that resembles the accompanying screen appears.

```
A>dir

 Volume in drive A has no label
 Directory of  A:\

COMMAND   COM    17792   10-20-83    12:00p
ANSI      SYS     1664   10-20-83    12:00p
FORMAT    COM     6912   10-20-83    12:00p
CHKDSK    COM     6400   10-20-83    12:00p
SYS       COM     1680   10-20-83    12:00p
DISKCOPY  COM     2576   10-20-83    12:00p
DISKCOMP  COM     2188   10-20-83    12:00p
COMP      COM     2534   10-20-83    12:00p
EDLIN     COM     4608   10-20-83    12:00p
MODE      COM     3139   10-20-83    12:00p
FDISK     COM     6369   10-20-83    12:00p
BACKUP    COM     3687   10-20-83    12:00p
RESTORE   COM     4003   10-20-83    12:00p
PRINT     COM     4608   10-20-83    12:00p
RECOVER   COM     2304   10-20-83    12:00p
ASSIGN    COM      896   10-20-83    12:00p
TREE      COM     1513   10-20-83    12:00p
GRAPHICS  COM      789   10-20-83    12:00p
```

This display is not explained in detail in this manual. The things to note are that filenames appear in the first column and their extensions appear in the second column. The third column displays the file size and the fourth column displays the date the file was created.

The name on the first column often is the one used to retrieve a file for use by an application program. The extension on the second column often is assigned by the application program to distinguish the data file according to its use. For example, SuperCalc assigns the extension CAL to all its spreadsheet files. In referring to a file from DOS, however, you must use both the filename and its extension, separated by a period (.). So, a SuperCalc file called MYFILE must be referred to as MYFILE.CAL.

At this point you are probably still pretty hazy about terms like **file** and **filename.** Don't worry for the time being. These will become clearer to you as you go through the rest of this manual. To continue, turn the computer off, since you will not be doing anything else on the computer in this section.

8. Take the disks out of the drives.

9. Turn OFF the computer and monitor.

COPY COMMAND

To copy some files that are on one disk onto another, you use the COPY command. Although there are many options in copying files, only the procedures needed for making backup copies of a file are discussed here. That is, you will learn how to copy a file from one disk to another and to use either the same name or a different name.

The idea is that you have a disk that contains data files from which you want to make backup copies. You want to copy these data files onto the disk you formatted earlier. Since you do not yet have any data files, just remember this section for reference later when you are ready to make backup copies.

The following are the steps you follow:

1. Insert the disk containing the data files in drive A.

2. Insert the formatted disk in drive B.

3. Type **COPY A:filename B:** and press ENTER.

   ¤ The filename is the name of the file on the disk in drive A you want to copy onto the formatted disk in drive B. The filename used here must be the complete name (both the filename and the extension). When this command is entered, DOS creates a file by the same name on the disk in drive B and copies the contents to it. (The original file stays intact.) If there already is a file by the same name on the disk in drive B, it is overwritten; that is, the new information replaces the old.

If you want to copy a file on a disk in drive A (filename1) onto a file with a different name (filename2) on drive B, type **COPY A:filename1 B:filename2** and press ENTER.

You can use the DIR command to make sure that the file you copied has been recorded on the other disk.

ERASE COMMAND

To remove an unwanted file from a disk, you use the ERASE command. The format is **ERASE filename,** where the filename is the complete name of the file to be removed. As part of the filename, you also can specify the drive that holds the source file. For example, if you want to remove a file named FILE with the extension DBF from a disk in drive B, type ERASE B:FILE.DBF and press ENTER. If the drive is not specified, the default drive is assumed.

Care must be taken when you issue this command so that you don't inadvertently remove a file you want to keep.

RENAME COMMAND

The RENAME command is used to rename a file on a disk. Its format is **RENAME filename1 filename2,** where filename1 is the old name and filename2 is the new name. Again, these names must be complete names and may include the drive specification (for filename1). Otherwise, the file is assumed to be on the disk in the default drive.

It is best not to depend on the default drive setting. Get into the habit of specifying the drive with the filename. This will reduce accidental erasure of files and may eliminate many hours of frustration.

EXECUTING PROGRAMS

Whenever a program in this manual is to be executed, the following procedure must be followed:

1. Boot up the computer with a disk containing DOS.

2. Remove the DOS disk from drive A.

3. Insert the program disk in drive A. This might be the WordPerfect, SuperCalc, or the dBASE III Plus disk that is supplied with the manual.

4. For WordPerfect, change the default drive to B.

5. Type the program name and press ENTER. The program name is specified in each module, but they are A:WP for WordPerfect, SC3 for SuperCalc, and DBASE for dBASE III Plus. This loads the program into the main memory and starts to execute it.

   Now you are ready to tackle different software. Don't be afraid. If you can use your toaster, you can use a computer!

Lab Procedures

IMPORTANT THINGS TO REMEMBER

The following three, important suggestions are provided to guide you in the use of computer labs:

1. Read the lesson BEFORE you come to the lab.

2. NO SMOKING, DRINKING, or EATING in the lab.

3. In general, you should not turn the computer switch ON until you have a disk in the disk drive.

GETTING STARTED

1. Make sure you have all the disks you need for the lesson.

2. If you are using a printer, learn how it works before you start.

3. If you are using a disk to store data, make sure to label it promptly with a felt-tip pen. If the disk has to be formatted beforehand, do so.

4. If the monitor switch is separate from the computer power switch. Be sure to turn it ON.

5. Follow the instructions given in each lesson.

6. If you are to boot up the computer with a software disk, insert the disk containing the software in the disk drive. Turn the computer power switch ON.

DURING THE LESSON

1. Read before asking questions.

2. Be brave and try different things.

3. Enjoy.

AT THE END OF A LESSON

1. Make sure you have saved the information on a disk.

2. Remove disks from the drives, but not while the red light in front of the disk drive is ON.

3. Turn OFF both the monitor and the computer.

FAILURE CHECKLIST

Here are some common lab problems and their possible causes and solutions.

Nothing works. Check mechanical connections such as power cords and cables. If you suspect anything, report it to the aide or instructor.

Disk drive stays on continuously. 1. No disk in the drive. Turn the computer OFF and insert one. 2. Drive door not closed. Turn the computer OFF and close it.

Won't print. Make sure printer is turned ON and is ready to print.

File is not on the disk. 1. Read over the instructions on how to save a file. Some require that you verify your request to save, especially when you are saving with a filename that already exists on the disk. You may have to do the work over again. 2. You might have forgotten your filename. See the software instructions to find out how to look at all the filenames on disk or exit to DOS and use the DIR command.

I'm typing it right, but the computer gives me a "Bad command or file name" message. Check to see if you are pressing the SHIFT key when you should not; or not pressing it when you should.

Something is strange. 1. Read the instructions again. 2. Make sure you have the right disk in the right disk drive. 3. If all else fails, turn the computer OFF, reboot, and start again.

WordPerfect

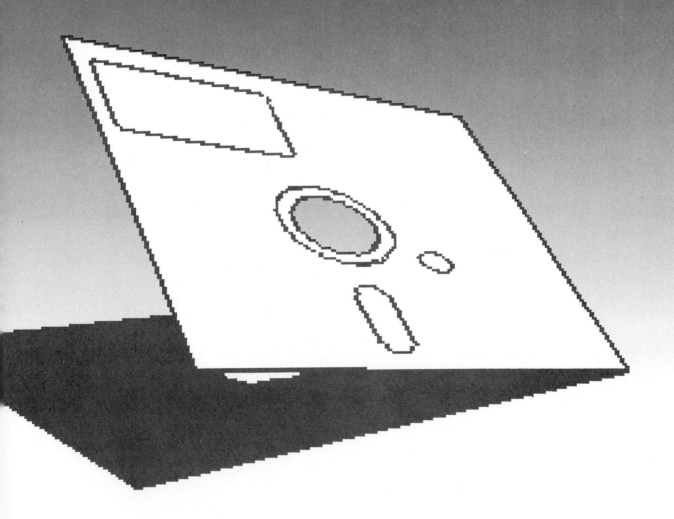

Lesson 1

ORIENTATION

In the next three lessons, you will get a taste of what you can do with a word processing program—in this case one called **WordPerfect.** A word processing program helps you create, modify, and print text. You can:

◻ Insert, delete, or change characters, words, lines, or whole chapters in a document.

◻ Print out a text in a printing format adjusted to your specifications, includ‐ ing automatic page numbering, headers, and footers.

◻ Print out form letters or other repetitive documents, with names, addresses, and other personalizing information inserted.

STARTING OFF

1. Insert the WordPerfect program disk in drive A and a formatted data disk in drive B.

2. Following the DOS A> prompt, type **B:** and press ENTER to change the default drive to B.

   In this way, when WordPerfect needs the data disk to store or retrieve documents, it looks automatically at the disk in drive B.

31

3. Type **A:WP** and press ENTER. The A, W, and P can be entered either in upper- or lowercase letters.

□ The WordPerfect 4.2 Training Version copyright message and the explanation on how the training version differs from the regular version appear on the screen.

The training version is limited in the following ways:

- Saved documents are limited in size to about 4000 characters.

- Printed output is unlimited, but occasionally contains the notation ***WPC**.

- Advanced printing features are not available.

- You cannot select a printer. LPT1 (PRN) is the only port that can be used for printing.

4. Press any key to continue.

□ A welcome message from WordPerfect is displayed. In a regular version of WordPerfect, this screen is not displayed once a printer has been selected (for use with your copy of WordPerfect). Since the training version does not allow you to select the printer, this screen is displayed every time.

If you have a template for the function keys, place it over the function keys.

If you do not have a template, press the F3 function key. You will see a display of what a template shows. When you are satisfied, press the SPACE BAR to return to a normal screen.

5. Press any key to continue. You will see the following:

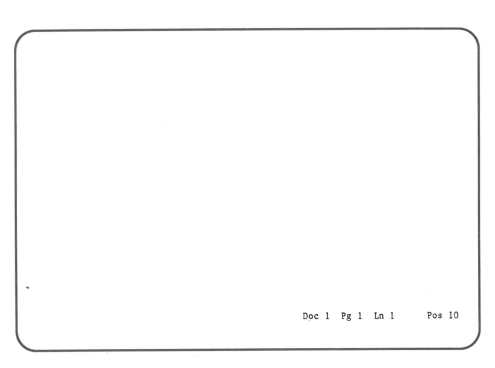

Doc 1   Pg 1   Ln 1   Pos 10

This is the screen on which you can enter new text, review what you have already entered, or change what is there. Of course, since you have not entered anything yet, it is blank.

The blinking underline character is the **cursor.** The cursor shows the position on the screen at which your entries are made.

The bottom line of the screen is the **status line.** The status line displays the position of the cursor. It is currently on page 1 of the first document. You can work on two documents at the same time in WordPerfect. This feature is illustrated in the next lesson. The cursor is on line 1, but position (or column) is 10! Why is it not on position 0 or 1? This is because of the default settings for the left and right margins, which are 10 and 74 respectively. WordPerfect presets certain screen and page formats so that you can just start typing. These settings can be changed at any time, but do not worry about this right now because this topic, too, is discussed in detail in the next lesson.

ENTERING TEXT

To enter text, use your IBM PC just as you would a typewriter. As you enter a character, it appears at the cursor position, and the cursor moves to the right one position. However, unlike the keyboard on a typewriter, this keyboard does not require entry of a carriage return as you fill up a line on the screen. Just keep on typing because, when the cursor gets beyond the right margin (remember the default setting), it will reappear at the left margin setting, one line down. When you come to the end of a paragraph, the ENTER key must be pressed. The ENTER key breaks the line and moves the cursor to the left margin, one line down. You have to press the ENTER key once at the end of a paragraph or twice if you want to insert a blank line between paragraphs in the text.

If your text fills up the screen, the text will **scroll up**—that is, a new line will appear at the bottom of the screen, and the uppermost line will disappear from view.

CORRECTING ERRORS

If you make a mistake when you are typing text, you may delete unwanted characters by pressing the BACKSPACE key, which is the left arrow key found just above the ENTER key. You can then retype the text.

UPPERCASE LETTERS

To enter uppercase letters, simply hold the SHIFT (large up arrow) key down while you press the character—as you would on a typewriter. If you want to type several characters in uppercase, as when you enter a title, press the CAPS LOCK key, just as you would do with the shift lock key on a typewriter. To get back into lowercase, simply press the CAPS LOCK key again. When you enter certain special characters, you have to hold the SHIFT key down regardless of whether the CAPS LOCK key has been pressed.

You can tell whether you are in the uppercase mode or lowercase mode by looking at the word **Pos** on the status line. When you are in the uppercase mode, the word appears in all uppercase, that is **POS**. When you are in the lowercase mode, it appears as **Pos**.

PRACTICE TIME 1-1

Enter the following text:

```
The concept behind word processing is a fascinating
one. The typewriter has become archaic, stricken by a
single technological blow—the technology made possible
by invention of the microprocessor. The concepts of
training and productivity have changed, too. The more
productive worker is the one who can insert text
changes, make corrections, and otherwise process text
rewrites efficiently. We no longer train people to
type 60-plus words per minute, error free.
```

As you typed in this paragraph, you might have noticed the phenomenon called **word wrap**. This means that as the text gets to the right margin, a word that is too long to fit on the line is moved down to the next line. Words are not split between two lines. This feature is included to make reading and text creation easier.

WORDPERFECT COMMANDS

Before you go any further, look at the way commands are entered in WordPerfect. Commands are the way you get the attention of the WordPerfect program. Many of the commands are given through use of the function keys, by themselves or in conjunction with the **Ctrl**, **Shift**, and **Alt** keys. When you see CTRL/F3, for example, you are to hold down the key marked **Ctrl** and press the F3 function key; and when you see ALT/F4, you hold down the key marked **Alt** and press the F4 function key.

This is where a function key template helps you. It is hard to remember what combination generates which key. If you place the template over the function keyboard, there is no need to memorize all the combinations.

There are other keys, such as arrow keys on the numeric keyboard, that also are used to issue commands, again either by themselves or in conjunction with the three keys previously mentioned.

Some commands are toggles. That means the command turns a feature ON and OFF each time you enter it. Others display a menu. A menu, like a menu in a restaurant, offers a choice of commands for the user. Still other commands begin a feature that is ended when the ENTER key is pressed. Some commands require additional information from you, such as a name to call a document.

If the command requires that you enter a number in response to a menu, use the numbers at the top of the keyboard, and not the ones on the numeric keyboard.

If you make a mistake and press the wrong command, you can "undo" the command in most cases by pressing the cancel key, which is the **F1** function key.

Not all commands are covered in this manual. Furthermore, the manual explains just what is needed for a particular lesson. Many options and features are available in WordPerfect which can be explored on your own after you understand the basic commands.

CURSOR MOVEMENT

Suppose, as you read what you typed earlier, you find a mistake or, better yet, you decide to change the text to include an improvement. If the change you want to make is at the beginning of the text, and if you use the BACKSPACE key to erase all unwanted characters starting at the cursor position, you will have to retype almost the whole text. This is no improvement over using a typewriter. A word processor has a better way. But, to make corrections like this, you need to learn how to move the cursor without affecting the text.

Press the UP ARROW key. The cursor moves up one line. Press the RIGHT ARROW key. The cursor moves to the right one position.

To move the cursor, use the four arrow keys located on the numeric keyboard to the right of the main keyboard. The cursor will move in the direction of the arrow, one position at a time.

If you have a long text, you cannot see all of it on the screen at any one time. With the UP and DOWN ARROW keys, you can read new information or retrieve information that has scrolled off the screen. If you keep on pressing the UP ARROW key, the screen will scroll down (that is, new lines will appear at the top); and if you keep on pressing the DOWN ARROW key, the screen will scroll up (new lines will appear at the bottom).

It also is possible to move the cursor a little faster. All you have to do is hold the key down, and the key will start repeating. If you hold down the DOWN ARROW key, the cursor will zoom down the page. You can return to the top of the page using the UP ARROW key. You will notice, however, that you cannot move the cursor past the beginning or the end of the text.

PRACTICE TIME 1-2

Try using the up, down, right, and left cursor movement commands.

You can move the cursor to the left or right, one word at a time, by holding down the CTRL key and pressing the LEFT and RIGHT ARROW keys, respectively.

PRACTICE TIME 1-3

1. Position the cursor on the *a* in "and" on the fourth line of the text.

```
The concept behind word processing is a fascinating one.  The
typewriter has become archaic, stricken by a single technological
blow--the technology made possible by invention of the
microprocessor.  The concepts of training and productivity have
changed, too.  The more productive worker is the one who can
insert text changes, make corrections, and otherwise process text
rewrites efficiently.  We no longer train people to type 60-plus
words per minute, error free.




                                        Doc 1  Pg 1  Ln 4      Pos 52
```

2. Enter CTRL/RIGHT ARROW repeatedly until the cursor reaches the end of the text.

3. Now, enter CTRL/LEFT ARROW repeatedly until the cursor is at the beginning of the text.

You can move the cursor to the beginning of the document by pressing the **HOME** key twice and then pressing the **UP ARROW** key, and to the end of the document by pressing the **HOME** key twice and then pressing the **DOWN ARROW** key.

PRACTICE TIME 1-4

1. Move the cursor to the end and then to the beginning of the document.

2. Place the cursor somewhere in the middle of the document.

3. Press the *HOME* key twice, then press either the *LEFT ARROW* or the *RIGHT ARROW* key. Do this several times, alternating LEFT and *RIGHT ARROW* keys. What happens?

You also can scroll the text up or down one page at a time by using the **PgUp** and **PgDn** keys, found on the numeric keyboard. The text you see on the screen right now is not long enough for you to try these keys. Just remember them for the future.

DELETING TEXT

As you recall, if you make a mistake in typing text, you can correct it immediately in this way:

◻ Press the BACKSPACE key to remove unwanted characters.

◻ Type the correct text.

You may delete unwanted characters anywhere in the text in this way:

◻ Move the cursor to the immediate right of the characters you wish to delete.

◻ Press the BACKSPACE key to erase unwanted characters.

◻ Type the correct text.

The BACKSPACE key removes the character to the left of the cursor. You can remove the character the cursor is on in this way:

◻ Press the Delete (**DEL**) key, which is found on the bottom right corner of the keyboard.

◻ Remove the word the cursor is on by holding down the **CTRL** key and pressing **BACKSPACE**.

◻ Remove the text from the cursor to the end of line by entering **CTRL/End**, that is, hold down the **CTRL** key and press the **END** key, found on the numeric keyboard.

RETRIEVING DELETED TEXT

If you realize you didn't mean to remove the text after you've deleted it, you can restore it by using the Cancel key, which is the **F1** function key. WordPerfect saves up to three deletions. When you restore the text, however, it is inserted at the cursor position, not where you deleted the text.

1. Position the cursor at the beginning of the document using **HOME, HOME,** and **UP ARROW** keys.

2. Delete the first line of text by using **CTRL/END**. Do not move the cursor.

3. Press the **F1** function key.

   ◻ The deleted line re-appears, highlighted. The following message appears at the bottom of the screen:

   `Undelete 1 Restore; 2 Show Previous Deletion: 0`

   Your options are:

   0 Cancel the command. Just press ENTER.
   1 Restore the highlighted text at the cursor position.
   2 Show what was deleted previously.

3. You want to restore this text. Type **1** (do not press ENTER).

   ◻ The text is restored.

MOVING TEXT

If you want to move a section of text, or **block** of text, such as a sentence, from one location to another, you must first mark the block.

You will now mark the last sentence you entered ("We no longer train people to type 60-plus words per minute, error free.") and place it after the third sentence.

1. Move the cursor to the first character of the last sentence; that is, to the character **W** of the word "We."

2. Enter the Block command, which is **ALT/F4** (hold down the ALT key and press the F4 function key).

   ◻ The word **Block on** flashes on the status line.

3. Move the cursor to the blank space immediately following the last sentence.

   ◻ The last sentence is now highlighted. That is, the block is marked.

   If you marked the wrong block, just press the Cancel key—the F1 function key. Then you can repeat steps 1 to 3.

```
The concept behind word processing is a fascinating one.  The
typewriter has become archaic, stricken by a single technological
blow--the technology made possible by invention of the
microprocessor.  The concepts of training and productivity have
changed, too.  The more productive worker is the one who can
insert text changes, make corrections, and otherwise process text
rewrites efficiently.  We no longer train people to type 60-plus
words per minute, error free._




Block on                              Doc 1  Pg 1  Ln 8      Pos 39
```

4. Enter the Move command, which is **CTRL/F4**. The following message is
   displayed on the status line:

   1 Cut Block; 2 Copy Block; 3 Append; 4 Cut/Copy
   Column; 5 Cut/Copy Rectangle: 0

   WordPerfect is asking if you want to "cut" the block or "copy" the block,
   among other options that are not discussed here. When you "cut" a block, it
   is physically moved out of the present location; whereas when you "copy,"
   the original text stays where it is and a copy of it can be inserted
   elsewhere.

5. You want to "cut" it. Type **1** (do not press ENTER).

   □ The block disappears.

6. Move the cursor to where you want to insert this sentence. In your case, to
   the space just before the fourth sentence—that is, immediately before the
   word "The."

7. Enter the Move command, **CTRL/F4,** again. The following message
   appears:

   Move 1 Sentence; 2 Paragraph; 3 Page;
   Retrieve 4 Column; 5 Text; 6 Rectangle: 0

8. You are retrieving text, or option **5**. Type **5** (no ENTER).

  ▫ The marked block is moved to the cursor position.

```
The concept behind word processing is a fascinating one.  The
typewriter has become archaic, stricken by a single technological
blow--the technology made possible by invention of the
microprocessor.  The concepts of training and productivity have
changed, too. We no longer train people to type 60-plus words per
minute, error free. The more productive worker is the one who can
insert text changes, make corrections, and otherwise process text
rewrites efficiently.




                                        Doc 1  Pg 1  Ln 5      Pos 24
```

You may have to insert or delete spaces to make the document look good, but do not be concerned about the text format right now.

PRACTICE TIME 1-5

Mark the sentence just moved above. Then, move it back to its original position.

BLOCK

Block is used for much more than just moving text. Once you mark a block, you can make the whole block appear in uppercase or lowercase, make the block come out in bold characters or underlined, delete the block, and much, much more. Refer to the WordPerfect manual to learn these features. Right now, you will delete a block.

1. Mark the text "—the technology made possible by invention of the microprocessor."

```
    The concept behind word processing is a fascinating one.  The
    typewriter has become archaic, stricken by a single technological
    blow--the technology made possible by invention of the
    microprocessor._ The concepts of training and productivity have
    changed, too.  The more productive worker is the one who can
    insert text changes, make corrections, and otherwise process text
    rewrites efficiently.  We no longer train people to type 60-plus
    words per minute, error free.




    Block on                            Doc 1  Pg 1  Ln 4      Pos 24
```

2. Press the **BACKSPACE** key. The following message appears on the status line:

Delete Block (Y/N) N

The cursor will be on **N**. If you just press ENTER, you have answered N.

3. You want to delete the block, so you have to answer Y. Type **Y** (but do not press ENTER).

   ▫ The block is deleted.

Even this block can be restored by using the F1 function key.

INSERTING TEXT

If you need to insert a word in the middle of a sentence, or a sentence in the middle of a paragraph, position the cursor where you want to begin inserting the text, then look at the status line. If you see the word **Typeover**, press the Insert (**INS**) key found to the left of the DEL key. When you press the INS key, the word **Typeover** disappears. Then you can start typing whatever you want to insert at the cursor position.

When **Typeover** is not on, any text in "front" of the cursor (to the right) is pushed across the line to make room for your insertion. When Typeover is on, however, the character you type replaces the character the cursor is on.

The Insert is a toggle command. The feature is turned on and off each time you press the INS key.

PRACTICE TIME 1-6

1. Place the cursor at the blank space after the word "corrections," in the second to the last sentence.

2. Insert " *move blocks of text,*". (Do not move the cursor.)

REWRITE THE SCREEN

You probably noticed that, as you inserted characters, the text in front of the cursor was pushed across the line but not down to the next line. As a result, some of the text was not visible on the screen. However, you will notice that, as soon as you move the cursor, the screen is rewritten so that the changes fit into the format of specified margins.

So, press any arrow key.

```
The concept behind word processing is a fascinating one.  The
typewriter has become archaic, stricken by a single technological
blow.  The concepts of training and productivity have changed,
too.  The more productive worker is the one who can insert text
changes, make corrections, move block of text, and otherwise
process text rewrites efficiently.  We no longer train people to
type 60-plus words per minute, error free.




                                    Doc 1  Pg 1  Ln 5      Pos 57
```

SAVING YOUR WORK

The text that you have just entered is stored in the main memory of the computer. If you quit for the day and turn off the computer, you will lose that text. To keep the text for future use, you must save your file on a disk.

There are a couple of ways to save your work. One method is shown now; another is covered in the next lesson.

1. Press the Exit key, which is the **F7** function key. The following message appears on the status line:

   Save Document? (Y/N) Y

   The cursor will be on Y. You want to save the document. You can simply press ENTER.

2. Press ENTER. The following appears on the status line:

   Document to be Saved:

   You are to enter a name under which the document is to be saved.

A valid name for the document, known as the filename, is one to eight characters in length, followed by an optional extension. The extension is a period (.) and one to three additional characters. Do not use an asterisk (*), colon (:), or question mark (?) in your filename and do not begin a filename with a period.

Use the name **MYFILE**.

3. Type **MYFILE** and press ENTER.

   ▫ The message **Saving B:\MYFILE** appears on the status line as the red light in front of disk drive B goes on.

   ▫ When the light in front of the drive goes off, the following message appears on the status line:

   ```
   Exit WP? (Y/N) N
   (Cancel to return to document)
   ```

   WordPerfect is asking if you want to exit the WordPerfect program. If you answer Y, you are back in DOS. If you answer N, you remain in WordPerfect but the document you are working on is erased from the main memory. That is, you are ready to start on another document. If you want to stay in WordPerfect and continue working on the same document, press the Cancel key, the F1 function key.

4. Select **N** so that you remain in WordPerfect but with a clean sheet of paper. Then press ENTER.

   ▫ A blank WordPerfect screen appears.

   Many people who are saving a file for the first time worry about whether the file has really been saved on the disk. You can check the disk directory first to see if your file's name is on it. Then you can check the contents of the file by loading it back into the computer.

5. Enter the List Files command, which is the **F5** function key. The status line displays the following message:

   ```
   Dir  B:\*.*
   ```

   The cursor will be on B.

   WordPerfect is asking if you want to display files on the disk in drive B. You do.

6. Press ENTER.

    □   A list showing the files stored on the disk in drive B is displayed.

```
11/22/86  19:51              Directory B:\*.*
Document Size:          0                          Free Disk Space:    361472

. <CURRENT>      <DIR>                   .. <PARENT>      <DIR>
MYFILE                  425  11/22/86 19:50
```

```
1 Retrieve; 2 Delete; 3 Rename; 4 Print; 5 Text In;
6 Look; 7 Change Directory; 8 Copy; 9 Word Search; 0 Exit: 6
```

MYFILE, as you can see, is one of the files stored on the disk. So there is a file with your filename on the disk. Does that mean it is the right file? You can check the content by retrieving it, or loading it back in the main memory.

7. Use the arrow keys to highlight listing for MYFILE.

8. The options presented at the bottom of the screen show that **1** is used to retrieve the document. Type **1** (no ENTER).

    □   The text appears on the screen. This text file is stored on the disk. It will not be erased even when you turn the computer off. You can always load it back into the computer (booted with the IBM DOS and running WordPerfect) by using the series of commands described earlier. You will be using this file during the next lesson.

TERMINATING YOUR SESSION

This is the end of this lesson. There is no need to save the text again. You will use the following procedure to quit.

1. Enter the Exit command, **F7**.

2. Type **N** to indicate that you do not wish to save the document.

3. Type **Y** to indicate that you want to exit WordPerfect.

4. When you see the DOS prompt, remove the disks from the disk drives.

5. Turn OFF both the monitor and the computer.

Lesson 2

ORIENTATION

At the end of this lesson, you will use all the WordPerfect commands you have learned to enter a text on the computer. After you enter it, you will save the text on a disk and get a printout (hard copy).

There are, however, some additional things you need to learn first. For one thing, you need to know how to get a printout of the text. You also need to learn some commands that will cause your computer to print the text in the format you want.

Your IBM PC should be booted up with the DOS and WordPerfect started (type A:WP at the B> prompt), with the data disk from the last lesson in drive B.

You will start by getting a printout. You can get a printout of a document that is on the computer (one that has been retrieved and is displayed on the screen) or a document that is stored on the disk. Right now, you will print a document that is stored by the computer.

PRINTOUT OF A STORED DOCUMENT

Begin by retrieving a document file from disk into memory. The file to retrieve is MYFILE, which you saved at the end of the last lesson. You retrieved it once before, at the end of the last lesson, by using the List Files command, F5, and the retrieve option. You will use a different method this time.

1. Enter the Retrieve command which is **SHIFT/F10**.

   ◻ The message **Document to be Retrieved:** appears on the status line.

2. You are to enter the name of the file you need. Type **MYFILE** and press ENTER.

   ◻ The text from the previous lesson is displayed on the screen.

3. Make sure that your printer is turned ON and is ready to use.

4. Enter the Print command, which is **SHIFT/F7.** The following is displayed on the status line:

   ```
   1 Full text; 2 Page; 3 Options; 4 Printer Control;
   5 Type-thru; 6 Preview: 0
   ```

   Option 6 will let you see on the screen what your document will look like when it is printed.

5. You want to print the entire document, which is option 1. Type **1** (no ENTER).

   ◻ The text for MYFILE starts to print. Notice the word ***WPC**, which is inserted by the training version of WordPerfect.

FORMAT OPTIONS

You might have noticed that the text was printed just about the way it was displayed on the screen. The only difference is that the text is "right justified," or aligned at the right margin by having the proper number of spaces embedded between words. Since the screen display and print formats you used were preset by WordPerfect (you were using the default settings), the format you got may have been different from what you had in mind.

You can change any of the default settings by entering **codes** in the document. There are different codes that set margins, spacing, tab settings, and other elements of a document. These codes tell WordPerfect how the document should look on the screen or on the printout. Codes are embedded in the text and affect the text that follows, until another code is embedded to change the format again. It is possible to view both the text and the embedded codes at any time, and you will be doing this a little later. You can delete embedded codes just as you would delete any character.

There are three different formats to consider: line format, page format, and print format. Line format includes tab settings, margins, and spacing. Page format includes the size of printed page, top margin, vertical centering of text, and page numbering. Print format includes lines per inch and justification (alignment of text on the right margin). The latter two formats do not affect the way the text is displayed on the screen, just the way it is printed.

Line Format

You will work with line format first.

1. Enter the Line Format command, which is **SHIFT/F8**. The following is displayed on the status line:

   ```
   1 2 Tabs; 3 Margins; 4 Spacing; 5 Hyphenation;
   6 Align Char: 0
   ```

2. You want to look at three items: tabs, margins, and spacing. Type 1 (no ENTER) to look at tabs.

   ¤ The following appears on the bottom half of the screen.

   ```
   The concept behind word processing is a fascinating one.  The
   typewriter has become archaic, stricken by a single technological
   blow.  The concepts of training and productivity have changed,
   too.  The more productive worker is the one who can insert text
   changes, make corrections, move block of text, and otherwise
   process text rewrites efficiently.  We no longer train people to
   type 60-plus words per minute, error free.
   ```

   ```
   L....L....L....L....L....L....L....L....L....L....L....L....L....L....L....L...
   01234567890123456789012345678901234567890123456789012345678901234567890123456 78
            20        30        40        50        60        70        80
   Delete EOL (clear tabs); Enter number (set tab); Del (clear tab);
   Left; Center; Right; Decimal; .= Dot leader; Press EXIT when done.
   ```

A ruler line is shown that displays all column numbers. On the dotted line, "L" entries indicate where the tabs are set initially. They are preset for every five spaces. To set a tab, all you have to do is to type the column number. To clear a tab, you move the cursor to the L you wish to delete and press the DEL key. If you want to clear all tabs, enter the Delete EOL command which is **CTRL/END**.

3. Press the Exit key, **F7**, to exit the tab screen.

   If you want to see the tab settings while you are working on a document, you can display the **tab-ruler line** at the bottom of the screen.

4. Enter the Screen command, which is **CTRL/F3**. The following options appear on the status line:

   ```
   0 Rewrite; 1 Window; 2 Line Draw;
   3 Ctrl/Alt keys; 4 Colors; 5 Auto Rewrite: 0
   ```

   The message and options displayed are not explained here, since they do not pertain to the current topic.

5. Type **1** (no ENTER) for Window.

   ▫ The message **# Lines in this Window: 24** appears on the status line.

6. Press the **UP ARROW** key, then ENTER.

   ▫ The Tab-Ruler line is displayed at the bottom of the screen.

```
The concept behind word processing is a fascinating one.  The
typewriter has become archaic, stricken by a single technological
blow.  The concepts of training and productivity have changed,
too.  The more productive worker is the one who can insert text
changes, make corrections, move block of text, and otherwise
process text rewrites efficiently.  We no longer train people to
type 60-plus words per minute, error free.




B:\MYFILE                            Doc 1  Pg 1  Ln 1      Pos 10
[    ▲    ▲   ▲    ▲    ▲   ▲    ▲    ▲    ▲   ▲    ▲  ]▲    ▲    ▲
```

A triangle indicates a tab setting; a bracket ([or]) indicates a margin setting. When a tab and margin setting are in the same position, a brace ({ or }) is displayed.

Leave the tab-ruler line on the screen as you look at the margin settings.

7. Place the cursor at the beginning of the document using **HOME, HOME,** and **UP ARROW**.

8. Enter the Line format command, **SHIFT/F8**.

9. Type **3** to look at the margin settings. The following is displayed on the status line:

    [Margin Set] 10 74 to Left =

The default setting for the left margin is 10 and the right margin is 74. Change them to 20 and 60.

10. Type **20** and press ENTER.

    □ Now a prompt asks for the right margin.

11. Type **60** and press ENTER.

    □ The first column of the screen is now the column 20 of the printed document. The width of the text on the screen shrinks.

    □ The tab-ruler line indicates the new margin settings as braces, since they fall at the same positions as tabs.

The margin settings will remain at 20 and 60 until you embed new codes to change them. If you want to know what the margin settings are at a specific position in the text, leave the tab-ruler line in view at the bottom of the screen and move the cursor to that position. The tab-ruler line always indicates the tab and margin settings at the cursor position.

Next, you are ready to look at one more item in the Line format: spacing.

12. Enter **SHIFT/F8** and type **4**.

    □ The message **[Spacing Set] 1** appears on the status line. It is now on single spacing, or 1. If you want double spacing, type 2; if you want triple spacing, type 3. You can try changing it on your own. Just make sure to set it back to 1 before going on.

Page Format

1. Enter the Page Format command, which is **ALT/F8**.

   ¤ The following page format menu is displayed.

```
Page Format

        1 - Page Number Position

        2 - New Page Number

        3 - Center Page Top to Bottom

        4 - Page Length

        5 - Top Margin

        6 - Headers or Footers

        7 - Page Number Column Positions

        8 - Suppress for Current page only

        9 - Conditional End of Page

        A - Widow/Orphan

Selection: 0
```

2. You will look at the page length and top margin to examine the default values. Type **4**.

   ¤ The following is displayed.

```
Page Length

      1 - Letter Size Paper: Form Length = 66 lines (11 inches)
          Single Spaced Text lines = 54 (This includes lines
          used for Headers, Footers and/or page numbers.)

      2 - Legal Size Paper: Form Length = 84 lines (14 inches)
          Single Spaced Text Lines = 72 (This includes lines
          used for Headers, Footers and/or page numbers.)

      3 - Other (Maximum page length = 108 lines.)

Current Settings

      Form Length in Lines (6 per inch):  66

      Number of Single Spaced Text Lines: 54




Selection: 0
```

Currently the settings are 66 for page length and 54 lines of text per page. If you want to change the setting, you can type 1 (letter paper, which is the current setting), 2 (for legal size paper), or 3 (if you'd like to set it to something else). Since you do not wish to change any setting, just press ENTER.

3. Press ENTER.

   ◻ The page format menu appears again.

4. Type **5**.

   ◻ The message **Set half-lines (12/inch) from 12 to** appears on the bottom line.

   The top margin is currently set to 1 inch. Again, you do not wish to change this default.

5. Press the Exit key, **F7**, twice to get back to the document.

Print Format

1. Enter the Print Format command, which is **CTRL/F8**.

   ◻ The following print format menu appears on the screen.

```
Print Format
      1 - Pitch                        10
          Font                          1

      2 - Lines per Inch                6

   Right Justification                 On
      3 - Turn off
      4 - Turn on

   Underline Style                      5
      5 - Non-continuous Single
      6 - Non-continuous Double
      7 - Continuous Single
      8 - Continuous Double

      9 - Sheet Feeder Bin Number       1

      A - Insert Printer Command

      B - Line Numbering               Off

Selection: 0
```

The number of characters per inch is the **Pitch**. **Right Justification** determines if the right margin will be aligned. As you can see, the pitch is **10**. That is, currently, the printer prints 10 characters to an inch, and the Right Justification is ON. Although the screen display does not reflect it, when the document is printed, the right margin is made even by inserting the required number of spaces between words.

You want to change the justification setting.

1. Type **3** to select "no justification."

   ◻ The word **ON** that appeared to the right of Right Justification changed to **OFF**.

2. Press ENTER to get out of the Page Format menu.

PRACTICE TIME 2-1

1. Get a printout of the document on the computer and compare it with the previous printout.

2. Change the Right Justification back to ON (by typing 4 on the Print Format menu).

REVEALING CODES

Before going any further, you want to look at the embedded codes.

1. Enter the Reveal Codes command, which is **ALT/F3**.

    ¤   The tab-ruler line moves to the middle of the screen, and beneath it is the same text that appears above the tab-ruler line, except with embedded codes revealed.

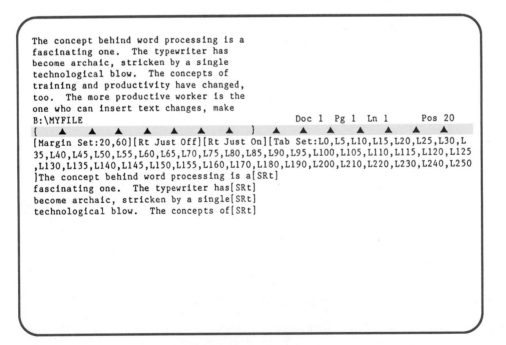

```
The concept behind word processing is a
fascinating one.  The typewriter has
become archaic, stricken by a single
technological blow.  The concepts of
training and productivity have changed,
too.  The more productive worker is the
one who can insert text changes, make
B:\MYFILE                              Doc 1  Pg 1  Ln 1      Pos 20
{     ▲    ▲    ▲    ▲    ▲    ▲    }    ▲    ▲    ▲    ▲    ▲    ▲
[Margin Set:20,60][Rt Just Off][Rt Just On][Tab Set:L0,L5,L10,L15,L20,L25,L30,L
35,L40,L45,L50,L55,L60,L65,L70,L75,L80,L85,L90,L95,L100,L105,L110,L115,L120,L125
,L130,L135,L140,L145,L150,L155,L160,L170,L180,L190,L200,L210,L220,L230,L240,L250
]The concept behind word processing is a[SRt]
fascinating one.  The typewriter has[SRt]
become archaic, stricken by a single[SRt]
technological blow.  The concepts of[SRt]
```

You can see the codes embedded in the rest of the document by scrolling. Use the arrow keys.

The only setting you've changed so far was the margin and it was done at the beginning of the document. Thus, the code **[Margins Set:20,60]** is embedded in the text. Other settings that you looked at but did not change, such as TAB, embedded a long code. Since you turned the justification ON and then OFF, you see **[Rt Just OFF]** followed by **[Rt Just ON]**. If you changed spacing, there are codes indicating that, too. The code **[HRt]** (Hard Return) shows where you pressed the ENTER key. The code **[SRt]** (Soft Return) shows where the wordwrap took place.

The current cursor position is indicated by a blinking underline. The cursor location code moves around when you move the cursor with the arrow keys. It is even possible to move the cursor in between different codes.

It was mentioned earlier that it is possible to remove an embedded code as though it were a character. Use this capability to clean up this mess. You will start by changing the margin settings back to the default value.

2. Place the cursor to the right of the margin code, **[Margins Set:20,60]**. Use the arrow keys.

3. Press the **BACKSPACE** key.

   ◻ The margin code disappears and the text above the tab-ruler line widens. When you deleted the code for the new margin setting, the text went back to the default margin setting, which is 10,74.

PRACTICE TIME 2-2

Delete some other codes as well, such as [Tab Set...], [Rt Just Off], [Rt Just On], etc. Leave [HRt] and [SRt] only.

4. Press the **SPACE BAR**, to return to normal screen.

SWITCH SCREEN

To illustrate the remaining topics in this manual, you will start a second document without erasing the first from the main memory.

1. Enter the Switch command, which is **SHIFT/F3**.

   ◻ A blank WordPerfect screen appears. Notice the status line. You are now in **Doc 2**.

You can switch from one document to the other by using the Switch command.

2. Shift back to **Doc 1** by entering **SHIFT/F3**.

   ◻ The first document is displayed again. You can work on it if you choose to do so.

3. Shift back to **Doc 2**. You will enter a new document.

LINE INDENTATION

Suppose you want to indent the first line of a paragraph five spaces. You accomplish this by setting the tab stop five spaces in from the left margin. Then, before you type the text, you press the TAB key, just as you would on a typewriter.

The default setting for the tab is every five positions, as you can see on the tab-ruler line.

1. Enter the following text. Make sure to indent the first line of the paragraph five spaces by using the TAB key.

```
    When a computer is instructed to do a job, it handles
the task in a very special way. It accepts the
information. It stores the information until it is ready
to use it. It processes the information. Then it gives
out the processed information.
```

Now look at the embedded codes to see what was inserted.

2. Enter the Reveal Codes command, **ALT/F3**.

   ◻ The following is displayed below the tab-ruler line.

```
            When a computer is instructed to do a job, it handles the
        task in a very special way.  It accepts the information.  It
        stores the information until it is ready to use it.  It processes
        the information.  Then it gives out the processed information.




                                                Doc 2  Pg 1  Ln 4      Pos 72
        {     ▲    ▲    ▲    ▲    ▲    ▲    ▲    ▲    ▲    ▲    ]▲    ▲    ▲
        [TAB]When a computer is instructed to do a job, it handles the[SRt]
        task in a very special way.  It accepts the information.  It[SRt]
        stores the information until it is ready to use it.  It processes[SRt]
        the information.  Then it gives out the processed information.
```

Notice the code **[TAB]** that was embedded at the beginning of the paragraph. Should you decide not to indent the first line of this paragraph anymore, you can change it by deleting the tab code (place the cursor to the right of [TAB] and press the BACKSPACE key).

3. Return to the normal screen by pressing the **SPACE BAR**.

PARAGRAPH INDENTATION

Sometimes, you need to indent a whole paragraph for emphasis, as you do when you are quoting from a book. What you want to do is change the value of the left margin for a little while. You can reset the margins (Line format) but there is an easier way.

1. If it isn't already there, place the cursor at the end of the text by pressing **HOME, HOME,** and the **DOWN ARROW** key.

2. Press the ENTER key as many times as needed to insert a blank line.

3. Press the Indent key, which is the **F4** function key.

   ▫ The cursor moves to the right five spaces.

Every time you press the **F4** function key, the left margin is indented to the next tab stop setting. The left margin setting remains indented until ENTER is pressed.

4. Type the following:

    This entire paragraph is to be indented five spaces. Make up some sentences and keep on typing until the paragraph is long enough to take up several lines.

5. Press ENTER.

   ◻ The cursor jumps back to the original left margin, indicating that the paragraph indentation is no longer in effect.

   Now, check to see see what codes were embedded this time.

6. Enter the Reveal Codes command, **ALT/F3**.

   ◻ The following is displayed below the tab-ruler line.

```
      This entire paragraph is to be indented five spaces.  Make
      up some sentences and keep on typing until the paragraph is
      long enough to take up several lines.




                                   Doc 2  Pg 1  Ln 9      Pos 10
  {
                                        ]
  [->Indent]This entire paragraph is to be indented five spaces.  Make[SRt]
  up some sentences and keep on typing until the paragraph is[SRt]
  long enough to take up several lines.[HRt]
```

The indentation code embedded at the beginning of the paragraph is **[->Indent]**. Delete it and see what happens.

7. Place the cursor to the right of the indentation code.

8. Press the BACKSPACE key.

 ¤ The text above the tab-ruler line, is no longer indented.

9. Press the SPACE BAR to return to normal screen.

 Now, indent it again.

10. Place the cursor at the beginning of the paragraph.

11. Enter the Indent command, **F4**, and press the **DOWN ARROW** key.

 ¤ The paragraph is indented again.

 If you have a function key template, you will notice that there are two Indent commands: F4 and SHIFT/F4. F4 generates the code [->Indent] and it indents the left margin to the next tab setting. SHIFT/F4 generates the code [->Indent<-] and it indents both the left margin (to next tab setting) and the right margin (the same number of spaces as the left margin indentation).

CENTERING TEXT

There are times when you need to center a text, such as when you enter a title. Follow the instructions below to try this.

1. Send the cursor to the beginning of the text using **HOME, HOME,** and **UP ARROW**.

2. Press ENTER a couple of times to insert blank lines, and then place the cursor on the first line.

3. Enter the Center command, which is **SHIFT/F6**.

 ¤ The cursor jumps to the middle of the line.

4. Type **TITLE FOR THIS TEXT** and press ENTER.

 ¤ The title is centered.

```
                        TITLE FOR THIS TEXT


      When a computer is instructed to do a job, it handles the
task in a very special way.  It accepts the information.  It
stores the information until it is ready to use it.  It processes
the information.  Then it gives out the processed information.

      This entire paragraph is to be indented five spaces.  Make
up some sentences and keep on typing until the paragraph is
long enough to take up several lines.
```

```
                                  Doc 2  Pg 1  Ln 2      POS 10
```

PRACTICE TIME 2-3

1. Reveal the codes. Can you tell what codes were embedded for centered text? There is a [C] where the text to be centered starts and a [c] where the text to be centered ends. [C] and [c] work together. If you delete one, the other is deleted as well.

2. Return to normal screen.

SAVING A FILE

Suppose you decide to save this file (second document) on a disk very quickly before working with it some more. You can do this with the Save command.

1. Enter the Save command, the **F10** function key.

   ▫ The message **Document to be Saved:** appears on the status line followed by the cursor.

2. Type a filename, say **FILE2**, that you make up yourself and press ENTER.

▫ The second document is saved on the data disk in drive B with filename **FILE2**, and the document still is displayed on the screen.

When you are working on a document, it is a good idea to save it to a disk periodically. Remember, the document you are working with is in the main memory of the computer, which is not a permanent storage. You can lose the document.

UNDERLINE

Suppose you want to underline the title. Since it has already been typed in, you have to mark the title as a block and then give the Underline command.

Do you remember how you mark a block?

1. Move the cursor to the first character you want underlined. In this case, *T* of "TITLE."

2. Enter the Block command, **ALT/F4**.

3. Move the cursor to the space beyond the last character to be underlined.

   ▫ The title is highlighted.

4. Enter the underline command, the **F8** function key.

   ▫ The block, or the title in this case, is now underlined. That is, when the document is printed, the title is underlined.

If you have a color or graphics monitor, underlined text is displayed as a separate color or in reverse video. If you have a monochrome monitor, it may be a good idea to change the setting for the screen color. That is, enter the Screen command (CTRL/F3), select option 4-Color, option 2-single color monitor, and then exit (F7).

The embedded codes for underline are [U], at the beginning of the underlined text, and [u], at the end of the underlined text. You can reveal the codes and verify if you wish.

If you decide to underline characters as you are typing them in, you can enter the Underline command, **F8**. Then, the characters that follow are underlined, until you enter the Underline command again.

5. Send the cursor to the end of the document (**HOME, HOME, DOWN ARROW**) and press the ENTER key twice to insert a blank line.

6. Type **This text is to be underlined**, then enter the Underline command, F8.

If you were to reveal the codes at this point, you see **This text is to be underlined [U]_[u]** with the cursor ( ) flashing. When you type a character at this point, it is inserted between [U] and [u], causing it to be underlined. When you enter the Underline command again, the cursor is moved to the right of [u].

7. Type **starting now** and enter the Underline command.

When the document is printed, the indicated text is underlined.

PRACTICE TIME 2-4

Change the text of Document 2 in the following manner:

1. Send the cursor to the beginning of the document.

2. Change the left margin setting to 20.

3. Change the right margin setting to 60.

4. Delete the second and third paragraphs. You can mark them as a block and then press BACKSPACE. Make sure to reply correctly to questions on the status line.

5. Insert ENTERs and numberings so that the text looks like the following.

```
              TITLE FOR THIS TEXT

     When a computer Is Instructed to do a job, it
handles the task In a very special way.

1. It accepts the Information.
2. It stores the Information until It is ready to
   use It.
3. It processes the Information.
4. Then It gives out the processed Information.
```

"HANGING" PARAGRAPH FORMAT

When you number a sentence and the sentence runs on to more than one line, the turnover lines look better indented. For example, item 2 in the list should look like this:

```
2. It stores the information until it is
   ready to use it.
```

When a sentence or item is in this format, it is said to be in **"hanging"** **paragraph** format. A hanging paragraph indents all but the first line of the paragraph.

Since the indentation is dependent on the tab setting, you will start by putting tab stops at positions 20 and 24 prior to the first line that needs to be reformatted.

1. Place the cursor on the blank line above the line starting with the number "1" (1. It accepts the information).

2. Enter the Line Format command, **SHIFT/F8**.

3. Type **1** for Tabs.

4. First, you will clear all tabs. Enter the Delete to EOL command, **CTRL/END**.

   ▫ All L tab markers disappear.

5. Type **20** and press ENTER to set tab stop at position 20.

   ▫ An "L" appears at position 20.

6. Type **24** and press ENTER to set tab stop at position 24.

   ▫ An "L" appears at position 24.

7. Press the Exit key, the **F7** function key, to return to the normal screen.

   ▫ The tab-ruler line shows a left brace at 20, a triangle at 24, and a right bracket at 60.

   Now you are ready to change the format of those numbered paragraphs with turnover lines; that is, multiple lines.

8. Place the cursor on the "2" of "2. It stores the information..."

9. Press the Indent key, **F4**.

   ◻ The first line of the paragraph moves to the first tab setting.

10. Now, release the margin (for the first line) by pressing **SHIFT/TAB**.

    ◻ The first line jumps back to the left margin.

11. Press the **DOWN ARROW** key.

    ◻ The format changes to hanging paragraph.

12. Do the same for "4."

    Reveal the embedded codes. Each time you pressed F4, [->Indent] was inserted, and each time you pressed CTRL/TAB, the code [<-Mar Rel:4] was inserted.

PRACTICE TIME 2-5

Save the document by using the Exit command, F7. Since you have saved this document once before, WordPerfect asks you if you want to replace the document already on the disk (with the same name). If you choose not to replace the existing document with the current one, that is, if you want to keep both the document already on the disk *and* this modified document, you have to enter another filename.

After you have saved Document 2, WordPerfect asks you if you want to *Exit Doc 2? (Y/N).* Answer *N.* (If you had answered Y, Doc 1 would have been displayed on the screen and you would have been asked if you want to save Doc 1, etc. before you can exit WordPerfect.

You should have the blank screen for Doc 2 displayed.

Below is a short essay titled "Idea Processing." You are to do the following:

1. Start a document (as Doc 2).

2. Set the margins to 15 and 65.

3. Make sure the text is justified.

4. Type the text, including all the embedded format commands necessary. Your text need not look exactly like the one shown here.

5. Save the text on the disk.

6. Print the document.

   As mentioned previously, the training version inserts the word *WPC in your printed document. Don't let it bother you.

IDEA PROCESSING

The phrases "word processing" and "data processing" are becoming more and more prevalent in common language. In the mid-1970s, who owned a word processor? What these phrases actually refer to is idea processing. With the recent growth in computer technology available to consumers, idea processing has evolved rapidly.

In many ways, idea processing has opened previously inaccessible avenues for businesses and individuals:

* Point-of-entry data terminals in a store can immediately register sales and provide data for efficient inventory and management decisions.

* Financial models can show a board of directors the cold figures that, in past times, were available only _after_ the decision making had taken place.

* Form letters no longer need to be typed individually and use so much secretarial time.

* Since businesses and individuals can obtain immediate access to a variety of data sets over phone lines, the possibilities for idea processing seem limited by the mind only.

And the mind is indeed the crucial element in idea processing. For, without an accurate financial model, the best available data are worthless; without proper thought, inventory and management decisions can be detrimental to the company's well-being; without a specific and detailed method for _how_ data are to be processed, access to timely data is worthless.

When you are through,

1. If you have not already exited WordPerfect, do so.

2. When you see the DOS prompt, remove the disks from the disk drives.

3. Turn OFF both the monitor and the computer.

Lesson 3

ORIENTATION

Say you have to do an essay for your English class. You wrote and typed it yesterday. You read it again today and hate it. What do you do now? You will have to edit it and possibly retype it. Does that sound familiar? If you had used the word processor, you would still hate your essay, but editing it and getting a printed copy would not be nearly so much work.

In this lesson, you simulate such a situation, starting with the text you prepared in the last lesson. But first, you have to correct the spelling errors and get rid of double words. You will do this using a feature of WordPerfect called the Speller.

SPELLER

The Speller helps you proof the document on the screen by comparing each word in your document with a list of correctly spelled words, known as a dictionary. On a regular version of WordPerfect, the dictionary contains more than 100,000 words. However, on this training version, the dictionary contains just those words necessary for you to get through the lessons and projects found at the end.

Your IBM PC should be booted up and WordPerfect started. Your data disk should be in drive B.

1. Retrieve the document file containing "Idea Processing" from the disk by using the Retrieve key, **SHIFT/F10**.

2. Enter the Speller command, which is **CTRL/F2**. The following is displayed on the status line:

```
Check: 1 Word; 2 Page; 3 Document; 4 Change
Dictionary; 5 Look Up; 6 Count
```

You enter 1 to check the spelling of the word the cursor is on; 2 to check spelling of the words on the page the cursor is on; and 3 to check the entire document. If you want to cancel the spelling check operation, enter the Cancel key, **F1**.

3. You want to check the entire document. Type **3** (no ENTER).

   ◻ The message * **Please Wait** * appears at the bottom of the screen until the Speller finds a word that is not on the dictionary. After a while, the screen displays the following:

```
                         IDEA PROCESSING

        The phrases "word processing" and "data processing"
        are becoming more and more prevelent in common
        language.  In the mid-1970´s, who owned a word
        processor?  What these phrases actually refer to is
        idea processing.  With the recent growth in in
        computer technology available to consumers, idea
        processing has rapidly evolved.


     =====================================================================

        A. prevalent           B. prevalent






     Not Found!  Select Word or Menu Option (0=Continue): 0
     1 Skip Once; 2 Skip; 3 Add Word; 4 Edit; 5 Look Up; 6 Phonetic
```

The word "prevelent" is highlighted and the message at the bottom tells you that it was not found in the dictionary. Just below the double line is a list of possible alternate spellings. This list includes those words in the dictionary that are different by a single letter or two letters typed out of sequence. (Sometimes, as the Speller program searches the list, a word on the list qualifies to be shown on the screen by meeting two different criteria. That is why the word "prevalent" appears twice.)

If a word on the alternative list is the correctly spelled word, type the letter preceding it. Option 1, SKIP ONCE, leaves this word alone, and goes on to find the next word not found in the dictionary. Option 2, SKIP, causes the Speller to ignore all other occurrences of the word. Option 3, ADD WORD, is used if the word currently highlighted is spelled correctly and you want to add it to the dictionary. Option 4, EDIT, lets you correct the spelling of the word manually. Options 5 and 6 are not discussed here.

4. Since either choice on the alternative list is correct, type **A** (no ENTER).

   ▫ The misspelled word is replaced by the selected word from the alternative list.

   ▫ Now **1970s** is highlighted, and the following appears on the bottom line.

   ```
   1  2 Skip;  3 Ignore  words  containing  numbers;
   4 Edit
   ```

5. You will select option 3. Type **3** (no ENTER).

   ▫ The double words **in in** are now highlighted with the following message on the bottom line.

   ```
   Double Word!  1  2 Skip;  3 Delete  2nd;  4 Edit;
   5 Disable  double  word  checking
   ```

6. You will select option 3 to delete the second occurrence of **in**. Type **3** (no ENTER).

PRACTICE TIME 3-1

1. Continue to correct the spelling errors in the document. When you are finished, the Speller displays the number of words checked.

2. Save the corrected document.

THESAURUS

One more feature that is available in many word processors should be mentioned: the thesaurus. Many times, when you are writing a document, you need help finding a word so you can express yourself more clearly. The thesaurus displays synonyms and other words that point to the same idea.

The thesaurus that is available on the training version is limited. It is used here only to give you an idea of what it can do.

1. Place the cursor on the word **rush** of "Form letters no longer need to be typed in a rush ..."

2. Enter the Thesaurus command, **ALT/F1**. The following screen appears:

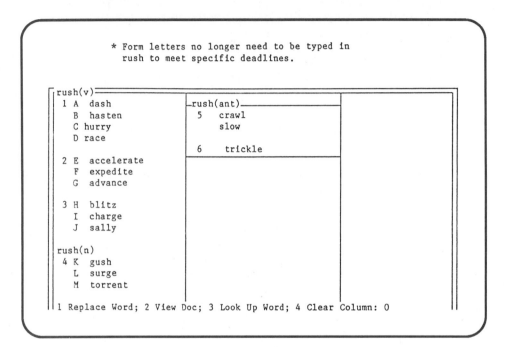

```
              * Form letters no longer need to be typed in
                rush to meet specific deadlines.

 rush(v)
   1 A  dash            rush(ant)
     B  hasten            5    crawl
     C  hurry                  slow
     D  race
                          6    trickle
   2 E  accelerate
     F  expedite
     G  advance

   3 H  blitz
     I  charge
     J  sally

 rush(n)
   4 K  gush
     L  surge
     M  torrent

 1 Replace Word; 2 View Doc; 3 Look Up Word; 4 Clear Column: 0
```

The screen displays those words you might want to use instead of "rush." The category **rush (v)** indicates "rush" used as a verb, (n) indicates "rush" used as a noun, and the **(ant)** category shows those words that have meanings opposite to "rush," or antonyms. Within each category, the words are divided into **subgroups**, or groups of words with the same connotation.

Those words that have a dot in front of them, such as "hurry" and "race," are **headwords**. That means they can be looked up in the thesaurus.

3. Type **C** (no ENTER) to look up "hurry."

    ¤ The second column displays those words that are found in the thesaurus under "hurry."

4. Type **4** (no ENTER) to get rid of the column for the word "hurry."

    You decide that the word "hurry" will do fine in place of "rush."

5. Type **1** (no ENTER) to indicate that you want to replace the word "rush" with a word on the screen.

6. Type **C** (no ENTER) to indicate "hurry."

   ¤ The document is displayed again, and the word "rush" has been replaced by "hurry."

7. Save the changed document.

In the box that follows, you will see the text for "Idea Processing" marked with changes you want to make.

1. Make your changes and recheck the document for spelling errors.

2. Save your edited document on disk.

3. Print the edited document.

4. Do the usual end-of-lesson procedure.

IDEA PROCESSING

The phrases "word processing" and "data processing" are becoming more and more prevalent in common language. In the mid-1970s, who owned a word processor? What these phrases actually refer to is idea processing. With the recent growth in computer technology available to consumers, idea processing has rapidly evolved.1

In many ways, idea processing has opened previously inaccessible avenues for businesses and individuals:

* Point-of-entry data terminals in a store can immediately register sales and provide data for efficient inventory and management decisions.

* Financial models can show a board of directors the cold
  figures which, in past times, were only available after
  the decision-making had taken place.

*Form letters no longer need to be typed in a hurry to meet
  specific deadlines.

* Since businesses and individuals can obtain immediate
  access to a variety of data sets over phone lines, the
  possibilities for idea processing seem limited by the
  mind only.

And the mind is indeed the crucial element in idea
processing. For, without an accurate financial model, the
best available data are worthless; without proper thought,
inventory and management decisions can be detrimental to the
company's well-being; without a specific and detailed method
for how data is to be processed, access to timely data is
worthless.

Project 1

1. Enter the following text using WordPerfect.

2. Check the spelling.

3. Save the text on a disk.

4. Produce a printout.

```
                        HEAVY METAL


     Imagine a metal fabricating shop consisting of a team of
robots linked by a computer. A new job is entered into the
computer, which determines the sequence of fabrication steps
and then schedules the tasks. Remember, the new job is added
to an existing job load. The computer schedules jobs by
priority (completion date) and station availability.

     Most stations are general-purpose. One robot can drill,
mill, or lathe metal blocks. Another can cut or form sheets
of metal to specifications. Some stations are for
specialized purposes, such as painting or coating.

     The shop of the future is far more productive than any in
existence today. Machines are always heavily used and
throughput is optimized. The work goes on 24 hours a day,
seven days a week. Humans are allowed into the shop only to
service the machines.

     The humans who service the machines will carry
specialized diagnostic computers. These computers plug into
the robots and check them out. If any problems are noted,
the computer instructs the human how to fix them and checks
the work to make sure it was done correctly!
```

Project 2

1. Enter the following letter using WordPerfect.

2. Check the spelling.

3. Save the letter on a disk.

4. Produce a printout.

```
                                    1728 Forest Road
                                    Takoma Park, Maryland
                                    March 27, 19—



Mr. Gary Bradshaw
Computer Parts Shop
1234 Byte Street
Golden, Colorado 81234

Dear Mr. Bradshaw:

Please accept my order for the following items:

    50 boxes of diskettes @12.50          $625.00
    10 printer interface boards @89.95     899.50
    15 cartons of 9 1/2 x 11" computer
       paper (15#) @29.00                  435.00
    24 printer ribbons @11.95              286.80
                                          --------
                                         $2246.30

My check for $2246.30 is enclosed.

                                    Yours very truly,



                                    Keiko Pitter


KMP/mtf
Enclosure
```

Project 3

1. Enter the following text using WordPerfect.
2. Check the spelling.
3. Save the text on a disk.
4. Get a printout.

Eighty days ago, they gave me this artificial brain transplant, the first attempt of its kind.

Seventy days ago, when I awoke from the coma, my mind (memory banks, now) was blank. I didn't know a thing. They gave me books, microfilms, and even an occasional diskette to supply me with what I had to know.

Sixty days ago, they added solar power cells so I could unplug myself and walk around.

Fifty days ago, I enrolled at the university, and forty days ago I finished the requirements for my Ph.D. in cybernetics. I knew more than all the professors there who had designed my artificial brain.

Thirty days ago, I completed my treatise on hybrid organic-artificial intelligence, which will earn me a Nobel Prize. The major conclusions were:

1. Hybrid organic-artificial intelligence (HOAI) enhances learning ability, performance, concentration, and productivity.

2. HOAI allows the user a minimum of excuses that prohibit or delay project completion: sleep, food, and exercise are allowed at optimum rates.

3. Humanity's problems of overpopulation, pollution, food and energy shortages, and conflicts cannot be solved without HOAI-assisted research and plan implementation.

Twenty days ago, I addressed the United Nations General Assembly and Security Council on the optimum use of HOAI for global reformation.

Then, ten days ago, I saw the light. My original plan would
work, but this new alternative is much more efficient.

That is why you, my friends, are here today. You have just
awakened and your memory banks are blank, but with the
education you will receive in the next twenty days, we will
be able to attack humanity's greatest problems together.

WordPerfect
Command Summary

This section is a quick reference for WordPerfect commands covered in this
manual. This is not a complete list of all WordPerfect commands. However,
some commands that were not covered in the lessons are listed here for your
convenience. Try them on your own.

Commands	Key(s)
Block	ALT/F4
Bold	F6
Center	SHIFT/F6
Cancel	F1
Delete (ch to left)	BACKSPACE
Delete (ch cursor is on)	DEL
Delete (wd cursor is on)	CTRL/BACKSPACE
Delete EOL	CTRL/END

Exit		F7
Format	Line	SHIFT/F8
	Page	ALT/F8
	Print	CTRL/F8
Help		F3
Indent		F4
Justification		CTRL/F8, 3 or 4
List Files		F5
Margin		SHIFT/F8,3
Margin Release		CTRL/TAB
Move	cursor	arrow keys
	a word at a time	CTRL/RIGHT or LEFT ARROW
	to beg of doc.	HOME,HOME,UP ARROW
	to end of doc	HOME,HOME,DOWN ARROW
Move text		CTRL/F4
Print		SHIFT/F7
Retrieve doc from disk		SHIFT/F10
	also use	F5, highlight, 1
Retrieve deleted text		F1
Reveal Codes		ALT/F3
Save		F10
	also use	F7
Screen		CTRL/F3
Spacing		SHIFT/F8,4
Spell		CTRL/F2
Switch		SHIFT/F3
Tab (set/rel)		SHIFT/F8,1
Tab Ruler Line		CTRL/F3,1,UP ARROW
Thesaurus		ALT/F1
Typeover (toggle)		INS
Underline		F8

SuperCalc3

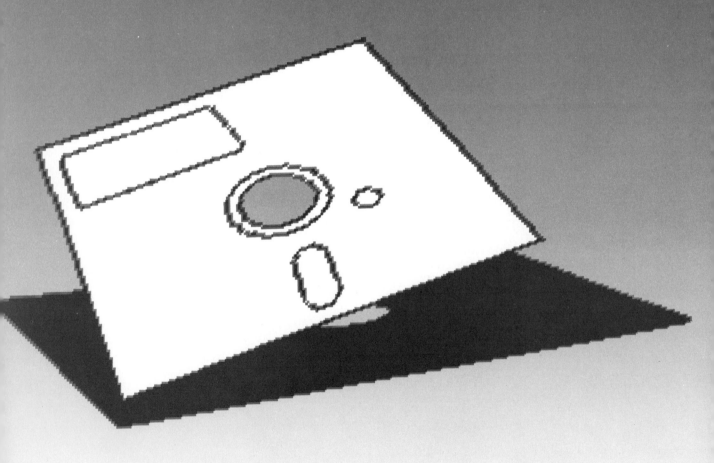

Lesson 1

THE ELECTRONIC SPREADSHEET

A lot of the problems encountered in running a business can be solved with the use of a calculator, a pencil, and a sheet of paper. The work, however, usually involves many hours of tedious calculations and recalculations—precisely the kind of need that can best be met with the aid of a computer.

This is where an **electronic spreadsheet** program such as SuperCalc3 comes in. SuperCalc3 lets the computer be the pencil, the sheet of paper, and the calculator. The main memory of the computer becomes the sheet of paper, and the monitor screen is the window through which you can view your work. The keyboard becomes the pencil. The formulas and values used in the calculations can be stored in the computer, and the computer can be instructed to do the calculations as needed. If there is a need for recalculation, only the changes need be entered.

You might wonder what good it would do you to learn how to use a spreadsheet program. After all, you might not work for a business. Well, you can use spreadsheets in other areas as well.

- With a spreadsheet, teachers can keep track of student grades on exams and homework. The computer can be instructed to figure out the class average, total score, student's average, and so on.

- The electronic spreadsheet can be used to do the household budget. Did you ever wonder if you could afford to buy a new car? If you save $20 a month this year and increase the amount by 5 percent each year, how much can you save in five years? What if you increase the amount by 8 percent instead? Using the SuperCalc3 program, you can figure these things out, quickly.

To use the SuperCalc3 program, you, of course, have to learn the terminology and commands for this specific program. Begin when you are ready.

STARTING OFF

Following the DOS A> prompt, type **SC3** and press RETURN. The S and C can be entered in either upper- or lowercase letters. You will then see the following displayed on the monitor screen:

```
                        SuperCalc3(tm)
                        Version  2.1E
                         I B M    P C
                       (8087 not present)
                       S/N-000000, IBM DOS

                         Copyright 1985

              COMPUTER ASSOCIATES INTERNATIONAL, INC.




                   FOR EDUCATIONAL USE ONLY




     Enter "?" for HELP or <RETURN> to start.
     F1=Help; F2=Cancel    FOR EDUCATIONAL USE ONLY
```

This screen identifies the program. Note the message: **FOR EDUCATIONAL USE ONLY.** The second line from the bottom tells you to enter ? for assistance or press the RETURN key (otherwise known as the ENTER key) to start. Press the RETURN key.

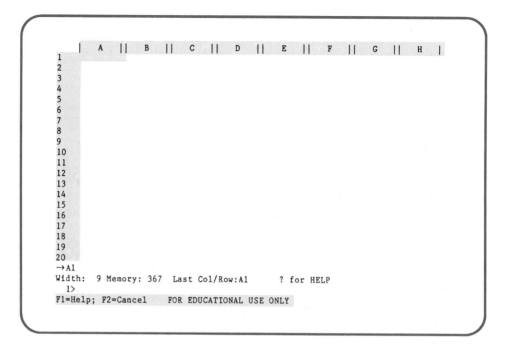

MENU LINE

Your screen is now a window to an electronic worksheet. The very bottom line on the screen is the **menu line.** This line displays commands that can be entered by depressing specific keys on the function keyboard. Currently, the F1 function key can be pressed to obtain on-screen help. You can try pressing it. Just follow the instructions on the screen and you will eventually return to this display. The F2 function key can be used to cancel a command that has been entered. Since you have not yet entered a command, pressing the F2 key will not produce any result. Needless to say, the message **FOR EDUCATIONAL USE ONLY** is displayed only on the educational version of SuperCalc3.

STATUS LINES

The three lines above the menu line are the **spreadsheet status lines.** The topmost line is called the **current cell status line.** It displays information on data entered. The second status line is called the **global status line.** It displays such information as the width of all columns and the amount of main memory still available for use. The third line is the **entry line.** The blinking underline is the **edit cursor.** Data to be entered in the spreadsheet are displayed on the entry line, and the edit cursor shows the position on the entry line where the character you type is displayed.

The screen is divided into rows and columns. Rows are numbered (1, 2, 3, ...), and columns are lettered (A, B, C, ...). Each intersection of a row and a column is referred to as a **cell** (A1, B3, C17).

CURSOR MOVEMENT

The reverse video rectangle (a bright, solid bar) you see at the cell A1 (column A, row 1) is the cursor. You can enter data on the spreadsheet at the cell where the cursor is located. This cell is referred to as the **current cell.** If you want to enter data elsewhere (in this case, other than A1), you must move the cursor to the entry position.

To move the cursor, use the four arrow keys located on the numeric keyboard to the right of the main keyboard. The cursor will move in the direction of the arrow.

1. Press the four arrow keys to move the cursor around.

   ◻ As you move the cursor, notice two things on the current cell status line, or the top line of the spreadsheet status lines.

   First, the location of the current cell is displayed. If you ever wonder about the location of your cursor, look on this line.

   Second, the arrow that appears to the left of the current cell position changes to point the direction that corresponds to the arrow key you pressed last. The arrow indicates the current direction in which the cursor will move automatically.

2. Press the RETURN key.

   ◻ The cursor moves one cell in the direction of the arrow.

3. Press an arrow key in a direction different from the one displayed on the current cell status line.

   ◻ The arrow on the current status line changes accordingly.

4. Press the RETURN key.

   ◻ Again, the cursor moves one cell in the direction of the arrow.

   To move the cursor back to cell A1, the easiest way is to press the **HOME** key. The HOME key is the lowercase 7 on the numeric keyboard.

PRACTICE TIME 1-1

Use the four arrow keys and the RETURN key to move the cursor around. Make sure to notice the current status line. When you are satisfied, move the cursor back to cell A1.

SPREADSHEET SIZE

Now, press the RIGHT arrow key 10 times, then the DOWN arrow key 25 times. Notice that the column and row headings change. The cursor can move to the right beyond column H and can move down below row 20. That is, the worksheet doesn't contain just eight columns and 20 rows. There are 63 columns, labelled A, B, C, . . . X, Y, Z, AA, AB, AC . . . AX, AY, AZ, BA, BB, BC . . . BK. And there are 254 rows. Because of the space limitation imposed by your screen size, however, you can see only as many rows and columns as your screen can display at any one time.

```
 1    X    X    X    X    X    1
 1                             1
 1                             1
 1                             1
 1                             1
 1                             1
 1                             1
 1                             1
 1                             1
 1                             1
 1                             1
 1                             1
```

In the accompanying illustration, the rectangle represents the whole SuperCalc spreadsheet. The X-marked area represents the size of the portion you see on the screen (columns A to H, rows 1 to 21). Obviously, you see only a small part of the spreadsheet at any one time.

As you continue pressing the RIGHT arrow key, new columns appear to the right, and the leftmost columns disappear. You are **scrolling** to the right. That is, you are moving the viewing area to the right. As you continue pressing the DOWN arrow key, new rows appear on the bottom, and the top rows disappear; you are scrolling down, moving the viewing area down. It is as though you are looking at a map with a magnifying glass. You see just one portion of the overall spreadsheet at a time, but you can move the viewing window around to look at the whole display.

If you want to move the cursor around a little faster, just hold the arrow key down and it will start repeating. Try this.

GOTO COMMAND (=)

Sometimes you want to move your cursor to a particular cell without having to press the key a certain number of times or hold it down; there is a way. Use the GOTO command by following the instructions below. If you make an error typing, you can either press the F2 function key to erase an entry completely or you can press the Backspace key (BKSP key—left arrow key located above the RETURN key) to back up and retype.

1. Type the GOTO character, =. Do not press the RETURN key.

   ▫ The following message appears on the global status line.

   > Enter cell to jump to.

2. The symbol => appears on the entry line, followed by the edit cursor. Enter the description of the cell in which you want to position the cursor. Then, press the RETURN key. For example, if you want to go to the cell C7, type **C7** and press RETURN.

   ▫ The cursor moves to the cell C7. The current cell status line shows you the cursor position.

PRACTICE TIME 1-2

Move the cursor directly by using =.

As you learn different commands in SuperCalc, remember: look at the global status line. Each time you press a key, the global status line tells you what you can type next. **There is nothing like experimenting to learn all the features of a software package.**

SLASH COMMANDS (/)

When you work with a spreadsheet, you are either inserting data to be processed or giving an immediate command for the SuperCalc program to carry out. When you make entries at the current cell, you are inserting data. When you give an instruction for SuperCalc to carry out, such as moving data or printing the spreadsheet on a printer, you are giving an **immediate command.**

An immediate command in SuperCalc starts with a slash (/). Hence, they also are referred to as slash commands.

1. Press / (no RETURN). The global status line reads:

```
Enter   A,B,C,D,E,F,G,I,L,M,O,P,Q,R,S,T,U,
V,W,X,Z,/,?
```

Each of the keys, **A, B, C,** through **?,** is a keystroke for a different command. Here is a brief explanation of what each key means:

A	Arrange
B	Blank
C	Copy
D	Delete
E	Edit (change)
F	Format
G	Global
I	Insert
L	Load
M	Move
O	Output
P	Protect
Q	Quit
R	Replicate (copy)
S	Save
T	Title
U	Unprotect
V	View
W	Window
X	eXecute
Z	Zap
/	data management
	help on slash commands

For a more detailed explanation of these commands, type ? or press the F1 function key. These commands are explained in more detail as each is encountered.

BLANK COMMAND (/B)

2. Press **B** (no RETURN). This command allows you to remove the content of a cell or of the entire spreadsheet.

    ▫   The current cell status line displays the command you entered, /Blank, followed by the edit cursor.

    ▫   The global status line reads:

```
Enter range, or *graph-range
```

The global status line always tells what you are to type next. In this case, it tells you that you are to specify which cells you want emptied. The second option is not discussed here. You want to clear the entire spreadsheet, so you specify **ALL**.

3. Type **ALL** and press the comma (,) key.

    ▫   If there were any entries, they have been removed. As you become more familiar with the SuperCalc commands, you will not need to pause to look at the global status line after you enter each character. For example, you will be able to clear the screen by entering **/BALL,**.

You also can erase information on the entire spreadsheet by using the Zap command (/Z). The Zap command works a little differently from the Blank command, however. It is discussed in a later lesson.

You will now learn how to prepare a spreadsheet by working on a simple personal budget for one month. Say you are a student and you have a certain amount of income each month. You might have a part-time job and/or you might be getting an allowance from your parents. The sum of these will be your "Income."

You also have a certain amount of expense each month. Maybe you buy your own clothing or pay your bus fare. You will budget a certain amount for "Expense."

The money you have left over after subtracting your expense from your income will be categorized as "Leisure" money in your budget. This is the money you can spend to have fun.

In subsequent lessons, you will add more entries, subdivide the general categories, and expand the budget to cover 12 months.

TEXT ENTRIES

You can make two different kinds of entries at a cell: **Text** or **Numeric Data.** The numeric data can be used for calculations, whereas the text cannot.

In setting up a spreadsheet, you begin with text entries that identify the data items in each row, or row headings. Your simple budget will have just three entries initially: **income, expense,** and **leisure.** You will enter these three words as row headings.

To enter an uppercase character in your text entry, hold the SHIFT key down while you press the character, just as you would do on a typewriter. If you want to type the whole entry in uppercase, press the CAPS LOCK key. To get out of all uppercase, simply press the CAPS LOCK key again. To enter special characters (nonalphabetic shifted characters), hold the SHIFT key down even if the CAPS LOCK key has already been pressed.

1. After you blank the screen (using **/BALL,)**, move the cursor to A1.

2. Type in the word **Income**. If you mistype a letter, press the BKSP key to back up and make corrections.

   ◻ The entry line reads **7>Income** followed by the edit cursor. The number that appears at the beginning of the entry line changes as you type the text. Remember, you have not pressed the RETURN key.

3. Press the BKSP key.

   ◻ The entry line now reads **6>Incom** followed by the edit cursor. Use of the backspace key has caused the **e** to be deleted.

   ◻ The number that appears at the beginning of the entry line is called the column count. It points to the position on the entry line where the next character typed would be placed (where the edit cursor is positioned).

4. Type **e** again and press RETURN.

   ◻ This moves your cursor one cell over in the direction indicated on the current cell status line, and the text **Income** remains at A1. If the arrow had pointed up or left, the cursor would not have moved.

   ◻ The word **TEXT** appears at the right end of the current cell status line.

   ◻ The information on the entry line disappears.

5. Move the cursor back to cell A1. If your cursor never moved off cell A1, just leave it where it is. The current cell status line reads:

```
<- A1          Text="Income
```

When you point to a cell with the cursor (make that cell the current cell), the current cell status line identifies that cell and its contents. In this case, cell A1 contains the text **"Income.** (Notice the absence of a closing quote.)

6. Move the cursor to cell A2 by pressing the DOWN arrow key, and type in the text **Expense.**

   ▢ Your input appears on the entry line. Note the column count.

7. Press RETURN.

   ▢ The cursor moves to cell A3.

   ▢ The information on the entry line disappears.

   ▢ The word TEXT appears on the current cell status line.

   ▢ The word Expense appears in cell A2.

CORRECTING ENTRY ERROR AT A CELL

If you make a wrong entry at a cell, you have two correction options:

   ▢ You can correct your error by placing the cursor at the cell and typing the correct entry, followed by RETURN.

   ▢ You can erase the entry (blank the cell) by placing the cursor at the cell and pressing **/B**, followed by RETURN.

In either case, make sure that you have not started a slash command before you start the process. You can cancel the command already in progress by pressing the F2 function key.

PRACTICE TIME 1-3

Enter the text "Leisure" at cell A3.

8. Move the cursor to cell B1.

NUMERIC DATA

Now, you will enter values for income, expense, and leisure. That means you want numbers (such as 150, 2, and 37) to appear in cells. You won't necessarily be entering the values that will appear at those positions, however. As you will see, you can enter a formula that will be used to calculate the value for entry to the corresponding cell.

In preparing your simple budget, assume that your monthly income is $250.

9. With B1 as the current cell, enter the value **250.**

◻   The entry line shows **4>250**, followed by the edit cursor.

◻   There is nothing in the current cell.

10. Press the RETURN key.

◻   The information on the entry line disappears.

◻   The number **250** appears, right justified, at cell B1.

◻   The cursor moves one cell in the direction of the arrow on the current cell status line.

PRACTICE TIME 1-4

In your budget, assume your monthly expenses are $150. Enter the value 150 at cell B2.

ENTERING FORMULAS

Instead of entering a value at cell B3, you will enter a formula that will cause the computer to calculate the money you have left over for leisure. The formula will be: **income value minus expense value.** That is, the formula is to determine the value at B1 minus the value at B2, or B1 minus B2. The difference will be entered as the value of your leisure budget.

When a formula is entered, the formula itself will appear on the entry line as the content of that cell. At the cell, however, what appears will be the result of evaluating the formula.

In a formula, + is the operator used to indicate addition, - is for subtraction, * is for multiplication, and / is for division. These operators are evaluated from left to right. As in ordinary mathematics, multiplication and division take precedence over addition and subtraction unless the latter operations are enclosed in parentheses. Example:

6+4/2 will result in 8, whereas **(6+4)/2** will result in 5.

11. The formula for your leisure budget is B1-B2. With the cursor at cell B3, type **B1-B2** and press RETURN.

    ◻ The information on the entry line disappears.

    ◻ Cell B3 shows the number **100**, which is the result of evaluating the formula (250 - 150).

    ◻ The cursor moves one cell in the direction of the arrow.

12. Move the cursor to cell B3 again. The current cell status line reads

    <= B3 Form=B1-B2

    ◻ This message indicates that the entry cell B3 contains the formula B1-B2.

13. Press the UP arrow key.

    ◻ The cursor moves to cell B2.

14. Type in some number other than 150, say 175, and press RETURN. Did you notice what happened to the number at B3? If you missed it, type in another number.

    ◻ The number at B3 changes. The computer saves the formula for the value at B3. This cell always will display the difference between the values at B1 and B2. Thus, the computer recalculates B3 every time you change the value at B1 or B2.

    Are you beginning to see the power of SuperCalc?

    As you wrote this formula, you may have had to check on which cell contained the number for income and which cell contained the expense. If this had been a large spreadsheet, you may have had trouble remembering which cell contained which value. If the cells you wanted had scrolled off the window, you would have had to move the cursor to find them; when you found them, you would have had to note their positions, move the cursor back to the cell where you wanted to make the entry, and then enter the formula. The SuperCalc program can make this process a little easier. (Of course, that may depend on your point of view.)

15. Put the cursor at B3 and enter **/B**, followed by the RETURN to clear the entry at cell B3.

16. Press the **ESC** key.

   ▫ The notation **3>B3** appears on the entry line followed by the edit cursor.

17. Press the UP arrow twice to put the cursor at the cell where the value of the income appears.

   ▫ Look at the entry line. It now reads **3>B1**, followed by the edit cursor. After pointing the cursor at (or moving it to) the cell of the value you want to include in the formula, you simply continue the formula by typing an arithmetic operation symbol such as -, +, *, or /.

18. Now, press the - key.

   ▫ The cursor jumps back to B3. The cell in which you are entering the formula.

19. Now, enter the second part of the formula by pointing to it with the cursor. Press the UP arrow key once to place the the cursor at the cell containing the value for the expense item.

   ▫ The entry line now reads **6>B1-B2**, followed by the edit cursor. This is the formula you want.

20. To enter the formula as it is shown on the entry line, press the RETURN key

   ▫ The information on the entry line disappears.

   ▫ The cell B3 displays the appropriate value.

   You can see that the results of pointing to cells with the cursor, known as the **point function**, are the same as for typing those cell numbers in directly from the keyboard.

21. Enter the value **150** at B2.

   Here is a question for you: What if you want to enter a text that is in the format of a formula, such as B1-B2?

   To enter a text that can be taken as a formula, you need to place a quotation mark (") at the beginning. The quote will not appear as part of the text. Do not place a closing quotation mark unless you want it as part of the text.

PRACTICE TIME 1-5

1. Change the heading for the third row from *Leisure* to *-Net-*.

2. You have just decided to put 25 percent of the money you have left over after deducting your expenses from your income into your savings account. That is, you will save 25 percent of the value of your Net, or .25*B3. On the fourth row of the spreadsheet, enter the label "Savings" and the formula for evaluating the amount to put in the savings account.

3. You would still like to know how much money you have to spend for leisure. On row 5, enter the label "Leisure" and the formula used to calculate it. The formula for leisure is the value for Net minus the value for Savings, that is, B3-B4. Your screen should look like this:

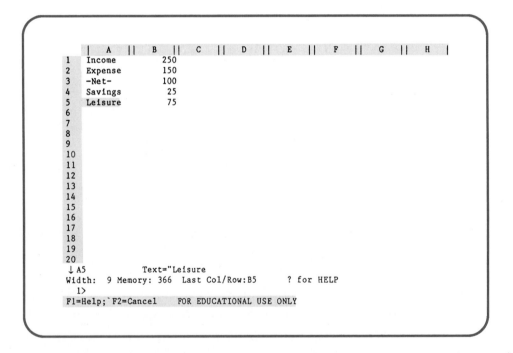

The spreadsheet you see in front of you is in the main memory of the computer. When you turn the computer off, all the information will be gone. Since you will be using this spreadsheet in the next two lessons, you must save it on a disk. You will also want to get a printout of the spreadsheet.

To understand the procedure for saving and printing, you will have to learn a little more about the SuperCalc command structure.

As you recall, all immediate commands start with a slash (/). When you enter a slash, the global status line shows you the characters used for the various commands. When you enter a character, if more information is needed to carry out that command, the global status line shows you the options for the subcommands.

SAVING FILE (/S)

Now, save the spreadsheet.

1. Type **/S** (no RETURN).

   ◻ The entry line shows **7>/Save,** followed by the edit cursor. The global status line now reads:

   ```
   Enter File Name (or <RETURN> for directory)
   ```

   You have to enter a **filename** at this point, or press the RETURN key to obtain more information about the data disk you are using. The latter option is not discussed here, but you can try on your own.

   Since you can save more than one spreadsheet on a disk, each spreadsheet on the same disk must have a unique name. The saved information is called a disk file, and the name that identifies the file is called a **filename.**

   A valid filename can be from one to eight characters in length. The filename characters must be either letters or numbers. When you enter the filename, the extension **.CAL** is added by the SuperCalc program. For example, if you were to call the file **MYFILE**, it is stored as **MYFILE.CAL**. Letters may be entered in upper- or lowercase, but are converted to upper case.

   To continue, use the filename **MYFILE**.

2. Type **MYFILE** and press RETURN.

   ◻ The entry line shows **14>/Save,MYFILE,** followed by the edit cursor.

   ◻ The global status line now reads:

   ```
   A(ll), V(alues), OR P(art)?
   ```

   You want to save the entire spreadsheet. Hence, the option to follow is A(ll). Enter only the first character.

3. Type **A** (no RETURN).

□ The global status line shows the message **Saving** briefly.

□ The disk drive should go on. After a few seconds, the drive will quiet down, and the red light will go off.

Your work is safely stored on the disk.

PRINTING (/O)

Now, follow these steps to print the spreadsheet.

1. Make sure you are working with an IBM-PC that is connected to a printer. Also, make sure that the printer is turned ON and is ready for use.

2. Type **/O** for Output.

    □ The entry line displays **9>/Output,** followed by the edit cursor. The global status line reads:

    ```
    D(Isplay) or C(ontents) report?
    ```

The program wants to know whether you want to print what is displayed on the screen or the actual content of each cell (such as the formula). You want to print what is displayed.

3. Type **D** (no RETURN).

    □ The entry line shows **17>/Output,Display,** followed by the edit cursor. The global status line reads:

    ```
    Enter range
    ```

You want to print the entire spreadsheet (which is not very big at this point), or All of it.

4. Type **ALL,** (ALL followed by a comma).

    □ The entry line now shows **21>/Output,Display,ALL,** followed by the edit cursor. The global status line reads:

    ```
    P(rinter), S(etup), C(onsole), or D(Isk)
    ```

You want the output delivered on the printer, or **P.**

5. Type **P** (no RETURN).

◻ The spreadsheet starts to print.

◻ The current cell status line informs you that if you want to stop printing, you can press the F2 function key.

◻ When printing is completed, the global status line shows the message **End of Report...Press any key to continue.**

6. Press any key.

This is the end of the lesson. To quit properly, follow this procedure.

1. Type **/Q** (no RETURN).

◻ The entry line reads **7>/Quit,** followed by the edit cursor.

◻ The global status line reads:

```
EXIT SuperCalc3? Y(es), N(o), or T(o)
```

2. Type **Y** for Yes (no RETURN).

3. Take the disk out of the disk drive.

4. Turn OFF both the computer and the monitor.

Lesson 2

ORIENTATION

What do you think about SuperCalc now? It is a rather powerful program. If you feel somewhat lost and confused, don't forget that it takes many hours of actually working with the program on the computer before you become a proficient user.

Your IBM PC should be booted up with the DOS and SuperCalc should be started (type SC3 at the A> prompt).

In this lesson, you will load the SuperCalc file you prepared in the first lesson into the computer's memory and will learn new commands to extend the basic principles.

LOADING A FILE (/L)

First, you will load the file from the disk.

1. Type **/L** for **Load.**

   ▫ The entry line reads **7>/Load,** followed by an edit cursor.

   ▫ The global status line displays the following:

   ```
   Enter File Name (or <RETURN> for directory)
   ```

98

At this point, you could simply type whatever filename you gave at the end of the previous lesson (with or without the extension .CAL) and press the RETURN key. But, suppose you forgot the name of the file.

2. Press the RETURN key.

   ❑ The SuperCalc3 Directory Options Menu appears. Under the second heading, DATA DRIVE & DIRECTORY OPTIONS, the last command is the message **S(ee) .CAL filenames & graph names.**

3. Type **S** (no RETURN).

   ❑ All the spreadsheet and graph files on your data disk are displayed. The filename you used the last lesson is **MYFILE.** Do you see it listed with the extension .CAL?

4. Press the F2 function key to return to the spreadsheet.

5. Now, start over again. Type **/L** for Load.

6. Type **MYFILE,** (MYFILE followed by a comma).

   ❑ The entry line now reads **14>Load,MYFILE,** followed by the edit cursor.

   ❑ The global status line reads:

   ```
   A(ll), P(art), C(onsolidate), or * for graphs
                      only
   ```

   You want to load the entire file, or A(ll). Other options are not discussed in this manual.

7. Type **A** (no RETURN).

   ❑ The spreadsheet you prepared during the previous lesson will appear.

   Move the cursor to cell B1. If the number at B1 is not 250, type 250 and RETURN.

INSERT COMMAND (/I)

Right now, you have values for income, expense, net, savings, and leisure for one month. You will now project these entries for 12 months. You will enter the figures for the second month in column C, for the third month in column D, and so on. To identify the values easily, you will put headings on these columns.

Column headings should go on row 1. Do you see a problem? Row 1 already has some entries. You could erase the whole spreadsheet and start over again, putting income in row 2, expense in row 3, net in row 4, and so on. However, there is an easier way. You can insert a row.

1. Enter /I for insert.

   ❑ The entry line reads **9>Insert,** followed by the edit cursor.

   ❑ The global status line reads:

$$\text{R(ow) or C(olumn)?}$$

SuperCalc wants to know if you want to insert a row or a column.

2. Type **R** for row.

   ❑ The entry line now reads **13>/Insert,Row,** followed by the edit cursor.

   ❑ The global status line displays:

$$\text{Enter Row Range}$$

The program wants to know how many rows to insert, and where. You want to insert just one row at row 1.

3. Type **1** for inserting a row at row 1 and press RETURN.

   ❑ All the information on the spreadsheet moves down one row and row 1 opens up.

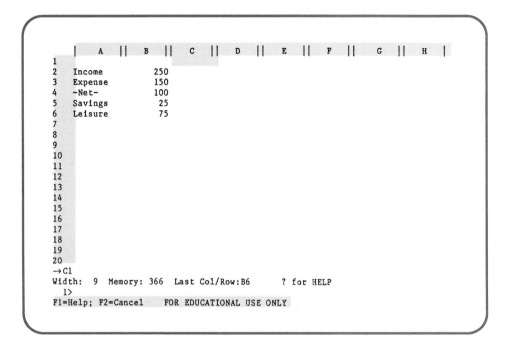

```
       |  A  || B  || C  || D  || E  || F  || G  || H  |
    1
    2  Income       250
    3  Expense      150
    4  -Net-        100
    5  Savings       25
    6  Leisure       75
    7
    8
    9
   10
   11
   12
   13
   14
   15
   16
   17
   18
   19
   20
  →C1
  Width:  9  Memory: 366  Last Col/Row:B6      ? for HELP
    1>
  Fl=Help; F2=Cancel      FOR EDUCATIONAL USE ONLY
```

4. Now, proceed with putting headings on the columns. Enter the text **Month** at cell A1.

5. Enter **1** at cell B1 as a column heading.

   Now you are going to enter 2 at C1, 3 at D1, . . . ,12 at M1. To do this, you could press the RETURN key, make an entry, press the RETURN key, make an entry, and so on. But, try another way. Each entry is one greater than the previous entry. The entry at C1 is the entry at B1 plus 1; the entry at D1 is the entry at C1 plus 1; and so on. So, you could enter the formula B1+1 at C1, C1+1 at D1, and so on.

6. Enter **B1+1** at cell C1 and press RETURN.

   ◻ The cell C1 shows the value 2.

   Now, think for a moment. You will have to enter the formula C1+1 at cell D1, D1+1 at cell E1, and on up to L1+1 at M1. How tedious to enter the same formula over and over. It's a lot of work. And you only need to do this 11 times. What if you were doing the budget for the next 60 months?

REPLICATE COMMAND (/R)

There is an easier way; use the **replicate** command. This command can be used to make copies of, or to replicate, formulas, texts, numbers, blank entries, and so on across columns, down rows, and wherever you want.

   7. With the cursor at C1, type **/R** to enter the replicate mode.

      □ The entry line reads **12>/Replicate,** followed by the edit cursor.

      □ The global status line reads:

From? (Enter Range)

The SuperCalc program wants to know what to copy. You want to copy the formula at C1, that is, the range is C1 to C1. All you have to do is press RETURN. Replicating a range of entries will not be discussed here.

   8. Press RETURN.

      □ The entry line now reads **15>/Replicate,C1,** followed by the edit cursor.

      □ The global status line displays:

```
To? (Enter Range), then <RETURN>; or <,>
for Options
```

So far, you've told the SuperCalc program to copy the formula at C1. Now it wants to know where to copy to? You are entering headings for 12 months (columns B to M). Since you've already inserted headings for columns B and C, the target range is D1 to M1. You could type in the range D1.M1, but this time you will point to the cells with the cursor. This method is discussed in lesson 1.

   9. Press the ESC key.

      □ The entry line now shows **17>Replicate,C1,C1** followed by the edit cursor.

  10. Press the RIGHT ARROW key once.

      □ The entry line now shows **17>/Replicate,C1,D1** This sets the beginning of the TO range to D1.

 11. Now type a period (.).

□ The entry line now shows **20>/Replicate,C1,D1:D1** followed by the edit cursor.

Pressing the period once produces a colon (:) on the entry line. The period tells the SuperCalc that the next cell entered will be the second part of the TO range.

12. Now press the RIGHT ARROW key nine times (until the cursor rests on M1).

□ The entry line now reads **20>/Replicate,C1,D1:M1** followed by the edit cursor. If you move too far with the RIGHT ARROW key, you can move back with the LEFT ARROW key.

13. Press RETURN.

□ The cursor appears at C1 and the numbers appear in the columns D to M.

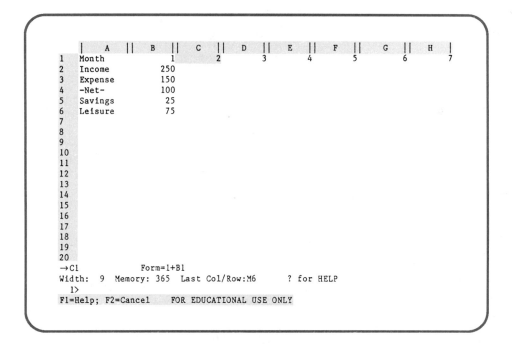

```
        |    A    ||   B    ||   C    ||   D    ||   E    ||   F    ||   G    ||   H    |
   1    Month          1         2        3        4        5        6        7
   2    Income       250
   3    Expense      150
   4    -Net-        100
   5    Savings       25
   6    Leisure       75
   7
   8
   9
  10
  11
  12
  13
  14
  15
  16
  17
  18
  19
  20
  →C1              Form=1+B1
  Width:   9   Memory: 365   Last Col/Row:M6       ? for HELP
     1>
  F1=Help; F2=Cancel     FOR EDUCATIONAL USE ONLY
```

Now your columns have headings.

PRACTICE TIME 2-1

Insert a blank line at row 2.

```
           |   A  ||   B  ||   C  ||   D  ||   E  ||   F  ||   G  ||   H  |
        1  Month            1        2        3        4        5        6        7
        2
        3  Income        250
        4  Expense       150
        5  -Net-         100
        6  Savings        25
        7  Leisure        75
        8
        9
       10
       11
       12
       13
       14
       15
       16
       17
       18
       19
       20
       →C1              Form=1+B1
       Width:  9  Memory: 365  Last Col/Row:M7      ? for HELP
          1>
       Fl=Help; F2=Cancel    FOR EDUCATIONAL USE ONLY
```

REPEATING TEXT (')

Now, you want to make the spreadsheet look good. You will put a line across the spreadsheet at row 2 to separate the headings from the values.

14. With the cursor at A2, type ' (apostrophe). This is the repeating text command.

   □ The entry line reads **2>'** followed by the edit cursor.

15. You are to enter the character(s) you want repeated across a field. Any character(s) can be used. Type - (hyphen) and press RETURN.

   □ The hyphen is repeated not only in cell A2, but in all cells to the right of cell A2, all the way until the end of the spreadsheet.

To terminate the repeating hyphens in a row, you must enter an apostrophe (') in the cell to the right of the cell in which you want hyphen entries terminated. You want hyphens terminated as of column M. Therefore, you must enter an apostrophe at cell N2.

16. Move the cursor to cell N2. Type ' (apostrophe), and press RETURN.

   ◻ The cursor jumps back to M2. The hyphens terminate as of cell M2.

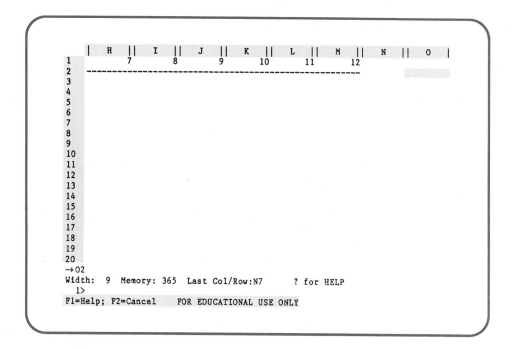

FORMAT COMMAND (/F)

Initially, every column in the spreadsheet is nine characters wide; that is, nine characters are displayed at each cell. This is indicated on the global status line. Changing the column width requires changing the format in which the data items are presented. Hence, you can change the column width of the entire spreadsheet using the format command.

17. Type **/F** for format change.

   ◻ The entry line reads **9>Format,** followed by the edit cursor.

   ◻ The global status line displays the following:

   ```
   Enter Level: G(lobal), C(olumn), R(ow), E(ntry)
   or D(efine)
   ```

SuperCalc wants to know if the format is to be changed on the entire spreadsheet (Global), column(s), row(s), one cell (entry) or for another option that you define. You want to change the entire spreadsheet, or global.

18. Type **G** for global.

   ▫ The entry line reads **16>Format,Global,** followed by the edit cursor.

   ▫ The global status line displays the following:

   ```
   Deflne  Formats:  (I,G,E,$,R,L,TR,TL,TC,*,
   U(1-8),H,D,column  wldth)
   ```

   Each of the keys, I, G, E, and so on is a keystroke entry for a different format. Only the options used in this exercise are discussed. You can get the explanations of each of these options by pressing the **F1 function key.**

19. You can change the column width by entering the number to which you want the width set. You will change it to a number other than 9, say 12. Type 12 and press RETURN.

   ▫ Columns get wider. Notice that only six columns are displayed on the screen instead of the eight columns that were there before. Notice also that even though the column width changed from 9 to 12 places, row 2 is still filled with hyphens.

20. Type **/FG4** and press RETURN to make all the columns narrower.

   ▫ Now you can see 28 columns on the screen.

   Notice column A, where all the headings are. Only four characters are displayed. When you change the width of a cell, the value or the text stored is not affected. The change affects only the number of characters displayed on the spreadsheet. For a column width set to n:

   • If a text is stored at that cell, the first n characters are displayed. However, if the cells to the right are blank, the excess characters are placed in adjacent columns.

   • If a value is stored at that cell, and the number of digits to the left of the decimal is more than n, the value is displayed as scientific notation. Numbers to the right of the decimal point are truncated (dropped).

PRACTICE TIME 2-2

Change the column width to 7.

A column width of 7 is sufficient for all the numeric data on the spreadsheet. However, that may not be wide enough for the row headings in column A. So, change the width only of column A.

21. Type **/F** for format change. Entry line messages will not be shown anymore, and the message displayed on the global status line will be shown only if needed.

22. You want to change the format for a column. Type C for column.

23. The column for which you want to change the format is A. Type **A,** (A followed by a comma).

24. You are to enter the column width just as you did with the global change. You will set the width to 10. Type 10 and press RETURN.

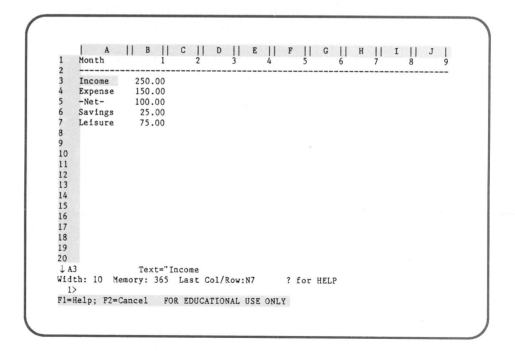

```
        |    A   ||   B  ||   C  ||   D  ||   E  ||   F  ||   G  ||   H  ||   I  ||  J  |
    1   Month           1       2       3       4       5       6       7       8       9
    2   ----------------------------------------------------------------------------------
    3   Income     250.00
    4   Expense    150.00
    5   -Net-      100.00
    6   Savings     25.00
    7   Leisure     75.00
    8
    9
   10
   11
   12
   13
   14
   15
   16
   17
   18
   19
   20
    ↓ A3                Text="Income
   Width: 10  Memory: 365  Last Col/Row:N7        ? for HELP
     1>
   F1=Help; F2=Cancel    FOR EDUCATIONAL USE ONLY
```

You will now enter the income for the next 12 months. You already have the value for the first month. You can replicate this value if you know that your income will not change for the next 12 months. When you are doing a budget, however, you often like to see what would happen if your income increases (or decreases). In other words, you may want to change the value. If you enter the actual values, you will have to change the value at all 12 cells every time a change is made (or perhaps replicate the value again). If you use a formula that makes each entry dependent on the entry for the previous month, changing the values for income will be simple.

You will use the formula B3 for the cell C3, C3 for the cell D3, and so on. In this way, if you change the income for January, you also automatically change the income for the next 11 months. If you want to change the income for June through December, you have to change only the value for June, and the rest are changed automatically.

1. Enter the formula **B3** at cell C3.

2. With the cursor on cell C3, enter **/R** to replicate the formula.

3. Press RETURN to indicate the FROM range.

4. Enter **D3.M3** followed by a RETURN to indicate the TO range.

5. Assume that you think your income will increase by $25 a month starting in July. You want to take that into consideration in preparing the budget. Place the cursor at cell H3 (Income for July), enter 275, and press RETURN.

   ◻ Values shown as income for July to December change to 275.

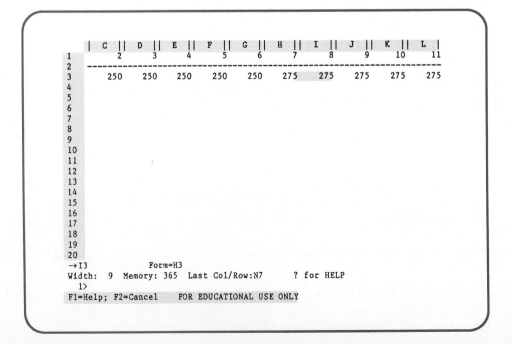

PRACTICE TIME 2-3

Use the replicate command to do the same with the Expense, Net, Savings, and Leisure headings. The following guide should help you.

TO REPLICATE

1. Position the cursor at the entry position you want to replicate.

2. Press /R to start the replicate command.

3. Press RETURN to indicate that the formula to replicate is in the current cell.

4. Point the cursor at the first entry position where you want the formula replicated (make sure to press the ESC key to start the process). Press . (period) and point to the last position (or you can type in the entry cells).

5. Press RETURN.

   HINTS: For Expense, enter the formula B4 at cell C4 and replicate that formula. For Net, Savings, and Leisure, replicate the formula at B5, B6 and B7, respectively.

At this point, consider the ways by which you can change the display format. Methods for changing the column width have been covered. Now you will learn how to change a format in which values are displayed in each cell. You can, for instance, change the whole worksheet (a global change) to an integer format (whole numbers only). Note that the value at cell H6 is 31.25.

1. Enter /FG for global format change.

   ¤ The global status line shows the different format options available.

2. Since you want to change the entire spreadsheet to integer format (whole numbers only), type I and press RETURN.

   ¤ Notice that in column H, under Savings, the value used to be 31.25. It is now 31.

Since you are dealing with money in this spreadsheet, you probably want your values to show two places to the right of the decimal point. This format is known as "dollars and cents," or $.

3. Enter **/FG** for global format change.

4. Type **$,** for dollars and cents, and press RETURN.

   ◻ All values on the screen show two places to the right of the decimal. Do you see a problem? Even the column headings show two places to the right of the decimal.

You can change the format of a particular row, column, or entry also.

5. With the cursor at cell B1, enter **/F** for format change.

   ◻ The global status line shows:

   ```
   Enter Level: G(lobal), C(olumn), R(ow), E(ntry)
   or D(efine)
   ```

6. You want to change the format of a row. Type **R** for Row. The global status line reads as follows:

   ```
   Enter row range of 1 to 254
   ```

7. Now you specify the range, which is just row 1. Type **1,** (1 followed by a comma).

   ◻ The global status line shows the options.

8. Type **I** for Integer format and press RETURN.

   ◻ The format of the numerical values in row 1 is changed to integer. The value displayed at cell B1, for example, is 1 instead of 1.00.

This is the end of another lesson. Save your spreadsheet for use during the next lesson. When you are saving the spreadsheet, however, you have to be careful in choosing the filename.

If you use the same filename you used at the end of the last lesson, the current spreadsheet will replace the existing contents of the disk file. This may be acceptable in some situations. By using a different filename, both the old and new spreadsheets will be stored on the disk.

The SuperCalc program makes sure that you don't accidentally replace an existing disk file. If you enter a filename that already exists on the disk, the global status line will display:

```
File already exists: C(hange name), B(ackup) or
O(verwrite)?
```

If you type **O**, the new spreadsheet will replace the contents of the file with the same name. If you type **B**, the extention .CAL on the existing file (the one before you made changes) is changed to .BAK and the changed file is saved with the extension .CAL. If you type **C**, the program lets you change the filename you have just entered. You will have to choose a different filename, since both the spreadsheets from lessons 1 and 2 will be used in the next lesson.

PRACTICE TIME 2-4

Save your spreadsheet file by using a filename other than MYFILE.

You also are to print your spreadsheet. Before you start on this, however, you need to know the following.

The number of columns you can print on a sheet of paper depends on the width of the paper or the number of characters the printer can print on one line. If you are using a 9-1/2-by-11-inch paper with a printer that has a capacity of 80 characters per line, you can print only eight columns (with a column width of nine characters) at a time. If there is a ninth column, it will print on the next row down or overstrike the row just printed.

In the last lesson, you printed the entire spreadsheet (All). This time you have to specify the range, or print the spreadsheet in sections by dividing it into rectangles. The range is specified by indicating the top left corner cell and the bottom right corner cell of the rectangle, separated by a period.

In your case, divide the spreadsheet into two sections. The first section will have A1 and H7 as the top left and bottom right corners, and the second section will have I1 and M7 as the top left and bottom right corners.

PRACTICE TIME 2-5

Print the spreadsheet in two sections.

As you did at the end of lesson 1:

1. Type **/QY** to get out of SuperCalc.

2. Take the disk out of the disk drive.

3. Turn OFF both the computer and the monitor.

Lesson 3

ORIENTATION

In the previous lesson, you may have noticed that one of the advantages of an electronic spreadsheet is that you can add or delete information without having to redo the entire spreadsheet. In this lesson, you will carry that principle even further. You will load the SuperCalc file you prepared in the previous lesson, calculate totals through use of a function, and replicate vertically (down a column) instead of horizontally (across a row). You will learn how to change the display format on the screen by freezing the titles (headings) and splitting the screen.

At the end of this lesson, you will still not know everything about SuperCalc. But you will know enough to be able to prepare most spreadsheets. In fact, you will get a chance to prepare a simple spreadsheet containing student examination scores.

Your IBM-PC should be booted up and SuperCalc started.

Now, load the file that contains the spreadsheet from the previous lesson and begin.

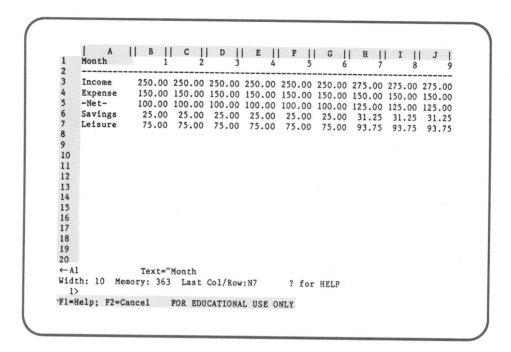

```
    |    A   ||  B  ||  C  ||  D  ||  E  ||  F  ||  G  ||  H  ||  I  ||  J  |
 1  Month         1      2      3      4      5      6      7      8      9
 2  ------------------------------------------------------------------------
 3  Income    250.00 250.00 250.00 250.00 250.00 250.00 275.00 275.00 275.00
 4  Expense   150.00 150.00 150.00 150.00 150.00 150.00 150.00 150.00 150.00
 5  -Net-     100.00 100.00 100.00 100.00 100.00 100.00 125.00 125.00 125.00
 6  Savings    25.00  25.00  25.00  25.00  25.00  25.00  31.25  31.25  31.25
 7  Leisure    75.00  75.00  75.00  75.00  75.00  75.00  93.75  93.75  93.75
 8
 9
10
11
12
13
14
15
16
17
18
19
20
←A1              Text="Month
Width: 10  Memory: 363  Last Col/Row:N7      ? for HELP
   1>
`F1=Help; F2=Cancel     FOR EDUCATIONAL USE ONLY
```

SUM FUNCTION

For column N, you decide to enter totals. You want to enter the total income, total expense, total net income, total savings, and total leisure money. To enter the total income at N3, for instance, you can enter the formula B3+C3+D3+E3+F3+G3+H3+I3+J3+K3+L3+M3. That's a long formula. Suppose you had to find the total income for 60 months? As you might have guessed, there is an easier way to total numbers. You can use the SUM function.

1. With the cursor at N3, enter **SUM(** (SUM followed by the left parenthesis).

   ◻ You are to indicate what values you want totaled. These values are known as the "arguments." The arguments you enter can be:

   - A range of cells, such as **SUM(B3.M3).** (A period serves as a delimiter again, separating the beginning of the range from the end.)

   - A list of specific cells separated by commas, such as **SUM(B3,C3,D3).**

   - Any combination of: ranges of cells, lists of cells, numbers, and formulas, such as **SUM(B3.B7,B9,4,7*C9).**

2. In your case, you want to enter a range of cells. You want to total the values on row 3, columns B to M. Enter **B3.M3)** and press RETURN.

☐ The cell N3 is filled with > entries.

In the previous lesson, it is stated that, if the number to be displayed has more digits than the column width, the entry either is truncated (to the right of the decimal) or displayed in scientific notation. However, you made a global format change to display all values in dollars and cents, that is, to display all numbers with two places to the right of the decimal point. Apparently, the sum to be displayed at cell N3 has more digits (including the decimal point) than the column width of 7. Since the program cannot change the format, it displays > symbols to tell you that you need to make the width wider for column N.

PRACTICE TIME 3-1

Change the width of Column N to 10.

☐ The number 3150.00 appears at the cell N3.

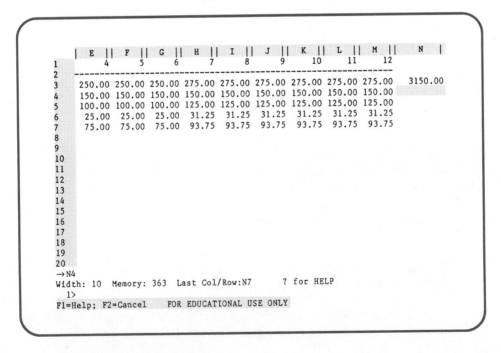

```
        | E || F || G || H || I || J || K || L || M ||  N  |
           4     5     6     7     8     9    10    11    12
 1
 2   --------------------------------------------------------------
 3   250.00 250.00 250.00 275.00 275.00 275.00 275.00 275.00 275.00   3150.00
 4   150.00 150.00 150.00 150.00 150.00 150.00 150.00 150.00 150.00
 5   100.00 100.00 100.00 125.00 125.00 125.00 125.00 125.00 125.00
 6    25.00  25.00  25.00  31.25  31.25  31.25  31.25  31.25  31.25
 7    75.00  75.00  75.00  93.75  93.75  93.75  93.75  93.75  93.75
 8
 9
10
11
12
13
14
15
16
17
18
19
20
→N4
Width: 10  Memory: 363  Last Col/Row:N7     ? for HELP
   1>
Fl=Help; F2=Cancel     FOR EDUCATIONAL USE ONLY
```

BUILT-IN FUNCTIONS

SuperCalc has several built-in functions that can be performed automatically to assist you in manipulating data. The names used to refer to these functions are "reserved" and may not be used for other purposes within SuperCalc. For example, when you type SUM, SuperCalc knows that you are referring to the SUM function. Each function performs a calculation on the values specified in your instruction (the arguments), and produces a numeric result. A function can be used as a numeric entry by itself or it can be used as part of a formula, such as **.25*SUM(A1.A6)**.

Many built-in functions are available. Some of the functions are listed in the command summary to this module.

REPLICATE A FORMULA

You will now replicate the formula at N3 down the column. Until now, you have replicated only an entry across a row. Replicating a formula down a column works much the same way.

3. With the cursor at N3, type **/R** for replicate.

4. Since you are replicating the entry at just one cell, press RETURN.

5. The TO range now is down the column. It is N4 to N7. Enter **N4.N7** and press RETURN.

   ▫ Corresponding numbers appear in column N.

```
     | E  || F  || G  || H  || I  || J  || K  || L  || M  ||  N   |
   1     4     5     6     7     8     9    10    11    12
   2  ------------------------------------------------------------
   3  250.00 250.00 250.00 275.00 275.00 275.00 275.00 275.00 275.00   3150.00
   4  150.00 150.00 150.00 150.00 150.00 150.00 150.00 150.00 150.00   1800.00
   5  100.00 100.00 100.00 125.00 125.00 125.00 125.00 125.00 125.00   1350.00
   6   25.00  25.00  25.00  31.25  31.25  31.25  31.25  31.25  31.25    337.50
   7   75.00  75.00  75.00  93.75  93.75  93.75  93.75  93.75  93.75   1012.50
   8
   9
  10
  11
  12
  13
  14
  15
  16
  17
  18
  19
  20
  → N3              Form=SUM(B3.M3)
  Width: 10   Memory: 363   Last Col/Row:N7      ? for HELP
     1>
  F1=Help; F2=Cancel    FOR EDUCATIONAL USE ONLY
```

6. You can move the cursor down and examine the current cell status line to make sure the formula to calculate the row total is entered at each of cells N4 to N7.

7. You have not yet put a heading on column N. Do that right now. Move the cursor to N1, type the text **Total,** and press RETURN.

   ◻ The text **Total** appears at N1.

JUSTIFYING TEXT

Does anything about the text bother you? Text entries do not line up right above all the values for the totals. Also, there is no space between text items and the heading **12** on column M. This is because numeric values are displayed right justified whereas the text items are displayed left justified on a spreadsheet. You can change this format.

8. Type **/F** for format change.

9. This time you want to change the format on just one cell. Type **E** for entry.

   ◻ The global status line asks you to enter the range.

10. The cell in which you want to change the format is N1. Type **N1,** (N1 followed by a comma).

11. The text is to be right justified, or TR. Type **TR** for TextRight and press RETURN.

   ◻ The word **Total** is now displayed right justified at cell N1.

```
      | E ||   F  ||  G  ||  H  ||   I  ||  J  ||  K  ||  L  ||  M ||    N  |
1     | 4      5      6      7       8      9     10     11    12      Total
2     -------------------------------------------------------------------------
3     250.00 250.00 250.00 275.00 275.00 275.00 275.00 275.00 275.00   3150.00
4     150.00 150.00 150.00 150.00 150.00 150.00 150.00 150.00 150.00   1800.00
5     100.00 100.00 100.00 125.00 125.00 125.00 125.00 125.00 125.00   1350.00
6      25.00  25.00  25.00  31.25  31.25  31.25  31.25  31.25  31.25    337.50
7      75.00  75.00  75.00  93.75  93.75  93.75  93.75  93.75  93.75   1012.50
8
9
10
11
12
13
14
15
16
17
18
19
20
↑ N1      TR       Text="Total
Width: 10  Memory: 363  Last Col/Row:N7      ? for HELP
    1>
F1=Help; F2=Cancel     FOR EDUCATIONAL USE ONLY
```

PRACTICE TIME 3-2

Insert hyphens at N2.

FREEZE TITLES COMMAND (/T)

Scroll your screen so that column N appears. At this point, you cannot see column A, the row headings. Without the headings, can you tell which value is which? Since this is a small spreadsheet, you may not have any trouble identifying the values. But if you were working with a large spreadsheet containing rows and rows of data, you might find it difficult to remember which row contains what data. To eliminate this problem, you can "freeze" the row headings (known as "titles") on the screen so that they will not scroll off.

1. Move the cursor to column A, to cell A1.

2. Enter /T for freezing the title. The global status line reads:

    H(oriz.), V(ert.), B(oth) or C(lear)

At any time, if you want to see a detailed explanation of the options, press the F1 function key.

3. You want to freeze titles on column A, which is vertical. Enter V (no RETURN). This command freezes the columns at and to the left of the cursor position.

   Now press the RIGHT ARROW key at least 10 times. As the screen scrolls to the left (look at the column texts at the top), column A stays on the screen. These headings are "frozen" on the screen. You can move the cursor to those cells that are frozen by using the goto (=) command.

4. Enter **/TC.** This command unfreezes the title.

5. With the cursor at A2, enter **/TH** for horizontal freeze. This command freezes the rows at and above the cursor position.

   Press the DOWN ARROW key at least 21 times. As the screen scrolls up, notice that rows 1 and 2 stay on the screen.

6. Enter **/TC** to unfreeze the title.

7. With the cursor at A2, enter **/TB.** This command freezes both the columns at and to the left of the cursor position and the rows at and above the cursor position.

   Press the arrow keys in all directions. Notice that both column headings and row headings are frozen.

8. Unfreeze by entering **/TC.**

WINDOW COMMAND (/W)

There are times when it is convenient to see two different sections of the spreadsheet at the same time. Freezing the title is one way. But, with the /T command, the same set of information stays in view all the time. Also, you can freeze rows or columns only at, to the left, or above the cursor position.

    Another method is the **/W** (window) command. As you recall, the monitor screen is the window to the spreadsheet. The **/W** command lets you split the screen so that you can view two portions of the spreadsheet at the same time.

1. Position the cursor on column E, cell E1.

2. Type **/W** for window. The global status line reads:

```
H(oriz.), V(ert.), C(lear Split), S(ynch.) or
U(nsynch.)
```

3. You will split the screen vertically. Enter V (no RETURN). This command splits the screen just to the left of the column at which the cursor is positioned.

   ▫ The cursor remains on cell E1. The screen is split as shown here:

```
      |   A   ||  B  ||  C  ||  D  |       |  E  ||  F  ||  G  ||  H  ||  I  |
   1  Month       1     2     3 1      4     5     6     7     8
   2  --------------------------- 2   -----------------------------------
   3  Income   250.00 250.00 250.00 3   250.00 250.00 250.00 275.00 275.00
   4  Expense  150.00 150.00 150.00 4   150.00 150.00 150.00 150.00 150.00
   5  -Net-    100.00 100.00 100.00 5   100.00 100.00 100.00 125.00 125.00
   6  Savings   25.00  25.00  25.00 6    25.00  25.00  25.00  31.25  31.25
   7  Leisure   75.00  75.00  75.00 7    75.00  75.00  75.00  93.75  93.75
   8                                8
   9                                9
  10                               10
  11                               11
  12                               12
  13                               13
  14                               14
  15                               15
  16                               16
  17                               17
  18                               18
  19                               19
  20                               20
  → E1            Form:D1+1
  Width:  7  Memory: 363  Last Col/Row:O7      ? for HELP
     1>
  F1=Help; F2=Cancel    FOR EDUCATIONAL USE ONLY
```

4. Press an arrow key several times.

   ▫ As the screen on the right scrolls, the screen on the left remains stationary.

JUMPING BETWEEN WINDOWS

5. Type ; (semicolon) (no RETURN).

   ▫ The cursor jumps over to the left screen.

   Typing ; moves the cursor to its last position on the other window.

6. Press an arrow key several times.

▫ As the screen on the left scrolls, the screen on the right remains stationary.

7. Scroll the screen so that the screen on the left shows columns A to D, rows 1 to 20; and the screen on the right shows columns J to N, rows 1 to 20.

With window split vertically, if you enter **/WS** for synchronous (with cursor in either screen), both screens scroll together up and down (sideways if they are split horizontally).

To get out of **/WS,** enter **/WU** for unsynchronous.

```
      |    A   ||  B   ||  C   ||  D   |      |   J   ||   K   ||   L   ||   M   ||    N    |
   1  Month          1      2      3  1         9      10      11      12      Total
   2  ---------------------------------  2     -------------------------------------------
   3  Income     250.00 250.00 250.00  3     275.00 275.00 275.00 275.00      3150.00
   4  Expense    150.00 150.00 150.00  4     150.00 150.00 150.00 150.00      1800.00
   5  -Net-      100.00 100.00 100.00  5     125.00 125.00 125.00 125.00      1350.00
   6  Savings     25.00  25.00  25.00  6      31.25  31.25  31.25  31.25       337.50
   7  Leisure     75.00  75.00  75.00  7      93.75  93.75  93.75  93.75      1012.50
   8                                    8
   9                                    9
  10                                   10
  11                                   11
  12                                   12
  13                                   13
  14                                   14
  15                                   15
  16                                   16
  17                                   17
  18                                   18
  19                                   19
  20                                   20
  →N1       TR      Text="Total
  Width: 10  Memory: 363  Last Col/Row:07       ? for HELP
    1>
  F1=Help; F2=Cancel     FOR EDUCATIONAL USE ONLY
```

8. Move the cursor to the left screen and change the value at B3 to 260.

▫ Values affected by the change in entry at B3 are recalculated. You can view the effect of the change on the entries at column N.

While the values are being recalculated, the word **Calculating** appears on the global status line.

9. Enter **/WC** to display a single window.

PRACTICE TIME 3-3

1. Split the screen as shown:

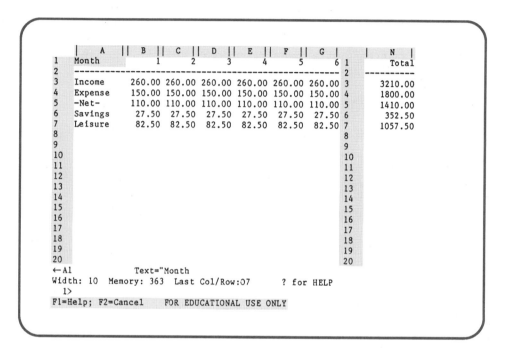

```
      |    A   ||  B  ||  C  ||  D  ||  E  ||  F  ||  G  |     |    N   |
 1   Month            1      2      3      4      5      6  1      Total
 2   ------------------------------------------------------  2   ----------
 3   Income      260.00 260.00 260.00 260.00 260.00 260.00  3    3210.00
 4   Expense     150.00 150.00 150.00 150.00 150.00 150.00  4    1800.00
 5   -Net-       110.00 110.00 110.00 110.00 110.00 110.00  5    1410.00
 6   Savings      27.50  27.50  27.50  27.50  27.50  27.50  6     352.50
 7   Leisure      82.50  82.50  82.50  82.50  82.50  82.50  7    1057.50
 8                                                          8
 9                                                          9
10                                                         10
11                                                         11
12                                                         12
13                                                         13
14                                                         14
15                                                         15
16                                                         16
17                                                         17
18                                                         18
19                                                         19
20                                                         20
←A1              Text="Month"
Width: 10  Memory: 363  Last Col/Row:07       ? for HELP
  1>
F1=Help; F2=Cancel     FOR EDUCATIONAL USE ONLY
```

2. Adjust the right screen so that column N is displayed.

3. Place the cursor on the left screen.

4. Freeze the title on column A by using the /T command.

With the display set in this format, you can identify each value. Also, you can see how the totals are affected by changing various entries.

PRACTICE TIME 3-4

1. Save your spreadsheet on a disk. Be cautious in selecting a filename.

2. Create a printout of the spreadsheet. You have to print the spreadsheet in sections.

CELL CONTENT OUTPUT

When you enter **/O** to obtain output and enter **D** for the display option, an image of the screen display is output (on printer, console, or wherever you specify). It is difficult for someone else to tell by looking at the output whether you entered an actual value or a formula to obtain a value at a cell.

1. Make sure you are using a computer connected to a printer, and the printer is ON and ready to use.

2. Clear the spreadsheet by typing **/ZY** (Zap command).

    Whereas the Blank command clears the contents of a spreadsheet but leaves the format alone, the Zap command clears both the contents and the format (such as column width and data display structures).

    Printing the entry at each cell, one cell per line, uses a lot of paper. If you have a spreadsheet that uses columns A through N (14 columns) and rows 1 through 9 (9 rows), it will take 14 times 9, or 126 lines, to list all the entries. At 66 lines per 11-inch page, that's two pages. For demonstration purposes, it might be best to use a small spreadsheet like the one you prepared in SuperCalc Lesson 1.

3. Load the spreadsheet you saved at the end of SuperCalc Lesson 1.

4. Type **/O** for output.

    At this point, rather than asking for D(isplay), you ask for the program to output the content of each cell.

5. Type C for content.

6. You want to output the content for the entire spreadsheet, or All. Type **ALL,** (ALL followed by a comma).

    You want your output sent to the printer.

7. Type **P** for printer (no RETURN).

    □ The printer lists the content of each cell:

    ```
    SuperCalc      ver. 2.1E
    Income
    A1             = "Income
    B1             = 250
    A2             = "Expense
    ```

B2	= 150
A3	= "-Net
B3	= B1-B2
A4	= "Savings
B4	= .25*B3
A5	= "Leisure
B5	= B3-B4

This display is followed by the message **FOR EDUCATIONAL USE ONLY.**

This type of printout is referred to as the printout of the contents as opposed to the printout of the display.

Now you will design a spreadsheet by yourself. It will keep track of six students and their scores on three exams. It is to contain the following:

1. Student names.

   Hint: You might put last names and first names in separate columns.

2. Scores for three exams.

3. The total score for each student. This is the sum of the three exams.

4. The average for each student. This is the sum of the three exam scores divided by 3.

   Hint: You can use the AVERAGE function. It works like SUM. You enter AVERAGE(argument) where the argument can be specific cells, a range of cells, or a combination of both.

5. The class average for each exam. This is the total of scores for the six students, divided by 6. Use the following data:

STUDENT NAME		EXAM 1 (100)	EXAM 2 (100)	EXAM 3 (100)
ADAMS	JOHN	97	88	91
COX	KAREN	82	79	95
JOHNSON	MAX	68	80	77
POWERS	GREG	80	84	75
SANDERS	MARY	94	89	98
WARNER	MIKE	72	80	83

Use your imagination and creativity and design a spreadsheet that will be easy for someone to understand. You may want to put all the spreadsheet display values in integer format.

You will save the spreadsheet and get printouts of both the spreadsheet display and content.

Your spreadsheet might look like this:

Student Name		Exam 1 (100)	Exam 2 (100)	Exam 3 (100)	Total (300)	Average
Adams	John	97	88	91	276	92
Cox	Karen	82	79	95	256	85
Johnson	Max	68	80	77	225	75
Powers	Greg	80	84	75	239	80
Sanders	Mary	94	89	98	281	94
Warner	Mike	72	80	83	235	78
Class Average		82	83	87		

Don't forget, you are to enter the formulas for totals and averages, not the actual values.

When you are done with the lesson:

1. Type **/QY** to get out of SuperCalc.

2. Take the disk out of the disk drive.

3. Turn OFF both the computer and the monitor.

Project 1

You are interested in keeping track of your automobile's gasoline mileage (miles per gallon). Each time you get gas for your automobile, you note its mileage and the amount of gasoline you add. You want to calculate the miles per gallon.

Use the following as a guide and prepare a spreadsheet. Use the data provided.

Date	Miles	Gallons	mpg
Nov. 6	8943		
Nov. 18	9296	19.0	
Nov. 30	9643	20.0	
Dec. 7	9951	19.4	
Dec. 20	10296	18.3	
Jan. 1	10592	17.7	
Jan. 12	10966	20.1	
Jan. 21	11354	20.7	
Feb. 2	11732	19.6	
Feb. 14	12097	20.2	
Feb. 24	12475	19.2	
Mar. 6	12821	20.4	

Hints: On November 18, the mpg is the miles (9296 - 8943) divided by the gallons (19.0).

Save the spreadsheet. Produce printouts of both the spreadsheet display and the content.

Project 2

You are starting a lawn/garden care service and you want to establish prices for the services you offer. You want to make sure you make a profit even if costs change. The three standard services you offer are lawn seeding, monthly lawn care (mowing and fertilizing), and yard clean-up (pruning and raking). The yards you serve are all about the same size.

- Seeding takes 4 hours of labor, 7 pounds of seeds, 6 pounds of fertilizer, and 1 round trip in the truck.

- Monthly lawn care takes 2 hours of labor, 2 pounds of fertilizer, 1 gallon of weeder, 1 cubic yard of disposal, and 5 round trips in the truck.

- Yard clean-up takes 3 hours of labor, 4 cubic yards of disposal, and 2 round trips in the truck.

When you have found the total cost of a service, you add 15% profit to arrive at your charge for the service.

Initially, your costs are:

Labor:	$10.00 per hour
Seed:	$ 2.25 per pound
Fertilizer:	$ 0.75 per pound
Weeder:	$ 9.00 per gallon
Disposal:	$ 3.00 per cubic yard
Truck:	$ 2.00 per round trip

You can use SuperCalc to find the prices you will charge customers and to update the prices as costs to you change.

ASSIGNMENT A

Use the following as a guide and prepare a spreadsheet.

		Seeding		Lawn Care		Clean-Up	
Item	Unit Cost	No. of Unit	Cost	No. of Unit	Cost	No. of Unit	Cost
Labor	10.00 / hr	4					
Seed	2.25 / lb	7					
Fertil	0.75 / lb	6					
Weeder	9.00 / gal	0					
Dispos	3.00 / yd	0					
Truck	2.00 /trip	1					
Total Cost							
.15 Profit							

Charge for Service

1. Enter the labels and values shown in the table.

2. Individual cost is calculated by multiplying the number of units by the unit cost.

3. For total costs, use the **SUM** function to total the values in each column.

4. The profit is the total cost multiplied by .15.

Save the spreadsheet on a disk. Get printouts of both the spreadsheet display and contents.

ASSIGNMENT B

After a month of service, you realize that it takes 2.5 hours of labor per month for lawn care, and the cost of disposal has been raised to $3.25 per cubic yard.

Make the changes, save the spreadsheet, and get printouts of the spread-sheet display and contents.

SuperCalc Commands

This section is a quick reference for SuperCalc commands. This is not a complete list of all SuperCalc commands.

SPREADSHEET STATUS LINES

1. **Current Cell Status Line.** Displays information on the current cell: its location, format (integer, dollars and cents, ...), and the content (as opposed to what is displayed).

2. **Global Status Line.** Displays information identifying various aspects of the spreadsheet: column width, amount of main computer memory still available, the rightmost column and the lowest row that contain data, and a reminder for Help. Also, as a command is entered, this line displays a message that describes the command sequence (save, replicate, and so on) and the options at that point in the command sequence. Look at this line. It tells you what you can do.

3. **Entry Line.** Displays characters as they are typed. Also, this line displays the commands that have been entered.

CURSOR MOVEMENT

1. **Arrow keys.** The arrow keys located on the numeric keyboard move the cursor one position in the direction of the arrow.

2. **Goto command.** Direct movement of the cursor

    =coordinate <RETURN>

    where coordinate gives the screen location to which you want to move the cursor.

    Example: =B4 <RETURN>

CORRECTING MISTAKES

1. **/ZY** clears the entire worksheet.

2. The **F2** function key cancels a command or entry.

3. **/B** <RETURN> erases the entry at the current cell.

4. The **BKSP** key (left arrow key located above the RETURN key) erases the characters to the left of the cursor.

COMMANDS

(Use the F1 function key or ? after typing / to get a description of these commands.)

/A   The **Arrange** command—sorts cells in ascending or descending order.

/B   The **Blank** command—removes or empties contents of cells or graphs. Specify range.

/C   The **Copy** command—duplicates graphs or contents and displays format of cells.

/D   The **Delete** command—erases entire rows or columns.

/E   The **Edit** command—allows editing of cell contents.

/F   The **Format** command—sets display format at Entry, Row, Column, or Global levels.

/G   The **Global** command—changes global display or calculation options.

/I   The **Insert** command—adds empty rows or columns.

/L   The **Load** command—reads spreadsheet or portion from disk into the workspace.

/M   The **Move** command—inserts existing rows or columns at new positions.

/O   The **Output** command—sends display or cell contents to printer, screen, or disk.

/P   The **Protect** command—prevents future alteration of cells.

/Q   The **Quit** command—ends use of the SuperCalc program.

/R   The **Replicate** command—reproduces contents of partial rows or columns.

/S   The **Save** command—stores the current spreadsheet on disk.

/T   The **Title** command—locks upper rows or left-hand columns from scrolling.

/U   The **Unprotect** command—allows alteration of protected cells.

/V   The **View** command—displays data as pie, bar, line, area, X-Y, or Hi-Lo graphics.

/W   The **Window** command—splits the screen display.

/X   The **eXecute** command—accepts commands and data from an .XQT file.

/Z   The **Zap** command—erases spreadsheet and format settings from workspace.

//   Additional commands   //D accesses Data Management options.

FUNCTIONS

This is not a complete list of all functions available in SuperCalc. See the SuperCalc manual for details.

ABS	Absolute value
ACOS	Arccosine
AND	Logical AND
ASIN	Arcsine
ATAN	Arctangent
AVERAGE	Average
COS	Cosine
COUNT	Count how many
ERROR	Forces all entries referencing the coordinate to display ERROR
EXP	Natural exponent
FALSE	Logical value FALSE
IF	Logical IF
INT	Integer
ISERROR	Is value ERROR?
ISNUM	Is value NUM?
ISDATE	Is value DATE?
ISTEXT	Is value TEXT?
LN	Natural Logarithm
LOG10	Base 10 logarithm
LOOKUP	Look up a value in a table
MAX	Maximum value on a list
MIN	Minimum value on a list
MOD	Modulus
NA	Forces all entries referencing the coordinate to display NA (Not Available)
NOT	Logical NOT

NPV	Net Present Value
OR	Logical OR
PI	PI (3.1415926536)
RANDOM	Random value
ROUND	Rounds off
SIN	Sine
SQRT	Square root
SUM	Sum of list of value
TAN	Tangent
TRUE	Logical value TRUE

Computer Associates (Publisher) Program License Agreement
Reduced Function SuperCalc3 Computer Program (Program)
(IBM PC & 100% IBM PC Compatible Version)

YOU SHOULD CAREFULLY READ THE FOLLOWING TERMS AND CONDITIONS BEFORE USING THE WORKBOOK OR THE PROGRAM DISKETTE. YOUR INITIAL USE OF THE WORKBOOK OR THE PROGRAM DISKETTE INDICATES YOUR ACCEPTANCE OF THESE TERMS AND CONDITIONS. IF YOU DO NOT AGREE WITH THEM, YOU SHOULD PROMPTLY RETURN THE WORKBOOK AND THE PROGRAM TO MITCHELL PUBLISHING, INC. (MITCHELL) OR THE PLACE OF PURCHASE FOR A REFUND.

The Workbook and its related materials (Workbook) and the software Program (Program), which are components of the package produced by Mitchell, contains, in part, copyrighted materials which are the property of Publisher and Publisher licenses their use by you only in conjunction with your authorized use of the Workbook. You assume responsibility for the selection of the Program to achieve your intended results, and for the installation and use of, and results obtained from the program.

LICENSE

You may in conjunction with your use of the Workbook:

(a)   use the Program on a single machine;

(b)   copy the Program into any machine readable or printed form for backup purposes in support of your use of the Program in accordance with this Agreement. (Certain programs, however, may include mechanisms to limit or inhibit copying. They are marked "copy protected");

(c)   modify the Program and/or merge it into another program for your use. (Any portion of the Program merged into another program will continue to be subject to the terms and conditions of this Agreement);

You must reproduce and include the copyright notice on any copy, modification or portion merged into another program.

You may not reverse assemble or reverse compile the Program.

You may not use, copy, modify or transfer the Program or any copy, modification or merged portion, in whole or in part, except as expressly provided for in this Agreement.

You may not sublicense, rent or lease the Program.

CHARGES

The charges applicable to the Program will be paid to Publisher by Mitchell.

TERM

You may terminate this Agreement at any time by destroying the Program together with all copies, modifications and merged portions in any form. It will also terminate if you fail to comply with any term or condition of this Agreement. You agree upon termination to destroy the Program together with all copies, modifications and merged portions in any form.

DISCLAIMER OF WARRANTY

THE PROGRAM IS PROVIDED "AS IS" WITHOUT WARRANTY OF ANY KIND, EITHER EXPRESS OR IMPLIED, INCLUDING, BUT NOT LIMITED TO, THE IMPLIED WARRANTIES OF MERCHANTIBILITY AND FITNESS FOR A PARTICULAR PURPOSE. THE ENTIRE RISK AS TO THE QUALITY AND PERFORMANCE OF THE PROGRAM IS WITH YOU. SHOULD THE PROGRAM PROVE DEFECTIVE, YOU (AND NOT PUBLISHER) ASSUME THE ENTIRE COST OF ALL NECESSARY SERVICING, REPAIR OR CORRECTION. SOME STATES DO NOT ALLOW THE EXCLUSION OF IMPLIED WARRANTIES, SO THE ABOVE EXCLUSION MAY NOT APPLY TO YOU. THIS WARRANTY GIVES YOU SPECIFIC LEGAL RIGHTS AND YOU MAY ALSO HAVE OTHER RIGHTS WHICH VARY FROM STATE TO STATE.

LIMITATION OF REMEDIES

IN NO EVENT WILL PUBLISHER AND/OR MITCHELL, BE LIABLE TO YOU FOR ANY DAMAGES OR ANY LOST PROFITS, LOST SAVINGS OR OTHER INCIDENTAL OR CONSEQUENTIAL DAMAGES ARISING OUT OF THE USE OF OR INABILITY TO USE THE PROGRAM EVEN IF PUBLISHER OR MITCHELL HAS BEEN ADVISED OF THE POSSIBILITY OF SUCH DAMAGES, OR FOR ANY CLAIM BY ANY OTHER PARTY.

SOME STATES DO NOT ALLOW THE LIMITATION OR EXCLUSION OF LIABILITY FOR INCIDENTAL OR CONSEQUENTIAL DAMAGES SO THE ABOVE LIMITATION OR EXCLUSION MAY NOT APPLY TO YOU.

GENERAL

You agree that you will look only to Mitchell, and not to Publisher, for any support, maintenance, assistance or the like with respect to the Program's use in conjunction with the Workbook and that Publisher shall have no liability to you in relation to this program.

Any attempt to sublicense, rent, lease or, except as expressly provided for in this Agreement, transfer any of the rights, duties or obligations hereunder is void.

This Agreement will be construed under the Uniform Commercial Code of the State of New York.

dBASE III PLUS

Lesson 1

THE DATABASE MANAGEMENT SYSTEM

In businesses, schools, and even private homes, a great deal of information must be maintained. Information on correspondence must be stored, kept up to date, and retrieved as the need occurs. When paper documents are involved, this information is usually kept in a file cabinet and is arranged in some kind of sequence. Any method used to organize information (manual or automated) must allow for its easy retrieval.

Should the information be in alphabetical order or should it be in numerical sequence? That all depends on how you intend to retrieve the information. Say, for example, that you are to create a file on students. Should the file be in alphabetical order by student name or in numerical sequence by student number? You have to consider which you will be doing more often: retrieving by student name or by student number? You decide to file by student name, since you look up students by names more often.

But what do you do if someone asks for information by student number? You need to have a cross-reference. If you find out later that you need to look up all the students in a particular class, you will have to create another cross-reference. Your filing system could become very complicated. It has been said that anybody can file; but the retrieving takes a little doing!

A *database management system (DBMS)* is a set of computer programs that provides a means for storing, updating, and retrieving information. You can use a database management system in many ways. In its simplest use, the system stores information in a file, such as a file on all students, with an individual record for each student. In a student file, a record might consist of several fields of information, depending on the application. In a student record, the fields might consist of student name, student number, and class number, among others.

More sophisticated uses of database management systems involve manipulating the files more efficiently than is possible through manual updating of records. The manual system requires individual processing of each record. A computer system might provide a program that uses a transaction file to update master files, say for inventory. In this instance, a transaction file consists of records with data items that affect inventory status. These transaction records must be used to transform, or alter the content of, the inventory records.

dBASE III Plus is a database management system with these simple and sophisticated capabilities. You keep information in files and you may retrieve the records that match the conditions you specify. In the example of student files, you could retrieve the record for any student if you were given the name or student number, or you could retrieve the names of all the students in any particular class. If you would like a printed report on students, alphabetized and by classes, you could produce that, too.

dBASE III Plus is a very powerful program capable of record retrieval, automatic updating, and report generation. With dBASE III Plus, you also can write programs that enable others, less familiar with computers, to perform data entry and retrieval.

This manual covers only the simple commands of dBASE III Plus and explains just what is needed for a particular lesson. Many options and features available in dBASE III Plus can be explored on your own after you understand the basic commands. The lessons in this manual introduce the student to dBASE III Plus and to database management system uses in general. After completing these lessons, you should find it easier to learn additional features of dBASE III Plus and to work with other database management systems and file management systems.

STARTING OFF

1. Insert dBASE III Plus Sampler Demo Disk #1 in drive A of an IBM PC or compatible microcomputer that has been booted with DOS.

2. Following the DOS A> prompt, enter DBASE and press RETURN. The entry can be typed in either upper- or lowercase letters.

   ◻ A screen display reminds the user of copyright and license protection. At the bottom is the message:

```
Press Enter to assent to the License
Agreement and begin dBASE III Plus
```

3. Remove Sampler Disk #1 from the disk drive and put it back in its envelope.

4. Insert Sampler Disk #2 in drive A and a formatted data disk in drive B. Make sure to close the door of each disk drive.

5. Press ENTER to begin use of dBASE III Plus.

The dBASE III Plus Assistant, or ASSIST, appears:

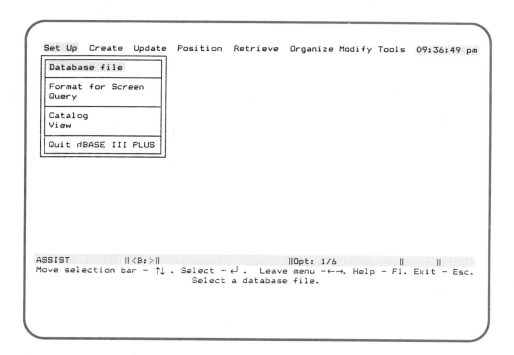

```
Set Up  Create  Update  Position  Retrieve  Organize Modify Tools   09:36:49 pm

  ┌─────────────────────┐
  │ Database file       │
  ├─────────────────────┤
  │ Format for Screen   │
  │ Query               │
  ├─────────────────────┤
  │ Catalog             │
  │ View                │
  ├─────────────────────┤
  │ Quit dBASE III PLUS │
  └─────────────────────┘




ASSIST           ‖<B:>‖                        ‖Opt: 1/6‖            ‖       ‖
Move selection bar - ↑↓ .  Select - ↵ .   Leave menu -←→. Help - F1. Exit - Esc.
                         Select a database file.
```

At the top of the screen is the ASSIST **menu bar** showing eight menu choices and the current time. The first choice, **Set Up**, is highlighted, and below it is a **pull-down menu** containing six options.

Near the bottom of the screen are three lines of information that are always present while you are using dBASE III Plus.

The first line is the status bar. It is highlighted, and divided into six areas. This first area shows where you are: it says ASSIST, indicating that you are in the ASSIST mode.

The second area shows <B:>, indicating that drive B is the default drive. That is, drive B contains the disk on which the file you create will be stored. On the dBASE Sampler, the default drive is pre-set to B. When you use the regular version of dBASE III Plus, the default is set initially to drive A. With the commercial version, you will have to change the default drive. At this point, verify that B: is your default drive setting. If necessary, use the **SET DEFAULT TO** command to select drive B. See the dBASE III Plus manual for more specific information.

The third area shows the database file you are using right now. It is blank, indicating that there is no file in use.

The next area shows **Opt: 1/6.** It indicates the option or current record number and the total number of options or records in the file.

The last two areas indicate when the insert (Ins) and Caps Lock keys are active.

Below the status bar line is the **navigation line.** It indicates the keystrokes that you may enter, and their effects.

The last line is the message line. It gives a brief description of the option on the pull-down menu that is highlighted.

6. Move the highlight to all the options on the top, using the LEFT and RIGHT ARROW keys.

   ▢ As you move the highlight and select different options, the pull-down menu blanks and another pull-down menu appears under the highlighted area on the menu bar.

   ASSIST, or the Assistant, is a feature of dBASE III Plus that leads new users (and experienced ones) by the hand to show them the use of various commands. The menu that you see on the screen is the main ASSIST menu. Just as a menu in a restaurant tells you which dishes are available, this menu shows you the functions that are available to you at this point. The pull-down menu that is displayed when an option on the menu bar is selected shows further options you have within the highlighted category. Again, to make a selection, you move the highlight, this time with the UP and DOWN ARROW keys, and press RETURN.

7. With any selection on the menu bar, move the highlight on the pull-down menu, using the UP and DOWN ARROW keys. Note that the message at the bottom line, the message line, changes each time you move the highlight. If there is a further selection to be made, another menu, or the sub-menu, is displayed. You make a selection with the UP and DOWN ARROW keys.

   NOTE: The RIGHT and LEFT ARROW keys are used to make selections on the menu bar. All other menu selections are made with the UP and DOWN

ARROW keys. The advantage of such a menu-driven system is that there is no need for you to memorize and type in all the commands.

dBASE III Plus can be used without ASSIST. You can get out of ASSIST at any time by pressing the ESC key from the main ASSIST menu.

8. From the ASSIST menu, press the ESC key.

  □ A dot appears, preceded by the word (DEMO) and followed by the blinking cursor. The word (DEMO) appears only in the sampler or the demonstration version of dBASE III Plus.

The dot, or the dot prompt, means that dBASE III Plus is ready for a command. The cursor shows where the characters you enter will appear on the screen. The status bar shows that the cursor is on the command line and the message line indicates that you are to enter a dBASE III Plus command.

  □ You can enter a command now. However, you haven't a clue of what to enter. At least with ASSIST, you can see the available commands, and the navigation and message lines give you brief directions on what you can do.

In these lessons, you will be entering all your commands through ASSIST. Keep in mind that any commands you enter through ASSIST can be entered from the dot prompt without ASSIST. However, the reverse is not true. Not all commands that can be entered from the dot prompt are available through ASSIST. As you become more familiar with the dBASE III Plus commands, you may try entering them from the dot prompt. As you enter commands in ASSIST, the display shows you the equivalent dot prompt command on the Action Line. This is explained later. Now, back to ASSIST.

9. From the dot prompt, type **ASSIST** and press ENTER. The ASSIST menu is displayed.

CREATE COMMAND

You must now indicate whether you are creating a new database file or using an existing one. You will create a new file. However, before doing so, you need to know some things about dBASE III Plus and some considerations in designing your files.

dBASE III Plus acts on database files. A single file can consist of up to one billion records (if disk space is available). Each record can contain up to 128 fields of information, or 4,000 characters, whichever is more limiting. It is not necessary for one file to contain all your information. One file can reference information in a different file. For example, an inventory file does not have to include the name and address of the vendor for each part in stock, but can reference the vendor by having a field containing vendor number. The vendor number, in turn, also can appear as a field in a separate vendor file. In this way, each vendor name and address is entered only once, in the vendor file, rather than including vendor names in records for inventory items.

Within dBASE III Plus each record is made up of a set of fields. Each field must be given a field name, which you make up to describe the content of the field. Field names consist of one to 10 characters, made up of letters (A-Z), numbers (0-9), and the underscore character (_). Each field name must begin with a letter. Letters that are entered in lowercase form are converted automatically to uppercase for all field names, file names, and dBASE commands. You may enter these as upper- or lowercase, but they are converted to uppercase for display.

There are five types of fields in dBASE III Plus. The type of information contained in the field and the types of operations that can be performed on the data depend on the field type. The field types and their uses are:

Character fields store character strings (names, telephone numbers, employee numbers, item descriptions, etc.). Strings can be compared, indexed, and sorted. But they cannot be modified by or used in arithmetic expressions.

Numeric fields store numbers, either as integers (whole numbers), or real numbers (including decimals). Regardless of how a number is displayed, it maintains 12 digits of accuracy. Numeric fields can be manipulated mathematically.

Logical fields each hold a single character, which serves as a **flag** indicating either true or false. Logical true is represented by T, t, Y, or y. Logical false is represented by F, f, N, or n. Logical fields can be tested in programs to select an appropriate processing sequence.

Date fields store date entries in the format 01/02/88 (MM/DD/YY). Dates can be sorted and indexed. They may be entered from the keyboard or specified as the current date. Numbers may be added or subtracted from dates to make new dates, and one date may be subtracted from another to yield the number of elapsed days or the length of a time period. There are ways for the user to determine the day of the week, the calendar month, and the year from a date field.

Memo fields are designed to hold large blocks of textual information, and can be up to 5,000 characters long, though each field uses only as much disk space as its content requires. Memo fields cannot be used to sort or index a file, and cannot be manipulated, except by using the screen editor. They can be read, printed, and modified. Memo fields are actually kept in different files, rather than in the database file. However, this is not noticeable when you are using database information.

The widths, or capacities, of Memo, Logical, and Date fields always are specified automatically. For Character fields, you need to specify the maximum number of characters in each field. For Numeric fields, you need to specify both the total number of characters and the number of places to the right of the decimal point.

Now, you will create a database that contains customer information. It will contain the names, addresses, telephone numbers, and credit account balance for all the customers, one customer per record. Since you may wish to use only first names (or last names) at times, you decide to store names in two fields. Summarizing the decisions you have made thus far, the fields in the record are:

FIELD NO.	CONTENTS
1	first name
2	last name
3	street address
4	city
5	state
6	zip code
7	telephone number
8	balance

You have to name each field and also decide what type of data each should contain. As a rule, if a field consists of numbers that are not manipulated mathematically, it is better to establish a character field.

The first and last names, address, city, and state should be character fields, since each will store both alphabetic and numeric characters. Although the zip code is a number, it should be a character field because you won't use it in mathematical expressions. Similarly, the telephone number might be expressed as (916) 983-1295. If you want to include the parentheses, space, and hyphen, then you must specify it as a character field. This is best because the telephone number will not be used for computation. The balance field must be specified as a numeric field.

Each field also needs to have a defined width. The width should be at least as large as the longest expected entry. You could choose the following field names, types, and widths:

FIELD NO.	NAME	TYPE	WIDTH	DEC
1	FIRST_NAME	CHARACTER	12	
2	LAST_NAME	CHARACTER	12	
3	ADDRESS	CHARACTER	30	
4	CITY	CHARACTER	15	
5	STATE	CHARACTER	2	
6	ZIP	CHARACTER	5	
7	TELEPHONE	CHARACTER	14	
8	BALANCE	NUMERIC	7	2

The last field is a numeric field that requires definitions of both width (7) and decimal positions (2). In calculating the width of the field, you need to account for the decimal point as one position and the minus sign as another position. By defining it as a field of width seven with two digits to the right of the decimal point, you are allowing it to be as large as 9999.99 or as negative as -999.99.

CREATING A FILE

To create a database file, the CREATE command is used. This allows you to name the file and to set up its structure. The structure is established by designating names, widths, and types for all fields within the record.

1. From the ASSIST main menu, select the second option on the menu bar, CREATE, by pressing the RIGHT ARROW key until it is highlighted.

2. Press ENTER to select the highlighted option. The pull-down menu shows six options. Database file is highlighted. A sub-menu, with drive letters, appears to the right of the pull-down menu. You are to select the drive that will store the database file. You want to select drive B:, which is already highlighted.

3. Press ENTER to select the highlighted option, B:. A message indicates that you are to enter a filename.

To create a new database file, you need to specify a filename. The name should reflect the contents of the file. A valid filename is any name from 1 to 8 characters long, consisting of letters (all lowercase letters are interpreted as uppercase letters), numbers, or any of the following symbols: !, @, #, $, %, ^, &, (,), -, _ , and ~. You should not specify an extension (a period followed by one to three additional characters) for the filename, since the extension .DBF is assigned to all database files.

Since you intend to store information on customers on the file, you decide to name the file ACCOUNTS.

4. Enter **ACCOUNTS.** If you make a mistake, use the Backspace key to delete your error and then retype. The following screen is displayed.

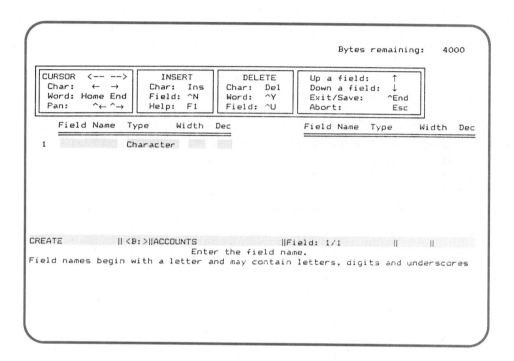

After you enter a filename, you are prompted to enter the structure of the database file. The structure describes the order in which fields are to appear in the file and also specifies field names, types, and widths, if necessary.

At the top, the number of bytes (characters) remaining is displayed. Just below are several helpful cursor control commands for use in creating the structure. The status bar shows the filename and number of fields that already are defined. Near the center of the screen, on the left side, are four titles: Field Name, Type, Width, and Dec. Beneath these is the number 1. This refers to the first field. The cursor is positioned on the line with the number 1, underneath the title Field Name.

5. Type FIRST_NAME. You hear a beep and the cursor jumps to the next field, which contains the word Character.

When you fill an entry completely (as, for example, the entry for field name, FIRST_NAME, that contains the maximum of 10 characters), dBASE III Plus automatically moves to the next entry and emits a beep.

You want the field to be a Character field, so you need only to press ENTER to go to the next entry.

6. You accept the default of Character by pressing ENTER. The cursor jumps to the Width column. You decided earlier that the field is to be 12 characters wide.

7. Enter 12 and press ENTER. Field 2 appears. The status bar updates the number of defined fields and bytes remaining.

Look at the screen. The cursor shows where you are. The editing and cursor navigation menu at the top of your screen shows all the commands to move the cursor and insert or delete items.

PRACTICE TIME 1-1

Enter the structure of the first seven fields, according to the information given here.

FIELD NO.	NAME	TYPE	WIDTH
1	FIRST_NAME	CHAR	12
2	LAST_NAME	CHAR	12
3	ADDRESS	CHAR	30
4	CITY	CHAR	15
5	STATE	CHAR	2
6	ZIP	CHAR	5
7	TELEPHONE	CHAR	14

Stop when the eighth field is displayed.

8. Type the last field name, **BALANCE** and press ENTER. Numeric field definitions are entered much as you do character field data, but you also specify the decimal field.

   ◻ The cursor jumps to the Type column. You want to make this a numeric field.

9. Press the SPACE BAR repeatedly. All the available field types are dis-played. You can stop when Numeric is displayed again. The type now reads Numeric.

10. Press ENTER. The cursor jumps to the Width column.

11. Enter 7 and press ENTER to go on. The cursor jumps to the Decimal column.

12. Enter 2 in the last column.

When you have entered the eighth field, the program prompts you for the structure of the ninth field. Since you are finished entering field structures, you will leave this mode.

13. Enter **Ctrl/End** (hold down the Ctrl key while you press the End key) to end creating structures. The bottom of the screen contains the message:

Hit ENTER to confirm. Any other key to resume

14. Press ENTER to confirm that you are finished. The screen displays the message:

Input data records now? (Y/N)

Now that you have created the structure of the file, the program is asking whether you want to enter data into the file. You have the option of either doing so or leaving the file empty. You will enter data now.

ENTERING DATA

15. Press the Y key to indicate that you will enter data. **Do not press ENTER.** You see the following blank form, or the template, on the screen.

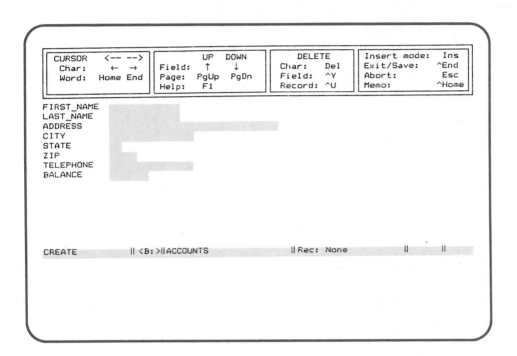

The screen is now designed to help you enter data into your file. The status bar shows that you have not yet entered any records. At the top are on-screen aids to help you to move the cursor, insert, and delete. In the middle of the screen are the names of the fields in the leftmost column and some highlighted areas of various widths to the right of the field names. These highlighted areas are the widths you specified for the respective fields, and these are the positions at which you will enter the information for the various fields in the first record. If you make a mistake, you can use the cursor movement keys to go back and correct the information. For example, if you key in an incorrect letter, you can use the backspace key to delete it, and then key the correct character. (Note that the BACKSPACE key deletes the character to the left of the cursor, while the Del key deletes the character the cursor is on.) You will now enter the data on customers.

The first customer is Robert Castillo, who lives at 112 South Broadway, Sparks, NV 89431. His phone number is (702) 358-0020, and his balance is 247.50.

16. With the cursor next to FIRST_NAME, type Robert in the first field and press ENTER to move to the next field. You are now making entries in the database. Unlike field names, the entries are not changed to uppercase. Enter them in upper- and lowercase letters, as they appear.

17. In the LAST_NAME field, enter Castillo and press ENTER to move to the next field. If you notice an error on a previous field, use the UP ARROW key to position the cursor at the point where the error occurs. Retype the entry.

18. Enter the street address, 112 South Broadway, in the ADDRESS field, and Sparks in the CITY field. After each entry, press ENTER to move to the next field.

19. In the STATE field, enter NV. Without your pressing ENTER, there is a beep and the cursor moves to the next field. Remember: When you fill a field, dBASE III Plus automatically moves the cursor to the next field. The beep should alert you in case you have misentered data.

20. Next, enter 89431 in the ZIP field, and (702) 358-0200 in the TELEPHONE field.

21. Finally, type 247.50 in the BALANCE field, and press ENTER. A blank template appears.

   ▫ The status bar now shows that you have entered one record. You are ready to enter the second record.

Do you have the idea yet? If the entry for a field is as long as the field length, the computer beeps and moves to the next field automatically. Otherwise, you press ENTER to go to the next field. If you make a mistake, either use the backspace key to erase the character to the left of the cursor and enter the correction, or use the arrow keys to position the cursor and retype the entry.

PRACTICE TIME 1-2

The remaining customer entries are given below. You are to enter them into the data base.

If you get out of the entry mode by mistake and end up back in the ASSIST main menu, position to UPDATE and select the APPEND option. You will be able to enter data from where you left off.

Name:	Harold Smith	Julio Chavez
Address:	885 North McCarran	225 Forest Hill Road
City,State,Zip:	Reno, NV 89512	Truckee, CA 95734
Telephone:	(702) 788-9120	(916) 968-2335
Balance:	29.75	782.38

Judy Davenport
555 Timber Lane
Truckee, CA 95734
(916) 966-0722
178.90

Larry Fisher
315 California Avenue
Reno, NV 89509
(702) 329-4405
278.98

Irene Orwell
12575 Sun Valley Blvd.
Sun Valley, NV 89433
(702) 673-9800
860.00

Jennifer Bacon
975 Lake Drive
Chilcoot, CA 95926
(916) 477-6705
142.45

Jonathan Handel
1001 East Fourth Street
Reno, NV 89501
(702) 786-0905
76.24

Cindy Beard
P.O. Box 10733
Reno, NV 89510
(702) 323-6220
923.40

Chico Juarez
72 Mill Road
Floriston, CA 96111
(916) 479-3205
312.12

Abdel Ahmed
417 Miner Street
Virginia City, NV 89440
(702) 847-3562
9.80

Sandy O'Dell
2219 Carson Highway
Carson City, NV 89701
(702) 234-0776
4.49

Mandy Vario
P.O. Box 37
Dayton, NV 89403
(702) 246-0171
442.45

When you have finished entering data, press ENTER again to exit the data entry mode. You return to the ASSIST menu.

BROWSE COMMAND

You have just finished entering the names, addresses, telephone numbers, and account balances of customers. Perhaps you would like to check the entries to verify that they were captured correctly. You can do so by using the BROWSE command. The BROWSE command allows you to look at all the data in all the records, and to modify the information if you choose. The data are displayed in a multi-record format; that means one record per line on the screen.

1. Select the Update option on the menu bar.

2. Select the Browse option on the pull-down menu and press ENTER. The following screen is displayed:

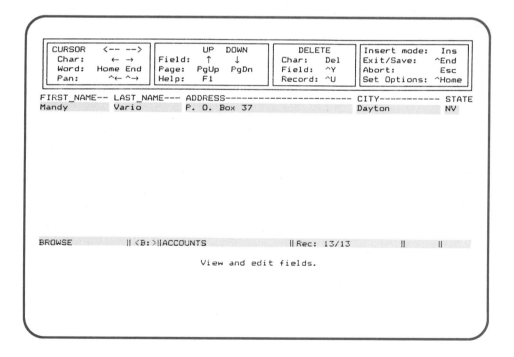

```
┌─────────────────┬───────────────────┬──────────────────┬──────────────────────┐
│ CURSOR   <-- -->│           UP  DOWN │   DELETE         │ Insert mode:   Ins   │
│ Char:      ← →  │ Field:    ↑    ↓   │ Char:     Del    │ Exit/Save:     ^End  │
│ Word:  Home End │ Page:   PgUp  PgDn │ Field:    ^Y     │ Abort:         Esc   │
│ Pan:    ^← ^→   │ Help:     F1       │ Record:   ^U     │ Set Options: ^Home   │
└─────────────────┴───────────────────┴──────────────────┴──────────────────────┘
 FIRST_NAME-- LAST_NAME--- ADDRESS----------------------- CITY----------- STATE
 Mandy        Vario        P. O. Box 37                   Dayton          NV




 BROWSE         || <B:>||ACCOUNTS                    || Rec: 13/13        ||     ||
                          View and edit fields.
```

3. Notice that only the last record entered in the file is displayed. Press the UP ARROW key repeatedly. Soon, records 1 through 11 are displayed on the screen.

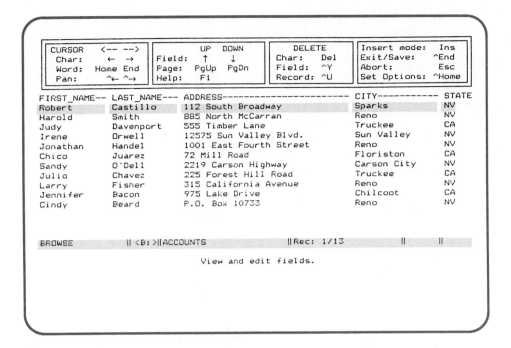

CURSOR	<-- -->		UP DOWN		DELETE		Insert mode:	Ins
Char:	← →	Field:	↑ ↓	Char:	Del	Exit/Save:	^End
Word:	Home End	Page:	PgUp PgDn	Field:	^Y	Abort:	Esc
Pan:	^← ^→	Help:	F1	Record:	^U	Set Options:	^Home

```
FIRST_NAME-- LAST_NAME--- ADDRESS--------------------- CITY---------- STATE
Robert       Castillo     112 South Broadway           Sparks         NV
Harold       Smith        885 North McCarran           Reno           NV
Judy         Davenport    555 Timber Lane              Truckee        CA
Irene        Orwell       12575 Sun Valley Blvd.       Sun Valley     NV
Jonathan     Handel       1001 East Fourth Street      Reno           NV
Chico        Juarez       72 Mill Road                 Floriston      CA
Sandy        O'Dell       2219 Carson Highway          Carson City    NV
Julio        Chavez       225 Forest Hill Road         Truckee        CA
Larry        Fisher       315 California Avenue        Reno           NV
Jennifer     Bacon        975 Lake Drive               Chilcoot       CA
Cindy        Beard        P.O. Box 10733               Reno           NV


BROWSE              || <B: >||ACCOUNTS            ||Rec: 1/13          ||      ||
                              View and edit fields.
```

When the edit-cursor move menu shows at the top, dBASE III Plus displays only 11 records. To display the entire file, press the F1 function key. The menu at the top disappears and you can see all the records. Press the F1 key a second time to get the menu back.

Only the first five fields are displayed. To see the other fields to the right, or pan to these fields, hold down the CTRL key while you press the RIGHT ARROW key (denoted CTRL/RIGHT ARROW). To move back to previous fields, you use CTRL/LEFT ARROW.

If you notice any mistakes, now is a good time to correct them. Use the cursor movement keys to position the cursor at the proper field and then enter the correct data. You will notice that what you type replaces the existing entries in the same position.

PRACTICE TIME 1-3

Practice moving around the file using the cursor move and pan commands until you become familiar with the commands given on the edit-cursor move menu and you can place the cursor in any field you choose.

SCREEN PRINTOUTS

There are several ways to get hard copies of the information when you are in dBASE III Plus. The simplest way is explained here. Other ways are described in subsequent lessons.

1. Check that the printer is on and ready to print.

2. Turn off the help menu by pressing the F1 function key, since you do not want the menu to show up in the printout.

3. Position the data on the screen so the leftmost field is displayed and all the records are displayed.

4. When you want a printout of the information on the screen, you press the PrtSc (Print Screen) key while holding down the SHIFT key.

   Since the record is wider than the screen width, you will need to pan to the right and get a second printout of the file for side by side display.

5. Turn OFF the printer when finished.

SUM, AVERAGE

Now you are ready to do some fancy but easy information retrieval from the database file.

1. Exit BROWSE by entering CTRL/END. The ASSIST menu is displayed.

2. Select Retrieve on the menu bar.

3. Select Sum on the pull-down menu and press ENTER. A sub-menu appears to the right. Execute the command option that already is highlighted. You will see this same sub-menu a number of times during the next lesson. It will not be discussed here.

4. Accept the highlighted option by pressing ENTER. The following appears at the bottom of the screen.

   13 records summed

   BALANCE

   4288.46

The program summed up the BALANCE field on all 13 records and printed the result on the screen.

5. Now try the AVERAGE function. Press any key to get back to the ASSIST menu. Retrieve is already selected.

6. Select Average and press ENTER.

7. Press ENTER to select the highlighted option. The following is displayed at the bottom of the screen.

> 13 records averaged
>
> BALANCE
>
> 329.88

The program calculated the average amount for the BALANCE field for the 13 records.

8. Press any key to get back to the ASSIST menu.

COUNT

The Count option in Retrieve gives the number of records contained in the file. Try it on your own.

ENDING THE SESSION

You are now to the end of the first lesson. The database file you have been working with is still in RAM memory of the computer. If you remove the disks and turn off the computer, you will lose the data. Thus, it is necessary to tell the program that you are quitting, so the program can save any open files in memory. You will do so now.

1. Select the **Set Up** option on the menu bar.

2. Select the last option, **Quit dBASE III Plus,** and press ENTER. The disk drive turns on and the program proceeds to save any open files. When dBASE III Plus has finished the housekeeping chores, you see the DOS prompt, A>.

3. Remove the disks from both drives.

4. Turn OFF the monitor if it has a separate control.

5. Turn OFF the computer.

Lesson 2

ORIENTATION

In completing the first lesson, you created and entered some information into a database file. You used the BROWSE command to view the contents of the file, and you found out how to use the COUNT, SUM, and AVERAGE functions. Finally, you learned how to print a screen image. In this lesson, you retrieve records and arrange records in alphabetic or numeric order according to content of one or more fields. You also learn how to print records and fields selected from a file. These commands are used widely in applications of dBASE III Plus. By using them yourself, you should begin to feel more comfortable with the database package.

You need two dBASE III Plus Sampler disks and the data disk on which you saved the file during the previous lesson. Turn on the computer and start up dBASE III Plus as you did in the first lesson. Make sure to insert the data disk in drive B. You should see the ASSIST menu on the screen.

The first thing you normally want to do is to let the program know which database file you plan to use. Now, do you remember the name of the file you created in the first lesson? dBASE III Plus has a command that allows you to see the names of files on your disk.

DIRECTORY

1. Select the option **TOOLS** by using the RIGHT ARROW key.

2. Select the option **Directory** by using the DOWN ARROW key and press ENTER.

   ▢ A submenu appears listing disk drives to the left.

3. Select the drive B, which already is highlighted, and press ENTER.

   ▢ The disk drive submenu is replaced with one giving 10 options for file type. dBASE III Plus is asking you if you want to display the names of only a specific type of files or all filenames. dBASE III Plus generates nine different file types, identified by the extensions in their filenames. Database files have the extension .DBF. As other file types are introduced, they will be described.

   Right now, you want to display only the database files.

4. Select **.dbf Database Files,** which already is highlighted, and press ENTER.

   ▢ The screen shows the names of the database files that are on your default drive, drive B. ACCOUNTS.DBF is listed.

5. Press any key to continue. The ASSIST menu is displayed.

   Database files on a disk are like a collection of files (in file folders) in a file cabinet. When you want to use a file that is in a file cabinet, you get the folder from the cabinet, place it on your desk, and open the folder to begin using the file. When you are finished using the file, you place all the papers back in the folder, close the folder, and place it back in the file cabinet. Similarly, to use a database file that is on disk, you need to place it in the computer's memory so that it is open for you to work with. This process is called **opening a file.** A file is opened when you select it for use. When a file is no longer needed, it should be recorded back on the disk so that its changes are recorded properly. This is called **closing the file.** A file is closed automatically either when you specify another file for review or when you enter exit dBASE III Plus.

OPENING A FILE

1. You want to open the file ACCOUNTS. From ASSIST menu, select **Set Up.**

2. Select **Database File** and press ENTER.

3. Press ENTER again, since drive B, where the disk containing your database disk is located, already is highlighted.

◻ All the names of database files on the disk in drive B are displayed.

4. Select **ACCOUNTS.DBF** and press ENTER. The following message is displayed.

> **Is the file indexed? [Y/N]**

This feature is discussed later in this lesson.

5. Type **N.** There is no need to press ENTER.

◻ The status bar shows the file named ACCOUNTS has been opened.

THE DISPLAY COMMAND

If you do not remember the data entered into the file during the first session, you can use the DISPLAY command to review file content. The DISPLAY command allows you to look at the data in the file. You cannot change data or enter new records through use of the DISPLAY command.

1. From the ASSIST menu, select **Retrieve.**

2. Select **Display** and press ENTER.

◻ A submenu appears to the right. The submenu shows five options you have at this point. The first option carries out the command DISPLAY. Carry out the command right now to see what happens.

3. With **Execute the Command** highlighted, press ENTER.

◻ Only the first record is displayed. The other options in the submenu let you specify what you want displayed. The program keeps track of all the records and their record numbers. Furthermore, there is a record pointer that is moved as the program carries out the command. When you issue the DISPLAY command without the other options set, the program displays only the record to which the pointer is set, or the **current record.** The pointer currently is set to the first record.

4. Now, specify other options. Press any key to continue work in ASSIST.

5. Select **Display** (in **Retrieve**), and press ENTER.

6. Select **Specify Scope** and press ENTER.

▫ A submenu appears below the previous menu. Use this menu to specify the scope of your display. If the scope is omitted, the display refers only to the current record. Right now, you want to see all the records.

7. Select **ALL** and press ENTER.

▫ The words **Specify Scope** change coloring on the menu, indicating that you have set the scope. This selection no longer is available for the current DISPLAY command option.

8. Select **Execute the Command** and press ENTER. The following screen appears.

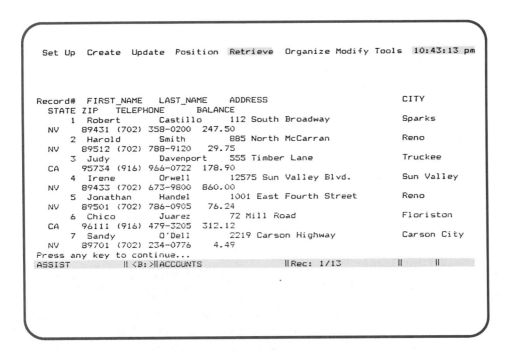

The contents of the first seven records in the file are displayed on the screen, two lines per record. At the bottom is the message:

Press any key to continue...

9. Press any key.

▫ The screen scrolls up and the last five records of the file are displayed. The screen is merely an output device, not a record of everything that exists in memory. If the screen is full and the program has more information to display on the screen, the screen scrolls up. That means the information on the screen moves up one line, so that the bottom line is available for the new information to be displayed. The information that was previously on the top line of the screen has scrolled off the screen.

10. Press any key to go back to the ASSIST menu.

THE HELP COMMAND (F1)

You may wonder just how to use a command for certain results or, in your case, how to enter the command you used in ASSIST from the dot prompt. You could look for a description of the command in the dBASE III Plus manual. But there is an easier way to get much of the information you might usually need.

Try this with the DISPLAY command.

1. From the ASSIST menu, select **Retrieve.**

2. Select **DISPLAY,** but do not press ENTER.

3. Press the F1 function key. The following screen appears.

```
 Set Up  Create  Update  Position  Retrieve  Organize Modify Tools  10:48:08 pm
     ┌──────────────────────────────────────────────────────────────────┐
     │                             DISPLAY                                │
     │   DISPLAY shows specified records and fields using the active database file │
     │   or view.  The listing pauses periodically and prompts for a key press.    │
     │                                                                    │
     │       Command Format:  DISPLAY [<scope>] [<expression list>]       │
     │                           [FOR <condition>] [WHILE <condition>]    │
     │                           [OFF] [TO PRINT]                         │
     │                                                                    │
     └──────────────────────────────────────────────────────────────────┘




 ASSIST          || <B:>||ACCOUNTS              ||Rec: EOF/13      ||      ||
                  Press any key to continue work in ASSIST.
                  Display the contents of this database file.
```

The F1 function key displays the help message for the command you have highlighted on the ASSIST menu. The screen is designed to be self-explanatory, although it can take a certain amount of experience before you can understand all the options. The parts enclosed in brackets, [], are optional. The words given in upper case are **keywords.** A keyword is a reserved word that dBASE III Plus recognizes as a part of a command. Keywords are used to indicate certain options of the command. They include: ALL, TO PRINT, OFF, FIELDS, FOR, and WHILE.

In the DISPLAY command, everything except the command itself is enclosed in brackets and is optional. Thus, you can specify how much detail you want to be displayed. The commands and their functions are summarized below.

[<scope>]	Allows the user to choose a scope for display. If the scope is omitted, the display refers only to the current record. Possible entries for scope are ALL, NEXT n, and RECORD n, where n is a number. NEXT n means to display the next n records, beginning with the current record, and RECORD n means to display only record number n.
[FIELDS <field list>]	Allows you to name the fields you want displayed. The field list is a series of field names to be displayed, separated by commas.
[FOR <condition>]	All records that meet the specified condition are displayed.
[WHILE <condition>]	All records are displayed until the first record is reached in which the specified condition is not met, and all subsequent records are not displayed, regardless of whether they meet the condition.
[OFF] and [TO PRINT]	Not available in the demonstration version of dBASE III Plus.

4. Press any key to go back to the ASSIST menu.

5. With **Retrieve/Display** selected, press ENTER.

   Look at the line just above the status bar, known as the **Action Line.** It shows **Command: DISPLAY.** The ASSIST tells you the dot prompt command equivalent of the command you are currently executing in ASSIST. Between the Action Line and the help you can get when you press the F1 key, you should be able to learn the dot prompt command.

6. Press the ESC key to go back to the ASSIST menu.

RECORD POINTER

As noted previously, dBASE III Plus keeps track of the records in the database file. For example, you could ask the system to display record 3 if you choose. dBASE III Plus also has a record pointer, which points to the "current" record. This record pointer is moved by GOTO, SEEK, and DISPLAY commands.

In the previous section, when you entered the DISPLAY command without other options set, only the first record was displayed. That was because the first record was the current record, the one the record pointer was set to. Now, try again, as follows:

1. From the ASSIST menu, select **Retrieve.**

2. Select **Display** and press ENTER.

3. Press ENTER to "execute the command."

   ▢ The screen shows the headings of the fields in the file, but no data.

   When the DISPLAY ALL command is carried out, as a record is displayed, the record pointer moves down the records in the file. When the entire file is displayed, the record pointer is below the last record in the file. The fourth area on the status bar shows EOF/13 meaning that the record pointer is on EOF (End of File) of 13 records.

   To review file content, you need to reposition the record pointer, probably to the beginning of the file.

4. Press any key to go back to the ASSIST menu.

THE GOTO COMMAND

5. Select **Position** on the menu bar.

6. Select the last option, **Go to Record** and press ENTER.

   ▢ A submenu appears to the right with three options: **TOP, BOTTOM,** and **RECORD.** TOP sends the record pointer to the beginning of the file. BOTTOM sends the record pointer to the end of the file. RECORD sends the pointer to the record you specify.

7. Select TOP and press ENTER.

   ▢ The ASSIST menu is displayed again. But the fourth area on the status bar shows **1/13.** This means the record pointer is on the first of 13 records.

PRACTICE TIME 2-1

1. Display the current record. The first record, for Robert Castillo, should be displayed.

2. Change the position of the record pointer and display the current record again. Do this several times until you feel comfortable.

3. Make sure to get back to the ASSIST menu.

DISPLAYING SELECTED RECORDS

So far, you have not indicated which fields in the record you want displayed. Hence, all the fields in the record at the record pointer were shown. As an option, you also may select fields to be displayed.

1. Select **Retrieve** on the menu bar.

2. Select **Display** on the pull-down menu and press ENTER. The third option on the submenu is for specifying the fields.

3. Select **Construct a field list** and press ENTER. Another submenu appears to the left, listing all the fields of the record. A box in the middle gives information about the field that is highlighted.

   ▫ You are to specify which fields you want displayed. Say that you want to display only the first name, last name, and telephone number for all the customers. Fields will be displayed in the order in which they were selected.

4. Select **FIRST_NAME** and press ENTER.

   ▫ The coloring of FIRST_NAME on the submenu changes, indicating that this field has been selected for display. The cursor moves to the next field.

5. Similarly, select and ENTER fields **LAST_NAME** and **TELEPHONE**.

6. Press either the LEFT ARROW or the RIGHT ARROW key to leave this menu.

   ▫ The selection **Construct a field list** has changed coloring on the submenu.

PRACTICE TIME 2-2

1. Specify ALL as your scope.

2. Execute the command.

The following is displayed.

```
  Set Up  Create  Update  Position  Retrieve  Organize Modify Tools  10:55:12 pm




Record#  FIRST_NAME   LAST_NAME    TELEPHONE
    1    Robert       Castillo     (702) 358-0200
    2    Harold       Smith        (702) 788-9120
    3    Judy         Davenport    (916) 966-0722
    4    Irene        Orwell       (702) 673-9800
    5    Jonathan     Handel       (702) 786-0905
    6    Chico        Juarez       (916) 479-3205
    7    Sandy        O'Dell       (702) 234-0776
    8    Julio        Chavez       (916) 968-2335
    9    Larry        Fisher       (702) 329-4405
   10    Jennifer     Bacon        (916) 477-6705
   11    Cindy        Beard        (702) 323-6220
   12    Abdel        Ahmed        (702) 847-3562
   13    Mandy        Vario        (702) 246-0171
ASSIST          || <B:>||ACCOUNTS              ||Rec: 1/13        ||          ||
                 Press any key to continue work in ASSIST.
```

You also have the option of specifying only some of the records, rather than all of them. If you want to select some records, you must first position the record pointer at the top of the file, since the search for a selection begins at the current record.

PRACTICE TIME 2-3

Position the record pointer at the beginning of the file.

Suppose you want the telephone numbers for all the customers who live in California. You can use the **Build a search condition** option on the submenu.

7. You are to display fields FIRST_NAME, LAST_NAME, and TELEPHONE for those customers who reside in California. Select **Retrieve** on the menu bar.

8. Select **Display** on the pull-down menu and press ENTER.

9. Select **Construct a field list** and press ENTER.

10. Select FIRST_NAME, LAST_NAME, and TELEPHONE fields to be displayed and press either the LEFT or RIGHT ARROW key.

11. Select **Build a search condition** and press ENTER.

   ¤ A submenu appears that lists all the fields in the record, and a box in the middle describes the field that is highlighted.

12. You want to select all the records for which STATE field is "CA." Choose **STATE** and press ENTER.

   ¤ · A submenu appears listing all the logical operators.

13. You are looking for the equals condition. Select = **Equal To** and press ENTER. The following message appears:

   `Enter a character string (without quotes):`

14. You want the records for which the state is equal to CA. Type CA (no ENTER).

   ¤ The computer beeps and a submenu appears to the right of the screen asking if there is more than one condition to be met by the records selected. There are no other conditions.

15. Select **No more conditions** and press ENTER.

   ¤ Note the Action Line above the status bar. As you set different options in DISPLAY, the Action Line presents the equivalent command that you would use from the dot prompt.

16. Select **Execute the command** and press ENTER.

   ¤ Four records are displayed. When you enter the comparison value, it must match exactly, both with regard to the character string, and with regard to upper- and lowercase letters. The DISPLAY command is really handy for finding certain records in a file.

THE DISPLAY STRUCTURE COMMAND

When you are interested in displaying some fields in your database file, there may be a problem if you have forgotten the field names. There are several ways you could find out the field names. One way is to display the structure of the file. This gives the field names, types, and widths.

1. From the ASSIST menu, select **Tools** on the menu bar.

2. Select **List structure** on the pull-down menu and press ENTER. The following message is displayed:

   Direct the output to the printer? [Y/N]

3. dBASE III Plus wants to know if you want this information printed. You want it on the screen. Type **N** (no ENTER). The following screen is displayed:

```
   Set Up   Create   Update   Position   Retrieve   Organize Modify Tools   10:59:21 pm




   Structure for database: B:ACCOUNTS.dbf
   Number of data records:      13
   Date of last update    : 10/04/86
   Field  Field Name  Type        Width   Dec
       1  FIRST_NAME  Character      12
       2  LAST_NAME   Character      12
       3  ADDRESS     Character      30
       4  CITY        Character      15
       5  STATE       Character       2
       6  ZIP         Character       5
       7  TELEPHONE   Character      14
       8  BALANCE     Numeric         7      2
   ** Total **                      98
   ASSIST            || <B:>||ACCOUNTS              ||Rec: EOF/13        ||       ||
                          Press any key to continue work in ASSIST.
```

4. Press any key to return to ASSIST.

PRACTICE TIME 2-4

Use the DISPLAY command to accomplish the following tasks. Remember, you may have to reposition the record pointer at the top of the file between DISPLAY commands.

1. Display all the customer names.

2. Display all records, but only the last name, first name, and balance for each customer.

3. Display only the fields last name, first name, and balance for only those records with balances of less than or equal to $500.00.

4. Display all fields for record number 6.

THE SORT COMMAND

Sometimes, it is necessary to arrange the records of a file in a particular sequence. A file consisting of records on the golfers' scores at a tournament might be arranged in ascending order (from lowest to highest) to find out who finished in which place. As an alternative, it might be necessary to print the names in alphabetical order. Such arranging of records in a particular order is called **sorting.** There are two ways in which dBASE III Plus arranges files in order. You will be introduced to both methods.

The first way is the SORT command, which sorts a file on one or more fields, in ascending or descending order, as you choose. The accompanying diagram shows how SORT works. The filenames shown in these boxes only serve to indicate that two files are involved.

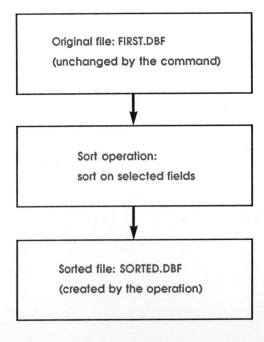

Original file: FIRST.DBF

(unchanged by the command)

Sort operation:

sort on selected fields

Sorted file: SORTED.DBF

(created by the operation)

When the SORT command is performed on a file in use, a new database file is created that consists of all the data in the original database file. However, the records in the new file are arranged in the sorted sequence. If you change the content of records or add records to the original file, the sorted file is not updated unless you issue the SORT command again.

The sorted file is created on disk. That is, it is not open. If you want to use the sorted file, you have to specify it for use. If the new file has the same name as an existing database file, it overwrites the previous contents.

You will now SORT the ACCOUNTS file so that the entries are alphabetical by last name. You will call the sorted file CUSTNAME.

1. From the ASSIST menu, select **Organize** on the menu bar.

2. Select **Sort** on the pull-down menu and press ENTER.

   ▫ A submenu listing all the field names is displayed, along with a box describing the field name that is highlighted.

3. dBASE III Plus wants to know which field to sort on. You want the file alphabetized by last name. Select **LAST_NAME** and press ENTER.

   ▫ The coloring of LAST_NAME changes on the submenu, indicating that the field has been selected.

4. Press either the RIGHT or LEFT ARROW key to leave the menu.

   ▫ A submenu showing disk drives appears to the right.

5. You want the sorted file created on the data disk in drive B. Select B:, which already is highlighted, and press ENTER.

   ▫ A box appears in the middle requesting that you enter the name for the sorted file to be created on the disk in drive B.

6. Type **CUSTNAME** and press enter. After a few seconds, the following message appears just above the status bar:

   `100% Sorted    13 Records sorted`

7. The file ACCOUNTS still is open. CUSTNAME is stored on disk. To see what happened, you need to open file CUSTNAME. Press any key to continue work in ASSIST. From the ASSIST menu, select **Set Up** on the menu bar.

8. Select **Database file** on the pull-down menu and press ENTER.

9. Select drive **B:** and press ENTER.

10. Select **CUSTNAME.DBF** and press ENTER.

11. Type **N** (no ENTER) in response to the question: **Is the file indexed?**

    ▢ The status bar indicates that CUSTNAME is the file in use. The first
      file you were using was closed safely. It now resides on disk only.

12. Display just the last name for all records.

    ▢ The file is in alphabetical order by last name.

```
   Set Up  Create  Update  Position  Retrieve  Organize Modify Tools  11:06:31 pm




   Record#  LAST_NAME
         1  Ahmed
         2  Bacon
         3  Beard
         4  Castillo
         5  Chavez
         6  Davenport
         7  Fisher
         8  Handel
         9  Juarez
        10  O'Dell
        11  Orwell
        12  Smith
        13  Vario
   ASSIST           || <B:>||CUSTNAME              ||Rec: 1/13          ||        ||
                       Press any key to continue work in ASSIST.
```

If you were to sort the file ACCOUNTS the second time, this time in ascending
order by balance, you have to specify the usage of the ACCOUNTS file again.
Also, you can place the sorted file on the file CUSTNAME once more, but when
you do, you overwrite the existing information.

     You also can sort on multiple fields. That is, you can specify more than one
field as the sort key. If there are several records with identical values for the
first field, the second field is used to break the tie. For example, suppose you
would like a list by city and state (all cities in one state, with states in
alphabetical order, followed by all cities in the next state, and so on). You
want the file sorted by state and city, in that order. In ASSIST, as you specify

the sort fields, make sure to select fields in the order you want the sort performed. In the example just stated, make sure to select STATE first, then CITY.

PRACTICE TIME 2-5

1. Sort the file ACCOUNTS by zip code and place the sorted file on CUSTZIP.

2. Sort the file ACCOUNTS by state and city, and place the sorted file on CUSTCITY.

Make sure to display the sorted file to check the results.

THE INDEX COMMAND

In addition to the SORT command, dBASE III Plus contains an **INDEX** command that performs sequencing in a different way. While SORT performs the sort once and creates a new database file, INDEX creates an index file (extension .NDX) that keeps the original file sorted all the time, even if you change an entry or enter a new record that affects the sequencing of the file.

Indexing updates the file's sequence each time a command is issued. The actual records in the file are still in their original positions. But, for all practical purposes, the .NDX file set the sequence of records displayed on the screen or accessed by a command. That is, the records are accessed in their **logical** order, according to some sequence, rather than in the physical order in which they were entered.

Indexing a file requires two steps. First, you INDEX the file, establishing an .NDX file for one (only one) field. If you wish, you can INDEX the file several times, establishing different .NDX files for different fields. Second, you have to specify which index file is being used. You can have more than one index file active at a time, but only the first index file is the master index, used for sequencing. The other active index files are used to keep them current if any changes are made to the database file. This may seem confusing at first, but you should be able to get the hang of it fairly soon. You will now index the file ACCOUNTS on last names.

1. Make sure that ACCOUNTS is in use.

2. From the ASSIST menu, select **Organize** on the menu bar.

3. Select **Index** on the pull-down menu and press ENTER.

    ▫   A box appears in the middle of the screen asking you for the name of the field to index on.

4. You want to index on the LAST_NAME field. Type **LAST_NAME** and press ENTER.

    ▫   A submenu listing disk drives appears to the right.

5. You want the .NDX file to be created on the disk in drive B. Select the highlighted option, **B:** and press ENTER.

    ▫   A box appears asking you to enter a name for the .NDX file.

6. You will call this file **LAST.** Type **LAST** and press ENTER. The following message appears on the screen:

    100% Indexed   13 Records Indexed

    So far, you have set up an index file, LAST.NDX, which you can use to place your database file in alphabetical order by last name. You will now see how to make the index file active so it can continually keep ACCOUNTS alphabetized. dBASE III Plus automatically sets the index file just created active. If any other index files were active when you created a new index, they are no longer active.

7. From the ASSIST menu, select **Set Up** on the menu bar.

8. Select **Database file** on the pull-down menu and press ENTER.

9. Select drive **B:** and press ENTER.

10. Select **ACCOUNTS.DBF** and press ENTER.

11. To the question **Is the file indexed?,** answer by typing **Y** (no ENTER).

    ▫   A submenu listing all the .NDX files appears on the screen.

12. Select **LAST.NDX** and press ENTER.

    ▫   The word **Master** appears next to LAST.NDX, indicating that the ACCOUNTS file is sequenced by this index. Other .NDX files you might make active at this time will only be used to keep them updated.

13. Now, check to see whether you have alphabetized the file. Use RIGHT or LEFT ARROW key to exit the submenu.

14. Display fields LAST_NAME and FIRST_NAME on all records in the file ACCOUNTS.

15. To be sure that the index file is always working, check to see what happens if you change an entry that affects the sequencing of the file. You will see this in BROWSE. From the ASSIST menu, select **Update** on the menu bar.

16. Select **Browse** on the pull-down menu and press ENTER.

17. Only the very last record is displayed. Press UP ARROW key repeatedly until all 13 records are displayed.

18. Using the DOWN ARROW key, place the cursor on the record for Castillo.

19. Using the RIGHT or LEFT ARROW keys, place the cursor on C of Castillo. Then type **Woodrum.**

20. Press the UP ARROW key once.

    What happens when you move the cursor off the record you changed? Are the names in alphabetical order? They were before you changed Castillo to Woodrum.

21. When you understand how the file behaves, change Woodrum's last name back to Castillo and again press the UP ARROW key once.

22. Press **CTRL/END** to get back to ASSIST.

PRACTICE TIME 2-6

1. Index the file ACCOUNTS on city. Call the .NDX file CITY.

2. Make CITY.NDX and LAST.NDX active, with CITY.NDX as the master.

THE SEEK COMMAND

Earlier, you learned how to move the record pointer to a specific record with the GOTO command. That command lets you point only to a record number, the beginning of the file, or the end of the file. It does not let you point to a record by specifying its content. For example, given a database file on inventory, you may want to point to a record that contains a specific part number. When a file is indexed, you can use the SEEK command to locate a record containing a specific expression for the field that is indexed.

You will now move the record pointer to the record that contains Dayton as the city. Make sure you have specified the ACCOUNTS file for use and CITY.NDX as the active, master index file.

1. From the ASSIST menu, select **Position** on the menu bar.

2. Select **Seek** on the pull-down menu and press ENTER. The following message appears:

Enter an expression:

dBASE III Plus wants to know what expression for the field CITY you are looking for. You are looking for the city of Dayton. Since Dayton is not numeric, it must be enclosed in either apostrophes or quotes (' or ").

3. Type **'Dayton'** and press ENTER.

4. Press any key to get back to the ASSIST menu.

5. Now that the record pointer is positioned, check to see if it is on the record with CITY='Dayton.' Select **Retrieve** on the menu bar.

6. Select **Display** on the pull-down menu and press ENTER.

7. Select **Execute the command,** which already is highlighted, and press ENTER.

   ◻ Mandy Vario's record is displayed. She lives in Dayton.

PRACTICE TIME 2-7

1. Make the index files LAST (master) and CITY active.

2. Use the SEEK command to locate the record for Jennifer Bacon.

3. Display fields LAST_NAME, FIRST_NAME, and TELEPHONE for her record.

4. Get a screen printout using SHIFT/PrtSc.

The SEEK command is a fast way to search through large database files. You could imagine how effective that would be if you had a database of 10,000 railroad cars and wanted to find the record of a car with a particular number.

THE LIST COMMAND

There is a command similar to DISPLAY that you can use to get a printout of records in the database file. The **LIST** command allows you to select the records and fields you want displayed or printed. As with DISPLAY, you need to determine the **scope** of the printout. The default here is **ALL.** That is, if you were to LIST without specifying the scope, all the records would be displayed or printed. You also **Construct a field list** just as you did with DISPLAY to specify which fields you want displayed or printed; and **Build a search condition** to specify which selected records you want.

Now, print fields FIRST_NAME, LAST_NAME, and TELEPHONE for all customers who live in California.

1. From the ASSIST menu, select **Retrieve** on the menu bar.

2. Select **List** on the pull-down menu and press ENTER.

   □ A submenu similar to the one in DISPLAY appears. You should know what to do at this point.

3. Select **Construct a field list** and press ENTER.

4. Select FIRST_NAME, LAST_NAME, and TELEPHONE—in that order.

5. Press the RIGHT or LEFT ARROW key to leave the menu.

6. Select **Build a search condition** and press ENTER.

7. Select **STATE** and press ENTER.

8. Select **= Equal to** and press ENTER.

9. Type **CA** (no ENTER).

10. Select **No more conditions** and press ENTER.

11. Select **Execute the command** and press ENTER. A box appears with the question:

    ```
    Direct the output to the printer? [Y/N]
    ```

If you answer **N**, LIST works like DISPLAY and shows the selected records on the screen. You want them to be printed.

12. Make sure the printer is turned on and ready.

13. Type **Y** (no ENTER).

    ◻ The selected records are printed on the printer.

THE DELETE COMMAND

A database is dynamic. One of the features of dBASE III Plus is the ability to update data in the database, to keep information current. You have seen some of the features dBASE III Plus uses to build and maintain files. Now you will find out how dBASE III Plus handles the deletion of individual records in a database.

You have just found out that Larry Fisher does not want to do business with you anymore. He paid up the balance, and there is no purpose in continuing to carry his record in the database. You will delete it.

1. From the ASSIST menu, select **Update** on the menu bar.

2. Select Delete on the pull-down menu and press ENTER.

    ◻ The same submenu you saw in using the DISPLAY and LIST commands appears. However, the **Construct a field list** option has a different shading to indicate this option is not available.

3. You want to delete the record for which LAST_NAME = Fisher. Select **Build a search condition** and press ENTER.

4. Select **LAST_NAME** and press ENTER.

5. Select **= Equal To** and press ENTER.

6. Type **Fisher** and press ENTER.

7. Select **No more conditions** and press ENTER.

8. Select **Execute the command** and press ENTER.

    ◻ The message **1 record deleted** appears at the bottom of the screen.

9. Press any key to return to the ASSIST menu.

10. Execute DISPLAY ALL. (You should know how to do this by now.)

Larry Fisher's record is still there, preceded by an * (asterisk). This indicates that it has been marked for deletion.

THE RECALL COMMAND

The DELETE command marks the record for deletion. In this marked state, you can change your mind and restore the record. This is done with the RECALL command. The RECALL command is reached through **Update** and **Recall.** Since Larry Fisher's record is the only one marked for deletion, you can RECALL all records marked for deletion.

PRACTICE TIME 2-8

Try figuring out the RECALL command on your own. After you have reinstated Larry Fisher's record, delete it again.

THE PACK COMMAND

Now, consider how to remove the record from the file permanently. This is done with the PACK command. The PACK command can require extensive processing time, especially on large files, so it is advisable to mark all records that are to be deleted, and then to perform PACK once. Make sure that the record for Larry Fisher is marked for deletion.

1. From the ASSIST menu, select **Update,** then **Pack.** Press ENTER.

   ◻ Since your file was not very big, you get the following messages back almost immediately:

```
           12 records copied
     Rebuilding index - B:CITY.ndx
         100% Indexed      12 Records indexed
     Rebuilding index - B:LAST.ndx
         100% Indexed      12 Records indexed
```

The file now contains 12 records instead of 13. Also, the two active index files were updated as well.

THE APPEND COMMAND

Now that you only have 12 customers, you advertise frantically for more business. In the process, you recruit not one, but two new customers. Now you need to add them to the database. To do so, you use the APPEND command. Since your database is indexed (and the index files are active), it doesn't matter where you add the new records. APPEND adds records physically at the bottom of the file, but you can retrieve them in any order you want logically.

1. From the ASSIST menu, select **Update,** then **Append.** Press ENTER.

   ❑ The empty template that appeared when you first entered data reappears. You are to enter the data into these fields. When you are finished with the first record, pressing ENTER brings a second blank form for data entry. After you finish the second record, and see the third form, use CTRL/END to exit, saving data.

PRACTICE TIME 2-9

Enter the following data into the database:

John Chodes
885 Greenstone Drive
Reno, NV 89512
(702) 323-5005
balance 378.45

Jim Winston
784 Rhinestone Road
Reno, NV 89503
(702) 747-8997
balance 0.00

Use *Display all* to see that the records are indexed by last name.

This is the end of the second lesson. You will close the database file that has been in use and then shut down the computer.

1. From the ASSIST menu, select **Set Up.**

2. Select **Quit dBASE III Plus** from the pull-down menu and press ENTER.

3. Remove both disks from the drives.

4. Turn OFF the computer, monitor, and printer.

Lesson 3

ORIENTATION

So far, you have seen several features that are common to most database management systems. That is, most systems have ways to enter data, sort records on one or more fields, view data, and obtain printouts. Another common feature is generation of printouts formatted according to your specifications. In this lesson, you learn to prepare labels and reports from information in the database.

Two types of printouts can be **formatted,** or laid out on paper according to a specific design. A **label** output lets you indicate which fields are to be placed on each line, and how many columns of labels are to be printed on each page. A good example of the use of a label output is to produce mailing labels from the information in a database.

The second type of output, the **report,** produces table-style output, with titles at the top of each page and column and the content of each column reflecting fields in the database.

For this lesson, you need the same two dBASE III Plus Sampler disks and the data disk you have used previously. Begin by booting the system; enter the correct date and time, then enter the dBASE III Plus program. Make sure to insert the data disk in drive B. The ASSIST menu should be displayed on the screen.

CREATING LABELS

A **label** is a formatted output of one or more fields printed into specified blocks on a page. For example, a variety of gummed label sheets can be used with most printers. Some sheets contain a series of 1-by-3-inch labels, either one, two, or three labels across. Other sheets contain various label sizes. Labels also come on continuous forms. The labels do not need to be mailing labels. They could be inventory labels, labels for internal distribution within an office or company, or any other type of information from a selected set of records that meets a particular need.

dBASE III Plus has a flexible label printing capability that can handle many different label-making needs. Two steps are required to produce labels. The first step involves designing a label file, which is saved and can be used repeatedly. The label file describes how the output is formatted on the page, and which fields are to be printed on each label. Label files on disk have the extension .LBL. A label file does not contain the actual labels, but rather lists the fields to be used to produce the different lines in the label. The second step is the actual printing of the labels.

1. Specify the database file ACCOUNTS for use with active index files LAST.NDX (Master) and CITY.NDX.

2. From the ASSIST menu, select **Create** on the menu bar.

3. Select **Label** on the pull-down menu and press ENTER.

4. Select **B:** as the drive for the label file and press ENTER. The following message appears on the screen:

   Enter the name of the file:

   You may have multiple label files, either serving different database files or formatting different types of labels for a particular database file. Each of these files must have a unique filename. You will now enter the label filename, ACCOUNTS.

   The two files, ACCOUNTS.DBF and ACCOUNTS.LBL, have different extensions, which indicate their different purposes. If you have only one label file for a particular database file, it may be helpful to give it a name that avoids confusion with other database files on the data disk.

5. Type **ACCOUNTS** and press ENTER. The following screen displays the label file structure.

```
 Options                   Contents                   Exit  11:29:10 pm

 Predefined size:       3 1/2 x 15/16 by 1

 Label width:           35
 Label height:          5
 Left margin:           0
 Lines between labels:  1
 Spaces between labels: 0
 Labels across page:    1



 CURSOR    <-- -->   Delete char:   Del   Insert row:    ^N   Insert:      Ins
 Char:      ←   →    Delete word:   ^T    Toggle menu:   F1   Zoom in:   ^PgDn
 Word:    Home End   Delete row:    ^U    Abandon:       Esc  Zoom out:  ^PgUp

 CREATE LABEL    ||<B:>||B:ACCOUNTS.LBL       ||Opt: 1/7        ||        ||
          Position selection bar −↑↓ .  Select − ↵ .  Leave menu −←→.
          Select a standard label size: (Width x Height by Number across).
```

The box at the top contains some parameters to establish the size and
spacing of the labels. The limits and defaults (already defined for labels
measuring 3-1/2-by-15/16-inch) for these parameters are shown in the
accompanying table.

Label Defaults

Parameter	Limits	Default size
Width of label:	1 - 120	35 characters
Height of label:	1 - 16	5 lines
Left margin:	0 - 250	0
Lines between labels:	0 - 16	1
Spaces between labels:	0 - 120	0
Number of labels across:	1 - 5	1

If you are using 1-by-3-1/2-inch labels in a strip, the default probably is
appropriate for you. For now, however, you will be printing onto the usual
printer paper, so you will see how to program the printing of multiple
labels per line. For example, suppose you had a sheet of 1-by-4-inch labels
two across on a line. This means an 8-1/2-by-11-inch sheet contains 22

labels. Also, suppose your printer prints 10 characters per inch. You want to change the default shown on your screen so that there are two labels across and 5 spaces between labels.

6. Select **Spaces between labels** by using the DOWN ARROW key and press ENTER.

   ◻ An arrow appears next to the value 0.

7. Type **5** and press ENTER.

8. Press the DOWN ARROW key once more to select **Labels across page** and press ENTER.

9. Type **2** and press ENTER.

10. Press the RIGHT ARROW key to continue.

    ◻ A box appears to the right for you to specify label content.

    ◻ You accepted the default value of five lines in the label. Thus, the screen shows five lines. dBASE III Plus requires all information in the labels to be character fields. If you have other types of fields, you need to enter the appropriate conversion functions, as indicated in the accompanying table.

Conversion Functions

Type of Field	Conversion Function
numeric	STR() keeps only the integer part
date	DTOC() if you want date printed
date	CDOW() if you want day of week
date	CMONTH() if you want month printed

Thus, if you have a numeric field, BALANCE, it is entered into the label as STR(BALANCE), but the fraction (cents) part is lost.

You are producing mailing labels. You would like them to have the name on the first line, street address on the second, and city, state, and zip code on the third line.

Note: When you place two or more fields on a single label line, dBASE III Plus separates the entries by a single blank, removing trailing blanks as necessary.

To indicate the content of any line, you simply enter the field names, or functions containing field names, for each line. If more than one field is to be printed in a line, separate the field names with commas.

11. Press ENTER to select the first line.

12. Type **FIRST_NAME, LAST_NAME** and press ENTER.

13. Press the DOWN ARROW key to select the second line; then press ENTER.

14. Type **ADDRESS** and press ENTER.

15. Press the DOWN ARROW key to select the third line, then press ENTER.

16. Type **CITY, STATE, ZIP** and press ENTER.

17. The label format specification is complete. Press the RIGHT ARROW key.

    ¤ A submenu appears to the right asking if you want to save this label file.

18. Select **Save** and press ENTER.

    ¤ You have prepared the label form. Now, you are ready to print your labels.

19. From the ASSIST menu, select **Retrieve.**

20. Select **Label** from the pull-down menu.

21. Specify that the label file is to reside in drive B by selecting **B:**. Press ENTER.

    ¤ The names of all the label files on the disk in drive B are displayed.

22. Select **ACCOUNTS.LBL** and press ENTER.

    ¤ The ever familiar submenu appears on the screen.

23. With **Execute the command** highlighted, press ENTER.

24. A message appears in the middle of the screen asking if you want your output sent to the printer. Try this option. Make sure that the printer is turned on and ready to use.

25. Type **Y** (no ENTER).

□ The labels are printed.

26. Press any key to get back to the ASSIST menu.

Once you get used to the questions that dBASE III Plus is asking, you can set up a label file and have it print either all the records in a file or only certain selected records.

PRACTICE TIME 3-1

Create mailing labels for those customers residing in California.

Hint: You do not need to create a new .LBL file.

CREATING REPORTS

The other type of printout is the Report. Creating reports also takes two steps. The first step is to design a report file, and the second step is the actual printing. Report files on disk have the extension .FRM.

You will now prepare a report containing customer names and balances. You will include their telephone numbers, so that you can call them, if you wish. It is important that you have an idea of what kind of report you want to produce. Some planning with pencil and paper is necessary before you complete the task on the computer.

At the top, the report heading can range from a simple "Customer Account Balances" to a more elaborate heading of one to four lines. The columns of the report should contain the first name, last name, telephone number, and the balance. You would like the balance field totaled at the bottom. The report might look something like the accompanying illustration.

```
                  Customer Account Balances

   Customer Name              Telephone          Balance
   ----------------------------------------------------------
   John          Chodes        (702) 323-5005      378.45
                     .
                     .
                     .
```

You want to index the report by the balance amount; that is, you want customer names listed in ascending order by balance amount. The report fields can have simple headers, or titles, as illustrated.

The first step is to get the records in the right sequence.

PRACTICE TIME 3-2

Index your database file ACCOUNTS by BALANCE. You can call the .NDX file whatever you wish. Make sure this index is the master index of the file.

1. From the ASSIST menu, select **Create.**

2. Select **Report** on the pull-down menu and press ENTER.

3. Select **B:** as the disk to store the report file by pressing ENTER.

4. The screen instructs you to enter a file name, which can consist of 1 to 8 letters or digits. Type **BALANCES** and press ENTER. The following screen is displayed:

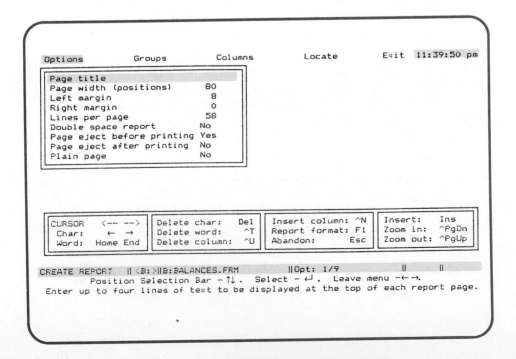

```
 Options          Groups          Columns          Locate      Exit  11:39:50 pm

  ┌─────────────────────────────────┐
  │ Page title                      │
  │ Page width (positions)   80     │
  │ Left margin              8      │
  │ Right margin             0      │
  │ Lines per page           58     │
  │ Double space report      No     │
  │ Page eject before printing Yes  │
  │ Page eject after printing  No   │
  │ Plain page               No     │
  └─────────────────────────────────┘




 ┌──────────────────┐┌──────────────────┐┌─────────────────────┐┌──────────────────┐
 │CURSOR  <-- -->   ││Delete char:   Del││Insert column:  ^N   ││Insert:     Ins   │
 │Char:    ←   →    ││Delete word:   ^T ││Report format:  F1   ││Zoom in:   ^PgDn  │
 │Word:  Home End   ││Delete column: ^U ││Abandon:       Esc   ││Zoom out:  ^PgUp  │
 └──────────────────┘└──────────────────┘└─────────────────────┘└──────────────────┘

 CREATE REPORT   || <B:>||B:BALANCES.FRM        ||Opt: 1/9        ||       ||
          Position Selection Bar - ↑↓ .  Select - ↵ .  Leave menu -←→.
 Enter up to four lines of text to be displayed at the top of each report page.
```

In the bottom box are the edit and cursor move commands. At the top is a box containing various parameters for the report. The top line in the box, which is highlighted, lets you enter the title for the report.

5. Press ENTER.

   □ A box appears with several blank lines. You may enter up to four lines of 80 characters each for a heading to be placed at the top of each page. At the end of each line, press the ENTER key to move to the next line. When you have completed your entry, press CTRL/END.

6. Type **Customer Account Balances** and press ENTER.

7. Press CTRL/END.

   The parameters presented in the menu are self-explanatory. A report on 8-1/2 inch wide paper usually will have a line width of 80 characters. The left and right margins are used to keep the report from going all the way to the edges of the paper. Similarly, the choice of 58 lines per page allows eight lines (four each) for the top and bottom margins. You also have the option of double spacing the report, if you choose. You will go ahead and use the pre-set values of these parameters.

8. Select **Columns** on the menu bar. The following screen appears:

```
  Options              Groups          Columns          Locate          Exit   11:45:50 pm
                         ┌──────────────────────────────────────────────────┐
                         │ Contents                                          │
                         │ Heading                                           │
                         │ Width                         0                   │
                         │ Decimal places                                    │
                         │ Total this column                                 │
                         └──────────────────────────────────────────────────┘



       ┌─Report Format─────────────────────────────────────────────────────────┐
       │>>>>>>>>>-------------------------------------------------------------- │
       │                                                                        │
       │                                                                        │
       └────────────────────────────────────────────────────────────────────── ┘
  CREATE REPORT   || <B:>||B:BALANCES.FRM          ||Column: 1       ||       ||
        Position selection bar -   .   Select -   .   Prev/Next column - PgUp/PgDn.
        Enter a field or expression to display in the indicated report column.
```

The final task of designing the report is to lay out the headers and contents of the various fields in the report. Initially, the report has a width of 80 character spaces, of which eight are taken by the left margin (unless you changed the margins in **Options**). For each column of the report, or the report field, you enter field names. If you need to see the edit-cursor move menu, press the F1 key. You press the F1 key a second time to get back to this screen.

The first line within the box at the bottom shows the number of columns taken up by the left margin and the number remaining. The > characters on the left show character spaces reserved for the margin, and the hyphens show columns left for the fields you can specify.

The top box contains parameters to specify the content of a report field. Try the first column.

9. With **Contents** highlighted, press ENTER.

   ▢ An arrow appears within the highlight, followed by the cursor.

10. You are to enter a field name. You want the first name to appear in the first column. Type **FIRST_NAME** and press ENTER.

   ▢ The field width specified changes to 12.

   ▢ X entries appear in the bottom box.

11. Enter the column heading "Customer Name." Select **Heading** and press ENTER.

   ▢ A box opens up for you to enter the heading.

12. Type **Customer Name** and press ENTER twice, type 13 hyphens (-) and press CNTRL/END.

   ▢ The width changed to 13, since this heading takes up 13 positions.

Notice that the header you entered now appears on the first line, followed by a blank space. The program makes sure that there is at least one blank space between each field. The X entries at the bottom show the actual field width.

NOTE: You can set the width to a larger value to allow more spaces between the report fields.

You have now specified the first report field.

13. Press the **PgDn** key to go to the next report field.

   □ Another blank box appears at the top. The fourth area on the status bar shows that you are now working with report column 2.

14. With **Contents** highlighted, press ENTER.

15. Type **LAST_NAME** and press ENTER.

   □ The width changes to 12 and X entries appear in the bottom box.

16. Select **Heading** and press ENTER.

17. Press ENTER, type 15 hyphens (-), and press CTRL/END.

PRACTICE TIME 3-3

Enter the other two report fields, TELEPHONE and BALANCE. TELE-PHONE will have the heading Telephone with 25 hyphens (-) on the second line.

BALANCE will have the heading Balance with 9 hyphens (-) on the second line. Notice that, since BALANCE is a numeric field, this box contains *Decimal places* and *Total this column* as added options. You will use the preset, or the default, value 2 to specify required decimal places and Yes for the total.

18. You have specified all the report fields. Now, save this report file. Select **Exit** on the menu bar by using the RIGHT ARROW key.

19. The pull-down menu asks you if you want to save the file. Select **Save** and press ENTER.

20. Now you complete the second step: print the report. From the ASSIST menu, select **Retrieve.**

21. Select **Report** and press ENTER.

22. Select **B:** and press ENTER to indicate that the report file is found in drive B.

   □ A submenu appears that lists all the .FRM files on the disk in drive B.

23. Select **BALANCES.FRM** and press ENTER.

24. With **Execute the command** highlighted, press ENTER.

   □   A message appears asking you if you want output sent to the printer.

25. Make sure that the printer is turned on and is ready to use.

26. Type **Y** (no ENTER).

   □   The report is printed. If you do not select Y, the output will be sent to your screen.

In these examples, you did not specify a scope, build a search condition, or build a scope condition in producing reports. You could have. Just as you did in the labels output, you could have used the submenu to make reports for only those customers from California, or only those customers who owe you more than $500.00. Remember, any options with dim coloring are not available to you at that point.

PRACTICE TIME 3-4

Design, create and print a report that lists all customers from Nevada who owe you more than $300.00. The report is to contain the customer name, address, and balance.

There are many, many more features available in dBASE III Plus. You have only scratched the surface. You should try entering various commands without ASSIST. ASSIST helps you to get started, but is limited and cumbersome for entering commands.

End the session by:

1. From the ASSIST menu, select **Set Up** on the menu bar.

2. Select **Quit dBASE III Plus** on the pull-down menu and press ENTER.

3. Remove the disks from both drives.

4. Turn OFF the monitor, computer, and printer.

Project 1

1. Create a home inventory file that includes the following items: item name, brand, model, serial number, date purchased, purchase price, and location.

2. Enter at least 15 records of information into the database (for example, furniture, jewelry, camera equipment, appliances, and sporting goods).

3. Create a report that prints the item name, date purchased, and purchase price.

4. Print the report, with the items sorted by purchase price.

Project 2

1. Create a database file for membership in your school's public service club. The database should contain name, address, telephone number, and office held.

2. Enter at least 10 records in the file, including at least five officers.

3. Design and create a label form for printing mailing labels three across (labels measure 2-1/2-inches-by-1-inch).

4. Print two sets of labels on regular paper. One set should include all the club members. The other set should include only the club officers.

Project 3

You have decided to start a dating service. You are going to create a file containing information on all the people who register with your service. Your file contains the following information on each person: name, address, telephone number, sex, age, color of hair, color of eyes, height, weight, favorite sport, favorite color, favorite food, and hobby.

1. Create a database file and enter information for at least 10 males and 10 females. Be sure that some of the people like pizza.

2. Design a label form for printing address labels.

3. Print address labels for all clients.

4. Design a report form for printing information on possible dates for a client. The report should contain name, telephone number, age, favorite sport and food, and hobby.

5. You have just received a call from a male who wishes to find a date. He wants to date someone between 5' 2" and 5' 5" who has brown hair and who loves to eat pizza. Print a report of possible dates for him.

dBASE III Plus Commands in ASSIST

Set Up

Database File	Opens a database file that exists on disk and optionally sets one or more index files active.
Format for Screen	Not covered.
Query	Not covered.
Catalog	Not covered.
View	Not covered.
Quit dBASE III PLUS	Ends the session of dBASE III PLUS.

Create

Database File	Creates a database file, defines its structure, and allows entry of records.
Format	Not covered.
View	Not covered.
Query	Not covered.
Report	Creates a report form that contains the information on report layout.
Label	Creates a label form that contains information on the label layout and fields.

Update

Append	Adds records to the database file.
Edit	Allows editing (modifying) of database records, viewed one record at a time.
Display	Lists specified records and fields to the monitor or printer, pausing when the screen is filled.
Browse	Displays the database in a multiple record format, one row per record.

Replace	Not covered.
Delete	Marks specified records for deletion from the database file.
Recall	Unmarks specified records.
Pack	Copies all unmarked records, creating a new version of the same database file, but without any marked records.

Position

Seek	Quickly locates an expression in the field for which the database is indexed in the master index file.
Locate	Not covered.
Continue	Not covered.
Skip	Not covered.
Goto Record	Positions the record pointer at the beginning or end of the open database file, or at any specified record.

Retrieve

List	Displays specified fields and records to the monitor or printer, without any pauses.
Display	Displays specified fields and records to the monitor, with pauses when the screen is filled.
Report	Uses a report form to prepare a report containing selected records.
Label	Uses a label form to prepare labels from selected records.
Sum	Sums a numeric field for specified records in a database.
Average	Averages a numeric field for specified records in a database.
Count	Counts the number of records in a database that meet specified conditions.

Organize

Index	Creates an index file (.NDX) that keeps the database file organized on an expression (usually a single field), even when changes are made to the database file.
Sort	Creates a copy of the database file that is sorted on one or more fields, in ascending or descending order.
Copy	Not covered.

Modify

Database file	Not covered. Makes changes to the structure of the database.
Format	Not covered.
View	Not covered.
Query	Not covered.
Report	Not covered. Makes changes to an existing report form (.FRM).
Label	Not covered. Makes changes to an existing label form (.LBL).

Tools

Set drive	Sets the default drive for the data disk.
Copy file	Not covered. Copies files, such as for backup purposes.
Directory	Displays the names of files on the data disk.
Rename	Not covered. Renames a disk file.
Erase	Not covered. Deletes a disk file.
List structure	Displays to monitor or printer the structure of the active database file.
Import	Not covered.
Export	Not covered.